THE ESSENTIAL HISTORY OF
ARSENAL

FOREWORD BY BOB WILSON

RAB MacWILLIAM AND KEVIN CONNOLLY

First published in 2003
by Headline Book Publishing
for WHSmith, Greenbridge Road, Swindon SN3 3LD

10 9 8 7 6 5 4 3 2 1

ISBN 0 7553 1267 8

Design by designsection, Frome, Somerset

All photographs in the book by Colorsport apart from page 29 (top) and 31
from Popperfoto. Programmes on pages 96 and 114 supplied by Tomàs at
theauldshillelagh.com

Text by Rab MacWilliam
Statistics and Great Players by Kevin Connolly

Printed and bound in Great Britain by Clays Ltd, St Ives PLC, Bungay, Suffolk

HEADLINE BOOK PUBLISHING
A division of Hodder Headline
338 Euston Road
London NW1 3BH

www.headline.co.uk
www.hodderheadline.com

Contents

Foreword
By Bob Wilson

I was an Arsenal player for 11 seasons, from 1963 to 1974, and goalkeeping coach from 1976 to 2003. You'd think I would know all there was to know about one of football's greatest clubs. I was confident I did until I read Rab MacWilliam's and Kevin Connolly's *Essential History of Arsenal*. All the essential facts really are here but it is the generous sprinkling of fascinating anecdotes which enhance this book and make it a must for any football historian, let alone every follower of Arsenal FC.

It is a club which, since Herbert Chapman's visionary approach, has always attempted to include a special style in the manner in which it conducts itself. Many clubs have attempted to copy the 'Arsenal way' but without success. There has always been great respect for Arsenal's ability,

in moments of great triumph, to laugh louder than most, and in defeat, to cry softer than most. Respect and admiration remains throughout football and long may it do so. This history of a marvellous club will leave all those who love being a part of it with a feeling of great pride and satisfaction.

Bob Wilson

Below: Bob Wilson celebrates after Arsenal's 'Double' in 1970-71. Previous page: (main) the athletic and fearless Wilson and (right) diving into the feet of a crowd of players to save the day, here denying Manchester United's George Best, 19 December 1970.

Chapter One: 1886-1919
From Woolwich to Highbury

In 1886, Woolwich Arsenal, based in a largely nondescript suburb of London just south of the River Thames, was a supplier of military munitions to the all-powerful and pervasive British Empire. Men came from across the country to secure work in the factory but the arrival of two skilled artisans from Nottingham that year was to be the catalyst for the emergence of one of the most famous names in world football – Arsenal Football Club.

Fred Beardsley and Morris Bates had transferred from the ordnance works in Nottingham to the Arsenal and met up with a new workmate, Scots-born David Danskin from Kirkcaldy, and Danskin's friends Elijah Watkins, Richard Pearce and John Humble. A love of the relatively new sport of Association Football united the men and, although the dominant sports in the South of England were rugby and cricket (unlike the increasingly football-obsessed Midlands and the North), they resolved to start up a football club. At the time, and until relatively recently, factories worked a five-and-a-half day week, with Saturday afternoon a day of relaxation, an ideal time to play their favoured sport away from the pressures and toil of the workplace.

Beardsley, a goalkeeper, and Bates had both played for Nottingham Forest who were one of the leading clubs of the era, and needed no second invitation to become involved with the fledgling club. As a ball was obviously needed, Danskin asked for subscriptions from various workers and received 15 payments of 6d (2.5p). He himself added three shillings (15p) to the total and a ball was acquired. The name they chose for the club was Dial Square, after one of the workshops at Woolwich and, having selected a team with Danskin as left back and captain, they played their first match on 11 December 1886.

Their opponents were Eastern Wanderers on a bog of a pitch across the Thames on the Isle of Dogs and, although there appears to have been some confusion over the result, an enthused Dial Square claimed a 6-0 victory. The game of football then was a very different affair. The pitch had no markings other than a centre line, crossbars were not required (a tape would sometimes be used), the goalkeeper could hold the ball anywhere on the pitch and players did not have to wear the same strip colours. One can understand how misunderstandings may have resulted. Buoyed by their success the club held a meeting in the Royal Oak public house in Plumstead, close to the Arsenal, on

Christmas Day 1886 to plan the future. They decided to adopt a more impressive name in keeping with their ambitions and so Dial Square was dropped for Royal Arsenal. They also considered that a unified strip colour would be helpful to the team's cohesion, so Beardsley contacted Nottingham Forest and requested the loan of a strip. Forest sent them plain red strips and a ball, and the club played in these colours until Herbert Chapman in season 1932-33 added the white neckband and arms. The club were known then, as now, as the 'Reds'.

Royal Arsenal are Born

Their first game as Royal Arsenal was against Erith on 8 January 1887 on their home pitch, the somewhat unregal Plumstead Common, where they secured a 6-1 win, and they played ten matches that season, winning seven and losing two. The following season they expanded the fixture list, playing 24 games and winning 14. They were, however, beaten on 19 November 2-1 by Tottenham Hotspur on Tottenham Marshes, the first salvo in a battle which continues 120 years later. By season 1888-89, they were nevertheless regarded as the best team in London – a list also containing Tottenham, Millwall, Fulham and QPR – and they reached the final of the London Senior Cup only to lose 2-0 to Clapton.

However, Royal Arsenal's star was in the ascendant and by season 1889-90 they were being hailed as the 'Football Champions of the South'. They won three cups that season. They were beaten by Old Westminsters 2-1 in the London Senior but gained their revenge by beating the same team 3-1 in the London Charity, watched by 10,000 spectators, and they also picked up the Kent Senior and Kent Junior trophies. They also reached the fourth and final preliminary round of the FA Cup but were defeated 5-1 at home by the celebrated Swifts.

'Home' at this point was no longer Plumstead Common. After a move to the Sportsman Ground, owned by a local pig breeder, on Plumstead Marshes in 1887, they moved to the Manor Ground the following year where military wagons acted as grandstands when there was a large crowd. In 1890 they moved yet again, to the nearby Invicta Ground which possessed a stand accommodating 3,000 spectators and a terrace with room for another 1,500.

Royal Arsenal had some fine players but the heavy defeat by Swifts had revealed the gulf in class between the amateur and the professional game. The line-up included such stalwarts as the Scottish full backs Jamie McBean and Peter Connolly (both from Kirkcaldy like Danskin), with David Howat, Joseph Bates and William Julian the half backs. Up front were Richard Horsington, Scots-born Humphrey Barbour, with experience at Third Lanark and Airdrie, and utility man Henry Offer. However, the legalization by the Football Association of professionalism in 1885 and the formation of the Football League in 1888 had led to dominance by the northern clubs and the best players moved to the professional clubs. Of the original members of the League none were from the South as the ethos of the London FA was emphatically one of amateurism.

Due to their relatively impressive performance in the previous season's FA Cup, Royal Arsenal were granted an exemption from qualifying for the competition's preliminary rounds in 1890-91, but a 2-1 home defeat by Derby (Derby scoring a dubious winner in the last few minutes) saw them out in the first round. Their finances were given a boost, however, by the visit of Scottish champions Hearts and Nottingham Forest over the Easter weekend, with large crowds turning up for both friendlies. Hearts won 5-0 and Forest also triumphed, 5-1. It was now clear that Royal Arsenal could not compete with the larger professional teams unless things changed.

In the light of this, at the 1891 AGM at the Windsor Castle Music Hall a vote was taken on turning professional and it was carried by a large margin. This decision was nearly disastrous and had the potential to finish off the club almost before it had begun. They were immediately expelled from the London FA and banned from all southern club competitions, leaving Royal Arsenal with only the FA Cup and a series of friendlies against Midlands and northern clubs. Again exempted from FA Cup preliminaries, they were knocked out in the first round by Small Heath (now Birmingham City) 5-1 in Birmingham in January 1892. Travelling to Birmingham, Crewe, Sheffield and Bolton was sapping morale and eroding the team's competitive spirit.

The following month Royal Arsenal called a meeting of London clubs to suggest the formation of a Southern League. Twelve clubs agreed: Chatham, Luton, Swindon, Marlow, Millwall, West Herts (now Watford), Reading, Royal Arsenal, Crouch End, Old St Marks, Chiswick Park and Ilford. The London FA disapproved and, under pressure, the clubs' commitment to the idea withered. In 1893 the Southern League was finally formed and became a successful competition, but by now Arsenal had moved on.

The Football League

The Football League had inaugurated a Second Division in 1892 which was started with 12 clubs. At the end of the

Harry Storer played a season for the Arsenal in goal in the late 1800s and played for an English League select in 1895.

season, the League decided to increase the number of clubs to 15 and, with relegated Bootle resigning from the League in a fit of pique and Accrington refusing to play in a lower division, there were five new places coming up for grabs. The five clubs voted into the Second Division were Liverpool, Newcastle, Rotherham Town, Middlesbrough Ironopolis and Royal Arsenal, making the London team the first southern club to play in the Football League.

Sensing that Royal Arsenal could now be about to make serious money, the owner of the Invicta Ground, George Weaver, raised the rent from £200 to £350 per annum and Royal Arsenal refused to pay the extra. The club took the decision to turn itself into a limited liability company and buy back the old Manor Ground which, after development, had a total capacity of 20,000. The new company – The Woolwich Arsenal Football and Athletic Company Ltd – had a nominal share capital of £4,000 and the club had a new name, Woolwich Arsenal. (The Football League continued to call them Royal Arsenal for another three years.)

Woolwich Arsenal began this new phase in their brief history with a home game against fellow newcomers Newcastle, drawing 2-2, with Walter Shaw scoring the club's first-ever league goal. Newcastle, however, beat them 6-0 away and the predictable pattern of home victory and away defeat continued through the season. Again, the problems of unreliable and arduous travel arrangements combined with second-rate, uncomfortable overnight accommodation took their toll. They concluded their first league season, however, with a respectable ninth place: winning 12, losing 12 and drawing four games.

The club faced further problems in that several of their better players were being lured away by some of the bigger, more successful northern clubs. Although

An early Woolwich Arsenal team from 1895, l-r: back row – Boyle, Powell, Storer, Caldwell, Hollis (trainer); middle row – Davis, Jenkyns, Ward; front row – Mills, Hare, Buchanan, O'Brien, Mortimer.

men such as captain and right back Joe Powell (who was to die in an accident against Kettering in a reserve match in 1896), Scottish outside right Gavin Crawford and keeper Charlie Williams displayed loyalty to the club, Williams' replacement between the posts, Harry Storer, remained for one season, as did Caesar Llewellyn Jenkyns, who captained the club in 1895-96. Storer became the first Arsenal player to gain a representative honour when he was selected for the English League v Scottish League in April 1895 and Jenkyns has the distinction of being the first Arsenal international when he was capped for Wales v Scotland the following year. With the absence both of top players and consistent winning performances, supporters stayed away, gates fell and the situation appeared bleak.

In 1896-97 Arsenal suffered the worst season in their history when they finished tenth in the Second Division. Not only did they incur their highest-ever defeat when they lost 8-0 at Loughborough, they were also eliminated from the FA Cup in the final qualifying round by lowly Millwall from the Southern League. Something had to be done to arrest the decline. The board took a decision to hire the club's first-ever manager and appointed Scotsman Thomas Mitchell from Blackburn Rovers to the job. He remained in the post for only a few months and was succeeded by George Elcoat from Stockton, but matters improved and Arsenal finished in fifth place in 1897-98 and seventh in 1898-99. The arrival of Harry Bradshaw as manager in 1899 was to add further impetus to Arsenal's ambitions. With a team which was largely Scottish (at one time eight out of the regular first XI hailed from over the border), they gained revenge over Loughborough with a 12-0 victory, still their highest-ever league win. Arsenal also battled over five games against New Brompton in the third qualifying round of the FA Cup before losing 1-0.

Events off the pitch, however, were adversely affecting the club's income. The Boer War, which lasted from 1899 to 1902, meant that several players were drafted to South Africa and that Saturday afternoon shifts at Woolwich Arsenal were reinstated, leading to other players being unavailable for matches. Some, such as Gavin Crawford, had to be sold in an attempt to balance the books. The financial shortfall was ameliorated by Mr G.H. Leavey, a Plumstead outfitter, who advanced £400 to the club to ease its problems. He apparently never received his money back but he was rewarded with a complimentary seat at the 1930 Cup final against Huddersfield. A long-term loan, indeed.

In 1900-01 Tottenham became the first southern club to win the FA Cup, an indication that the North's tight grip on English football was loosening. That season, Arsenal advanced beyond the first round of the FA Cup for the first time, beating Blackburn Rovers 2-0. This was also their first victory over a First Division side. The team was now becoming known for its inventive, quick passing, speedy interception and intelligent movement, largely a function of its Scottish contingent. Bradshaw had bought the massive goalkeeper Jimmy Ashcroft from Gravesend United (he became the first Arsenal player to be capped by England, in 1905-06) and right back Archie Cross from Dartford. He had also raided Scotland again to acquire the services of full backs Jimmy Jackson (from Newcastle United) and David McNichol. Jackson was appointed captain and the centre half was Percy Sands, known as the 'third back', predating Herbert Chapman and Charlie Buchan's defensive strategy by nearly 30 years.

In 1901-02, Arsenal achieved their highest league placing to date, ending in fourth place. Bradshaw had augmented the team with Scottish left half Roddy McEachrane, centre forward Bill Gooing and inside right John Coleman. Later in the year he bought again, adding Irish inside left and expert penalty taker Tommy Shanks and wingers Tommy Briercliffe and Bill Linward. Bradshaw clearly had promotion in his sights.

Promoted to the Top Flight

Promotion was the reward for his astute expenditure and man-management skills in 1903-04. Unbeaten at home all season and drawing only their last two games, Arsenal scored 65 home goals and conceded only five, finishing in second spot in the Second Division. They battled with Preston in the first half of the season but Manchester United surged through in the early spring to present a close challenge. At Arsenal's last home match, against Port Vale, they required just one point to be sure of promotion and ground out a goalless draw to confirm their elevation to the top division. Celebrating fans invaded the Manor Ground pitch at the end of the game, delighted that their local works team had taken less than 20 years to reach the pinnacle of the English game. The team during the season included: Ashcroft, Cross, Jackson, Dick, Sands, McEachrane, Briercliffe, Coleman, Gooing, Shanks, Linward.

For their opening season in Division One, Arsenal had a new manager, Harry Bradshaw having been seduced away by Southern League Fulham. Phil Kelso, a tough Scotsman who had been managing Hibernian, stepped into the breach and immediately began buying new players, including Charlie Satterthwaite, a 16-stone centre forward with a powerful shot; Tommy Fitchie, a Scottish inside left amateur who came from Norwood; professional hairdresser Bobby Templeton, a brilliant, mercurial Scottish left winger; Bert Freeman, an elegant centre forward; and outside right Bill Garbutt. In their first season Arsenal finished in tenth place, although they could only score 36 goals.

In 1905-06 burly Scottish international Jimmy Sharp, not the fastest of players but possessed of a shrewd positional brain, had replaced Jimmy Jackson

Jimmy Ashcroft, the Woolwich Arsenal goalkeeper, makes a save against Everton while playing at the Plumstead ground in 1905.

at left back alongside Archie 'Baldie' Gray at right back. The half back line remained Dick, Sands and McEachrane. Arsenal progressed to their first-ever FA Cup semi-final, defeating West Ham and Watford on their way to an unexpected 5-0 home win over mighty Sunderland in the fourth round. It is reported that young Charlie Buchan watched the game, having sold a schoolbook for 3d to afford the ticket, and his fine career was to span both these clubs. After disposing of Manchester United in the quarter-final they took on Newcastle in the semi-final at Stoke. Arsenal played well against a full team of internationals, Freeman hitting the crossbar in the first half, but Newcastle's superior strength and skill saw them run out 2-0 winners.

The following season they again reached the FA Cup semi-final (they would not repeat this feat for another 20 years). This time they faced Sheffield Wednesday in Birmingham. Garbutt headed the opener from a Satterthwaite cross but Wilson equalized for Wednesday from a free kick after Ashcroft had collided with him. Arsenal's resistance crumbled and Wednesday proceeded to the final, 3-1. Arsenal also led the League by late October, dropping only three points out of 18, but fell away in February, losing four games, and ended in seventh place.

In spite of Arsenal's relative success, they were again experiencing financial problems. The club's location was perhaps the most pressing issue. Plumstead was too far away from central London and difficult to reach by train. By 1909 Chelsea and Tottenham were also in the First Division while Fulham and Clapton (now Leyton) Orient played in the Second. These clubs' grounds were

Scotsman Phil Kelso became manager in 1904 when Arsenal finally won promotion to the top flight.

easier for the average fan to reach, and Arsenal's gates began to decline, so the club had again to sell off their better players. Kelso had resigned as manager and one of new manager George Morrell's first tasks was to oversee the departures of Ashcroft and Garbutt to Blackburn Rovers, Coleman and Freeman to Everton, Scottish centre forward Peter Kyle to Aston Villa and Jimmy Sharp to Rangers. Joe Shaw, who was to serve at Highbury in various capacities until 1956, was available to replace Sharp, but the club had lost four forwards.

New Financial Support

By the end of the 1909-10 season Arsenal were in a parlous financial state, not helped by scoring only 37 goals and avoiding relegation by two points. Then a saviour arrived in the shape of one Mr (soon to become Sir) Henry Norris, property developer, chairman of Fulham FC and Mayor of Fulham. Something of a force of nature, Norris had an irresistible personality and would not tolerate any disagreement if his mind was made up. His forceful opinions and frequent blunt rudeness could be offset by a plausible charm, should the situation demand it. There is little doubt that by buying the club he saved Arsenal from bankruptcy. He proposed to the Football League in 1910 that Arsenal amalgamate with Fulham. When this was rejected, he suggested that Arsenal share Craven Cottage. When this was also turned down, he turned his mind to the possibility of moving the club away from Plumstead.

The arrival of Alf Common in 1910 helped to generate enthusiasm among the supporters. Common, an overweight inside forward and something of a practical joker, had been the first £1,000 transfer when he was sold from Sunderland to Middlesbrough in 1905, but he was now over 30 and his first season was a poor one. In the League Arsenal started badly but improved to end in tenth place, which was also their position the following season, 1911-12. At the end of the season the skilful right half Andy Ducat, who would also represent England at cricket, had to be sold, as did centre forward Jackie Chalmers. The next season, 1912-13, was a catalogue of disasters for Arsenal. They finished in bottom spot in the First Division, five points behind Notts

George Morrell took over as manager but was to see Arsenal relegated in the 1912-13 season.

County, and won only three games, losing 23. They also went 23 games without a win between end-September and early March. The top scorer was Charlie Randall with four goals while the other 26 goals were shared among 13 players. Arsenal were relegated, and the rumour was that they only had £19 in the bank. The situation was clearly desperate.

Relegation and a New Ground

Meanwhile, Norris and his fellow director William Hall had been scouring London looking for suitable sites for the new Arsenal ground. They finally settled on land owned by St John's College of Divinity in Highbury, North London. The site, then used by the college for tennis, cricket and football, was close to public transport – several bus routes and Gillespie Road underground station – and was available. Norris entered into extended negotiations with the Ecclesiastical Commissioners, finally agreeing a 21-year lease on a six-acre site for a £20,000 fee. The deed of transfer was signed by the Archbishop of Canterbury. A condition was that no games could be played on Christmas Day or Good Friday, but this stipulation lasted only until 1925 when Arsenal bought the entire site for £64,000.

Objections were raised by a number of interested parties, principally local residents protesting about the arrival of 'undesirable elements' and by the local league clubs, Tottenham and Clapton Orient. Both clubs claimed that the new ground was too close to their own stadiums and the matter was referred to a special League Management Committee held on 13 March. The Committee found in Arsenal's favour, stating: 'In view of the fact that a considerable number of clubs in the League have changed their ground without application to, or consent from, the League, this Committee is unanimously of the opinion that they have no right to interfere with the proposal of Woolwich Arsenal to remove its ground to Gillespie Road.'

Work began on the new stadium, using mud from the newly-built Piccadilly Line for the terraces on three sides of the ground and the erection of an East Stand. The pitch had to be levelled – the north end of the pitch had to be raised by 11ft while the southern end had to be lowered by 5ft. In spite of the fact that the ground was far from ready, the first game at Highbury kicked off on 6 September 1913 against visitors Leicester Fosse. Centre forward George Jobey scored Arsenal's first goal at Highbury with a header and Andy Devine scored the club's second in a 2-1 win. During the game Jobey twisted his ankle and was carried to his lodgings on a milk cart. The team for this historic match was: Lievesley, Shaw, Fidler, Grant, Sands, McKinnon, Greenaway, Hardinge, Jobey, Devine, Winship.

The new faces this season included keeper Joseph Lievesley, England football and cricket international 'Wally' Hardinge, left back Joseph Fidler and outside right Jock Rutherford, whose superstition was always to be last on to the pitch, even once refusing the captaincy for this reason. Long-serving left half Roddy McEachrane was also replaced by Angus McKinnon, a fellow Scot. Arsenal were very unlucky not to go back to Division One in their first relegated season. On the last day they were level with Bradford in second place, well behind leaders, Notts County. Arsenal beat Glossop 2-0 while Bradford's 4-1 win over Blackpool gave the Yorkshire club promotion by 0.09 of a goal.

War was declared against Germany on 4 August 1914, but the league and FA Cup competitions continued as the general belief was that the hostilities would be concluded by Christmas. As the 1914-15 season continued, interest in football declined as the press criticized players for not enlisting. Attendances dropped dramatically and the government imposed an entertainment tax on matches, forcing players' wages down. Arsenal ended in fifth place in the Second Division. From 1915-16 until 1918-19 Arsenal competed in the London Combination, as both the League and FA Cup were discontinued for the duration of the war. Like other clubs Arsenal were forced to field 'guest' players, as most of the normal playing staff were in France or otherwise engaged in the war effort. As a tragic illustration of the situation, Bob Benson, a full back who had signed from Sheffield United in 1913, attended a game against Reading in February 1916 and volunteered to stand in for Joe Shaw who was involved in munitions work. Benson, who had not played the game for nearly a year, soon became dizzy and left the field supported by trainer George Hardy. He died in Hardy's arms in the dressing room.

At the end of the 1914-15 season George Morrell was sacked as manager as economies had to be made. Norris had put nearly £150,000 into Arsenal, the move to Highbury had cost £50,000 and more money was needed to finish the stand. When football kicked off again after World War I, in season 1919-20, Arsenal were in debt to the tune of £60,000, but the determined chairman Henry Norris was yet again to prove equal to the task before the new season began.

Chapter Two: 1919-34
Chapman Takes Over

In May 1919 Norris appointed Leslie Knighton as the new manager of Arsenal. Knighton had acquired a reputation as a resourceful man-manager at Huddersfield Town and Manchester City and Norris immediately laid down his requirements. Knighton's task was to turn Arsenal into the most successful club in the country but with scant resources. At a time when the average transfer fee was around £3,000, Knighton was forbidden to spend more than £1,000 on a single player and he would have to build the team without a scouting network. His resourcefulness and ability to spot potential were to be tested to the full.

The first step on the road to greatness was to gain promotion to Division One. The manner in which Norris achieved this still rankles with fans of Tottenham after all these years. The Football League decided to increase the number of clubs in Division One from 20 to 22 for 1919-20, the first season after the war. This meant that there was now room in the upper reaches for four Division Two clubs. Derby County and Preston North End were promoted at the end of 1914-15, so they automatically took two of the spots. Chelsea and Tottenham were relegated that season so there was a strong argument in favour of these two London clubs taking the other two places. At a meeting of the League Committee, Chelsea were unanimously voted back into Division One. They had finished second-bottom and may not have been relegated at all had a match on Good Friday 1915 between Manchester United and Liverpool not been fixed. Liverpool lost 2-0 and eight players, four from each side, were convicted of throwing the game. If Manchester United had lost, they would have gone down instead of Chelsea, so popular sentiment was with the Stamford Bridge club.

One place remained. Arsenal were in fifth place in Division Two, ahead of Birmingham City on goal average, so it seemed they had little chance of promotion ahead of Wolves in third place and Tottenham. However, utilizing his usual blend of disingenuous charm and Machiavellian manipulation, Norris adroitly canvassed all the members of the committee and, in particular, the president John McKenna to allow Arsenal the place. McKenna made a speech vigorously supporting Arsenal's promotion, based mainly on the club's long service in the League. Wolves had been in the League seven years longer than Arsenal, and had finished above them in Division Two, but for some inexplicable reason this did not appear to afford them primacy. When the votes were counted, Arsenal led the list with 18 while

Tottenham, whom logic might suggest would have the stronger case for promotion, could only muster eight. What happened behind the scenes to sway the committee, and particularly McKenna, remains to this day a mystery, but the result was a triumph for Norris and Division One football for Arsenal.

Knighton now had to construct a team capable of remaining there. Of the pre-war old guard, Angus McKinnon, Jock Rutherford and Joe Shaw were still in place. Billy Blyth, a Scot who could play in the inside forward and wing half positions, had joined the club in 1914. Knighton, denied the resources of other clubs, had to use persuasion and guile to attract players. He signed Alf 'Doughie' Baker, a utility player who played in every position except goal in his 12 seasons with the club, by meeting him at the pithead after his shift at Ilkeston colliery while representatives of Sunderland and Aston Villa awaited Baker at his home. Tom Whittaker, a half back and qualified engineer who was to become a great servant of the club as trainer and manager, also joined that first season, as did outside left Joe Toner from Belfast United and small centre forward Henry White from Brentford. Arsenal finished in tenth place in the League that season, a creditable position given the severe constraints on Knighton.

Knighton Brings in New Players

Knighton continued to cajole and convince players of the virtues of joining Arsenal and over the following two seasons signed outside left Jimmy Paterson, a doctor with a practice in Clapton, Northeast London, who had enjoyed a distinguished career with Rangers and Queen's Park; Reg Boreham, an amateur inside left from Wycombe Wanderers; Billy Milne, a Scottish wing half who would become Arsenal's first-team trainer in 1947; Irish full backs Andy Kennedy and Alex Mackie (Mackie, something of an eccentric, spent his first £5 weekly wage packet on a pet monkey); and Bob John, a half back from Caerphilly, whom Knighton snatched from under the nose of an unhappy Cardiff City and who would make 421 league appearances for Arsenal until his retirement in 1937. Although they made ninth place in Division One in 1920-21, in 1921-22 they were 17th in the League. This was the only season under Knighton's management that Arsenal progressed further than the second round of the FA Cup, when they played Preston North End away in a fourth round replay and lost 2-1 after extra-time.

In 1922-23 Arsenal's 11th position in the League was largely due to the goals of Scotsman Bob Turnbull who had joined the club as a full back but was converted by Knighton to centre forward. His total of 20 included nine in four games between Christmas and New Year. The following season Arsenal crashed to 19th in the League, two spots away from relegation and one point ahead of relegated Chelsea. Even the signing of Welsh centre forward Jimmy Brain, who

Manager Leslie Knighton was given few resources to make Arsenal a title-winning side and he was unable to bring the club success in Division One.

would score 125 league goals in his seven years at the club, did not lift the gloom around Highbury.

Norris was becoming concerned, not only about his financial investment in the club but also about the poor performances on the pitch. The team, although containing quality players, seemed to lack confidence and to play as 11 individuals rather than as a unit. Under Knighton the 'goals against' column had exceeded the 'goals for' column in every season and the players seemed to capitulate too easily to adversity, lacking the stomach for a fight. It appeared that Knighton's days in charge were numbered. Knighton had not helped his cause by ignoring Norris' instruction that no player should be acquired if he was under 5ft 8in or weighed less than 11 stone. He had spotted a highly skilful, 5ft tall winger, 'Midget' Moffat, playing for Workington and signed him when Norris was holidaying in France. When Norris returned, Moffat was sold to Luton Town.

Season 1924-25 was even worse, with Arsenal ending up third from bottom in the League, although seven points clear of second bottom Preston North End, and again failing in the FA Cup. They played West Ham in the first round of the Cup and, before the game, Knighton was approached by a doctor who suggested that he give his players some pep pills. Assured that they were not harmful, Knighton took them from the doctor and handed them to the players an hour before kickoff. The game was abandoned due to fog. The players complained about the unpleasant taste, excessive thirst and too much unfocused energy. Phil Soar and Martin Tyler's *Official History of Arsenal* quotes Knighton as saying, 'Getting the boys back to Highbury that afternoon was like trying to drive a flock of lively lions.' The pills came out again for the replay but the fog again rolled in and the effects were the same. The players reluctantly took the pills for a third time before the next match. West Ham controlled the first half, but when the pills kicked in, Arsenal went on the rampage but couldn't score. For the next replay, the players refused the pills and the game ended 2-2, both goals coming from Jimmy Brain. West Ham won the decider at Stamford Bridge 1-0.

Towards the end of the 1924-25 season Knighton was dismissed. Although Knighton had managed to keep Arsenal in Division One, his lack of success in

Jimmy Brain was Arsenal's most productive striker of the 1920s and stayed long enough to pick up a championship medal in 1931.

bringing trophies to Highbury had persuaded Norris that Arsenal needed a change of manager. Knighton's Arsenal career had not been helped by Norris's transfer policy (Norris had twice tried to convince the League that there should be a general transfer ceiling of £1,650) but he had failed to weld a collection of reasonably talented players into a cohesive team and paid the price.

Norris placed an advert in the *Athletic News*, 11 May 1925, which stated: 'Arsenal Football Club is open to receive applications for the position of Team Manager. He must be experienced and possess the highest qualifications for the post, both as to ability and personal character.' The job, however, had already been offered to and accepted by Herbert Chapman who was to revolutionize football and take Arsenal to heights which Norris and the club could at the time barely imagine.

Herbert Chapman Arrives

A stocky, ruddy-faced, seemingly unprepossessing character, Chapman can nonetheless be regarded as one of the greatest managers in football history and in many ways he invented the modern game. During his nine years at Highbury he turned a dormant, failing club into one of the best sides in the world, through a combination of steely resolve, determination, tactical insight, commercial nous and astute man-management. He commanded the utmost respect from his players and the staff at Highbury and he was a true footballing innovator.

An engineer by training, Chapman had a relatively undistinguished playing career as an inside forward – the only things that stood out about him on the pitch were the yellow football boots he wore – and he played for ten clubs before taking over at Northampton Town in 1907. He achieved promotion the following season and eventually moved to Leeds City in 1912 where he reinvigorated the club. Following an FA investigation into alleged illegal payments to players, Leeds City were liquidated in 1919 and Chapman suspended, although there is little evidence that he was personally involved in any shenanigans. He came back to football in 1921 as manager of Huddersfield Town. The Yorkshire club had reached the FA Cup final in 1920, but were beaten by Aston Villa, and Chapman was in charge when Huddersfield won the Division One title two years in succession, 1923-24 and 1924-25. He was approached by Norris in April 1925 and signed in May for the princely sum of £2,000 per annum.

When Chapman took over at Arsenal, he was aware that, with its populous and relatively prosperous hinterland, the club could become one of the giants of the game. However, he had to find the players to help him achieve his grand ambitions. One such was Charlie Buchan, a star inside forward of the era. He had played a few games for Woolwich Arsenal as an amateur youth but walked out of the club when manager George Morrell refused to pay him 11 shillings which Buchan claimed he was owed in expenses. Buchan joined Orient and then Sunderland for £1,000. A tall, strong player with a silken touch on the ball and particularly effective in the air, Buchan was England captain and had scored over 200 goals for Sunderland. Shortly after taking over at Highbury Chapman walked into Buchan's sports shop in Sunderland (this being the days of the maximum wage, players often augmented their salaries in other ways) and proclaimed: 'I've come to sign you for Arsenal.' Sunderland demanded £4,000 for their star player, but Henry Norris balked at this, pointing out that Buchan was 33 years old. An intriguing compromise was reached whereby Arsenal were to pay £2,000 plus £100 for every goal Buchan scored in his first season – he scored 20 league and cup goals in his first season so Sunderland got their money.

Another newcomer was Bill Harper, a Scottish international keeper from Hibs, for £5,000. Something of a showman on the pitch with his daring saves and athletic leaps, Harper was particularly known for the distance he could kick a ball. As ex-heavyweight champion in the Scots Guards, he could also look after himself in those days of thundering tackles and crunching shoulder charges. Chapman then moved Jimmy Brain to centre forward, where in the forthcoming season he would break the club scoring record with 34 goals, and switched Billy Blyth to left half, teaming him up in the half back line with Alf Baker and Jack Butler.

At the beginning of Chapman's first season the offside law had been changed – there now had to be only two defenders between attacker and goal when the ball was kicked, rather than three. The old system had become stultifying, with often 40 stoppages for offside per game, and some teams, in particular Newcastle United whose centre half Bill McCracken was a prime exponent, perfected the offside trap. A story tells of a visiting team drawing into Newcastle station and the guard blowing his whistle. 'Blimey. Offside already,' cracked a player. This season was to see an increase in the number of goals – at the rate of a goal a match – and fewer stoppages and crowd numbers increased. On the opening day of the season Aston Villa put ten past Burnley, setting the trend for the remainder of the campaign.

Unlike today, the centre half then was normally an attacking player who left defence to the full backs. After being crushed 7-0 away by Newcastle, Arsenal began to rethink this role. *The Times* noted: 'Hitherto The Arsenal have owed most to their defenders but the Newcastle United forwards played at such a speed and, moreover, were so exact in their placing of the ball that weaknesses that had not been suspected appeared.' To remove these 'weaknesses' Buchan, in particular, argued for the centre half to become a defender and to link up with the full backs in defence (what became known as the 'stopper' system) in order to stem the flood of goals after the offside change. This would require an inside forward to drop back to provide the link between defence and attack and also the full backs to move wide to force the opposing wingers to stay on the wing and not cut inside. This was effectively the end of the old 2-3-5 system and its replacement by 3-3-4, later to be refined to more of a 3-4-3 formation. Chapman was persuaded by Buchan's arguments and tried the system the following Monday at Upton Park with Scotsman Andrew Neil playing the role of midfield creator and provider. Arsenal beat West Ham 4-0 and the new tactics appeared to work. The results improved as Chapman's first season went on.

In February 1926 he bought Joe Hulme from Blackburn. Hulme, an outside right, was reputed to be the fastest player in British football and he also had a ferocious shot. He was to be a critical component in the all-conquering side which the manager was assembling. By the end of the campaign Arsenal finished second in Division One, behind Huddersfield who had won the title for the third year in succession. Arsenal's tally of 52 points was their highest ever and also the highest ever for a London club. They had also enjoyed their best FA Cup run since 1906-07, defeating Wolves, Blackburn and Aston Villa before falling 2-1 to Swansea in the sixth round. The club announced a record profit of £6,500. Chapman's first season in charge had been a successful one.

The following season Arsenal could only achieve a mid-table place. Chapman continued with his team building and bought Tom Parker from Southampton as his new right back and, the following season, his captain. Parker was an intelligent reader of the game and had good positional sense. To fill the left wing slot, Chapman acquired Charlie Jones from Nottingham Forest. Jones was later moved to right half. Jack Lambert, a big, bustling centre forward, arrived from Doncaster Rovers and he was to score nearly 100 league goals in his eight years with the club. Buchan and Chapman had agreed that Jack Butler, although a skilful player, was by nature and experience an attacking centre half and, as such, not ideally suited to the new 'stopper' system. To bring solidity and consistency to the centre of defence Chapman paid Oswestry £200 in December for the tall, red-haired Herbie Roberts. Although not as

Charlie Buchan was Chapman's first signing and became his inspirational leader on the pitch.

comfortable on the ball as Butler and unable to kick the ball very hard, Roberts was happy to remain in defence and he was highly effective in the air. Although it took him a couple of seasons to supplant Butler, 'Copper' Roberts would be at the heart of the defence throughout the great years of the 1930s. Welsh international Dan Lewis, who joined Arsenal from Clapton Orient in 1924, had largely taken over from Harper in goal during the season.

Although their final league position was poor, season 1926-27 was all about the FA Cup. In the third round, they beat Sheffield United 3-2, the winner coming from a splendid Hulme strike in their first win at Bramall Lane for 20 years. Port Vale were next and, although Parker scored an own goal and gave away a penalty, Buchan and a last-minute Brain goal ensured a 2-2 draw. Buchan scored the only goal in the Highbury replay. The fifth round saw Liverpool lose 2-0 at Highbury, Buchan and Brain again the scorers. Butler opened the scoring against Wolves at Highbury in the sixth round with a wind-assisted header from outside the box and Blyth scored another in the 2-1 win. In the semi-final at Stamford Bridge, only the third semi-final in Arsenal's history, Buchan scored the winner in their 2-1 victory over Southampton and Arsenal were in the final for the first time.

The First FA Cup Final

Their opponents were Cardiff City, who had lost 1-0 to Sheffield United in the final two years before. Cardiff had eight internationals in their team and the game was officiated by a referee resplendent in a natty black sports jacket and matching black bow-tie. In a ragged, disjointed encounter played on a greasy pitch, Arsenal had most of the game, winning all eight corners, although the match was dominated by the two defences. In the 73rd minute, Cardiff centre forward Hugh Ferguson attempted a speculative shot. Keeper Lewis dropped on his right knee to block the ball but it slipped out of his grip. In attempting frantically to pull the ball back, Lewis knocked it over the line with his elbow, and Cardiff were one up, which remained the score till the final whistle.

Under the heading 'A Tragic Blunder' *The Times* reported: 'a heart-rending moment for the goalkeeper and the helpless back alongside – not to mention the rest of the Arsenal team'. After the game, a distraught Lewis threw his medal on to the ground but it was handed back to him by Bob John. The goal was blamed on a combination of the ball being polished by the lush Wembley turf and Lewis's shiny new jersey. For the 1930 final, keeper Charlie Preedy wore an unwashed jersey, an Arsenal tradition which continued in finals up to the 1950s. The 1927 final was the first to be broadcast live on radio and was also the only time that the Cup left England.

This season 29-year-old Tom Whittaker had been appointed first-team trainer after George Hardy had made the mistake of shouting tactical instructions to the players in a game against Port Vale. Chapman took exception to Hardy usurping his authority and he was relegated to the reserves. Whittaker was to become one of the country's top physiotherapists. After an accident had ended his playing career in 1925 Whittaker studied anatomy, massage and advanced methods of treating injuries, including electrical treatment and sunray lamps. A modest, popular man, he worked hard to ensure players were at the peak of their fitness and his services were sought by sportsmen across the country. Cliff Bastin, soon to become a Highbury legend, remarked, 'Men who under other hands would have remained on the injured list for three or four weeks, Tom would have fit again in three or four days.' When young left back Eddie Hapgood joined the club in 1927, it was noticed that he would become dizzy after heading the wet, heavy ball of the time and would occasionally faint. Whittaker found out he was a vegetarian and immediately forced him to eat meat. Hapgood's heading confidence improved. The elegant, two-footed defender was to become one of English football's finest ever full backs and made over 400 appearances in his 11-year career at Highbury.

Season 1927-28 was not a particularly memorable one with Arsenal finishing tenth in the League, although they did again reach the FA Cup semi-final, beating West Bromwich Albion, Everton, Aston Villa and Stoke City before being eliminated 1-0 by Blackburn. The last league game of the season was against Everton at Goodison. 'Dixie' Dean needed to score three if he was to beat George Camsell's record of 59 league goals set the previous season. Dean got his hat-trick and achieved the record, which still stands today. Although Arsenal's new defensive system was in place, they let in 86 league goals over the season, scoring 82.

At the end of the season, the massively influential Charlie Buchan retired to take over as sports correspondent for the *News Chronicle*. Chapman now had to face the problem of who would replace his talisman. One of the biggest names in English football was David Jack, a tall, elegant, if rather aloof

England international inside forward who played for Bolton Wanderers. He scored the first-ever goal at Wembley in Bolton's win over West Ham in the 'White Horse' final of 1923 and he picked up another winner's medal in 1926. Chapman enquired after Jack's availability and was told he was not for sale, although Bolton eventually settled on £11,500, almost twice the existing transfer record. Bob Wall, Chapman's young, newly-appointed personal assistant, tells the story in his book *Arsenal From The Heart* of their meeting with Bolton officials at London's Euston Hotel: 'We arrived at the hotel half an hour early. Chapman immediately went into the lounge bar. He called the waiter, placed two pound notes in his hand and said, "George, this is Mr Wall, my assistant. We shall be joined by guests. They will drink whatever they like. See that our guests are given double of everything but Mr Wall's whisky and dry ginger will contain no whisky and my gin and tonic will contain no gin."' Chapman's ruse worked, as the deal was done with the increasingly inebriated Bolton contingent for £11,500, the first five-figure transfer, and Jack became an Arsenal player. Chapman said to Wall, 'Well, that's your first lesson in football. You now know how to conduct a transfer.'

By now, Arsenal were becoming known as 'The Bank of England' club with critics accusing them of trying to buy success, a far cry from the restrictive transfer policy of earlier years. Norris, meanwhile, had been forced out of football in February after he lost a libel action against the FA who had accused him of financial irregularities. His role as chairman of the club was taken over by Sir Samuel Hill-Wood and the man who had the vision to hire Chapman died in 1934.

Arsenal's high spending policy, however, had still not been translated into success on the pitch. Although Jack scored 25 league goals in 1928-29, the club ended in ninth position in the League, but they reached the sixth round of the FA Cup, losing 1-0 to Aston Villa. On his appointment as manager Chapman had predicted that it would take him five years to mould Arsenal into a dominant side. As ever, the manager was to be proved correct in his assessment. He was about to put into place the final pieces of his masterplan with the acquisition of the little

David Jack, a celebrated England international, was brought to Highbury for a record fee.

Scottish footballing genius, Alex James, and the young goalscoring winger, Cliff 'Boy' Bastin. Arsenal were about to enter the most glorious era in their history.

The Glory Years Begin

Chapman had gone to watch a Third Division South match between Watford and Exeter City in May 1929 to watch a player named Barnett. However, he was more impressed by the skill, control and speed of a young Exeter City inside forward, 16-year-old Cliff Bastin, and travelled to Devon to sign him up for Arsenal. At first the youngster was reluctant to make such a dramatic move, partly because he did not want to jeopardize his benefit at Exeter, but he eventually agreed. He was struck by Chapman's jovial but determined presence, saying, 'There was an aura of greatness about Chapman. I was impressed by him straight away.' The commissionaire at Highbury refused to let him into the stadium on his arrival, suspecting he was a young fan searching for autographs, and Joe Shaw had to come up from the dressing room to vouch for Bastin's credentials. He made his debut for the club against Everton in October and, although rested for a number of games, scored his debut goal against Sheffield Wednesday in January 1930. Chapman had demonstrated his prescience by moving Bastin from inside left to the left wing, a position in which Bastin had not played since he was nine years old but in which he was to revel over the coming years. He ended his first season with 21 league appearances and seven goals.

Bastin had been capped by England Schoolboys at the tender age of 14 and he possessed prodigious talent. He had electric pace, an ice-cool temperament and a tactically astute brain which, combined with his immaculate passing skills and his predatory eye for goal, made him the complete forward. He was to hold the Arsenal all-time goalscoring record (176) until overtaken by Ian Wright in the late 1990s.

A month after Chapman's capture of the young winger, Bastin was joined in the Arsenal forward line by Alex James. James was one of the legends of British football, having been orchestrator of the 'Wembley Wizards' Scottish team which thrashed England 5-1 the previous year. He joined Preston North End from Raith Rovers in 1925 and had scored over 60 goals for the Lancashire side (the team was described as 'Alex James and ten others'). To the surprise of many, including the Football League who held an inquiry, James was transferred to Arsenal for the relatively low sum of £8,750 and Chapman's arrangement of a job in Selfridge's may have influenced the Scottish playmaker's decision to move south. James was short, pugnaciously self-confident and a sublime dribbler and passer of the ball as well as an effective finisher, and he was about to become

50 Greatest Players

CHARLIE BUCHAN Inside right

Born: Plumstead, 22 September 1891

Joined Arsenal: 1925   **From:** Sunderland

Debut: 29 August 1925 v Tottenham Hotspur, League

Appearances: 120   **Goals:** 56

Left Arsenal: 1928 (retired)

Charlie Buchan was Herbert Chapman's first signing for Arsenal. The fee was £2,000 plus £100 for every goal he scored in his first season. This novel arrangement ensured that Buchan, and Arsenal, were rarely out of the headlines, as he netted 20 times. The long-striding Buchan was a subtle, creative player and a prolific scorer. He was also club captain and Chapman's leader on the pitch. Ironically, Buchan had joined Woolwich Arsenal in 1909 as an amateur but never played a senior game for them. He left after a row over expenses, moving via Leyton to a glittering career with Sunderland, with whom he earned a championship medal and six England caps.

the heart of the Arsenal side which swept all before it in the 1930s. James's role with Arsenal was not to score goals but to act as the critical link between attack and defence. He did take time to settle into this new system at Arsenal who, in spite of their recent signings, ended the 1929-30 season in 14th place in Division One with their expensively assembled strike force scoring only 78 goals.

The FA Cup, though, was a different matter. In January 1930 the Gunners, as they were increasingly becoming known, entertained Chelsea in the third round. Bastin and Lambert scored in the 2-0 victory. James was coming under criticism from the Highbury crowd and, in James's interests, Chapman had dropped him in favour of Len Thompson. He was still out of the team for the fourth round tie against Birmingham, who managed a 2-2 draw at Highbury. The Saturday before the replay, Chapman woke up James, who had been confined to bed by the club doctor, and said, 'Get up, Alex. You're coming to Highbury to train. You're going to win the match for us.' James played and, with his confidence restored, was soon back to peak form. As Chapman said, 'He has justified every hope and expectation.' An Alf Baker penalty was the only score at St Andrews. They then met Middlesbrough, Lambert and Bastin scoring one apiece in a 2-0 win at Ayresome Park. The Gunners then beat West Ham 3-0 (Lambert 2 and Baker) in the sixth round at Upton Park.

Hull City, then bottom of the Second Division, were to provide the opposition in the semi-final, seemingly an easy tie for the London side. However, after only

15 minutes at Elland Road a fluffed clearance from keeper Dan Lewis was volleyed back over his head by Hull's Howieson into the net. On the half hour Eddie Hapgood conceded an own goal. Arsenal piled on the pressure in the second half to no avail until, in the 70th minute, Jack pulled a goal back from a Hulme cross. With only seven minutes left, Bastin ran onto a ball from James and equalized. In the replay Joey Williams, replacing the injured Hulme, crossed for Jack to volley the only goal of the match and Arsenal were back at Wembley to play Huddersfield Town, with seven internationals in the Yorkshire club's side. Two weeks before the final, Arsenal beat Sheffield Wednesday 8-1, their biggest win to date in Division One, and then drew 6-6 with Leicester City. The recent signing from Sunderland, centre forward David Halliday, scored four goals in the Leicester game but this display was still not enough for him to replace Jack Lambert in the striker's position.

A Trophy at Last

The 1930 FA Cup final, remembered for the appearance overhead of the *Graf Zeppelin*, saw Arsenal win their first major trophy. Man of the match was Alex James, with *The Times* stating: 'The Arsenal won the match because they had an inside forward (James) who could develop the attack and press it home to the utmost.' The *Daily Mail* agreed, running the headline 'James the Master Player'.

Chapman's tactics had been vindicated, but so much depended on Alex James, the small, exuberant figure in the over-sized shorts sweeping crossfield passes out to Hulme and short, accurate balls to Bastin on his left. Both wingers ('the flying columns') would cut in and shoot, with Lambert also on hand to convert and to pick up anything loose. James was the pivot of Chapman's system and the audacious little Scotsman was becoming the darling of the Arsenal crowd. Although many opposing fans found their style of play 'boring', and the system essentially was a defensive one, their speed on the counter-attack was breathtaking and their goalscoring was ruthless. Chapman was fond of saying 'you can attack too long' and believed that, by inviting the opposition to attack, space was created for a breakaway through James and Arsenal's raiding forwards. In his book *Herbert Chapman on Football*, the manager wrote: 'It is impossible to divorce defence from attack. One is as important as the other,' and his ideal was 'seven men in attack and eight in defence'.

The manager held regular Friday meetings with his players, discussing his tactics and footballing philosophy and demonstrating moves on a magnetic table top. The players were encouraged to air their views on tactics and a strong camaraderie was developing in the side. As Chapman said, 'It is no use for a

Great Matches

FA CUP FINAL **Wembley, 26 April 1930**

Arsenal 2   **Huddersfield Town 0**   **Attendance: 92,486**
James
Lambert

The 1930 FA Cup final was the first final in which the teams emerged from the
tunnel side-by-side. It is remembered as the 'Zeppelin Final', when the menacing
Graf Zeppelin floated over the pitch and tipped its nose in salute to George V,
who raised his hat. It is also recalled for a splendid piece of opportunism from
Alex James. In the 17th minute James took a quick free kick while still bent
over the ball, the ball finding Bastin. In a tactic agreed before the match,
Bastin sped off down the wing, passed the ball back to James who scored in
the corner of the net. Huddersfield, stung by this impertinence, went on the
attack. Charlie Preedy, in goal for the injured Lewis, caused nervous moments
for his defence by continually advancing from his line. Bastin later noted, 'To call his display
erratic would be a miserable understatement.' However, with seven minutes remaining, a
long clearance from James in the besieged Arsenal half found Lambert in the centre circle.
The big centre forward turned two defenders, ran half the length of the pitch and scored
from the edge of the area past the out-of-position Huddersfield keeper Turner. Lambert ran
back to his own half to celebrate with his team-mates. Captain Tom Parker picked up the
cup from the King and both sides shared the banquet and celebrations that evening.

Arsenal: Preedy, Parker, Hapgood, Baker, Seddon, John, Hulme, Jack, Lambert, James, Bastin

Huddersfield Town: Turner, Goodall, Spence, Naylor, Wilson, Campbell, Jackson, Kelly,
Davies, Raw, Smith

Referee: T. Crew

*Top: Arsenal captain
Tom Parker carrying
the trophy. Left:
FA Cup winners 1930,
l-r: back – Baker,
Lambert, Preedy,
Seddon, Hapgood,
John; middle –
Chapman, Jack,
Parker, James,
Whittaker; front –
Hulme, Bastin.*

manager to do all the talking. Every man should be encouraged to talk and express his views without a fear that he will hurt anyone's feelings. I am always looking for new ideas. I would borrow one from a programme boy at Highbury if it were a good one.' With his talented squad now psychologically attuned to Chapman's positive philosophy, the coming season was to be the most successful one so far in the club's history.

Brimming with confidence and self belief, Arsenal roared into season 1930-31, unbeaten in their first nine games before slipping up against Derby County away in October. By early November Aston Villa were on top on goal average but Arsenal went top on the eighth of the month after an emphatic 5-2 win over Villa at Highbury, the scorers being Bastin (2), Jack (2) and Lambert. They were now scoring freely. One-nil down with 30 minutes remaining against Chelsea in late November at Stamford Bridge, Arsenal demonstrated their determination and resilience by scoring five without further reply, three coming from Jack. A 7-1 win over Blackpool at Highbury over Christmas, Jack and Brain both scoring hat-tricks, was followed by a 9-1 rout of Grimsby Town in January, with Jack netting four and Lambert claiming a hat-trick. Young left half George Male made his debut in the Blackpool match.

The goals continued to flow in February when Lambert scored another three in the 7-2 defeat of Leicester and it was Bastin's turn for the match ball

50 Greatest Players

JIMMY BRAIN Centre forward

Born: Bristol, 11 September 1900

Joined Arsenal: 1923   **From:** Ton Pentre

Debut: 25 October 1924 v Tottenham Hotspur, League

Appearances: 231   **Goals:** 139

Left Arsenal: 1931   **For:** Tottenham Hotspur

Honours won with Arsenal: Division One championship 1931

Jimmy Brain was Arsenal's most lethal striker of the 1920s. A coal miner before turning professional with South Wales club Ton Pentre, he had previously been on Cardiff City's books as an amateur. Leslie Knighton signed him for Arsenal in August 1923. Brain finished top scorer in four of the next five seasons after breaking into the team in 1924. He set a club record with 34 league goals in 1925-26, netted 31 in the following campaign and 25 in 1927-28, forming a formidable partnership with Charlie Buchan. Brain lost his place to Jack Lambert at the end of the 1929-30 season, though he started 16 league games in the 1930-31 title success. He went on to play for Tottenham, Swansea and Bristol City and later managed Cheltenham Town.

Pre-season training before the 1930-31 campaign when Arsenal won their historic first title. The line-up includes: Preedy, Parker, Hapgood, Baker, Seddon, John, Hulme, Jack, Lambert, James, Bastin and (centre front), Tom Whittaker.

after the 6-3 win over Derby County the following week. The team's pride was dented in mid-March in Birmingham when Jack scored a consolation goal in their 5-1 defeat by Aston Villa, seeking revenge for the Highbury encounter in November. They won seven of their last nine games, drawing the other two, and the league title was secured at Highbury with two games to go. Liverpool were the visitors and Roberts betrayed his nerves by slicing a cross into his own net after only two minutes. However, Lambert equalized and then Jack and Bastin made the final score 3-1. Arsenal were now seven points ahead of Aston Villa and were champions of Division One for the first time in their history.

First-time Champions

The statistics for this magnificent season make remarkable reading. This was the first time that the league title came south, breaking the stranglehold of the northern and Midland clubs. Arsenal ran up a record 66 points out of a possible 84 and suffered only four defeats in 42 games. They scored 127 goals which would have been a record had not Aston Villa, seven points behind, scored one more. Their tally of 60 away goals, however, was a record as were the 33 away points they acquired. They failed to score in only one game and in 17 games they scored four or more. Also, Jack Lambert set a new club scoring record with 38 goals. Boring Arsenal? Hardly.

Their FA Cup run was less glorious. They squeezed past Villa 3-1 in a third round replay, with Lambert's second goal bursting the ball, but were knocked out in the next round 2-1 by Chelsea. But, with Chapman's seemingly unstoppable team firm in defence, creative in midfield and lethal in attack, who would bet against both trophies coming to Highbury in season 1931-32? The

50 Greatest Players

DAVID JACK Inside right

Born: Bolton, 3 April 1899

Joined Arsenal: 1928   **From:** Bolton Wanderers

Debut: 20 October 1928 v Newcastle United, League

Appearances: 206   **Goals:** 123

Left Arsenal: 1934   **For:** Southend United (manager)

Honours won with Arsenal: Division One championship 1931, 1933, 1934;

FA Cup winner 1930; 5 England caps

Arsenal smashed the British transfer record to sign David Jack to Highbury in October 1928. Herbert Chapman had earmarked the £11,500 inside forward to fill the gap left by Charlie Buchan's departure. Jack had already gained two FA Cup winner's medals with Bolton, scoring the first-ever goal in a Wembley final in 1923. Jack was a brilliant dribbler and clinical finisher. He was top scorer with 25 league goals in his first season at Highbury and weighed in with 31 as the Gunners won the championship two years later. He was also the first Arsenal player to captain England. He left Highbury at the age of 35 to go into management with Southend. He spent later spells in charge at Middlesbrough and Dublin club Shelbourne.

'Double' had only been won twice – by Preston in 1888-89 and Aston Villa in 1896-97 – and Chapman was determined that Arsenal would be the third.

However, Arsenal began badly in season 1931-32. They lost their first game at home 1-0 against newly-promoted West Bromwich Albion and did not win until the fifth match. Results were patchy and, having lost three games in succession over the Christmas period, they were five points behind leaders Everton. They now had a new keeper, Frank Moss, who was reserve goalkeeper at Oldham when he was spotted by Chapman who acquired him for £3,000. A brave, agile player, he took over in November from Harper who moved to Plymouth Argyle.

Arsenal were faring better in the FA Cup. They disposed of Lancashire Combination side Darwen 11-1 in the third round and then defeated Plymouth and Portsmouth to face Huddersfield in the sixth round. In the second minute the unlikely figure of centre half Herbie Roberts headed in the only goal of the game. In the semi-final at Villa Park, the Arsenal defence held out bravely against a sprightly Manchester City attack until, in the last minute with Chapman already planning tactics for the replay, Bastin crossed to Lambert who hooked the ball from the by-line to a waiting Bastin who made the result 1-0 with a low shot. They were to meet Newcastle United in the final on 23 April.

In the League the situation had improved somewhat and, by the time they played West Ham at the end of March, they were only three points behind Everton. Disaster struck at Upton Park when Alex James collided with West Ham's big centre half Jim Barrett in the second minute and badly damaged his ligaments. Chapman had James back at Highbury for Tom Whittaker's attention before the game ended. Without James, Arsenal won only one of their next five games before the Cup final. The day before the game James had a fitness test at the Brighton training camp. Although he appeared back to normal, Whittaker tackled him strongly just to be sure and James winced in pain. The Scottish maestro would not appear in the next day's final.

Chapman had to make changes because of his playmaker's unavailability. Bastin was moved back to inside left and George Male was brought in at left half, his first appearance in the FA Cup. Arsenal went ahead in the 11th minute when John headed in a loose ball. On the stroke of half-time, Newcastle centre half Davison sent a long ball up the wing for Jimmy Richardson to chase. As the ball appeared to go over the by-line, the Arsenal defence relaxed and began to turn away. However, Richardson hooked the ball into the centre, Jack Allen

---

50 Greatest Players

TOM PARKER Right back

Born: Woolston, Hampshire, 19 November 1897

Joined Arsenal: 1926   **From:** Southampton

Debut: 3 April 1926 v Blackburn Rovers, League

Appearances: 292   **Goals:** 17

Left Arsenal: 1933   **For:** Norwich City (manager)

Honours won with Arsenal: Division One championship 1931;

FA Cup winner 1930

Tom Parker was another of Herbert Chapman's early signings and one of the most consistent. He was ever-present during his first three full seasons and played 155 consecutive games between April 1926 and December 1929. He succeeded Charlie Buchan as skipper and lifted Arsenal's first major trophy when they won the FA Cup in 1930. He also captained the Gunners' first title-winning side the following year. Parker was noted as a sound defender with a cool head and shrewd positional sense. He was a deadly accurate penalty taker too. He left Highbury in March 1933 to manage Norwich and rejoined Southampton as boss in 1937. He had another spell in charge at Norwich before finishing his football career as Southampton's chief scout.

put it in the net and the referee awarded a goal. The Arsenal players looked astonished but sportingly did not appeal. Newsreel pictures later confirmed that the whole of the ball had gone over the line before Richardson's foot connected with it. Buoyed by their good fortune, Newcastle went on the attack in the second half and Allen wrapped it up for the Geordies with a second goal.

In the League, although Arsenal took seven points from their last four games, Everton became champions by two points. In a season which had promised so much Arsenal came away with nothing. In his book *Forward Arsenal*, Bernard Joy suggests the reason for their failure to retain the league title was over-confidence, in that they had too many players, including wing halves, in attack and left too much space in midfield for the opposition to exploit. In the latter part of the season, the absence of James was also a problem. Arsenal were to learn from their mistakes and were to become unquestionably the dominant force in the land over the next three seasons.

The Titles Keep Coming

Chapman had by now stamped his authority and personality on Arsenal and to most observers he was the club. As well as his tactical insights, in his thinking he was far ahead of most others in the game. His enthusiasm for shirt numbers (which he introduced against Liverpool in 1928 until told to desist by the Football League, but which were made compulsory in 1939) and floodlit games; his advocacy of a 10-yard penalty semi-circle, his appeal for goal judges and two referees and his desire so see more clubs promoted and relegated, all mark him out as an innovator. He also suggested the creation of a full-time national team manager, with full powers of selection, a role which would not be filled in England until the appointment of Alf Ramsey in 1963.

He was also active off the pitch. He oversaw the development of increased banking at the North Bank in 1931 where, in the course of construction, a horse and cart had fallen into a hole. The horse was destroyed and its remains left where they lay. A new West Stand was built, designed by Claude Waterlow Ferrier. Previously uncovered terracing, the west side of the ground was transformed into the most advanced grandstand in England, with seating for 4,000 and standing room for a further 17,000, at a cost of £50,000. It was opened in December 1932. He also commissioned a 12ft diameter 45-minute clock to be erected on the North Bank. When the FA objected, he changed it to a 60-minute timepiece. It was transferred to the south of the ground in 1935, hence the Clock End. And perhaps his greatest publicity coup lay in persuading London Transport (or London Electric Railway as it was then known) to change the name of Gillespie Road station on the Piccadilly Line, just behind the North Bank, to Arsenal. It

50 Greatest Players

JACK LAMBERT Centre forward

Born: Rotherham, 22 May 1902

Joined Arsenal: 1926   **From:** Doncaster Rovers

Debut: 6 September 1926 v Bolton Wanderers, League

Appearances: 159   **Goals:** 109

Left Arsenal: 1933   **For:** Fulham

Honours won with Arsenal: Division One championship 1931;
FA Cup winner 1930

Jack Lambert was one of Arsenal's most wholehearted strikers, a physically powerful and determined finisher who complemented the skilful players around him. Herbert Chapman signed him for £2,500 from Doncaster in the summer of 1926. He made his big breakthrough in the 1929-30 season, beating off competition from Jimmy Brain and Dave Halliday to establish himself and score the second goal in the Gunners' FA Cup final win over Huddersfield. He set a club record of 38 league goals the next year as Arsenal won the championship. He added 26 more in 1931-32 but lost his place to Ernie Coleman the following season. He had a brief spell with Fulham before retiring. He returned to Arsenal to manage the 'nursery' team at Margate.

was opened on 5 November 1932, and Arsenal celebrated by beating Wolves 7-1 at Molineux, the goals coming from his celebrated stars, Lambert, Jack and Bastin.

Chapman had every reason to face season 1932-33 with optimism. Alex James was fully back from injury and Chapman had found a new centre forward – Ernie Coleman, from Grimsby – to cover for and perhaps replace Jack Lambert. Tall, graceful full back Leslie Compton had also joined in April, making his debut in place of Tom Parker at the away draw with Aston Villa. Compton was to become a dependable stand-in right back over the next few years. Early in the season Chapman called in left half George Male and announced, 'George, you're going to be a right back.' An astonished Male tried to argue but Chapman had made his mind up. Later, Male recounted, 'By the time Chapman was finished with me I was convinced that I was not merely a full back but the best in the country.' He was to establish a brilliant full back partnership with Eddie Hapgood for Arsenal and England, for whom they played together on 14 occasions. Parker was to play only five games in 1932-33 before giving way to Male and retiring to become manager of Norwich in March.

The team that won the 1932-33 championship, l-r: back row – Male, Les Compton, Moss, Roberts, Hapgood; front row – Hulme, Jack, Stockill, James, Bastin, John.

Although their average age was nearly 30, the rest of Chapman's team were fit and raring for another assault on the league title. However, in their first home game of the season they again lost to West Bromwich Albion but held their nerve to produce a 12-game unbeaten run, eventually losing away to Aston Villa. The run included a home match against Derby in October when, with Arsenal ahead 3-1 through Coleman (2) and Hulme, centre half Roberts turned the ball twice into his own net within one minute from crosses by Dally Duncan. The game ended 3-3. After the Villa defeat Arsenal went five further games without loss and the final match in the run – against Sheffield United at Highbury on Christmas Eve – was won 9-2, with five coming from Lambert, his highest tally in a game. Arsenal were now six points in front. Although they suffered a surprise defeat at home by Leeds in the next match, by April they were ahead of Villa and Sheffield Wednesday, both with games in hand. These two contenders visited Highbury in April and both were beaten, leaving Arsenal in pole position. They faced Chelsea in late April at Stamford Bridge requiring a win for the title, and a goal from Jack and two from Bastin in their 3-1 victory meant that they had won the league title for the second time in three years. They scored 118 goals, 26 more than Villa, the next highest, and Bastin's tally of 33 became a record for a winger.

Arsenal may have dominant been in the League, but disaster was awaiting them in the FA Cup. On 14 January they travelled away in the third round to meet Walsall from the Third Division North in what was to prove one of the biggest giant-killing acts in the history of the competition. With Hapgood injured, Hulme off form and John, Lambert and Coleman all down with flu, Chapman selected four players – Tommy Black, Norman Sidey, Billy Warnes and Charlie Walsh – of whom only one, Sidey, had ever played for the first team and that was only in one game. Walsh was so nervous that he put his boots on without his socks. On a narrow pitch, with 11,000 partisan spectators crowding on to the touchline, Walsall refused to be cowed by Arsenal's reputation and produced a gutsy, performance. In the 60th minute Allsop headed in a corner to put Walsall 1-0 ahead and five minutes later Black gave away a penalty and Sheppard scored from the spot. Centre forward Walsh fluffed two excellent chances and the game ended 2-0 amid uproar and wild celebration from Walsall's supporters.

Arsenal had the chances to win but couldn't take them and Bastin remarked, 'Never have I seen Chapman look so miserably unhappy.' An embarrassed and ashamed Arsenal slunk back to London. Chapman was criticized for not taking the game seriously enough and he retaliated by transferring Black, Walsh and Warnes within a month, although Sidey was retained. Fans of Rangers will draw immediate comparisons with manager Scot Symon's similar treatment of Jim Forrest and George McLean after the Glasgow club's humiliating 1-0 first round cup defeat by Berwick Rangers in 1967.

Chapman realized that his squad was becoming an aging one and in April 1933 he acquired Ray Bowden from Plymouth as a successor to Jack, who was to play only 14 games in 1933-34 and retire in May to manage Southend. Ralph Birkett, an outside right from Torquay, arrived to take over from Hulme. Peter

50 Greatest Players

ALEX JAMES Inside left

Born: Mossend, Lanarkshire, 14 September 1901

Joined Arsenal: 1929   **From:** Preston North End

Debut: 31 August 1929 v Leeds United, League

Appearances: 259   **Goals:** 27

Left Arsenal: 1937 (retired)

Honours won with Arsenal: Division One championship 1931, 1933, 1934, 1935; FA Cup winner 1930, 1936; 4 Scotland caps

To an older generation, Alex James was the greatest Gunner of them all. Herbert Chapman signed him for £8,750 in the summer of 1929, then converted the little Scot from an attacking inside forward to the midfield general who plotted Arsenal's domination of the English game. James, in his trademark baggy long shorts, dictated the tempo and turned defence into attack, firing long passes to release flying wingers Hulme and Bastin or through balls for the central strikers. His opening goal in the 1930 FA Cup final against Huddersfield also set the Gunners on the way to their first major honour. His retirement in 1937 left an impossible gap to fill. He became a football writer, then returned to Highbury after the war to coach the juniors.

Dougall, a Scottish inside left, was introduced as cover for James. Dougall had the ball-playing virtuosity of his fellow Scot but lacked James's distribution skills. Pat Beasley, who had arrived in 1931 from Stourbridge, was introduced into the first team on the left wing when Bastin pulled inside into the inside left position. Lambert moved to Fulham in October and, with Coleman's form inconsistent, Chapman needed another centre forward. He bought the blond-haired Jimmy Dunne, an Irish international from Sheffield United with exceptional ability in the air, as a replacement striker.

Chapman Passes Away

Newly-promoted Tottenham made the running early in 1933-34 but Arsenal took over the lead in November. They won all three of their Christmas matches and a draw with Birmingham on 30 December saw them move four points ahead of the pack. Early in January Chapman contracted what he felt was a heavy cold. Against medical advice he attended a third-team match in Guildford and fell ill after the game. At 3am on 6 January he died of pneumonia at the age of 55. Everyone in football was stunned and the team were devastated. *The Times* said: 'Association Football is not so rich in personalities that it can afford to lose

50 Greatest Players

HERBIE ROBERTS Centre half

Born: Oswestry, 19 February 1905

Joined Arsenal: 1926 **From:** Oswestry Town

Debut: 18 April 1927 v Aston Villa, League

Appearances: 333 **Goals:** 5

Left Arsenal: 1938 (retired)

Honours won with Arsenal: Division One championship 1931, 1933, 1934, 1935; FA Cup winner 1936; 1 England cap

Herbie Roberts was the first of the great defensive 'policemen' centre halves as Herbert Chapman developed new tactics to deal with the change in the offside law. 'Copper' Roberts trained as a gunsmith and began his career with his home town club. Arsenal paid Oswestry £200 for him in December 1926. He missed the 1930 FA Cup final through injury but established himself in the Gunners' title-winning team the following season. Tall, powerful and unruffled, he was a regular for the next seven years, but he was forced to retire after suffering a severe knee injury in a match against Middlesbrough in October 1937. He later became trainer to Arsenal's 'nursery' side at Margate.

The team that won the 1933-34 championship, l-r: back row – Sidey, Dunne, Moss, Male, John; front row – Hill, Bowden, Jones, James, Bastin, Hapgood.

such a man as Herbert Chapman. He did his sides the inestimable service of making them think about the game and the results of his teaching were obvious on the field of play.' There was a huge crowd at his funeral at Hendon four days later, the pall bearers being Jack, Lambert, Hapgood, Bastin, Hulme and James.

On the day of his death Arsenal drew 1-1 at Highbury against Sheffield Wednesday, the goal coming from Bastin who said, 'I suppose Arsenal gave quite a good display that day, considering the game was an unimportant incident and Chapman's death a terrible reality.' Reaction soon set in among the players and they lost their next three games in a row, but they got back to winning ways in February. One of the games they lost was against Tottenham when 68,828 crammed into Highbury to set a record mid-week attendance. Arsenal lost 3-1, their first home defeat of the season. The 2-1 home win over Blackburn in February saw Arsenal take over the top position from Derby and they consolidated their lead with a fine 3-2 victory against Wolves with debutant centre forward Ted Drake, recently acquired from Southampton, scoring on his first appearance for the club. Drake scored again in their fine victory over Huddersfield in early April, and they picked up seven of the last ten points to ensure the league championship, three points ahead of Huddersfield. Arsenal had also reached the sixth round of the Cup, Dunne scoring the only goal in the third round match against Luton and he scored two more in the 7-0 rout of Palace in the next round. Derby were then beaten 1-0 but Aston Villa won 2-1 in the sixth round.

Although Arsenal's second consecutive league title was deserved, they had scored only 75 goals, their lowest total since 1924-25, the year of Knighton's sacking. Alex James had been injured in the first game of the season against Birmingham and played in only 22 league games, so the absence of his creative

Great Managers – 1925-34

HERBERT CHAPMAN

One of the true visionaries in the history of football, Herbert Chapman was the force behind Arsenal's domination of English football in the 1930s. After a relatively undistinguished playing career, and spells as manager at Northampton Town and Leeds City, Chapman took over at Huddersfield Town and led the Yorkshire club to two league titles in the 1920s. He was appointed Arsenal manager in 1925 and his revolutionary tactics – including the development of the 'stopper' centre half and his emphasis on speedy counter-attacking – saw Arsenal become the first southern club to win the FA Cup, beating Huddersfield in the 1930 FA Cup final. His acquisition of Alex James and Cliff Bastin were masterstrokes: the guile of James and the speed and goalscoring prowess of Bastin were critical to Arsenal's league title win in 1930-31. The following year Chapman's team narrowly failed to win the 'Double' but they won the league title for a second time in 1932-33.

A masterful reader of the game, a shrewd motivator and an untiring publicizer of the club, Chapman invented the modern Arsenal. He involved the players in tactical and team discussions, ensured that they were fully aware of the roles they had to play and inspired self belief and confidence in his legendary side. An innovator, and a man decades ahead of his time, he can be seen as the father of modern football. Relentless in his dedication to Arsenal, Chapman ignored the advice of club doctors at the beginning of 1934 not to attend so many matches, and he contracted what he thought was a heavy cold while watching a third-team game. He died of pneumonia on 6 January 1934 at the age of 55, his passing mourned throughout football. His legacy continues to this day, with his bust sculpted by Jacob Epstein occupying centre stage in the East Stand entrance at Highbury.

trickery goes some way to explaining the goals shortfall. Also, the team was rebuilding and they used six different players in the centre forward position. In the following season, however, the presence of Ted Drake in the striker role was to ensure that goals were not going to be a problem.

Behind the scenes, George Allison had been appointed managing director/secretary after Chapman's sudden death, while the day-to-day running of the club had been left in the hands of Tom Whittaker and Joe Shaw. The club had received over 200 applications for the manager's job but, at the end of the season, the board appointed Allison in the role. Chapman may have gone but Allison was to continue the great manager's winning ways.

Chapter Three: 1934-56
The Allison and Whittaker Years

George Allison had been involved with the club since their Woolwich days. He had been honorary editor of the programme (under the soubriquet 'Gunner's Mate') and was invited to join the board in the early 1920s. Now 51 years old, he was a respected broadcaster and journalist and had been BBC commentator at the 1927 Arsenal v Cardiff FA Cup final. However, he had never played the game at a senior level and had no direct experience of football management. As Bernard Joy, who played under him, stated: 'He was tactful, friendly and good-hearted. But he fell short in his handling of footballers and lacked the professional's deep understanding of the game.' Tom Whittaker and Joe Shaw assumed day-to-day control of the dressing room and the team.

Perhaps mindful of the words addressed to him by Chapman the previous season – 'The team is played out, Mr Allison. You must rebuild' – Allison had acquired two wing halves, Jack Crayston and Wilf Copping, to refresh his aging team. There had been a clear-out of older players, including Lambert, Jack, Jones and Coleman, and Allison had to rebuild. Crayston, acquired from Bradford and known as 'Gentleman Jack', was a tall, imposing right half, excellent in the air and the possessor of an awesomely long throw. Copping, an international left half ex-miner bought from Leeds, was a fearsome competitor whose ferocity was enhanced by his refusal to shave on match days. Labelled 'the Ironman', his motto was 'the first man in a tackle never gets hurt'.

Bob Wall tells a story about Crayston and Allison at a pre-match briefing session before a Sheffield Wednesday game. 'Several times he (Allison) reminded the players that the Wednesday inside forward was likely to be the danger man. Each time he noticed that Jack Crayston was trying to say something. "Not now, Jack. Let me say my piece and you can say yours," said Allison. Eventually he ended his briefing and turned to Jack. "Now what is it you wish to say, Jack?" to which he replied, "Only, Mr Allison, that the inside forward you want us to watch was transferred to Bolton five weeks ago."'

Arsenal's second game in Allison's first full season in charge resulted in a resounding 8-1 win over Liverpool at Highbury, with Drake and Bowden plundering hat-tricks and Crayston netting on his debut. By the end of the year they had lost only five games out of 21 and had scored four or more goals on eight occasions, including beating Wolves 7-0 (Drake scoring four) and Leicester 8-0 (Drake claiming a hat-trick). In January they played three league and two Cup matches without conceding a single goal. This was in spite of a protracted injury list throughout the season, with players such as Hulme, Beasley, Copping and Hapgood out for long stretches. The reserve team was strong, however, and Leslie Compton, Norman Sidey and Scottish international wing half Frank 'Tiger' Hill were able stand-ins.

England played world champions Italy on 14 November at Highbury. The England team contained no less than seven Arsenal players including Ted Drake and, although it was billed as 'Drake's Armada', it soon became known as the 'Battle of Highbury'. Drake broke Luisito Monti's foot early on and the game degenerated into an exhibition of punching, kicking and general mayhem on the Italians' part. The game ended 3-2 in England's favour and the England dressing room resembled a field hospital after the game, with Hapgood suffering a broken nose.

In the early spring Allison brought in inside forward Bobby Davidson from St Johnstone and outside right Alf Kirchen, a £6,000 buy from Norwich. Davidson scored on his debut against Stoke on 20 February and played in the FA Cup sixth round tie against Sheffield Wednesday on 2 March, when Arsenal were knocked out of the competition 2-1. In his first game on 6 March, Kirchen scored twice in the 6-0 defeat of Tottenham, a game which was dominated by the skills of Peter Dougall, replacing the injured Alex James. A month previously James had scored a hat-trick against Sheffield Wednesday to the astonishment of his team-mates. Wednesday were perhaps over-confident in their belief that the diminutive Scotsman could not score and closely marked the forwards. James then used the gaps to his advantage. His feat was even sweeter as his son had scored seven goals for his school side that morning and taunted his dad: 'That's more than you've scored all season.' 'Right, I'll show you,' thought James.

Three in a Row

The next game was a crucial match. Sunderland were one point behind in the League but Arsenal had two games in hand and there were 11 games to play. Sunderland came to Highbury on 9 March and were held to a 0-0 draw in front of a massive 73,295 crowd. The advantage now lay clearly with Arsenal. The following week against Everton at Goodison, Moss dislocated his shoulder, had it set and came back on the left wing, with Hapgood taking over in goal. An unmarked Moss cut in and scored a superb goal, leaving the final score 2-0. Reserve keeper Alex Wilson kept goal for the rest of the season and the injury eventually led to Moss retiring from football in 1936.

Arsenal were unbeaten in their next eight matches, including an 8-0 win over Middlesbrough, where Drake scored another four, and won the title four points ahead of Sunderland.

By winning their third title in succession Arsenal had equalled Huddersfield's record set the previous decade, a resounding tribute to the builder of both teams, the late Herbert Chapman. The season had been a triumph for Ted Drake who scored a total of 42 goals, by some distance the league's leading goalscorer, and Arsenal hit 115, 25 more than runners-up Sunderland. The Football League presented the club with a magnificent silver shield to commemorate their achievement.

Season 1935-36 was something of an anti-climax. Perhaps this was inevitable as no side could maintain this blistering pace indefinitely. The team seemed unconvincing and tired and, although the injury list was a long one, several of the team, particularly James and Roberts, were now veterans and lacked the pace of old. Nonetheless, despite their inconsistent form, attendances at Highbury were higher than ever, with average crowds of just under 60,000.

The Gunners started promisingly enough with a 3-1 win over Sunderland at Highbury but won only one of their next six games. On 2 November they lost 2-1 away to Brentford, who would prove a 'bogey' team over the coming years. This shock to the system woke the team up and they embarked on a seven-game unbeaten run, including a 7-1 win over Aston Villa on 14 December at Villa Park. This game produced a remarkable performance by Ted Drake who scored all seven! Despite a strapped-up knee, each of his first six shots resulted in a goal, three in the first half and three more within 12 minutes of the restart. Although marked by virtually the entire Villa defence, Drake claimed his seventh at the end with a left-foot shot from a Bastin cross.

At the end of December Arsenal met league leaders Sunderland at Roker Park. In a stunning display from the Sunderland forwards, Arsenal were 4-1 down at half-time. Drake and Bowden scored shortly after the interval but Sunderland went further ahead. Bowden pulled one back in the 75th minute but Sunderland held onto their 5-4 lead till the whistle. Sunderland were now *Denis Compton, who also played cricket for England.*

eight points ahead and Arsenal's championship expectations were over. Sunderland won the League 11 points ahead of Arsenal in lowly sixth place.

In their three-year domination of the League, Arsenal had never gone further than the sixth round of the FA Cup. The 'Double' appeared too difficult, even for a team of Arsenal's quality. The one year they won the FA Cup, 1930, they were 14th in the League. By January, with league hopes effectively gone, they could concentrate on the Cup. Memories of the Walsall debacle were in the air on 11 January when they faced Third Division Bristol Rovers in the third round. The jitters were compounded when Rovers went 1-0 ahead by half-time. Arsenal settled down, however, and won the tie 5-1. Liverpool were next and, with Sidey capably replacing the injured Roberts, Bowden and Hulme gave Arsenal a 2-0 victory. Against Newcastle in the fifth round, a team they had never beaten in the Cup, a thrilling contest ended 3-3. Arsenal comfortably won the replay at Highbury, Bastin scoring twice. Barnsley were efficiently defeated 4-1 in the sixth round and a Bastin strike was the only goal of the game against Grimsby in the semi-final.

Dependable Defence Wins the Cup

The final was against Second Division Sheffield United on 25 April, with Arsenal regarded as favourites. United went on the attack and as early as the first minute Wilson dropped a high cross and had to be quick to smother Pickering's shot. By half-time the score remained 0-0. Arsenal's performance improved in the second half and in the 74th minute James found Bastin on the wing. He crossed and a low left-foot shot from Drake gave Arsenal the lead. Dodds almost equalized in the last minute when his header hit the bar, but Arsenal held on to their 1-0 margin. The FA Cup was back at Highbury, although United had acquitted themselves well in the game and could have won. *The Times* reported: 'Arsenal's defence proceeded to be its usual dependable self... the forward line, on the other hand, never really found itself'. The team was: Wilson, Male, Hapgood, Crayston, Roberts, Copping, Hulme, Bowden, Drake, James, Bastin.

However, the cup win could not conceal the fact the Arsenal were now a fading team. Psychologically, a game against the Gunners was no longer seen as quite as daunting a task as it would have been a couple of seasons ago. Also, Arsenal's tactics had been rumbled and other clubs had prepared their own retaliatory systems. Had Chapman still been in charge he would no doubt have dreamt up some new method of countering the opposition, but Allison was not as tactically astute and he continued with the Arsenal system even although several of the players, James included, were past their best.

The 1936 FA Cup-winning team, l-r: back row – Copping, Male, Crayston, Wilson, Roberts, Drake, Hapgood; front – Allison, Hulme, Bowden, James, Bastin, Whittaker.

As if to signal their relative decline, they won only two out of their first nine games in 1936-37 and did not manage an away goal until mid-October, when Davidson and young left winger and swashbuckling England cricket international Denis Compton both scored in the 2-0 defeat of Charlton. By the end of October they lay 17th in the table with only 11 points from 12 games. However, things picked up in November when they won all four games, including a game at Highbury against Middlesbrough when they came back from 3-1 down to win 5-3. They then took five points out of six over Christmas and by early January they were on top of the League.

In the FA Cup they won their first two round matches emphatically, despatching Chesterfield away 5-1 and Manchester United 5-0 at Highbury. Drake scored four in their 7-1 destruction of Burnley, but they went down 3-1 to West Bromwich Albion in the sixth round at the Hawthorns in a game in which Drake was injured and subsequently out for the rest of the season. Charlton were now league leaders but a win over Liverpool at Highbury four days after the West Bromwich game saw Arsenal reclaim the top spot. Manchester City had become the form team and they were to drop only four points from their last 20 games. With Arsenal only one point ahead of City, the visit to Maine Road on 10 April was critical. Roberts and Drake were both injured. Kirchen replaced Drake and tall amateur centre half Bernard Joy, a teacher, came in for Roberts, but Arsenal were defeated 2-0. They finished the season in third place behind champions Manchester City and Charlton.

Arsenal's season had been marred by a frustrating tendency to drop points at home. Although they lost only one game at Highbury (against Manchester City in December), they drew as many as they won (10). Also, the cause had not been helped by Drake's absence at the tail end of the season (although

Drake scored 20 goals in his 26 appearances). But Arsenal were in need of new blood, a situation underlined at the end of the season when Alex James admitted to the inevitable and retired, having played only 19 league games. Bob John and Herbie Roberts also ended their playing careers, Roberts after an injury sustained against Middlesbrough in October.

The middle of 1937-38 saw other departures: Bobby Davidson went to Coventry, Ray Bowden to Newcastle and Jackie Milne to Middlesbrough, while Joe Hulme moved to Huddersfield in January. The great team of the early 1930s was breaking up and Allison had to find replacements, particularly a creative midfielder to carry on James's role. New faces included 17-year-old forward Reg Lewis, who scored on his league debut, and 5ft 7in centre forward Eddie Carr. In goal George Swindin was taking over from Wilson although Frank Boulton, who was to leave at the end of the season, was also vying for the job. The defence and midfield were largely intact, with Joy now taking over as centre half and Bastin, Drake and Kirchen remaining in the forward line.

Arsenal won their first three games and by January they were in third place behind leaders Brentford and Wolves. They had eliminated Bolton 3-1 in the third round of the FA Cup and faced Wolves in the fourth round. In a game

50 Greatest Players

JOE HULME Outside right

Born: Stafford, 26 August 1904

Joined Arsenal: 1926   **From:** Blackburn Rovers

Debut: 6 February 1926 v Leeds United, League

Appearances: 372   **Goals:** 124

Left Arsenal: 1938   **For:** Huddersfield Town

Honours won with Arsenal: Division One championship 1931, 1933, 1935; FA Cup winner 1930, 1936; 9 England caps

Joe Hulme was reckoned to be the quickest forward in the Football League when Herbert Chapman signed him. His explosive pace and accurate crosses set up a stack of goals for the Gunners. Unlike most wingers of the time, he also loved to cut in and shoot. He passed double figures in the League for four consecutive seasons, peaking at 20 goals in 1932-33. He spent nearly 12 years at Highbury before ending his career at Huddersfield. He became the first man to play in five Wembley FA Cup finals when he turned out for them against Preston in 1938. Hulme spent four years managing Tottenham after the war, then became a football writer.

Ted Drake who finished as top scorer for the Gunners in each of the five seasons he played at Highbury.

described by Joy as 'one of the most memorable in Arsenal's annals', Arsenal decided to counter the aerial dominance of Wolves' centre half Stan Cullis by keeping their crosses low. The ploy worked as early as the first minute, when Bastin whipped in a low ball and Drake mis-kicked into the net. Inside left Bryn Jones equalized for Wolves on half-time but Kirchen scored the winner from a tight angle in the second period.

In mid-February, Preston eliminated Arsenal from the competition, 1-0. By now Brentford's league challenge had collapsed and after the Wolves game Arsenal lost only one of their next nine matches. With six games to go, they were three points ahead of Wolves and Preston but they lost twice (to Brentford) and drew over Easter but remained on top on goal average.

'They've Lost Eddie!'

On the last day of the season Wolves were one point ahead and played Sunderland while Arsenal entertained Bolton, a game which kicked off 15 minutes after the Wolves match. With Arsenal 4-0 up and the game approaching its conclusion, Joy saw a 1-0 result go up on the scoreboard. '"They've lost, Eddie!" I shouted to Eddie Hapgood.' Indeed they had, and Arsenal won the championship by one point. Their 52 points was the league's lowest total since 1919 when Division One was extended from 20 to 22 clubs.

On 4 August 1938, Allison broke the English transfer record fee (set by Chapman's acquisition of David Jack) when he paid Wolves a sum of £14,000 for 5ft 6in Bryn Jones, Wolves' Welsh international forward. Allison felt that he now had his replacement for Alex James. Skilful though Jones was, however, he was essentially an attacking player and never quite managed to emulate the Scotsman's scheming, creative role in the team. Bastin opined, 'Bryn just did not have it in him to become the general and prime mover of the Arsenal attack. He never pretended to be anything but an extremely efficient attacking player.'

Also, Jones was a quiet, reserved personality, a far cry from the ebullient James, and he was uneasy about his celebrity and being constantly under the

The 1937-38 championship-winning team, l-r: back – Pryde, Crayston, Joy, Swindin, Male, Drake, Whittaker (trainer); front – Griffiths, Carr, Hapgood, Allison (manager), Drury, Bastin, Copping.

spotlight. The 1938-39 season was an unexceptional one, with Arsenal winning five out of their last six games, the last being against Brentford, their first win over the Bees in eight games. This game, incidentally, was used for a feature film – *The Arsenal Stadium Mystery* – shot at Highbury over the summer. Brentford played the fictitious 'Trojans'. Arsenal's FA Cup run was brief – they were eliminated at Stamford Bridge in the third round 2-1. Although Jones was in brilliant form during Arsenal's summer tour of Scandinavia when they won all seven of their games, his suitability as Arsenal's creative midfielder was never proven. Britain declared war against Germany on 3 September and English league football was to go into hibernation for seven seasons.

The Second Great War

As soon as the war began, Highbury was commandeered by the Civil Defence as an ARP (Air Raid Protection) post and the team moved to White Hart Lane. They were to play all their home wartime games at the Lane, Tottenham obviously having decided to forgive the events of 1919. Due to a ban on the assembly of large crowds, the maximum capacity was set at 22,000. Virtually all the Arsenal squad were called up, with the exception of Bastin whose increasing deafness rendered him unfit for service. Bastin became an Air Raid Warden at Highbury. In 1940 Italian radio broadcast a report that Bastin had been shot down over the Gulf of Taranto and had surrendered, which must have come as a surprise to him as he went about his duties at the stadium.

Only three Division One games had been played before the declaration of war and thereafter the game was divided into regional leagues. Arsenal won the Regional League South in 1939-40 and again in 1941-42. In the latter season they also reached Wembley in the Football League War Cup and drew 1-1, Denis Compton scoring for Arsenal. They lost the replay 2-1. They reached Wembley again in 1942-43 when they defeated Charlton 7-1, four of the goals coming from the speedy Reg Lewis. The team was: Marks, Scott, L. Compton, Crayston, Joy, Male, Kirchen, Drake, Lewis, Bastin, D. Compton. The importance of the various competitions was becoming increasingly diluted as the war wore on as many players were sent overseas and their places taken by guest players. Indeed, when Arsenal played Aldershot in 1942, the Aldershot team was composed of such internationals as Stan Cullis, Tommy Lawton and Joe Mercer, the town being the main base of the British army. Nonetheless, Arsenal recovered from being 4-1 down at half time to win 7-4.

Early in 1943-44, Alf Kirchen and Jack Crayston retired from the game due to injury, and they were followed shortly after by Ted Drake, the victim of a slipped disc. Eddie Hapgood also left the club and would soon take over as manager of Blackburn Rovers. However, full back Laurie Scott had broken into the team and Denis Compton was emerging as a useful left winger. Centre forward Reg Lewis had made the position his own, emphasized by his total of 39 league goals in 1942-43. The versatile, assured full back Walley Barnes, who would play in virtually every position for

50 Greatest Players

TED DRAKE Centre forward

Born: Southampton, 16 April 1912

Joined Arsenal: 1934   **From:** Southampton

Debut: 24 March 1934 v Wolverhampton Wanderers, League

Appearances: 182   **Goals:** 136

Left Arsenal: (retired, through injury in wartime match)

Honours won with Arsenal: Division One championship 1935, 1938; FA Cup winner 1938; 5 England caps

Dashing Ted Drake was one of the most glamorous players of the 1930s. A powerful leader of the line, he was signed by George Allison for £6,500 to solve Arsenal's scoring problems during the 1933-34 season. He responded by netting 42 league goals in 1934-35, a club record that still stands. He also holds the Gunners record for most goals in a game – all seven in an amazing 7-1 win at Aston Villa in 1935-36. One of his most important goals for Arsenal was the FA Cup final winner against Sheffield United later that season. Drake finished top scorer in each of his five full seasons at Highbury. His career was ended by a spinal injury in a wartime game at Reading, but he went on to become a successful manager, guiding Chelsea to their only league championship in 1954-55.

Arsenal in his 12 years at the club, made his debut in 1943. Barnes had been recommended by Tom Parker at Southampton and as one of Arsenal's finest postwar players, cost the club nothing.

In November 1945 Moscow Dynamo arrived in London for a short British tour. The mysterious Russians drew 3-3 with Chelsea and then annihilated Cardiff 10-1. Arsenal, fielding six 'guests' (including the two Stans, Matthews and Mortensen) as several of the regular team were still away on wartime duties, entertained Dynamo in thick fog at Highbury. Dynamo insisted on their own ref and he lined up on one touchline with his two linesmen on the other. The Russians scored almost immediately but were 3-2 down by half-time, Mortensen scoring twice for Arsenal. Bernard Joy, who played in the match, was particularly impressed by the Russians' speed and fast, interconnected passing game – known as 'passovotchka' – and mused that this was exactly the system which British teams employed nearly 50 years ago before modern tactical systems took over. During the interval the Russians poured their tea on the floor, perhaps suggesting their distrust of their hosts, and filled their cups with vodka. Although visibility was now under 20 yards the game continued and the final score was 4-3 to Dynamo. They played their final game against Rangers – a 2-2 draw – and left Britain as abruptly as they arrived.

50 Greatest Players

WILF COPPING Left half

Born: Middlecliffe, 17 August 1909

Joined Arsenal: 1934   **From:** Leeds United

Debut: 25 August 1934 v Portsmouth, League

Appearances: 185   **Goals:** 0

Left Arsenal: 1939   **For:** Leeds United

Honours won with Arsenal: Division One championship 1935, 1938; FA Cup winner 1936; 13 England caps

Wilf Copping was a stern-tackling wing half who supplied the bite to complement Jack Crayston's guile. His refusal to shave on match days added to his iron man aura. He gave one of his finest displays when England beat World Cup winners Italy 3-2 in the 'Battle of Highbury' in 1934. A former miner, he was an £8,000 signing from Leeds where he had already won six caps. He gave Arsenal nearly five seasons' service before returning to Leeds. Copping retired from football during wartime. He later coached the Belgium team and had spells as trainer or coach with Southend, Bristol City and Coventry City.

Earlier in the year Arsenal had been embarrassingly beaten 6-1 in the FA Cup third round by West Ham. Ironically, their best performance came from keeper George Swindin, replacing George Marks who was to transfer to Blackburn Rovers at the beginning of the 1946-47 season. Arsenal and league football returned to Highbury to find the ground damaged by the wartime years. The North Bank roof had burnt down in 1941 and the south end of the ground had been damaged by a 1,000lb bomb. On top of this, the club were in debt to the tune of £200,000 and had to ensure good attendances to keep going.

Of the pre-war team only Bernard Joy, George Male and Cliff Bastin remained. Jimmy Logie, a 5ft 4in Scottish inside forward (and another Alex James according to Allison), had joined the club in 1939 and was now a regular. Other new faces were right half Paddy Sloan, centre forward Ian McPherson, soon to become outside right, and amateur Dr Kevin O'Flanagan who had represented Ireland at football and rugby. The first game in season 1946-47 was against Wolves at Molineux. The score was 0-0 at half-time but Arsenal collapsed to a 6-1 defeat. In the first postwar match at Highbury, with Leslie Compton now at centre half in place of Bernard Joy, they lost again, 3-1 to Blackburn Rovers. They did not win at Highbury and by December were second bottom, only 0.142 of a goal ahead of Huddersfield. One bright spot, however, was the goalscoring of Reg Lewis who scored 11 times in the first ten games. Also Walley Barnes returned from serious injury in November and performed well against Tom Finney in a 2-0 defeat by Preston. Cliff Bastin, however, had retired after a 5-2 defeat by Manchester United in September, the legendary winger having played 392 games for the club.

The one position which Allison desperately needed to fill was left half. The 33-year-old international left half Joe Mercer had decided to leave Everton, after a dispute with the club, to concentrate on his grocery business. Allison paid the Liverpool club £7,000 for his services and, although Mercer's natural inclination was an attacking one, Whittaker persuaded him to adopt a more defensive role. His arrival was to spark a much-needed revival in Arsenal's fortunes. The revival was aided by another acquisition two weeks later, that of 35-year-old centre forward Ronnie Rooke from Fulham. Allison welcomed him with the words 'Ronnie, we're in trouble. We've got to get goals, by hook or by Rooke'. With the consistent Swindin in goal and a settled half back line of Sloan, Compton and Mercer, Rooke scored the only goal in a 1-0 win over Charlton in December and Arsenal lost only one of their next eight games. The run included a 6-2 win over Manchester United at Highbury in early February, Rooke claiming a hat-trick. Arsenal ended the

50 Greatest Players

EDDIE HAPGOOD Left back

Born: Bristol, 24 September 1908

Joined Arsenal: 1927   **From:** Kettering Town

Debut: 19 November 1927 v Birmingham City, League

Appearances: 434   **Goals:** 2

Left Arsenal: 1945 (retired)

Honours won with Arsenal: Division One championship 1931, 1933-35, 1938; FA Cup winner 1930, 1936; 30 England caps

Eddie Hapgood was England's greatest left back of the inter-war years. He played more internationals than any other England player of the period, skippering the team in most of them. Herbert Chapman plucked him from the obscurity of Kettering for a bargain £1,000 in October 1927. Hapgood made the left back slot his own at the end of the 1928-29 season and was a fixture in the side until the outbreak of war. He succeeded Tom Parker as Gunners skipper in 1932. Hapgood was noted as an elegant, constructive but hugely solid defender, who led by example. He played his last game for the Gunners during the final year of wartime football. He later managed Blackburn and Watford before returning to the West Country as boss of Bath City.

season in 13th place, their lowest position since 1929-30. In the FA Cup they played Chelsea in a three-game third round clash, eventually falling 2-0 to two Tommy Lawton goals at White Hart Lane.

Whittaker Takes Over

In May, George Allison, wearied by his efforts, stepped down from the post of manager. The players petitioned the board to appoint Tom Whittaker to the job and the trainer assumed control of the team. Whittaker was a popular choice within the club and Joe Shaw returned from Chelsea where he had been assistant manager to assume a similar role at Arsenal. Whittaker added two new players to his squad. Red-haired, Scottish international right half Archie Macaulay was acquired from Brentford and tall right winger Don Roper came from Southampton. Roper was a confident, two-footed player and an excellent crosser of the ball.

The 1947-48 season was a memorable one for the Gunners. They won their first six games, including an impressive 2-1 win over Manchester United at Highbury, crowned by a magnificent 35-yard strike from Rooke.

In the final match of that sequence, at home to Bolton, they won 2-0 with only nine men for most of the game. Lewis and centre half Alf Fields were both injured and in those days there were no substitutes. In the following game, away to Preston, club captain Leslie Compton was back. In Mercer's autobiography *The Great Ones*, he tells how in the dressing room before the match Whittaker threw the ball to Compton. Compton then threw it to acting captain Mercer with the words, 'Lead us out, Joe. You haven't been doing too badly in the job so far.' Under Mercer's leadership Arsenal did not lose a game until a 1-0 away defeat by Derby in late November.

Mercer and Macaulay had devised the 'retreating' defence system, based on Mercer's observations of basketball games during the war. Mercer writes, 'When an inside forward got the ball in midfield and had time to control it, instead of going towards him we would retreat. Invariably he would run on to us and try to play it into a packed defence, when we could pick up the ball at our leisure.' It may not have been pretty, and was denounced as negative in the newspapers, but it was certainly effective.

On New Year's Day 1948, Arsenal, after their 1-0 win over Bolton, were five points clear in Division One. Later in the month they travelled to Maine Road to play Manchester United, in front of a Football League record crowd of 83,260, and obtained a 1-1 draw. They then beat their other two close competitors, Preston and Burnley, both by 3-0 with the Burnley game witnessing the return of Denis Compton on the left wing. Arsenal were now eight points clear and cruising. In early March Alex Forbes, a Scottish international wing half and close friend of Archie Macaulay, who had assisted Whittaker in negotiating the transfer, made his debut at inside left against Wolves at Highbury and scored in the Arsenal 5-2 win. Ironically, Forbes, who had been bought as a long-term replacement for Mercer, would eventually replace Macaulay in the team. Later in the month a Rooke hat-trick and two from Compton contributed to the 7-0 rout of Middlesbrough. By the time Arsenal faced Huddersfield at Leeds Road on 10 April there were still five league games remaining. However, such was Arsenal's supremacy that a win would bring the title back to Highbury.

Consistency Brings Another Title

A goal from Roper gave Arsenal a point in the 1-1 draw but, as the other contenders Manchester United, Burnley and Derby all lost, Arsenal were now champions. On the last day of the season Arsenal humbled Grimsby Town 8-0 at Highbury, with Rooke scoring four and becoming the league's highest scorer with 33. Centre half Lionel Smith, who would convert to left

The 1947-48 championship-winning team, l-r: back row – Forbes, Macaulay, Scott, Swindin, Milne (trainer), Barnes, Mercer, McPherson; front row – Roper, R. Lewis, Rooke, Jones, D. Compton, L. Compton.

back from the following season, made his debut in the game. Arsenal won the title by seven points, scoring 81 goals and conceding only 32. Although Arsenal had been surprisingly eliminated at the first hurdle in the FA Cup by Division Two side Bradford Park Avenue, it was none the less a triumphant season for the Gunners. The defensive prowess of Mercer and Macaulay, the scheming of little Jimmy Logie and Rooke's goalscoring had all contributed in great measure to Arsenal's sixth league title. Consistency was also an important factor, with only 18 players being used throughout the season. The regular team that season was: Swindin, Scott, Barnes, Macaulay, L. Compton, Mercer, Roper, Logie, Lewis, Rooke, McPherson.

In May, 6ft inside forward Doug Lishman arrived from Walsall but 1948-49 was something of a lacklustre season for Arsenal. They started badly in the League, winning only four of their first ten games and by September they were in 18th place. They hit form in the Charity Shield against Manchester United in October, however, scoring three times in the first three minutes through Lewis, the veteran Jones and Rooke, and the game ended 4-3 in the Gunners' favour. By Christmas Arsenal had risen to fifth in the League and they remained there till the end of the season. In the FA Cup they had their first-ever cup encounter with Tottenham and secured a 3-0 win to meet Derby in the fourth round. With Leslie Compton injured, Mercer moved to centre half but Derby won the match 1-0.

Early in 1949 Sam Hill-Wood died and he was replaced as chairman by Sir Bracewell Smith, Mayor of London and chairman of Wembley Stadium. Through prudent spending and cost controls, the postwar debt of £200,000 had been largely eliminated and gate receipts of £150,000 in 1947-48 also contributed to the club's healthy financial position. On the pitch, however,

Arsenal maintained their less than impressive league form, losing four out of their first five games in 1949-50. Their one win was 2-1 away at Stamford Bridge with new centre forward Peter Goring, bought earlier in the year from Cheltenham, scoring on his debut. Goring quickly became known as 'the butcher's boy' after his previous occupation. He replaced Ronnie Rooke – scorer of 68 goals in 88 Division One games – who left the club for Crystal Palace. In what was a nondescript league season, Arsenal finished in sixth place, but the real excitement was in the FA Cup.

Freddie Cox, a fast, direct outside right, had joined the club in September from Tottenham and he teamed up in attack with Logie, Lewis, Goring and McPherson for Sheffield Wednesday's visit to Highbury in the third round tie in early January. Keeper George Swindin had forecast that all Arsenal's games in the competition would be played in London and his prediction had begun promisingly. It took Arsenal until the last minute to score the only goal, through Lewis, and they were again at home against Division Two's Swansea for the fourth round. The Welsh side put up a plucky performance and a Walley Barnes penalty saved Arsenal from embarrassment and ensured a 2-1 win. Again drawn at Highbury in the fifth round, they defeated Burnley 2-0, Lewis and Denis Compton doing the damage.

50 Greatest Players

JACK CRAYSTON Right half

Born: Grange-over-Sands, Lancashire, 9 October 1910

Joined Arsenal: 1934   **From:** Bradford Park Avenue

Debut: 1 September 1934 v Liverpool, League

Appearances: 184   **Goals:** 17

Left Arsenal: 1945 (retired)

Honours won with Arsenal: Division One championship 1935, 1938; FA Cup winner 1936; 8 England caps

Jack Crayston was another of George Allison's early signings. Crayston had recovered from a broken leg to become Bradford's star. An elegant attacking wing half, he was strong in the air – and one of the earliest long-throw experts. He was a fixture in the Gunners' side until the outbreak of war and made his England debut in December 1935. Severe varicose veins during wartime ended his playing career. He joined the Arsenal coaching staff and became Tom Whittaker's assistant in 1947. He took over as manager after Whittaker's death in 1956 but resigned after 18 months in charge.

Swindin's forecast was now appearing uncannily accurate as Arsenal were drawn once more at Highbury for the sixth round, the opponents this time being Division Two's Leeds United. Lewis made sure of their semi-final status by scoring the game's only goal and they faced Chelsea at White Hart Lane on 18 March. Two-nil down after 25 minutes through two Roy Bentley goals, Arsenal retaliated with a slice of outrageous good fortune just before the interval. Cox took a corner from the right and curved the ball with the outside of his right foot. The ball dipped over Chelsea keeper Harry Medhurst and was in the net before the keeper could stop it. In the 75th minute Denis Compton on the left prepared to take a corner. His brother Leslie ran upfield, ignoring Joe Mercer's signals to move back into defence, and his forehead connected with his brother's cross to cannon the ball into the net, the impact forcing him into a backward somersault. In the replay four days later, again at White Hart Lane, the match was goalless after normal time. In the 14th minute of extra-time a Cox solo run ended with a low, left-foot shot from 18 yards and Arsenal were back at Wembley.

The opposition in the final on 29 April were Liverpool, who had already beaten Arsenal in both their league encounters that season. The match was played in pouring rain but this did not prevent Arsenal turning in an efficient, confident performance. The Gunners went ahead in the 18th minute when Logie stabbed a clever ball into space for Lewis who had anticipated the pass. The inside left sped through the defence and sent a low shot into the net with the outside of his right foot. Arsenal, in a changed strip of old gold with white collars, were commanding the game and Forbes was ably marking Liverpool's dangerous forward, Billy Liddell. At half-time Denis Compton,

FA Cup-winning side 1950, l-r: back row – Whittaker, Scott, Swindin, Barnes, Milne; middle row – D. Compton, Goring, Forbes, Mercer, Lewis, L. Compton; front row – Logie, Cox.

who had already made his mind up to retire at the end of the season, knocked back a whisky and, suitably fortified, returned to the fray in the second half. In the 63rd minute, Goring, having one of his finest games for the club, crossed from the left. Cox backheeled and Lewis, again, buried the ball in the net from 15 yards. Mercer, who had the previous evening received the Football Writers' Player of the Year award, collected the trophy from King George VI. *The Times* commented: 'Seldom can Arsenal have performed as well this season,' and the FA Cup came back to Highbury for a third time.

'To us the Cup; to Arsenal the Glory'

Arsenal started the 1950-51 season reasonably well, winning five of their first ten games. After a 2-1 away defeat by Newcastle towards the end of September, however, they embarked on a run of nine games losing only one point. By early December they were three points clear in the League. The season's turning point was against Stoke at Highbury on Christmas Day when big centre forward Lishman broke his leg. Lishman, who had found the net 16 times, including four against Sunderland, would be out until the last two games of the season. In the same match, keeper Swindin suffered a knee injury which would sideline him for three months. Swindin's place was filled by reserve keeper Ted Platt and also by recent signing Welshman Jack Kelsey whose association with the club was to last for almost another 40 years. Kelsey, who possessed the largest hands in British football, made his debut against Charlton in February, unfortunately letting in five goals. His confidence would soon recover, however.

With their goalscorer out of action Arsenal stuttered and for the second half of the season they could only manage less than one point per game. They were two points behind leaders Tottenham in early February but then lost three in succession, to West Brom, Charlton and Manchester United, and were effectively out of the running. They had also gone out of the FA Cup to Manchester United in the fifth round, and finished the season in fifth place, 13 points behind winners Tottenham, the old enemy's first-ever league title.

By the beginning of the next season Welshman Ray Daniel had replaced Leslie Compton, who had made his English international debut the previous year at the age of 38, in the centre half position. Cliff Holton, who had joined Arsenal four years previously as a half back, was moved to centre forward, and Arthur Milton was promoted from the reserves to outside right. Milton was also a successful batsman with Gloucestershire. At the end of September a postwar Highbury attendance of over 72,000 witnessed a 1-1 draw with Tottenham, while three weeks later they beat Charlton 3-1 at the

50 Greatest Players

CLIFF BASTIN Outside left

Born: Exeter, 14 March 1912

Joined Arsenal: 1929   **From:** Exeter City

Debut: 5 October 1929 v Everton, League

Appearances: 392   **Goals:** 176

Left Arsenal: 1946 (retired)

Honours won with Arsenal: Division One championship 1931, 1933-35, 1938; FA Cup winner 1930, 1936. 21 England caps

Cliff 'Boy' Bastin was the young prodigy of his time. An England Schoolboy star, he played in Exeter's league team when he was only 15. Herbert Chapman snapped him up for Arsenal in a £2,000 deal in May 1929. Less than a year later, he had established himself in the Gunners' team and collected his first major honour, an FA Cup winner's medal against Huddersfield. Bastin will always be remembered for his scoring feats from the wing. His 33 league goals in 1932-33 were a record for a winger and his tally of 176 in League and Cup set a club record bettered only by Ian Wright in 1997-98. He also scored 12 for England. The war ended Bastin's glittering career. He retired in 1947, hampered by a knee injury and increasing deafness.

Valley without the services of Smith, Barnes and Daniel, all on international duty. Lishman had recovered from his broken leg and was back in sharpshooting form, claiming three home hat-tricks in succession in October and November. A Christmas Day 4-1 win over Portsmouth saw Arsenal take the lead in the League.

The Highbury floodlights were now in place and the season was punctuated by a series of evening friendlies under the lights. Israeli side Hapoel drew a crowd of 50,000 in the autumn while 10,000 had to be turned away from a game against Rangers. In the FA Cup, Arsenal had progressed to the sixth round at the expense of Norwich, Barnsley and Leyton Orient who had reached the fifth round for the first time in their history. Logie and Forbes were both injured for the sixth round tie against Luton, and Arthur Shaw and Milton took their places. Milton scored in the 3-2 win and Chelsea were again opponents in the semi-final. The two teams met on 5 April at White Hart Lane with Cox scoring in a 1-1 draw. In the replay, two more from Cox and one from Lishman gave Arsenal a 3-0 victory and a place in the final against Newcastle.

The injury list was now a growing one, the latest addition being Daniel with a broken wrist and Arsenal had played eight games in 17 days. However, with three matches (including the final) remaining, Arsenal were level on points with Manchester United and the talk was of the 'Double', the first in modern times. However, in the penultimate game they were defeated by West Brom while Manchester United beat Chelsea 3-0 the same evening. In order to win the title Arsenal had to beat Manchester United 7-0 in the last game, but the Gunners went down 6-1 and United had the title.

Arsenal lined up against Newcastle in the final at Wembley on 3 May with Logie and Roper carrying bruised thighs while Daniel's arm sported a plastic covering ('if we win the Cup tomorrow they can break my arm in four places, for all I care', said the redoubtable Welshman). Lishman almost scored from an overhead shot in the third minute and Arsenal began impressively. However, in the 34th minute Barnes, who had badly twisted his leg, had to go off and Arsenal were down to ten men. Roper moved to right back and Arsenal played with four forwards. With Mercer particularly outstanding in his excellent tackling, covering and passing, Arsenal performed heroically to deny the Newcastle attack. Late in the second half, Arsenal pressed forward and a Lishman header from a corner hit the crossbar and bounced over. With five minutes to go, and Roper lying injured on the edge of the box, Bobby Mitchell crossed for Chilean forward George Robledo to head into the net in off the post and Newcastle had won the Cup. Arsenal were universally praised for their courageous, whole-hearted performance, with Stan Seymour, the vice-chairman of Newcastle, commenting: 'To us the Cup; to Arsenal the glory.' A proud Mercer said, 'Always I thought that football's greatest honour was to captain England. I was wrong. It was to captain Arsenal today.'

Barnes's injury was serious enough for him to miss out the entire 1952-53 season, his place taken variously by John Chenhall and Joe Wade. Arsenal won their first two games – against Aston Villa and Manchester United – but won only one of their next six. However, a 5-1 away win at Liverpool, winger Ben Marden scoring twice, started a run of six unbeaten games, culminating in a 6-4 away victory over Bolton. By mid-February, with Arsenal well placed in the League and due to face Blackpool in the sixth round of the FA Cup, the talk at Highbury was again of the 'Double', but an away league defeat at Blackpool and a home defeat by the same team in the Cup a week later put paid to that. A 4-1 home win over Bolton in mid-April saw Arsenal lead the League while a draw at Cardiff maintained their leadership, one point ahead of Wolves and two ahead of Preston. Preston beat the Gunners 2-0 at Deepdale on 25 April and, with Wolves defeated by Tottenham, the race could

Great Matches

LEAGUE DIVISION ONE   Highbury, 1 May 1953

Arsenal 3   **Burnley 2**   Attendance: 51,500
Forbes   Mercer o.g.
Lishman   Elliott
Logie

This vital, title-deciding match got off to the worst possible start when Joe Mercer deflected a Roy Stephenson centre into his own net in the third minute. Arsenal had no option other than to tear into the attack. Within a minute Alex Forbes equalized with a 25-yard drive. Then Lishman volleyed home a Roper cross and Logie made the score 3-1 with a flick from five yards. In the second half Arsenal massed in defence and kept the marauding Burnley forwards at bay. With 15 minutes to go, Burnley made it 3-2 and the tension in the Arsenal camp was unbearable. With Mercer dominant in defence and Swindin producing some remarkable saves, Arsenal held their lead to the end, the referee finally echoing the whistling from the Gunners' frantic support. They had won the championship by 0.099 of a goal and the celebrations began at Highbury. Arsenal had now become league champions for the seventh time – more than any other team in English history. The supporters, however, would have to savour their triumph as it would be 17 years before another trophy would come to Highbury.

Arsenal: Swindin, Wade, Smith, Forbes, Daniel, Mercer, Roper, Logie, Goring, Lishman, Marden

Burnley: Thompson, Aird, Winton, Adamson, Cummings, Brown, Stephenson, McIlroy, Holden, Shannon, Elliot

Referee: R. Leafe

Players from the 1952-53 championship-winning squad, l-r: back row – Daniel, Forbes, Swindin, Smith, Shaw; front row – Goring, Oakes, Mercer, Wade, Lishman, Roper.

hardly be closer. Preston and Arsenal were level on points, with Arsenal having the better goal average, with one game each left on the fixture list.

More Title Glory

In Preston's last game against Derby, a Tom Finney penalty was the difference between the sides and Arsenal had to win their last game against Burnley two days later, the evening before the FA Cup final, to snatch the title. Mercer commented afterwards that 'we played 4-2-4 that day with a vengeance' and Bob Wall remembered that he sat 'immediately behind Tom Whittaker and long before the end there was a pile of half-smoked cigarettes discarded at his feet and another at mine'. At the end of a nerve-racking evening, Arsenal had won the seventh league title in their history.

In the summer of 1953 Alex James succumbed to cancer at the premature age of 51, his death observed in an obituary in *The Times* . The loss of the brilliant little Scotsman may have affected the club as they lost six of their first eight matches in the 1953-54 season, including a 7-1 trouncing by Sunderland at Roker Park, and drew the other two. After this collapse, Arsenal propped up the table. Bill Dodgin, a 6ft 4in centre half bought from Fulham where his father was manager, had made his debut towards the end of the previous season and replaced Ray Daniel who moved to Sunderland. The Sunderland game saw Swindin's last appearance for the club and Jack Kelsey took over in goal. Walley Barnes was back from injury, although not yet fully fit, but he played in less than half the games that season.

Whittaker attempted to bolster his attack of Holton, Lishman and Roper with the acquisition in September of ex-England international centre forward and national hero Tommy Lawton, now 34 years old and player-manager of Brentford, but the gamble did not work. Lawton could not command a regular place and he scored only one goal in his nine appearances in the season. The season was largely undistinguished, with Arsenal putting together a good run in the autumn and moving to seventh spot, but collapsing to 12th place at the end of the campaign. The FA Cup was also disappointing. Two goals from Roper contributed to their 5-1 third round win over Aston Villa but they crashed 2-1 at Highbury to Norwich City in the fourth round.

On 10 April 1954 Mercer broke his leg in a collision with team-mate Joe Wade in a game at Highbury against Liverpool. As he was carried off on a stretcher, he lifted himself up and waved to the crowd, as if accepting that his long career was finally over. The popular captain received a standing ovation. Mercer's playing career was indeed at an end and he went on to manage Sheffield United, Manchester City and England. Making his debut

50 Greatest Players

GEORGE MALE Right back

Born: West Ham, 8 May 1910

Joined Arsenal: 1929   **From:** Clapton

Debut: 27 December 1930 v Blackpool, League

Appearances: 314   **Goals:** 0

Left Arsenal: 1948 (retired)

Honours won with Arsenal: Championship medals 1933-35, 1938; FA Cup winner's medal 1936; 19 England caps

George Male and Eddie Hapgood formed one of English football's finest full back partnerships, for club and country. Yet Male, once an amateur with Clapton, joined Arsenal as a left half. Herbert Chapman spotted that Male's defensive qualities made him the ideal replacement for veteran right back Tom Parker. The manager persuaded him to switch positions and he took over from Parker in 1932-33. The hard-tackling defender was a fixture until the outbreak of war, giving one of his finest displays in Arsenal's 1936 FA Cup final win over Sheffield United. He played on until 1948, retiring after the final game of the Gunners' sixth championship season. He later coached Arsenal's juniors and scouted the Gunners' forthcoming opponents.

in the same game was young Welsh forward, Derek Tapscot, a small, energetic player from Barry Town, who scored twice in Arsenal's 3-0 win.

Season 1954-55 was equally disappointing. Arsenal got off to a terrible start, winning only five of their first 20 games, and by December they were second from bottom in the League. New players arrived, with inside forward Jimmy Bloomfield making his first appearance in an away defeat at Everton in August and towering centre half Jim Fotheringham taking over from Dodgin in November. The team steadied itself and took three points from Chelsea in two games over Christmas and by Easter had lost only one out of 11 games. By now Jimmy Logie had departed for Gravesend and Arthur Milton had joined Bristol City. Milton was replaced by speedy right winger Danny Clapton. The Gunners took all six points from their three games over Easter to reach fifth position in the League but lost three out of their last four. The final placing in the League was ninth. They were also knocked out of the FA Cup in the fourth round by Wolves.

Although Lawton scored a hat-trick in the opening home game of the 1955-56 season, a 3-1 win over Cardiff City, he scored only three more before his move to Kettering Town in February. Another notable departure later in the season was Doug Lishman who moved to Nottingham Forest. Lishman had scored 137 goals for the club in his eight years' loyal service at Highbury. Wingers Gordon Nutt and Mike Tiddy joined the club early in the season from Cardiff City and hard-tackling right back Stan Charlton and young centre forward Vic Groves arrived from Leyton Orient in November. The team was becoming a younger one but the lack of maturity and experience showed once again in the League.

Although Arsenal won seven of their last eight games, they could only finish in fifth place in the League. They also received a serious fright in the FA Cup third round tie against Southern League side Bedford Town. Following a sensational 2-2 draw at Highbury, Arsenal were 1-0 down at Bedford with five minutes to go, when Groves equalized and Tapscott headed in the winner in extra-time. The Gunners' interest in the tournament came to an end in the sixth round when they were beaten 3-1 at Highbury by Birmingham City.

An era came to an end on 24 October 1956 when Tom Whittaker died at the age of 59 from a heart attack at London's University College Hospital.

50 Greatest Players

LES COMPTON Centre half/Full back

Born: Woodford, 12 September 1912

Joined Arsenal: 1932   **From:** Hampstead Town

Debut: 25 April 1932 v Aston Villa, League

Appearances: 270   **Goals:** 6

Left Arsenal: 1952 (retired)

Honours won with Arsenal: Division One championship 1948; FA Cup winner 1950; 1 England cap

Les Compton joined Arsenal as a full back but his pre-war opportunities were limited by the form of George Male and Eddie Hapgood. He switched to centre half, and occasionally centre forward, during wartime football, then became the cornerstone of the Gunners' postwar defence. He played five times for England in wartime 'internationals' but only once thereafter – when he became the oldest player to make an England debut, against Wales at the age of 38! 'Big Les' was noted for his steadiness, strength in the air and long-term commitment to the Gunners. He retired in 1952 and later joined the Highbury coaching staff. He also played county cricket for Middlesex.

Great Managers – 1947-56

TOM WHITTAKER

A hugely respected and universally popular figure at Highbury, Tom Whittaker was an Arsenal man for nearly 40 years. He joined the club as a 19-year-old centre forward in 1919 and represented Arsenal as a left half and left back throughout his playing career, which was terminated by a knee injury he received while playing for the Football Association in Australia in the summer of 1925. A keen student of the latest advances in physiotherapy and training techniques, Whittaker was appointed assistant trainer at Highbury in 1926 and succeeded George Hardy as trainer in February 1927. In 1946, after his demobilization, he became assistant manager to George Allison, and the pair's astute acquisition of Joe Mercer and Ronnie Rooke staved off the threat of relegation in 1946-47. Allison resigned in June 1947 and Whittaker took over as manager. In his first season in charge Whittaker led Arsenal to the league championship. In 1950 he guided the Gunners to FA Cup triumph, beating Liverpool 2-0 in the final, and in 1952-53, the Gunners won the league title for the seventh time, winning the last game of the season and securing the championship on goal average. In the autumn of 1956 Whittaker was diagnosed with nervous exhaustion and was admitted to hospital where, in October, this loyal club servant died of a heart attack.

When he took over from Chapman, Whittaker remarked with ominous prescience, 'Herbert Chapman worked himself to death for the club and if is to be my fate I am happy to accept it.' Joe Mercer commented that Whittaker 'was the best thing that ever happened to me'. In his book *End of an Innings* Denis Compton summed up the feelings of many of the players, saying, 'I shall always feel a particular sense of gratitude and admiration for Tom Whittaker. He was a great and kindly man.'

The new manager was to be Jack Crayston but he was not to emulate the stirring achievements of the Chapman/Whittaker regimes. Indeed, Arsenal were about to enter a barren period which would not bear fruit until the arrival of Bertie Mee and the triumphs of 1970 and 1971.

Chapter Four: 1956-70
The Barren Years

'Gentleman' Jack Crayston took over the manager's seat at Highbury in November 1956. Crayston had been an elegant wing half for the Gunners, making over 200 appearances for the club between 1934 and 1939, and he had joined the coaching staff in 1946 as assistant manager to Whittaker. The fatal pressures on Whittaker led the Arsenal board to split the secretary/manager job into two, with Bob Wall taking up the position of secretary.

Crayston's promotion sparked off a good run for Arsenal who went unbeaten for ten league games, rising from 11th to third. In early January Don Roper returned to Southampton having spent ten years at Highbury but a new forward, Scotsman David Herd, had emerged through the ranks to claim the regular centre forward slot. Herd, an energetic player with a powerful right-foot shot, was the son of Scottish international Alex Herd and had made his senior debut at the age of 17 at Stockport County playing alongside his dad. In the FA Cup Herd scored six times in the first four matches but Arsenal were eliminated 2-1 at Highbury in a sixth round replay against West Bromwich Albion. In the League they finished in a reasonable fifth place, the competition being won by Manchester United. Two links with the past were broken during the season, with the retirement of Joe Shaw and the death of George Allison.

Vic Groves, whose brief Arsenal career had been dogged by injury and disaffection with a section of the crowd, was fully recovered for the start of the 1957-58 season and he teamed up effectively in attack with David Herd. Defensive deficiencies, however, saw Arsenal finish the campaign having conceded 85 goals, their highest since 1927-28, and end the campaign in a lowly 12th position. They were also knocked out of the FA Cup in the third round, dramatically going down 3-1 to Northampton Town away.

One game that season, however, is remembered by older Gunners fans as one of the finest matches ever seen at Highbury. The visitors were Manchester United and the fabulously promising 'Busby Babes'. The outstanding display of football was United's last game in England before the tragic air crash crash.

At the end of what was a deeply disappointing season, Jack Crayston, disillusioned by not having the money to invest in the transfer market, resigned as manager at a board meeting in May 1958. In July George Swindin was revealed as the new manager. Although the first choice for the board was Joe

Great Matches

LEAGUE DIVISION ONE   **Highbury, 1 February 1958**

Arsenal 4	Manchester United 5	Attendance: 63,578
Herd	Edwards	
Bloomfield 2	Charlton	
Tapscott	Taylor 2	
	Viollet	

The visitors in this enthralling match were Manchester United – the 'Busby Babes' – who had won the League in the previous two seasons. United were magnificent in the first half, running up a 3-0 lead by the interval through Duncan Edwards, a fierce volley from young Bobby Charlton and an opportunistic goal from Tommy Taylor. Arsenal fought back in the second period, drawing level in an incredible three minutes. In the 58th minute David Herd volleyed in from a David Bowen lob. Then Jimmy Bloomfield netted twice, the second from a diving header. Four minutes later Viollet put United 4-3 ahead and within seven minutes an angled shot from Taylor gave United a 5-3 advantage. All was not over, however, and Derek Tapscott reduced United's winning margin to one in the 77th minute. United defended desperately until the final whistle and the score was 5-4 to the northern side. The game marked United's last appearance in England before the team was destroyed by the Munich air disaster, in which five of the team that day – captain Roger Byrne, Duncan Edwards, Tommy Taylor, Mark Jones and Eddie Colman – died in the crash.

Arsenal: Kelsey, Stan Charlton, Evans, Ward, Fotheringham, Bowen, Groves, Tapscott, Herd, Bloomfield, Nutt

Manchester United: Gregg, Foulkes, Byrne, Colman, Jones, Edwards, Morgans, Bobby Charlton, Taylor, Viollet, Scanlon

Referee: G. Pullen

Mercer, Mercer decided to take over at Aston Villa. Swindin, a single-minded Yorkshireman and ex-Arsenal goalkeeper, had done well at Peterborough United and was regarded as a man who could take the ailing club forward.

George Swindin Returns as Manager

He embarked on a clearout of some of the players, with Fotheringham, Tapscott (scorer of 62 league goals for Arsenal), Tiddy and Holton all leaving the club. He paid Preston £27,000 for the abrasive, self-confident Scottish international wing half Tommy Docherty who scored on his debut against Burnley, the only goal he ever notched for the club. A fellow Scottish international, Jackie Henderson, an explosive attacker who normally occupied the left wing position, also joined from Wolves. Like Docherty, Henderson scored in his first game for Arsenal, netting two headers in a home 4-3 win over West Brom at Highbury. The fast, incisive Irish left back Billy 'Flint' McCullough also arrived at Highbury from Portadown as a replacement for Dennis Evans. McCullough was to be a regular in the position until the emergence of the combative Peter Storey in the mid-1960s.

Arsenal began the season in impressive home form, winning their first six games at Highbury. Herd also scored four in a 6-1 demolition of Everton in September. Young, fair-haired inside forward John Barnwell broke into the first team in November and was to prove a useful addition to the attacking line-up. However, three defeats in December and a bad, non-winning run of seven games in March and April could not be redeemed by winning their last three games. They finished the season in third place, the title going to Stan Cullis's Wolves. In the FA Cup, Jack Kelsey suffered a broken arm in a fifth round replay against Sheffield United in mid-November and the Gunners were knocked out 3-0. Deputy keeper Jim Standen took over in goal for the remainder of the season.

Swindin continued to buy in talent, hoping to secure some consistency in his squad. In April 1959 he spent £42,000 to acquire Mel Charles, a robust, versatile player, from Swansea Town. Charles – brother of the much-lauded John Charles, the 'Gentle Giant' of Leeds, Juventus and Wales – had suspect knees, however, and spent much of his brief Highbury career recovering from cartilage operations. The injury list was a long one over season 1959-60 and included Docherty breaking an ankle in October in a match against his old club, Preston. Arsenal lost five games in succession in November and December and lost four out of their last six league games to finish 13th in the League, 16 points behind leaders Burnley. On top of this humiliation, they went out of the FA Cup in the third round, losing the second replay 2-0 to Rotherham United. Arsenal had hit their lowest placing in the League for 13 years, when Swindin was the regular custodian, and the situation was bleak.

Arsenal's beleaguered state was thrown into starker relief by the pre-eminence of Tottenham Hotspur, the old enemy just up London's Seven Sisters Road. With supreme footballing talents such as Danny Blanchflower, Cliff Jones and John White, manager Bill Nicholson was parading the finest team in the club's history and he was about to win the first 'Double' in modern times over the following season. An unhappy and demoralized Arsenal side, and their many disenchanted fans, would find this painful to behold.

Meanwhile, player power was finally beginning to make itself felt in English football. Until now, players were not only subject to the maximum wage (£20 per week) but also to the iniquitous 'retain and transfer' system, where the clubs decided when and to where a player could transfer. A

50 Greatest Players

REG LEWIS Inside forward/Centre forward

Born: Bilston, Staffordshire, 7 March 1920

Joined Arsenal: 1937   **From:** Margate

Debut: 1 January 1938 v Everton, League

Appearances: 175   **Goals:** 116

Left Arsenal: 1953 (retired)

Honours won with Arsenal: Division One championship 1948;
FA Cup winner 1950

Reg Lewis will always be remembered for scoring the two goals that sank Liverpool in the 1950 FA Cup final. He was one of the most consistent scorers in the Gunners' history. His best years were lost to the war, otherwise he may well have beaten Cliff Bastin's scoring record. He was top scorer in three of his four full postwar seasons, including a haul of 29 league goals in 28 appearances in 1946-47. Lewis's family moved to South London when he was a small boy. He developed with amateur club Nunhead before joining Arsenal's 'nursery' side at Margate. He made his first-team debut in December 1937 and netted seven goals in 15 league appearances the following season. He retired in 1953 and later worked in insurance.

player's registration was sufficient to bind him to the club in perpetuity. George Eastham, one of the most skilful and sought-after inside forwards of his generation, was questioning this fundamental restraint of trade. Eastham was determined to leave Newcastle United after a number of acerbic disputes, having given the Geordie club four years of his playing career. Relations between Eastham and the club had clearly deteriorated to the point of no return when Newcastle manager Charlie Mitten described the player as 'the guy with the biggest head, the shortest arms and the deepest pockets in the business'.

Supported by the Professional Footballers Association, spearheaded by Jimmy Hill, Eastham challenged 'retain and transfer', but he was not to win his landmark victory until July 1963, when the High Court found in his favour and legalized fixed-term contracts, by which time the maximum wage had also gone the way of this archaic piece of industrial relations, unique to the world of professional football. In 1960, however, Eastham had agreed with Newcastle that he could leave the club if they received an offer of £25,000 plus two proven international forwards to replace him. Arsenal, desperate to find a playmaker to help them compete with Spurs, the new North London masters, offered Newcastle Jimmy Bloomfield as part payment (it was no surprise that an upset Bloomfield decided to leave for Birmingham City soon after Eastham's arrival) and then £47,500 for the slightly-built but extravagantly-gifted forward. Eastham joined the Gunners in October 1960, having received a munificent £20 signing-on fee.

The new inside left made his mark on his first appearance for Arsenal on 10 December, scoring twice in the 5-1 home defeat of Bolton Wanderers. Two weeks later, 19-year-old Ulster-born wing half Terry Neill made his debut in a match against Sheffield Wednesday, also scoring in his first game. Later in the season, 5ft 5in Welsh forward Arfon Griffith appeared in the red and white for the first time. However, in the spring the influential Tommy Docherty took up a post as first-team coach at Chelsea (managed by ex-Gunner Ted Drake) while coach Ron Greenwood was appointed to the manager's role at West Ham. This coming and going seemed to affect the team and they could only manage 11th, in the League, a long way and 25 points behind Nicholson's rampant Spurs. Progress in the FA Cup was equally disappointing, the Gunners going out 2-1 to Sunderland in the third round.

The following season was not much of an improvement, although Mel Charles began to show his goalscoring prowess, netting six in his first five games including two in a 4-3 defeat by Spurs. Centre half Laurie Brown joined from Northampton Town and big winger Alan Skirton ('the Highbury Express'), who had joined 18 months earlier from Bath City, had recovered from a long layoff due to tuberculosis. Skirton began to demonstrate his scoring touch and was to finish the season as top scorer with 21 goals. Other new faces included winger Johnny MacLeod, bought from Hibs for £40,000 and tough wing half Eddie Clamp, but Arsenal exited from the FA Cup in the fourth round, defeated 1-0 at Old Trafford by Manchester United. Ipswich, managed by Alf Ramsey, won the League for the first time in their history and the Gunners ended up in tenth place. Swindin had chopped and changed his team and had injected much

Jack Kelsey won 41 caps for Wales, a record for a British keeper at the time.

69

50 Greatest Players

JOE MERCER Left half

Born: Ellesmere Port, 9 August 1914

Joined Arsenal: 1946   **From:** Everton

Debut: 30 November 1946 v Bolton Wanderers, League

Appearances: 273   **Goals:** 2

Left Arsenal: 1954 (retired)

Honours won with Arsenal: Division One championship 1948, 1953; FA Cup winner1950

Joe Mercer was one of the most inspirational skippers in Arsenal history. He was one of George Allison's last – and shrewdest – signings for the Gunners. Everton thought Mercer's best days were behind him when he made a £7,000 move to Highbury in November 1946. Instead, he played on until a broken leg ended his career in April 1954. Tom Whittaker switched Mercer to a more defensive role than he played for Everton and he thrived. His experience and influence on the players around him laid the foundations for two championships and an FA Cup success. He later became a title-winning manager with Manchester City.

new blood, but he had not managed to create a winning formula. The situation was exacerbated by the successes enjoyed by Spurs and a saddened and disappointed Swindin resigned at the end of the season.

Billy Wright Comes In

Swindin's successor was Billy Wright, appointed to the job in May 1962. Wright, who had no managerial experience, was nonetheless one of Britain's biggest sporting stars. Wright had spent his career with Wolverhampton Wanderers whom he had captained three times to the league title and he had gained a record 105 caps for England, captaining his country for 90 of them, and had played in 70 consecutive internationals. He had also been voted Footballer of the Year and been awarded a CBE. His marriage to Joy Beverley, one of the country's biggest pop stars as part of the Beverley Sisters, further cemented his position as one of the nation's top personalities.

Wright moved quickly to dispel the bleak mood around Highbury by acquiring the services of Joe Baker from Torino for £70,000. Baker was a flamboyant centre forward with speedy acceleration and tight ball control, and he had made footballing history by being the first man to be capped for

England while playing outside the Football League (with Hibernian). Wright's new attacking line-up comprised Baker the marksman, flanked by the equally lethal, lean figure of Geoff Strong and the artistic skills of George Eastham, supported on the wings by the small Geordie teenager George Armstrong and Alan Skirton. The team appeared as strong as any other club in the League. Young Terry Neill was appointed captain and the omens for the 1962-63 season seemed more than favourable. One black cloud, however, was the retirement of Jack Kelsey due to an injury received while playing for Wales in a friendly against Brazil. Kelsey was replaced in goal by Ian McKechnie, a 21-year-old Scot.

The new manager began his Arsenal career with a 2-1 away victory at Leyton Orient, the goals coming from Baker and Strong. Baker scored again in the next game, a 2-0 home win against Birmingham City. However, over the next 11 games they won only one, although an exciting 4-4 draw in October with Spurs saw the appearance in the first team of young forward David Court who scored two and made another while deputizing for the injured Baker. Baker ended the streak with a hat-trick in a 5-4 defeat of Wolves at the end of October. Strong and Baker finished the campaign with 52 goals between them, but the defence leaked goals and Arsenal could only secure seventh place in the League. As quoted in the *Official History of Arsenal*, Strong said, 'Our partnership blended well and it was, I think, the start of playing two central strikers at the club. The goals flowed. But unfortunately we kept letting them in at the other end.'

The goals continued to flow in season 1963-64, with Baker and Strong scoring 31 apiece, but the defence continued to diminish their efforts, letting in 82 goals, nearly twice as many as champions Liverpool who scored only two more than Arsenal during the season. Tall, fair-haired Scottish centre half Ian Ure had joined the club at the beginning of the season and keeper Jim Furnell had arrived from Liverpool. Ure had been the central defender for the Dundee team which had reached the semi-final of the European Cup the previous season where they lost to AC Milan. After a shaky start Ure,

Ian Ure was brought in from a successful Dundee to patch up the leaky defence.

71

Billy Wright had had a successful career at Wolves, acquired 105 England caps and married a Beverley Sister. Sadly, he was not a success as manager of Arsenal.

an excellent header of the ball but less confident on the ground, settled down in defence for the Gunners but could do little about their defensive profligacy. In spite of the claims of other keepers at the club – McKechnie, McClelland, Burns and a young Bob Wilson – Furnell became the main goalminder, even although he let in five goals at Anfield on the last day of the season against his old club.

Two of the modern Arsenal legends arrived at the club in 1964. To strengthen his defence, Wright paid £35,000 in the spring to buy the classy, intelligent right back Don Howe from West Bromwich Albion. Howe, an England international, made his debut in the opening game of the 1964-65 season at Anfield, the first game to be screened on BBC TV's *Match of the Day* Saturday night programme. Liverpool's 3-2 win in the fixture was partly achieved by Liverpool winger Peter Thompson running Howe ragged. Howe quickly recovered from this initial, highly public setback. In October, Scottish international wing half Frank McLintock arrived from Leicester City for £80,000. McLintock, then an attacking midfielder who was not afraid to speak his mind on the pitch, was to develop into the defensive captain of the 1971 'Double' team. Other members of the 'Double' side who received outings in the first team during the season were centre forward John Radford, left-footed central defender Peter Simpson and midfielder Jon Sammels. Top scorer in the season was again Joe Baker who did not miss a match and claimed 25 goals, while his erstwhile partner Geoff Strong was transferred to Liverpool in November 1964. The season remained a period of transition for the Gunners, who plummeted to 13th in the League and were humiliatingly eliminated from the FA Cup in the fourth round away to Peterborough United.

The situation deteriorated even further in season 1965-66. Another of the class of 1971, Peter Storey, broke through into the first team as left back to replace Billy McCullough, but Joe Baker departed to join Nottingham Forest in February and the scoring duties were left to John Radford and George Eastham. Wingers George Armstrong and Alan Skirton did what they could to help plunder the goals but the side was again let down by defensive shortcomings. There was increasing friction in the dressing room and arguments between players on the pitch. Wright was losing control. Arsenal ended the season with 12 wins out of 42 games and 14th position in the League, their worst since 1929-30, and they were knocked out of the FA Cup by Blackburn in the third round. The nadir was reached on Thursday 5 May 1966 when, in a game against Leeds, they attracted a crowd of only 4,544 to Highbury for a league game, losing 3-0. The supporters were voting with their feet against Wright and the players.

The inevitable occurred when Wright returned from holiday at the end of the season and, to no one's surprise, was sacked by chairman Denis Hill-Wood. A chastened and unhappy Wright, who confessed that he was not tough enough with his players and who was probably too genial a man for a job which demanded ruthless decision-making, moved to become Head of Sport and Outside Broadcasts at ATV in Birmingham. Arsenal, with three managers in ten years and no silverware in the Highbury trophy cabinets, looked again for a man who could lead them to the heights their history deserved.

Billy Wright Out, Bertie Mee in

The appointment in June 1966 of Bertie Mee as the new manager surprised the media and the players, as well as the man himself. Mee had been Arsenal's physiotherapist for the past six years but, although highly respected for his training skills throughout the game, he had no management experience. His playing career had been an undistinguished one, with spells at Derby County and Mansfield Town, but he had a successful military career as well as having conducted courses and lectures for the FA over the previous 20 years.

Smallish in stature, he was a disciplinarian, an efficient organizer and delegator and an expert in motivation and man management. Aware that his appointment was something of a gamble by the Arsenal board, Mee asked for a 12-month trial period. If he failed, he would get his old job back. To help him in understanding and applying the tactical side of the game, he persuaded his old friend Dave Sexton to join him from Fulham as coach. The players quickly took to Sexton

Joe Baker, who finished as top scorer in his four seasons at Arsenal.

George Eastham, the classy forward who played his part in creating the legislation that was to abolish the maximum wage for professional footballers. He is seen here in action against Newcastle on 2 October, 1965. Arsenal won 1-0.

whose positive approach, footballing knowledge and enthusiasm for the game readily transmitted itself to a team demoralized by the failures of recent years. He set about turning Arsenal into a tight, cohesive unit, strong in defence, creative in midfield and quick on the break, a team which would bring success back to Highbury.

Mee's philosophy was that he preferred committed, hard-working team players to erratic, if gifted, individuals. George Eastham, therefore, was the first to suffer the effects of the new regime and he was transferred to Stoke in August. In Mee's first game in charge, Alan Skirton scored twice in the 3-1 away win over Sunderland at Roker Park but the winger was the next to leave, joining Blackpool in September. West Ham, with recent World Cup-winning heroes Martin Peters, Geoff Hurst and Bobby Moore, were the visitors to Highbury for the first home game of the season and were beaten 2-1, both goals coming from Radford. The next game was a 1-0 win over Villa and Arsenal were unbeaten until the fifth league fixture, going down 3-1 to the old foe at White Hart Lane.

Arsenal entered the League Cup for the first time, attracted to the tournament because the final was now to be held at prestigious Wembley instead of home and away and also because the winners would gain automatic admission to next season's Fairs Cup. They made heavy weather, however, of their first round, taking three games to beat Third Division Gillingham. Inside forward Tommy Baldwin scored four times in the three games but was transferred shortly after to Chelsea in part exchange for forward George Graham. A well-built, elegant player, with a smooth first touch and an excellent header of the ball, Graham had an impressive scoring record with Chelsea. His creative, almost arrogant play compensated for his lack of acceleration and he soon became known as 'Stroller'.

Mee added to his mix of talents with the purchase of the muscular, voluble full back Bob McNab from Huddersfield Town and striker Colin Addison from Nottingham Forest. McNab would become an integral part of the 1971 side but Addison found it difficult to fit in at Highbury and moved to Sheffield United 15 months later. McNab had been offered the opportunity to move to Liverpool but turned them down. An angry Bill Shankly told him, 'You never could play, anyway. You'll regret it joining these fancy Dans down in London.'

After the Spurs defeat, Arsenal went off the boil and won only two of their next 15 games, recovering at the end of the season to seventh place by virtue of an unbeaten run in their last 12 encounters. In the FA Cup they beat Bristol Rovers and Bolton (Radford scoring a hat-trick in the replay), but lost to Birmingham City in the fifth round. Nonetheless, Mee was putting into place the makings of a very good side. Regulars in the team now included the dependable and popular winger Geordie Armstrong; tough

50 Greatest Players

GEORGE SWINDIN Goalkeeper

Born: Doncaster, 4 December 1914

Joined Arsenal: 1936   **From:** Bradford City

Debut: 3 September 1936 v Brentford, League

Appearances: 294

Left Arsenal: 1954   **For:** Peterborough United

Honours won with Arsenal: Division One championship 1938, 1948, 1953; FA Cup winner 1950

George Swindin was yet another Gunners star whose best years were interrupted by the war. He was signed from Bradford City for £4,000 in April 1936. He played enough games to gain a championship winner's medal in 1937-38, but really established himself in postwar football. He was Arsenal's first-choice keeper until injury struck him early in the 1952-53 season, though he returned for the closing seven league matches.

After 18 years at Highbury, he was given a free transfer to join Peterborough as player-manager the following season. After three non-league championships with Peterborough, he returned to Highbury, succeeding Jack Crayston as manager in 1958. He resigned in 1962 and later took charge at Norwich.

defender Peter 'Snoutie' Storey; passionate midfielder Frank McLintock; attacking left back Bob McNab; tall, intelligent centre forward John Radford; stylish George Graham; creative inside forward Jon Sammels; and calm central defender Peter 'Stan' Simpson, with a sure left foot. The 1971 'Double' side was coming together.

It was now becoming clear that, although the defence was settling down well, a goalscorer was needed. Graham had topped the Arsenal scoring list during the season with 11, but the next three highest were Sammels, Armstrong and McLintock, all notionally midfielders. Mee set to work to find his man. Season 1967-68 began unsteadily with two wins in the first five games, but four wins in succession (including a 5-3 defeat of Fulham with Radford picking up another hat-trick) during September helped morale. Dave Sexton's departure to become manager of Chelsea early in the season dismayed several of the players who had benefited from the coach's insights. He was replaced by 33-year-old reserve coach Don Howe, whose playing career for the Gunners had been cut short when he broke his right leg playing against Blackpool in 1966.

It took some while for Howe to stamp his authority on the disaffected team. However, according to McLintock, quoted in David Tossell's *Seventy-One Guns*, at a training session, 'Don said, "Right, I have had enough of you lot. I am Don Howe. Dave Sexton has gone. I am the coach and from now

50 Greatest Players

JACK KELSEY Goalkeeper

Born: Swansea, 19 November 1929

Joined Arsenal: 1949   **From:** Winch Wen

Debut: 24 February 1951 v Charlton Athletic, League

Appearances: 351

Left Arsenal: 1962 (retired)

Honours won with Arsenal: Division One championship 1953; 41 Wales caps

Jack Kelsey was unfortunate to reach his peak when the Gunners were going through one of their most disappointing spells since the early 1920s. He established himself in the side, deputizing for the injured George Swindin during the 1952-53 championship campaign. That was to be his only medal with the Gunners. He won his first Wales cap in 1954 and starred in their run to the 1958 World Cup quarter-finals. His total of 41 caps set a record at the time for a British goalkeeper. Kelsey's career was ended when he suffered a back injury diving at the feet of Brazil striker Vava in an international friendly. After a six-month fight to recover, he was forced to retire.

50 Greatest Players

JIMMY LOGIE Inside forward

Born: Edinburgh, 23 November 1919

Joined Arsenal: 1939   **From:** Lochore Welfare

Debut: 9 January 1946 v West Ham United, FA Cup

Appearances: 326   **Goals:** 76

Left Arsenal: 1955   **For:** Gravesend & Northfleet

Honours won with Arsenal: Division One championship 1948, 1953; FA Cup winner 1950; 1 Scotland cap

Jimmy Logie was one of Arsenal's finest postwar schemers. He was at the centre of the Gunners' triumphs under Tom Whittaker. Scottish and small, like Alex James, he joined the Gunners just before war broke out. He made his senior debut in the FA Cup against West Ham in 1946 and was a regular for the next eight seasons. Besides his creative talents, he was also a frequent scorer. Probably his most important goal was the third in the Gunners' 3-2 win over Burnley which clinched the 1952-53 title. Like James, Logie went curiously unrecognized by the Scotland selectors. After retiring from football, he worked as a porter in Smithfield meat market, a far cry from the riches of modern stars.

on you will do what I say. Right, come on! We are going to do double laps. Go, Go!" And from then on you could tell he was in charge.' Howe moved the players away from Sexton's man-marking system and introduced a zonal defence, to which the players eventually found it easier to adapt.

In the League Cup the Gunners dismissed Coventry, Reading and Blackburn to face Burnley in the quarter-final. At Turf Moor Burnley went 2-0 ahead in the first ten minutes but two from Graham and one from McLintock gave Arsenal a 3-2 lead at half-time. McNab was sent off in the second half and Burnley equalized shortly before the end. McNab's replacement in the following week's replay was a young, stocky, Irish full back, brought up just round the corner from Highbury. Pat Rice was a hard-working, committed defender, who perhaps lacked some of the finer footballing skills and delicacy but he was to become a Highbury fixture over the coming years. Goals apiece from Radford and Neill ensured a 2-1 win. In the semi-final two wins over Second Division Huddersfield Town meant that Arsenal would face Leeds in the final on 2 March at Wembley.

Don Revie's Leeds United were one of the top teams in England but were unpopular with football fans throughout the country. Although a highly skilful

50 Greatest Players

GEORGE EASTHAM Midfielder

Born: Blackpool, 23 September 1936

Joined Arsenal: 1960   **From:** Newcastle United

Debut: 10 December 1960 v Bolton Wanderers, League

Appearances: 223   **Goals:** 41

Left Arsenal: 1966   **For:** Stoke City

Honours won with Arsenal: 19 England caps

George Eastham was among the most elegant midfield schemers of his time. A frail, slight inside forward, he joined the Gunners for £47,500 after a wrangle with Newcastle that eventually ended in a far-reaching court judgement. Eastham scored twice on his debut and quickly established himself as Arsenal's linchpin. In the first two years of Billy Wright's reign, he masterminded one of the league's most prolific attacks. Unfortunately, Arsenal were nowhere near as strong in defence. Eastham's skills made him an England regular for three seasons, but he fell out of favour at Highbury as the Gunners slid down the table in 1965-66. He moved on that summer as Bertie Mee introduced a new managerial regime.

side – with creative players such as Billy Bremner, Johnny Giles, Eddie Gray and Peter Lorimer – their aim was to win at all costs. Their methods were often underhand and even brutal, and opposing players complained of being kicked, elbowed and stamped on in their bruising encounters with Revie's side. The Wembley game was a hard-fought one and was settled when Eddie Gray swung in a left-foot corner. Arsenal keeper Furnell was impeded and distracted by Leeds' tallest two players, Jack Charlton and Paul Madeley, at the near post (a favourite Leeds spoiling tactic). Graham headed out, but the ball fell to Terry Cooper who volleyed in for the only goal of the match.

In the FA Cup Arsenal reached the fifth round, losing 2-1 to Birmingham in a replay. Bobby Gould, a new signing from Coventry City for an Arsenal record fee of £90,000, scored. Mee was now hoping he had found a new goalscorer. Furnell had dropped a long shot into his own net in the first game against Birmingham, causing the replay. He was dropped for the replay and the game marked the assumption of the regular goalkeeping spot by ex-teacher Bob Wilson, who had nearly left the club after being demoted to the third team two years previously. Wilson, whose speciality was diving at the feet of attackers to snatch the ball, was to be ever-present in the team of 1971. In a late spurt, Arsenal won their last five games in the League to finish in ninth place.

Season 1968-69 saw Arsenal's best league start for years, beginning with a 2-1 win over Tottenham at White Hart Lane, their first win at Spurs' ground for 11 years. They then set off on an nine-game unbeaten run which came to a halt with a 2-0 defeat at Elland Road. The team was now bedding down and producing some confident performances and, later in the season, the introduction of George Graham to a left-sided midfield role, where his lack of pace was less of a problem, made fuller use of his creative gifts. Between late November and early January they won six games in succession in the League, but they tailed off later in the season and won only two out of the last seven to end in fourth place, 11 points behind winners Leeds. They also reached the fifth round of the FA Cup but lost away 1-0 to West Bromwich Albion.

In the League Cup, they again reached the final. Dispensing with Sunderland, Scunthorpe, Liverpool and Blackburn, they met Spurs in the two-legged semi-final. At Highbury a late goal from Radford gave Arsenal a 1-0 lead to take to White Hart Lane, where goals from Jimmy Greaves and Radford produced an aggregate 2-1 win for the Gunners. The final took place on 15 May at Wembley against unfancied Third Division Swindon Town.

Heavy rain had turned the pitch into a quagmire and playing conditions were dreadful. On top of this, over half the team were still suffering the after-effects of flu. Arsenal immediately went on the attack but the cloying surface sapped the players' energies. A botched backpass from the hapless Ian Ure to Wilson in the 34th minute was seized on by Roger Smart and Swindon were 1-0 up. With

50 Greatest Players

JOE BAKER Centre forward

Born: Liverpool, 17 July 1940

Joined Arsenal: 1962   **From:** Torino

Debut: 18 August 1962 v Leyton Orient, League

Appearances: 156   **Goals:** 100

Left Arsenal: 1966   **For:** Nottingham Forest

Honours won with Arsenal: 3 England caps

Joe Baker was Billy Wright's first major signing for Arsenal. For three years he gave terrific value for the £70,000 fee. He was skilful, predatory and a tough competitor, as much bigger centre backs discovered. He finished top scorer, or joint top, in each of his four seasons at Highbury. Even though he left for Forest in February 1966, he still topped Arsenal's goals tally for the 1965-66 campaign. Baker's understanding with George Eastham brought him a host of goals. He also forged a potent partnership with Geoff Strong, until his fellow striker was transferred to Liverpool. But, like Eastham, Baker fell out of favour as the Gunners slipped down the table in 1965-66 and his hopes of a place in England's World Cup squad disappeared.

just a few minutes remaining of the match Swindon keeper Peter Downsbrough made one of his few mistakes and kicked a clearance against Bobby Gould, who converted the opportunity with his head. In the 15th minute of extra-time Swindon forward Don Rogers scored from a corner and in the second period Rogers ran half the length of the pitch before scoring Swindon's third past Wilson. Against the run of play, the underdogs had won their only major trophy and there was an enormous sense of disappointment among the Arsenal players. McLintock, in particular was devastated as this was his fourth major final and the fourth in which he had collected the runners-up medal.

Changes were made for the start of the 1969-70 season. The increasingly criticized Ian Ure moved to Manchester United and Arsenal bought tall Welshman John Roberts from Swansea Town as his replacement in the centre half position. A gangling, skinny local lad, Charlie George – a product of the North Bank and soon to become its darling – made his first appearance for Arsenal in the opening game of the season against Everton and the lanky forward scored in the third game, a 1-0 away win against West Bromwich Albion. George, who had been coached by Bob Wilson at Holloway School, was a quick, strong, self-confident player with a touch of genius on the ball and an ability to score important goals. His winning goal in the 1971 FA Cup final has passed into Highbury legend.

The team suffered a dire run of results between the end of August and late October when they could fashion only one win out of 12 league games. They were also knocked out of the League Cup in the third round after a 1-0 replay against Everton. The 13th game, however, saw Radford score a hat-trick in the 5-1 crushing of Crystal Palace at Selhurst Park. Bobby Gould had not performed as well as Mee had hoped and the emergence of George had made him redundant. Gould was dropped from the side, put on the transfer list and was to join Wolves at the end of the season. To add to the gloom, in January Arsenal were beaten 3-2 in a third round FA Cup replay by Blackpool. The season was not running to plan.

That month, 19-year-old outside right, Peter Marinello, arrived from Hibernian for £100,000. A long-haired George Best lookalike, Marinello was hailed as one of the outstanding players of the future, a view which appeared to hold credence when he scored on his debut against Manchester United, running fully 50 yards with the ball and rounding Alex Stepney to slot the ball into the net. However, commercial and media pressures on the photogenic young Scot, allied to his youth and immaturity, cut short his long-term potential. His first-team chances were also not helped by Armstrong's

Great Matches

INTER-CITIES' FAIRS CUP FINAL		Highbury, 28 April 1970

Arsenal 3	**Anderlecht 0**	**Attendance: 51,612**

Kelly
Radford
Sammels

Arsenal won 4-3 on aggregate

The first game in the two-legged final was at the Parc Astrid Stadium in Brussels against Anderlecht, with their world-class players Jan Mulder and Paul Van Himst. Arsenal were 3-0 down to the fast-raiding Belgian team when substitute Ray Kennedy, with his first touch of the ball, headed in to make the final score 3-1. This away goal was vital as, in the event of an aggregate draw, away goals counted double. Arsenal only had to win 2-0 at Highbury to lift the trophy. In front of a 51,612 crowd on 28 April, Arsenal took the game to Anderlecht, mindful of the quick counter-attacking abilities of the Belgian side. In the 26th minute, Eddie Kelly collected the ball on the edge of the penalty area and unleashed a savage 20-yard strike to put Arsenal 1-0 ahead on the night. Midway through the second half Radford powerfully headed home a McNab cross from the left. Two minutes later Sammels scored the third from a clever ball from George. The Gunners held on to win their first trophy for 17 years and Highbury went wild. Delighted supporters flooded on to the pitch to salute their heroes and the partying began in North London. McLintock had broken his personal jinx and he was carried shoulder-high around the pitch, brandishing the trophy in triumph.

Arsenal: Wilson, Storey, McNab, Kelly, McLintock, Simpson, Armstrong, Sammels, Radford, George, Graham

Anderlecht: Trappeniers, Heylens, Martens, Nordahl, Velkeneers, Kialunda, Desanghere, Devrindt, Mulder, Van Himst, Puis

Referee: G Kunze

John Radford headed Arsenal's second midway through the second half.

consistent form on the wing. Marinello remained with the club until 1973 but featured little in Mee's plans. In the next game, against Chelsea, another 19-year-old forward, Ray Kennedy, made his first full appearance. Kennedy's impact at the club would far exceed that of Marinello's.

A decent run in February and March helped Arsenal move up the table. By this time McLintock had been convinced by Howe and Mee that his best position was at centre half, where he gradually displaced John Roberts and Terry Neill. McLintock's No. 4 shirt was assumed by 18-year-old Glaswegian Eddie Kelly, a quick-thinking, talented midfielder. The league season gradually petered out and Arsenal ended in 12th place. The season, however, was all about European success.

European Triumph

Earlier in the season, Arsenal drew Glentoran in the first round of the Fairs Cup and won 3-0 at Highbury, although they were beaten 1-0 in Northern Ireland. Charlie George revealed another side of his game when he was sent off in the second match for insulting a linesman, and he was consigned to the reserves for three months. Sporting Lisbon were next and a penalty save in Portugal from Geoff Barnett, bought in October as a deputy for Bob Wilson, helped Arsenal take home a clean sheet. Two goals at Highbury from George Graham contributed to the Gunners' 3-0 win.

Jon Sammels scored the only goal in the aggregate 1-0 win over Rouen in round three. In early March goals from Sammels and Radford secured a 2-0 victory over Dinamo Bacau in Romania. Radford, George and Sammels all scored twice, with Graham claiming the other in the 7-1 win at Highbury. The semi-final was to be against the emergent Ajax team of Johan Cruyff, Rudi Krol and Gerrie Muhren who were to win the European Cup three years in succession between 1971 and 1973, with the first leg at Highbury. George opened the scoring against a defensive Dutch team with a long-range shot in the first half. Marinello was replaced by Armstrong and Sammels, in fine scoring form, added another in the second half. Then Graham was fouled in the penalty area and George demonstrated his maturity by calmly scoring from the spot, his first-ever penalty for the club. In Amsterdam, Arsenal went down 1-0 to a Muhren strike but progressed 3-1 on aggregate to the final.

Arsenal returned from the first leg with a 3-1 deficit but took Anderlecht by storm in the second leg to triumph 3-0. Geoffrey Green in *The Times* wrote, 'It will be a night every Arsenal supporter will remember. They have waited long enough.' Don Howe sensed the importance of the win later that night when he commented, 'This can be the big breakthrough. We can go on and on and on from here.' The following season was to realize every word of Howe's prediction.

Chapter 5: 1970-71
The 'Double'

The 'Double' – winning the English Football League championship and FA Cup in the same season – had only been achieved three times since the League was established in 1888-89. Preston North End were the first club to clinch both trophies. 'The Invincibles' achieved the feat in that first season, winning all their games, albeit in a 12-team league. The following decade Aston Villa replicated Preston's dominance, winning both competitions in 1896-97. As the 20th century progressed and the number of clubs entering the competitions grew in number, it seemed increasingly unlikely that the 'Double' was a realistic goal. Spurs' triumph in 1960-61, however, demonstrated that it remained a possibility, although with the League Cup and European competitions now flourishing alongside the two other venerable tournaments, by 1970 the consensus was that the chances of a club pulling off the prize were remote. As the season began Arsenal, 12th in the League the previous year and knocked out of the FA Cup in the third round, appeared unlikely winners of even one, never mind both, of the competitions. But this was to be the club's finest year in their history to date.

The defeats of Ajax and Anderlecht – two of Europe's top clubs – en route to their Fairs Cup victory instilled a sense of self belief in Bertie Mee's team and created a camaraderie and team spirit at Highbury which had been absent for nearly 20 years. Having triumphed in Europe, domestic success was next on the agenda. Chelsea, Manchester City and Everton were only some of the strong teams they had to overcome, but the main threat throughout the season was to be Leeds United, regarded by many as one of the finest sides in Europe.

The First Half

A confident Arsenal began the 1970-71 season at Goodison Park, home to Everton who had won the previous year's title by nine points. In the first big test for Mee's rejuvenated team, Peter Simpson was missing, awaiting a cartilage operation and Jon Sammels was also injured. John Roberts replaced Simpson and Peter Storey moved into midfield, where he was to spend the remainder of his hugely influential season, with Pat Rice replacing him at right back.

Everton, with their English international forward Joe Royle and organized from midfield by Howard Kendall, Alan Ball and Colin Harvey, surged into

Midfielder Peter Storey played a huge part in Arsenal's 'Double'-winning season.

the attack and were rewarded with the first goal, a diving header from Royle within half an hour. The Merseysiders were on top but a breakaway from Radford with 20 minutes to go found George who equalized, although he broke two bones in his ankle in a collision with keeper Gordon West. George was stretchered off and was not to return to first-team duties for nearly six months. With six minutes to go, Wilson deflected a Tommy Wright cross onto the inside of his post, Ball (soon to join the Gunners) deflected the ball and Johnny Morissey put Everton ahead. With the game close to conclusion, Roberts found Graham in space and the Scottish midfielder levelled the score with a deft chip. Arsenal left Goodison with a deserved point.

West Ham at Upton Park were next. Marinello was in midfield and Kennedy in for George, with Storey moved back to the right back role to replace an injured Rice. In spite of Jimmy Greaves's repeated incursions, Arsenal held on to collect another away point in a 0-0 draw. At a hot Highbury in late August, Manchester United were the visitors for Arsenal's first home game of the season. A crowd of 54,000 watched Arsenal go ahead in the 14th minute, when a McNab free kick was headed on by Kelly to an unmarked Radford and the big centre forward converted. Four minutes later a low shot from Radford made the score 2-0. George Best was, as usual, ably policed by Storey, although the Northern Ireland winger forced Wilson into a brave diving save at his feet. A Radford volley from a Kennedy header gave Arsenal a 3-0 lead and United keeper Alex Stepney, hurt in the collision with Radford, left the pitch, giving his jersey to David Sadler. The stand-in was beaten by a Graham header from an Armstrong cross and Arsenal had a comfortable 4-0 win.

Newly-promoted Huddersfield Town put up stronger resistance than expected when they came to Highbury in the next game. Wilson had to be alert to keep out the Town forwards although Kennedy settled matters with a 75th minute header and Arsenal remained unbeaten. They did, however, suffer their first defeat of the season at Stamford Bridge four days later. In a bad-tempered, fast and furious match, John Hollins (another Gunner-in-waiting) picked up a pass from Ron Harris and lobbed the ball over Wilson. The ball hit the crossbar, rebounded and a determined Hollins chased it and scored, the goal receiving ITV's Golden Goal of the Season award. McLintock berated McNab for not preventing Hollins from reaching the rebound, but the left back had slipped at the crucial moment. Kelly equalized with a header early in the second half but Irish full back Paddy Mulligan scored the winner, and his first-ever league goal, when he slotted home from a Peter Osgood pass.

On 1 September, Leeds, boasting a 100 per cent record to date, arrived at Highbury. The two titans of the English game slugged out a goalless draw in what was, unsurprisingly, a closely-contested and ugly match. The unpleasant side of Leeds's game surfaced in the 24th minute when Bremner barged into McNab from behind and, seconds later, McNab retaliated by kicking the little Scotsman. As Bremner lay on the turf, apparently feigning injury, McNab was sent off, to the consternation of his team-mates who surrounded the referee. Rice was in particularly effective form, which could explain why he was badly fouled by Terry Cooper who was cautioned. Mee exonerated his players after the game, saying, 'This was the best performance I have ever seen by an Arsenal team against a side the calibre of Leeds.' Tottenham, having won only two of their first seven games, rolled over at Highbury in the next game. Arsenal won 2-0, the scorer being Armstrong, who scored from close range against reserve keeper Ken Hancock and then turned home a Kelly cross.

Three days later Arsenal contested their first game in the League Cup, drawing away 0-0 to Bobby Robson's Ipswich Town, with McLintock and Wilson having to be at their most resilient. Back in the League, they then travelled to Burnley, who had not scored in their previous five games and were bottom of the table. Before five minutes had elapsed Kennedy had headed Arsenal into the lead but Wilson was then forced into producing some athletic keeping. Under pressure, John Roberts headed a Dave Thomas corner into his own net, but the centre half atoned with ten minutes to go by releasing Radford for the winner. The Gunners were now third equal in the League with Crystal Palace, two points behind Leeds and one behind Manchester City.

Two weeks before the start of the season, UEFA had decided that, for the first time, the holders of the Fairs Cup would be admitted into the following season's tournament to defend the trophy. Arsenal were, therefore, back in Europe and were drawn to meet Lazio in Rome for the first leg, the first time the Gunners had faced an Italian team in competition. Fireworks and flares lit the Roman sky as the team walked out to an intimidating reception at the Olympic Stadium on

18 September. Within five minutes of the second half Arsenal were 2-0 ahead. Kelly crossed to find Radford's head and Kelly again supplied Radford at the near post for the second. Lazio, however, equalized in the last six minutes, both from Giorgio Chinaglia, the second a penalty. After the game both sides met at a restaurant for a meal. Kennedy, needing some air, went outside and was attacked by a Lazio player. This was the signal for mayhem. The fighting began inside the restaurant, spilling out onto the pavement. McNab was pinned against an iron grille, Armstrong thrown against the side of the team bus and Marinello tossed over a car. Mee ushered the players onto the coach, glad to get them away from the angry Lazio mob, incensed by Arsenal's dominance of the game.

As a somewhat prosaic contrast to the Lazio game and the punch-up, Arsenal entertained West Bromwich Albion at Highbury the following Saturday. The Baggies scored twice – through Reid and Tony 'Bomber' Brown (who was to end the season as the league top scorer) – but they were overwhelmed 6-2, with Graham in sparkling form and scoring twice. The other goals came from Kennedy (2), Armstrong and an own goal from Len Cantello.

The Fairs Cup second leg against Lazio was held in midweek in front of a 53,000 crowd at Highbury. Radford scored from a Storey cross in the tenth minute and, with 17 minutes remaining, Armstrong made it 2-0 on the night, turning Storey's pass into the net. Five Italians were cautioned by referee Rudi Glockner, the referee in the thrilling 1970 World Cup final. Lazio, far from the star-studded side of today, were relegated from Serie A at the end of the season.

Stoke City had become a tough nut to crack. Under Tony Waddington, the team, with such industrious players as John Ritchie, Jimmy Greenhoff and Mike Pejic,

George Armstrong, on a typically surging run down the wing, seen here bursting through the Newcastle defence on 10 October 1971 when Arsenal won 1-0. Armstrong appeared 621 times for Arsenal and few could claim to have worn the red shirt with more pride.

had beaten league leaders Leeds United 3-0 two weeks previously. The weekend after the Lazio win Arsenal had to travel to the Potteries and by half-time they were 2-0 down to two Ritchie goals, aided by slip-ups from Roberts and Mclintock. Perhaps the Lazio euphoria had taken the team's mind off basic defensive skills. Whatever the reason, an uncharacteristically nervous display by Wilson – at fault for two more goals in the second half – helped Stoke to a 5-0 win.

Before the next game, at home to Nottingham Forest, Wilson, a part-time television analyst, appeared on BBC's Saturday lunchtime football programme and discussed the goals he had let in against Stoke. Mee was furious about Wilson's betrayal of information which should have remained inside the club and let Wilson know his feelings. It did not affect the keeper's performance in the Forest game, however, as he hardly saw the ball. Kennedy scored in the 15th minute and with half an hour remaining he had claimed his first senior hat-trick. Armstrong scored another for a 4-0 win.

Arsenal had beaten Ipswich 4-0 in the League Cup second round replay the previous week (with two each from Kennedy and Radford) and met Second Division Luton Town in the third round at a sell-out Kenilworth Road. Ex-Gunner David Court gave away a free kick in the 26th minute and Graham headed in at the near post for the only goal of the game. Newcastle, who had not won at home since the first day of the season, were the opposition at St James's Park the following Saturday and, although 'Pop' Robson put the Geordies ahead, Graham exploited an error by centre half Ollie Burton to level the score. The return game against Everton at Highbury the next Saturday was, unlike the opening game of the season, a one-sided affair. The Gunners were 2-0 ahead after 20 minutes through two Kennedy headers. Kelly, with a rasping drive from the edge of the area and Storey, from the penalty spot, after Roger Kenyon had handled in the box, added two more.

In the Fairs Cup, Arsenal had been drawn to play Sturm Graz with the first leg at Highbury. Sturm Graz had successfully persuaded UEFA that it would be more sensible to get the first game over with in Austria, given the rapidly worsening weather in the country. In spite of Mee's disparaging comments about Sturm – likening them to a Second Division team – on 21 October the Austrian side secured a 1-0 win, although possibly not a big enough cushion for the return at Highbury in two weeks' time. On Saturday the Gunners travelled to Coventry, who had ex-Arsenal player Geoff Strong in their ranks. Radford scored twice (breaking his wrist while falling after the second) and Graham capitalized on a Strong mistake with four minutes to go in the 3-1 result.

In midweek an enthralling, end-to-end game in the fourth round of the League Cup against Crystal Palace resulted in a 0-0 draw and on 31 October

Derby County, managed by Brian Clough, came to Highbury. Kelly intercepted a back pass from England centre half Roy McFarland in the 37th minute to open the scoring and a Radford header, his tenth goal of the season, made the final score 2-0. By now, the beginning of November, Arsenal were still in four competitions and only two points behind leaders Leeds in the League.

Arsenal continued their presence in the Fairs Cup during the following week, when they beat Sturm Graz in the second leg 2-0 on the night and 2-1 on aggregate, but they made heavy going of it. Although Kennedy scored early on, the team missed numerous chances to finish off the Austrians. After 90 minutes, the referee added on five minutes of injury time and in the last minute Sturm defender Reiter handled on the line from a Graham volley. Storey held his nerve to score from the spot and Arsenal were through.

Blackpool were having a poor season, with only two wins to date, and would be relegated at the end of the campaign. Arsenal came away from Bloomfield Road on 7 November with a 1-0 win, after Radford headed in from an Armstrong cross, but the Gunners were criticized in the media for what was perceived as their cautious, defensive play and their over-utilization of the long ball. Perhaps the criticism affected them in midweek, when they lost their first game in ten months at Highbury and were knocked out of the League Cup by Crystal Palace in the fourth round replay. They again squandered scoring opportunities after Gerry Queen had given Palace the lead, and a rash foul by John Roberts on Queen resulted in Bobby Tambling scoring from the spot. By chance, Palace were the next visitors to Highbury in the League. Radford put the Gunners ahead from a rebound, but another Roberts error, when he lost his balance, allowed Alan Birchenall to equalize in a 1-1 result.

Mee dropped the gaffe-prone Roberts from the away match at Ipswich on 21 November and Peter Simpson came back into the team to resume his partnership with McLintock. Roberts was to make only one more league appearance that season, although he had generally been a significant factor in the Gunners' success to date. Also left out of the team was an off-form George Graham, replaced by Jon Sammels making his first appearance of the season. Ipswich attacked throughout the game and probably should have won, were it not for young keeper Laurie Sivell dropping an Armstrong shot in injury time and letting the ball fall over his line. Mee admitted that Arsenal had been lucky, and a more forthright Bobby Robson fumed, 'I can't believe it. We pulverized them.'

In the next game, against Liverpool at Highbury, for all their domination Arsenal could not find the net until Graham came on for Kelly in the 65th minute. Six minutes later, the Scottish midfielder, unhappy at his relegation to the bench, slipped a Tommy Smith tackle, played a quick one-two with

Sammels and volleyed the return from 12 yards past Ray Clemence for a superb goal. He also made the second nine minutes later, flicking the ball to Kennedy who shot and Radford converted the rebound. Bill Shankly claimed afterwards that both goals were offside, but replays demonstrated that Graham's masterly effort was perfectly legitimate although the second was dubious. Graham's rehabilitation was complete.

On 2 December Belgian part-timers Beveren Waas were easily overcome 4-0 at Highbury in the Fairs Cup third round fourth leg. On the Saturday following, Arsenal played Manchester City on a terrible, muddy pitch, with Howe asking his players to 'keep it simple'. McLintock and Simpson effectively controlled the dangerous forwards Franny Lee and Mike Summerbee and Wilson was in outstanding form. After the game the keeper said that it was the best he had played in his career. Arsenal won 2-0, both goals coming in the last 15 minutes from Armstrong and Radford.

An attacking Arsenal laid siege to the Wolves goal at Highbury on 12 December. Graham, and Radford with his left foot from a rebounded Sammels header, did the damage in a 2-1 win, Derek Dougan pulling one back for Wolves. The following Saturday the Gunners visited Old Trafford. Manchester United, a pale shadow of the team which had won the European Cup three seasons previously, could only attract a crowd of 33,000. With 35 minutes elapsed Arsenal were three goals ahead, through a McLintock half-volley on the six-yard line, a long-range Graham header from an Armstrong corner and another header from Kennedy. Wilson had to be brave to save from the feet of Best and to parry a Charlton shot and Carlo Sartori scored for United just before half-time, the final goal of the game. An emphatic and commanding victory by Arsenal was marred when Wilson was struck by a coin thrown from the Stretford End, although the keeper magnanimously asked the referee not to include the incident in his match report.

A 0-0 draw against Southampton at a snow-covered Highbury, with Saints' young Scottish keeper Eric Martin defying all Arsenal's attempts at goal, was the last game of 1970.

The Second Half

Halfway through this memorable season, Arsenal were three points behind Leeds in the League with a game in hand. The Gunners' next game was to be in the third round of the FA Cup against the giantkillers of the Southern League, Yeovil Town. In the event, Yeovil proved no match for Arsenal. Two Radford headers and a Kennedy strike gave Arsenal an easy 3-0 win. A week later in the League, West Ham, without Jimmy Greaves and Bobby Moore

Bob Wilson was the bravest of keepers and inspirational throughout the 'Double' campaign, appearing in every match.

who were both dropped after ignoring a curfew at Blackpool the previous week, lined up at Highbury. McNab was replaced by 22-year-old Sammy Nelson, a Northern Ireland left back who was to become a crowd favourite at Highbury throughout much of the 1970s. Graham and Kennedy were the scorers in the 2-0 win over the Hammers.

A Leeds defeat by Spurs, courtesy of two Martin Chivers goals, had narrowed the Yorkshire club's lead to one point over Arsenal, who had a game in hand. In the next game at Huddersfield, the home team went ahead after McLintock had his nose broken by a flying elbow. Kennedy equalized early in the second half but McLintock was adjudged to have handled in the box with six minutes left, although the offence was committed outside the area. Frank Worthington scored from the spot and Arsenal had lost two valuable points.

Fratton Park was the next venue on 23 January in the fourth round of the FA Cup where a determined Second Division Portsmouth ran out onto a muddy pitch in front of a 40,000 crowd. In the 35th minute a Radford shot was apparently saved by keeper John Milkins until a vociferous protest to the referee by the Arsenal players resulted in the official checking with his linesman. Informed that the save had been executed by left back George Ley, he awarded a penalty, which was converted by Storey. Pat Rice left the pitch with an ankle injury in the second half and ex-Everton striker Mike Trebilock equalized in the last minute for Pompey to set up a replay at Highbury.

At the end of the month an assured Liverpool display at Anfield secured a 2-0 win over the Gunners, although the score would certainly have been greater had Wilson not been in top form. John Toshack and Tommy Smith were the scorers for Liverpool. On the same day a Leeds win over Manchester City set up a gap of five points at the top of the table.

The FA Cup fourth round replay at Highbury against Portsmouth was a physical, bad-tempered affair, with Portsmouth's Brian Bromley sent off towards the end. Charlie George had finally returned from injury in his first appearance since August and replaced Graham. Pompey took the lead early on but a brilliant run and 20-yard shot from George in the 15th minute restored parity. A Simpson volley 20 minutes later gave Arsenal the lead but Ley made the score 2-2 early in the second half. A late Storey penalty saw Arsenal progress to the fifth round.

Five days later Manchester City came to Highbury and keepers Joe Corrigan and Wilson were both kept busy, Wilson in particular making two crucial saves from Colin Bell. The game was goalless until, with four minutes to go, Simpson shot from 25 yards, Corrigan fumbled the ball and Radford scored from the rebound. As quoted in the *Arsenal Official History*, Mee remarked, 'Following up on other people's shots is what we demand of John Radford. To make what looks like a useless run in the last few minutes takes character.' With Leeds losing at Liverpool, Arsenal were now only three points behind.

On 17 February Arsenal met Manchester City again, this time at Maine Road in the fifth round of the FA Cup. On a greasy pitch Arsenal went ahead in the 17th minute when George smashed in a free kick from the edge of the box. Early in the second half Radford played a through ball into space. George picked it up, accelerated past the City defence and sidefooted a low right-foot shot into the net from 15 yards. Bell pulled one back but the match ended 2-1 in Arsenal's favour. Three days later Ipswich visited Highbury in the League. The Gunners stormed into a 3-0 lead by half-time, the goals coming from George, Radford and McLintock. It was a different game in the second half. Ex-Arsenal winger Jimmy Robertson spurred a strong fightback from the Suffolk side, scoring two and having one disallowed. Arsenal were happy to settle for a 3-2 win. A week later they faced Derby at the Baseball Ground and were not so fortunate, going down 2-0 to goals from Roy McFarland and Kevin Hector, whom McLintock described as the trickiest forward he had played against.

The media knives were now out for Arsenal. Never the most popular club in England, they were again accused of defensive play and of being unfit to become league champions. Leeds were now seven points ahead, although the Gunners had two games in hand. Stung by the press criticism, Arsenal produced a supremely confident display three days later at Wolves. Kennedy headed in from an Armstrong pass in the first minute, Radford scored on the half hour and Kennedy claimed the third just after half-time with a right-foot shot. With 12 games remaining in the League, Arsenal were five points behind with a game in hand. Leeds, meanwhile, had crashed out of the FA Cup 3-2 at the hands of Fourth Division Colchester United, one of the most sensational results in Cup history.

On a freezing, blustery day, Arsenal met Leicester City on 6 March in the FA Cup quarter-final and were lucky to come away from Filbert Street with a 0-0 draw, Wilson making the save of the match in the 70th minute when he dived full-length to divert a shot from Rodney Fern. Arsenal had now played

Ray Kennedy in the Inter-Cities' Fairs Cup quarter-final first leg against FC Koln, on 9 March 1971. Arsenal went on to win 2-1.

46 competitive matches and the 47th was against FC Koln at Highbury three days later in the quarter-final of the Fairs Cup. McLintock opened the scoring but Thielen equalized before half-time, netting from a corner. With 20 minutes left on the clock, Storey shot through a ruck of players to give Arsenal a 2-1 win, not the most encouraging of scorelines to take to West Germany for the second leg.

The increasingly crowded fixture list saw the Gunners at Selhurst Park four days later to play Crystal Palace, something of a bogey team this season, in the League. Graham made his first start for six weeks, replacing Sammels, and in the 20th minute he headed in a McLintock cross. Sammels came on for George in the second half and he met a header from another McLintock cross to make the final score 2-0. Sammels, always the butt of a section of the Highbury crowd, was to make only two further appearances as a substitute for the rest of the season and he left Arsenal for Leicester City in the summer. Leicester came to Highbury on the Monday after the Palace game for the FA Cup quarter-final replay. A 57,000 crowd filled the stadium to watch a closely-contested match, the only goal coming in the 45th minute when George headed in an Armstrong corner past Peter Shilton. The odds were now dropping on the 'Double'.

The following weekend Arsenal entertained Blackpool in the League. A sprightly Wilson kept out the spirited attacks from the Blackpool forwards and his opposite number Neil Ramsbottom was also on fine form. Just after half-time, however, Ramsbottom let a Graham cross slip out of his grasp and Storey headed into the net, his first senior goal with his head. Since his move to midfield at the start of the season, Storey, despite the constant media criticism of his battling, combative style, had been one of the staunchest players in the team. He was to be rewarded with the first of his 19 England caps the following season.

Within three days the Gunners were in Cologne for the Fairs Cup quarter-final second leg tie. In a game littered with controversial decisions by referee Constantin Petres, Werner Biskup scored from the spot when Kappelmann fell over after contact with McNab in the fourth minute. Rice, George and Kennedy were booked and the Germans went through on away goals. Mee commented after the game 'the childish histrionics of some of the West Germans is bringing the game into disrepute'.

At the weekend, Arsenal met Stoke City (their nemesis earlier in the season) at Hillsborough in the FA Cup semi-final, and found themselves 2-0 down by half-time. A Storey clearance rebounded off Denis Smith's boot into the net, and then George was guilty of a badly judged back-pass which was intercepted by John Ritchie for the second goal. However, in the 60th minute Kennedy chipped backwards into the area and Storey connected with an instinctive right-foot shot for Arsenal's first goal. Then, two minutes into injury time, a McLintock header from an Armstrong cross was handled by John Mahoney in the Stoke area. With Wilson on his knees in prayer, Storey proved once again to be Arsenal's saviour when he scored the penalty with the inside of his right foot past Gordon Banks. The replay was held four days later at Villa Park. With Arsenal in total control, they went ahead from an early 15-yard header from Graham and shortly after the interval Radford supplied Kennedy for his first goal in seven games. Arsenal won 2-0 and were to meet Liverpool in the final.

Arsenal's hectic cup and league schedule meant that, although they were now six points behind Leeds, they had three games in hand on the leaders, whom they still had to meet at Elland Road at the end of April. Chelsea came to Highbury on 3 April, with over 62,000 in attendance. Early in the second half a clever George dummy from an Armstrong cross confused the Chelsea defence and Kennedy capitalized to put Arsenal ahead. A left-foot shot from the same player doubled the score after a neat one-two between George and Radford. In midweek at Highbury Kennedy claimed his 25th goal of the season in the 1-0 defeat of Coventry.

The Gunners were now faced with having to play five league games within 15 days before their encounter with Leeds. Radford opened the scoring at Southampton on the following Saturday but Terry Paine equalized for Saints shortly after. McLintock scored the winner early in the second half. The next game, away against Forest, resulted in a 3-0 win for Arsenal, the goals coming from McLintock, Kennedy and George. The title race was now wide open. Leeds could only manage to draw their last two games and were only two points ahead while Arsenal had two games in hand.

On 17 April the visitors were Newcastle. With the Geordies lying deep in defence, Arsenal found it difficult to break through until the 81st minute when

George picked up a clearance from a Simpson free kick and scored with a stunning 20-yard left-foot shot. That same day West Bromwich Albion beat Leeds 2-1 at Elland Road, where a hotly-disputed Albion goal sparked off a pitch invasion. Arsenal were now on top on goal average. Three days later a George penalty was the only goal against relegated Burnley and Arsenal had won nine league games in succession, dropping only one goal. A 2-2 draw with West Brom at the Hawthorns, Asa Hartford scoring for both clubs and Tony Brown equalizing late in the game, took some of the shine off Arsenal's progress but they were now one point clear at the top with a game in hand.

Lying in wait on 26 April at Elland Road were Leeds in what was a crucial game for both clubs. A crowd of 48,000 packed the stadium and Arsenal produced a brilliant defensive performance. With the game heading to a goalless draw, Alan Clarke found Jack Charlton in what appeared to be an offside position on the edge of the six-yard line. The big defender needed two attempts but scored with the second. The goal was given and Arsenal players protested to the referee. George was booked for kicking the ball into the stand, although TV evidence indicated that McNab had played Charlton onside. 'Never was a defeat less deserved,' said Mee. Leeds were now back on top. Against Stoke at Highbury in the penultimate league game, Storey went off with an ankle injury early in the second half. He was replaced by Kelly who scored from a Radford pass 12 minutes later for the game's only goal. Leeds, however, had also won and the championship race was going to the wire.

The League Title

The last game of the campaign was, appropriately, against Tottenham at White Hart Lane on Monday 3 May. Spurs were third in the League, had won the League Cup and needed to win to be sure of Europe the following season. Spurs' natural antipathy to the Gunners was compounded by the need to get both points. As a cocky Alan Mullery commented, 'Arsenal have got as much chance of being handed the title by Spurs as I have of being given the Crown Jewels.' The mathematics were complicated: if Arsenal won, they would have the title with 65 points to Leeds' 64; if they were beaten, Leeds would win; and, under the then-existing goal average system, if it was a 0-0 draw Arsenal would win while a scoring draw would give the title to Leeds.

The Times described the game as 'a magnificent battle in which attack from both sides was the order of the day... it was attack and counter-attack all the way with action flowing the length and breadth of White Hart Lane'. A late header by Ray Kennedy broke the deadlock and saw Arsenal win the first part of the historic double.

Great Matches

LEAGUE DIVISION ONE **White Hart Lane, 3 May 1971**

Arsenal 1 **Tottenham Hotspur 0** **Attendance: 51,992**
Kennedy

Thousands thronged the Tottenham High Road and White Hart Lane was packed to capacity, with tens of thousands more locked out on this thrilling finale to the league season. Such was the mass of humanity that the referee, Kevin Howley, had to abandon his car a mile from the ground and walk to the stadium. With the referee's whistle barely audible in the noise, the match kicked off and Arsenal went on the attack, although Martin Peters went close twice in the first half. A pulsating game continued in the second period, both teams

Frank McLintock celebrates with ecstatic fans as Arsenal win the clash with North London rivals Spurs, and with it the first leg of the 'Double'.

creating but failing to convert scoring opportunities. With three minutes remaining Pat Jennings punched away a Radford cross but only as far as Armstrong on the left side of the penalty box. The little winger crossed again and Kennedy rose to bullet a header into the net over the despairing Jennings and Cyril Knowles. Spurs tried desperately to equalize and Wilson had to be quick to save a corner in the dying seconds. Then it was all over, and Arsenal had won the eighth league title in their history. Thousands of their supporters surged on to the pitch, and such was the bedlam that nearly half an hour after the final whistle some of the players had still not made it back to the dressing room. The first leg of the 'Double' was now secure but they still had to play Liverpool at Wembley in five days time to achieve footballing immortality.

Arsenal: Wilson, Rice, McNab, Kelly, McLintock, Simpson, Armstrong, Graham, Radford, Kennedy, George

Tottenham Hotspur: Jennings, Kinnear, Knowles, Mullery, Collins, Beal, Gilzean (Pearce), Perryman, Chivers, Peters, Neighbour

Referee: K. Howley

Great Matches

FA CUP FINAL   **Wembley, 8 May 1971**

Arsenal 2   **Liverpool 1**   **Attendance: 100,000**
Kelly   Heighway
George

In the final, Arsenal met Liverpool, the team that would soon become the dominant force in English and European football. Gradually Arsenal assumed the upper hand in the first half and there were close calls on goal in both halves, but the game edged inexorably to a nail-biting extra-time period. Two minutes into the first period of extra-time, with the players feeling the draining effects of the heat and cramp, Heighway burst through on the Liverpool left past Rice and Kelly. Wilson moved off his line, anticipating a cross to Toshack, and Heighway shot in between the keeper and the near post to put Liverpool ahead. With four minutes remaining of the first period Radford lobbed the ball over his shoulder into the Liverpool area, Kelly touched it on through a forest of legs, Graham swiped at the ball and it rolled into the Liverpool net for the equalizer. Graham appeared to claim the goal but it was later credited to Kelly.

With nine minutes to go, and both tired sides looking to a replay, Radford found George and the long-haired Arsenal star unleashed a right-foot shot from 20 yards which took a slight deflection off Lloyd and rocketed into the Liverpool net. The image of George lying on the pitch, his arms aloft in triumph, remains one of the most memorable in the club's history. The final whistle went and Arsenal had won the 'Double'. McLintock led his exhausted team-mates up the steps to the royal box, collected the trophy from the Duke of Kent and the celebrations began.

Arsenal's first goal in the final – Eddie Kelly pokes the ball through the crowd of players in the box and George Graham takes a swing at it as it goes past. Kelly is awarded the goal after the match. Arsenal are level with Liverpool at 1-1...

Arsenal: Wilson, Rice, McNab, Storey (Kelly), McLintock, Simpson, Armstrong, Graham, Radford, Kennedy, George

Liverpool: Clemence, Lawler, Lindsay, Smith, Lloyd, Hughes, Callaghan, Evans (Thompson), Heighway, Toshack, Hall

Referee: N. Burtenshaw

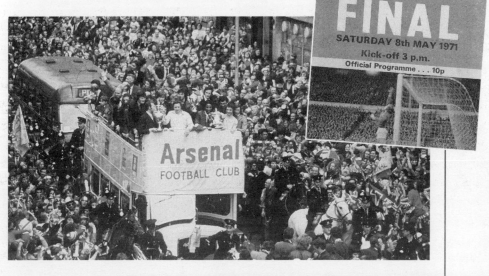

Above: Charlie George scores the unforgettable second goal that seals the 'Double' for Arsenal. Below: John Radford and Bob Wilson hold the FA Cup at the front of the celebration bus that weaves its way through the massed crowds.

ARSENAL v LIVERPOOL
FOOTBALL ASSOCIATION CHALLENGE
CUP COMPETITION

FINAL
SATURDAY 8th MAY 1971
Kick-off 3 p.m.
Official Programme . . . 10p

The 'Double'-winning squad from 1970-71, l-r: back row – Wright (trainer/physio), McNab, Storey, Simpson, Barnett, Wilson, Roberts, Kennedy, Marinello, Howe (coach); front – George, Radford, Armstrong, Sammels, McLintock, Mee (manager), Rice, Kelly, Graham, Nelson.

Saturday 8 May was unusually hot for the time of year with temperatures inside Wembley soaring into the nineties as Arsenal prepared for their 51st game of the league and Cup season. Peter Storey was back from the ankle injury he had received at Stoke and the line-up, with the exception of Eddie Kelly, was the same as against Tottenham earlier in the week.

The 'Double'

The teams played out a nerve-jangling 90 minutes with no score and then entered a period of extra-time that has passed into the annals of Highbury history, culminating in Charlie George's winning goal and famous 'arms aloft' celebration. An historic 'Double' had been completed.

Although they had perhaps not possessed the most skilful players in the Gunners' history, their determination and tireless dedication had brought the team to the pinnacle of the English game. As Mee commented, 'Technically there were certain deficiencies but our other qualities were superb.' The team's success was also a function of its consistency. Wilson, McLintock and Armstrong had played in every league game during the season; Radford, Rice and Kennedy had only missed one each; and Storey and McNab were absent on just two occasions. The whole had been gloriously more than the sum of its parts and selfless teamwork, planned and fostered by backroom men Mee and Howe, had once again brought triumph to Highbury.

Chapter Six: 1971-86
The Neill and Howe Era

In early July 1971, amid the continuing euphoria of the previous season, Don Howe shocked Mee and the players by accepting the manager's job at West Bromwich Albion. He took with him first-team trainer George Wright and the board fulminated at what they perceived to be West Brom's underhand tactics in luring the 'Double' tactician away from Highbury. Steve Burtenshaw was promoted to head coach.

Arsenal opened the 1971-72 season with two wins but lost the next three. Plagued by injuries, suspensions and the loss of form of key players through the autumn, they were knocked out of the League Cup by Sheffield United in early November and then humiliated by Wolves 5-1 at Molineux ten days later. They bounced back after this reversal, however, by setting off on a 14-game unbeaten run which lasted until March when they lost in succession to Manchester City, Newcastle and Leeds. The squad had been reinforced in December by the arrival of Alan Ball. The industrious, technically gifted midfielder who had played in England's World Cup-winning team in 1966, came from Everton for a Football League record of £220,000.

In the European Cup for the first time, Arsenal brushed aside Norway's Stromgodset 7-1 and then eliminated Grasshoppers Zurich 5-0 to set up a meeting with Ajax, Europe's best side and European Cup holders. With Ball ineligible for both games, Arsenal went ahead with an early Kennedy goal at a packed Olympic Stadium in Amsterdam, but two goals from Gerrie Muhren gave Ajax a 2-1 lead to take to Highbury. Radford was suspended for the return, his place taken by Marinello. The young winger wasted

Fiery redheaded midfielder Alan Ball was bought from Everton for £220,000.

Charlie George peaked at Arsenal in the early 1970s as the team claimed the Fairs Cup and the 'Double'. His celebration after the goal which won the 1971 'Double' remains a classic footballing image.

an easy opportunity in the first minute and a misjudged header from Graham back to Wilson 15 minutes later eluded the keeper. Ajax were 3-1 in front, a lead which remained until the final whistle. Ajax were to win the European Cup for the second year in succession, beating Inter Milan 2-0 in the final.

In the FA Cup the Gunners faced Derby in the fifth round, having beaten Swindon and Reading in earlier rounds. It took three games to progress against Brian Clough's side, who were to win the League this season for the first time in their history. Two goals from George secured a draw at the Baseball Ground and the replay at Highbury ended goalless after extra-time. A Kennedy strike in the third game was enough to see Arsenal through to the sixth round. Second Division Leyton Orient, who had remarkably recovered from being 2-0 down against Chelsea at Brisbane Road in the previous round to win 3-2, were the opponents, and a Ball goal at the Orient ground was the only score.

For the second year in succession Arsenal were drawn against Stoke City at Villa Park in the semi-final. George and Radford played up front while Kennedy was on the bench, the young striker off form and feeling the effects of two bruising seasons. Armstrong put Arsenal ahead but Wilson tore his cartilage in a collision. The keeper stayed on the pitch but could not prevent a Simpson own goal. With 15 minutes remaining, Wilson went off and was replaced by Radford, with Kennedy filling the centre forward's position, and Arsenal held on for the draw. With Geoff Barnett in goal for the replay, George equalized a Jimmy Greenhoff penalty and Radford scored the winner. In the final at Wembley on 6 May a diving Alan Clarke header from a Mick Jones cross early in the second half was the only excitement in a poor game, and Leeds won the FA Cup for the only time in their history.

Arsenal finished their league programme with a 0-0 draw against Liverpool – a result which helped to hand the league title to Derby – and a 2-0 defeat by Spurs. They ended the campaign in fifth place, one slot below qualification for the UEFA Cup. The Gunners had been unable to replicate the consistency of the previous season and the 'Double' team was soon to unravel.

Season 1972-73 saw the arrival of tall, stopper centre half Jeff Blockley as a long-term replacement for McLintock. McLintock and several of his team-mates were angered by the acquisition and Mee was to describe this as his biggest mistake, particularly as Blockley found it difficult to settle into the team and became a target for a section of the crowd. Although they won their first three league games, their autumn form was patchy and they were knocked out of the League Cup 3-0 by Norwich in November. Four days later a 5-0 defeat at Derby sparked off a run of 11 unbeaten games. From early March until the end of the season they lost only two matches and

50 Greatest Players

FRANK McLINTOCK Midfielder/Centre back

Born: Glasgow, 28 December 1939

Joined Arsenal: 1964   **From:** Leicester City

Debut: 6 October 1964 v Nottingham Forest, League

Appearances: 403   **Goals:** 32

Left Arsenal: 1973   **For:** Queens Park Rangers

Honours won with Arsenal: Division One championship 1971;
FA Cup winner 1971; Fairs Cup winner 1970;
Footballer of the Year 1971; 6 Scotland caps

Frank McLintock's place in Arsenal history is assured as the skipper of the 'Double' side, the club's most inspiring captain since Joe Mercer. McLintock arrived at Arsenal as an attacking wing half but achieved his greatest feats as a centre back. He made the switch at Don Howe's suggestion after the Gunners' defeat in the 1968-69 League Cup final. By the end of the 1969-70 season, his partnership with Peter Simpson was firmly cemented as the Gunners won the Fairs Cup. McLintock was relatively small for a central defender, but his reading of the game meant he was rarely caught out by taller strikers. He was a fine covering defender and a strong tackler. It was a surprise when Arsenal let him go in the spring of 1973 and he played for four more seasons with QPR.

finished in second place behind Liverpool. Arsenal were also knocked out of the FA Cup 2-1 by Second Division Sunderland at the semi-final stage. George scored for the Gunners but the unhappy Blockley was blamed for giving away the winning goal. Sunderland went on to beat Leeds in the final.

Marinello made 13 appearances during the season but the Scot's disappointing career with the Gunners came to an end in the summer when he joined Portsmouth. The inspiration behind the 'Double', Frank McLintock, had also said his farewells to Highbury in April when he joined QPR, where he would enjoy a further four successful and productive years. Alan Ball took over as captain. George Graham was another departure and became Tommy Docherty's first signing at ailing Manchester United. The exit of these two senior players seemed to indicate problems within the club. Head coach Steve Burtenshaw was next to exit Highbury when he resigned after a 5-0 defeat at Bramall Lane by Sheffield United. Burtenshaw had not been able to move out of Don Howe's shadow and he was replaced by Bobby Campbell who had been coach at QPR when they won promotion to Division One.

The fact that confidence was plummeting was dramatically illustrated in October 1973 when the Gunners, fielding nine of the 'Double' side, were knocked out of the League Cup 1-0 by Tranmere Rovers at Highbury. By the end of the year Arsenal had won only eight league games and they were to win only five more before the season finished. Arsenal finished in tenth place, 20 points behind victorious Leeds. Their FA Cup run had also been undistinguished, having been knocked out by Aston Villa 2-0 in the fourth round. One bright spot, however, was the emergence of 17-year-old, left-sided midfielder Liam 'Chippy' Brady from the youth team. Brady, soon to become one of Arsenal's finest-ever player, made his debut as substitute in a 1-0 win over Birmingham City in October and made 13 full appearances in the first team during the season.

In the summer of 1974 Bob Wilson retired to start a career in television. Wilson had bided his time at Highbury, joining the club in 1963 and not making the keeper's position his own until 1968. However, his courageous performances in the 'Double' season had confirmed him as one of the finest keepers in British football. He was succeeded by Jimmy Rimmer, an agile, dependable player from Manchester United. Another 'Double' hero also left the club. Ray Kennedy, whose 26 goals had been so important in the 1970-71 season, joined Liverpool for £200,000 in Bill Shankly's last transfer negotiation. Shankly's successor Bob Paisley converted the off-form and overweight striker into a midfield player, in which position he was to revive

50 Greatest Players

BOB WILSON Goalkeeper

Born: Chesterfield, 30 October 1941

Joined Arsenal: 1963   **From:** Wolves (amateur)

Debut: 26 October 1963 v Nottingham Forest, League

Appearances: 308

Left Arsenal: 1974 (retired)

Honours won with Arsenal: Division One championship 1971;
FA Cup winner 1971; Fairs Cup winner 1970; 2 Scotland caps

Trained to be a PE teacher, Bob Wilson became one of
Arsenal's finest goalkeepers – and one of the bravest. His
trademark save was a headlong dive at an onrushing striker's
feet. After playing for Loughborough Colleges and Wolves, he
joined the Gunners, first as an amateur, in the summer of
1963. He made his senior debut that October, but was
confined to the reserves until the end of 1967-68 when
Bertie Mee gave him the chance to take over from Jim Furnell. Wilson seized the opportunity
and firmly established himself in 1968-69, starting every match. He was injured at the
start of the following season, but returned to play in the Fairs Cup victory and was ever-
present again in the 'Double' campaign. He retired in 1974 to become a TV commentator.

his career for club and country. A replacement striker arrived at Highbury in
August 1974 in the shape of Brian Kidd, joining from newly-relegated
Manchester United. As a 19-year-old, he had scored for United in the 1968
European Cup final in their 4-1 win over Benfica. Kidd was tall, slim and
left-sided and was to play alongside Radford.

Arsenal began the 1974-75 season without their captain and playmaker
Alan Ball who had broken his ankle on a pre-season tour of Holland. The
season began well enough – Kidd scoring the only goal against Leicester at
Filbert Street – but rapidly deteriorated. Although they beat Manchester City
4-0 at Highbury in the third game, with two coming from Kidd, they then
went ten games without a win. They were also knocked out of the League
Cup 2-1 by Leicester. In October Mee purchased 31-year-old central
defender Terry Mancini from QPR. A member of a famous London boxing
family, the balding player – known as 'Henry' for obvious reasons – was a
comedian and raconteur and quickly became a great favourite of the
Highbury faithful. Two months later Scottish midfielder Alex Cropley
arrived from Hibs for £150,000. Small in stature, Cropley was nonetheless

a tough, determined player, rugged in the tackle. He was to break his leg after only seven games and would be sidelined until 1975-76.

Younger players, such as forwards Brian Hornsby and Wilf Rostron, and midfielders Trevor Ross and John Matthews were being blooded in the first team alongside the old guard but results continued to range from the erratic to the poor. Kelly saved Arsenal's blushes in the third round of the FA Cup when his goal secured a draw with lowly York City at Highbury. A Kidd hat-trick secured progress in the 3-1 replay win at Bootham Crescent. Two strikes from Armstrong contributed to the club's 3-0 win over Coventry in a fourth round replay, and it took three games to defeat Leicester in the fifth round, Radford scoring the winner.

Before the sixth round Ball and McNab had been sent off in a 2-1 defeat at Derby County, the first time since the war that two players from the same club had been sent off in Division One. Arsenal refused to appeal on their behalf and a disaffected Ball now felt his future with Arsenal was a limited one. The opinionated redhead proclaimed, 'Arsenal and I can never be the same again.' Alan Taylor scored twice for West Ham in the Cup game as Arsenal went out of the competition 2-0 at Highbury. West Ham were

50 Greatest Players

RAY KENNEDY Striker

Born: Seaton Delaval, Northumberland, 28 July 1951

Joined Arsenal: 1968   **From:** Port Vale (apprentice)

Debut: 29 September 1969 v Glentoran, Fairs Cup

Appearances: 212   **Goals:** 71

Left Arsenal: 1974   **For:** Liverpool

Honours won with Arsenal: Division One championship 1971; FA Cup winner 1971; Fairs Cup winner 1970

Ray Kennedy was a powerful, brave striker, very strong in the air, who rose through the youth ranks to make crucial contributions to the Fairs Cup victory and the 'Double'. His late strike as a substitute against Anderlecht gave Arsenal a vital away goal in the final and paved the way for triumph at Highbury. The next season, he replaced the injured Charlie George after the first game and finished top scorer with 26 goals, forming a heavyweight partnership with John Radford. Like George, he never quite touched those heights again, though he did finish top scorer in 1971-72. A move to Liverpool, and a switch to midfield, revived his career and he won a host of medals at Anfield.

winners again at Upton Park on the last day of the season as a dispirited and demoralized Arsenal slumped to 16th place in the League, their lowest position since 1924-25.

It was now clear that Bertie Mee's days were numbered. More senior players departed over the summer. Bob McNab, a left back stalwart, moved to Wolves on a free transfer, his place going to Sammy Nelson, and Charlie George, who had been at loggerheads with the club over the previous two seasons and had been transfer-listed, joined Derby for £90,000. George was a rare talent who never quite lived up to his promise. A combination of volatile temperament and injuries had not helped his cause at Highbury but a total of 179 appearances and 49 goals in his six years at the club was significantly less than his prodigious abilities warranted. Angered by the club's perilous position and their attitude to his sending-off against Derby, Ball opened the season with a transfer request and he was dropped for the three opening games, with Kelly being handed the captaincy. On Ball's return he scored in the 2-1 home defeat of Norwich, but wins were few and far between for the Gunners in this season, one of the worst in their Division One history.

Not only were the Gunners eliminated by Everton in the League Cup in the opening round, they suffered a similar indignity in the third round of the FA Cup, losing 3-0 to Wolves at Molineux. In his book *So Far So Good*, Liam Brady comments, 'Once again, our season was dead – just a dreary, worrying relegation battle.' Their league form was certainly a matter for concern, conceding 53 goals against 47 scored and losing their last three games to end up in 17th position in the League, a massive 24 points behind a resurgent Liverpool. Indeed, relegation was a serious prospect with only four games remaining, but a Mancini winning goal – a second-half header from a left-wing cross, his only goal ever for Arsenal – helped them to a 2-1 win over Wolves who were relegated.

Although the season was a dire one, two new young players were establishing themselves in the first team. Along with the rapidly maturing and increasingly influential Liam Brady, Frank Stapleton and David O'Leary were to help drag Arsenal out of the mire over the next few years. Twenty-year-old Stapleton was a quiet, introverted personality but also a hard-working, talented centre forward, while O'Leary, like Stapleton and Brady an Irishman from the Arsenal youth team, was a 17-year-old, tall, pacy defender with a cultured touch on the ball.

Before the end of the campaign, Bertie Mee had announced his intention to retire at the end of the season. At an emotional press conference in March, the man who had brought success back to Highbury after 17 barren years

Great Managers – 1966-76

BERTIE MEE

A small, modest but determined man, Bertie Mee became manager of Arsenal in June 1966 after the undistinguished reign of Billy Wright. Mee had been trainer and physiotherapist at Highbury since 1960 and his appointment was something of a surprise. An expert at motivation and man-management, however, he turned round the ailing fortunes of the Gunners and the club reached the final of the League Cup in 1966-67 and 1968-69, losing on both occasions. With the invaluable assistance of head coach Don Howe, and players like George Graham, Bob McNab, John Radford and Frank McLintock, Mee led the Gunners to their first major trophy in 17 years when they defeated Anderlecht over a two-leg final to win the European Fairs Cup in 1970. The following year, 1970-71, Mee became only the second manager in the 20th century to win  the 'Double'. Unsurprisingly, Mee was voted Manager of the Year. Although his team reached the FA Cup final the following year, going down to Leeds, Mee then oversaw a period of relative decline with the 'Double' team breaking up and Mee unable to bring in adequate replacements. In March 1976 he announced his retirement and ended his football career as general manager and director of Watford. He died in October 2001.

announced that he could no longer function as club manager and that the time had come to find a replacement. After a search lasting nearly three months – which included offering the job to Yugoslavian coach Miljan Miljanic and Crystal Palace manager Terry Venables – the board found their man and Terry Neill was on his way back to Arsenal.

The Terry Neill Years

Only 34 years of age, articulate and self-confident, the Northern Irishman had spent 11 years at the club, making 275 appearances, before leaving in 1970 to take over as player-manager at Hull City. He moved in 1974 to become Tottenham manager and, as an Arsenal man through and through, it was not difficult to tempt him away from White Hart Lane. He took with him Wilf Dixon as chief coach and Bobby Campbell, whom the senior players had proposed as the new manager, left the club shortly after his arrival. Several of his old team-mates – such as Rice, Armstrong, Storey, Radford and Simpson – were still at the club, and Neill was to struggle to assert his authority. Neill states in his book *Revelations of a Football Manager,* 'A number of the older players, led by club captain Alan Ball, were opposed to my appointment and I knew I had to make changes.' Armstrong, in particular, had a distant and unhappy relationship with the new manager. The little winger was to last only one further season and left at the end of 1976-77 to join Leicester City, having made 500 league appearances for the Gunners.

There were also other significant comings and goings. Brian Kidd had left the club for Manchester City shortly before Neill's appointment. To replace him Neill acted quickly to prise striker Malcolm Macdonald away from Newcastle United. Macdonald, revered as 'Super Mac' at St James's Park, had disagreements with Newcastle manager Gordon Lee and he was acquired for £333,333 at the beginning of the 1976-77 season. A powerful, stocky forward with pace and acceleration, Macdonald was a fearsome goal-getter for Newcastle and, although only just over 5ft 8in tall, he was also excellent in the air. He had been converted from full back at his first club, Fulham, and had moved to Newcastle via Luton Town. He immediately stated that he would claim 30 goals in his first season and he finished only one behind his target, teaming up in attack with Frank Stapleton. With no room for Radford, the 'Double' centre forward was transferred in December to West Ham for £80,000. Radford's total of 149 goals in his 14 years at Highbury affords him the distinction of being Arsenal's third highest-ever goalscorer, behind Ian Wright and Cliff Bastin.

Other departures over the season included the argumentative Alan Ball ('Ball and Neill did not get on. It was as simple as that,' says Brady) who moved to Southampton in December for £60,000. In September, Terry Mancini joined Aldershot. In the same month Alex Cropley moved to Aston Villa and 'Double' hero Eddie Kelly joined up with old team-mate Frank McLintock at Queens Park Rangers. Another long-serving member of the class of 1970-71, Peter Storey, with 501 Arsenal appearances under his belt, became a Fulham player in March 1977. Storey had not turned up for training for ten consecutive days the previous spring and had been suspended by the club.

As for the newcomers, centre half Pat Howard came from Newcastle to replace Mancini but he was to last less than a season. Howard's tenure of the centre half position was ended when Neill discovered that one of his old players, Willie Young, was available for transfer from Spurs. The ginger-haired, 6ft 3in Scottish stopper joined the Gunners in March 1977 for £80,000 and established the centre of defence alongside David O'Leary.

Malcolm Macdonald joined the forward line in 1976-77. The feisty 'Super Mac' scored 29 goals that season.

Powerful in the air, but often erratic in his distribution, Young was to become a cult favourite with the Arsenal fans, particularly for his eccentric forays upfield and his subduing effect on opposing centre forwards. An infinitely more subtle player had arrived at Highbury three months earlier. Alan Hudson was regarded as one of the most skilful midfielders in the English game. The 25-year-old had moved from Chelsea to Stoke and, in December, to Arsenal for £200,000. His sublime touch, close control and peerless passing were, however, not always accompanied by a high work rate and he had a tendency to drift out of games. Something of a playboy and bon viveur, Hudson's career had been a controversial one and his first season was to be marred by being sent home with Macdonald from a summer tour of Australia amid stories of drinking before a game. He was suspended and placed on the transfer list.

Neill's first season in charge saw Macdonald beginning to vindicate his transfer fee with two hat-tricks, against Newcastle at home and Birmingham away. After the Birmingham match, however, they fell away and went ten games without a win, the streak broken by a 3-0 win over Leicester in early April. O'Leary scored twice with the third coming from Graham Rix on his debut in the first team. Rix was a 19-year-old, curly haired, Yorkshire-born midfielder who was to team up with Liam Brady on the left side of the park over the coming three years. Arsenal lost only two more games in the run in and ended in eighth spot in the League.

In the League Cup Arsenal needed three games to defeat Blackpool in the third round and they knocked out Chelsea in round four, winning 2-1 in front of over 50,000 at Highbury, the goals coming from Trevor Ross and

Stapleton. Interest in the competition ceased in the fifth round at Loftus Road, Arsenal going down 2-1 to Queens Park Rangers. The FA Cup was also less than rewarding. Macdonald scored twice in the 3-1 win over Coventry in the fourth round and, although Macdonald scored again in the fifth round at Ayresome Park, Middlesbrough won 4-1.

That first season had been a torrid one for Neill and it was obvious that the senior players lacked the necessary respect for the new manager. His position had not been helped by his injudicious remarks to the media, in particular when, after a 3-0 defeat by Middlesbrough in February, he commented of his increasingly disaffected squad, 'This was the worst Arsenal performance since I took over as manager. We could not have beaten 11 dustbins on that display.' Neill now needed a buffer between him and the squad and the existing coach Wilf Dixon appeared, to the players, to offer only unsophisticated and tedious tactical analysis.

The summer of 1977 saw the return to Highbury of Don Howe as head coach. Neill turned to the experienced trainer after he had been rebuffed by Dave Sexton who had taken over as manager of Manchester United. Chairman Denis Hill-Wood was less than happy about Howe's return to Highbury, given Howe's abrupt departure to West Bromwich Albion in 1971, but under Howe discipline and teamwork quickly became the watchwords at Highbury and morale improved almost immediately. Indeed, O'Leary commented in

50 Greatest Players

CHARLIE GEORGE Striker/Midfielder

Born: Islington, 10 October 1950

Joined Arsenal: 1966   **From:** School

Debut: 9 August 1969 v Everton, League

Appearances: 179   **Goals:** 49

Left Arsenal: 1975   **For:** Derby County

Honours won with Arsenal: Division One championship 1971; FA Cup winner 1971; Fairs Cup winner 1970

Charlie George will always be remembered in one famous image, lying flat out, arms in the air, after scoring the Wembley winner against Liverpool that clinched the 'Double'. Once a Holloway Schoolboy, he stepped off the North Bank to star for the Gunners. He played in the team that won the Fairs Cup, then, after an injury in the first game of the 'Double' season, returned to add goals from midfield on the league and Cup run-ins. He seemed set for a glittering career, but injuries and disagreements with Bertie Mee meant he never fulfilled his immense potential. He was in and out of the side until a move to Derby.

his autobiography *My Story* that Howe's arrival meant 'the start of a new era for one of the game's great clubs'. Brady agreed, saying 'never in my life have I witnessed such a change in so many players in such a short space of time'. Howe was now to concern himself with coaching and tactics while Neill was to take over administration and dealings with the outside world, not the taciturn Howe's forte.

Neill pulled off a masterstroke in August when he persuaded Pat Jennings, the Spurs and Northern Ireland keeper, to join Arsenal. Spurs' manager Keith Burkenshaw had deemed Jennings to be past his best at the age of 32 and let him go for £45,000. The unflappable and agile keeper, with the biggest hands in British football and an unerring positional sense, was to remain first choice at Highbury for the next eight years and confound Burkenshaw's innacurate predictions. In front of Jennings, right back and 'Double' survivor Pat Rice was captain and he was paired with Sammy Nelson, with Young and O'Leary the central defenders. In November Trevor Ross was transferred to Everton, his position on the right of midfield assumed by David Price, a blond haired, ex-captain of England Schoolboys who had fought through from the youth team. An arrival that month was the Afro-haired Alan Sunderland, a quick and incisive forward who cost £220,000 from Wolves and who would score a memorable goal at the end of the following season.

Arsenal progressed well in the League Cup in 1977-78, defeating Manchester United 3-2 in August at Highbury, Macdonald scoring two. They then defeated Southampton and Hull City to set up a fifth round encounter with Manchester City. Jennings in goal, and a scintillating display by substitute Hudson, inspired a 0-0 draw at Maine Road and the replay was settled by a Brady penalty at Highbury. The Gunners were, however, eliminated from the competition after Liverpool won 2-1 at Anfield and held Arsenal to a goalless draw at Highbury.

In the FA Cup the strike force of Stapleton and Macdonald both scored two in the third round demolition of Sheffield United at Bramall Lane. They then knocked out Wolves, Walsall and Wrexham and eliminated Leyton Orient 3-0 in the semi-final, Macdonald again scoring twice. Ipswich, in the first FA Cup final in their history, were the opponents at Wembley on 6 May. Arsenal had one of their better seasons, winning half of their league games and drawing a further ten to secure fifth place, 12 points behind leaders Nottingham Forest, and were regarded as favourites. However, Ipswich were the better side on the day although Arsenal were carrying injuries to Brady, Sunderland, Rice and Macdonald, with a disappointing Brady substituted by

Rix. Ipswich's Roger Osborne scored the only goal with 14 minutes remaining. Neill commented, 'We have learnt from this defeat and we will be back next season more determined than ever.'

Over the summer Macdonald had operations on his injured knees and he only managed four games in August 1978, and one at the end of the season, before he had to retire through injury. His two years at Highbury had resulted in an impressive 57 goals. In October, the out-of-favour Alan Hudson departed for Seattle Sounders in a £120,000 deal and his role as Brady's playmaker partner was assumed by a fast-improving Graham Rix. The new season started badly, Arsenal suffering two draws and two losses, including a surprise but deserved away 3-1 elimination by Rotherham in the opening round of the League Cup. Things, however, picked up and the Gunners embarked on a ten-game undefeated run (including seven wins) between late October and Christmas.

The last game in the sequence was a superb 5-0 defeat of Spurs at White Hart Lane on 23 December, with Brady in stunning form. Sunderland scored a hat-trick, Stapleton added another from a Brady cross and Brady netted

50 Greatest Players

JOHN RADFORD Striker

Born: Hemsworth, Yorkshire, 22 February 1947

Joined Arsenal: 1962   **From:** School

Debut: 21 March 1964 v West Ham United, League

Appearances: 481   **Goals:** 149

Left Arsenal: 1976   **For:** West Ham United

Honours won with Arsenal: Division One championship 1971; FA Cup winner 1971; Fairs Cup winners 1970; 2 England caps

John Radford was a hard man who shouldered the striking burden when football was at its most physical and tackles from behind were commonplace. Another youth team product, he was powerful, tenacious and particularly dangerous in the air. He came to the fore in 1968-69 when he scored 19 goals, including the two that beat Tottenham in the League Cup semi-finals, and won his first England cap. The following season, he headed Arsenal's second goal in the 3-0 victory over Anderlecht that won the Fairs Cup. But he will be best remembered for his partnership with Ray Kennedy during the 'Double' season when they netted 47 goals between them, 21 for Radford. His tally of 149 goals makes him the third-highest scorer in Arsenal history.

with a magnificent curling shot with the outside of his left foot from the edge of the box. By early January Arsenal were in fourth place and another good run early in the new year maintained their challenge to leaders Liverpool. In April one of the jokers in the Arsenal team, Sammy Nelson, deflected a shot into his own net in a game against Coventry at Highbury. The Irishman atoned for this lapse in the second half by scoring the equalizer and saving the point. He promptly dropped his shorts and mooned the crowd, incurring a fine and suspension from Arsenal and further punishment from the football authorities. Five games without a win at the end of the programme left Arsenal in a final seventh position.

Earlier in the season Stapleton scored five (one a headed own goal) in the aggregate 7-1 crushing of Locomotiv Liepzig in the first round of the UEFA Cup. Yugoslav side Hadjuk Split won 2-1 in Split in the next round (Brady scoring for the Gunners) and at Highbury, with Brady and two Yugoslavs sent off, Willie Young, of all people, scored the only goal with a delightful chip over the keeper from the edge of the box. This put Arsenal through on away goals. One-nil down to Red Star Belgrade in the next round, they were 1-0 up

50 Greatest Players

GEORGE ARMSTRONG Winger

Born: Hebburn, County Durham, 9 August 1944

Joined Arsenal: 1961   **From:** School

Debut: 24 February 1962 v Blackpool, League

Appearances: 621   **Goals:** 68

Left Arsenal: 1977   **For:** Leicester City

Honours won with Arsenal: Division One championship 1971;

FA Cup winner 1971; Fairs Cup winner 1970

George Armstrong was one of the most wholehearted players ever to wear an Arsenal shirt. He was unlucky to be England's best winger at a time when wingers were out of fashion. Another who rose through the youth ranks, 'Geordie' seemed to have energy to burn as he made his trademark runs down the right. He was also a pinpoint crosser who chipped in with valuable goals. Questions had been raised about Armstrong's future when the Gunners signed Peter Marinello in 1970. But he saw off the challenge to play crucial roles in the Fairs Cup success and the 'Double' campaign, going on to hold the club's appearance record for many years. After spells coaching in the Middle East, he returned to Arsenal as reserve team coach. He died in 2000 after collapsing at the training ground.

in the second leg with eight minutes to go when Red Star scored to knock the Gunners out of the tournament.

In the middle of one of the coldest winters in years, Arsenal benefited from their undersoil heating to continue playing while other clubs suffered cancellations. On 6 January they lined up at a frozen Hillsborough to face Third Division Sheffield Wednesday, managed by Jack Charlton, in the third round of the FA Cup. With Jennings being pelted by snowballs from home fans, they secured a 1-1 draw. Back at Highbury only a last-minute effort from Brady kept Arsenal in the competition in another 1-1 draw. In the replay at Leicester (protected from the elements by a hot air balloon on the pitch) another draw resulted after extra-time, and in the third replay at Leicester, yet again the result was a draw. Stapleton scored twice and Young claimed the other in the 3-3 draw, although Brady missed a penalty. In the final match Stapleton and midfielder Steve Gatting (brother of England cricket captain Mike) both scored in the 2-0 win, after 540 minutes of the marathon tie.

During the month Brian Talbot, a determined and skilful midfielder who had played for Ipswich in the previous year's final, joined Arsenal and scored in the 2-0 defeat of Notts County in the fourth round. The Gunners met reigning champions Nottingham Forest in the fifth round and were under constant pressure throughout the game. A relieved Arsenal made it through 1-0, courtesy of a late Stapleton header. In a sixth round replay against Southampton, with Charlie George playing for the Saints, Sunderland scored twice in the 2-0 win, and Stapleton and Sunderland scored in the semi-final 2-0 win over Wolves.

Unforgettable FA Cup Triumph

On 12 May at a sweltering Wembley Arsenal faced Manchester United in the FA Cup final, with 100,000 in the stadium and millions more watching on TV. Unlike the previous year's final the Arsenal team was fully fit including, ominously for Manchester United, PFA Player of the Year, Liam Brady. In a match that swung first one way, then the other, and back again, it was a scintillating last five minutes that saw the memorable final decided. Although all the Arsenal players had coped manfully with United, the game belonged to Brady who had been a constant threat and who created all three goals. As the *Daily Telegraph* commented, 'It is wholly appropriate that Brady was in at the death of United's hopes since he had hit them hard early on then shoved them forwards to disaster just before half-time.' Pat Rice collected the trophy from Prince Charles and Arsenal had won their fifth FA Cup.

Still only 23 years old, the magnificent Brady was now regarded as one of the finest midfielders in the world. Not long after the final he announced his

Great Matches

FA CUP FINAL

Arsenal 3
Talbot
Stapleton
Sunderland

Manchester United 2
McQueen
McIlroy

Wembley, 12 May 1979

Attendance: 100,000

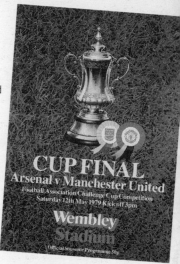

In a sweltering Wembley Stadium, Liam Brady, the recently crowned PFA Player of the Year, served notice of his intentions in the 11th minute by surging across the pitch and sending a square ball to Stapleton who found Price in the area. The midfielder cut back the ball from the goalline and Talbot and Sunderland arrived to slide it into an empty net. The credit for the goal was given to Talbot. Although United centre half Gordon McQueen had the ball in the Arsenal net before half-time, it was adjudged a hand ball. Two minutes from the interval, Brady again wriggled through United's defence and crossed for Stapleton to head into the corner of the net. Arsenal appeared in command.

In the second half Young was effectively policing United's dangerous centre forward Joe Jordan while Brady continued to set up attacks with his perceptive ventures forward. With five minutes remaining, and the Arsenal fans preparing to celebrate victory, a tiring David Price was substituted to make way for central defender Steve Walford which appeared to disrupt the rhythm of the team. Almost immediately, United winger Steve Coppell sent a free kick into the Arsenal box, Jordan knocked it back and McQueen stuck out a leg to score. Two minutes later a Coppell long ball found Sammy McIlroy running into the Arsenal box. McIlroy evaded the desperate attentions of Walford and O'Leary and slid the ball with his left foot under Jennings for the equalizer. But there was more to come in this amazing last five minutes. Brady moved forward diagonally into the United half and crossed to Rix running into position on the left. Brady said after the game, 'I was so tired, I dreaded extra-time. So I tried to take the ball into their half.' Rix sent in a high cross which eluded keeper Gary Bailey and Sunderland at the far post sealed the Cup for Arsenal, placing the ball low into the net. The final whistle blew and the 'five-minute final' was over.

Arsenal: Jennings, Rice, Nelson, Young, O'Leary, Talbot, Price (Walford), Rix, Brady, Stapleton, Sunderland

Manchester United: Bailey, Nicholl, Albiston, Buchan, McQueen, Coppell, Macari, McIlroy, Thomas, Greenhoff, Jordan

Referee: R. Challis

From the top: In a tangle of limbs, Brian Talbot slides in to score the first goal; Frank Stapleton powers in goal number two; Alan Sunderland scores the last-gasp winner and Arsenal win the amazing 'five-minute final'.

intention to leave Arsenal at the end of 1979-80 to test his talents in Europe against the continent's best players. Although Arsenal tried to hold on to this special and irreplaceable talent, the young Irishman had made up his mind, but he still had much to offer the Gunners in the coming season.

In July, the veteran midfielder, John Hollins, joined Arsenal for £75,000 from Queens Park Rangers, having played previously for Chelsea. The 33-year-old came on as a substitute for Brady in their their first game of 1979-80, a 4-0 away win over Brighton. The team won only two of their next 11 league matches but rallied and, between early October and the end of March, the Gunners lost only three league games. This season, however, was mainly about cup competitions.

In the League Cup they beat Leeds 7-0 at Highbury in a magnificent display in a second round replay in early September. Sunderland claimed a hat-trick while a desperate Leeds defence conceded two penalties in the second half, both converted by the masterful Brady. Stapleton and Nelson scored the others. However, they succumbed 4-3 to Swindon away in the fifth round in November, giving away two own goals from Walford and Hollins.

In the first leg of the European Cup-Winners' Cup in September they encountered tough Turkish side Fenerbahce at Highbury and a late strike from Young added to an earlier Sunderland goal to give the Gunners a 2-0 lead. They managed to hold Fenerbahce to 0-0 in Istanbul and met East Germany's Magdeburg in round two. Young and Sunderland were again the scorers at Highbury and a 2-2 draw in Magdeburg set them up for the third round against Gothenburg in March, where Young was again on the scoresheet in their 5-1 win. They were to meet Juventus, with Italian internationals Bettega, Tardelli, Zoff and Gentile, at Highbury on 9 April for the first leg of the Cup-Winners' Cup semi-final.

Two days before the semi-final, an injury-ravaged Arsenal put out a below-strength team in a league game at White Hart Lane, resting Stapleton, Sunderland, Jennings, Rix, Nelson and Price and including such players as young Irish full back John Devine, striker Paul Vaessen and 17-year-old, left-sided midfielder Paul Davis who made his first-team debut. Spurs had refused Arsenal's request to move the game until after the semi-final and Arsenal retaliated by winning 2-1. The elegant Davis, who was to become a long-serving crowd favourite, impressed everyone with his skills and distribution.

At Highbury Juventus went ahead when Cabrini's penalty was saved by Jennings but the Italian scored from the rebound in the 11th minute. Juventus then attempted to close the game down and resorted to ugly tactics. In the 20th minute Bettega launched himself into a disgraceful, over-the-top tackle on O'Leary who was carried off and Tardelli was dismissed for a foul on Brady, the Italian midfielder's second yellow card. An incensed Neill said after the game, 'We have taken the studs out of O'Leary's legs and given them back to Bettega.' With less than five minutes to go Bettega, harrassed by Stapleton, headed into his own net and justice was done. The game ended 1-1.

Three days after the game Arsenal met Liverpool in the FA Cup semi-final at Hillsborough. The Gunners had disposed of Cardiff, Brighton, Bolton and Watford to reach this stage. A 0-0 draw saw them replay four days later at Villa Park, a draw again being the outcome. Before the next replay there was the small matter of the second leg against Juventus. On 23 April Arsenal lined up against Juventus at the Stadio Communale in Turin, where no European side had won for the last ten years. The teams were welcomed onto the pitch by a massive wall of sound from the crowd of over 66,000, most of whom had come to celebrate a win on away goals from the 'Zebras'.

Juventus had clearly decided on a goalless draw and formed a virtually impregnable wall, against which Brady and the Arsenal forwards battered with little success. Chances were few and, given Juventus's defensive sterility, there was little attacking football. However, with less than two minutes remaining Rix sent over a high cross from the left and Vaessen, on as a

50 Greatest Players

PETER SIMPSON Centre back

Born: Gorleston, Norfolk, 13 January 1945

Joined Arsenal: 1960   **From:** School

Debut: 14 March 1964 v Chelsea, League

Appearances: 477   **Goals:** 15

Left Arsenal: 1978   **For:** New England Teamen (USA)

Honours won with Arsenal: Division One championship 1971;
FA Cup winner 1971; Inter-Cities' Fairs Cup winner 1970

Peter Simpson was unlucky enough to reach his peak at the same
time as Bobby Moore and Norman Hunter. Otherwise he would
have played many times for England. A youth team product,
he made his senior debut in 1964. But he really prospered
after tightening up his approach under the influence of Bertie
Mee. Simpson was a strong tackler, who radiated calm on the
pitch. He also had a classy left foot which enabled him to
play his way out of trouble. He missed the first 17 league games of the 'Double'
campaign because of a cartilage injury but was ever-present for the rest of the season.
His central partnership with Frank McLintock was at the heart of the Gunners' success.

---

substitute for Price, nodded the ball into the net. The crowd were stunned
and the Gunners were through to the final. The Arsenal fans in the ground
were pelted with bottles and missiles, but this was one of the club's finest
nights in European football. As Neill remarked, 'The performance of my
players showed what a remarkable bunch they are. I am so proud of them.'
As a footnote, hero Vaessen was forced to give up the game after serious knee
injury two years later and he was found dead in sad circumstances in 2001
at the age of 39.

Four days later, they played their second replay against Liverpool in the
Cup semi-final, Sunderland scoring within 12 seconds and Dalglish
extending the epic tie again by equalizing for a 1-1 result. The fourth match
at Coventry on 1 May finally squeezed Arsenal through to the FA Cup final,
Talbot heading in the only goal of the game. Waiting for them at Wembley
were Second Division West Ham. A weary Arsenal took to the Wembley
pitch on 10 May and were 1-0 down by the 13th minute, when a Stuart
Pearson mis-hit shot deflected off Trevor Brooking's head, only the third
headed goal of Brooking's career and a fluke at that. West Ham closed ranks
but could have added another if Willie Young had not deliberately and

cynically brought down young forward Paul Allen in a clear scoring position three minutes from the end. The FA Cup went to East London. In this exhausting season, however, Arsenal still had three games to play,

The Gunners travelled to the Heysel Stadium in Brussels to meet Valencia in the European Cup-Winners' Cup final on 14 May, their 16th match in 46 days. Valencia were managed by Alfredo di Stefano and contained such footballing luminaries as Argentine international striker Mario Kempes and West Germany's Rainer Bonhof. The game was a tense affair which went into extra-time and finished goalless. *The Times* described the game as 'a finely balanced match in which Arsenal demonstrated to the full the character and strength many doubted they still possessed after 67 demanding matches'. The winner would now be decided by the lottery of penalties. Both Kempes and Brady missed with their opening efforts. After another nine successful conversions, the score was 5-4 and Rix had to score from his. Valencia keeper Carlos Pereira moved before Rix made contact but he guessed correctly and saved. Rix was inconsolable and Valencia had won the Cup.

Brady Departs

With two league games remaining Arsenal still had an opportunity to enter the following season's UEFA Cup. Although they beat Wolves 2-1 at Highbury, they crumbled in their final game at Middlesbrough, remarkably their 70th game of the season, going down 5-0 to end in fourth place in the League and out of European competition the next season. From a possible cup 'Double' only nine days previously, the Gunners ended a long and arduous campaign with nothing to show for their troubles, a season of failure but one which had been characterised by determination and bravery. In *My Story*, O'Leary

Liam Brady was one of the finest talents to have worn an Arsenal shirt and he left Highbury at just 24 years of age in search of European challenges.

50 Greatest Players

LIAM BRADY Midfielder

Born: Dublin, 13 February 1956

Joined Arsenal: 1971   **From:** School

Debut: 6 October 1973 v Birmingham City (sub), League

Appearances: 306   **Goals:** 59

Left Arsenal: 1980   **For:** Juventus

Honours won with Arsenal: FA Cup winner 1979; 27 Republic of Ireland caps

Liam Brady was one of the most gifted midfielders in Arsenal history. Another youth team product, he made his senior debut in October 1973 and established himself the following season. After Alan Ball's departure in December 1976, Brady became the Gunners' playmaker and revelled in the role. Small, slight, but deceptively strong, his majestic left foot could open up the tightest defence. He was the brains behind Arsenal's run to three successive FA Cup finals and the 1980 Cup-Winners' Cup final. His departure left a gap that Arsenal could not fill until the rise of a new generation of midfield players under George Graham. Meanwhile, Brady was a big hit in Italy, first with Juventus, then with Internazionale. He returned to Highbury in 1996 as head of youth development.

quotes Howe as saying in the dressing room after the Middlesbrough game, 'We've had a tremendous year. We've won nothing but we've still got a heck of a lot to celebrate on the way home. Well done every one of you.'

True to his word Liam Brady left Arsenal in the summer of 1980 to join Juventus for a fee of £600,000 which, as he was out of contract, was the maximum Arsenal could receive under UEFA rules. Brady was to prove a major success in Italian football, playing for four clubs before his swansong with West Ham whom he joined in 1986. There are many fans who believe that with Brady's departure, and also that of Frank Stapleton at the end of the following season, the club had lost not only its finest two players but also its will to succeed. The early 1980s were far from disastrous but generally lacked both flair and consistency, with Neill and Howe looking for stopgap solutions to longer-term problems on the pitch and unable to bring the success which the crowd increasingly demanded. Attendances gradually declined during the first half of the decade as players came and went without arousing too much in the way of excitement.

In August 1980 Neill paid £1,250,000 to Queens Park Rangers for their 19-year-old striker, Clive Allen, the previous season's Division One leading scorer. Before he had played a league game for the club Allen was transferred to Crystal Palace in exchange for Palace's England international left back

50 Greatest Players

PAT RICE Right back

Born: Belfast, 17 March 1949

Joined Arsenal: 1964 **From:** School

Debut: 2 December 1967 v Burnley (sub), League

Appearances: 527 **Goals:** 13

Left Arsenal: 1980 **For:** Watford

Honours won with Arsenal: Division One championship 1971;
FA Cup winner 1971, 1979; 49 Northern Ireland caps

Pat Rice was one of the most determined players of his
generation. He was not the most naturally gifted, but few worked
harder to reach the top. He grew up in Islington and rose
through the Gunners' youth ranks. He was an FA Youth Cup
winner in 1966. His chance came at the start of the 'Double'
campaign when Peter Storey was switched from right back to
midfield anchor. Rice missed only one game that season and
became a fixture for the next decade, for club and country. He played in five FA Cup finals,
skippering the Gunners to three consecutive Wembley appearances between 1978 and
1980. He ended his playing days at Watford but rejoined Arsenal in 1984 as youth coach.

Kenny Sansom. Although there were murmurs about the situation having
been pre-arranged between the clubs, the Arsenal explanation was that the
form of the existing strikers, Sunderland and Stapleton, was such that Allen
would find it difficult to break through. So why buy him in the first place?
Whatever the truth of the matter, Sansom was a fine acquisition. Although
only 5ft 6in, he was a speedy, classy defender and his arrival meant the end
of Sammy Nelson's Highbury career. Nelson would move to Brighton at the
season's end and Sansom would occupy the left back position until replaced
by Nigel Winterburn in 1988. Another arrival was Scottish keeper George
Wood from Everton. Wood was to prove a capable deputy for Jennings and
he took over from the Irishman for two months in the autumn of 1980 when
Jennings was injured. At the beginning of 1980-81 veteran right back Pat
Rice moved to Watford and O'Leary was handed the captaincy, an honour
indeed for the 22-year-old defender.

In contrast to the previous season, progress in the cup competitions in
1980-81 was brief. Arsenal were knocked out of the League Cup in
November by Spurs in the fourth round, 1-0 at White Hart Lane. In January
they were eliminated from the FA Cup 2-0 by Everton in the third round. In

the League their form was patchy and by the middle of March they were languishing in mid-table having won only three of their previous 15 games. The arrival that month of tough-tackling, Welsh international midfielder Peter Nicholas, for £400,000 from Crystal Palace, however, seemed to spark a revival and Arsenal finished the season with nine unbeaten games, seven of them wins. Their late push helped them finish in third spot and a place in the UEFA Cup the following season.

Shortly before the 1981-82 season kicked, off Frank Stapleton, his contract now at an end, accepted an offer from Manchester United and moved to Old Trafford. The enigmatic Irishman was one of the finest centre forwards to have played for Arsenal and he scored 109 goals in his six years in the first team. His departure angered and dismayed many fans who felt that he had opted for money over loyalty and also that the club should have made more of an effort to hold on to him. Like Brady, he left a vacancy which was to prove difficult to replace. Neill said that their going was 'a tragedy of monumental proportions for the club. I worked tirelessly to keep them but was helpless'. At the beginning of 1981-82 Neill bought bustling centre forward John Hawley from Sunderland but, in spite of 14 appearances over the season, he only scored three goals and left the club in 1983.

Other new faces this season included the tall, 20-year-old central defender Chris Whyte whose arrival in the first team in a 1-0 home win over Manchester City in October signalled the end of Willie Young's time with Arsenal. Crowd favourite Young joined Nottingham Forest in November for £175,000. Whyte's

Irish centre forward Frank Stapleton whose departure to Manchester United was a blow to the struggling 1980s team.

50 Greatest Players

FRANK STAPLETON Striker

Born: Dublin, 10 July 1956

Joined Arsenal: 1972   **From:** School

Debut: 29 March 1975 v Stoke City, League

Appearances: 299   **Goals:** 108

Left Arsenal: 1981   **For:** Manchester United

Honours won with Arsenal: FA Cup winner 1979; 24 Republic of Ireland caps

Frank Stapleton was a constant threat in the air, highly mobile and adept at playing with his back to goal. Another who rose from the youth ranks, he played in four FA Cup finals for the club. His departure in 1981, for a tribunal-set £900,000, was a major blow to the Gunners, who struggled to replace him until Alan Smith's arrival six years later. He finished top scorer in each of his first three seasons at United, rubbing salt into Arsenal's wounds. Stapleton made his debut in 1975 and established himself the following season. He developed rapidly alongside Malcolm Macdonald, then formed an effective partnership with Alan Sunderland as the Gunners won the FA Cup in 1979. He headed the second goal in their 3-2 Wembley win over Manchester United.

first game also saw the league debut of 18-year-old Raphael Meade who scored the only goal of the game. Stewart Robson, a 17-year-old, competitive defender-cum-midfielder, made his first appearance against West Ham in December. Defenders Sansom and O'Leary were virtually ever-present in defence throughout the season, as were Rix and Talbot in midfield and Sunderland in attack, while Wood took over in goal for Jennings for the second half of the season.

This season saw the introduction of three points for a win, with only one for a draw. The Gunners' league campaign started badly, winning only three of their first 11 games, before a six-game winning streak between the end of October and mid-January. They stuttered again between mid-February and April but a late burst of five wins in the last seven games saw them finish fifth, 16 points behind Liverpool but good enough for a place in the UEFA Cup. They fell again at the first hurdle in the FA Cup, losing 1-0 to Spurs at White Hart Lane in early January, and they had been eliminated from the League Cup 3-0 by Liverpool in the fourth round at a replay at Anfield. The first-team debut of Raphael Meade was against Panathinaikos in the UEFA Cup in Greece in September and the young striker scored with his first touch when he came on as a substitute, in the 2-0 win. Young forward Brian McDermott scored the other. After winning 1-0 at Highbury in the second leg, they lost 1-0 at Winterslag in the first leg of round two and a 2-1 win at Highbury, through Hollins and Rix, in the second leg meant they were eliminated on away goals.

After another disappointing season Neill moved again into the transfer market. Ex-Nottingham Forest forward Tony Woodcock arrived at Highbury in the summer of 1982 from Cologne for £500,000. He was closely followed by Lee Chapman, another £500,000 buy, from Stoke. Woodcock was to remain a regular in the side until 1986 while Chapman was to prove something of a disaster on the pitch, scoring only three goals in 19 games, and he left the club in December 1983. Neill described the acquisition of Chapman as 'the biggest transfer mistake of my career'. Arsenal's league form was again wretched and they won only six games by Christmas. The arrival in December of Vladimir Petrovic, a hugely talented, midfield schemer from Red Star Belgrade, seemed to offer hope, but the Yugoslav was frequently played out of position and found it difficult to deal with the pace of the First Division. Against the player's (and many of the fans') wishes, he moved to Antwerp at the end of the season. Neill said, 'He had a good touch and a lot of skill and the crowd took to him immediately... [but] I had to act in the interests of the club.'

A 5-2 humbling by a dominant Spartak Moscow at Highbury in late September had ended Arsenal's interest in the UEFA Cup and the Russian side was sportingly given a standing ovation by the Arsenal support. However, they progressed well in the other two knockout tournaments. In the League (now renamed Milk) Cup they reached the semi-final against Manchester United, only to lose 6-3 on aggregate. In the FA Cup they again met Manchester United in the semi-final but lost again, this time going down 2-1 at Villa Park with Woodcock scoring the only Arsenal goal. In the League results improved slightly (although they were crushed 5-0 at White Hart Lane in April) and ten more wins found the Gunners in tenth position at the campaign's end.

It seemed that Arsenal were turning into a mid-table team, not good or consistent enough to win the championship but too strong to be relegated. This state of affairs was becoming unacceptable to the board, now under the chairmanship of Peter Hill-Wood whose father Denis had died two years previously, and Neill's position was coming under close scrutiny. Neill responded to his critics in June 1983 by buying the 21-year-old Celtic forward Charlie Nicholas who had just broken the Scottish scoring record for a season with over 50 goals. Nicholas, an audacious talent with a cheeky charisma, soon became a North Bank favourite, not least because he had turned down offers from Manchester United and Liverpool to come to Highbury. On song, his skills were unparalleled in the team but, as with many players of his ilk, he suffered from inconsistency and less than total application.

Arsenal won their first two matches of 1983-84, Nicholas scoring both in the 2-1 away defeat of Wolves, but then lost in the same week to Manchester United and Liverpool, both at Highbury. Throughout the autumn the league form was erratic, losing at home to Coventry and Sunderland (a game in which 17-year-old centre half Tony Adams made his debut) but beating Aston Villa 6-2 at Villa Park, Woodcock scoring five goals in the match. After a poor performance at Filbert Street on 26 November when they lost 3-0 to Leicester City, Neill lambasted his players, saying, 'They don't seem to know what it is to hunger for goals or glory.' The situation rapidly deteriorated three days later when they were beaten 2-1 at home in the Milk Cup by Third Division Walsall, an uncanny repetition of the shock defeat by the same club 50 years previously. Two more league defeats followed – against West Brom and West Ham – and on 16 December Neill was called before the chairman and asked to leave. He recalls, 'Peter Hill-Wood said, "I suppose you know why you're here?" I thought to myself, "I know I'm Irish but I'm not that dumb."' Neill had limited success in the transfer market, had failed to win the respect of several of his players and under his reign Arsenal had won nothing for almost four years. But most importantly of all, he had been unable to replace the two star players, Brady and Stapleton, whose talents had been critical to the club's fortunes in the late 1970s.

Other important changes had been occurring behind the scenes. In 1983 David Dein, a 36-year-old commodity broker, had joined the Arsenal board. A wealthy and successful North London businessman, Dein was far from the stereotypical formal, patrician director of the past. Not only did he attempt to involve himself in team affairs, he also took a much more commercial view than had previously been the case of the club's longer-term profit potential. Dein was one of the first directors in British football to understand the possibilities of merchandising, licensing and TV rights, and his vision for the club was vindicated in the 1990s.

Howe Gets his Opportunity

On 17 December Don Howe took over as caretaker manager, although he was not formally confirmed in the job until the following spring. His stewardship started brightly with a 3-1 home win over Watford (Raphael Meade claiming a hat-trick) and a 4-2 defeat of Spurs at White Hart Lane, Meade and Nicholas scoring two apiece. He also had a new centre half, Tommy Caton, whom Neill had acquired from Manchester City for £500,000 just days before his

Big Pat Jennings served eight seasons at Highbury after Tottenham no longer had room for him.

departure. Although they were knocked out of the FA Cup in the third round 3-2 at Middlesbrough, and lost again to Manchester United and Liverpool in the early spring, Arsenal put together three consecutive wins in late March and early April. The attack had been reinforced in February with the arrival of the 31-year-old England centre forward Paul Mariner, a strong frontman with a powerful header. Three more victories by the end of the season gained Arsenal sixth place in the League, arguably a respectable position after such a traumatic season.

Season 1984-85 was Pat Jennings's last season. John Lukic, a tall shotstopper with a prodigious kick, took over in December and the amiable Irishman retired at the end of the season. Viv Anderson, a stylish, pacy right back and the first black player to gain a full cap for England, arrived from Nottingham Forest for £250,000 to partner Kenny Sansom. After a shaky start, Arsenal won eight of their nine games in September and October, including 3-1 against Liverpool and 1-0 against Everton (the eventual league champions) at home, and they led the table. In the Milk Cup they went down embarrassingly to Oxford United 3-2 at Oxford in the third round. In the League an inconsistent second half of the season left Arsenal in seventh place. In the FA Cup, a 7-2 crushing at Highbury of Hereford United in a third round replay was followed by an ignominious expulsion from the competition at York, the Gunners going down 1-0 to a last-minute penalty from Keith Houchen.

Howe was experiencing similar problems to his predecessor, namely the lack of quality goalscorers. Woodcock led the season's tally but he only amassed 13 goals in all competitions. Nicholas scored 12, but this contribution was

50 Greatest Players

PAT JENNINGS Goalkeeper

Born: Newry, 12 June 1945

Joined Arsenal: 1977   **From:** Tottenham Hotspur

Debut: 20 August 1977 v Ipswich Town, League

Appearances: 326

Left Arsenal: 1985 (retired)

Honours won with Arsenal: FA Cup winner 1979; 42 Northern Ireland caps

Pat Jennings proved Tottenham wrong after he was snapped up by old Northern Ireland colleague Terry Neill for Arsenal. Spurs thought Jennings was past his best. Instead, he played on for eight more years, appearing in four FA Cup finals for the Gunners and shining for Northern Ireland in the 1982 World Cup finals. He had reputedly the biggest hands in English football and used them to dominate his box. Strong on crosses and a brilliant shot stopper, he gave many memorable displays. At the age of 39, he finally gave way to John Lukic in the second half of the 1984-85 season.

significantly below initial expectations. Attendances at Highbury were in decline and frustration was almost palpable on the terraces.

Season 1985-86 – Arsenal's 100th year – was to be Don Howe's last at Highbury. In the Milk Cup Arsenal reached a fifth round replay at Highbury only to exit 2-1 to Aston Villa on 4 February. Howe played an off-form Mariner out of position instead of the club's recent signing Steve Williams. On 5 March they met Luton Town on the plastic pitch at Kenilworth Road for a fifth round FA Cup second replay and crashed out 3-0. Although they were progressing satisfactorily in the League, after their 3-0 home win over Coventry on 22 March – their fourth consecutive win – Don Howe asked to be released from his contract. He had heard that the Arsenal board were sounding out Terry Venables about leaving Barcelona and taking over at Highbury. Howe perceived this to be an affront to his dignity and, with some justification, something of a stab in the back. The probability, however, was that he was not going to be offered a new contract anyway.

The season ended with Arsenal in seventh place in the League and it had been seven long years since the club had won a trophy. However, on 14 May 1986 George Graham was appointed the new manager and he was about to bring back success and silverware to the famous old club.

Chapter Seven: 1986-96
Graham Returns

George Graham – the 'Stroller' of the 1971 team – had enjoyed a successful four years in management at Millwall before returning to Highbury. Although a diffident, laid-back personality in his playing career, Graham had evolved into a single-minded disciplinarian as a manager. Several of the senior players had mixed socially with Graham, but he made his position clear when, according to Tony Adams's book *Addicted,* he told them, 'I don't mind if you call me George by mistake at first, but I want to be known as boss.' His experience in coaching at Crystal Palace and Queens Park Rangers and in man-management and team building at Millwall had equipped him well for his new challenge. Tactically astute, and aware of what was required at Highbury, Graham set to work on restructuring the team.

With no room in his philosophy for overpaid, ageing stars – and with Arsenal over £1 million in debt – he quickly disposed of Woodcock to Cologne and Mariner to Portsmouth, with both players out of contract anyway, and he turned to the younger players to form the core of his team. Young Tony Adams, who was described by Graham as a future England captain, became his regular centre half, playing in every game in 1986-87. Adams teamed up with O'Leary, the only remaining player in the squad who had appeared in the 1979 FA Cup final, in the centre of defence, flanked by Viv Anderson and captain Kenny Sansom, with Lukic making the goalkeeping position his own. The temperamental but highly skilful Steve Williams and the fast, exciting David Rocastle, a right-sided player with a powerful shot, made up the midfield alongside the elegant Paul Davis, with an injured Graham Rix ceding his place in October to the tall, speedy Martin Hayes. The 6ft 5in, 20-year-old Niall Quinn, who had scored on his debut in December 1985 in the 2-0 home win over Liverpool, utility forward Ian Allinson and fans' favourite Charlie Nicholas roamed up front.

Graham's first acquisition was red-haired attacker Perry Groves (nephew of former Arsenal captain Vic Groves) from Colchester in September. Graham dampened down false expectations by stating that the team was not yet strong enough to challenge seriously for the league title, although the first game of the season – a 1-0 home win over Manchester United, the scorer being Nicholas – aroused optimism among the home support. The old goalscoring

Niall Quinn, the towering young Irishman, who scored on his debut in 1985, against Liverpool.

problem raised its head, however, in September when Arsenal went four games without finding the net. A Williams goal direct from a corner against Everton in early October ended the drought and they won nine out of their next ten matches to lead the League by early December. On 27 December Arsenal celebrated their centenary, Quinn scoring in a 1-0 win over Southampton. In early January, and still leading the League, Arsenal travelled away to play Spurs, with whom they had drawn 0-0 earlier in the season. Two-nil up at half-time through Adams and a Davis free kick, the Gunners held on to win 2-1, an important symbolic victory in terms of their championship aspirations.

Spurs and the Semi-final Saga

In the Littlewoods (League) Cup Arsenal reached the semi-final, a two-legged tie against a talented Spurs side, at Highbury on 8 February. Without an injured Anderson, replaced by Gus Caesar, and a suspended Rocastle, Arsenal went down 1-0 to a Clive Allen goal. Caesar had a nightmare against a rampant Chris Waddle and was substituted by young Michael Thomas, an ex-England Under-21 captain playing his first game in the senior side.

Three weeks later at White Hart Lane Williams was injured and replaced by Thomas in midfield. Spurs went ahead through Clive Allen in the first half after a Lukic error and at half-time Arsenal were 2-0 down on aggregate. Kenny Sansom recounts in his book *Going Great Guns*, 'Spurs announced on their public address system how the fans should apply for tickets to the final and the message boomed into our dressing room. Then they switched on their old FA Cup final song "Spurs are on their way to Wembley", and that took the lads' determination over the top.' A revitalized Arsenal scored within five minutes of the restart, Anderson knocking the ball in from close range. Midway through the second half a Rocastle cross found Quinn and the big forward did well to score and equalize the tie on aggregate. Three days later the third game kicked off at White Hart Lane. That Arsenal came

Great Matches

LEAGUE CUP SEMI-FINAL REPLAY		**White Hart Lane, 4 March 1987**

Arsenal 2   **Tottenham Hotspur 1**   **Attendance: 41,055**
Allinson   Allen
Rocastle

Arsenal lost the first leg 1-0 at Highbury and won 2-1 in the second leg at White Hart Lane to equalize the tie on aggregate. Three days later the third game kicked off at White Hart Lane, Spurs' manager David Pleat having won the toss for choice of grounds. With 10,000 Arsenal fans packed into the ground Clive Allen put Spurs ahead in the second half. In the 82nd minute, Ian Allinson, on for an injured Nicholas, gathered a long ball from Davis in the area and sent a shot through Richard Gough's legs and under Ray Clemence at the near post for his first goal of the season. Arsenal threw Anderson, Allinson and Rocastle forward to join Quinn in attack and Spurs were now up against it. In injury time, Rocastle picked up a blocked shot from Allinson and scored the winner with his left foot under Clemence. Over the 300 minutes of the tie, Arsenal had led for only one of them. The Arsenal fanzine *One-Nil Down, Two-One Up* was named after this historic victory, which was a classic example of how courage and character can overcome a technically more gifted side.

Arsenal: Lukic, Anderson, Sansom, M. Thomas, O'Leary, Adams, Rocastle, Davis, Quinn, Nicholas (Allinson), Hayes

Tottenham Hotspur: Clemence, D. Thomas, M. Thomas, Ardiles, Gough, Mabbutt, C. Allen, P. Allen, Waddle, Stevens, Claessen (Galvin)

Referee: J. Worrall

away the victors is a tribute to the determination and resilience of George Graham's team.

A 2-0 defeat by Manchester United in the League at the end of January saw Arsenal start a run of nine league games without a win and, although they picked up in April and May, they could only manage fourth place at the end of the season. They were also knocked out of the FA Cup by Watford at the quarter-final stage. But they had reached the final of the Littlewoods Cup and were drawn against favourites Liverpool at Wembley on 5 April. Ian Rush scored from a Craig Johnston pass in the 23rd minute and just before half-time Nicholas scrambled in the equalizer. With seven minutes remaining, substitute Groves sped down the left and passed to Nicholas who swung at the ball, mishit it but the ball rolled past Bruce Grobbelaar into the net. Graham commented afterwards, 'We have often played better, but the prize at the end made it one of Arsenal's more memorable performances.'

Charlie Nicholas scores the first of his two goals in the 1987 League Cup final for Arsenal's first trophy in eight years.

The team that had brought back the first trophy to Highbury for eight years was: Lukic, Anderson, Sansom, Williams, O'Leary, Adams, Rocastle, Davis, Quinn (Groves), Nicholas, Hayes (Thomas).

Despite trophy-winning goals, Charlie Nicholas had fallen out of favour with Graham and, after playing only three games at the start of season 1987-88, he was dropped and sold to Aberdeen in January. Viv Anderson also departed in July to Manchester United. Over the summer, the manager had spent £750,000 on buying tall centre forward Alan Smith from Leicester City (Smith actually signed in the spring but was loaned back to Leicester for the remainder of the season), busy midfielder Kevin Richardson for £200,000 from Watford and spiky, tough-tackling left back Nigel Winterburn from Wimbledon for £350,000. Winterburn, however, made his appearances this season in the right back slot. A promising teenage forward, Paul Merson, had come through the youth system and made his senior debut in November 1986.

The first game of the 1987-88 season was a 2-1 home defeat by Liverpool, followed by a 0-0 draw at Old Trafford. Smith got off his mark with a hat-trick in the 6-0 win over Portsmouth and between 12 September and 14 November the Gunners were on a roll, winning ten games in succession to lead the League briefly. Unhappily this was followed by only one win in the next 11 games, a run which included consecutive defeats by Manchester United and Liverpool. They finished the season with six wins in their last 14 games to end up in sixth position. Goalscoring continued to be a problem with the top scorer being

Smith with only 11 goals, followed by Thomas with nine. Martin Hayes had also proved to be something of an enigma. The tall front man who had scored 19 goals in 35 league games the previous season could only manage one in 27 starts in 1987-88.

Arsenal had beaten Manchester United 2-1 in the fifth round of the FA Cup in front of a 54,161 crowd but were knocked out in the next round 2-1 by Nottingham Forest. They did, however, reach the final of the Littlewoods Cup, having beaten Everton 3-1 in the semi-final and scored 15 while only conceding one goal en route to Wembley, where they were led out on 24 April by new captain Tony Adams who was to assume the leadership of the team until his retirement in 2002.

A poor performance by Arsenal allowed Brian Stein to put little-fancied Luton Town ahead 1-0 by the interval. Substitute Hayes equalized in the 75th minute and five minutes later Arsenal were ahead when Smith scored between keeper Andy Dibble and the post. Then Smith hit the bar and Hayes shot against the post from the rebound. In the 82nd minute, Rocastle was tripped in the box and Winterburn's penalty, his first for the club, was athletically saved by Dibble. With five minutes remaining a hashed clearance by Gus Caesar, having a nervous game throughout, was seized on by Danny Wilson for Luton's equalizer. With virtually the last kick of the game, Stein scored the winner for Luton, the only major honour in the club's history.

Graham was, unlike his counterparts at Manchester United and Liverpool, parsimonious in his transfer market dealings but, by the beginning of the 1988-89 season, he had a title-winning team in place. Graham Rix signed for Caen, Steve Williams joined Luton, while Sansom was relegated to the reserves and eventually moved to Newcastle in December 1988 after nearly 400 appearances and an outstanding career with the club. Winterburn replaced him as left back and the right back position was occupied by Lee Dixon, a tenacious, attacking player bought from Stoke for £400,000 midway through the previous season. Brian Marwood, an excellent crosser of the ball and an intelligent winger, arrived from Sheffield Wednesday towards the end of the previous season for £600,000 and powerful, 6ft 3in centre back Steve Bould joined from Stoke for £390,000. The famous Arsenal back four were now in place in front of Lukic, with O'Leary competing with Bould for the fourth place. The strikeforce of Smith and Merson, the young forward now an integral part of Graham's team, was supported in midfield by Thomas and Richardson, with Rocastle and Marwood playing wide. Groves, Hayes and Davis (injured, however, for most of the season) were also to make their contributions this season.

Graham was developing a fast, fit, counter-attacking team with a solid defence and, in Alan Smith, an increasingly predatory striker.

Arsenal opened the season in style, Alan Smith scoring a hat-trick in the 5-1 away defeat of Wimbledon, and although they lost a couple of games – to Aston Villa and Sheffield Wednesday – by early November a 4-1 away crushing of Nottingham saw them move into second place in the League. In November they lost a second replay against Liverpool in the League Cup third round to go out of the competition. Three days later they were beaten 2-1 at the Baseball Ground by Derby but then embarked on an 11-game unbeaten run in the League. The run included five wins in succession – over Manchester United, Charlton, Aston Villa Tottenham and Everton – between 17 December and 14 January, and the Gunners were now five points ahead of second-placed Norwich in the League and 11 ahead of a distant Liverpool. They were, however, knocked out of the FA Cup in January in a third round replay at Highbury, beaten 1-0 by West Ham.

Smith had scored 17 league goals so far, assisted by seven from Merson, and Arsenal were becoming clear favourites for the league title. Their aspirations began to unravel, however, when they could only draw 0-0 with Queens Park Rangers at Loftus Road and they won only one out of their next five games. Meanwhile, Liverpool were winning all their matches and closing the gap. A 3-1 away win at Southampton restored the differential but at Old Trafford a 1-1 draw – Adams scoring with a header and then slicing the ball into his own

net in attempting to clear – narrowed the gap further. A 5-1 win over Sheffield Wednesday on the morning of 8 April put Liverpool on top of the League for the first time but Arsenal's 2-0 defeat of Everton that afternoon saw Arsenal reclaim the lead.

On 15 April Arsenal consolidated their pole position with a 1-0 win over Newcastle but the Hillsborough disaster that afternoon – when 96 people were crushed to death in the FA Cup semi-final between Liverpool

Kenny Sansom was a combative and reassuring presence at left back in almost 400 appearances for Arsenal.

and Nottingham Forest – put the title race into perspective. Arsenal postponed their next game as a mark of respect for the dead.

Arsenal won their next two matches – a 5-0 hammering of Norwich City, their biggest win of the season, and a 1-0 defeat of Middlesbrough – and met Derby County at Highbury. By this stage Arsenal were five points ahead of Liverpool, who had a game in hand. A Dean Saunders volley gave Derby the lead. With a few minutes remaining Adams pulled down Saunders in the area and the striker converted. Alan Smith pulled one back but the final score was 2-1 for Derby. Liverpool had beaten Wimbledon and were now favourites. Still unbeaten since New Year's Day, the Merseyside team only had to win their remaining matches to become champions and three days later they moved one point clear of Arsenal with a 2-0 defeat of Queens Park Rangers.

In a critical game the following day at Highbury against Wimbledon, Arsenal's penultimate game of the season, although Winterburn smashed in a 30-yard shot with his right foot to open the scoring, the Dons equalized through Alan Cork. A Merson second-half volley gave the lead back to Arsenal but a Paul McGee strike led to a 2-2 final score. Arsenal were now level on points with Liverpool who had a game in hand, against West Ham in midweek. Arsenal's title hopes were now being written off, with the *Daily Mirror* opining, 'Arsenal's championship dream is now all but over.' Although Arsenal had scored more goals the two teams were now level on points and goal difference, but Liverpool's 5-1 win over West Ham meant that the two contenders had to meet for the last game of the season at Anfield with the Gunners needing to win by two goals to claim the championship.

Champions Again

The match against Liverpool on Friday 26 May 1989 was of huge significance. Graeme Souness had dismissed the Gunners chances in the *Sun* while the *Daily Mirror* trumpeted, 'Arsenal do not have a prayer.' The kickoff that evening was delayed because many Arsenal fans were stuck in traffic jams, and when the Arsenal players ran on to the pitch they gave bouquets of flowers to the Liverpool fans, as a mark of respect for Hillsborough. In the dressing room Graham had told his team, 'Go out and play without fear because you've got nothing to lose. But just think of what there is to gain.' Arsenal came away with a famous victory and a new hero in Michael Thomas.

Arsenal started season 1989-90 with Graham professing faith in his existing squad. He had bought only one player, Siggi Jonsson, from Sheffield Wednesday for £475,000. A hefty pre-season schedule meant that a tired Arsenal team played Manchester United on the opening game of the season at Old Trafford

Great Matches

LEAGUE DIVISION ONE   **Anfield, 26 May 1989**

Liverpool 0   **Arsenal 2**   **Attendance: 41,728**
            Smith
            Thomas

Arsenal travelled to Liverpool on Friday 26 May 1989 for their most important game in 18 years, needing two goals for the championship. Virtually all the media had written off the team's chances. The Gunners had not won at Anfield on their last seven visits and Liverpool remained unbeaten since New Year's Day. The game began at a feverish pace and there were chances at both ends but at half-time there was still no score. Seven minutes after the restart Winterburn, dead ball taker in the absence of the injured Marwood, sent an indirect free kick into the Liverpool box after Ronnie Whelan had fouled Rocastle. Smith glanced a header past Grobbelaar and, although the Liverpool players complained he had not touched the ball, the referee gave the goal after consultation with the linesman.

 Arsenal continued to apply pressure but the game went into injury time and, amid the unbearable tension, Liverpool players began to congratulate each other and the Kop chanted 'Champions!'. In the 92nd minute Lukic threw to Dixon who sent a long upfield pass to Smith. The tall striker cleverly laid the ball off to Thomas, steaming up the inside right channel towards the Liverpool goal. Thomas tried to lob Nicol, the ball bounced back to him and he continued his run with Nicol and Houghton in desperate pursuit. Grobbelaar came out but at the last moment Thomas flicked the ball with the outside of his right foot

Above: Michael Thomas scores the goal that makes Arsenal league champions for 1988-89; above right: Tony Adams, Steve Bould and David O'Leary celebrate.

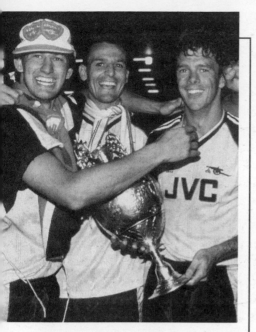

over the keeper's legs and into the net. Thomas, the architect of one of the most unforgettable and dramatic moments in English footballing history, somersaulted away in delight. The final whistle went amid scenes of pandemonium at Anfield and in the bars of North London. Despite throwing away what at one time was a 19-point lead over Liverpool, Arsenal had shown yet again their resolve and character to snatch a famous and almost unbelievable victory when it was most needed.

Liverpool: Grobbelaar, Ablett, Staunton, Nicol, Whelan, Hansen, Houghton, Aldridge, Rush (Beardsley), Barnes, McMahon

Arsenal: Lukic, Dixon, Winterburn, Bould (Groves), Adams, O'Leary, Thomas, Richardson, Rocastle, Merson (Hayes), Smith

Referee: D. Hutchinson

and were humbled 4-1. Rocastle headed in the Gunners' only goal from a Marwood cross in the second half and Caesar, on for Adams, was tormented by Mark Hughes. However, they won five out of their next six games, the run coming to an end with a 2-1 defeat by Tottenham away.

On 4 November Arsenal met Norwich at Highbury, when O'Leary's 622nd appearance for Arsenal broke George Armstrong's previous record. The Irishman was booked in the first half and at the interval Arsenal were 2-0 down. Quinn and Dixon made the score 2-2, Norwich scored a third and O'Leary equalized with a header, his first goal in the League for six years. Dixon scored the winner, converting a rebound from his penalty kick, and Smith was pushed when he ran into the net to celebrate. An undignified but harmless fracas erupted and the Gunners were to be fined £20,000 by the FA for their part in the incident.

Arsenal then won five out of their next six games, going down 2-1 to Liverpool at Anfield but beating Manchester United 1-0 through a Perry Groves goal. The following week Merson scored the only goal against Coventry at Highfield, sending in a beautiful chip over giant keeper Steve Ogrizovic from a tight angle outside the area. By 16 December they were the league leaders, two points ahead of second-placed Liverpool.

50 Greatest Players

KENNY SANSOM Left back

Born: Camberwell, 26 September 1958

Joined Arsenal: 1980   **From:** Crystal Palace

Debut: 16 August 1980 v West Bromwich Albion, League

Appearances: 394   **Goals:** 6

Left Arsenal: 1988   **For:** Newcastle United

Honours won with Arsenal: League Cup winner 1987; 77 England caps

Kenny Sansom was already England's left back when he joined the Gunners in a swap deal for £1.25 million striker, Clive Allen. Sansom was small, stocky and quick, a determined tackler and enthusiastic attacker. He was ever present in his first two seasons and missed only a handful of matches in eight seasons. He skippered Arsenal to League Cup victory over Liverpool in 1987, but lost the captaincy the following year after falling out with George Graham. Sansom was sidelined as Nigel Winterburn became the regular left back at the start of the 1988-89 season and he joined Newcastle two days before Christmas. He never played for England again. But he remains Arsenal's most-capped outfield player.

They stumbled over Christmas, however, going down to Southampton and Aston Villa in succession. In January they beat Tottenham at Highbury, Adams scoring the only goal, but they then went five games without scoring, including elimination from the fourth round of the FA Cup by Queens Park Rangers, now managed by Don Howe. In November they had been knocked out of the Littlewoods Cup 3-1 by Oldham, so the league title was now their only target, albeit a distant one. Between early March and the end of the season Arsenal could manage only another five wins and they ended in fourth place, well behind champions Liverpool.

Although Arsenal had lost only two games at Highbury they seemed lost on their travels, losing 13 away matches. Scoring was again a problem, with Smith netting only 13 and Merson next with nine. The defence had kept Arsenal in the hunt during the season, with 14 clean sheets in 38 league games. Marwood, Bould and Davis were also out injured for lengthy spells, and the team generally lacked the coherence and cohesion they had triumphantly demonstrated the previous season, with too many of the players off-form. There was a positive note, however, in the emergence towards the end of the season of powerful young striker Kevin Campbell who scored in the wins over Nottingham Forest and Derby in March. A disappointing season by the Gunners was, however, to be redeemed in 1990-91.

Niall Quinn had joined Manchester City in March and Kevin Richardson moved to Real Sociedad in the summer of 1990. George Graham realized that he had to strengthen his squad to have any realistic chance of the league title. In came tricky little Swedish winger Anders Limpar for £2.2 million from Italian club Cremonese to replace an increasingly injury-prone Marwood. John Lukic departed for Leeds United, much to the anger of many fans, but his replacement from Queens Park Rangers, David Seaman, costing a British record £1.3 million fee for a goalkeeper, was soon to gain the supporters' respect. Another newcomer was Andy Linighan, a centre back from Norwich, bought as support for Bould and Adams.

This season was to be a triumph for Arsenal and George Graham. 'There was a freshness to us from the outset of the season and a steely togetherness,' recalls Adams in his autobiography. Arsenal got off to a impressive start and Limpar, with his darting runs, accurate crossing and keen nose for goal, immediately became a crowd favourite. The Gunners went 14 games without defeat until they met Manchester United at Highbury in the fourth round of the Rumbelows (League) Cup on 28 November. In an amazing game United won 6-2, three goals coming from Lee Sharpe, and the score could easily have gone

50 Greatest Players

GRAHAM RIX Midfielder

Born: Doncaster, 23 October 1957

Joined Arsenal: 1974   **From:** School

Debut: 2 April 1977 v Leicester City, League

Appearances: 463   **Goals:** 51

Left Arsenal: 1988   **For:** Caen (France)

Honours won with Arsenal: FA Cup winner 1979; 17 England caps

Graham Rix announced his arrival with a goal inside 13 minutes of his debut against Leicester in 1977. He established himself the following season, when Rix, Brady and Nelson formed the most threatening left side triangle in English football. Frail, but stronger than he looked, Rix was a tricky dribbler, a fine long passer and an accurate crosser. It was his centre to the far post that set up Alan Sunderland's dramatic winner in the 1979 FA Cup final. He had the unenviable job of trying to take up Brady's mantle after the Irishman moved to Juventus – and did well enough to get himself into the England team for the 1982 World Cup finals. Unfortunately, injuries, particularly Achilles tendon trouble, plagued him in his latter years at Highbury.

Michael Thomas's goal in the final game of the 1988-89 campaign secured the league title for Arsenal and an enduring place for him in the Highbury Hall of Fame.

the other way. In one game Seaman conceded as many goals as he had done in the previous 17. The freakishness of the result was confirmed when Liverpool visited Highbury four days later. A Limpar-inspired display defeated the league champions 3-0, the goals coming from Merson, Dixon and Smith (now back to his best, with seven goals in five games).

Arsenal had met Manchester United on 20 October and Limpar scored a hotly disputed goal in the Gunners' 1-0 win, a heated affair as usual between the two clubs. A crunching Winterburn tackle on McClair led to the Scotsman retaliating and then all hell broke loose, with nearly every player on the pitch involved in the altercation, although it seemed that many players were simply trying to calm things down. Only Limpar and Winterburn were booked by the referee, but after the media-titled 'Battle of Old Trafford', Arsenal deducted two weeks' wages from the two cautionees as well as Davis, Thomas and Rocastle, hoping to prevent any further FA action. George Graham was fined, with Peter Hill-Wood stressing that the 'ultimate responsibility for conduct of the players lies with the manager'. Worse was to follow when, on 13 November, an FA commission fined Arsenal £50,000 and deducted two points from their league standing. The result of the decision left Liverpool eight points clear at the top.

An unbowed Arsenal continued on their unbeaten run, overcoming Derby, Sheffield United and Manchester City at Christmas, with a rejuvenated Smith scoring five goals over the three games. The Gunners, however, had now to cope with the absence of their talismanic skipper Tony Adams who had been sentenced at Southend Crown Court on 19 December to four months imprisonment for reckless and drunken driving, the result of an incident over the summer. It was a harsh, exemplary sentence but the indomitable Adams did his time unflinchingly and, having missed 13 games, he was back in the side for the fifth round FA Cup tie against Shrewsbury on 27 February. He was fully supported by Arsenal during his incarceration, with the club's managing director Ken Friar promising 'he will continue to be an Arsenal player and receive our full support'. Paul Davis took over the captain's armband.

Arsenal had beaten Sunderland in the third round of the FA Cup to set up a fourth round meeting with old foes Leeds United at Highbury on 27 January. The marathon went to four games and was settled at Elland Road where Merson and Dixon scored in the 2-1 win. Thomas scored the only goal in the fifth round at Shrewsbury and Adams and the fast-improving 'Super' Kevin Campbell were both on the scoresheet after the 2-1 defeat of Cambridge United in the sixth round at Highbury. The semi-final was to be against Tottenham.

Meanwhile, Arsenal had lost their unbeaten league record on 2 February. Chelsea won 2-1. Bould, taking over Adams's defensive mantle, and having an enormously influential season, had to go off at half-time with an injury, with young midfielder David Hillier dropping back out of position to replace him as centre back. Bould's absence almost certainly contributed to Arsenal's only league defeat of the season. Arsenal bounced back from this minor setback to crush Crystal Palace 4-0 in their next league game. Merson scored the only goal at Anfield in the next game to put Arsenal three points clear at

50 Greatest Players

MICHAEL THOMAS Midfielder/Right back

Born: Lambeth, 24 August 1967

Joined Arsenal: 1983   **From:** School

Debut: 14 February 1987 v Sheffield Wednesday, League

Appearances: 206   **Goals:** 30

Left Arsenal: 1991   **For:** Liverpool

Honours won with Arsenal: Division One championship 1989, 1991; League Cup winner 1987; 2 England caps

Michael Thomas's place in the history of Arsenal and English football was assured by his 'Roy of the Rovers' title decider at Liverpool in 1989. Thomas, another youth product, broke into the side when he was 19 and became a regular for the next four seasons. He settled down in midfield, but had begun as a full back and he was a dangerous attacker from either position. At his best, Thomas was an awesome box-to-box runner and clinical finisher. But his Arsenal career ended after a disagreement with George Graham in 1991 and he moved on, ironically, to Liverpool that December. He gained an FA Cup winner's medal in his first season with them yet rarely showed the form of his early days with Arsenal.

the top of the League, and the 'Double' was becoming a real possibility. Campbell scored twice in the 2-0 defeat of Leeds at Highbury and the muscular striker claimed another brace against Derby at the end of the month.

The FA Cup semi-final on 14 April was the first such game to be played at Wembley in English footballing history. Spurs were in financial trouble and they desperately needed the revenue that a final appearance would bring while Arsenal were now concentrating on the 'Double'. Within five minutes Paul Gascoigne scored one of the finest goals ever seen at the old stadium when he lashed a free kick past Seaman's outstretched fingertips from over 30 yards. Gary Lineker poached a second within 15 minutes and, although Smith headed one back for Arsenal, Lineker made sure of a 3-1 win for Spurs halfway through the second half.

The 'Double' dream had gone but Arsenal now had five games remaining, four of them at home, to secure the league title. Merson and Campbell scored in an uneasy 2-2 draw with Manchester City three days later and the Gunners were now three points ahead of Liverpool. After a 2-0 win over Queens Park Rangers, the lead remained three points. On 4 May Liverpool met Chelsea at Stamford Bridge at 3pm while Arsenal were to start their match at Roker Park at 5.30pm. Chelsea overcame Liverpool 4-0 and Arsenal ground out a 0-0 draw against Sunderland. Arsenal were now four points ahead of Liverpool with two games left to play.

Graham's Arsenal Celebrate Once More

On a warm Bank Holiday afternoon on Monday 6 May Liverpool faced Nottingham Forest at the City Ground with Arsenal fans glued to the radio or watching the game on TV, knowing that a defeat for the Anfield team would give the championship to the Gunners. And that's what happened, Ian Woan scoring the winner for Brian Clough's team. The game against Manchester United at Highbury that evening was a massive celebration. Smith scored the first goal after 20 minutes, converting a Dixon cross, and on half-time Smith again finished off a pass from Campbell. Smith completed his hat-trick with a penalty and, although Bruce scored for United, Arsenal were rampant. The last game of the season was against Coventry at Highbury. Limpar, at the end of a brilliant season for the impish winger, scored a dazzling hat-trick and Smith, Groves and a Trevor Peake own goal gave the new champions a 6-1 victory.

George Graham had done it again and was the toast of Highbury. His team, put together with relatively modest resources, had won their second title in three seasons. Seaman and the imperious back four had let in only 18 league goals throughout the season and had prevented the opposition scoring in 24

Arsenal celebrate with the Division One trophy after the match against Coventry, 11 May 1991, l-r: back – Peter Hill-Wood (chairman), George Graham (manager), Linighan, Merson, Groves, Winterburn, Smith, Seaman, O'Leary, Bould, Adams, Houston (coach), Thomas; front – Hillier, Campbell, Dixon, Limpar, Davis, Rocastle, Gary Lewin (physio).

games. Smith had demonstrated his supreme centre forward talents, as adept at holding the ball and laying off as at scoring. The rangy striker amassed 22 league goals, while his fellow attackers Merson and Campbell scored the same number between them. Davis had been an exceptional playmaker and Limpar had achieved superhero status, in particular for his sparkling contribution in the first half of the season. As ever with Arsenal, the whole had exceeded the sum of the parts. Nick Hornby summed up the season by writing, 'The club and the fans closed ranks and overcame, with a magnificently single-minded sense of purpose, almost unsurmountable difficulties all of their own making.'

Graham now had a new challenge ahead. The ban on English teams in European football after the Heysel disaster had expired the previous season and Arsenal, as champions, were back in the European Cup for the first time since 1971-72.

Once again Arsenal followed up a season of dominance with one of a perverse mixture of brilliance and ineptness. They drew the first game of 1991-92 at home against Queens Park Rangers, followed by two consecutive away defeats, to Everton and Aston Villa. They won their next two games at home, drew with Leeds at Elland Road, and then went down 2-1 to Coventry

Anders Limpar's silky skills endeared him to the fans in 1990-91. He scored a hat-trick in the last game of the season.

at Highbury. In the Coventry game Dixon scored a stunning long-range own goal within the first minute, with Seaman a spectator.

Bould was injured for the first half of the season and his reassuring presence was missed in defence, particularly as O'Leary was losing pace, Linighan had become unpredictable and Colin Pates was seemingly out of his depth. Dixon was inconsistent and became a target for the fans, and Seaman was also affected by the general lack of confidence around him. Davis and Rocastle ran the midfield, but Davis was replaced by Hillier in October after a row with Graham. He made only one further appearance during the season. Michael Thomas was transferred to Liverpool in December and promptly incurred a fine from the FA after publicly criticizing Graham's long-ball style and dictatorial attitude.

George Graham finally made a big-name signing in September, bringing in 28-year-old Ian Wright, an infectiously exuberant, goal-hungry striker, from Crystal Palace for £2.5 million. Initial concerns about why Arsenal needed another goalscorer – when Smith, Campbell, Limpar and Merson were at the club – were allayed when Wright scored on his debut against Leicester in the League Cup and then claimed a hat-trick in the 4-0 win over Southampton on 28 September. Wright scored again in the next game, a 3-2 home win over Chelsea, and the following game saw one of the goals of the season, when Rocastle shimmied through the Manchester United defence at Old Trafford and chipped over Peter Schmeichel from 30 yards in a 1-1 draw.

Back in Europe Smith scored four in Arsenal's 6-1 rout of Austria Memphis at Highbury on 18 September and a 1-0 defeat in Vienna saw them through to meet Benfica in the next round of the European Cup. Benfica's Brazilian star Isaias opened the scoring in Lisbon but Campbell equalized with a well-taken strike towards the end. Back at Highbury, with Wright ineligible to play, Colin Pates scored first (his only ever goal for Arsenal) but Benfica levelled the score. The game went into extra-time and the Portuguese club scored twice, the second beginning with an Isaias nutmeg on Adams, and Arsenal were knocked out of the tournament.

The previous week Arsenal had been beaten 1-0 in the League Cup by Coventry. They also hit a slump in their league form, winning only two of their next six matches, against Spurs and Everton. The Everton game confirmed Graham's astuteness in the transfer market when Wright scored all four in Arsenal's 4-2 win. Matters deteriorated when the Gunners gained only one point from three games over Christmas.

January was an even more wretched month. Not only did they fail to score in three consecutive games – their 2-0 defeat by Liverpool marking the debut of teenage midfielder Ray Parlour – they were also knocked out of the FA Cup in the third round away by Fourth Division Wrexham, 92nd in the Football League the previous season. Arsenal were the superior side throughout the game and were 1-0 ahead at half-time through Smith. With eight minutes to go Wrexham's Mickey Thomas thundered in a free kick to equalize and in the dying seconds Steve Watkin scored the winner for the Welsh club. Graham described the embarrassing defeat as 'the lowest point of my career'.

After the nadir of January, however, Arsenal went the rest of the season – 17 games – without defeat helped by the return of Bould in the 1-1 draw with Manchester United on 1 February. The old duo of Bould and Adams reformed their partnership and the forwards recovered their form. Later in the month Smith limped off in a game against Sheffield Wednesday with less than 20 minutes remaining and the score 1-1 and was replaced by Campbell. The substitution sparked a remarkable goal glut, Arsenal finishing 7-1 winners, with Campbell and Limpar picking up two apiece.

Other highlights towards the end of the season included a Merson hat-trick against Crystal Palace in April and a 4-0 defeat of Liverpool at Highbury later in the month, Wright claiming two and Limpar scoring with a breathtaking lob from the halfway line. The team had gleefully rediscovered its form of the previous season but had left it too late to challenge Leeds for the league title. Arsenal finished in fourth place.

The last game of the season was at home to Southampton and another Wright hat-trick contributed to the 5-1 win. The old North Bank terrace was to be knocked down over the summer and a new all-seater stand was to open for the beginning of season 1993-94. Thousands of Gooners staged a good-natured sitdown demonstration on the famous old terracing after the game and chanted 'You'll never take the North Bank' but the protest soon dwindled away. Progress, one felt, was inevitable and the new stand was to become one of the finest in the country, with seating for 12,5000. Cheered by the team's recent form, and by new hero Ian 'Wright, Wright, Wright!' who scored 24 league goals in 30 games during the season, the fans looked forward with considerable optimism to the coming campaign.

A Tale of Two Cups

In the event there is not a great deal to say about Arsenal's 1992-93 league season, other than that it was a serious disappointment and contrasted dramatically with their performance in the two cup competitions. The squad had changed little from the previous season although Rocky Rocastle had joined Leeds for £2 million in the summer and bustling midfielder John Jensen had arrived from Brondby, after opening the scoring for Denmark in their victorious European Nations Cup final against Germany in the summer. The only other newcomer this season was defender Martin Keown, acquired from Everton for £2 million in February. Ironically, ex-youth-team player Keown had left Arsenal shortly after Graham's arrival, irked by the new manager's refusal to pay him an extra £50 a week.

This season was the first year of the Premier League, a new competition run by the Football Association. While the North Bank redevelopment was taking place the club had erected a mural to hide the building works, which had cut capacity to 29,000. On the mural were painted thousands of faces, but it had to be amended when it was pointed out that none of the 'spectators' were black or, indeed, women. The mural was unveiled in time for the opening game of the season, against Norwich at Highbury, when Arsenal, 2-0 ahead at half time, collapsed to a 4-2 defeat. They won only three out of their first nine games, then won six in a row to go top of the League by early November.

A 3-0 defeat by Leeds later in the month ended the winning sequence and they did not win again until 16 January when Merson scored at Maine Road in the 1-0 defeat of Manchester City. Between then and the season's end they won only a further five to end in tenth spot in the new Premiership, an inauspicious start to the competition.

Powerful forward Kevin Campbell battles for possession.

The statistics made dismal reading. Arsenal, top league scorers in 1991-92, were bottom this season with only 40 goals. Wright was top scorer with 15 but Smith, Campbell and Merson could muster only 13 between them. Also, the team only won 15 out of their 42 games and their league position was their worst for ten years.

With the exception of Wright the forwards had an inconsistent season. Campbell's first touch was suspect, his control was clumsy and he had lost his scoring ability. Merson, increasingly erratic and out of condition, showed only flashes of his talent, while Limpar could not claim a regular place. The once prolific Smith continued to act as a supplier to Wright and managed only three league goals all season. In midfield Jensen had joined a young midfield of Parlour, Hillier and Ian Selley, while Davis did not play his first game until March.

The season was rescued by the Gunners' performance in the cups. In the League (now, wearingly, Coca-Cola) Cup, Arsenal scraped through the early rounds beating Millwall on penalties in a replay and then having to go again to a replay to knock out Derby. At a fog-bound Scarborough a Winterburn penalty was the only goal in the fourth round and two goals from Wright eliminated Nottingham Forest at Highbury in the fifth. In the semi-final a 5-1 aggregate saw off Crystal Palace and Arsenal faced Sheffield Wednesday in the final at Wembley on 18 April.

Smith was injured, Keown cup-tied and Dixon suspended and the midfield saw the return of Davis and the inclusion of Steve Morrow. John Harkes put Wednesday ahead early in the match but Merson equalized with a swerving shot from just outside the penalty area in the 20th minute. Midway through the second half, Merson crossed from the left and Morrow benefited from Carlton Palmer's confusion to rifle home the winner. In the post-match celebration on the pitch Adams lifted up Morrow and clumsily dropped him, and the Northern Ireland midfielder broke his arm. A contrite Adams lifted the League Cup and Arsenal had won their first trophy of the season.

50 Greatest Players

DAVID ROCASTLE Midfielder

Born: Lewisham, 2 May 1967

Joined Arsenal: 1983 **From:** School

Debut: 28 September 1985 v Newcastle United, League

Appearances: 275 **Goals:** 34

Left Arsenal: 1992 **For:** Leeds United

Honours won with Arsenal: Division One championship 1989, 1991; League Cup winner 1987; 14 England caps

David Rocastle, who died tragically from cancer in 2001, was one of the most popular Arsenal players of recent years. He rose through the youth ranks and his commitment to the Gunners always shone through. Don Howe gave him a senior debut at 18 and he became a regular under George Graham, who switched him from the centre to the right. A skilful midfielder with bags of energy, Rocastle's surges on the flank were a hallmark of the Arsenal attack in the late 1980s. He could also track back and tackle fearlessly. But his career went downhill after an injury early in the 1990-91 title campaign. He was sold to Leeds the following summer and rarely recaptured the sparkle of his early years at Highbury.

The FA Cup campaign began on 2 January away to Yeovil where Wright collected a hat-trick in the 3-1 win. The fourth round meeting with Leeds was a much nervier affair. Two-nil down at half-time, Arsenal rescued a replay with a 51st minute Parlour goal and a venomous 25-yard strike from Merson in the last ten minutes. At Elland Road they were 2-1 down with eight minutes remaining when Wright equalized and another Wright goal in extra-time put a relieved Arsenal through to the fifth round. Smith's goal in the match was his first since 7 November against Coventry, his 100th goal for Arsenal. Wright's two goals disposed of Nottingham Forest and, in the sixth round, Ipswich were beaten 4-2.

Spurs at Wembley were the opposition in the semi-final, an opportunity to gain revenge for 1991. In a tense game, Spurs attacked in the first half but Arsenal gradually gained the upper hand. Ten minutes from time Parlour was fouled by Justin Edinburgh just outside the box. Merson swung in the free kick and Linighan's run into the box took Gary Mabbutt and Neil Ruddock with him. '"Take them all inside," I told him,' said Adams later. The captain was left unmarked at the far post to power a downward header past Thorstvedt and the Gunners were in another final. 'That has to be the most important goal of my career,' said Adams and the fans in red-and-white celebrated in the stadium.

They were again to face Sheffield Wednesday at Wembley. In a poor game Wright scored first with a header in the 21st minute and David Hirst equalized with 20 minutes to go. Extra-time produced no further goals. In the replay the following Thursday, in front of a crowd of only 62,367, Wright again opened the scoring, running onto a through ball from Smith and flicking it over Chris Woods in the 33rd minute. A Chris Waddle volley in the 68th minute brought Wednesday back into the running and the game again went into extra-time. With penalties appearing inevitable, in the 119th minute the often maligned Andy Linighan rose to meet a Merson corner and thumped a header past Woods, the ball helped into the net by Nigel Worthington attempting to make a desperate clearance. Arsenal had become the first team ever to hold both of the cups.

Over the summer of 1993 David O'Leary, who had made 719 appearances for Arsenal in his 20 years with the club, departed for Leeds United while the only significant arrival was Eddie McGoldrick, an Irish international winger-cum-utility player for £1 million from Crystal Palace. The new North Bank stand opened at the beginning of season 1993-94 and by November the Clock End was also all-seater. There were few who would deny that Arsenal now had one of the most attractive and comfortable stadiums in Britain. They started the league season badly, going down 3-0 at Highbury to a Mick Quinn hat-trick against Coventry, but two days later a late Wright header gave them a 1-0 win at White Hart Lane. Limpar was dropped for the Spurs game and played only 11 matches that season before his transfer to Everton in March, after a number of disagreements with Graham. 'Anders and I could not get on the same wavelength,' said Graham in his autobiography.

Although the Gunners won four out of their next five league games, it seemed to the players that Graham was preoccupied with Europe that season, with league success secondary in his ambitions. On 15 September Arsenal travelled to play Odense in the first round of the Cup-Winners' Cup and, although the Danish side profited from a Keown own goal after 20 minutes, the Gunners came away with a 2-1 win. They qualified for the second round with a 1-1 draw at Highbury.

In October they ground out four 0-0 draws in succession and on the 20th of the month two goals from Wright and a stunning 25-yard free kick from Merson gave them a 3-0 lead over Standard Liege in the Cup-Winners' Cup second round at Highbury. In the return in Belgium, Arsenal, expected to defend their lead, produced a magnificent performance, winning 7-0 with the highlight being McGoldrick's run and rocket shot for the last goal. Graham commented in his book that it was 'one of the greatest attacking displays I have ever seen on an away ground'.

Three days later they were beaten 2-1 at Highbury by Aston Villa to go sixth in the League, 14 points behind leaders Manchester United. At the end of the month the Birmingham side also knocked them out of the League Cup in the fourth round at Highbury in a lacklustre display by the Gunners. Results were mixed in the League but, after a 3-0 defeat of Wimbledon on New Year's Day, Arsenal had moved to third in the League, albeit still 14 points behind United.

Progress in the FA Cup was little better. A last-minute Adams header squeezed them past Millwall at the New Den in the third round in early January but they came unstuck against Bolton Wanderers in the next round. A 2-2 draw at Bolton was followed by a 3-1 defeat at Highbury. Smith scored his first goal since November but Campbell's increasingly hapless form made him again a target for some of the home support.

Between early January and mid-February they played five league draws (including three 0-0 scorelines) in succession but Graham was again eyeing Europe, seemingly his obsession this season. On 2 March Arsenal travelled to Turin to face Torino in the Cup-Winners' Cup quarter-final and came away with a gritty goalless draw. In the second leg at Highbury a classic Davis free kick in the 66th minute found Adams at the far post and the captain scored the winner. Back in the League, Wright scored a hat-trick (his second in successive league matches) at the Dell in the 4-0 defeat of Southampton, but Arsenal won only three of their last ten league games to end in fourth spot in the League, 19 points behind leaders Manchester United.

At the end of March the Gunners faced French league leaders Paris St Germain in the semi-final of the Cup-Winners' Cup at the Parc des Princes in Paris. PSG had eliminated the mighty Real Madrid in the previous round and boasted players of the quality of David Ginola and George Weah. Early in the game the attractive football came from Arsenal with Jensen almost scoring his first goal for the club. With 35 minutes gone another Davis free kick was headed by Wright into the far corner of the net. At half-time the PA system played the Pet Shop Boys' 'Go West' and the Arsenal fans sang along to the tune with the words 'One-nil to the Arsenal'. Thus an enduring chant was born. Shortly after the interval Ginola equalized with a corner from a header and the game ended 1-1, an encouraging result for the team to take back to Highbury.

European Triumph

On 12 April at Highbury, a sea of red and white cards welcomed Arsenal onto the pitch in an electric atmosphere. Campbell, in for an unwell Merson, headed in a Dixon corner in the fifth minute and Arsenal were in command. Just before half-time Wright launched a reckless tackle on Alain Roche and, as he had already received a yellow card against Standard Liege, the striker would miss the final. A tearful Wright was virtually inconsolable at half-time until, as he narrates in his book *Mr Wright*, Lee Dixon said to him, 'Wrighty, pull yourself together, the boys need you.' He came out in the second half to help his team-mates to a famous 1-0 victory.

In the final against Parma, Arsenal defended well against the Italian side's international forward line and, having taken the lead with a Smith goal,

Great Matches

EUROPEAN CUP-WINNERS' CUP FINAL		Copenhagen, 4 May 1994
Arsenal 1	**Parma 0**	**Attendance: 33,765**
Smith		

Italian side Parma, with their international forwards Thomas Brolin, Faustino Asprilla and Franco Zola, lay in wait in the final in Copenhagen on 4 May. Arsenal, with 12,000 Gooners having made the trip, were very much the underdogs and Parma were holders of the Cup-Winners' Cup. Wright was out and Keown, Jensen and Hillier injured. The midfield comprised Davis, Selley and Morrow. Parma immediately went on the offensive, with Bould doing well to tackle Asprilla before he could shoot in the second minute, and Brolin hitting the post. In the 20th minute a Dixon throw was returned to the right back by Smith and Dixon tried to find Merson on the right. The ball was intercepted by sweeper Minotti who attempted an overhead clearance. The ball found Smith who chested it and volleyed with his left foot into the net for a great goal. The remainder of the game was all about Parma attacking with Arsenal producing a superb defensive display. Seaman, playing with the aid of pain-killing injections, pulled off an excellent save from Zola and Bould was immense in defence and deservedly Man of the Match. Arsenal showed spirit and determination against a technically superior team and held on to their one-goal lead until the final whistle.

Arsenal: Seaman, Dixon, Winterburn, Davis, Bould, Adams, Campbell, Morrow, Smith, Merson (McGoldrick), Selley

Parma: Bucci, Sensini, Minotti, Apollonio, Benarrivo, Crippa, Pin (Melli), di Chiara, Brolin, Asprilla, Zola

Referee: V. Krondi

Nigel Winterburn became a regular at left back after Kenny Sansom left in 1988.

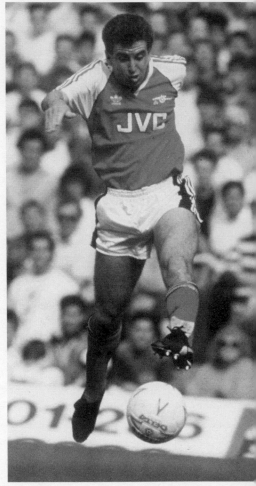

hung on to their narrow advantage to claim the trophy.

Season 1994-95 was something of a roller-coaster ride for the Gunners, with their domestic travails relieved by their European performances, and stories of financial irregularities hitting the headlines. True to form, Graham had made only one major signing over the summer, bringing Swedish midfield playmaker Stefan Schwarz to Highbury from Benfica for £1.75 million. Over the previous couple of seasons Graham had been criticized for the lack of creativity in his midfield. He claimed that he had a T-shirt printed with the words 'I am trying to buy a midfielder' and the arrival of Schwarz was his response to the criticisms.

At home the season was a depressing one. Although Arsenal won their first game 3-0 against Manchester City at Highbury, they failed to score in the next four matches. They began their defence of the Cup-Winners' Cup in September with a 6-1 aggregate defeat of Omonia Nicosia and met Brondby in Denmark in early November. Within 20 minutes Wright and Smith gave them a 2-0 lead although the Danes scored in the second half. At Highbury a fortnight later Brondby scored in the second minute and Wright equalized with a penalty. In the second half Selley restored Arsenal's advantage but Brondby scored again. Arsenal had to defend grimly for the rest of the game and were fortunate to survive a last-minute penalty appeal against Bould. They went through 4-3 on aggregate.

In his painfully honest book, *Rock Bottom*, Paul Merson described the Brondby game at Highbury as 'the moment my football career had reached the point of disaster… I knew I needed some sort of help'. Later in the month the troubled player publicly admitted to addiction to alcohol, drugs and gambling and he entered rehabilitation. He was supported by Arsenal and the Football Association and would not be back in the team until February.

In the League Arsenal won only three out of 17 games and none out of eight at Highbury, between 29 October and 11 February. A landmark was reached on New Year's Eve when John Jensen scored his first goal in 98 games in the 3-1 defeat by Queens Park Rangers and T-shirts immediately appeared with the legend: 'I saw Jensen score'. The domestic competitions mirrored the Gunners' league form. In January they were knocked out of the FA Cup by Millwall in a third round replay and eliminated from the League Cup 1-0 in the quarter-final by Liverpool.

Graham Leaves

Momentous events were occurring off the pitch. In December the *Mail on Sunday* alleged that Graham had taken 'bungs' when signing Jensen and Pal Lydersen. Graham protested that the money was unsolicited and that he had repaid it but on 21 February he was sacked as Arsenal manager. His eight-year reign had brought two league championships, two League Cups, one FA Cup and the European Cup-Winners' Cup to Highbury and he can be regarded as one of the most successful managers in Arsenal's history. First-team coach Stewart Houston was installed as caretaker manager.

One of Graham's last acts was to buy three players – teenage striker John Hartson from Luton, forward Chris Kiwomya from Ipswich and left winger Glen Helder from Vitesse Arnheim. On the evening of his sacking Kiwomya scored in the 1-0 defeat of Nottingham Forest at Highbury and Helder's sparkling display marked him out as the heir apparent to Limpar. Kiwomya also scored twice in Arsenal's next game, a 3-0 defeat of Crystal Palace. Unfortunately, neither of the players lived up to their early promise.

The Cup-Winners' Cup draw saw Auxerre visit Highbury for the quarter-final, where the French club equalized Wright's penalty goal within three minutes in the second half, the score ending 1-1. In France, Wright scored a magnificent goal in the 16th minute when he curled the ball over the Auxerre keeper from the right of the penalty area. Arsenal defended well to go through to the semi-final 2-1 on aggregate. In the League in March the Gunners lost all four of their matches, to plummet to 14th spot. However, they recovered some confidence when they beat Norwich 5-1, two coming from burly Welsh striker John Hartson, five days before the semi-final of the Cup-Winners' Cup.

Their opponents were Sampdoria, managed by Sven Goran Eriksson, at Highbury on 6 April. Seaman was heavily strapped and playing with pain-

50 Greatest Players

DAVID O'LEARY Centre back

Born: Stoke Newington, 2 May 1958

Joined Arsenal: 1973   **From:** School

Debut: 16 August 1975 v Burnley, League

Appearances: 719   **Goals:** 14

Left Arsenal: 1993   **For:** Leeds United

Honours won with Arsenal: Division One championship 1989, 1991; FA Cup winner 1979, 1993; League Cup winner 1987, 1993; 68 Republic of Ireland caps

David O'Leary played more games for Arsenal than any other Gunner in history, during a stay of 20 years. He made his debut at 17 and within a year was a first-team fixture. O'Leary was one of the most graceful defenders to wear the Arsenal shirt. Pacy, strong in the air and a fine reader of the game, he was also blessed with a cool head. He gave probably the best performance of his career in the 1980 Cup-Winners' Cup final when he marked Valencia's great Argentine striker Mario Kempes out of the game. He was also a major help to the young Tony Adams as he developed in the late 1980s. Fittingly, his last appearance for the Gunners came in the 1993 FA Cup final replay victory.

killing injections, Jensen was injured and Keown suspended. Early in the game keeper Walter Zenga dropped the ball over his line from a Bould headed flick, but the goal was disallowed for 'intimidation'. In the 35th minute Hillier's shot rebounded off the keeper and Bould stroked it into the net for his first goal of the season. Three minutes later the big centre back claimed his second goal of the season, heading in from a corner. In the second half Adams mishit a clearance and Vladimir Jugovic pounced to make the score 2-1. In the 70th minute a carefully-weighted through ball from Merson was latched onto by Wright and the striker clipped it past Zenga from 15 yards. With 11 minutes left Jugovic again scored for the Italians, leaving the final score 3-2.

Any lingering worries about relegation were eased with two league victories in mid-April, when they beat Ipswich 4-1 (three coming from Wright) and Aston Villa. Arsenal ended their league campaign in 12th place, their most disappointing finish for many years. Three days after the Villa match the Gunners travelled to Genoa to meet Sampdoria in the semi-final second leg. In the 13th minute Roberto Mancini lobbed Seaman from 20 yards while Arsenal fruitlessly appealed for an offside decision against Atillo Lombardo. Arsenal had to attack and they did, with Merson and Hartson going close in the first half. Early in the second half, Wright scrambled a Hartson header into the net to go 4-3 ahead on aggregate. With 15 minutes to go Wright was replaced by Kiwomya and within ten minutes Sampdoria were 5-4 in the overall lead, their two goals coming from Claudio Belluci. Arsenal appeared to be on their way out. However, in the 87th minute Bould was fouled 30 yards from the Sampdoria goal (and was booked for over-protesting). Schwarz sent a low shot through the wall and the ball evaded Zenga's grasp. The score was 5-5 and remained that way till the end of extra-time.

A place in the final would now be decided on penalties. Dixon scored and Mijhailovic's effort was saved by Seaman. McGoldrick sent his shot over the bar but Seaman again saved, this time from Jugovic. Hartson made it 2-0 but Mespero scored. Adams then increased the lead to 3-1 and Mancini converted his attempt. Merson missed and Lombardo had to score. Seaman, the hero of the hour, anticipated his shot, dived to his left and saved it with his upraised right arm. Arsenal were through to the final.

On 10 May the Gunners faced Real Zaragoza in the Parc des Princes in Paris to contest the Cup-Winners' Cup final. Linighan replaced the suspended Bould. Honours were even in a goalless first half, towards the end of which Keown and Winterburn were substituted by Hillier and Morrow. The Spanish side dominated the early part of the first half and in the 75th minute Argentinian striker Juan Esnaider scored with a left-foot volley into the corner of the net. Five minutes late Hartson equalized and the game went into extra-time. With seconds remaining ex-Spurs player Nayim spotted Seaman off his line and from fully 50 yards lofted the ball towards goal. Seaman frantically back-pedalled but was too late to stop the ball looping into the top of the net. He recalls in his book *Safe Hands*, 'Then Nayim did his party piece... as soon as he struck it I knew I was in trouble.' Seconds later the whistle blew and a stunned Arsenal team trailed off the pitch, their hold on the Cup-Winners' Cup prised away by a fine piece of individual opportunism.

Big Names Arrive at Highbury

On 15 June Bruce Rioch was appointed manager. Rioch, previously manager at Bolton Wanderers and captain of Scotland in the 1978 World Cup finals, was a tough disciplinarian but he also believed that football should be an elegant, passing game. Over the summer he welcomed to Highbury two of the world's most respected players.

Great Managers – 1986-95

GEORGE GRAHAM

Much to the surprise of many of his ex-'Double' team-mates, the previously laid-back 'Stroller' George Graham had evolved into a tough, formidable manager when he arrived at Arsenal from Millwall in 1986 to take over the hot seat from the increasingly beleaguered Don Howe. His firm, no-nonsense style propelled Arsenal to League Cup triumph in his first season in charge, two goals from Charlie Nicholas putting paid to Liverpool in the final.

A tactically astute disciplinarian, Graham's finest moment was probably on 26 May 1989 when, despite having frittered away a substantial lead over Liverpool in the League, his team won 2-0 at Anfield to claim the championship thanks to Michael Thomas's unbelievable injury-time goal. With his famous 'back four' and forwards Alan Smith, Paul Merson and Anders Limpar, Graham's Arsenal won the title again in 1990-91, losing only one game in the entire season. That was to be the Scotsman's last league success. Despite signing prolific striker Ian Wright at the beginning of the 1991-92 season, Graham showed little inclination to inject flair and swagger into the team and was happy to grind out results without recourse to the transfer market. However, under his stewardship Arsenal won the League and FA Cups in 1993 and beat Parma 1-0 in Copenhagen in 1994 to win the Cup-Winners' Cup, only the second European trophy in the club's history.

By the middle of the following season, however, it seemed that the time had come for a change at the top but the way it happened was a shock. In February 1995 Graham was fired by Peter Hill-Wood after an investigation into alleged financial irregularities in the transfer market. Graham protested his innocence but was banned from football for one year. He later enjoyed spells as manager of Leeds and Tottenham.

David Platt, reigning England captain, joined from Sampdoria. Platt, with 62 caps, had scored the extra-time goal, from a Gascoigne free kick, which had taken England into the 1990 World Cup quarter-final. A determined and skilful midfielder, he was particularly adept at bursting through defences to score some crucial goals. The second arrival was to rival Liam Brady as the greatest Arsenal player of modern times. Dennis Bergkamp was a brilliant forward with a subtle touch, exceptional technique and devastating goalscoring ability. Bergkamp, who had an unhappy time at his previous club Inter Milan, broke the club transfer record when he left the Italian giants in return for £7.5 million.

The two new acquisitions signalled to the fans and the world of football generally that Arsenal were now shredding their previously rigid wage and transfer policy in an attempt to introduce the flair, experience and international quality which they needed to compete at the highest level. The days of 'boring, boring Arsenal' were about to disappear. Platt, however, was dogged by injury in his first season and after he had opened his account for the club with a brilliant volley in the 1-1 draw at Highbury against Nottingham Forest in late August he was out of action after a cartilage operation until early November. Bergkamp, unquestionably one of the world's greatest footballers, played seven games before scoring, with question marks being raised over the wisdom of the purchase. On 23 September against Southampton, however, he showed the fans why he was worth the transfer fee. On a warm day at Highbury he scored his first goal with a splendid 12-yard volley into the Clock End. In the second half, he drifted past the Southampton defence to score with a sumptuous 20-yard shot which sent the North Bank into delirium. A superstar and Arsenal hero – 'Walking in a Bergkamp Wonderland' – had arrived.

To fans in the Upper East Stand, Rioch's tactics came as a pleasant surprise. The new passing policy meant that, instead of looking straight ahead to find the position of the ball, one had to lower one's gaze to the pitch. After years of long-ball football, the 'beautiful game' was now being unveiled at Highbury, although no prizes came their way that season. With the retirement of the unselfish crowd favourite 'Smudger' Smith due to injury

in the spring of 1995 after 345 appearances and 115 goals, Schwarz's move to Fiorentina and the departure of the increasingly maligned Kevin Campbell to Nottingham Forest over the summer, it seemed that there was a new mood at Highbury, one which boded well for the future.

Younger players were also coming through. Diminutive striker Paul Dickov was again given an

The skilful Paul Davis was a key component in George Graham's resurgent team of the late 1980s and early 1990s.

50 Greatest Players

PAUL DAVIS Midfielder

Born: Dulwich, 9 December 1961

Joined Arsenal: 1978   **From:** School

Debut: 7 April 1980 v Tottenham Hotspur, League

Appearances: 445   **Goals:** 37

Left Arsenal: 1995   **For:** Brentford

Honours won with Arsenal: Division One championship 1989, 1991; FA Cup winner 1993; League Cup winner 1987, 1993; European Cup-Winners' Cup winner 1994

Paul Davis was a skilful left-sided playmaker who seemed jinxed by injury every time he was close to an England call. Another youth-team product, he established himself in the early 1980s before becoming a key figure in Arsenal's revival under George Graham. A clever strategist and pinpoint passer, he formed potent midfield partnerships, first with Steve Williams, then with Mickey Thomas. He was sidelined for nearly a season after publicly criticizing Graham during 1991-92. But he was restored for the 1993 League Cup final win over Sheffield Wednesday and stayed in for the FA Cup victory over the Owls. His experience and ability to control the tempo were important factors in the Gunners' Cup-Winners' Cup success the following year.

opportunity after his first-team appearances the previous season. Winger Adrian Clarke and defender Scott Marshall also impressed in their few appearances, Marshall in particular filling in capably for the injured Bould and Adams in the latter part of the season. But Rioch had disagreements with several of the senior players, notably an unhappy Wright who submitted a transfer request in February. In his book, Seaman says, 'There is no doubt that the bad atmosphere between Rioch and some of the players did affect the team... we all realized that he was out of his depth as a manager.' Wright, however, ended the season as top goalscorer at the club.

The campaign was largely uneventful, with Arsenal knocked out of the FA Cup 1-0 in the opening round replay against First Division Sheffield United and exiting the League Cup in the semi-final on away goals against Aston Villa. In the League Arsenal began well with three successive wins in September but toiled in December and January. Four further wins in March and April – including Newcastle and Leeds – helped them to a final position of fifth in the table. Rioch, however, would not be with the Gunners for much longer and a footballing revolution would soon be under way in North London at Highbury.

Chapter Eight 1996-2001
Arsène Knows

Five days before the start of the 1996-97 season, Bruce Rioch was fired as manager. Rioch, whose 14-month reign was the shortest of any manager in Arsenal's modern history, was replaced by Stewart Houston as caretaker. On 22 September at a press conference Peter Hill-Wood formally unveiled the new manager, although his identity was by now common knowledge. Arsène Wenger, a seemingly austere and urbane Frenchman, was to take over the job. Although largely unknown to the average British fan, Wenger had enjoyed considerable success at Monaco and Japan's Nagoya Grampus Eight and was the epitome of the modern football manager. Articulate and fluent in several languages, Wenger was to introduce far-reaching tactical, dietary and training methods to the club and profoundly alter his players' attitudes to their responsibilities and to the game.

During the summer, John Jensen had returned to Brondby. New players included Senegal-born Patrick Vieira, a tall, long-limbed French midfielder who joined from AC Milan for £3 million, and Remi Garde, another French midfielder and utility player, who arrived on a Bosman transfer from Strasbourg. Both players had been signed on Wenger's recommendation. One of the great figures from the club's past, Liam Brady, returned to become head of youth development.

As a result of his exertions for England in Euro 96, Adams was out for the first six weeks of the season, which began with a 2-0 home win against West Ham at Highbury and they then went down 2-0 to Liverpool at Anfield before embarking on a ten-game unbeaten run. Adams returned to the team as a substitute for Dixon in the 2-0 away defeat of Middlesbrough, a game which also saw Vieira's first start in an impressive performance by the young player. Two weeks previously Adams had called a team meeting at London Colney and had informed his team-mates that he was an alcoholic. Adams remarks in his book *Addicted,* 'Andy Linighan very touchingly said to me "You've cracked it, Tone. You've taken the first step." And I had.'

Arsenal had met Borussia Mönchengladbach in the first round of the UEFA Cup at Highbury on 10 September and by half-time were 2-0 down. Wright and Merson scored in the second half but the game ended 3-2 in the German side's favour. Three days after the match Houston resigned to take over as manager at Queens Park Rangers (with Bruce Rioch his assistant) and Pat Rice assumed the caretaker role. Wenger was on the bench for the second leg in Germany on 25 September although Rice was still formally in charge, and Arsenal were again beaten 3-2, going out of the competition 6-4 on aggregate.

Wenger finally took over as manager for the 2-0 away win against Blackburn on 12 October, Wright scoring both, and they were unbeaten in their next three league games until a 1-0 defeat by Manchester United on 16 November. That month the Gunners were also eliminated from the League Cup 4-2 by Liverpool, the prolific Wright scoring twice in the 5-2 defeat of Stoke in the previous round and a further two at Anfield. In a dramatic match at a rain-soaked Highbury against Spurs on 24 November, a Wright penalty gave Arsenal a half-time 1-0 lead. Andy Sinton equalized in the 60th minute. With two minutes to go Bergkamp found Adams and the defender smacked in a left-foot volley. In injury time Wright crossed to Bergkamp who deftly killed the ball and lashed it past Ian Walker to make the final score 3-1 in front of an ecstatic North Bank. A week later at St James's Park Dixon opened the scoring against Newcastle with a 12th-minute diving header but Shearer levelled the score nine minutes later. Adams was sent off for a foul on Shearer but a 60th-minute strike from Wright gave Arsenal a 2-1 victory and they went to the top of the Premiership. A 2-1 away defeat by Nottingham Forest and two draws over the Christmas period, however, saw the Gunners drop to third place.

Wenger's Innovations

Meanwhile, Wenger had been introducing innovative techniques at the London Colney training ground. The Frenchman, a keen student of the latest scientific training methods, had introduced a new fitness regime, including hiring the services of a masseur and osteopath, vitamin injections, stretching exercises and warm-downs. He also changed the players' dietary habits, substituting such exotica as pasta, broccoli and steamed chicken for the traditional steak and chips. His methods, common at European clubs but rare in Britain, were to provide the players with added stamina and power. Wenger, who had an encyclopedic knowledge

The popular Ian Wright was a lethal striker and is number one on Arsenal's all-time scoring list with 184 goals in 287 appearances.

50 Greatest Players

ALAN SMITH Striker

Born: Birmingham, 21 November 1962

Joined Arsenal: 1987   **From:** Leicester City

Debut: 15 August 1987 v Liverpool, League

Appearances: 345   **Goals:** 115

Left Arsenal: 1995 (retired)

Honours won with Arsenal: Division One championship 1989, 1991; FA Cup winner 1993; League Cup winner 1993; European Cup-Winners' Cup winner 1994; 13 England caps

Alan Smith made his name alongside Gary Lineker at Leicester. He was George Graham's first major signing for Arsenal and gave excellent value for the £750,000 fee. Smith was an unselfish target man, brilliant at holding the ball under pressure and bringing colleagues into play. He was also a fine header of the ball and thrived on crosses. He finished First Division top scorer in each of Arsenal's title years under Graham. Smith's importance declined as the Gunners' tactics changed and they began to rely on Ian Wright. But he could still score vital goals, like the winner against Parma in the 1994 Cup-Winners' Cup final. He retired because of injury at the end of the following season. He now works as a journalist and pundit.

of world football, also provided new tactical insights and built on Rioch's introduction of the passing game. His increasingly fitter and faster team were soon to reach the heights of English football.

The team's form dipped, however, as in February they went out of the FA Cup 1-0 to Leeds at Highbury in the fourth round, and lost two league games in succession, both at home to Manchester United and Wimbledon. By the end of the month they had slipped to fourth in the Premiership. March saw the arrival of gangling 17-year-old French striker Nicolas Anelka from Paris St Germain for £500,000. The fee for the precociously talented youngster would in time prove to be something of a bargain. The previous month John Hartson, a talented but irascible figure on the pitch, had joined West Ham for £3.2 million.

In March, the Gunners stepped up their league challenge, winning three games in succession against Everton, Nottingham Forest and Southampton, all by 2-0, before losing 2-1 at Highbury against Liverpool. In this last match Robbie Fowler jumped over Seaman in the penalty box at the North Bank and the referee awarded a penalty. Fowler sportingly waved his arms to the referee to indicate that there had been no contact but the official was unmoved. Fowler took the kick, a half-hearted effort which almost indicated he didn't want to score. Seaman parried but a lurking Jason McAteer slotted in the rebound.

Arsenal won two games, including a battling 3-0 away defeat of Chelsea, and drew two more in April. In their penultimate match against Newcastle at Highbury they were beaten 1-0 and were now level on points and on goal difference with Newcastle and, with Manchester United having won the League, the battle was on between the two clubs for the second Champions League spot. Although Arsenal won their final match, Wright scoring two and Bergkamp one in the 3-1 win at Derby, Newcastle won 5-0 and were in the following season's European competition. Arsenal's third place guaranteed them European football in the UEFA Cup the coming season. A campaign which had promised much had delivered little. The Gunners' vulnerability to the top clubs (they had been beaten twice by Liverpool and Manchester United and lost at home to Newcastle) was a problem on which Wenger had to work.

A Beautiful Moment

The 'famous five' defence remained in place at the start of season 1997-98, but there had been other significant comings and goings. Paul Merson, after ten years and 422 appearances, had moved to Middlesbrough, a departure which surprised many fans. 'Merse' had always been a crowd favourite at Highbury and his transfer, at the age of 29, appeared unnecessary, almost counterproductive. Emmanuel 'Manu' Petit, a powerful, pony-tailed French international midfielder, arrived from Monaco, as did utility player Gilles Grimandi and Liberian forward Christopher Wreh. Little Dutch winger Marc Overmars, a member of the European Cup-winning Ajax side of the mid-1990s, moved to Highbury for £5 million in the close season. Other newcomers included 20-year-old Austrian keeper Alex Manninger, Portuguese left winger Luis Boa Morte and 18-year-old defender Matthew Upson from Luton for a record fee of £1 million for a teenager. Vieira was about to establish himself as the best central midfielder in the country alongside a revitalized Ray Parlour, with Platt still very much in contention and young Stephen Hughes making his contribution. Up front was the explosive partnership of Bergkamp and Wright.

By the end of the eighth game of the season Arsenal were unbeaten and were top of the Premiership. The games included a 3-3 draw with Leicester, Bergkamp scoring a superb hat-trick and securing the top three slots in BBC TV's 'Goal of the Month' competition for August. He described his third, the Goal of the Season and a piece of hypnotic brilliance, as 'the best goal I've ever scored'.

50 Greatest Players

PAUL MERSON Forward/Midfielder

Born: Harlesden, 20 March 1968

Joined Arsenal: 1984   **From:** School

Debut: 22 November 1986 v Manchester City (sub), League

Appearances: 422   **Goals:** 99

Left Arsenal: 1997   **For:** Middlesbrough

Honours won with Arsenal: Division One championship 1989, 1991; FA Cup winner 1993; League Cup winner 1993; European Cup-Winners' Cup winner 1994; 15 England caps

Paul Merson's battles with alcohol, drugs and gambling have been well documented, but he will always be remembered as one of the stars of George Graham's reign. Merson grabbed his chance at the start of the 1988-89 season after Arsenal failed to sign Tony Cottee. He hit ten league goals partnering Alan Smith as the Gunners won the title. He switched to wide right in the 1991 success, covering for the injured David Rocastle, then played the rest of his Highbury career as an attacking midfielder. He was voted Man of the Match in Arsenal's 1993 League Cup final victory over Sheffield Wednesday. A skilful, right-footed player, he scored many spectacular goals, with measured chips his trademark.

The stunning run of matches also included a 4-1 defeat of Bolton at Highbury where Wright scored a hat-trick to become Arsenal's all-time highest scorer; a 30-yard left-foot winner from Winterburn in the 3-2 defeat of Chelsea at Stamford Bridge; and a 4-0 crushing of West Ham, Overmars claiming two. They remained unbeaten in the League until their 3-0 defeat at Derby on 1 November although they had been surprisingly eliminated by PAOK Salonika in the first round of the UEFA Cup. The game after Derby was against Manchester United at Highbury. Bergkamp had collected five yellow cards and was suspended, his place taken by Anelka. Anelka promptly scored his first goal for the club and Vieira added another. United hit back with two goals from Teddy Sheringham. Vieira limped off to be replaced by Bould and Arsenal's change to a back three seemed to unsettle the United attack, with an increasingly ineffectual Giggs being substituted. Platt scored the winner, with a thumping header from a Parlour corner, to leave Arsenal only one point behind leaders United.

Arsenal, however, lost their cohesion in the next two games, going down to Sheffield Wednesday and Liverpool and, after beating Newcastle away, were

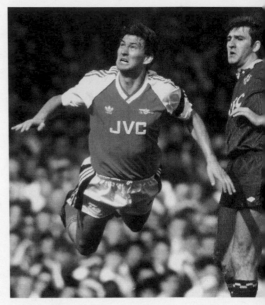

Tony Adams, captain for 14 years, picked up more trophies than any other skipper in Arsenal's history.

defeated again, this time by Blackburn with Adams at fault for two of the goals. After the game a no-holds-barred team meeting was held at which Adams spelled out to the foreign players their responsibilities. By the end of the year a 1-1 draw with Spurs left a gap of 13 points behind Manchester United. United, however, began to slip up. By early February the Gunners' 2-0 win against Chelsea at Highbury, both goals coming from Stephen Hughes, found them only six points behind the league leaders with a game in hand. The attack was now without Ian Wright, who had pulled a hamstring against Port Vale in an FA Cup game in mid-January, but Anelka was to prove a more than adequate replacement for the rest of the season.

Arsenal reached the semi-final of the League Cup and were in the fifth round of the FA Cup, having disposed of Port Vale, Middlesbrough and Crystal Palace. In the League Cup a 2-1 first leg win over Chelsea was overturned 3-1 at Stamford Bridge. In the FA Cup quarter-final they drew 1-1 with West Ham on 8 March, Anelka the scorer, to set up a replay at Upton Park later in the month. The following weekend the Gunners travelled to Old Trafford for a crucial match. The gap between the two sides was nine points but Arsenal had three games in hand. Manninger had taken over from an injured Seaman for the previous five games and the young Austrian had demonstrated his considerable abilities by keeping five consecutive clean sheets. He did it again against United, performing heroically in Arsenal's 1-0 win and making an exceptional save from Andy Cole. The winner came in the 79th minute when a rampaging Overmars received a Bergkamp flick, dissected the defence and slid the ball under Peter Schmeichel to seal a much-deserved and important victory. The title race was now wide open.

In the FA Cup Anelka scored just before half-time in the replay, with Bergkamp being sent off for elbowing Steve Lomas in the face in the 32nd minute. With six minutes to go, Hartson equalized for the Hammers and the game went to penalties. Arsenal squeezed through 4-3. In early April a Wreh goal against Wolves in the semi-final eased the Gunners into the final against Newcastle.

By 11 April eight games were left to clinch the title. Two goals from Anelka and a spectacular 25-yard shot from Vieira gave Arsenal a 3-0 lead over Newcastle at Highbury, although Warren Barton pulled one back late on, the first goal conceded by the Arsenal defence in ten games. Two days later Arsenal were three up within the first ten minutes at Blackburn, with two from Parlour and one from Bergkamp, and a dazzling run from Anelka, dummying the keeper and scoring, added a fourth for a 4-1 scoreline. Petit scored his first goal for the club in the 5-0 rout of Wimbledon at Highbury. With Manchester United being held by Newcastle at Old Trafford, Arsenal went top of the table and needed to win three of their next five matches to be champions.

At Barnsley on 26 April a brilliant Bergkamp curling shot from the edge of the area for his 22nd goal of the season and an Overmars strike were the only goals. The following Wednesday Bergkamp missed a first-half penalty against Derby at Highbury and then injured his hamstring. The Dutch master was out for the rest of the season. Petit scored the winner, swerving in a low shot from 25 yards. If Arsenal could beat relegation-threatened Everton on the following Saturday they would be champions.

The streets and bars around Highbury were buzzing as kickoff approached on 3 May and there was an almost palpable air of expectancy within the ground. In the sixth minute the stadium erupted when Slaven

50 Greatest Players

IAN WRIGHT Striker

Born: Woolwich, 3 November 1963

Joined Arsenal: 1991   **From:** Crystal Palace

Debut: 25 September 1991 v Leicester City, League Cup

Appearances: 287   **Goals:** 184

Left Arsenal: 1998   **For:** West Ham United

Honours won with Arsenal: Division One championship 1998; FA Cup winner 1993; League Cup winner 1993; 27 England caps

Ian Wright heads the Gunners' all-time leading scorers' list. He made an immediate impression on his arrival from Palace, with a hat-trick at Southampton. He scored another treble against the Saints on the last day of the 1991-92 season, to snatch the Golden Boot from Gary Lineker. Wright finished top scorer in all but his last season at Highbury. His goals propelled George Graham's Gunners to four cup finals, though he missed the 1994 Cup-Winners' Cup triumph over Parma through suspension. Wright was quick and brave and loved to play on the shoulder of the last defender. His temperament also earned him several bans, but Arsenal can never have had a more lethal goal predator.

Bilic, harassed by Adams, headed into his own net. Arsenal pressed forward against an already demoralized Everton side and less than 20 minutes later Overmars made it 2-0. Platt came on for Petit just before half-time, the Frenchman a victim of a two-footed tackle from Don Hutchison. Overmars added another in the 57th minute, running from the centre circle and scoring with a low shot. In the last minute with the chant of 'Champions' ringing around Highbury, Tony Adams, the indomitable heart of Arsenal, loped up the field, received a perfectly chipped pass from Bould, chested the ball down and smashed a left-foot half-volley into the Everton net for the Gunners' fourth goal. Adams stood in front of the North Bank, arms raised, a king receiving the adoration of his subjects. He wrote later, 'As the ball hit the net I just thought "Wow". It was a beautiful moment.' Adams led the players on a lap of honour, clutching the Premiership trophy.

The 'Double' Again

The 'Double' was still up for grabs and Arsenal seized their moment in the FA Cup final to secure a place in history with a 2-0 victory over Newcastle and record their second 'Double' season. The uncertainties post-George Graham had now been forgotten. Wenger had restored Arsenal to supremacy in English football, aided by the genius of Bergkamp, the speed and skill of Overmars, the lethal athleticism of Anelka, the midfield powerhouse of Vieira and Petit and, of course, the enduring 'famous five'. Other players, such as Hughes, Platt, Parlour and, earlier in the season, Wright, had all played important parts in the triumph. Arsenal appeared unstoppable but football is a perverse master, as the following season was about to prove.

In July 1998, record goalscorer Ian Wright left to join West Ham and David Platt retired from playing. Two new arrivals were Swedish international attacking midfielder Freddie Ljungberg, who joined early in the season after impressing in Sweden's 2-1 win over England in a Euro 2000 qualifier, and diminutive Argentinian international defender Nelson Vivas. Arsenal had a listless start to the season, winning their first match 2-1 at Highbury against Nottingham Forest but drawing their next three 0-0. They then drew again, 1-1 against Leicester, Hughes equalizing late on with a 30-yard strike.

Back in the European Cup (now misleadingly titled the Champions League) they were drawn in the first group against Lens, Panathinaikos and Dynamo Kiev. Arsenal had decided to play all their home matches at Wembley Stadium so that more fans could attend the games, although many supporters opposed the idea, citing travel difficulties and poor views of the pitch. On 16 September they met Lens in the north of France. The nippy French side caused problems

Great Matches

FA CUP FINAL		**Wembley, 16 May 1998**
Arsenal 2	**Newcastle United 0**	**Attendance: 79,183**
Overmars		
Anelka		

The 'Double' dream was still alive as Arsenal approached the FA Cup final on 16 May 1998. Captain Adams led the players onto the Wembley pitch in the warm sunshine. Bergkamp, the newly-crowned Football Writers' Player of the Year, was injured and he was replaced by Wreh. As the first half progressed, the pace of Anelka and Overmars was causing all sorts of problems in the Newcastle defence but the Frenchman missed two chances. Midway through the first half Petit lobbed over the defence and found Overmars sprinting towards goal. The Dutchman nodded the ball down and slid it with his left foot under the advancing keeper's legs for the opener. Newcastle came back into the game in the second half and Dabizas and Shearer both hit the woodwork.

In the 68th minute Parlour passed to a just onside Anelka who chested the ball, ran towards the goal and sent a shot from the right of the area into the corner of the Newcastle net. Both teams had further chances to score, but Arsenal never looked as though they were going to throw away a two-goal lead. The final whistle blew and the Gunners had famously achieved the second 'Double' in their history.

Arsenal: Seaman, Dixon, Keown, Adams, Winterburn, Vieira, Parlour, Petit, Overmars, Anelka, Wreh (Platt)

Newcastle United: Given, Pistone, Dabizas, Howey, Pearce (Andersson), Barton (Watson), Lee, Batty, Ketsbaia (Barnes), Shearer

Referee: P. Durkin

for the defence in the first half although Arsenal wasted scoring chances. Overmars put the Gunners ahead in the 51st minute but Lens equalized in injury time, a Tony Vairelles shot deflecting off Keown into the net.

Four days later they faced Manchester United and hit 'Double' form. With Vieira outstanding, they were two up by half-time through an early Adams header and an Anelka goal. The young Frenchman, however, was profligate and was substituted by Ljungberg in the second half. The Swede scored on his debut with a cheeky lob over Schmeichel for a 3-0 scoreline. Manninger replaced Seaman for the away game against Sheffield Wednesday on 26 September and conceded his first-ever Premiership goal in the 1-0 defeat. Keown and Di Canio were sent off after a clash (after which the volatile Di Canio famously pushed referee Paul Alcock, who fell over) and Vieira was accused of making an obscene gesture at the home support. He was fined

David Platt was to prove as determined a player in his red Arsenal jersey as when he played for England.

£20,000 by the FA for the incident. Keown's red card was later rescinded.

They played Panathinaikos at Wembley in midweek and again missed several chances, Anelka being particularly culpable. Adams and Keown scored in the second half, although substitute Mauro scored a consolation for the Greek team near the end. The following Sunday they outplayed Newcastle at Highbury, winning 3-0 but it could have been more had Newcastle keeper Shay Given not been in such splendid form. Bergkamp scored twice, his first goals of the season.

By the end of November Arsenal were out of Europe. Outplayed at Wembley by a sparklingly inventive Dynamo Kiev side, and in particular by forwards Andrei Shevchenko and Sergei Rebrov, the Gunners nonetheless went ahead in the 73rd minute when Bergkamp headed in from a Dixon cross, although Rebrov in injury time made the score 1-1. Two weeks later in Kiev, without Adams, Anelka, Bergkamp and Overmars, Arsenal were again overcome by Dynamo's attacking flair and were three down with six minutes to go. Hughes headed in a consolation for a 3-1 defeat.

In a match they had to win to progress in the tournament they next played Lens at Wembley with Petit suspended and Vieira and Bergkamp injured, but their European ambitions were ended by a 72nd minute goal from Michael Debeve in the 1-0 defeat. Ironically, in the final, meaningless match against Panathinikos in Greece, and fielding a makeshift team, Arsenal came away with an impressive 3-1 win, the scorers being Alberto Mendez, Boa Morte and Anelka. Adams commented 'injuries and suspensions proved that we needed a greater depth of squad next time round'.

The Gunners had also been bundled out of the League Cup 5-0 in the fourth round by Chelsea at Highbury. In their worst defeat for five years, Wenger fielded virtually a reserve side, with Bergkamp and Ljungberg the only regulars. In the League, by the time they faced Aston Villa on 19 December, they had lost only one of their previous nine matches, although their scoring rate had been unspectacular. Anelka, in particular, was missing chances and Wenger remarked after the early November 1-0 win over Everton 'we lack a bit of aggression in the box'. The situation was not helped by injuries to the pivotal Bergkamp.

At Villa Park, playing without an injured Adams, Arsenal were two ahead by half-time through Bergkamp and Anelka. However, Villa staged a comeback, winning the game 3-2 with the winner coming from Dion Dublin. The old 'Double' Arsenal blasted back the following weekend at Highbury against Leeds, now managed by David O'Leary. In a fast, counter-attacking contest, Arsenal gained their first league win in six games. Bergkamp opened the scoring and made the other two in the 3-1 win, for Vieira and Petit. Over Christmas they beat West Ham and Charlton 1-0, although Vieira was sent off in the latter game for the third time that season. The Gunners were undefeated in the League in January and on 6 February Bergkamp was back to his scintillating best, scoring and making two more in the 4-0 win at West Ham. January also saw the arrival of Nwankwo Kanu, a young, 6ft 5in Nigerian forward from Inter Milan, for £4.5 million. Kanu, who had captained Nigeria to triumph in the 1996 Olympics, had spell-binding control for such a big man and was to score some astonishing goals for the Gunners.

In the FA Cup they reached the fifth round on 13 April at Highbury against Sheffield United, having disposed of Preston and Wolves. With 13 minutes remaining, and the score 1-1, United's Lee Morris was felled by cramp and his keeper Alan Kelly kicked the ball into touch so that Morris could receive attention. Parlour restarted play by throwing the ball in the direction of Villa's corner flag, a conventional piece of good sportsmanship. However, Kanu, making his debut as a substitute, gathered the ball and crossed for Overmars to score. The Sheffield United bench were in uproar, with manager Steve Bruce threatening to lead his side off the pitch. Eventually the game restarted and ended 2-1. Kanu was mortified ('I just made a mistake') and Wenger sportingly offered a replay ten days later. When it was suggested that the tie be moved to Sheffield, Wenger declined saying 'We are sporting but not stupid.' Arsenal won the replay 2-1.

The Gunners continued their unbeaten run in February, drawing 1-1 at Old Trafford without Bergkamp and Petit who were both suspended, routing Leicester 5-0 and drawing 1-1 at Newcastle, Anelka scoring his 13th league goal of the season at St James's Park. The end of March found the Gunners four points behind leaders Manchester United. Three goals in the last ten minutes (two from Bergkamp) finished off Sheffield Wednesday. Parlour and

Bergkamp scored in the 2-0 defeat of Everton although Petit was again sent off, and they extended their unbeaten league run to 13 with a 2-0 win against Coventry. They also reached the FA Cup semi-final, beating Derby 1-0 through a Kanu goal, his first for his new club.

A 0-0 draw with a battling, relegation-threatened Southampton and a 1-0 win over Blackburn (where Keown was sent off, the ninth Arsenal dismissal this term) in early April meant that Arsenal were now only one point behind Manchester United, although United had a goal in hand. In the semi-final they met, of course, Manchester United. Vivas became the tenth Arsenal dismissee in the 0-0 draw. In the replay four days later Beckham opened the scoring with a 30-yard effort in the 17th minute. Bergkamp levelled in the 68th minute with a 25-yard deflection off Stam. Four minutes later Keane was sent off for a nasty tackle on Overmars. In injury time Parlour was brought down by Phil Neville in the box and Bergkamp's penalty was saved by Schmeichel. Three minutes into the second period of injury time, Giggs gathered a misdirected pass from Vieira, outpaced Keown, Dixon and Adams and smashed the ball into the net from the edge of the six-yard box for the winner.

A 5-1 scoreline against Wimbledon at Highbury five days later restored Arsenal's confidence, and it was followed by a comprehensive 6-1 hammering of Middlesbrough at the Riverside. In the latter match Kanu scored an extraordinary goal when he met a Dixon cross with a stunning back-heel volley into the astonished keeper's net, a demonstration of the luminous talent of the lanky Nigerian. This win put Arsenal one point ahead of United but a goal behind. Wins over Derby and Spurs in early May gave Arsenal a three-point lead with United having a game in hand. However, a defensive lapse towards the end of the penultimate game at Elland Road, with substitute Nelson Vivas out of position for Harry Kewell's cross, allowed Jimmy Floyd Hasselbaink to head in the only goal of the game in the 86th minute for the Gunners' fourth defeat of the season. Many had thought that O'Leary might go easy on his old club. He did anything but and, after this crucial setback, the championship race was now out of their hands. Arsenal had to beat Aston Villa at Highbury and hope that Spurs, now under the managership of George Graham, either won or drew at Old Trafford.

A wave of elation gripped Highbury on 16 May as news came through that Tottenham had taken the lead in the first half at Old Trafford when Les Ferdinand scored in the 23rd minute. However, two goals either side of half-time from United were almost inevitable. Kanu scored for Arsenal but the strike was academic as United held on to their 2-1 lead and won the title with 79 points to Arsenal's 78 – a long season ultimately decided in the last 45 minutes. With hindsight Wenger blamed their second place on dropping too many points in the autumn when his players were jaded after the exertions of the 'Double' season and the World Cup. Bergkamp, in particular, had taken several months to find his true form. But Wenger was about to enlarge his squad for another onslaught on the title in season 1999-2000.

Thierry Henry Arrives

In the summer of 1999 Steve Bould initiated the break-up of the famous Arsenal defence by joining Sunderland while Stephen Hughes went on loan to Fulham and eventually moved to Everton. Like other Arsenal youngsters Hughes was finding it difficult to break into the increasingly star-studded team and had to find his first-team football elsewhere. The petulant Anelka, increasingly at odds with the club and his team-mates, and at the centre of a protracted saga concerning his future, transferred to Real Madrid for a fee of £24 million, representing a more than useful £23.5 million profit for Arsenal. Arrivals included Silvinho, a left-sided Brazilian defender; Oleg Luzhny, a Ukrainian right back from Dynamo Kiev; Davor Suker, a Croatian striker who had won the Golden Boot at the 1998 World Cup; and 21-year-old French forward Thierry Henry, purchased from Juventus for £11 million.

By inclination a winger, Henry was to exploit his explosive pace and goalscoring instincts as a striker this coming season.

In August Arsenal won three of their six games, with Kanu and Bergkamp the strikeforce, but lost to Manchester United at Highbury and Liverpool at Anfield. They recovered from 1-0 down at home to Aston Villa in early September to win 3-1, Suker opening his Arsenal goal account with two and the other coming from Kanu. Henry scored his first Arsenal goal coming on as a substitute against Southampton at the Dell in the 1-0 win on 18 September.

In the Champions League Arsenal's group comprised Fiorentina, AIK Solna and Barcelona. They opened their European campaign in

Emmanuel Petit, along with Patrick Vieira, achieved a rare 'treble' in 1998: the English 'Double' followed by a World Cup winner's medal with France.

Florence where, although dominant for much of the match, they could only draw 0-0 and Kanu had an underhit penalty saved in the 80th minute. Their next game was against Swedish part-timers AIK at Wembley where goals in the last minute by Henry and Suker saved them the embarrassment of a 1-1 draw. The Gunners were outclassed in the first half in Barcelona in the third match and went 1-0 down to a Luis Enrique goal gifted by Vieira. They fought back courageously in the second half, although Grimandi was sent off and levelled the score through Kanu, the best player on the pitch.

In the League Arsenal went down 2-1 to West Ham on 3 October (Di Canio scoring both) and Vieira was sent off for the fourth time in his Arsenal career. Thereafter they were unbeaten in the League until 7 November at White Hart Lane when Spurs claimed their first win over Arsenal for four years. Ljungberg and Keown were controversially sent off by David Elleray in the 2-1 defeat and Vieira was booked. The French midfielder had already been fined £45,000 and banned for six weeks by the FA for his disciplinary record and for spitting at West Ham's Neil Ruddock, and his booking brought him another game's suspension. The result meant that Arsenal had now suffered four league defeats, as many as they lost in the entire previous season.

In October they were trailing 2-0 to Chelsea at Stamford Bridge until, in the last 15 minutes, Kanu claimed a hat-trick, the highlight being when he drifted past keeper Ed de Goey on the goalline and scored from a seemingly impossible angle. 'Kanu, that day, was on fire,' said Henry. Arsenal went second in the table, one point behind Leeds. In October they had also again been eliminated from the Champions League when, after an eventful 4-2 defeat at Wembley by Barcelona, the Gunners went down 1-0 in the fifth game to Fiorentina at Wembley. A glorious late strike from Gabriel Batistuta did the damage.

In the League they demolished Middlesbrough 5-1 on 20 November. Vieira had started his ban but Petit was outstanding in midfield. Overmars collected three and Bergkamp two in a dismissively dominant performance by the Dutchmen. Middlesbrough got their revenge ten days later when they knocked the Gunners out of the League Cup on penalties, a game which saw the appearance of Arsenal's youngest-ever player, Jerome Pennant at 16 years 319 days. In between these games Arsenal played their first match in the UEFA Cup beating Nantes 3-0 at Highbury. In the return in early December Nantes went ahead early in the game but Grimandi, Henry and Overmars made it 3-1 at half-time. An entertaining game finished 3-3 and Arsenal were through to the last 16, to be played in March.

Early December witnessed an impressive 3-0 win over Leicester although they lost again away from home against Coventry on Boxing Day to go eight

Nwankwo Kanu, the 6ft 5in Nigerian whose eccentric brilliance has delighted Arsenal fans. He captained the Nigerian football team to Olympic gold in 1996.

points off the lead. A 2-0 win over Leeds two days later, with Vieira back from suspension and Kanu again in outstanding form, preceded two draws in early January. On 15 January Bould returned to Highbury with Sunderland. Suker scored twice in the 4-1 win, his first an exquisitely-placed lob over the goalkeeper from the left side of the area. The result placed Arsenal on level points with Manchester United although the Gunners had played three more games. Four days later they were knocked out of the FA Cup on penalties in the fourth round by Leicester.

Arsenal played Manchester United at Old Trafford on 24 January without Kanu (on international duty), the injured Adams, Overmars and Bergkamp and the suspended Suker. Ljungberg caught Stam in possession early in the game and scored but United rescued a point with an equalizer in the 73rd minute from substitute Sheringham. However, between then and mid-March, when they lost 2-1 at Middlesbrough, they won only one of their five league games and lost three away games. Indeed they had not won away from Highbury since 4 December and Wenger admitted 'our inconsistency away from home has cost us the championship'. With no realistic hope of catching leaders Manchester United, who had opted out of the FA Cup to contest a meaningless tournament in South America, there remained the second spot in the Premiership and automatic entry into the Champions League and also the UEFA Cup, which they contested again in early March.

Deportivo la Coruna were the opponents on 3 March at Highbury where Arsenal overwhelmed the Spanish side with their pace and power. Dixon opened the scoring with a fifth-minute header from a Henry cross and Henry scored himself in the 30th minute. Djalminha scored for the visitors early in the second half but 15 minutes later Henry made the gap 3-1 with a header from a Petit cross. In the 78th minute Kanu nodded the ball forward through the defence, completely deceived the keeper with a nonchalant shimmy and walked the ball into the net for the fourth, a typical piece of insouciant magic from the Nigerian. Bergkamp wrapped up a 5-1 unassailable victory. A week later a 2-1 defeat in Spain put Arsenal through to play Werder Bremen in the quarter-final. In the first game at Highbury, Henry and Ljungberg scored in the 2-0 win. They won again in Germany a week later, 4-2, helped by an unlikely but welcome hat-trick from Parlour. Henry was sent off in the game, a ridiculous decision by the referee, but one which meant the Frenchman would miss the first leg of the semi-final.

In the League the Gunners won only their second game out of the last seven when they beat Spurs 2-1 at Highbury in mid-March. Their form then picked up and they won their next eight Premiership games in succession, culminating in the 2-1 home win over Chelsea in early May. The penultimate league game against Sheffield Wednesday was a 3-3 draw and the point ensured Arsenal of Champions League football the coming season. A 4-2 defeat by Newcastle in the final game hardly mattered. Arsenal finished in second place, 18 points behind Manchester United.

Without Henry, Arsenal won the first leg of the semi-final against Lens at Highbury. Bergkamp scored in the second minute and, in a poor performance from the home team, that was the only goal. Henry scored a superb goal just on the interval in Lens and Kanu added a second with four minutes to go in the 2-1 win. In the final they met Galatasaray on 17 May in Copenhagen against a background of street battles and stabbings between opposing fans. Gheorghe Hagi and Hakan Sukur were the main danger men for the Turkish team but, in a counter-attacking game, there was no score by full-time. Hagi was sent off in the third minute of extra-time for punching Adams in the back but Arsenal could not benefit from

The darting runs of Freddie Ljungberg have produced some fine goals for Arsenal.

their numerical advantage. The game went into penalties at the Turkish supporters' end. Suker and Vieira missed and Gheorghe Popescu's successful conversion gave the game and the trophy to Galatasaray. Arsenal, eliminated from their third tournament this season on a penalty shoot-out, again had nothing to show for another gruelling campaign. Kanu's skills, however, had been a revelation and, after a slow start, Henry had successfully made the transition from winger to striker, scoring 26 goals in all competitions. There was much for Wenger and his side to look forward to in the coming campaign and there were several more changes to be made to his squad.

More Frenchmen Arrive

Veteran left back Nigel Winterburn had lost his place to Silvinho and, after 13 years at Highbury and 579 appearances for the club, he signed a two-year contract with West Ham in the summer. Davor Suker also left for Upton Park. Marc Overmars and Manu Petit joined Barcelona for a combined total of £32 million. Wenger had tried to keep both players but they had decided that their chances of Champions League success were greater in Spain than in North London. The wages were higher, too. In came French international midfielder-cum-winger Robert Pires from Marseille for £6 million to replace Overmars. Pires had supplied the cross for David Trezeguet to score the golden goal in the Euro 2000 final against Italy. Cameroon international midfielder Lauren also joined for £7 million from Real Mallorca. In August, to augment his quality strikeforce, Wenger paid Bordeaux an Arsenal club record fee of £13 million for another French international, Sylvain Wiltord, who had ended the previous season as the French league top scorer. Wiltord, a busy little forward with close control, had equalized in the last minute of the Euro 2000 final.

On the opening day of the season at Highbury Arsenal inexplicably lost 1-0 to Sunderland, the goal coming when Seaman failed to hold a cross and Niall Quinn headed into the net. Arsenal were dominant throughout and could have scored six. In the last minute Vieira was sent off for retaliating when fouled by Darren Williams. Sunderland manager Peter Reid commented that the midfielder was 'desperately unlucky'. The Gunners beat Liverpool two days later at Highbury, their first win over the Scousers since 1994, with a debut goal from Lauren and a last-minute strike from Henry. Vieira was again dismissed for two yellow cards, both curious decisions by referee Graham Poll. The following day Wenger was charged by the FA with 'physical intimidation' of the fourth official and threatened with a 12-game touchline ban. He won his appeal in February.

50 Greatest Players

LEE DIXON Right back

Born: Manchester, 17 March 1964

Joined Arsenal: 1988   **From:** Stoke City

Debut: 13 February 1988 v Luton Town, League

Appearances: 614   **Goals:** 28

Left Arsenal: 2002 (retired)

Honours won with Arsenal: Division One championship 1989,
1991; Premiership 1998, 2002; FA Cup winner 1993, 1998;
European Cup-Winners' Cup winner 1994; 22 England caps

Lee Dixon was another hungry player who defied the years. He
started out in the lower divisions with Chester, then Bury, before
attracting attention at Stoke. He settled in during the latter
part of 1987-88, then became a fixture for the next 13 years.
He was the Gunners' penalty expert during the 1990-91 title
success, netting five times from the spot. That was the
season when he also established himself in the England team. Dixon had terrific pace,
great enthusiasm and seemed to get better and better as a defender as he grew older.
Few players used their experience to greater effect. He took his final bow as a
substitute when the Gunners won at Old Trafford to clinch the 2001-02 championship.

A thoroughly disenchanted Vieira nonetheless temporarily shrugged aside
his grievances to produce a majestic performance in the next game at
Highbury against Charlton Athletic. He also scored twice in the 5-3 thriller,
the other scorers being Henry (2) and Silvinho. Arsenal remained unbeaten
in their next three league matches and faced Manchester United at Highbury
on 1 October.

Before the United game they resumed their Champions League campaign,
their group comprising Sparta Prague, Shakhtar Donetsk and group
favourites Lazio. On 12 September a solo goal from Silvinho gave them a 1-0
win in Prague. The following week they were 2-1 down at home to Shakhtar
with six minutes remaining. The unlikely figure of Keown shouldered in to
level and he then scored the winner from close range. A Bergkamp-inspired
performance against Lazio at Highbury gave the Gunners a 2-0 win, both
goals made by the Dutchman and scored by Ljungberg. Arsenal now had
maximum points from their first three games.

They maintained their unbeaten streak against United by winning 1-0, the
goal coming in the 30th minute from Henry who, with his back to the goal

and 25 yards out, flicked up the ball and volleyed an unforgettable shot over a startled Barthez. It was Henry's first goal for six games and he scored another in the 1-0 defeat against Aston Villa in the middle of the month. An away 2-1 defeat of West Ham and a scintillating 5-0 demolition of Manchester City kept Arsenal in the title hunt. They also managed a 1-1 draw in Rome with Lazio. A Nedved shot in the 24th minute deflected off Silvinho for the opener and Pires levelled in the 88th minute with a curling shot over Paruzzi. Pires, with his darting runs, intelligent distribution and unselfish teamwork, was fast becoming an indispensable member of the team. They followed this up with a 4-2 defeat of Sparta Prague at Highbury although in the last group game away to Shakhtar they were outplayed in the Ukraine and defeated 3-0. Nonetheless, Arsenal were through to the second group stage.

Fielding a reserve side the Gunners were beaten 2-1 by Ipswich Town in the opening round of the League Cup on 1 November, the same day that Geordie Armstrong, the great winger and Arsenal servant, collapsed and died at the age of 56 at the London Colney training ground. Central defender Igors Stepanovs, a £1 million signing from Skonto Riga, scored on his debut against Leicester. Arsenal's 12-game unbeaten run came to an end in the middle of the month, losing 2-0 away to Everton, and they lost again a week later at Leeds, going down 1-0. Seven Arsenal players were booked in the bad-tempered affair and Vieira was charged with misconduct. Pires and Leeds manager David O'Leary confronted each other after the game, Pires complaining that O'Leary had blown kisses at him during the match. Arsenal were now eight points behind leaders Manchester United.

Their European opponents in the second group stage were Spartak Moscow, Bayern Munich and Lyons. Although Silvinho gave the Gunners the lead in the second minute, they collapsed to a 4-1 defeat in Moscow, with Spartak's tough, inventive attack taking advantage of Arsenal's poor defending on a freezing night. They then drew 2-2 at Highbury with Bayern Munich in a match they should have won. Two-nil ahead in the second half through Henry and Kanu, they allowed Bayern to equalize within 11 minutes. Arsenal, however, were still in with a chance as Lyons had beaten Spartak, and the group games were to resume in February.

Arsenal rediscovered their scoring touch in early December when they annihilated Newcastle 5-0 at Highbury, Parlour claiming a hat-trick with two in the last four minutes. 'We got smashed,' said manager Bobby Robson. Vieira saved a point in the next game away to Spurs, levelling with a header in the last minute for a 1-1 draw. Smarting from a 4-0 defeat by Liverpool on 23 December at Highbury, Arsenal destroyed Leicester on Boxing Day 6-1 with

Ray Parlour, an influential presence in the 1990s. He continues to turn in performances that make him an ever-reliable member of the Arsenal midfield.

Henry scoring a superb hat-trick. By the end of December, however, they remained eight points behind Manchester United.

The goals dried up again in January, which included a defeat by Charlton and two draws. A 2-0 home win over Bradford at the end of the month initiated a run of four league wins before they faced Manchester United on 25 February. At Old Trafford an abject defensive performance resulted in a humiliating 6-1 defeat for the Gunners. Lacking the steadying influence of Adams, Dixon and Keown, Stepanovs was guilty of dreadful, almost comic, defending and young left back Ashley Cole was taken off at half-time after being given a torrid time by Beckham. Manchester United were now 16 points ahead and United's title a formality. 'I think that's Arsenal finished now,' said Alex Ferguson.

There were, however, still in the FA Cup and the Champions League. Earlier in the month Arsenal had beaten Lyons 1-0 away courtesy of an Henry header and excellent goalkeeping from Seaman. On 21 February they drew 1-1 with the French side at Highbury, with Bergkamp scoring in the 37th minute, and one-time Wenger target Edmilson equalizing at the end, to leave them second in the group. One week before the Old Trafford debacle Arsenal played Chelsea in the fifth round of the FA Cup at Highbury, having earlier disposed of Carlisle and Queens Park Rangers. Wiltord came off the bench to score twice in the last 15 minutes in the 3-1 win.

With Adams and Dixon now back in the side, the Gunners beat West Ham 3-0 in the League in early March thanks to a first-half Wiltord hat-trick. On

6 March Henry scored the only goal in the 1-0 defeat of Spartak Moscow at Highbury, and one week later they succumbed 1-0 in Munich in the last group game. A fortunate Arsenal still qualified for the quarter-final of the Champions League due to Spartak drawing at home with Lyons.

One minute's silence was observed before the league game against Spurs at Highbury on 31 March as David 'Rocky' Rocastle had died earlier in the day of non-Hodgkin's lymphoma at the tragically young age of 33. The genial and popular midfielder had made 275 appearances for the club before his move to Leeds in 1992. The shock and sadness was reflected in the rigid observation of the silence at both ends of the ground. Arsenal's 2-0 victory was secured by a Pires curler and an Henry solo effort in the last 20 minutes.

Five days later Arsenal met Valencia, a counter-attacking Spanish side with an enviable defensive record, in the first leg of the quarter-final of the Champions League at Highbury. One-nil down at half-time to a Roberto Ayala goal, and with Valencia assuming control, Arsenal appeared in trouble. However, in the 58th minute Henry struck an emphatic equalizer from a Pires back-heel and two minutes later Parlour unleashed an unstoppable 25-yard shot to give Arsenal a 2-1 win on the night.

The euphoria evaporated in the return game two weeks later when John Carew headed in the only goal of the night at the formidable Mestalla Stadium in Valencia, and Arsenal were once again out of Europe. After the game a bitterly disappointed Patrick Vieira complained, 'We need some more quality players. Losing Manu and Marc Overmars was a mistake of the club.' Other observers felt that what was really required was a striker in the Ian Wright mould, a poacher in the box who could convert Arsenal's often breathtaking, elegant flowing movement into the goals their supremacy demanded.

Arsenal's capitulation to Valencia came as a surprise to those who had witnessed their ruthless 4-0 defeat of Manchester City just six days earlier in the League at Maine Road. The goals were all scored in the first 36 minutes of the match, with Ljungberg (2), Wiltord and Kanu the scorers, and City manager Joe Royle said, 'They were awesome and too bloody good for us.' With second place to play for in the League, Arsenal won their next three games and drew their penultimate match against Newcastle to secure second place and Champions League status the following season. Their final game was against Southampton, playing their last match at the Dell. Arsenal were beaten 3-2, the winner coming appropriately from local hero Matt Le Tissier in the 89th minute.

50 Greatest Players

TONY ADAMS Centre back

Born: Romford, 10 October 1966

Joined Arsenal: 1983   **From:** School

Debut: 5 November 1983 v Sunderland, League

Appearances: 665   **Goals:** 48

Left Arsenal: 2002 (retired)

Honours won with Arsenal: Division One championship 1989, 1991; Premeiership 1998, 2002; FA Cup winner 1993, 1998, 2002; League Cup winner 1987, 1993; European Cup-Winners' Cup winner 1994; 66 England caps

Tony Adams lifted more trophies than any other Arsenal skipper. He took over from Kenny Sansom in the spring of 1988 and held the job for 14 years. Adams revealed his often turbulent life and his recovery from alcoholism in his book *Addiction*. But he was always a massive presence and influence on the pitch. He made his first-team debut at 17 and became a regular under George Graham. An uncompromising defender, powerful in the air and a natural organizer, he was also a major threat in opponents' penalty areas. The 1993 FA Cup semi-final winner against Tottenham was one of many important goals he scored. Adams had also become a vital figure for England until increasing back pain forced him to quit international football.

A 2-1 win over Spurs in the FA Cup semi-final in early April brought Arsenal to the final against Liverpool at the Millennium Stadium in Cardiff on 12 May. Liverpool were defensively minded, and the Gunners, on top throughout, deservedly went ahead when Pires in the 72nd minute found Ljungberg who rounded the keeper and scored from six yards. Parlour came on as a substitute for Wiltord to protect the lead, and this was probably one of Wenger's rare errors. With seven minutes left on the clock Owen equalized with a half-volley and the little striker did it again in the 87th minute, taking advantage of a 70-yard pass from Patrik Berger to shoot low across Seaman for a final score of 2-1.

Yet again there was no new silverware in the Highbury trophy cabinet. It was suggested by some critics that the team lacked the motivation and desire to win and were fated to be perennial runners-up. As the new season approached, however, Arsenal were determined that this would be their year and that they would at last overturn the dominance of the increasingly arrogant and cocksure Manchester United.

Chapter Nine 2001-03
Another 'Double' Triumph

In his five years at Highbury, Wenger had enjoyed one season of real success. Although his team had at times proven themselves to be one of the classiest and most skilful sides in Europe, all too often they had lacked consistency both in defence and, Henry notwithstanding, attack. Midfield was less of a problem, with the peerless authority and vision of Vieira linking up with the tenacity and determination of Parlour, supported by the attacking thrust of Ljungberg and Pires. Wenger ('Arsène knows') moved over the summer to reinforce his squad.

In June he acquired midfielder Gio Van Bronckhorst from Rangers for £8.5 million. The Dutchman was bought to fill the void left by Petit on the left side of central midfield. To fill the role of 'the fox in the box' – a natural finisher in the penalty area – Wenger brought in young Franny Jeffers from Everton. And in his most audacious coup of all, English international centre back Sol Campbell

joined from Spurs, after ten years' service, on a free transfer to breathe new life into a creaking and increasingly disjointed defence. Other recruits included Junichi Inamoto (quickly nicknamed 'T-shirt' for his commercial appeal to the Far Eastern market) from Japan's Gamba Osaka, the Premiership's first Japanese player, and keeper Richard Wright from Ipswich, viewed as a long-term replacement for Seaman.

Vieira, however, appeared less than happy over the summer about Arsenal's prospects, reportedly stating that, 'I need to move because I need to win more trophies and I cannot see that happening at Arsenal.' Chairman Peter Hill-Wood retorted, 'He played in the team and should take some of the blame. It would have helped if he'd not been sent off quite so often.' Vieira was also accused of stabbing

England international Sol Campbell was drafted in to shore up the defence.

Wenger in the back, after the manager had plucked him from relative obscurity and turned him into one of the world's finest midfielders. The dispute was resolved in July when Vieira signed a new, improved contract.

Arsenal, whose title challenge had been crucially undermined the previous season by their poor away record, began 2001-02 by beating Middlesbrough 4-0 at the Riverside. Although Parlour was sent off early in the second half, Vieira was magnificent, his troubles of the summer forgotten. Three goals in the last three minutes, two from Bergkamp, sealed the victory. By the end of September Arsenal were on top of the Premiership after beating Derby 2-0 and Wright making his debut in goal. They had lost only one of their first seven games, 2-1 against Leeds.

They had also played their first three games in the Champions League. On 11 September in Spain, with the world numbed by the horrific collapse of the World Trade Centre in New York, the Gunners met Real Mallorca. Cole was sent off in the 11th minute and Mallorca scored the only goal from the subsequent penalty. Eight days later the Gunners staged a ragged performance to beat Schalke 04 3-2. In Greece on 26 September, with Upson in for Adams, they played dismally with hardly a shot on target in the 1-0 defeat by Panathinaikos in Greece. Two defeats in three games was a poor start to their campaign. At home in October, however, they beat Panathinaikos 2-1, both goals coming from Henry and Wright saving a penalty – 'Richard Wright, Wright, Wright!' sang the crowd. The following week Arsenal ensured their participation in the second group stage with a 3-1 win at Highbury over a defensive Mallorca, Henry scoring the third in injury time. A 3-1 defeat in Germany was academic. The last game saw the first start of the season for Brazilian midfielder Edu.

A win and two draws in the League maintained Arsenal's title challenge, although a link with the past was broken on October 23 when Bertie Mee, manager of the first 'Double' side, died at the age of 82. November began badly. One-nil ahead of Charlton at Highbury and seemingly coasting, Arsenal let in four goals in less than 20 minutes either side of half-time. Poor defending and goalkeeping and a wasteful attitude up front contributed to the 4-2 defeat. On 17 November they travelled to White Hart Lane where Campbell was vilified by his former fans, with chants of 'Judas' ringing around the stadium. Campbell coped well with the hostility and, with Henry injured, Pires took over the goalscoring mantle, netting with nine minutes to go. In the last minute Wright fumbled a Poyet shot and Spurs equalized.

The second Champions League stage began four days later. The Gunners were outplayed by the compact movement and neat interpassing of Deportivo La Coruna in Spain and were defeated 2-0, their sixth straight away defeat in Europe. Manchester United visited Highbury the following

50 Greatest Players

MARTIN KEOWN Centre back

Born: Oxford, 24 July 1966

Joined Arsenal: 1982, 1993   **From:** School, Everton

Debut: 23 November 1985 v West Bromwich Albion, League

Appearances: 430   **Goals:** 8

Left Arsenal: 1986   **For:** Aston Villa

Still at club

Honours won with Arsenal: Premiership championship 1998,
2002; FA Cup winner 1998, 2002, 2003; 43 England caps

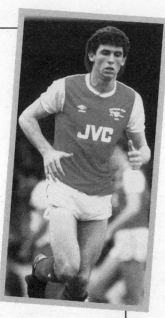

Martin Keown made his name as an Arsenal youngster in
1985-86 but joined Aston Villa after less than a season in the
first team. He moved on to Everton, before George Graham
brought him back to Highbury in a £2 million deal in
February 1993. Ironically, his centre back pairing with Tony
Adams stretched back to youth team days in the early 1980s.
Keown's pace has been his greatest asset, combined with fierce determination and
stern tackling. A 'Double' winner in 1998, he recovered from a serious leg injury to
form a combative partnership with Sol Campbell as the Gunners won another 'Double'
in 2001-02. He also forced his way back into the England squad in 1997 and played
four more years at international level.

weekend and left 3-1 losers. One-nil down at half-time, Arsenal equalized
with a Ljungberg lob over Fabien Barthez early in the second half. In the
80th minute Barthez kicked a clearance straight at Henry and the Frenchman
gratefully accepted the gift. 'Barthez is a Gooner' chanted the home crowd.
Five minutes later another Barthez error, dropping a ball from Vieira,
allowed Henry to score the third. Earlier in the month the Gunners had also
beaten United, although largely a reserve side, 4-0 in the League Cup,
Wiltord claiming a first-half hat-trick.

Their next opponents in the Champions League were Juventus at Highbury
on 4 December. Arsenal soaked up the early pressure and Vieira and Parlour
gradually assumed control of the midfield. Taylor and Upson were outstanding
and Ljungberg scored first from a Buffon rebound in the 21st minute. Six
minutes later Henry floated in a 22-yard free kick for the second. A second-half
own goal from Taylor, the ball bouncing off the young keeper's back into the
net, made it 2-1. With two minutes to go, Bergkamp twisted and turned the
Juventus defence before slipping a perfect pass to Ljungberg for the third goal.

Dennis Bergkamp was a player reborn when he came to Highbury in 1995. The flying Dutchman was oustanding in the 'Double' year of 1997-98 with 22 goals and the Footballer of the Year award.

Against Aston Villa at Highbury four days later Arsenal turned a 2-0 half-time deficit into a 3-2 win, Henry claiming the winner in the last minute of a thrilling second half. Arsenal moved into second place. December brought welcome news. Early in the month Wenger finally signed a four-year extension to his contract and formal permission was granted to build a new 60,000 seat stadium at Ashburton Grove, half a mile from Highbury, by Islington Council.

An essentially reserve side was eliminated from the League Cup 4-0 by Blackburn but two big games awaited the Gunners in December. The championship race was tight, with six points covering the top eight clubs, and Arsenal's main rivals were Newcastle and Liverpool, both of whom they had to face in consecutive weeks. A low shot from Pires in the 20th minute against Newcastle at Highbury on 18 December gave Arsenal the lead and they should have scored more. Parlour was sent off just before half-time and Newcastle equalized on the hour. With five minutes remaining, referee Graham Poll awarded a penalty against Arsenal after Campbell had cleanly tackled Laurent Robert in the box. Alan Shearer converted and Robert made it 3-1 in the last minute. Poll had to be given a police escort off the pitch, with an angry Henry in close attendance. Newcastle went top, level on points with Liverpool.

On the Title Trail

They then played Liverpool at Anfield where Arsenal had not won for nine years. Van Bronckhorst was sent of for 'diving' in the 36th minute – although the Dutchman had clearly slipped and immediately got up without claiming anything – but the game ended 2-1 in Arsenal's favour. Henry and Bergkamp were the scorers and Parlour was immense, taking over the midfield general role from the suspended Vieira. Wenger later remarked, 'That was the turning point for us; winning there with ten men convinced me we would win the championship.'

Arsenal went to the top of the table with a 2-1 defeat of Chelsea on Boxing Day, Campbell heading in his first goal for the club, and consolidated their position at the end of the year with a 2-1 defeat of Middlesbrough, Cole taking advantage of a clever chip from Bergkamp to score the winner with a diving header.

Amid stories in the media about the talismanic Vieira joining Real Madrid in the summer, Arsenal were unbeaten in their January league matches, although Ljungberg was injured in the 1-1 away draw against Leeds and would be out for eight weeks. They also qualified for the fifth round of the FA Cup, crushing Watford 4-2 at Vicarage Road and beating Liverpool 1-0 at Highbury. Bergkamp headed in the only goal of the game from a Henry cross in the 28th minute but the game was marred by the sending off of Keown and Bergkamp in the second half. Liverpool's Jamie Carragher was also dismissed after being hit by a coin and hurling it back into the crowd. In a Pires-inspired 3-2 defeat of Blackburn on 30 January, Keown picked up an injury which would sideline him for two months.

In early February against Southampton Cole joined the growing injury list and would be out of action for 11 games. Van Bronckhorst joined the walking wounded when he ruptured ligaments in the late February 4-1 win over Fulham and he was to miss the rest of the season. The second stage of the Champions League continued with an away trip to Bayer Leverkusen where a Pires goal gave Arsenal a 1-1 draw and a valuable point, although Parlour was sent off for the third time this season. In the return at Highbury on 27 February a stunning, attacking display by Arsenal gave them a 2-0 lead within the first

50 Greatest Players

DENNIS BERGKAMP Forward

Born: Amsterdam, 10 May 1969

Debut: 20 August 1995 v Middlesbrough, League

Joined Arsenal: 1995   **From:** Internazionale

Appearances: 314   **Goals:** 104

Honours won with Arsenal: Premiership championship 1998, 2002; FA Cup winner 1998, 2002, 2003; Footballer of the Year 1998; 79 Holland caps

Dennis Bergkamp has been two players in one: a creator and a finisher. He has been a prolific scorer, capable of great goals like his brilliant strike at Newcastle in the 2001-02 'Double' season. His slide-rule passes have also set up a host of chances for strike partners Nicolas Anelka and Thierry Henry. The former Ajax star resurrected his career at Highbury after a miserable time in Italy. His best season was 1998 when he finished top scorer with 22 goals and was voted Footballer of the Year. He capped the season with some brilliant displays at the World Cup, including a memorable winner against Argentina. He netted 37 goals in 79 games for his country and would have played more but for his fear of flying.

Ashley Cole settled in the Arsenal defence to become first choice for Wenger and for England manager, Sven Goran Eriksson.

seven minutes. Pires swept in the first goal and Henry finished off from a Wiltord low cross two minutes later. Vieira headed in the third in the 48th minute and Bergkamp lobbed the fourth towards the end for a 4-1 scoreline.

Bergkamp scored one of the goals of the season in the 2-0 away defeat of Newcastle in early March when he flicked the ball past Nikos Dabizas, spun round the defender and cooly despatched it past Shay Given, all in one glorious shimmying movement. Arsenal won all four of their league games in March and, after the 3-0 defeat of Charlton on 1 April – the goals coming within nine first-half minutes – they went top of the League with a game in hand. The Gunners had also reached the semi-final of the FA Cup, beating Gillingham and then Newcastle 3-0 in a replay at Highbury. Bergkamp was at his brilliant best, scoring one, making another and twice hitting the woodwork. Bobby Robson said, 'Arsenal had a genius on the pitch. We didn't.' Unfortunately, Pires, the inspiration behind Arsenal's success to date, suffered a bad knee injury which would keep him out for the rest of the season and make him miss the World Cup finals. They beat Middlesbrough in the semi-final in mid-April 1-0 courtesy of a Gianluca Festa own goal and were to meet Chelsea in the final on 4 May.

Arsenal played their last two European games in mid-March. Deportivo came to Highbury and outclassed the Gunners, with the Spanish side's speed, incisive passing and lethal counter-attacking giving them a deserved 2-0 win and the home fans' applause at the end of the match. It was Arsenal's first European defeat in 17 games at Highbury. A 1-0 away defeat by Juventus in front of a tiny crowd was irrelevant, as Bayer had beaten Deportivo and Arsenal had failed to qualify for the quarter-finals.

By the end of April, a run of four straight wins in the League after the Charlton game meant that Arsenal were now five points clear at the top of the Premiership and had only to draw their penultimate game at Old Trafford to become champions. 'We want to do it at Old Trafford,' said Wenger. The first part of the 'Double' was achieved on 4 May at the Millennium Stadium against Chelsea in the FA Cup final. In the 70th minute

Parlour, with the Chelsea defence backing off, curled in a superb shot from 25 yards for the opener. 'Usually they end up in the crowd but today it went in the top corner,' said the man from Romford. Nine minutes later Ljungberg scored his seventh goal in six games when he bent a shot round Cudicini from the edge of the box and Arsenal had won the Cup 2-0. In the post-match celebration the players gleefully genuflected to the besuited Robert Pires on the pitch, recognizing the massive contribution the injured Frenchman and Player of the Year had made to their season. The team was: Seaman, Lauren, Adams, Campbell, Cole, Wiltord, Parlour, Vieira, Ljungberg, Bergkamp, Henry.

A Third 'Double'

On 8 May at Old Trafford the Gunners, lacking Henry, Bergkamp and Adams, won the 'Double' for the third time in their history. Wiltord scored from a rebound in the 56th minute for the only goal of the game to ensure that the Gunners ended the season unbeaten in their league travels. Adams lifted the trophy at the last game, a 4-3 defeat of Everton at Highbury. To crown his exceptional season, Henry scored twice and won the Golden Boot. Despite being beset by injuries and suspensions throughout the season,

---

50 Greatest Players

PATRICK VIEIRA Midfielder

Born: Dakar, Senegal, 23 June 1976

Joined Arsenal: 1996   **From:** Milan

Debut: 16 September 1996 v Sheffield Wednesday (sub), League

Appearances: 315   **Goals:** 23

Honours won with Arsenal: Division One championship 1998, 2002; FA Cup winner 1998, 2002; 62 France caps

Patrick Vieira was one of Arsène Wenger's first signings for Arsenal and one of the shrewdest. A former Cannes midfielder, Vieira seized the chance after spending most of his time in Serie A on the Milan bench. He made an immediate impact in his debut and never looked back. Tall, strong, a powerful runner, accurate passer and strong tackler, he is recognized as one of the world's best midfielders. The responsibility of captaining the Gunners seems to have helped his disciplinary record too after several suspensions. He was one of the stars of France's Euro 2000 triumph and was voted French Footballer of the Year in 2001.

Great Matches

LEAGUE DIVISION ONE   **Old Trafford, 8 May 2002**

Manchester United 0   **Arsenal 1**   **Attendance: 67,580**
                              Wiltord

Four days after the FA Cup victory Arsenal travelled to Old Trafford for one of their most important games since Anfield in 1989. A draw or victory over Manchester United would give the Gunners their second 'Double' under Wenger and, as the Frenchman said, 'We want to do it at Old Trafford.' With Henry and Adams absent through injury, and an unfit Bergkamp on the bench, Arsenal ran on to the pitch to a cacophony of noise from the packed stadium. United made their intentions clear in the first half with some tough tackling, Keane in particular being culpable and receiving a yellow card for a wild tackle on Vieira. Neville and Scholes also found their way into the referee's book. A Wiltord shot was deflected wide but Seaman also made some good saves from Veron and then a Keane volley. An intense, high-energy first half ended goalless.

Early in the second half Kanu tested Barthez with a long-range shot and, shortly after, the keeper miskicked a clearance straight to Wiltord. The Frenchman bore down on goal but was well tackled by Wes Brown. In the 57th minute Ljungberg was fed by Wiltord and surged through the United defence but his shot was blocked. The ball rebounded to an unmarked Wiltord and the French forward scored what was to be the only goal of the game. Although Ruud van Nistelrooy came on, his arrival was too late. Arsenal gradually controlled what remained of the match, with their character and defensive determination

proving too much for a fading United side. The whistle blew and the Arsenal players danced in front of the visiting fans, celebrating the 'Double'. The balance of power in English football now appeared to have tipped away from Manchester towards North London.

Manchester United: Barthez, P. Neville, Brown, Blanc, Silvestre, Veron (van Nistelrooy), Keane, Scholes, Giggs, Forlan, Solskjaer

Arsenal: Seaman, Lauren, Keown, Campbell, Cole, Ljungberg, Parlour, Vieira, Edu, Wiltord, Kanu (Dixon)

Referee: P. Durkin

Sylvain Wiltord scored the only goal of the game to win Arsenal the 'Double' and how sweet it was that the title was clinched at Old Trafford, the home of Manchester United.

Wenger's team had played with irresistible flair, pace and power, to capture the ultimate English footballing prize. European success, however, remained elusive and was to be the manager's main priority for season 2002-03.

Tony Adams, who had served Arsenal for nearly 20 years, finally called it a day at the end of the season. The departures in the close season included Richard Wright, after playing only 12 league games, to Everton for £4.75 million, and Inamoto on a free transfer. In recognition of Seaman's continuing importance to the club, Wenger offered the pony-tailed keeper a one-year contract. Centre back Pascal Cygan arrived from Lille, while Brazilian World Cup-winning midfielder Gilberto Silva joined for £4.5 million from Atletico Mineiro. The good news in July was that the new stadium at Ashburton Grove was given the go-ahead by the High Court; the bad news was that Ljungberg, who had been so influential the previous season, was to miss the first month of the coming season with a hip injury picked up at the World Cup.

The 2002-03 season began with a 1-0 win over Liverpool in the Community Shield while the winning run, a record for the English top division of 14 successive games, came to an end against West Ham in August when they drew 2-2. Arsenal strolled past Birmingham and West Bromwich Albion and drew 1-1 away with Chelsea on 1 September. In this game Vieira was sent off and later charged with misconduct for allegedly insulting referee Andy D'Urso. His penalty was a two-match ban and a £25,000 fine. Arsenal won their next three league games (including a 2-1 home win over Manchester City, where an unpopular Anelka scored for City) and met Borussia Dortmund at Highbury in the Champions League on 17 September. A well-organized Borussia kept out a raiding Arsenal until Bergkamp scored in the 62nd minute. The final score was 2-0 after Ljungberg deftly finished off a brilliant counter-attacking move initiated by Seaman.

Arsenal were by now playing some marvellous football, characterized by the electric pace of Henry, the dazzling control and vision of Bergkamp, the surging runs of Ljungberg and the imperious authority of Vieira. It all came together in two games at the end of September. In their 4-0 thrashing of PSV Eindhoven in Holland on 25 September, Gilberto scored within 20 seconds – the fastest-ever goal scored in the tournament – and the other three came in the second half, Ljungberg and then Henry with two in the last ten minutes.

It is difficult to recall an English side ever playing with the sheer panache, artistic grace and ebullient skill which Arsenal displayed in their stunning 4-1 win over Leeds four days later at Elland Road, their 23rd consecutive away league win. In the ninth minute young Ivory Coast international midfielder

50 Greatest Players

DAVID SEAMAN Goalkeeper

Born: Rotherham, 19 September 1963

Joined Arsenal: 1990   **From:** Queens Park Rangers

Debut: 25 August 1990 v Wimbledon, League

Appearances: 560

Left Arsenal: 2003   **For:** Manchester City

Honours won with Arsenal: Division One championship 1991; Premiership 1998, 2002; FA Cup winner 1993, 1998, 2002, 2003; League Cup winner 1993; European Cup-Winners' Cup winner 1994; 75 England caps

David Seaman made more appearances, and won more honours, than any other Arsenal goalkeeper. He cost a then-British record fee for a goalkeeper, £1.3 million, when he arrived from QPR. He conceded just 18 league goals in his first season – as the Gunners won the 1990-91 championship – and regained his England place. He was his country's number one for a decade, probably reaching his peak during England's run to the Euro 96 semi-finals. He was at the heart of Arsenal's triumphs under George Graham and Arsène Wenger. He produced match-winning saves, often when he had been largely inactive, and his coolness inspired confidence in his defenders. His 2003 FA Cup semi-final save from Paul Peschisolido was one of his greatest ever.

Kolo Toure, acquired by Wenger in February, found Kanu who scored with a side-foot shot. Toure himself headed in a Henry cross 11 minutes later. Early in the second half Henry slipped the ball under Paul Robinson for the third and Kanu converted a clever pass from young winger Jerome Pennant with nine minutes remaining. Arsenal now appeared simply unbeatable.

Unbeatable Arsenal?

After a 1-0 win at Auxerre in early October, they defeated Sunderland 3-1 to set a record of 30 unbeaten Premiership games in succession. Everything, however, comes to an end, as they discovered two weeks later when 16-year-old substitute Wayne Rooney scored a 30-yard wonder goal in the last minute to defeat Arsenal 2-1 at Goodison. They were then defeated 2-1 at home by Auxerre, a game in which Pires returned to a rousing reception for his first game in seven months. In the next game, although on top throughout and creating 27 scoring opportunities, they went down to Blackburn 2-1 through a Dwight Yorke winner after Edu had scored an own goal and equalized with a free kick. Vieira and Henry were suspended and Blackburn keeper Brad Friedel had been in superb form. This supposedly invincible team then lost again, in a meaningless 2-1 defeat to Borussia Dortmund as they had already qualified for the next stage.

They rediscovered the winning habit in November, winning their next three league games, including a 3-0 win over Spurs at Highbury where Henry sprinted virtually the length of the pitch, avoiding and outwitting challenges and tackles, to score a perfectly-executed goal. Wenger said, 'A world class goal in an outstanding team performance. Clearly we've got our confidence back.' They stumbled again in their next match, a 3-2 defeat at Southampton, not helped by Campbell's dismissal and Cygan's uncertain performance, but stayed on top of the Premiership at the end of the month with a 3-1 defeat of Aston Villa. Henry was again sensational and Villa manager Graham Taylor said, 'You just feel they can score when they want to against anybody.'

Three days earlier Henry had proven his international class, if anyone had doubted, by scoring a hat-trick against Roma in Rome in the opening stage of the Champions League for a 3-1 win. His third goal was a majestic free kick and he became the only Arsenal player to score a hat-trick in the competition. With no Campbell, and young Stuart Taylor in goal, Arsenal were beaten 2-0 by Manchester United and then drew 1-1 with Spurs. When

50 Greatest Players

ROBERT PIRES Midfield

Born: Reims, France, 29 October 1973

Joined Arsenal: 2000   **From:** Marseille

Debut: 19 August 2000 v Sunderland (sub), League

Appearances: 138   **Goals:** 37

Honours won with Arsenal: Premiership championship 2002; FA Cup winner 2003; Footballer of the Year 2002; 54 France caps

Robert Pires's form on the left was crucial to Arsenal's 'Double' charge in 2001-02, when he was voted Footballer of the Year. He netted 13 goals and created many more before an anterior cruciate ligament ended his season in March and ruled him out of the World Cup finals. He returned to action in October and finished the season as second top scorer, with 16 goals – including the winner against Southampton in the FA Cup final. Pires joined Arsenal after creating France's Golden Goal winner for David Trezeguet against Italy in the Euro 2000 final. He spent much of his first season coming to terms with the physical demands of the Premiership, then blossomed to show his skill and flair. He is a fixture in his national side.

they beat West Brom 2-1 away on Boxing Day, with Jeffers scoring in his first start of the season, Arsenal were four points ahead of second-placed Chelsea. In their last game of the year they drew 1-1 at Highbury with a defensively-minded Liverpool, a second half penalty from Danny Murphy equalized by an Henry penalty after Jeffers fell over in the box.

On New Year's Day 2003 Arsenal were 3-0 up against Chelsea at Highbury until two defensive errors in the last five minutes produced a 3-2 scoreline to put the Gunners five points ahead. Bergkamp scored his hundredth goal for the club three days later in the 2-0 FA Cup third round defeat of Oxford United, and Henry claimed his hundred in the 4-0 away rout of Birmingham, Arsenal's best display since the Leeds game. An Henry hat-trick followed in the 3-1 defeat of West Ham on 19 January, and Liverpool twice came back from behind in the 2-2 draw at Anfield at the end of the month, their second coming from a controversial corner converted by Emile Heskey in the last minute.

A win and a draw early in the month saw Arsenal three points clear at the top. They had knocked non-league Farnborough out of the FA Cup 5-1 the previous month and met Manchester United in the fifth round at Old Trafford on 15 February. With the score 0-0 Giggs missed a sitter. An Edu free kick took a wicked deflection off David Beckham to put Arsenal ahead in the 35th minute and, with the Brazilian and Vieira outstanding in midfield, Edu released Wiltord

for the second goal with 12 minutes remaining. Yet another magnificent display by Henry a week later inspired Arsenal to a 5-1 win over Manchester City, four goals scored within the first 19 minutes. Despairing City defender Steve Howey observed, 'When they play like that you just can't stop them. It's awful. There are players coming at you from every direction.'

Europe was not proving so easy, with the more sophisticated European clubs increasingly aware of the imperative to retain possession and defend deep against the Gunners' devastatingly fast and penetrative counter-attacking style. They could only draw 1-1 at home on 18

David Seaman was England's and Arsenal's number one choice between the posts for over a decade, appearing 560 times for the Gunners.

---

50 Greatest Players

THIERRY HENRY Striker

Born: Paris, 17 August 1977

Joined Arsenal: 1999   **From:** Juventus

Debut: 7 August 1999 v Leicester City (sub), League

Appearances: 204   **Goals:** 112

Honours won with Arsenal: Premiership championship 2002; FA Cup winner 2002, 2003;
46 France caps

Thierry Henry is another who has prospered at Highbury after arriving from Serie A.
The £11 million signing had been a left winger with Monaco and Juventus, but Arsène
Wenger converted him into a striker and he has finished top scorer in each of his four
seasons at Highbury. He was Premiership top scorer in 2001-02 too. An eye-catching
forward of pace and breathtaking skill, he rarely scores mundane goals. His trademark
strike is the dart from the left flank to finish with his right foot. He is also a dead ball
expert from the left side. Henry is Arsenal's all-time leading scorer in Europe. His form
for the Gunners earned him a recall for France and he is now a fixture in the national
side. He was voted Man of the Match in the 2003 FA Cup final.

February against Ajax and, at the Amsterdam Arena a week later, coach Ronald
Koeman's defensive tactics afforded Ajax a goalless draw. Arsenal had now won
only once in seven Champions League games and to proceed had to beat Roma
at Highbury and hope that Ajax overcame Valencia in Amsterdam.

After their 2-0 win over Charlton on 2 March Arsenal were eight points
ahead and clear favourites to lift the Premiership title. In the FA Cup quarter-
final against Chelsea at Highbury on 8 March, although Cudicini saved a
first-half penalty from Henry, the French marksman controlled and turned in
one movement just on half-time to mesmerize the keeper and roll the ball
into the unguarded net for a 2-1 lead, after Jeffers had opened Arsenal's
account eight minutes earlier. A late strike from Frank Lampard made the
final score 2-2. In the replay at Stamford Bridge two weeks later John Terry
deflected a Vieira cross into his own net in the 25th minute. Cygan was sent
off but Wiltord scored the second two minutes later. A Lauren left-foot shot
with eight minutes to go gave the Gunners a 3-1 win and a semi-final place.

In March, Arsenal's European ambitions were again ended. On 11 March
a Vieira header early on gave Arsenal the lead at Highbury but, although
playmaker Francesco Totti was sent off in the 23rd minute, they conceded a
Cassano goal from a defence-splitting through ball from Emerson just before
half-time. Montella missed a clear chance for Roma by heading over the bar

at the death. In the Mestalla Stadium the following week, during the city's ear-splitting Festival of Fireworks, Valencia went ahead through a John Carew shot past Stuart Taylor in the first half, although Henry took advantage of a Pires pass after half-time to equalize with a curling shot into the far corner of the net. Carew scored again with a header in the second half and the game ended 2-1. A mediocre performance from a nervous and plainly dispirited Arsenal defence saw them lose 2-0 to Blackburn in the next league match, although a 2-1 win over Everton kept them two points ahead in the Premiership at the end of the month.

April began with a Toure own goal cancelling out an earlier Ljungberg strike in the 1-1 draw at Villa Park and they faced Manchester United at Highbury in the middle of the month. Now three points behind United before the game, although one goal ahead on goal difference and a game in hand, this was a game the Gunners had to win. Van Nistelrooy shot over Stuart Taylor in the 23rd minute and the ball ricocheted off Henry's leg to level the score early in the second half. The Frenchman slipped the offside trap to put Arsenal ahead in the 59th minute but a minute later sloppy defending by Arsenal allowed Giggs to equalize with a header. The score remained 2-2 and the championship race was now wide open.

Three days earlier in the FA Cup semi-final against Sheffield United Ljungberg put Arsenal ahead in the first half. With eight minutes to go Seaman produced a gravity-defying save from Paul Peschisolido, reminiscent of Gordon Banks's save against Pele in the 1970 World Cup finals, and the Gunners progressed to the Cup final. Henry scored his 30th goal of the season in the league match at the Riverside and Wiltord added a second in the 2-0 defeat of Middlesbrough on 19 April and they met relegation-threatened Bolton a week later at the Reebok Stadium desperately needing a win to keep in touch with leaders Manchester United.

Title Dreams Shattered

Arsenal's season, which promised so much less than two months previously, was now on a knife edge. The Gunners were 2-0 ahead – through Wiltord and Pires – early in the second half. However, French international striker Youri Djorkaeff struck a well-taken poacher's goal and then sent in a free kick which deflected off Keown's head into the net. The final score was 2-2 and a dejected Arsenal were now five points behind Manchester United with three games remaining in the title race. To stay in with a chance they had to beat Leeds at Highbury and hope that Manchester United would at least be held by Charlton the same day. Harry Kewell put Leeds ahead in the fifth

Great Managers – 1996- present

ARSENE WENGER

'Who?' was the question on many fans' lips when the tall studious-looking figure of Arsène Wenger was unveiled as the new Arsenal manager in September 1996. Little known to British football fans, the urbane Frenchman was nonetheless regarded as one of the finest coaches in the world, and he was to turn Arsenal into one of the most successful and exciting teams in British football. Wenger's acute tactical understanding, his emphasis on the correct diet and training techniques and his perceptive forays into the transfer market – including the acquisitions of Patrick Vieira, Emmanuel Petit, Nicolas Anelka and Marc Overmars – brought him the 'Double' in 1997-98. Wenger's methods, and his ability to balance domestic and foreign players and extend the playing careers of such stalwarts as Tony Adams and Ray Parlour, were turning Arsenal into the only English team capable of mounting an effective and prolonged challenge to Manchester United.

In 2001-02, playing some of the best football ever seen from an English side and bolstered by the stunning displays of Robert Pires, Thierry Henry and Freddie Ljungberg, Wenger's side again collected the 'Double', securing the league title at Old Trafford and winning the FA Cup with goals from Parlour and Ljungberg in the 2-0 defeat of Chelsea. In spite of a breathtaking start to season 2002-03, Wenger's side inexplicably fell away in the League but won the FA Cup beating Southampton in the final. Wenger commands total respect from the players, board and fans at Highbury, with the only question mark being Arsenal's poor record in Europe. But no doubt, as season 2003-04 approaches, he has already calculated how best to secure victory in the Champions League. After all, 'Arsène knows'.

minute with a ferocious left-foot shot from the edge of the box but Henry headed in a rebound from a Parlour effort 25 minutes later. Ian Harte's free kick restored Leeds's advantage just after half-time and Bergkamp equalized, converting a Pires pass in the 63rd minute. Young substitute Jermaine Pennant came on with 15 minutes remaining and, with two minutes of the game to go, Pennant lost the ball which made its way up to Mark Viduka, who won the game for Leeds with a blistering shot from the edge of the box.

Arsenal now had lost any chance of catching Manchester United, who had won anyway. Over the last two months, Arsenal's nervy and disorganized

Thierry Henry, the gifted Frenchman whose attacking flair lit up Arsenal's foward line and earned him the PFA Footballer of the Year award in 2003.

defending, owing much to the absence of Campbell and/or Keown, their rash of suspensions and injuries and the absence of a conventional, goal-poaching centre forward had terminally damaged their title aspirations.

They won their last two games – 6-1 against Southampton, with Pires and Pennant claiming hat-tricks and 4-0 against Sunderland, the goals coming from newly-crowned PFA Footballer of the Year Henry and a hat-trick from Ljungberg – and met Southampton in the FA Cup final on 17 May. A defensive Southampton were outplayed and Pires scored the only goal of the match, turning in a blocked Ljungberg shot in the 38th minute. Arsenal had retained the FA Cup but for many of the fans it was not sufficient compensation for a season which had begun so thrillingly but which had ended in such disappointment in the Premiership and in Europe.

It is conceivable that, if he stays at the club, Wenger will take over from the legendary Herbert Chapman as the greatest manager in Arsenal's history. His achievements to date at Highbury have been remarkable, including two 'Doubles' and the acquisition and fostering of such stellar talents as Henry, Pires and Vieira. Personally, he symbolizes the 'new' Arsenal – sophisticated, thoughtful, international in outlook and dedicated to football as a joyful spectacle. The development of the Ashburton Grove site – although recently escalating in cost and with uncertainty surrounding its conclusion – will eventually provide him and the club with the stage and the financing necessary in today's climate for domestic and ultimately European success. The days of 'clean sheets' and 'boring Arsenal' are, thankfully, long gone and Arsenal can now compete with the finest clubs in the world. One hundred and seventeen years after their humble origins as a factory team in southeast London, the Arsenal story continues.

THE ESSENTIAL HISTORY OF
ARSENAL

CLUB STATISTICS

The Arsenal Directory

Origins

- The club was formed in 1886 by munitions workers at Woolwich Arsenal – Scotsman David Danskin, his friends Jack Humble, Elijah Watkins and Richard Pearce, and two former Nottingham Forest players, Fred Beardsley and Morris Bates. Humble later became the 'historian' of the club's early years. The team were first known as Dial Square, after one of the workshops at the Arsenal. They played their first match, against Eastern Wanderers, on December 11, 1886. They changed their name to Royal Arsenal at a meeting on Christmas Day that year. Their first kit was a set of 11 red jerseys supplied by Beardsley and Bates's old club, Forest. Royal Arsenal became the first southern club to turn professional and the first to enter the Football League – as Woolwich Arsenal – in 1893.

Honours

- Champions: 1931, 1933, 1934, 1935, 1938, 1948, 1953, 1971, 1989, 1991, 1998, 2002
- FA Cup winners: 1930, 1936, 1950, 1971, 1979, 1993, 1998, 2002, 2003
- Football League Cup winners: 1987, 1993
- Fairs Cup winners: 1970
- European Cup-Winners' Cup winners: 1994

League and Premiership Record

- Division Two (old) 1893-1904
- Division One (old) 1904-1913
- Division Two (old) 1913-1919
- Division One (old) 1919-1992
- FA Premier League 1992-

Club Information

- Arsenal Stadium, Avenell Road, Highbury, London N5 1BU
- Telephone: 020 7704 4000
  Fax: 020 7704 4001
- Box office enquiries: 020 7704 4040
- Recorded ticket information: 020 7704 4242
- Commercial department: 020 7704 4100
- Website: www.arsenal.com
- Ground capacity: 38,200
- Year formed: 1886
- Turned professional: 1891
- Club nickname: The Gunners
- Previous grounds: 1886 Plumstead Common; 1887 The Sportsman Ground, Plumstead; 1888 The Manor Ground, Plumstead; 1890 The Invicta Ground, Plumstead; 1893 The Manor Ground, Plumstead
- Colours: Red shirts with white neck and sleeves, white shorts, white socks with red trim
- Change colours: Blue and light blue shirts with dark blue sleeves, dark blue shorts and socks

Managers

T.B. (Thomas) Mitchell (1897-98)

George Elcoat (1898-99)

Harry Bradshaw (1899-1904)

Phil Kelso (1904-08)

George Morrell (1908-15)

Leslie Knighton (1919-25)

Herbert Chapman (1925-34)

George Allison (1934-47)

Tom Whittaker (1947-56)

Jack Crayston (1956-58)

George Swindin (1958-62)

Billy Wright (1962-66)

Bertie Mee (1966-76)

Terry Neill (1978-83)

Don Howe (1984-86)

George Graham (1986-95)

Stewart Houston (caretaker 1995)

Bruce Rioch (1995-96)

Stewart Houston (caretaker 1996)

Arsène Wenger (1996-)

Records

- Biggest league win: 12-0 v Loughborough Town, Division 2, 12 March 1900
- Record points total (2 pts for a win): 66 from 42 matches, Division 1, 1930-31
- Record points total (3 pts for a win): 87 from 38 matches, Premiership, 2001-02
- Most league goals scored: 127 in 42 matches, Division 1, 1930-31
- Fewest goals conceded: 17 in 38 matches, Premiershhip, 1998-99

- Fewest league defeats: 1 in 38 matches, Division 1, 1990-91
- Most appearances (League, FA Cup, League Cup and Europe): David O'Leary, 719, 1975-93
- Most goals (League, FA Cup, League Cup and Europe): Ian Wright, 184, 1991-98
- Most league goals: Cliff Bastin, 150, 1929-46
- Most league goals in a season: Ted Drake, 42, 1934-35
- Most league goals in a match: Ted Drake, 7, v Aston Villa (a), 14 December 1935
- Most European goals: Thierry Henry, 26, 1999-
- Most international appearances as an Arsenal player: Kenny Sansom, 77 (of 86) for England, 1980-88
- Record attendance at Highbury: 73,295 v Sunderland (League), 9 March 1935
- Record attendance at Wembley: 73,707 v Lens (Champions League), 25 November 1998

Above left: Cliff Bastin, who scored the most league goals with 150. Above: Ian Wright who is the leading goalscorer with 184.

50 Greatest Players

This list is not intended to be definitive. Not many fans would agree on exactly the same choice of the greatest players ever to have donned an Arsenal shirt. The 50 listed here are our choices, taking into consideration their respective performances, their achievements as players and their dedication to the club. Whether or not you agree with our selection, it shows what a great variety of incredible talent has represented Arsenal Football Club over the years. Substitute appearances have been included in appearances total.

No. 1 Alex James (Inside left) – 259 appearances, 27 goals. (Above) The legendary Scot in the baggy shorts was the midfield general behind the Gunners' dominance in the 1930s (see page 37).
No. 2 Joe Mercer (Left half) – 273 appearances, 2 goals. The greatest skipper in Gunners' history, he led them to two championships and two FA Cup finals in six seasons (see page 70).
No. 3 Cliff Bastin (Outside left) – 392 appearances, 176 goals. 'Boy' Bastin won every major honour before his 20th birthday and held Arsenal's scoring record for nearly 60 years (see page 58).
No. 4 Ted Drake (Centre forward) – 182 appearances, 136 goals. Still holds the Gunners' record for the most league goals in a season and scored seven in one game against Aston Villa (see page 49).

No. 5 David O'Leary (Centre back) – 719 appearances, 14 goals. The cultured Irish central defender set a club appearance record during a 20-year career at Highbury (see page 152).
No. 6 Tony Adams (Centre back) – 665 appearances, 48 goals. Another inspiring captain, the rugged defender lifted more trophies than any other Arsenal skipper (see page 178).
No. 7 Eddie Hapgood (Left back) – 434 appearances, 2 goals. The most constructive full back of his time, a top-class defender and captain (see page 52).
No. 8 Liam Brady (Midfielder) – 306 appearances, 59 goals. 'Chippy' Brady was a playmaker with a left foot that could unpick the best defences in Europe (see page 119).
No. 9 Frank McLintock (Centre back) – 403 appearances, 32 goals. Switched from midfield to become a rock in defence and inspirational 'Double' team skipper (see page 101).
No. 10 Ian Wright (Striker) – 287 appearances, 184 goals. Arsenal's all-time top scorer, who led the goal charts in six of his seven seasons at Highbury (see page 163).
No. 11 Joe Hulme (Outside right) – 372 appearances, 124 goals. The fastest winger of his time and a prolific scorer for Herbert Chapman's Gunners (see page 46).
No. 12 David Jack (Inside right) – 206 appearances, 123 goals. Classy dribbler and deadly finisher who won three title medals (see page 32).
No. 13 George Armstrong (Winger) – 621 appearances, 68 goals. A bundle of energy who gave Arsenal 16 years of service (see page 112).
No. 14 Dennis Bergkamp (Forward) – 314 appearances, 104 goals. A stealthy subtle attacker, the Dutchman created as many goals as he scored (see page 183).
No. 15 Charlie Buchan (Inside right) – 120 appearances, 56 goals. Arsenal's first genuine superstar, and skipper in their first Wembley final (see page 27).
No. 16 Charlie George (Striker/Midfielder) – 179 appearances, 49 goals. Local boy who scored the Wembley winner that clinched the 1971 'Double' (see page 109).

No. 17 Jimmy Logie (Inside forward) – 326 appearances, 76 goals. Subtle Scottish playmaker, the brains of Tom Whittaker's successful Gunners (see page 77).

No. 18 Jack Kelsey (Goalkeeper) – 351 appearances. Britain's top keeper and Arsenal's star during the difficult days of the late 1950s (see page 76).

No. 19 Patrick Vieira (Midfielder) – 315 appearances, 23 goals. The driving force behind the Gunners' two 'Doubles' under Arsène Wenger (see page 185).

No. 20 David Seaman (Goalkeeper) – 560 appearances. Made more club appearances and won more honours than any other Arsenal keeper (see page 188).

No. 21 Thierry Henry (Striker) – 204 appearances, 112 goals. Pacy, imaginative France striker who specialises in scoring spectacular goals (see page 191).

No. 22 George Male (Right back) – 314 appearances, 0 goals. Tough tackling ex-wing half who partnered Hapgood for club and country (see page 62).

No. 23 Pat Rice (Right back) – 527 appearances, 13 goals. Determined defender who spanned two successful teams and played in six cup finals (see page 120).

No. 24 Jack Crayston (Right half) – 184 appearances, 17 goals. Elegant creative wing half and one of the earliest long throw experts (see page 55).

No. 25 John Radford (Striker) – 481 appearances, 149 goals. Determined striker, powerful in the air and third in Arsenal's all-time scorers list (see page 111).

No. 26 Les Compton (Defender) – 270 appearances, 6 goals. Pre-war full back, then rock-solid centre half for Whittaker's postwar team (see page 63).

No. 27 David Rocastle (Midfielder) – 275 appearances, 34 goals. Skilful, committed right-side midfielder who became a fans' favourite (see page 146).

No. 28 George Swindin (Goalkeeper) – 294 appearances. A consistently reliable keeper throughout an 18-year Arsenal career (see page 75).

No. 29 Tom Parker (Right back) – 292 appearances, 17 goals. Classy full back who skippered Gunners to their first cup and league honours (see page 33).

No. 30 Reg Lewis (Forward) – 175 appearances, 116 goals. Two-goal hero against Liverpool in the 1950 FA Cup final (see page 68).

No. 31 George Eastham (Midfielder) – 223 appearances, 41 goals. Frail but cultured inside forward playmaker of the early 1960s (see page 78).

No. 32 Lee Dixon (Right back) – 614 appearances, 28 goals. Gritty, pacy defender who was first choice for 13 seasons (see page 174).

No. 33 Michael Thomas (Midfielder/right back) – 206 appearances, 30 goals. Always to be remembered for his 1989 title winner at Anfield (see page 139).

No. 34 Jimmy Brain (Centre forward) – 231 appearances, 139 goals. Arsenal's record-breaking striker of the 1920s (see page 30).

No. 35 Martin Keown (Centre back) – 430 appearances, 8 goals. A quality defender during two spells with the Gunners (see page 181).

No. 36 Ray Kennedy (Striker) – 212 appearances, 71 goals. A hero of the 1970 Fairs Cup victory and top scorer in the 1971 'Double' season (see page 104).

No. 37 Alan Smith (Striker) – 345 appearances, 115 goals. Brilliant target man and Golden Boot winner in 1989 and 1991 (see page 159).

No. 38 Robert Pires (Midfielder) – 138 appearances, 37 goals. Wide midfielder with vision and an exceptional eye for goals (see page 189).

No. 39 Jack Lambert (Centre forward) – 159 appearances, 109 goals. Set a club scoring record in the 1931 title season (see page 35).

No. 40 Wilf Copping (Left half) – 185 appearances, 0 goals. A teak-tough defensive wing half and man marker of the 1930s (see page 50).

No. 41 Herbie Roberts (Centre half) – 333 appearances, 5 goals. The leading 'policeman' centre half of the late 1920s and early 30s (see page 38).

No. 42 Bob Wilson (Goalkeeper) – 308 appearances. Brave and consistent keeper for Bertie Mee's 'Double' winners (see page 103).

No. 43 Joe Baker (Centre forward) – 156 appearances, 100 goals. Arsenal's most prolific scorer of the early 1960s (see page 79).

No. 44 Graham Rix (Midfielder) – 463 appearances, 51 goals. Creative stalwart on the left of midfield for a decade (see page 137).

No. 45 Kenny Sansom (Left back) – 394 appearances, 6 goals. Won more England caps with Arsenal than any other player (see page 136).

No. 46 Frank Stapleton (Striker) – 299 appearances, 108 goals. One of the Gunners' finest all-round strikers (see page 122).

No. 47 Pat Jennings (Goalkeeper) – 326 appearances. Built a new career with Arsenal after Spurs thought he was over the hill (see page 126).

No. 48 Peter Simpson (Centre back) – 477 appearances, 15 goals. Composed defender at the heart of the 1971 'Double' team (see page 117).

No. 49 Paul Merson (Forward/Midfielder) – 422 appearances, 99 goals. Versatile attacker who blossomed under George Graham (see page 161).

No. 50 Paul Davis (Midfielder) – 445 appearances, 37 goals. Left-footed playmaker who served the Gunners for 15 years (see page 156)

Results and Tables 1889-2003

The following pages include details of every official match played by Arsenal, starting with the early FA Cup matches from 1889. From 1893-94 each season has its own page and is dated at the top. The opponents played at home are written in capital letters and appear in upper and lower case for away games. The date of the match, the score, Arsenal goalscorers and the match attendance are also included. Full league and cup appearances and the goalscorers are featured separately. The final league table is included at the bottom of each page as well as a Fact File which notes particularly interesting facts and figures for the season as well as any notable transfers etc.

The results of matches played during the war years, 1915-18 and 1939-45, are not included. During these years the official Football League programme was suspended.

Key: S – Supplementary round; QR – Qualifying round; Rd – round; R – replay; 2R – second replay; L – leg; 1L – first leg; F – final; SF – semi-final; SF/1L – semi-final first leg; QF – quarter-final; P – phase; Gp – group

Season 1889-90

Arsenal first competed in the FA Cup – as Royal Arsenal – in the 1889-90 season, four years before the club entered the Football League.

FA Cup

DATE	OPPONENTS	SCORE	GOALSCORERS	ATTENDANCE
Oct 5	LYNDHURST	(QR1) W 11-0	Barbour 3, Scott 3, Meggs 2, Robertson 2, Horsington	2,000
Oct 26	Thorpe*	(QR2) D 2-2	Barbour, Connolly	1,000
Nov 16	CRUSADERS	(QR3) W 5-2	Robertson 2, Scott, Connolly, Meggs	4,500
Dec 7	SWIFTS	(QR4) L 1-5	Meggs	6,000

*Royal Arsenal progressed to the third qualifying round after Thorpe withdrew from the competition.

Cup Appearances

PLAYER	CUP COMPETITION FA CUP	TOTAL
Barbour	4	4
Bates	3	3
Beardsley	2	2
Charteris	1	1
Connolly	4	4
Foster	2	2
Horsington	2	2
Howat	4	4
Julian	3	3
McBean	4	4
Meggs	4	4
Offer	2	2
Robertson	4	4
Scott	3	3
Stewart	1	1
Williams E.	1	1

Goalscorers

PLAYER	CUP COMPETITION FA CUP	TOTAL
Barbour	4	4
Meggs	4	4
Robertson H.	4	4
Scott	4	4
Connolly	2	2
Horsington	1	1

Season 1890-91

FA Cup

DATE	OPPONENTS	SCORE	GOALSCORERS	ATTENDANCE
Jan 17	DERBY COUNTY	(Rd1) L 1-2	Offer	8,000

Cup Appearances

PLAYER	CUP COMPETITION FA CUP	TOTAL
Barbour	1	1
Bee	1	1
Christmas	1	1
Connolly	1	1
Gloak	1	1
Howat	1	1
Julian	1	1
McBean	1	1
Meggs	1	1
Offer	1	1
Stewart	1	1

Goalscorers

PLAYER	CUP COMPETITION FA CUP	TOTAL
Offer	1	1

Season 1891-92

FA Cup

DATE	OPPONENTS	SCORE	GOALSCORERS	ATTENDANCE
Jan 16	Small Heath	(Rd1) L 1-5	Davie	4,000

Cup Appearances

PLAYER	CUP COMPETITION FA CUP	TOTAL
Bee	1	1
Buist	1	1
Connolly	1	1
Crawford	1	1
Davie	1	1
Graham	1	1
Howat	1	1
McBean	1	1
Peachey	1	1
Robertson	1	1
Shaw	1	1

Goalscorers

PLAYER	CUP COMPETITION FA CUP	TOTAL
Davie	1	1

Season 1892-93

FA Cup

DATE	OPPONENTS	SCORE	GOALSCORERS	ATTENDANCE
Oct 15	HIGHLAND LIGHT INFANTRY	(QR1) W 3-0	Elliott, Davie, Booth	5,000
Oct 29	CITY RAMBLERS	(QR2) W10-1	Henderson 3, Booth 3, Elliott 3, Davie	4,000
Nov 19	MILLWALL ATHLETIC	(QR3) W 3-2	Howat, Henderson, o.g.	12,000
Dec 10	CLAPTON	(QR4) W 3-0	Henderson, Booth, Crawford	4,000
Jan 21	SUNDERLAND	(Rd1) L 0-6		4,500

Cup Appearances

PLAYER	CUP COMPETITION FA CUP	TOTAL
Ambler	1	1
Bee	2	2
Booth	5	5
Buist	5	5
Crawford	2	2
Davie	3	3
Devine	1	1
Dyer	5	5
Elliott	5	5
Gemmell	3	3
Henderson	5	5
Howat	5	5
Jeffrey	5	5
McQuilkie	2	2
Powell	1	1
Rankin	3	3
Williams	1	1
Wood	1	1

Goalscorers

PLAYER	CUP COMPETITION FA CUP	TOTAL
Booth	5	5
Henderson	5	5
Elliott	4	4
Davie	2	2
Crawford	1	1
Howat	1	1
Opps' o.gs.	1	1

Season 1893-94

Football League Division Two

DATE	OPPONENTS	SCORE	GOALSCORERS	ATTENDANCE
Sep 2	NEWCASTLE UNITED	D 2-2	Shaw, Elliott	10,000
Sep 9	Notts County	L 2-3	Elliott, Shaw	7,000
Sep 11	WALSALL TOWN SWIFTS	W 4-0	Heath 3, Crawford	4,000
Sep 25	GRIMSBY TOWN	W 3-1	Elliott, Heath, Booth	2,000
Sep 30	Newcastle United	L 0-6		2,000
Oct 21	Small Heath	L 1-4	Henderson	3,000
Oct 28	LIVERPOOL	L 0-5		9,000
Nov 11	ARDWICK	W 1-0	Henderson	4,500
Nov 13	ROTHERHAM TOWN	W 3-0	Shaw 2, Elliott	3,000
Nov 18	Burton Swifts	L 2-6	Elliott, Shaw	1,500
Dec 9	Northwich Victoria	D 2-2	Shaw, Boyle	1,500
Dec 25	BURSLEM PORT VALE	W 4-1	Shaw, Booth, Henderson, Crawford	10,000
Dec 26	Grimsby Town	L 1-3	Buist (pen)	3,000
Dec 30	Ardwick	W 1-0	Henderson	4,000
Jan 1	Liverpool	L 0-2		5,000
Jan 6	Burslem Port Vale	L 1-2	Elliott	900
Feb 3	Lincoln City	L 0-3		2,000
Feb 6	Rotherham Town	D 1-1	Worrall	2,000
Feb 10	CREWE ALEXANDRA	W 3-2	Henderson 3	4,000
Feb 12	Walsall Town Swifts	W 2-1	Henderson, Elliott	2,000
Feb 17	LINCOLN CITY	W 4-0	Elliott 2, Bryan, o.g.	3,000
Feb 24	Middlesbrough Ironopolis	W 6-3	Shaw 3, Henderson 2, Davis	500
Mar 3	Crewe Alexandra	D 0-0		2,000
Mar 10	MIDDLESBROUGH IRONOPOLIS	W 1-0	Shaw	5,000
Mar 23	NORTHWICH VICTORIA	W 6-0	Jacques 2, Henderson 2, Heath, Howat	5,000
Mar 24	NOTTS COUNTY	L 1-2	Crawford	13,000
Mar 31	SMALL HEATH	L 1-4	McNab	6,000
Apr 14	BURTON SWIFTS	L 0-2		2,000

FA Cup

Oct 14	ASHFORD UNITED	(QR1) W 12-0	Elliott 3, Henderson 3, Booth 2, Heath 2, Crawford, Powell	3,000
Nov 4	CLAPTON	(QR2) W 6-2	Henderson 2, Cooper 2, Shaw, Elliott	2,500
Nov 25	MILLWALL	(QR3) W 2-0	Davis, Booth	20,000
Dec 16	2nd Scots Guards	(QR4) W 2-1	Henderson 2	9,000
Jan 27	SHEFFIELD WEDNESDAY	(Rd1) L 1-2	Elliott	15,000

League & Cup Appearances

PLAYER	LEAGUE	CUP COMPETITION FA CUP	TOTAL
Booth	16	5	21
Boyle	10		10
Briggs	2		2
Bryan	9		9
Buist	17	4	21
Burrows	6		6
Cooper	6	2	8
Crawford	21	5	26
Davis	26	5	31
Devine	2	1	3
Elliott	24	5	29
Gemmell	5		5
Heath	8	1	9
Henderson	23	4	27
Howat	27	4	31
Jacques	2		2
Jeffrey	22	4	26
Kirk	1		1
McNab	2		2
Powell	26	4	30
Shaw	17	4	21
Storrs	12	4	16
Williams C.	19	3	22
Williams W.	1		1
Worrall	4		4

Goalscorers

PLAYER	LEAGUE	CUP COMPETITION FA CUP	TOTAL
Henderson	12	7	19
Elliott	10	5	15
Shaw	11	1	12
Heath	4	2	6
Booth	2	3	5
Crawford	3	1	4
Jacques	2		2
Davis	1	1	2
Cooper		2	2
Boyle	1		1
Bryan	1		1
Buist	1		1
Howat	1		1
McNab	1		1
Worrall	1		1
Powell		1	1
Opps' o.gs.	1		1

Fact File

The club returned to their original home, the Manor Ground in Plumstead, for their first season in the Football League. Arsenal refused to pay a 75 per cent rent increase at the Invicta Ground and instead bought the Manor Ground outright for £4,000.

MANAGER: No professional manager
CAPTAIN: Joe Powell
TOP SCORER: James Henderson 19 (12 League)
BIGGEST WIN: 12-0 v Ashford United, 14 October 1893, FA Cup
HIGHEST ATTENDANCE: 20,000 v Millwall Athletic, 25 November 1893, FA Cup
MAJOR TRANSFER IN: Jimmy Boyle from Celtic

Final Division Two Table

		P	W	D	L	F	A	Pts
1	LIVERPOOL	28	22	6	0	77	18	50
2	SMALL HEATH	28	21	0	7	103	44	42
3	NOTTS CO	28	18	3	7	70	31	39
4	NEWCASTLE U	28	15	6	7	66	39	36
5	GRIMSBY T	28	15	2	11	71	58	32
6	BURTON SWIFTS	28	14	3	11	79	61	31
7	BURSLEM PORT VALE	28	13	4	11	66	64	30
8	LINCOLN C	28	11	6	11	59	58	28
9	WOOLWICH ARSENAL	28	12	4	12	52	55	28
10	WALSALL T SWIFTS	28	10	3	15	51	61	23
11	MIDDLESBROUGH I	28	8	4	16	37	72	20
12	CREWE ALEX	28	6	7	15	42	73	19
13	ARDWICK	28	8	2	18	47	71	18
14	ROTHERHAM T	28	6	3	19	44	91	15
15	NORTHWICH V	28	3	3	22	30	98	9

Season 1894-95

Football League Division Two

DATE	OPPONENTS	SCORE	GOALSCORERS	ATTENDANCE
Sep 1	Lincoln City	L 2-5	Heath, Mortimer	2,000
Sep 10	GRIMSBY TOWN	L 1-3	Boyd	4,000
Sep 15	Burton Swifts	L 0-3		3,000
Sep 22	BURY	W 4-2	Boyd 2, Henderson, O'Brien	8,000
Sep 29	MANCHESTER CITY	W 4-2	Boyd 3, Mortimer	5,000
Oct 6	LINCOLN CITY	W 5-2	Boyd 2, Mortimer 2, O'Brien	8,000
Oct 13	Newton Heath	D 3-3	Mortimer 2, Boyd	4,000
Oct 20	Rotherham Town	W 2-1	Boyle, Henderson	2,000
Oct 27	Notts County	D 2-2	Howat, Caldwell	2,000
Nov 3	NOTTS COUNTY	W 2-1	Henderson, O'Brien	11,000
Nov 10	Walsall Town Swifts	L 1-4	Boyle	1,500
Nov 24	Newcastle United	W 4-2	Sharpe, Crawford, O'Brien, Buchanan,	3,000
Dec 8	DARWEN	W 4-0	Mortimer, O'Brien, Henderson, Davis	8,000
Dec 15	Manchester City	L 1-4	Buchanan	5,000
Dec 25	PORT VALE	W 7-0	O'Brien 3, Davis, Buchanan, Sharpe, Henderson	8,000
Dec 26	Grimsby Town	L 2-4	Henderson, O'Brien	5,000
Jan 1	Darwen	L 1-3	Crawford	6,000
Jan 7	Leicester Fosse	L 1-3	Mortimer	3,000
Jan 12	NEWCASTLE UNITED	W 3-2	Buchanan, Meade, Crawford	5,000
Jan 19	Port Vale	W 1-0	Crawford	1,000
Jan 26	BURTON WANDERERS	D 1-1	Henderson	7,000
Feb 9	ROTHERHAM TOWN	D 1-1	Sharpe	3,000
Feb 23	BURTON SWIFTS	W 3-0	Mortimer 2, Buchanan	5,000
Mar 2	Bury	L 0-2		4,000
Mar 9	LEICESTER FOSSE	D 3-3	O'Brien, Sharpe, Mortimer	4,000
Mar 23	Crewe Alexandra	D 0-0		1,000
Mar 30	NEWTON HEATH	W 3-2	Mortimer, Buchanan, Crawford	6,000
Apr 6	CREWE ALEXANDRA	W 7-0	Buchanan 2, Davis, Boyle, O'Brien, Crawford, Hare	4,000
Apr 12	WALSALL TOWN SWIFTS	W 6-1	Hare 2, Mortimer 2, Buchanan, Crawford	6,000
Apr 20	Burton Wanderers	L 1-2	Hare	3,000

FA Cup

DATE	OPPONENTS	SCORE	GOALSCORERS	ATTENDANCE
Feb 2	Bolton Wanderers	(Rd1) L 0-1		7,000

League & Cup Appearances

PLAYER	LEAGUE	CUP COMPETITION FA CUP	TOTAL
Boyd	6		6
Boyle	28	1	29
Buchanan	25	1	26
Burrows	3		3
Caldwell	30	1	31
Crawford	29	1	30
Crozier	1		1
Davis	26	1	27
Hare	6		6
Hatfield	1		1
Heath	2		2
Henderson	15		15
Howat	28	1	29
Meade	3		3
Mortimer	22		22
O'Brien	27	1	28
Powell	27	1	28
Reece	1		1
Sharpe	13	1	14
Shaw	2	1	3
Stevenson	7		7
Storer	28	1	29

Goalscorers

PLAYER	LEAGUE	CUP COMPETITION FA CUP	TOTAL
Mortimer	14		14
O'Brien	11		11
Boyd	9		9
Buchanan	9		9
Crawford	7		7
Henderson	7		7
Hare	4		4
Sharpe	4		4
Boyle	3		3
Davis	3		3
Caldwell	1		1
Heath	1		1
Howat	1		1
Meade	1		1

Fact File

Goalkeeper Harry Storer became the first Woolwich Arsenal player to win representative honours when he played for the Football League against the Scottish League in April 1895. He was also a county cricketer for Derbyshire.

MANAGER: No professional manager

CAPTAIN: Joe Powell

TOP SCORER: Peter Mortimer 14 (all League)

BIGGEST WIN: 7-0 v Port Vale, 25 December 1894, League; 7-0 v Crewe Alexandra, 6 April 1895, League

HIGHEST ATTENDANCE: 11,000 v Notts County, 3 November 1894, League

MAJOR TRANSFERS IN: Harry Storer from Loughborough Town, Peter Mortimer from Leith Athletic, Henry Boyd from West Bromwich Albion

Final Division Two Table

		P	W	D	L	F	A	Pts
1	BURY	30	23	2	5	78	33	48
2	NOTTS CO	30	17	5	8	75	45	39
3	NEWTON HEATH	30	15	8	7	78	44	38
4	LEICESTER FOSSE	30	15	8	7	72	53	38
5	GRIMSBY T	30	18	1	11	79	52	37
6	DARWEN	30	16	4	10	74	43	36
7	BURTON W	30	14	7	9	67	39	35
8	WOOLWICH ARSENAL	30	14	6	10	75	58	34
9	MANCHESTER C	30	14	3	13	82	72	31
10	NEWCASTLE U	30	12	3	15	72	84	27
11	BURTON SWIFTS	30	11	3	16	52	74	25
12	ROTHERHAM T	30	11	2	17	55	62	24
13	LINCOLN C	30	10	0	20	52	92	20
14	WALSALL T SWIFTS	30	10	0	20	47	92	20
15	BURSLEM PORT VALE	30	7	4	19	39	77	18
16	CREWE ALEX	30	3	4	23	26	103	10

Season 1895-96

Football League Division Two

DATE	OPPONENTS	SCORE	GOALSCORERS	ATTENDANCE
Sep 2	GRIMSBY TOWN	W 3-1	Jenkyns, O'Brien, Gordon	6,000
Sep 7	MANCHESTER CITY	L 0-1		6,000
Sep 14	Lincoln City	D 1-1	Buchanan	1,200
Sep 21	LINCOLN CITY	W 4-1	Jenkyns, Mills, Gordon, Buchanan	6,000
Sep 28	Manchester City	L 0-1		9,000
Oct 5	ROTHERHAM TOWN	W 5-0	Gordon, Mortimer, Mills, Jenkyns, Buchanan	6,000
Oct 12	BURTON WANDERERS	W 3-0	McAvoy, Gordon, Mortimer	8,000
Oct 19	BURTON SWIFTS	W 5-0	Mortimer 2, Mills, Buchanan, Boyd	8,000
Oct 26	Rotherham Town	L 0-3		2,000
Nov 2	Notts County	W 4-3	Hare, Gordon 2, Boyd	8,000
Nov 9	NEWTON HEATH	W 2-1	Boyle, Hare	9,000
Nov 16	LIVERPOOL	L 0-2		10,000
Nov 30	Newton Heath	L 1-5	Hare	6,000
Dec 7	LEICESTER FOSSE	D 1-1	Boyd	5,000
Dec 14	Burton Wanderers	L 1-4	Boyd	5,000
Dec 21	Burton Swifts	L 2-3	Buchanan, Boyd	2,000
Dec 23	Crewe Alexandra	W 1-0	Boyd	3,000
Dec 25	BURSLEM PORT VALE	W 2-1	Buchanan, Mortimer	2,000
Jan 4	LOUGHBOROUGH TOWN	W 5-0	Boyd 2, Jenkyns, Powell, Buchanan	4,000
Jan 11	Liverpool	L 0-3		7,000
Jan 18	Newcastle United	L 1-3	Jenkyns (pen)	8,000
Jan 25	Leicester Fosse	L 0-1		6,000
Feb 15	Burslem Port Vale	W 2-0	Boyd, Haywood	1,000
Feb 29	Loughborough Town	L 1-2	Boyd	2,000
Mar 7	NOTTS COUNTY	W 2-0	Jenkyns, Haywood	6,000
Mar 14	Darwen	D 1-1	Crawford	3,000
Mar 21	CREWE ALEXANDRA	W 7-0	Boyd 2 (1 pen), Mortimer 3, Haywood, o.g.	5,000
Apr 4	Grimsby Town	D 1-1	Boyd	5,000
Apr 6	NEWCASTLE UNITED	W 2-1	Mortimer, Boyd	14,000
Apr 18	DARWEN	L 1-3	Haywood	4,000

FA Cup

Feb 1	Burnley	(Rd1) L 1-6	O'Brien	6,000

League & Cup Appearances

PLAYER	LEAGUE	CUP COMPETITION FA CUP	TOTAL
Ambler	1		1
Boyd	22	1	23
Boyle	10	1	11
Buchanan	17	1	18
Burrows	1		1
Caldwell	29	1	30
Crawford	27	1	28
Davis	24	1	25
Fairclough	9		9
Gilmer	3		3
Gordon	20		20
Hare	13	1	14
Hatfield	1		1
Haywood	9		9
Howat	1		1
Jenkyns	27		27
McAvoy	11	1	12
Mills	24	1	25
Mortimer	27		27
O'Brien	10	1	11
Powell	25		25
Russell		1	1
Storer	12		12
Ward	7		7

Goalscorers

PLAYER	LEAGUE	CUP COMPETITION FA CUP	TOTAL
Boyd	13		13
Mortimer	9		9
Buchanan	7		7
Gordon	6		6
Jenkyns	6		6
Haywood	4		4
Hare	3		3
Mills	3		3
O'Brien	2	1	3
Boyle	1		1
Crawford	1		1
McAvoy	1		1
Powell	1		1
Opps' o.gs.	1		1

Fact File

Centre half Caesar Llewellyn Jenkyns became the first Woolwich Arsenal player to gain an international cap when he played for Wales against Scotland at Dundee in March 1896.

MANAGER: No professional manager

CAPTAIN: Joe Powell

TOP SCORER: Henry Boyd, 13 (all League)

BIGGEST WIN: 7-0 v Crewe Alexandra, 21 March 1896, League

HIGHEST ATTENDANCE: 14,000 v Newcastle United, 6 April 1896, League

MAJOR TRANSFERS IN: Caesar Llewellyn Jenkyns from Small Heath, Adam Haywood from Swadlincote, Frank McAvoy from Ayr

MAJOR TRANSFER OUT: Harry Storer to Liverpool

Final Division Two Table

		P	W	D	L	F	A	Pts
1	LIVERPOOL	30	22	2	6	106	32	46
2	MANCHESTER C	30	21	4	5	63	38	46
3	GRIMSBY T	30	20	2	8	82	38	42
4	BURTON W	30	19	4	7	69	40	42
5	NEWCASTLE U	30	16	2	12	73	50	34
6	NEWTON HEATH	30	15	3	12	66	57	33
7	WOOLWICH ARSENAL	30	14	4	12	58	42	32
8	LEICESTER FOSSE	30	14	4	12	57	44	32
9	DARWEN	30	12	6	12	72	67	30
10	NOTTS CO	30	12	2	16	57	54	26
11	BURTON SWIFTS	30	10	4	16	39	69	24
12	LOUGHBOROUGH	30	9	5	16	40	66	23
13	LINCOLN C	30	9	4	17	53	75	22
14	BURSLEM PORT VALE	30	7	4	19	43	78	18
15	ROTHERHAM T	30	7	3	20	34	97	17
16	CREWE ALEX	30	5	3	22	30	95	13

Season 1896-97

Football League Division Two

DATE	OPPONENTS	SCORE	GOALSCORERS	ATTENDANCE
Sep 5	Manchester City	D 1-1	Haywood	8,000
Sep 12	WALSALL	D 1-1	Boyd	6,000
Sep 14	Burton Wanderers	W 3-0	O'Brien, Brock, Boyd	1,000
Sep 19	LOUGHBOROUGH TOWN	W 2-0	O'Brien, McAvoy	8,000
Sep 26	NOTTS COUNTY	L 2-3	Meade, McAvoy	9,000
Oct 12	BURTON WANDERERS	W 3-0	Haywood, Boyd 2	1,000
Oct 17	Walsall	L 3-5	Meade, Boyd (pen), Haywood	4,000
Oct 24	GAINSBOROUGH TRINITY	W 6-1	Boyd 2, Brock 2, Haywood, Russell	5,500
Nov 7	Notts County	L 4-7	Brock, Haywood, O'Brien, Boyd	3,000
Nov 14	Small Heath	L 2-5	McAvoy, Brock	3,000
Nov 28	GRIMSBY TOWN	W 4-2	O'Brien 2, Boyd, Brock	6,500
Dec 5	Lincoln City	W 3-2	O'Brien 2, Boyd	2,000
Dec 12	Loughborough Town	L 0-8		500
Dec 19	BLACKPOOL	W 4-2	Crawford 2, Haywood 2	6,000
Dec 25	LINCOLN CITY	W 6-2	O'Brien 2, Boyle, Meade 2, Russell	9,000
Dec 26	Gainsborough Trinity	L 1-4	Brock	3,000
Jan 1	Darwen	L 1-4	Russell	5,000
Jan 4	Blackpool	D 1-1	Brock	1,000
Jan 23	Newcastle United	L 0-2		6,000
Feb 13	Leicester Fosse	L 3-6	O'Brien 2, Haywood	6,000
Feb 20	BURTON SWIFTS	W 3-0	Haywood 2, Caie	5,000
Mar 13	Burton Swifts	W 2-1	Caie 2	1,000
Mar 22	Newton Heath	D 1-1	Brock	3,000
Mar 29	SMALL HEATH	L 2-3	Haywood, McAvoy	2,500
Apr 3	NEWTON HEATH	L 0-2		6,000
Apr 8	Grimsby Town	L 1-3	o.g.	1,000
Apr 16	NEWCASTLE UNITED	W 5-1	Brock, Boyle, O'Brien 2, Caldwell	7,000
Apr 17	LEICESTER FOSSE	W 2-1	Caie, Brock	5,000
Apr 19	DARWEN	W 1-0	O'Brien	8,000
Apr 28	MANCHESTER CITY	L 1-2	Russell	2,000

FA Cup

Dec 12	LEYTON	(QR4)	W 5-0	Meade, McAvoy 2, Duff, Farmer	3,000
Jan 2	CHATHAM	(QR5)	W 4-0	Haywood 2, Boyle, Meade	4,500
Jan 16	Millwall	(QR6)	L 2-4	Boyle, O'Brien	14,000

League & Cup Appearances

PLAYER	LEAGUE	CUP COMPETITION FA CUP	TOTAL
Anderson	12		12
Boyd	12		12
Boylan	11		11
Boyle	13	3	16
Brock	29	2	31
Buist	6		6
Caie	8		8
Caldwell	15		15
Carver	1		1
Cassidy	1		1
Crawford	26	2	28
Davis	20	2	22
Duff		1	1
Fairclough	17	1	18
Farmer	1	1	2
Harding		1	1
Haywood	26	2	28
Heath		1	1
Kane	1		1
Kington		1	1
Leather	8	2	10
McAvoy	18	1	19
McFarlane	5		5
Meade	8	3	11
O'Brien	26	2	28
Powell	8		8
Russell	23	2	25
Shrewsbury	2	3	5
Sinclair	26	2	28
Talbot	5		5
Whitfield	2		2
Wilson		1	1

Goalscorers

PLAYER	LEAGUE	CUP COMPETITION FA CUP	TOTAL
O'Brien	14	1	15
Haywood	11	2	13
Brock	11		11
Boyd	10		10
McAvoy	4	2	6
Meade	4	2	6
Caie	4		4
Russell	4		4
Boyle	2	2	4
Crawford	2		2
Caldwell	1		1
Duff		1	1
Farmer		1	1
Opps' o.gs.	1		1

Fact File

Joe Powell, the skipper in Woolwich Arsenal's first-ever league match, died through contracting blood poisoning and tetanus after breaking his arm in a reserve match against Kettering on 23 November 1896. Woolwich Arsenal suffered their record defeat when they crashed 8-0 in the League at Loughborough Town on 12 December 1896.

MANAGER: No professional manager

CAPTAIN: Joe Powell/Gavin Crawford

TOP SCORER: Paddy O'Brien 15 (14 League)

BIGGEST WIN: 6-1 v Gainsborough Trinity, 24 October 1896, League

HIGHEST ATTENDANCE: 9,000 v Notts County, 26 September 1896, League; 9,000 v Lincoln City, 25 December 1896, League

MAJOR TRANSFERS IN: P.A. Boylan from Greenock Volunteers, Tom Shrewsbury from Darwen

MAJOR TRANSFER OUT: Caesar Llewellyn Jenkyns to Newton Heath

Final Division Two Table

		P	W	D	L	F	A	Pts
1	NOTTS CO	30	19	4	7	92	43	42
2	NEWTON HEATH	30	17	5	8	56	34	39
3	GRIMSBY T	30	17	4	9	66	45	38
4	SMALL HEATH	30	16	5	9	69	47	37
5	NEWCASTLE U	30	17	1	12	56	52	35
6	MANCHESTER C	30	12	8	10	58	50	32
7	GAINSBOROUGH T	30	12	7	11	50	47	31
8	BLACKPOOL	30	13	5	12	59	56	31
9	LEICESTER FOSSE	30	13	4	13	59	57	30
10	WOOLWICH ARSENAL	30	13	4	13	68	70	30
11	DARWEN	30	14	0	16	67	61	28
12	WALSALL	30	11	4	15	54	69	26
13	LOUGHBOROUGH	30	12	1	17	50	64	25
14	BURTON SWIFTS	30	9	6	15	46	61	24
15	BURTON W	30	9	2	19	31	67	20
16	LINCOLN C	30	5	2	23	27	85	12

Season 1897-98

Football League Division Two

DATE	OPPONENTS	SCORE	GOALSCORERS	ATTENDANCE
Sep 1	GRIMSBY TOWN	W 4-1	Monteith, Steven, Farrell, White	6,000
Sep 4	Newcastle United	L 1-4	McGeoch	10,000
Sep 6	Burnley	L 0-5		3,000
Sep 11	LINCOLN CITY	D 2-2	Farrell, McAvoy	8,000
Sep 18	GAINSBOROUGH TRINITY	W 4-0	McGeoch 3, McAvoy	8,000
Sep 25	Manchester City	L 1-4	Brock	7,000
Oct 2	Luton Town	W 2-0	McAvoy, Davis	2,000
Oct 9	LUTON TOWN	W 3-0	Stuart, Brock, Davis	14,000
Oct 16	NEWCASTLE UNITED	D 0-0		12,000
Oct 23	LEICESTER FOSSE	L 0-3		7,000
Nov 6	Walsall	L 2-3	Hannah, Hunt	2,000
Nov 13	WALSALL	W 4-0	McGeoch 3, White	2,000
Nov 27	BLACKPOOL	W 2-1	Hannah, Davis	6,500
Dec 4	Leicester Fosse	L 1-2	Duff	3,000
Dec 18	Loughborough Town	W 3-1	Brock, Hannah, White	2,000
Dec 27	Lincoln City	W 3-2	Hunt 2, Brock	4,000
Jan 1	Blackpool	D 3-3	Devlin, 2 o.gs.	1,500
Jan 8	NEWTON HEATH	W 5-1	Hunt, Anderson, White, Brock, Hannah	8,000
Jan 15	Burton Swifts	W 2-1	Haywood, Hannah	2,000
Feb 5	MANCHESTER CITY	D 2-2	Davis, Brock	8,000
Feb 12	Grimsby Town	W 4-1	Hunt 2 (1 pen), Hannah 2	3,500
Feb 26	Newton Heath	L 1-5	Hunt	8,000
Mar 5	SMALL HEATH	W 4-2	Hannah 3 (1 pen), White	8,000
Mar 12	Darwen	W 4-1	White, Hunt, Brock, McGeoch	5,000
Mar 19	LOUGHBOROUGH TOWN	W 4-0	Hunt 2, Haywood, McAuley	5,000
Mar 26	Gainsborough Trinity	L 0-1		1,500
Apr 2	BURNLEY	D 1-1	Hunt	12,000
Apr 9	DARWEN	W 3-1	Brock 2, Haywood	5,000
Apr 11	BURTON SWIFTS	W 3-0	Hannah 2, Haywood	6,000
Apr 23	Small Heath	L 1-2	Hunt	3,000

FA Cup

DATE	OPPONENTS		SCORE	GOALSCORERS	ATTENDANCE
Oct 30	ST ALBANS	(QR3)	W 9-0	Hunt 3, Brock, Haywood, Steven, McGeoch, Davis, Farrell	3,000
Nov 20	SHEPPEY UNITED	(QR4)	W 3-0	Crawford, Haywood, Brock	6,000
Dec 11	NEW BROMPTON	(QR5)	W 4-2	Haywood, McAuley, Crawford, o.g.	5,500
Jan 29	Burnley	(Rd1)	L 1-3	Brock	6,000

League & Cup Appearances

PLAYER	LEAGUE	CUP COMPETITION FA CUP	TOTAL
Anderson	21	2	23
Brock	25	4	29
Caldwell	19	2	21
Clark	3		3
Crawford	19	4	23
Davis	23	3	26
Devlin	1		1
Duff	1		1
Farrell	19	3	22
Hannah	20	3	23
Haywood	26	4	30
Hunt	22	2	24
McAuley	23	4	27
McAvoy	15	1	16
McConnell	17	1	18
McGeoch	9	3	12
Monteith	6		6
Ord	30	4	34
Shrewsbury	1		1
Steven	5	1	6
Stuart	2		2
White	23	3	26

Goalscorers

PLAYER	LEAGUE	CUP COMPETITION FA CUP	TOTAL
Hunt	12	3	15
Hannah	12		12
Brock	9	3	12
McGeoch	8	1	9
Haywood	4	3	7
White	6		6
Davis	4	1	5
McAvoy	3		3
Farrell	2	1	3
McAuley	1	1	2
Steven	1	1	2
Crawford		2	2
Anderson	1		1
Devlin	1		1
Duff	1		1
Monteith	1		1
Stuart	1		1
Opps' o.gs.	2	1	3

Fact File

T.B. (Thomas) Mitchell became Woolwich Arsenal's first professional manager. A Scot from Dumfries, he had made his name as manager of Blackburn Rovers. He resigned in March 1898, after less than a year in charge, probably because of the club's acute financial position.

MANAGER: T.B. Mitchell
CAPTAIN: Gavin Crawford
TOP SCORER: Fergus Hunt 15 (12 League)
BIGGEST WIN: 9-0 v St Albans, 30 October 1897, FA Cup
HIGHEST ATTENDANCE: 14,000 v Luton Town, 9 October 1897, League
MAJOR TRANSFERS IN: Roger Ord from Middlesbrough Ironopolis, David Hannah from Dundee, Fergus Hunt from Darwen
MAJOR TRANSFERS OUT: Paddy O'Brien to Bristol City, P.A. Boylan to Morton, Jimmy Boyle to Dartford

Final Division Two Table

		P	W	D	L	F	A	Pts
1	BURNLEY	30	20	8	2	80	24	48
2	NEWCASTLE UNITED	30	21	3	6	64	32	45
3	MANCHESTER C	30	15	9	6	66	36	39
4	NEWTON HEATH	30	16	6	8	64	35	38
5	WOOLWICH ARSENAL	30	16	5	9	69	49	37
6	SMALL HEATH	30	16	4	10	58	50	36
7	LEICESTER FOSSE	30	13	7	10	46	35	33
8	LUTON T	30	13	4	13	68	50	30
9	GAINSBOROUGH T	30	12	6	12	50	54	30
10	WALSALL	30	12	5	13	58	58	29
11	BLACKPOOL	30	10	5	15	49	61	25
12	GRIMSBY T	30	10	4	16	52	62	24
13	BURTON SWIFTS	30	8	5	17	38	69	21
14	LINCOLN C	30	6	5	19	43	83	17
15	DARWEN	30	6	2	22	31	76	14
16	LOUGHBOROUGH	30	6	2	22	24	87	14

Season 1898-99

Football League Division Two

DATE	OPPONENTS	SCORE	GOALSCORERS	ATTENDANCE
Sep 3	Luton Town	W 1-0	Mitchell	2,000
Sep 5	Burslem Port Vale	L 0-3		5,000
Sep 10	LEICESTER FOSSE	W 4-0	White 2, Hunt 2	6,000
Sep 17	Darwen	W 4-1	Hunt, Dailly, White, Anderson	3,000
Sep 24	GAINSBOROUGH TRINITY	W 5-1	Dailly 2, McGeoch 2, Hunt	7,000
Oct 1	Manchester City	L 1-3	White	6,000
Oct 15	Walsall	L 1-4	Haywood	4,000
Oct 22	BURTON SWIFTS	W 2-1	McGeoch, Hunt (pen)	4,000
Nov 5	SMALL HEATH	W 2-0	White, Hunt	7,000
Nov 12	Loughborough Town	D 0-0		2,500
Nov 26	Grimsby Town	L 0-1		2,000
Dec 3	NEWTON HEATH	W 5-1	White 3, Hannah 2	7,000
Dec 10	New Brighton	L 1-3	White	1,500
Dec 17	LINCOLN CITY	W 4-2	Mitchell, Dailly, McConnell, Hunt	5,000
Dec 24	Barnsley	L 1-2	Hunt	2,000
Dec 31	LUTON TOWN	W 6-2	Haywood 3, Hunt 3	4,000
Jan 7	Leicester Fosse	L 1-2	Haywood	10,000
Jan 14	DARWEN	W 6-0	Haywood, Hannah 2, Shaw, White, Hunt	3,000
Jan 21	Gainsborough Trinity	W 1-0	Haywood	2,000
Feb 4	Glossop North End	L 0-2		2,000
Feb 11	WALSALL	D 0-0		3,000
Feb 13	GLOSSOP NORTH END	W 3-0	Anderson, Hunt, McGeoch	3,000
Feb 18	Burton Swifts	W 2-1	Shaw 2	2,500
Feb 25	BURSLEM PORT VALE	W 1-0	Shaw	6,000
Mar 4	Small Heath	L 1-4	Haywood	3,000
Mar 13	LOUGHBOROUGH TOWN	W 3-1	Cottrell, Shaw, McGeoch	2,000
Mar 18	BLACKPOOL	W 6-0	Cottrell 3, Hunt, Haywood 2	4,000
Mar 22	Blackpool	D 1-1	Cottrell	2,000
Mar 25	GRIMSBY TOWN	D 1-1	Hannah	3,500
Apr 1	Newton Heath	D 2-2	Cottrell, Haywood	5,000
Apr 3	MANCHESTER CITY	L 0-1		5,000
Apr 8	NEW BRIGHTON	W 4-0	Hunt, Cottrell 2, Haywood	3,000
Apr 15	Lincoln City	L 0-2		2,000
Apr 22	BARNSLEY	W 3-0	Shaw 2, Cottrell	4,000

FA Cup

Jan 28	DERBY COUNTY	(Rd1) L 0-6		20,000

League & Cup Appearances

PLAYER	LEAGUE	CUP COMPETITION FA CUP	TOTAL
Anderson	21		21
Brock	3		3
Clark	1		1
Cottrell	18		18
Dailly	8		8
Davis	18	1	19
Dick	30	1	31
Fyfe	7		7
Garton	5		5
Hamilton	1		1
Hannah	26	1	27
Haywood	23	1	24
Hunt	31	1	32
McAvoy	25	1	26
McConnell	20		20
McGeoch	26	1	27
McPhee	7	1	8
Mitchell	10		10
Moir	29	1	30
Ord	33	1	34
Shaw	16	1	17
White	16		16

Goalscorers

PLAYER	LEAGUE	CUP COMPETITION FA CUP	TOTAL
Hunt	15		15
Haywood	12		12
White	10		10
Cottrell	9		9
Shaw	7		7
Hannah	5		5
McGeoch	5		5
Dailly	4		4
Anderson	2		2
Mitchell	2		2
McConnell	1		1

Fact File

New manager George Elcoat also lasted only one season, but he made one major signing for Woolwich Arsenal – wing half John Dick from Airdire. Dick went on to play 284 games in a Woolwich career that lasted until 1910.

MANAGER: George Elcoat

CAPTAIN: John Dick

TOP SCORER: Fergus Hunt 15 (all League)

BIGGEST WIN: 6-0 v Darwen, 14 January 1899, League; 6-0 v Blackpool (H), 18 March 1899, League

HIGHEST ATTENDANCE: 20,000 v Derby County, 28 January 1899, FA Cup

MAJOR TRANSFERS IN: John Dick from Airdrie, Ernie Cottrell from Sheppey United

MAJOR TRANSFER OUT: Frank McAvoy to Brighton United

Final Division Two Table

		P	W	D	L	F	A	Pts
1	MANCHESTER C	34	23	6	5	92	35	52
2	GLOSSOP	34	20	6	8	76	38	46
3	LEICESTER FOSSE	34	18	9	7	64	42	45
4	NEWTON HEATH	34	19	5	10	67	43	43
5	NEW BRIGHTON TOWER	34	18	7	9	71	52	43
6	WALSALL	34	15	12	7	79	36	42
7	WOOLWICH ARSENAL	34	18	5	11	72	41	41
8	SMALL HEATH	34	17	7	10	85	50	41
9	BURSLEM PORT VALE	34	17	5	12	56	34	39
10	GRIMSBY T	34	15	5	14	71	60	35
11	BARNSLEY	34	12	7	15	52	56	31
12	LINCOLN C	34	12	7	15	51	56	31
13	BURTON SWIFTS	34	10	8	16	51	70	28
14	GAINSBOROUGH T	34	10	5	19	56	72	25
15	LUTON T	34	10	3	21	51	95	23
16	BLACKPOOL	34	8	4	22	49	90	20
17	LOUGHBOROUGH	34	6	6	22	38	92	18
18	DARWEN	34	2	5	27	22	141	9

Season 1899-1900

Football League Division Two

DATE	OPPONENTS	SCORE	GOALSCORERS	ATTENDANCE
Sep 2	LEICESTER FOSSE	L 0-2		10,000
Sep 9	Luton Town	W 2-1	Logan, Tennant	3,000
Sep 16	BURSLEM PORT VALE	W 1-0	Sanders	6,000
Sep 23	Walsall	L 0-2		3,000
Sep 30	MIDDLESBROUGH	W 3-0	Shaw 2, McCowie	6,000
Oct 7	Chesterfield	L 1-3	Aston	4,000
Oct 14	GAINSBOROUGH TRINITY	W 2-1	Hartley, Hunt (pen)	6,000
Oct 21	Bolton Wanderers	L 0-1		5,000
Nov 4	Newton Heath	L 0-2		5,000
Nov 11	SHEFFIELD WEDNESDAY	L 1-2	McCowie	7,000
Nov 25	SMALL HEATH	W 3-0	Aston 2, Dick	4,000
Dec 2	New Brighton	W 2-0	McCowie 2	4,000
Dec 16	BURTON SWIFTS	D 1-1	Gaudie	3,000
Dec 25	Lincoln City	L 0-5		6,000
Dec 30	Leicester Fosse	D 0-0		8,500
Jan 6	LUTON TOWN	W 3-1	Gaudie 2, Logan	2,500
Jan 13	Burslem Port Vale	D 1-1	Gaudie	2,000
Jan 20	WALSALL	W 3-1	Logan 2, Gaudie	3,000
Feb 3	Middlesbrough	L 0-1		6,000
Feb 10	CHESTERFIELD	W 2-0	Dick, McCowie	3,000
Feb 17	Gainsborough Trinity	D 1-1	McCowie	1,000
Feb 24	BOLTON WANDERERS	L 0-1		5,500
Mar 3	Loughborough Town	W 3-2	Logan, Gaudie, Tennant	800
Mar 10	NEWTON HEATH	W 2-1	Hunt, Dick	4,000
Mar 12	LOUGHBOROUGH TOWN	W12-0	Gaudie 3, Cottrell 2, Dick 2, Main 2, Tennant 2, Anderson	600
Mar 17	Sheffield Wednesday	L 1-3	McNichol	3,000
Mar 24	LINCOLN CITY	W 2-1	McCowie, Gaudie	2,500
Mar 31	Small Heath	L 1-3	Gaudie	3,000
Apr 7	NEW BRIGHTON	W 5-0	Main, Anderson, Gaudie 2, Logan	2,000
Apr 14	Grimsby Town	L 0-1		2,000
Apr 16	GRIMSBY TOWN	W 2-0	Tennant 2	3,000
Apr 21	Burton Swifts	L 0-2		1,500
Apr 23	Barnsley	L 2-3	Anderson, Lloyd	500
Apr 28	BARNSLEY	W 5-1	Lloyd 2, Gaudie 2, Dick	3,000

FA Cup

Oct 28	NEW BROMPTON	(QR3) D 1-1	Hunt	5,500
Nov 1	New Brompton	(R) D 0-0		2,000
Nov 6	New Brompton*	(2R) D 2-2	Aston, Hunt	2,000
Nov 8	New Brompton**	(3R) D 1-1	Aston	2,000
Nov 14	New Brompton†	(4R) L 0-1		3,000

*Played at Cold Blow Lane. **Played at White Hart Lane. †Played at Gravesend.

League & Cup Appearances

PLAYER	LEAGUE	CUP COMPETITION FA CUP	TOTAL
Anderson	22		22
Aston	11	4	15
Cottrell	1		1
Dick	33	5	38
Dunsbee	8	3	11
Gaudie	25		25
Graham	1		1
Hamilton	6		6
Hannigan	1	1	2
Hartley	5	4	9
Hunt	16	5	21
Jackson	28	5	33
Lloyd	18	1	19
Logan	23	1	24
McCowie	25	5	30
McNichol	30	5	35
Main	8		8
Moir	12	3	15
Murphy	27	5	32
Murrell	6		6
Ord	26	5	31
Sanders	4		4
Shaw	10	3	13
Spicer	2		2
Tennant	26		26

Goalscorers

PLAYER	LEAGUE	CUP COMPETITION FA CUP	TOTAL
Gaudie	15		15
McCowie	7		7
Dick	6		6
Logan	6		6
Tennant	6		6
Aston	3	2	5
Hunt	2	2	4
Anderson	3		3
Lloyd	3		3
Main	3		3
Cottrell	2		2
Shaw	2		2
Hartley	1		1
McNichol	1		1
Sanders	1		1

Fact File

Woolwich Arsenal's 12-0 win over Loughborough Town at the Manor Ground on 12 March remains the club's record league victory. Ironically, Loughborough had inflicted the Gunners' record defeat three seasons earlier.

MANAGER: Harry Bradshaw

CAPTAIN: Jimmy Jackson

TOP SCORER: Ralph Gaudie 15 (all League)

BIGGEST WIN: 12-0 v Loughborough Town, 12 March 1900, League

HIGHEST ATTENDANCE: 10,000 v Leicester Fosse, 2 September 1899, League

MAJOR TRANSFERS IN: Ralph Gaudie from Sheffield United, Paddy Logan from Notts County, Andy McCowie from Liverpool, Jimmy Jackson from Newcastle United

MAJOR TRANSFERS OUT: Alex McConnell to Queens Park Rangers, Archie McGeoch to Dundee

Final Division Two Table

		P	W	D	L	F	A	Pts
1	SHEFFIELD W	34	25	4	5	84	22	54
2	BOLTON W	34	22	8	4	79	25	52
3	BIRMINGHAM	34	20	6	8	78	38	46
4	NEWTON HEATH	34	20	4	10	63	27	44
5	LEICESTER F	34	17	9	8	53	36	43
6	GRIMSBY T	34	17	6	11	67	46	40
7	CHESTERFIELD T	34	16	6	12	65	60	38
8	WOOLWICH ARSENAL	34	16	4	14	61	43	36
9	LINCOLN C	34	14	8	12	46	43	36
10	NEW BRIGHTON T	34	13	9	12	66	58	35
11	BURSLEM PV	34	14	6	14	39	49	34
12	WALSALL	34	12	8	14	50	55	32
13	GAINSBOROUGH T	34	9	7	18	47	75	25
14	MIDDLESBROUGH	34	8	8	18	39	69	24
15	BURTON U	34	9	6	19	43	84	24
16	BARNSLEY	34	8	7	19	46	79	23
17	LUTON T	34	5	8	21	40	75	18
18	LOUGHBOROUGH	34	1	6	27	18	100	8

Season 1900-01

Football League Division Two

DATE	OPPONENTS	SCORE	GOALSCORERS	ATTENDANCE
Sep 1	GAINSBOROUGH TRINITY	W 2-1	Turner, Blackwood	8,000
Sep 8	WALSALL	D 1-1	Anderson J.	7,000
Sep 15	Burton Swifts	L 0-1		1,500
Sep 22	BARNSLEY	L 1-2	Main	7,000
Sep 29	CHESTERFIELD	W 1-0	Main	5,500
Oct 6	Blackpool	D 1-1	Blackwood	1,000
Oct 13	STOCKPORT COUNTY	W 2-0	Dick, Place	5,000
Oct 20	Small Heath	L 1-2	Coles	8,000
Oct 27	GRIMSBY TOWN	D 1-1	Turner	7,000
Nov 3	LEICESTER FOSSE	W 2-1	Blackwood, Gaudie	7,000
Nov 10	NEWTON HEATH	W 2-1	Anderson J., Turner	8,000
Nov 17	Glossop North End	W 1-0	Place	3,000
Nov 24	MIDDLESBROUGH	W 1-0	Blackwood	8,000
Dec 1	Burnley	L 0-3		4,000
Dec 8	BURSLEM PORT VALE	W 3-0	Blackwood, Place 2	7,000
Dec 15	Leicester Fosse	L 0-1		10,000
Dec 22	NEW BRIGHTON	W 2-1	Main, Gaudie	6,000
Dec 24	Walsall	L 0-1		4,000
Dec 29	Gainsborough Trinity	L 0-1		1,500
Jan 12	BURTON SWIFTS	W 3-1	Blackwood, Main, Turner	5,000
Jan 19	Barnsley	L 0-3		2,000
Jan 26	Lincoln City	D 3-3	Gaudie 2, Main	3,000
Feb 16	Stockport County	L 1-3	Turner	3,000
Feb 19	Chesterfield	W 1-0	Gaudie	2,000
Mar 2	Grimsby Town	L 0-1		2,500
Mar 9	LINCOLN CITY	D 0-0		3,000
Mar 16	Newton Heath	L 0-1		5,000
Mar 23	GLOSSOP NORTH END	W 2-0	Place, Tennant	3,000
Mar 30	Middlesbrough	D 1-1	Main	6,000
Apr 6	BURNLEY	W 3-1	Gaudie 2, Coles	4,000
Apr 8	BLACKPOOL	W 3-1	Gaudie, Low, Tennant	5,000
Apr 13	Burslem Port Vale	L 0-1		1,000
Apr 22	SMALL HEATH	W 1-0	Cottrell	3,500
Apr 27	New Brighton	L 0-1		1,500

FA Cup

Jan 5	Darwen	(S) W 2-0	Blackwood, Tennant	5,000
Feb 9	BLACKBURN ROVERS	(Rd1) W 2-0	Tennant, Low	11,000
Feb 23	WEST BROMWICH ALBION	(Rd2) L 0-1		20,000

League & Cup Appearances

PLAYER	LEAGUE	CUP COMPETITION FA CUP	TOTAL
Anderson J.	32	3	35
Ashcroft	32	3	35
Blackwood	17	1	18
Coles	27	3	30
Cottrell	5		5
Cross	3		3
Dick	33	3	36
Gaudie	22	3	25
Grieve	6		6
Jackson	32	3	35
Low	24	2	26
McCowie	3		3
McNichol	30	3	33
Main	20	3	23
Place	25		25
Spicer	2		2
Tennant	25	3	28
Turner	33	3	36
Wolfe	3		3

Goalscorers

PLAYER	LEAGUE	CUP COMPETITION FA CUP	TOTAL
Gaudie	8		8
Blackwood	6	1	7
Main	6		6
Place	5		5
Turner	5		5
Tennant	2	2	4
Anderson J.	2		2
Coles	2		2
Low	1	1	2
Cottrell	1		1
Dick	1		1

Fact File

Harry Bradshaw was considered one of the top managers of the time after his success at Burnley, whom he guided to the Second Division championship and third place in Division One. He would lead Woolwich Arsenal into the First Division in 1904.

MANAGER: Harry Bradshaw

CAPTAIN: Jimmy Jackson

TOP SCORER: Ralph Gaudie 8 (all League)

BIGGEST WIN: 3-0 v Port Vale, 8 December 1900, League

HIGHEST ATTENDANCE: 20,000 v West Bromwich Albion, 23 February 1901, FA Cup

MAJOR TRANSFERS IN: Jimmy Ashcroft from Gravesend United, John Blackwood from Celtic, Peter Turner from St Bernard's, Archie Cross from Dartford

MAJOR TRANSFERS OUT: Andy McCowie to Middlesbrough, Roger Ord to Luton Town, Paddy Logan to Reading

Final Division Two Table

		P	W	D	L	F	A	Pts
1	GRIMSBY T	34	20	9	5	60	33	49
2	BIRMINGHAM	34	19	10	5	57	24	48
3	BURNLEY	34	20	4	10	53	29	44
4	NEW BRIGHTON T	34	17	8	9	57	38	42
5	GLOSSOP	34	15	8	11	51	33	38
6	MIDDLESBROUGH	34	15	7	12	50	40	37
7	WOOLWICH ARSENAL	34	15	6	13	39	35	36
8	LINCOLN C	34	13	7	14	43	39	33
9	BURSLEM PV	34	11	11	12	45	47	33
10	NEWTON HEATH	34	14	4	16	42	38	32
11	LEICESTER F	34	11	10	13	39	37	32
12	BLACKPOOL	34	12	7	15	33	58	31
13	GAINSBOROUGH T	34	10	10	14	45	60	30
14	CHESTERFIELD T	34	9	10	15	46	58	28
15	BARNSLEY	34	11	5	18	47	60	27
16	WALSALL	34	7	13	14	40	56	27
17	STOCKPORT C	34	11	3	20	38	68	25
18	BURTON U	34	8	4	22	34	66	20

Season 1901-02

Football League Division Two

DATE	OPPONENTS	SCORE	GOALSCORERS	ATTENDANCE
Sep 2	BARNSLEY	W 2-1	Foxall, Swann	6,000
Sep 7	LEICESTER FOSSE	W 2-0	Anderson J., Briercliffe	10,000
Sep 14	Preston North End	L 0-2		6,000
Sep 21	BURNLEY	W 4-0	Briercliffe 2, Laidlaw, Foxall	10,000
Sep 28	Port Vale	L 0-1		3,000
Oct 5	CHESTERFIELD	W 3-2	Laidlaw, Anderson J. (pen), Logan	8,000
Oct 12	Gainsborough Trinity	D 2-2	Main, Owens	1,500
Oct 19	MIDDLESBROUGH	L 0-3		8,000
Oct 26	Bristol City	W 3-0	Briercliffe 2, Place	10,500
Nov 9	Stockport County	D 0-0		3,000
Nov 16	NEWTON HEATH	W 2-0	Owens, Briercliffe	5,000
Nov 23	Glossop North End	W 1-0	Foxall	3,000
Nov 30	DONCASTER ROVERS	W 1-0	Swann	10,000
Dec 7	Lincoln City	D 0-0		4,000
Dec 21	BURTON UNITED	L 0-1		4,000
Dec 25	BLACKPOOL	D 0-0		3,500
Dec 26	PORT VALE	W 3-1	Briercliffe, Gooing, Main	5,500
Dec 28	Barnsley	L 0-2		2,000
Jan 4	Leicester Fosse	L 1-2	Gooing	7,000
Jan 11	PRESTON NORTH END	D 0-0		8,000
Jan 18	Burnley	D 0-0		4,000
Feb 1	Chesterfield	W 3-1	Main, Dick, Anderson W.	2,000
Feb 8	GAINSBOROUGH TRINITY	W 5-0	Fitchie 2, Briercliffe 2, Gooing	7,000
Feb 15	Middlesbrough	L 0-1		8,500
Feb 22	BRISTOL CITY	W 2-0	Gooing 2	10,000
Mar 1	Blackpool	W 3-1	Anderson W., Dick, Edgar	3,000
Mar 8	STOCKPORT COUNTY	W 3-0	Gooing, Anderson W. 2	6,000
Mar 15	Newton Heath	W 1-0	Anderson W.	4,000
Mar 22	GLOSSOP NORTH END	W 4-0	Dick, Gooing 2, Briercliffe	6,000
Mar 29	Doncaster Rovers	L 0-1		3,000
Mar 31	WEST BROMWICH ALBION	W 2-1	Gooing, Main	10,000
Apr 5	LINCOLN CITY	W 2-0	Briercliffe, Fitchie	6,000
Apr 12	West Bromwich Albion	L 1-2	Main	8,878
Apr 19	Burton United	L 0-2		3,000

FA Cup

DATE	OPPONENTS		SCORE	GOALSCORERS	ATTENDANCE
Dec 14	LUTON TOWN	(S)	D 1-1	Jackson	10,000
Dec 18	Luton Town	(R)	W 2-0	Gooing, Place	3,000
Jan 25	NEWCASTLE UNITED	(Rd1)	L 0-2		15,000

League & Cup Appearances

PLAYER	LEAGUE	CUP COMPETITION FA CUP	TOTAL
Anderson J.	28	2	30
Anderson W.	13	1	14
Ashcroft	34	3	37
Briercliffe	34	2	36
Coles	32	3	35
Cross	15	2	17
Dick	28	3	31
Edgar	10	1	11
Fitchie	3		3
Foxall	31		31
Gooing	24	3	27
Jackson	33	3	36
Laidlaw	3		3
Logan	5		5
McNichol	20	1	21
Main	28	3	31
Owens	9	2	11
Place	17	3	20
Swann	7		7
Vaughan		1	1

Goalscorers

PLAYER	LEAGUE	CUP COMPETITION FA CUP	TOTAL
Briercliffe	11		11
Gooing	9	1	10
Anderson W.	5		5
Main	5		5
Dick	3		3
Fitchie	3		3
Foxall	3		3
Anderson J.	2		2
Laidlaw	2		2
Owens	2		2
Swann	2		2
Place	1	1	2
Edgar	1		1
Owens	1		1
Jackson		1	1

Fact File

Woolwich Arsenal's fourth place was their best finish yet in the Football League. Their success was based on a solid defence which conceded only 26 goals in 34 games and only nine at home.

MANAGER: Harry Bradshaw

CAPTAIN: Jimmy Jackson

TOP SCORER: Tommy Briercliffe 11 (all League)

BIGGEST WIN: 5-0 v Gainsborough Trinity, 8 February 1902, League

HIGHEST ATTENDANCE: 15,000 v Newcastle United, 25 January 1902, FA Cup

MAJOR TRANSFERS IN: Bill Gooing from Chesterfield, Abraham Foxall from Queens Park Rangers, Tommy Shanks from Brentford

MAJOR TRANSFERS OUT: John Blackwood to Reading, Ernie Cottrell to Watford, Peter Turner to Luton Town

Final Division Two Table

		P	W	D	L	F	A	PTS
1	WEST BROM	34	25	5	4	82	29	55
2	MIDDLESBROUGH	34	23	5	6	90	24	51
3	PRESTON NE	34	18	6	10	71	32	42
4	WOOLWICH ARSENAL	34	18	6	10	50	26	42
5	LINCOLN C	34	14	13	7	45	35	41
6	BRISTOL C	34	17	6	11	52	35	40
7	DONCASTER R	34	13	8	13	49	58	34
8	GLOSSOP	34	10	12	12	36	40	32
9	BURNLEY	34	10	10	14	41	45	30
10	BURTON U	34	11	8	15	46	54	30
11	BARNSLEY	34	12	6	16	51	63	30
12	PORT VALE	34	10	9	15	43	59	29
13	BLACKPOOL	34	11	7	16	40	56	29
14	LEICESTER C	34	12	5	17	38	56	29
15	NEWTON HEATH	34	11	6	17	38	53	28
16	CHESTERFIELD	34	11	6	17	47	68	28
17	STOCKPORT CO	34	8	7	19	36	72	23
18	GAINSBOROUGH T	34	4	11	19	30	80	19

Season 1902-03

Football League Division Two

DATE	OPPONENTS	SCORE	GOALSCORERS	ATTENDANCE
Sep 6	Preston North End	D 2-2	Connor, o.g.	9,000
Sep 13	PORT VALE	W 3-0	Briercliffe, Dick, Coleman	12,000
Sep 20	Barnsley	D 1-1	Coleman	2,000
Sep 27	GAINSBOROUGH TRINITY	W 6-1	Gooing 3, Connor, Coleman, Lawrence	10,000
Oct 4	Bristol City	L 0-1		12,024
Oct 11	BRISTOL CITY	W 2-1	Coleman, Hunt (pen)	16,000
Oct 18	Glossop North End	W 2-1	Coleman 2	1,000
Oct 25	MANCHESTER UNITED	L 0-1		12,000
Nov 1	MANCHESTER CITY	W 1-0	Gooing	12,000
Nov 8	BLACKPOOL	W 2-1	Bradshaw, Lawrence	8,000
Nov 15	Burnley	W 3-0	Anderson W., Gooing, Briercliffe	2,500
Nov 22	Doncaster Rovers	W 1-0	Gooing	5,000
Nov 29	LINCOLN CITY	W 2-1	Coleman, Briercliffe	14,000
Dec 6	Small Heath	L 0-2		10,000
Dec 20	Manchester City	L 1-4	Gooing	25,000
Dec 25	Burton United	L 1-2	Gooing	2,000
Dec 27	BURNLEY	W 5-1	Coleman 3, Briercliffe, Anderson W.	13,000
Jan 1	Stockport County	W 1-0	Gooing	2,000
Jan 3	PRESTON NORTH END	W 3-1	Gooing, Anderson W., Linward	12,000
Jan 10	Port Vale	D 1-1	Briercliffe	4,000
Jan 17	BARNSLEY	W 4-0	Shanks 2, Anderson W., Briercliffe	10,000
Jan 24	Gainsborough Trinity	W 1-0	Anderson W.	3,000
Jan 31	BURTON UNITED	W 3-0	Gooing, Shanks, Coleman	12,000
Feb 14	GLOSSOP NORTH END	D 0-0		10,000
Feb 28	STOCKPORT COUNTY	W 3-1	Lawrence, Coleman, Shanks	8,000
Mar 7	Blackpool	D 0-0		3,000
Mar 9	Manchester United	L 0-3		5,000
Mar 14	Chesterfield	D 2-2	Coleman 2	5,000
Mar 21	DONCASTER ROVERS	W 3-0	Linward, Coleman, o.g.	10,000
Mar 28	Lincoln City	D 2-2	Gooing, Linward	3,000
Apr 4	SMALL HEATH	W 6-1	Coleman 2, Linward 2, Gooing 2	15,000
Apr 10	CHESTERFIELD	W 3-0	Briercliffe, Gooing, o.g.	14,000
Apr 11	Leicester Fosse	W 2-0	Coleman, Gooing	10,000
Apr 13	LEICESTER FOSSE	D 0-0		12,000

FA Cup

Date	Opponent		Score	Goalscorers	Attendance
Dec 13	Brentford	(S)	D 1-1	Gooing	7,500
Dec 17	BRENTFORD	(R)	W 5-0	Coleman 2, Connor, Gooing, Anderson J.	3,000
Feb 7	SHEFFIELD UNITED	(Rd1)	L 1-3	Anderson W.	24,000

League & Cup Appearances

PLAYER	LEAGUE	CUP COMPETITION FA CUP	TOTAL
Anderson J.	8	2	10
Anderson W.	15	1	16
Ashcroft	34	3	37
Bannister	16	1	17
Bradshaw	1		1
Briercliffe	33	2	35
Coles	18	2	20
Coleman	30	3	33
Connor	14	2	16
Cross	14	1	15
Dick	26	3	29
Fitchie	1		1
Gooing	25	3	28
Hunt	3	1	4
Jackson	28	3	31
Lawrence	20	3	23
Linward	14		14
McEachrane	28	1	29
McNichol	21	2	23
Main	7		7
Shanks	14		14
Theobald	2		2
Wolfe	2		2

Goalscorers

PLAYER	LEAGUE	CUP COMPETITION FA CUP	TOTAL
Coleman	17	2	19
Gooing	16	2	18
Briercliffe	8		8
Anderson W.	5	1	6
Linward	5		5
Shanks	4		4
Lawrence	3		3
Connor	2	1	3
Bradshaw	1		1
Dick	1		1
Hunt	1		1
Anderson J.		1	1
Opps' o.gs.	3		3

Fact File

A run of away defeats in December, at Manchester City (champions), Small Heath (promoted) and Burton United, cost Woolwich Arsenal promotion. But their revival under Bradshaw was reflected in increased gates and a record home attendance for the FA Cup tie against Sheffield United.

MANAGER: Harry Bradshaw

CAPTAIN: Jimmy Jackson

TOP SCORER: Tim Coleman 19 (17 League)

BIGGEST WIN: 6-1 v Gainsborough Trinity, 27 September 1902, League; 6-1 v Small Heath, 4 April 1903, League

HIGHEST ATTENDANCE: 24,000 v Sheffield United, 7 February 1903, FA Cup

MAJOR TRANSFERS IN: Roddy McEachrane from West Ham United, Tim Coleman from Northampton Town

MAJOR TRANSFER OUT: John Anderson to Portsmouth, Fergus Hunt to Fulham

Final Division Two Table

		P	W	D	L	F	A	PTS
1	MANCHESTER C	34	25	4	5	95	29	54
2	SMALL HEATH	34	24	3	7	74	36	51
3	WOOLWICH ARSENAL	34	20	8	6	66	30	48
4	BRISTOL C	34	17	8	9	59	38	42
5	MANCHESTER U	34	15	8	11	53	38	38
6	CHESTERFIELD	34	14	9	11	67	40	37
7	PRESTON NE	34	13	10	11	56	40	36
8	BARNSLEY	34	13	8	13	55	51	34
9	PORT VALE	34	13	8	13	57	62	34
10	LINCOLN C	34	12	6	16	46	53	30
11	GLOSSOP	34	11	7	16	43	57	29
12	GAINSBOROUGH T	34	11	7	16	41	59	29
13	BURTON U	34	11	7	16	39	59	29
14	BLACKPOOL	34	9	10	15	44	59	28
15	LEICESTER FOSSE	34	10	8	16	41	65	28
16	DONCASTER R	34	9	7	18	35	72	25
17	STOCKPORT CO	34	7	6	21	38	74	20
18	BURNLEY	34	6	8	20	30	77	20

Season 1903-04

Football League Division Two

DATE	OPPONENTS	SCORE	GOALSCORERS	ATTENDANCE
Sep 5	BLACKPOOL	W 3-0	Gooing 2, Coleman	10,000
Sep 12	Gainsborough Trinity	W 2-0	Coleman 2	3,000
Sep 19	BURTON UNITED	W 8-0	Briercliffe 3, Coleman 2, Gooing, Shanks, Linward	12,000
Sep 26	Bristol City	W 4-0	Gooing 2, Coleman, Linward	14,000
Oct 3	MANCHESTER UNITED	W 4-0	Shanks, Coleman, Busby, Briercliffe	20,000
Oct 10	Glossop North End	W 3-1	Gooing 2, Coleman	1,000
Oct 24	Port Vale	W 3-2	Briercliffe, Shanks, Gooing	3,000
Oct 26	LEICESTER FOSSE	W 8-0	Shanks 3, Pratt 2, Gooing, Briercliffe, Busby	5,000
Oct 31	Barnsley	L 1-2	Briercliffe	6,000
Nov 7	LINCOLN CITY	W 4-0	Shanks 3, Coleman	16,000
Nov 21	CHESTERFIELD	W 6-0	Briercliffe, Shanks 2, Coleman, Linward, Gooing	10,000
Nov 28	Bolton Wanderers	L 1-2	Gooing	6,000
Dec 19	GRIMSBY TOWN	W 5-1	Shanks 4, Coleman	14,000
Dec 25	BRADFORD CITY	W 4-1	Shanks, Sands, Coleman 2	18,000
Dec 26	Leicester City	D 0-0		14,000
Jan 1	Stockport County	D 0-0		4,000
Jan 2	Blackpool	D 2-2	Shanks, Sands	3,000
Jan 9	GAINSBOROUGH TRINITY	W 6-0	Sands, Briercliffe, Gooing 2, Shanks, Coleman	10,000
Jan 16	Burton United	L 1-3	Briercliffe	2,500
Jan 30	Manchester United	L 0-1		40,000
Feb 27	BARNSLEY	W 3-0	Gooing, Shanks, Coleman	12,000
Feb 29	BURNLEY	W 4-0	Shanks 3, Gooing	4,000
Mar 5	Lincoln City	W 2-0	Dick, Shanks	5,000
Mar 12	STOCKPORT COUNTY	W 5-2	Coleman 2, Gooing, Linward 2	10,000
Mar 14	BRISTOL CITY	W 2-0	Coleman 2	10,000
Mar 19	Chesterfield	L 0-1		9,000
Mar 26	BOLTON WANDERERS	W 3-0	Gooing 2, Coleman	18,000
Apr 1	Preston North End	D 0-0		12,000
Apr 2	Burnley	L 0-1		5,000
Apr 4	GLOSSOP NORTH END	W 2-1	Coleman, Shanks (pen)	17,000
Apr 9	PRESTON NORTH END	D 0-0		28,000
Apr 16	Grimsby Town	D 2-2	Gooing, Coleman	6,000
Apr 19	Bradford City	W 3-0	Coleman, Bradshaw, Watson	12,000
Apr 25	PORT VALE	D 0-0		20,000

FA Cup

Dec 12	Bristol Rovers	(S) D 1-1	Dick	14,000
Dec 15	BRISTOL ROVERS	(R) D 1-1	o.g.	12,000
Dec 21	Bristol Rovers*	(2R) W 1-0	Briercliffe	10,000
Feb 6	FULHAM	(Rd1) W 1-0	Shanks	15,000
Feb 20	MANCHESTER CITY	(Rd2) L 0-2		30,000

*Played at White Hart Lane.

League & Cup Appearances

PLAYER	LEAGUE	CUP COMPETITION FA CUP	TOTAL
Anderson E.	2		2
Ashcroft	34	5	39
Bannister	2	3	5
Bradshaw	3		3
Briercliffe	27	5	32
Busby	5	1	6
Coleman	28	5	33
Coles	1		1
Cross	25	5	30
Dick	33	5	38
Gooing	34	5	39
Jackson	33	5	38
Linward	27	3	30
McEachrane	33	5	38
Pratt	8	2	10
Ransom	1		1
Sands	32	2	34
Shanks	30	4	34
Thorpe	10		10
Watson	6		6

Goalscorers

PLAYER	LEAGUE	CUP COMPETITION FA CUP	TOTAL
Shanks	24	1	25
Coleman	23		23
Gooing	19		19
Briercliffe	10	1	11
Linward	5		5
Sands	3		3
Busby	2		2
Pratt	2		2
Dick	1	1	2
Bradshaw	1		1
Watson	1		1
Opps' o.gs.		1	1

Fact File

Harry Bradshaw stunned Woolwich Arsenal after leading them to promotion. The club's first successful manager left them after accepting a lucrative offer from Fulham, then in the Southern League. Meanwhile, crowds at the Manor Ground hit new highs during this season. The 30,000 attendance for the FA Cup tie against Manchester City was a club record.

MANAGER: Harry Bradshaw

CAPTAIN: Jimmy Jackson

TOP SCORER: Tommy Shanks 25 (24 League)

BIGGEST WIN: 8-0 v Burton United, 19 September 1903, League; 8-0 v Leicester Fosse, 26 October 1903, League

HIGHEST ATTENDANCE: 30,000 v Manchester City, 20 February 1904, FA Cup

MAJOR TRANSFER IN: Percy Sands from Cheltenham Town

MAJOR TRANSFER OUT: Alex Main to Motherwell

Final Division Two Table

		P	W	D	L	F	A	PTS
1	PRESTON NE	34	20	10	4	62	24	50
2	WOOLWICH ARSENAL	34	21	7	6	91	22	49
3	MANCHESTER U	34	20	8	6	65	33	48
4	BRISTOL C	34	18	6	10	73	41	42
5	BURNLEY	34	15	9	10	50	55	39
6	GRIMSBY T	34	14	8	12	50	49	36
7	BOLTON W	34	12	10	12	59	41	34
8	BARNSLEY	34	11	10	13	38	57	32
9	GAINSBOROUGH T	34	14	3	17	53	60	31
10	BRADFORD C	34	12	7	15	45	59	31
11	CHESTERFIELD	34	11	8	15	37	45	30
12	LINCOLN C	34	11	8	15	41	58	30
13	PORT VALE	34	10	9	15	54	52	29
14	BURTON U	34	11	7	16	45	61	29
15	BLACKPOOL	34	11	5	18	40	67	27
16	STOCKPORT CO	34	8	11	15	40	72	27
17	GLOSSOP	34	10	6	18	57	64	26
18	LEICESTER FOSSE	34	6	10	18	42	82	22

Season 1904-05

Football League Division One

DATE	OPPONENTS	SCORE	GOALSCORERS	ATTENDANCE
Sep 3	Newcastle United	L 0-3		25,000
Sep 10	PRESTON NORTH END	D 0-0		25,000
Sep 17	Middlesbrough	L 0-1		15,000
Sep 24	WOLVERHAMPTON WANDERERS	W 2-0	Satterthwaite, Coleman	20,000
Oct 1	Bury	D 1-1	Briercliffe	8,000
Oct 8	ASTON VILLA	W 1-0	Gooing	32,850
Oct 15	Blackburn Rovers	D 1-1	Satterthwaite	10,000
Oct 22	NOTTINGHAM FOREST	L 0-3		20,000
Oct 29	Sheffield Wednesday	W 3-0	Crowe 2, Coleman	15,000
Nov 5	SUNDERLAND	D 0-0		30,000
Nov 12	STOKE	W 2-1	Crowe, Hunter	20,000
Nov 19	Derby County	D 0-0		12,000
Dec 3	Small Heath	L 1-2	Hunter	20,000
Dec 10	MANCHESTER CITY	W 1-0	Satterthwaite	16,000
Dec 17	Notts County	W 5-1	Fitchie 3, Satterthwaite 2	15,000
Dec 24	SHEFFIELD UNITED	W 1-0	Fitchie	20,000
Dec 26	Aston Villa	L 1-3	Satterthwaite	40,000
Dec 27	Nottingham Forest	W 3-0	Hunter, Briercliffe, Satterthwaite	16,000
Dec 28	Sheffield United	L 0-4		30,000
Dec 31	NEWCASTLE UNITED	L 0-2		30,000
Jan 7	Preston North End	L 0-3		13,000
Jan 14	MIDDLESBROUGH	D 1-1	Fitchie	15,000
Jan 21	Wolverhampton Wanderers	L 1-4	Briercliffe	8,500
Jan 28	BURY	W 2-1	Satterthwaite 2	11,000
Feb 11	BLACKBURN ROVERS	W 2-0	Fitchie, Briercliffe	15,000
Feb 25	SHEFFIELD WEDNESDAY	W 3-0	Satterthwaite, Coleman 2	20,000
Mar 4	Sunderland	D 1-1	Coleman	14,000
Mar 11	Stoke	L 0-2		4,000
Mar 18	DERBY COUNTY	D 0-0		15,000
Apr 1	SMALL HEATH	D 1-1	Hunter	20,000
Apr 5	Everton	L 0-1		12,000
Apr 8	Manchester City	L 0-1		18,000
Apr 15	NOTTS COUNTY	L 1-2	Templeton	12,000
Apr 22	EVERTON	W 2-1	Satterthwaite, Ducat	25,000

FA Cup

Feb 4	BRISTOL CITY	(Rd1)	D 0-0		25,000
Feb 8	Bristol City	(R)	L 0-1		10,000

League & Cup Appearances

PLAYER	LEAGUE	CUP COMPETITION FA CUP	TOTAL
Ashcroft	33	2	35
Bellamy	1		1
Bigden	7		7
Briercliffe	28	2	30
Buchan	8		8
Coleman	26	2	28
Cross	12		12
Crowe	4		4
Davidson	1		1
Dick	33	2	35
Ducat	10		10
Dwight	1		1
Fitchie	9		9
Gooing	11	1	12
Gray	26	2	28
Hunter	22		22
Jackson	29	2	31
Linward	6		6
McEachrane	24	2	26
Neave	3		3
Sands	31	2	33
Satterthwaite	30	2	32
Templeton	16	2	18
Watson	3	1	4

Goalscorers

PLAYER	LEAGUE	CUP COMPETITION FA CUP	TOTAL
Satterthwaite	11		11
Fitchie	6		6
Coleman	5		5
Briercliffe	4		4
Hunter	4		4
Crowe	3		3
Ducat	1		1
Gooing	1		1
Templeton	1		1

Fact File

The new manager was Phil Kelso, previously boss of Hibernian. He made his priority signing forwards who would consolidate Woolwich Arsenal's place in the top division. One of those signings, Charlie Satterthwaite, scored the club's first goal in Division One, against Wolverhampton Wanderers on 24 October, 1904. The visit of Aston Villa on 8 October set a new attendance record for the Manor Ground.

MANAGER: Phil Kelso

CAPTAIN: Jimmy Jackson/John Dick

TOP SCORER: Charlie Satterthwaite 11 (all League)

BIGGEST WIN: 5-1 v Notts County, 17 December 1904, League

HIGHEST ATTENDANCE: 32,850 v Aston Villa, 8 October 1904, League

MAJOR TRANSFERS IN: Charlie Satterthwaite from West Ham United, Bobby Templeton from Newcastle United, Andy Ducat from Southend United, Archie Gray from Hibernian

MAJOR TRANSFERS OUT: Bill Gooing to Northampton Town, Bill Linward to Norwich City, Jimmy Buchan to Hibernian

Final Division One Table

		P	W	D	L	F	A	Pts
1	NEWCASTLE U	34	23	2	9	72	33	48
2	EVERTON	34	21	5	8	63	36	47
3	MANCHESTER C	34	20	6	8	66	37	46
4	ASTON VILLA	34	19	4	11	63	43	42
5	SUNDERLAND	34	16	8	10	60	44	40
6	SHEFFIELD U	34	19	2	13	64	56	40
7	SMALL HEATH	34	17	5	12	54	38	39
8	PRESTON NE	34	13	10	11	42	37	36
9	SHEFFIELD W	34	14	5	15	61	57	33
10	WOOLWICH ARSENAL	34	12	9	13	36	40	33
11	DERBY CO	34	12	8	14	37	48	32
12	STOKE	34	13	4	17	40	58	30
13	BLACKBURN R	34	11	5	18	40	51	27
14	WOLVERHAMPTON W	34	11	4	19	47	73	26
15	MIDDLESBROUGH	34	9	8	17	36	56	26
16	NOTTINGHAM F	34	9	7	18	40	61	25
17	BURY	34	10	4	20	47	67	24
18	NOTTS CO	34	5	8	21	36	69	18

Season 1905-06

Football League Division One

DATE	OPPONENTS	SCORE	GOALSCORERS	ATTENDANCE
Sep 2	LIVERPOOL	W 3-1	Coleman, Satterthwaite, Blair	20,000
Sep 9	Sheffield United	L 1-3	Blair	16,000
Sep 16	NOTTS COUNTY	D 1-1	Fitchie	16,000
Sep 18	PRESTON NORTH END	D 2-2	Fitchie 2	12,000
Sep 23	Stoke	L 1-2	Fitchie	15,000
Sep 30	BOLTON WANDERERS	D 0-0		20,000
Oct 7	Wolverhampton Wanderers	W 2-0	Coleman 2	9,000
Oct 14	Blackburn Rovers	L 0-2		10,000
Oct 21	SUNDERLAND	W 2-0	Blair, Bellamy (pen)	13,000
Oct 28	Birmingham City	L 1-2	Crowe	16,000
Nov 4	EVERTON	L 1-2	Coleman	18,000
Nov 11	Derby County	L 1-5	Satterthwaite	6,000
Nov 18	SHEFFIELD WEDNESDAY	L 0-2		20,000
Nov 25	Nottingham Forest	L 1-3	Freeman	8,000
Dec 2	MANCHESTER CITY	W 2-0	Freeman 2	16,000
Dec 9	Bury	L 0-2		8,000
Dec 16	MIDDLESBROUGH	D 2-2	Bellamy, Freeman	12,000
Dec 23	Preston North End	D 2-2	Neave 2	10,000
Dec 25	NEWCASTLE UNITED	W 4-3	Ducat 2, Fitchie 2	20,000
Dec 27	Aston Villa	L 1-2	Fitchie	30,000
Dec 30	Liverpool	L 0-3		15,000
Jan 1	Bolton Wanderers	L 1-6	Satterthwaite	30,000
Jan 6	SHEFFIELD UNITED	W 5-1	Coleman 2, Fitchie, Garbutt, Ducat	10,000
Jan 20	Notts County	L 0-1		8,000
Jan 27	STOKE	L 1-2	Neave	10,000
Feb 10	WOLVERHAMPTON WANDERERS	W 2-1	Freeman 2	10,000
Feb 17	BLACKBURN ROVERS	W 3-2	Coleman 2, Bellamy (pen)	8,000
Mar 3	BIRMINGHAM CITY	W 5-0	Satterthwaite 2, Coleman, Sharp, Freeman	25,000
Mar 17	DERBY COUNTY	W 1-0	Neave	20,000
Mar 21	Everton	W 1-0	Garbutt	8,000
Mar 24	Sheffield Wednesday	L 2-4	Sharp (pen), Fitchie	15,000
Apr 2	NOTTINGHAM FOREST	W 3-0	Neave 2, Freeman	10,000
Apr 7	Manchester City	W 2-1	Satterthwaite 2	12,000
Apr 13	ASTON VILLA	W 2-1	Coleman, Freeman	30,000
Apr 14	BURY	W 4-0	Ducat, Coleman, Satterthwaite 2	20,000
Apr 16	Newcastle United	D 1-1	Garbutt	25,000
Apr 21	Middlesbrough	L 0-2		12,000
Apr 25	Sunderland	D 2-2	Satterthwaite, Coleman	8,000

FA Cup

DATE	OPPONENTS		SCORE	GOALSCORERS	ATTENDANCE
Jan 13	WEST HAM UNITED	(Rd1)	D 1-1	Sharp (pen)	18,000
Jan 18	West Ham United	(R)	W 3-2	Ducat, Satterthwaite, Garbutt	12,000
Feb 3	WATFORD	(Rd2)	W 3-0	Freeman, Coleman, Fitchie	11,000
Feb 24	SUNDERLAND	(Rd3)	W 5-0	Garbutt 2, Fitchie, Sands, Coleman	30,000
Mar 10	Manchester United	(QF)	W 3-2	Freeman 2, Coleman	26,500
Mar 31	Newcastle United*	(SF)	L 0-2		19,964

*Played at the Victoria Ground.

Fact File

Woolwich Arsenal reached the FA Cup semi-final for the first time. They had never previously advanced beyond the second round. Goalkeeper Jimmy Ashcroft created another record for the club when he became their first player to be picked for England. He won three caps.

MANAGER: Phil Kelso

CAPTAIN: John Dick/Roddy McEachrane

TOP SCORER: Tim Coleman 15 (12 League)

BIGGEST WIN: 5-0 v Birmingham City, 3 March 1906, League; 5-0 v Sunderland, 24 February 1906, FA Cup

HIGHEST ATTENDANCE: 30,000 v Aston Villa, 13 April 1906, League; 30,000 v Sunderland, 24 February 1906, FA Cup

MAJOR TRANSFERS IN: Bert Freeman from Aston Villa, Bill Garbutt from Reading, Jimmy Sharp from Fulham

MAJOR TRANSFERS OUT: John Hunter to Portsmouth, Jimmy Jackson to Leyton

League & Cup Appearances

PLAYER	LEAGUE	CUP COMPETITION FA CUP	TOTAL
Arnold	2		2
Ashcroft	35	6	41
Bateup	1		1
Bellamy	17		17
Bigden	25	6	31
Blair	12		12
Coleman	28	6	34
Cross	15	6	21
Crowe	2		2
Dick	16		16
Ducat	15	2	17
Fitchie	22	5	27
Freeman	17	4	21
Garbutt	19	6	25
Gray	28	1	29
Grice	1		1
Kemp	2		2
McDonald	2		2
McEachrane	31	6	37
Neave	18		18
Sands	26	6	32
Satterthwaite	18	1	19
Sharp	35	5	40
Templeton	17	6	23
Theobald	14		14

Goalscorers

PLAYER	LEAGUE	CUP COMPETITION FA CUP	TOTAL
Coleman	12	3	15
Freeman	9	3	12
Satterthwaite	10	1	11
Fitchie	9	2	11
Neave	6		6
Garbutt	3	3	6
Ducat	4	1	5
Bellamy	3		3
Blair	3		3
Sharp	2	1	3
Crowe	1		1
Sands		1	1

Final Division One Table

		P	W	D	L	F	A	Pts
1	LIVERPOOL	38	23	5	10	79	46	51
2	PRESTON NE	38	17	13	8	54	39	47
3	SHEFFIELD W	38	18	8	12	63	52	44
4	NEWCASTLE U	38	18	7	13	74	48	43
5	MANCHESTER C	38	19	5	14	73	54	43
6	BOLTON W	38	17	7	14	81	67	41
7	BIRMINGHAM	38	17	7	14	65	59	41
8	ASTON VILLA	38	17	6	15	72	56	40
9	BLACKBURN R	38	16	8	14	54	52	40
10	STOKE	38	16	7	15	54	55	39
11	EVERTON	38	15	7	16	70	66	37
12	WOOLWICH ARSENAL	38	15	7	16	62	64	37
13	SHEFFIELD U	38	15	6	17	57	62	36
14	SUNDERLAND	38	15	5	18	61	70	35
15	DERBY CO	38	14	7	17	39	58	35
16	NOTTS CO	38	11	12	15	55	71	34
17	BURY	38	11	10	17	57	74	32
18	MIDDLESBROUGH	38	10	11	17	56	71	31
19	NOTTINGHAM F	38	13	5	20	58	79	31
20	WOLVERHAMPTON W	38	8	7	23	58	99	23

Season 1906-07

Football League Division One

DATE	OPPONENTS	SCORE	GOALSCORERS	ATTENDANCE
Sep 1	Manchester City	W 4-1	Kyle 2, Coleman, Satterthwaite	18,000
Sep 3	Bury	L 1-4	Kyle	9,000
Sep 8	MIDDLESBROUGH	W 2-0	Satterthwaite 2	20,000
Sep 15	Preston North End	W 3-0	Satterthwaite 2, Bellamy	12,000
Sep 22	NEWCASTLE UNITED	W 2-0	Kyle 2	30,000
Sep 29	Aston Villa	D 2-2	Satterthwaite, Coleman	45,000
Oct 6	LIVERPOOL	W 2-1	Neave 2	30,000
Oct 13	Bristol City	W 3-1	Bigden, Ducat, Neave	22,000
Oct 20	NOTTS COUNTY	W 1-0	Coleman	25,000
Oct 27	Sheffield United	L 2-4	Kyle, Satterthwaite	18,816
Nov 3	BOLTON WANDERERS	D 2-2	Satterthwaite 2	20,000
Nov 10	Manchester United	L 0-1		25,000
Nov 17	STOKE	W 2-1	Kyle, Coleman	10,000
Nov 24	Blackburn Rovers	W 3-2	Freeman 2, Coleman	12,000
Dec 1	SUNDERLAND	L 0-1		20,000
Dec 8	Birmingham City	L 1-5	Sands	19,000
Dec 15	EVERTON	W 3-1	Satterthwaite, Kyle, Coleman	16,000
Dec 22	Derby County	D 0-0		7,000
Dec 26	BURY	W 3-1	Kyle 2, Satterthwaite	8,000
Dec 29	MANCHESTER CITY	W 4-1	Coleman 2, Garbutt, Kyle	15,000
Jan 1	Sheffield Wednesday	D 1-1	Kyle	16,000
Jan 5	Middlesbrough	L 3-5	Coleman, Sharp, Neave	15,000
Jan 19	PRESTON NORTH END	W 1-0	Coleman	12,000
Jan 26	Newcastle United	L 0-1		35,000
Feb 9	Liverpool	L 0-4		20,000
Feb 16	BRISTOL CITY	L 1-2	Satterthwaite	18,000
Mar 2	SHEFFIELD UNITED	L 0-1		12,000
Mar 16	MANCHESTER UNITED	W 4-0	Satterthwaite 2, Kyle, Coleman	6,000
Mar 27	Bolton Wanderers	L 0-3		5,000
Mar 29	SHEFFIELD WEDNESDAY	W 1-0	Satterthwaite	25,000
Mar 30	BLACKBURN ROVERS	W 2-0	Sands, Coleman	8,000
Apr 1	ASTON VILLA	W 1-0	Garbutt, Satterthwaite, Freeman	20,000
Apr 6	Sunderland	W 3-2	Freeman 2, Sands	12,000
Apr 10	Everton	L 1-2	Satterthwaite	8,000
Apr 13	BIRMINGHAM CITY	W 2-1	Freeman, Coleman	18,000
Apr 15	Stoke	L 0-2		5,000
Apr 17	Notts County	L 1-4	Freeman	5,000
Apr 27	DERBY COUNTY	W 3-2	Coleman, Garbutt, Freeman	6,000

FA Cup

DATE	OPPONENTS		SCORE	GOALSCORERS	ATTENDANCE
Jan 12	Grimsby Town	(Rd1)	D 1-1	Garbutt	10,000
Jan 16	GRIMSBY TOWN	(R)	W 3-0	Satterthwaite, Sands, Garbutt	6,000
Feb 2	BRISTOL CITY	(Rd2)	W 2-1	Hynds, Kyle	31,300
Feb 23	BRISTOL ROVERS	(Rd3)	W 1-0	Neave	22,000
Mar 9	Barnsley	(QF)	W 2-1	Satterthwaite, Neave	13,871
Mar 23	Sheffield Wednesday*	(SF)	L 1-3	Garbutt	36,000

*Played at St Andrews.

League & Cup Appearances

PLAYER	LEAGUE	CUP COMPETITION FA CUP	TOTAL
Ashcroft	35	6	41
Bateup	3		3
Bellamy	11		11
Bigden	37	6	43
Blair	1		1
Coleman	34	6	40
Cross	16	1	17
Dick	1		1
Ducat	4		4
Ferguson	1		1
Freeman	12		12
Garbutt	25	6	31
Gray	23	5	28
Hynds	13	4	17
Kyle	29	6	35
Low	3		3
McEachrane	34	6	40
Mordue	3		3
Neave	33	6	39
Sands	24	2	26
Satterthwaite	38	6	44
Sharp	36	6	42
Theobald	2		2

Goalscorers

PLAYER	LEAGUE	CUP COMPETITION FA CUP	TOTAL
Satterthwaite	17	2	19
Coleman	14		14
Kyle	13	1	14
Freeman	8		8
Neave	4	2	6
Garbutt	3	3	6
Sands	3	1	4
Bellamy	1		1
Bigden	1		1
Ducat	1		1
Sharp	1		1
Hynds		1	1

Fact File

This was the best season yet in Woolwich Arsenal's history. Seventh place was their highest-ever position in the Football League and they reached the FA Cup semi-finals for the second year running.

MANAGER: Phil Kelso
CAPTAIN: Roddy McEachrane
TOP SCORER: Charlie Satterthwaite 19 (17 League)
BIGGEST WIN: 4-0 v Manchester United, 16 March 1907, League
HIGHEST ATTENDANCE: 31,300 v Bristol City, 2 February, 1907, FA Cup
MAJOR TRANSFER IN: Peter Kyle from Tottenham Hotspur
MAJOR TRANSFER OUT: Bobby Templeton to Celtic

Final Division One Table

		P	W	D	L	F	A	Pts
1	NEWCASTLE U	38	22	7	9	74	46	51
2	BRISTOL C	38	20	8	10	66	47	48
3	EVERTON	38	20	5	13	70	46	45
4	SHEFFIELD U	38	17	11	10	57	55	45
5	ASTON VILLA	38	19	6	13	78	52	44
6	BOLTON W	38	18	8	12	59	47	44
7	WOOLWICH ARSENAL	38	20	4	14	66	59	44
8	MANCHESTER U	38	17	8	13	53	56	42
9	BIRMINGHAM	38	15	8	15	52	52	38
10	SUNDERLAND	38	14	9	15	65	66	37
11	MIDDLESBROUGH	38	15	6	17	56	63	36
12	BLACKBURN R	38	14	7	17	56	59	35
13	SHEFFIELD W	38	12	11	15	49	60	35
14	PRESTON NE	38	14	7	17	44	57	35
15	LIVERPOOL	38	13	7	18	64	65	33
16	BURY	38	13	6	19	58	68	32
17	MANCHESTER C	38	10	12	16	53	77	32
18	NOTTS CO	38	8	15	15	46	50	31
19	DERBY CO	38	9	9	20	41	59	27
20	STOKE	38	8	10	20	41	64	26

Season 1907-08

Football League Division One

DATE	OPPONENTS	SCORE	GOALSCORERS	ATTENDANCE
Sep 2	NOTTS COUNTY	D 1-1	Garbutt	10,000
Sep 7	BRISTOL CITY	L 0-4		14,000
Sep 9	Bury	L 2-3	Neave, Kyle	10,000
Sep 14	Notts County	L 0-2		7,000
Sep 21	MANCHESTER CITY	W 2-1	Sharp, Coleman	12,000
Sep 28	Preston North End	L 0-3		12,000
Oct 5	BURY	D 0-0		14,000
Oct 12	Aston Villa	W 1-0	Neave	25,000
Oct 19	LIVERPOOL	W 2-1	Lee 2	15,000
Oct 26	Middlesbrough	D 0-0		18,000
Nov 2	SHEFFIELD UNITED	W 5-1	Kyle 2, Coleman, Neave, Satterthwaite C.	12,000
Nov 9	Chelsea	L 1-2	Satterthwaite C.	65,000
Nov 16	NOTTINGHAM FOREST	W 3-1	Kyle 2, Coleman	8,000
Nov 23	Manchester United	L 2-4	Kyle, Garbutt	15,000
Nov 30	BLACKBURN ROVERS	W 2-0	Satterthwaite C., Sands	7,500
Dec 7	Bolton Wanderers	L 1-3	Coleman	10,000
Dec 14	BIRMINGHAM	D 1-1	Coleman	3,000
Dec 21	Everton	D 1-1	Coleman	10,000
Dec 25	NEWCASTLE UNITED	D 2-2	Kyle, Freeman	25,000
Dec 28	SUNDERLAND	W 4-0	Lewis 2, Neave 2	6,000
Dec 31	Sheffield Wednesday	L 0-6		9,000
Jan 1	Sunderland	L 2-5	Kyle, Neave	20,000
Jan 4	Bristol City	W 2-1	Freeman, Coleman	15,000
Jan 18	Manchester City	L 0-4		25,000
Jan 25	PRESTON NORTH END	D 1-1	Sands	6,000
Feb 8	ASTON VILLA	L 0-1		12,000
Feb 15	Liverpool	L 1-4	Coleman	18,000
Feb 22	MIDDLESBROUGH	W 4-1	Lewis 2, Lee, Freeman	7,000
Feb 29	Sheffield United	D 2-2	Freeman, Lewis	8,000
Mar 7	CHELSEA	D 0-0		30,000
Mar 14	Nottingham Forest	L 0-1		14,000
Mar 21	MANCHESTER UNITED	W 1-0	Lee	18,000
Mar 28	Blackburn Rovers	D 1-1	Ducat	12,000
Apr 4	BOLTON WANDERERS	D 1-1	Satterthwaite J.	10,000
Apr 11	Birmingham	W 2-1	Lewis, Lee	15,000
Apr 17	Newcastle United	L 1-2	Neave	30,000
Apr 18	EVERTON	W 2-1	Mordue, Lee	15,000
Apr 20	SHEFFIELD WEDNESDAY	D 1-1	Lewis	16,000

FA Cup

Jan 11	HULL CITY	(Rd1)	D 0-0		15,000
Jan 16	Hull City	(R)	L 1-4	Kyle	17,000

League & Cup Appearances

PLAYER	LEAGUE	CUP COMPETITION FA CUP	TOTAL
Ashcroft	36	2	38
Bateup	2		2
Bigden	6		6
Coleman	26	2	28
Cross	11		11
Dick	17		17
Ducat	18	2	20
Freeman	15	1	16
Garbutt	8	1	9
Gray	30	2	32
Hoare	10		10
Kyle	23	2	25
Lee	18		18
Lewis	13		13
McEachrane	38	2	40
Mordue	23	2	25
Neave	35	2	37
Rodger	1		1
Sands	34	2	36
Satterthwaite C.	21		21
Satterthwaite J.	5		5
Sharp	32	2	34
Shaw	2		2
Theobald	3		3

Goalscorers

PLAYER	LEAGUE	CUP COMPETITION FA CUP	TOTAL
Kyle	8	1	9
Coleman	8		8
Lewis	8		8
Neave	7		7
Lee	5		5
Freeman	4		4
Satterthwaite C.	3		3
Garbutt	2		2
Sands	2		2
Ducat	1		1
Mordue	1		1
Satterthwaite J.	1		1
Sharp	1		1

Fact File

Phil Kelso resigned as Woolwich Arsenal faced a financial crisis which forced them to sell their best players. The team slid down the table and out of the FA Cup to a Second Division side. Gates slumped, travelling was expensive as Arsenal was one of only two London teams in the First Division – and the club had previously spent heavily in the transfer market.

MANAGER: Phil Kelso

CAPTAIN: Percy Sands

TOP SCORER: Peter Kyle 9 (8 League)

BIGGEST WIN: 5-1 v Sheffield United, 2 November 1907, League

HIGHEST ATTENDANCE: 30,000 v Chelsea, 7 March 1908, League

MAJOR TRANSFER IN: Charlie Lewis from Maidstone United

MAJOR TRANSFERS OUT: Bert Freeman to Everton, Tim Coleman to Everton, Peter Kyle to Aston Villa

Final Division One Table

		P	W	D	L	F	A	Pts
1	MANCHESTER U	38	23	6	9	81	48	52
2	ASTON VILLA	38	17	9	12	77	59	43
3	MANCHESTER C	38	16	11	11	62	54	43
4	NEWCASTLE U	38	15	12	11	65	54	42
5	SHEFFIELD W	38	19	4	15	73	64	42
6	MIDDLESBROUGH	38	17	7	14	54	45	41
7	BURY	38	14	11	13	58	61	39
8	LIVERPOOL	38	16	6	16	68	61	38
9	NOTTINGHAM F	38	13	11	14	59	62	37
10	BRISTOL C	38	12	12	14	58	61	36
11	EVERTON	38	15	6	17	58	64	36
12	PRESTON NE	38	12	12	14	47	53	36
13	CHELSEA	38	14	8	16	53	62	36
14	BLACKBURN R=	38	12	12	14	51	63	36
14	WOOLWICH ARSENAL=	38	12	12	14	51	63	36
16	SUNDERLAND	38	16	3	19	78	75	35
17	SHEFFIELD U	38	12	11	15	52	58	35
18	NOTTS CO	38	13	8	17	39	51	34
19	BOLTON W	38	14	5	19	52	58	33
20	BIRMINGHAM	38	9	12	17	40	60	30

Season 1908-09

Football League Division One

DATE	OPPONENTS	SCORE	GOALSCORERS	ATTENDANCE
Sep 2	EVERTON	L 0-4		10,000
Sep 5	Notts County	L 1-2	Neave	13,000
Sep 7	Everton	W 3-0	Neave, Lee, Raybould	10,000
Sep 12	NEWCASTLE UNITED	L 1-2	Greenaway	18,000
Sep 19	Bristol City	L 1-2	Greenaway	16,000
Sep 26	PRESTON NORTH END	W 1-0	Fitchie	12,000
Oct 3	Middlesbrough	D 1-1	Sands	20,000
Oct 10	MANCHESTER CITY	W 3-0	Raybould 2, Lee	12,000
Oct 17	Liverpool	D 2-2	Satterthwaite, Neave	20,000
Oct 24	BURY	W 4-0	Raybould 3, Satterthwaite	9,500
Oct 31	Sheffield United	D 1-1	Lee	15,000
Nov 7	ASTON VILLA	L 0-1		20,000
Nov 14	Nottingham Forest	W 1-0	Hoare	10,000
Nov 21	SUNDERLAND	L 0-4		12,000
Nov 28	Chelsea	W 2-1	Greenaway, Lewis	50,000
Dec 5	BLACKBURN ROVERS	L 0-1		12,000
Dec 12	Bradford City	L 1-4	Fitchie	24,000
Dec 19	MANCHESTER UNITED	L 0-1		10,000
Dec 25	Leicester Fosse	D 1-1	Satterthwaite	16,000
Dec 26	LEICESTER FOSSE	W 2-1	Fitchie 2	20,000
Dec 28	Sheffield Wednesday	L 2-6	Fitchie, Hoare	12,000
Jan 2	NOTTS COUNTY	W 1-0	Hoare	10,000
Jan 9	Newcastle United	L 1-3	Hoare	27,500
Jan 23	BRISTOL CITY	D 1-1	Hoare	10,000
Jan 30	Preston North End	D 0-0		8,000
Feb 13	Manchester City	D 2-2	Lewis, Ducat	20,000
Feb 20	LIVERPOOL	W 5-0	Beney 3, Satterthwaite (pen), Lewis	15,000
Feb 27	Bury	D 1-1	Lewis	12,000
Mar 13	Aston Villa	L 1-2	Fitchie	20,000
Mar 17	MIDDLESBROUGH	D 1-1	Hoare	9,000
Mar 20	NOTTINGHAM FOREST	L 1-2	Neave	10,000
Mar 27	Sunderland	L 0-1		7,500
Apr 1	SHEFFIELD UNITED	W 1-0	Fitchie	8,000
Apr 3	CHELSEA	D 0-0		20,000
Apr 10	Blackburn Rovers	W 3-1	Lee, Neave, Lewis	5,000
Apr 12	SHEFFIELD WEDNESDAY	W 2-0	Lee, o.g.	12,000
Apr 17	BRADFORD CITY	W 1-0	Lee	14,000
Apr 27	Manchester United	W 4-1	Lee 2, Fitchie, Lewis	30,000

FA Cup

DATE	OPPONENTS		SCORE	GOALSCORERS	ATTENDANCE
Jan 16	Croydon Common*	(Rd1)	D 1-1	Fitchie	20,000
Jan 20	CROYDON COMMON	(R)	W 2-0	Raybould, Ducat	15,000
Feb 6	MILLWALL	(Rd2)	D 1-1	Lewis	32,000
Feb 10	Millwall	(R)	L 0-1		16,285

*Played at the Crystal Palace.

League & Cup Appearances

PLAYER	LEAGUE	CUP COMPETITION FA CUP	TOTAL
Beney	8		8
Chisholm	3		3
Cross	12		12
Curle	3		3
Dick	5		5
Ducat	33	4	37
Fitchie	21	2	23
Gray	33	4	37
Greenaway	36	4	40
Hoare	11	2	13
Lee	17		17
Lewis	23	2	25
McDonald	38	4	42
McEachrane	36	4	40
McKinnon	2		2
Maxwell	2		2
Neave	25	3	28
Raybould	26	4	30
Sands	32	4	36
Satterthwaite	18	3	21
Shaw	28	4	32
Theobald	3		3
Thomson	3		3

Goalscorers

PLAYER	LEAGUE	CUP COMPETITION FA CUP	TOTAL
Fitchie	9	1	10
Lee	8		8
Lewis	6	1	7
Raybould	6	1	7
Hoare	5		5
Neave	5		5
Satterthwaite	4		4
Beney	3		3
Greenaway	3		3
Ducat	1	1	2
Sands	1		1
Opps' o.gs.	1		1

Fact File

Arsenal achieved their best-ever League position despite their financial crisis – though their points total was six fewer than in 1907 and they lost seven home games. New manager George Morrell was used to making do on a tight budget. He had been in a similar situation with Scottish club Morton.

MANAGER: George Morrell

CAPTAIN: Percy Sands

TOP SCORER: Tom Fitchie 10 (9 League)

BIGGEST WIN: 5-0 v Liverpool, 20 February 1909, League

HIGHEST ATTENDANCE: 32,000 v Millwall, 6 February 1909, FA Cup

MAJOR TRANSFERS IN: Angus McKinnon from Petershill, Sam Raybould from Sunderland, Tom Fitchie from Queen's Park

MAJOR TRANSFERS OUT: Jimmy Sharp to Rangers, Jimmy Ashcroft to Blackburn Rovers, Bill Garbutt to Blackburn Rovers, James Bigden to Bury

Final Division One Table

		P	W	D	L	F	A	Pts
1	NEWCASTLE U	38	24	5	9	65	41	53
2	EVERTON	38	18	10	10	82	57	46
3	SUNDERLAND	38	21	2	15	78	63	44
4	BLACKBURN R	38	14	13	11	61	50	41
5	SHEFFIELD W	38	17	6	15	67	61	40
6	WOOLWICH ARSENAL	38	14	10	14	52	49	38
7	ASTON VILLA	38	14	10	14	58	56	38
8	BRISTOL C	38	13	12	13	45	58	38
9	MIDDLESBROUGH	38	14	9	15	59	53	37
10	PRESTON NE	38	13	11	14	48	44	37
11	CHELSEA	38	14	9	15	56	61	37
12	SHEFFIELD U	38	14	9	15	51	59	37
13	MANCHESTER U	38	15	7	16	58	68	37
14	NOTTINGHAM F	38	14	8	16	66	57	36
15	NOTTS CO	38	14	8	16	51	48	36
16	LIVERPOOL	38	15	6	17	57	65	36
17	BURY	38	14	8	16	63	77	36
18	BRADFORD C	38	12	10	16	47	47	34
19	MANCHESTER C	38	15	4	19	67	69	34
20	LEICESTER FOSSE	38	8	9	21	54	102	25

Season 1909-10

Football League Division One

DATE	OPPONENTS	SCORE	GOALSCORERS	ATTENDANCE
Sep 1	Aston Villa	L 1-5	Lewis	12,000
Sep 4	SHEFFIELD UNITED	D 0-0		10,000
Sep 11	Middlesbrough	L 2-5	Beney 2	12,000
Sep 18	Bolton Wanderers	L 0-3		20,000
Sep 25	CHELSEA	W 3-2	Lee 2, Greenaway	15,000
Oct 2	Blackburn Rovers	L 0-7		10,000
Oct 7	Notts County	L 1-5	Neave	10,000
Oct 9	NOTTINGHAM FOREST	L 0-1		8,000
Oct 16	Sunderland	L 2-6	Greenaway, Lawrence	10,000
Oct 23	EVERTON	W 1-0	Thomson	10,000
Oct 30	Manchester United	L 0-1		20,000
Nov 6	BRADFORD CITY	L 0-1		10,000
Nov 13	Sheffield Wednesday	D 1-1	Lawrence	10,000
Nov 20	BRISTOL CITY	D 2-2	Buckenham, Greenaway	8,000
Nov 27	Bury	W 2-1	Greenaway, Steven	7,000
Dec 4	TOTTENHAM HOTSPUR	W 1-0	Lawrence	18,000
Dec 11	Preston North End	W 4-3	Buckenham 2, Neave 2	6,000
Dec 18	NOTTS COUNTY	L 1-2	Lewis	10,000
Dec 25	NEWCASTLE UNITED	L 0-3		20,000
Dec 27	LIVERPOOL	D 1-1	McKellar	15,000
Jan 1	Liverpool	L 1-5	Neave	25,000
Jan 8	Sheffield United	L 0-2		17,000
Jan 22	MIDDLESBROUGH	W 3-0	Buckenham, Neave, Lawrence	8,000
Jan 29	BOLTON WANDERERS	W 2-0	Greenaway, Ducat	10,000
Feb 12	BLACKBURN ROVERS	L 0-1		7,500
Feb 26	SUNDERLAND	L 1-2	Ducat	8,000
Mar 2	Nottingham Forest	D 1-1	Buckenham	5,000
Mar 7	Everton	L 0-1		6,000
Mar 12	MANCHESTER UNITED	D 0-0		5,000
Mar 19	Bradford City	W 1-0	Beney	14,000
Mar 25	Newcastle United	D 1-1	Lewis	20,000
Mar 26	SHEFFIELD WEDNESDAY	L 0-1		8,000
Mar 28	Chelsea	W 1-0	McGibbon	40,000
Apr 2	Bristol City	W 1-0	Lawrence	8,000
Apr 9	BURY	D 0-0		10,000
Apr 11	ASTON VILLA	W 1-0	McGibbon	8,000
Apr 16	Tottenham Hotspur	D 1-1	McGibbon	39,800
Apr 23	PRESTON NORTH END	L 1-3	Ducat	10,000

FA Cup

Jan 15	WATFORD	(Rd1) W 3-0	McKellar, Lewis 2	8,668
Feb 5	Everton	(Rd2) L 0-5		30,000

League & Cup Appearances

PLAYER	LEAGUE	CUP COMPETITION FA CUP	TOTAL
Bassett	1		1
Beney	8	1	9
Buckenham	21		21
Cross	9	2	11
Dick	7		7
Drain	2		2
Ducat	29	2	31
Fisher	2		2
Gray	13		13
Greenaway	36	2	38
Heppinstall	18		18
Hoare	1		1
Lawrence	25	1	26
Lee	6		6
Lewis	28	2	30
McDonald D.	25	1	26
McDonald H.	36	2	38
McEachrane	32	2	34
McGibbon	4		4
McKellar	3	2	5
McKinnon	8		8
Neave	21	2	23
Oliver	1		1
Sands	12		12
Satterthwaite	4		4
Shaw	29	1	30
Steven	7		7
Thomson	30	2	32

Goalscorers

PLAYER	LEAGUE	CUP COMPETITION FA CUP	TOTAL
Buckenham	5		5
Greenaway	5		5
Lawrence	5		5
Neave	5		5
Lewis	3	2	5
Beney	3		3
Ducat	3		3
McGibbon	3		3
Lee	2		2
McKellar	1	1	2
Steven	1		1
Thomson	1		1

Fact File

Woolwich Arsenal's tally of 37 league goals was the lowest by any club since the First Division was increased to 20 teams in 1905. They escaped relegation largely thanks to a 1-0 win at Chelsea, who went down instead. Star player was wing half Andy Ducat who won three England caps during the season.

MANAGER: George Morrell

CAPTAIN: Percy Sands/Joe Shaw

TOP SCORER: Billy Buckenham 5 (all League), David Greenaway 5 (all League), Walter Lawrence 5 (all League), David Neave 5 (all League), Charlie Lewis 5 (3 League),

BIGGEST WIN: 3-0 v Middlesbrough, 22 January 1910, League; 3-0 v Watford, 15 January 1910, FA Cup

HIGHEST ATTENDANCE: 20,000 v Newcastle United, 25 December 1909, League

MAJOR TRANSFER IN: Walter Lawrence from Crystal Palace

MAJOR TRANSFER OUT: Tom Fitchie to Glossop North End

Final Division One Table

		P	W	D	L	F	A	Pts
1	ASTON VILLA	38	23	7	8	84	42	53
2	LIVERPOOL	38	21	6	11	78	57	48
3	BLACKBURN R	38	18	9	11	73	55	45
4	NEWCASTLE U	38	19	7	12	70	56	45
5	MANCHESTER U	38	19	7	12	69	61	45
6	SHEFFIELD U	38	16	10	12	62	41	42
7	BRADFORD C	38	17	8	13	64	47	42
8	SUNDERLAND	38	18	5	15	66	51	41
9	NOTTS CO	38	15	10	13	67	59	40
10	EVERTON	38	16	8	14	51	56	40
11	SHEFFIELD W	38	15	9	14	60	63	39
12	PRESTON NE	38	15	5	18	52	58	35
13	BURY	38	12	9	17	62	66	33
14	NOTTINGHAM F	38	11	11	16	54	72	33
15	TOTTENHAM H	38	11	10	17	53	69	32
16	BRISTOL C	38	12	8	18	45	60	32
17	MIDDLESBROUGH	38	11	9	18	56	73	31
18	WOOLWICH ARSENAL	38	11	9	18	37	67	31
19	CHELSEA	38	11	7	20	47	70	29
20	BOLTON W	38	9	6	23	44	71	24

Season 1910-11

Football League Division One

DATE	OPPONENTS	SCORE	GOALSCORERS	ATTENDANCE
Sep 1	MANCHESTER UNITED	L 1-2	Rippon	15,000
Sep 3	Bury	D 1-1	Rippon	10,000
Sep 10	SHEFFIELD UNITED	D 0-0		14,000
Sep 17	Aston Villa	L 0-3		20,000
Sep 24	SUNDERLAND	D 0-0		15,000
Oct 1	OLDHAM ATHLETIC	D 0-0		12,000
Oct 8	Bradford City	L 0-3		26,000
Oct 15	BLACKBURN ROVERS	W 4-1	Neave 2, Lewis, Chalmers	11,500
Oct 22	Nottingham Forest	W 3-2	Chalmers 2, Greenaway	8,000
Oct 29	MANCHESTER CITY	L 0-1		10,000
Nov 5	Everton	L 0-2		15,000
Nov 12	SHEFFIELD WEDNESDAY	W 1-0	Chalmers	10,000
Nov 19	Bristol City	W 1-0	Chalmers	8,000
Nov 26	NEWCASTLE UNITED	L 1-2	Chalmers	14,000
Dec 3	Tottenham Hotspur	L 1-3	Chalmers	16,000
Dec 10	MIDDLESBROUGH	L 0-2		10,000
Dec 17	Preston North End	L 1-4	Common	6,000
Dec 24	NOTTS COUNTY	W 2-1	Chalmers, Hoare	8,000
Dec 26	Manchester United	L 0-5		35,000
Dec 31	BURY	W 3-2	Ducat, Hoare, Chalmers	7,000
Jan 7	Sheffield United	L 2-3	Hoare, o.g.	12,000
Jan 28	Sunderland	D 2-2	Ducat (pen), Lewis	10,000
Feb 11	BRADFORD CITY	D 0-0		10,000
Feb 18	Blackburn Rovers	L 0-1		20,000
Feb 25	NOTTINGHAM FOREST	W 3-2	Ducat, Chalmers, Hoare	10,000
Mar 4	Manchester City	D 1-1	Greenaway	20,000
Mar 6	Oldham Athletic	L 0-3		7,000
Mar 11	EVERTON	W 1-0	Chalmers	10,000
Mar 15	ASTON VILLA	D 1-1	Hoare	6,000
Mar 18	Sheffield Wednesday	D 0-0		7,000
Mar 25	BRISTOL CITY	W 3-0	Common 2, Flanagan	10,977
Apr 1	Newcastle United	W 1-0	Chalmers	18,000
Apr 8	TOTTENHAM HOTSPUR	W 2-0	Chalmers, Common	24,583
Apr 14	LIVERPOOL	D 0-0		20,277
Apr 15	Middlesbrough	D 1-1	Neave	14,000
Apr 17	Liverpool	D 1-1	Chalmers	20,000
Apr 22	PRESTON NORTH END	W 2-0	Hoare, Chalmers	9,092
Apr 29	Notts County	W 2-0	Common 2	6,000

FA Cup

Jan 16	Clapton Orient	(Rd1) W 2-1	Chalmers, Hoare	9,519
Feb 4	Swindon Town	(Rd2) L 0-1		14,861

League & Cup Appearances

PLAYER	LEAGUE	CUP COMPETITION FA CUP	TOTAL
Bateup	28	2	30
Burdett	10		10
Calder	1		1
Calvert	1		1
Chalmers	29	2	31
Common	29	2	31
Ducat	33	2	35
Flanagan	9	1	10
Gray	26	2	28
Greenaway	22		22
Heppinstall	5		5
Hoare	14	2	16
Lewis	34	2	36
Logan	11		11
McDonald D.	1		1
McEachrane	30	2	32
McKinnon	10		10
Neave	15	1	16
Peart	7		7
Quayle	1		1
Rippon	9		9
Sands	31	2	33
Shaw	35	2	37
Shortt	4		4
Thomson	17		17
Winship	6		6

Goalscorers

PLAYER	LEAGUE	CUP COMPETITION FA CUP	TOTAL
Chalmers	15	1	16
Hoare	6	1	7
Common	6		6
Ducat	3		3
Neave	3		3
Greenaway	2		2
Lewis	2		2
Rippon	2		2
Flanagan	1		1
Opps' o.gs.	1		1

Fact File

A run of 11 unbeaten games at the end of the season pulled Woolwich Arsenal clear of relegation danger. They won six and conceded only three goals. The club's top signing, Alf Common, had become England's first £1,000 player when he moved from Sunderland to Middlesbrough in 1905.

MANAGER: George Morrell

CAPTAIN: Percy Sands/Joe Shaw

TOP SCORER: Jackie Chalmers 16 (15 League)

BIGGEST WIN: 4-1 v Blackburn Rovers, 15 October, 1910, League

HIGHEST ATTENDANCE: 24,583 v Tottenham Hotspur, 8 April 1911, League

MAJOR TRANSFERS IN: Jackie Chalmers from Clyde, Alf Common from Middlesbrough

MAJOR TRANSFERS OUT: Hugh McDonald to Oldham Athletic, Walter Lawrence to Crystal Palace

Final Division One Table

		P	W	D	L	F	A	Pts
1	MANCHESTER U	38	22	8	8	72	40	52
2	ASTON VILLA	38	22	7	9	69	41	51
3	SUNDERLAND	38	15	15	8	67	48	45
4	EVERTON	38	19	7	12	50	36	45
5	BRADFORD C	38	20	5	13	51	42	45
6	SHEFFIELD W	38	17	8	13	47	48	42
7	OLDHAM ATH	38	16	9	13	44	41	41
8	NEWCASTLE U	38	15	10	13	61	43	40
9	SHEFFIELD U	38	15	8	15	49	43	38
10	WOOLWICH ARSENAL	38	13	12	13	41	49	38
11	NOTTS CO	38	14	10	14	37	45	38
12	BLACKBURN R	38	13	11	14	62	54	37
13	LIVERPOOL	38	15	7	16	53	53	37
14	PRESTON NE	38	12	11	15	40	49	35
15	TOTTENHAM H	38	13	6	19	52	63	32
16	MIDDLESBROUGH	38	11	10	17	49	63	32
17	MANCHESTER C	38	9	13	16	43	58	31
18	BURY	38	9	11	18	43	71	29
19	BRISTOL C	38	11	5	22	43	66	27
20	NOTTINGHAM F	38	9	7	22	55	75	25

Season 1911-12

Football League Division One

DATE	OPPONENTS	SCORE	GOALSCORERS	ATTENDANCE
Sep 2	LIVERPOOL	D 2-2	Flanagan, Chalmers	12,000
Sep 9	Aston Villa	L 1-4	Common	24,000
Sep 16	NEWCASTLE UNITED	W 2-0	Flanagan, Common	17,000
Sep 23	Sheffield United	L 1-2	Common	9,000
Sep 30	OLDHAM ATHLETIC	D 1-1	Lewis	11,000
Oct 7	Bolton Wanderers	D 2-2	Chalmers 2	20,000
Oct 14	BRADFORD CITY	W 2-0	Common, Ducat	11,873
Oct 21	Preston North End	W 1-0	Common	8,000
Oct 28	Manchester City	D 3-3	Ducat, Randall, Common	25,000
Nov 4	EVERTON	L 0-1		15,000
Nov 11	West Bromwich Albion	D 1-1	Hoare	13,900
Nov 18	SUNDERLAND	W 3-0	Randall 3	3,000
Nov 25	Blackburn Rovers	L 0-4		15,000
Dec 2	SHEFFIELD WEDNESDAY	L 0-2		8,000
Dec 9	Bury	L 1-3	Chalmers	10,000
Dec 16	MIDDLESBROUGH	W 3-1	Chalmers 2, Randall	11,000
Dec 23	Notts County	L 1-3	Calvert	6,000
Dec 25	Tottenham Hotspur	L 0-5		47,100
Dec 26	TOTTENHAM HOTSPUR	W 3-1	Lewis, Randall, Winship	22,000
Dec 30	Liverpool	L 1-4	Flanagan	16,000
Jan 1	Manchester United	L 0-2		20,000
Jan 6	ASTON VILLA	D 2-2	Winship, Common	6,000
Jan 20	Newcastle United	W 2-1	Common, Flanagan	18,000
Jan 27	SHEFFIELD UNITED	W 3-1	Common 2, Greenaway	10,299
Feb 10	BOLTON WANDERERS	W 3-0	Flanagan, Common, Lewis	14,000
Feb 17	Bradford City	D 1-1	Randall	10,000
Feb 24	Middlesbrough	W 2-0	Common, Ducat (pen)	13,000
Mar 2	MANCHESTER CITY	W 2-0	Common, Randall	12,000
Mar 9	Oldham Athletic	D 0-0		8,000
Mar 16	WEST BROMWICH ALBION	L 0-2		15,000
Mar 23	Sunderland	L 0-1		5,000
Mar 27	Everton	L 0-1		10,000
Apr 5	MANCHESTER UNITED	W 2-1	Common 2	15,507
Apr 6	Sheffield Wednesday	L 0-3		5,000
Apr 8	PRESTON NORTH END	W 4-1	Ducat; Greenaway, Common 2	10,066
Apr 13	BURY	W 1-0	Ducat (pen)	8,000
Apr 22	BLACKBURN ROVERS	W 5-1	Grant J. 3, Flanagan 2	8,000
Apr 27	NOTTS COUNTY	L 0-3		10,000

FA Cup

Jan 13	Bolton Wanderers	(Rd1) L 0-1		24,635

League & Cup Appearances

PLAYER	LEAGUE	CUP COMPETITION FA CUP	TOTAL
Burdett	18		18
Calvert	1		1
Chalmers	19	1	20
Common	36	1	37
Crawford	7	1	8
Ducat	33	1	34
Flanagan	33		33
Grant G.	1		1
Grant J.	4		4
Gray	5		5
Greenaway	23		23
Hoare	3		3
Lewis	29	1	30
McEachrane	18	1	19
McKinnon	22		22
McLaughlan	3		3
Neave	4		4
Peart	34	1	35
Randall	27	1	28
Roose	13		13
Sands	34	1	35
Shaw	36	1	37
Thomson	7		7
Winship	8	1	9

Goalscorers

PLAYER	LEAGUE	CUP COMPETITION FA CUP	TOTAL
Common	17		17
Randall	8		8
Flanagan	7		7
Chalmers	6		6
Ducat	5		5
Grant J.	3		3
Lewis	3		3
Greenaway	2		2
Winship	2		2
Calvert	1		1
Hoare	1		1

Fact File

Woolwich Arsenal inflicted the heaviest defeat of the season on champions Blackburn Rovers, 5-1. Off the field, the Football League rejected new chairman Sir Henry Norris's proposals for Woolwich Arsenal to amalgamate or ground share with his 'other' club Fulham. That led Norris to seek a new home for Arsenal.

MANAGER: George Morrell

CAPTAIN: Percy Sands/Joe Shaw

TOP SCORER: Alf Common 17 (all League)

BIGGEST WIN: 5-1 v Blackburn Rovers, 22 April 1912, League

HIGHEST ATTENDANCE: 22,000 v Tottenham Hotspur, 26 December 1911, League

MAJOR TRANSFER IN: Charlie Randall from Newcastle United

MAJOR TRANSFER OUT: Willis Rippon to Brentford

Final Division One Table

		P	W	D	L	F	A	Pts
1	Blackburn R	38	20	9	9	60	43	49
2	Everton	38	20	6	12	46	42	46
3	Newcastle U	38	18	8	12	64	50	44
4	Bolton W	38	20	3	15	54	43	43
5	Sheffield W	38	16	9	13	69	49	41
6	Aston Villa	38	17	7	14	76	63	41
7	Middlesbrough	38	16	8	14	56	45	40
8	Sunderland	38	14	11	13	58	51	39
9	WBA	38	15	9	14	43	47	39
10	Woolwich Arsenal	38	15	8	15	55	59	38
11	Bradford C	38	15	8	15	46	50	38
12	Tottenham H	38	14	9	15	53	53	37
13	Manchester U	38	13	11	14	45	60	37
14	Sheffield U	38	13	10	15	63	56	36
15	Manchester C	38	13	9	16	56	58	35
16	Notts Co	38	14	7	17	46	63	35
17	Liverpool	38	12	10	16	49	55	34
18	Oldham Ath	38	12	10	16	46	54	34
19	Preston NE	38	13	7	18	40	57	33
20	Bury	38	6	9	23	32	59	21

Season 1912-13

Football League Division One

DATE	OPPONENTS	SCORE	GOALSCORERS	ATTENDANCE
Sep 2	MANCHESTER UNITED	D 0-0		10,000
Sep 7	Liverpool	L 0-3		30,000
Sep 14	BOLTON WANDERERS	L 1-2	Winship	13,000
Sep 16	ASTON VILLA	L 0-3		6,805
Sep 21	Sheffield United	W 3-1	Randall 2, McLaughlan	20,000
Sep 28	NEWCASTLE UNITED	D 1-1	McLaughlan	18,000
Oct 5	Oldham Athletic	D 0-0		7,500
Oct 12	CHELSEA	L 0-1		20,000
Oct 19	SUNDERLAND	L 1-3	McLaughlan	10,000
Oct 26	Bradford City	L 1-3	Hanks	7,000
Nov 2	MANCHESTER CITY	L 0-4		8,000
Nov 9	West Bromwich Albion	L 1-2	Greenaway	15,980
Nov 16	EVERTON	D 0-0		10,000
Nov 23	Sheffield Wednesday	L 0-2		14,000
Nov 30	BLACKBURN ROVERS	L 0-1		9,000
Dec 7	Derby County	L 1-4	Flanagan	10,000
Dec 14	TOTTENHAM HOTSPUR	L 0-3		13,000
Dec 21	Middlesbrough	L 0-2		10,000
Dec 25	NOTTS COUNTY	D 0-0		7,000
Dec 26	Notts County	L 1-2	Graham	12,000
Dec 28	LIVERPOOL	D 1-1	Graham (pen)	9,070
Jan 1	Sunderland	L 1-4	Lewis	22,000
Jan 4	Bolton Wanderers	L 1-5	Flanagan	10,000
Jan 18	SHEFFIELD UNITED	L 1-3	Randall	6,000
Jan 25	Newcastle United	L 1-3	Duncan	20,000
Feb 8	OLDHAM ATHLETIC	D 0-0		9,000
Feb 15	Chelsea	D 1-1	Burrell	15,000
Mar 1	BRADFORD CITY	D 1-1	Burrell	10,000
Mar 8	Manchester City	W 1-0	Lewis	15,000
Mar 15	WEST BROMWICH ALBION	W 1-0	Sands	8,000
Mar 21	Manchester United	L 0-2		20,000
Mar 22	Everton	L 0-3		10,000
Mar 24	Aston Villa	L 1-4	Randall	30,000
Mar 29	SHEFFIELD WEDNESDAY	L 2-5	Devine, Grant	5,000
Apr 5	Blackburn Rovers	D 1-1	Devine	6,000
Apr 12	DERBY COUNTY	L 1-2	Lewis	4,000
Apr 19	Tottenham Hotspur	D 1-1	Grant	20,000
Apr 26	MIDDLESBROUGH	D 1-1	Stonley	3,000

FA Cup

Jan 11	Croydon Common	(Rd1) D 0-0		8,000
Jan 15	CROYDON COMMON	(R) W 2-1	Duncan, Graham	9,000
Feb 1	LIVERPOOL	(Rd2) L 1-4	Lewis	8,653

League & Cup Appearances

PLAYER	LEAGUE	CUP COMPETITION FA CUP	TOTAL
Burrell	17	1	18
Common	12		12
Crawford	19		19
Devine	11		11
Duncan	3	2	5
Evans	1	1	2
Fidler	13		13
Flanagan	22	3	25
Ford	3		3
Graham	12	3	15
Grant G	13		13
Greenaway	27	3	30
Groves	3		3
Hanks	4		4
King E	11	2	13
Lewis	24	3	27
McDonald H.	18	3	21
McEachrane	7	2	9
McKinnon	29	1	30
McLaughlan	13		13
Payne	3		3
Peart	16	2	18
Randall	15		15
Sands	28	1	29
Shaw	38	3	41
Spittle	6		6
Stonley	10		10
Thomson	25	3	28
Wilson	1		1
Winship	14		14

Goalscorers

PLAYER	LEAGUE	CUP COMPETITION FA CUP	TOTAL
Randall	4		4
Lewis	3	1	4
McLaughlan	3		3
Burrell	2		2
Graham	2	1	3
Devine	2		2
Flanagan	2		2
Grant	2		2
Duncan	1	1	2
Greenaway	1		1
Hanks	1		1
Sands	1		1
Stonley	1		1
Winship	1		1

Fact File

This was the worst season in the club's history with only three league wins and 26 goals, their lowest-ever totals. The club's points total of 18 was another unwanted record. Off the field, Norris had agreed a 21-year lease, costing £20,000, on a site in Highbury which was to be developed into Arsenal's new home.

MANAGER: George Morrell

CAPTAIN: Percy Sands/Joe Shaw

TOP SCORER: Charlie Randall 4 (all League), Charlie Lewis 4 (3 League)

BIGGEST WIN: 3-1 v Sheffield United, 21 September 1912, League

HIGHEST ATTENDANCE: 20,000 v Chelsea, 12 October 1912, League

MAJOR TRANSFER IN: Stephen Stonley from Oldham Athletic

MAJOR TRANSFERS OUT: Andy Ducat to Aston Villa, Alf Common to Preston North End

Final Division One Table

		P	W	D	L	F	A	Pts
1	SUNDERLAND	38	25	4	9	86	43	54
2	ASTON VILLA	38	19	12	7	86	52	50
3	SHEFFIELD W	38	21	7	10	75	55	49
4	MANCHESTER U	38	19	8	11	69	43	46
5	BLACKBURN R	38	16	13	9	79	43	45
6	MANCHESTER C	38	18	8	12	53	37	44
7	DERBY CO	38	17	8	13	69	66	42
8	BOLTON W	38	16	10	12	62	63	42
9	OLDHAM ATH	38	14	14	10	50	55	42
10	WBA	38	13	12	13	57	50	38
11	EVERTON	38	15	7	16	48	54	37
12	LIVERPOOL	38	16	5	17	61	71	37
13	BRADFORD C	38	12	11	15	50	60	35
14	NEWCASTLE U	38	13	8	17	47	47	34
15	SHEFFIELD U	38	14	6	18	56	70	34
16	MIDDLESBROUGH	38	11	10	17	55	69	32
17	TOTTENHAM H	38	12	6	20	45	72	30
18	CHELSEA	38	11	6	21	51	73	28
19	NOTTS CO	38	7	9	22	28	56	23
20	WOOLWICH ARSENAL	38	3	12	23	26	74	18

Season 1913-14

Football League Division Two

DATE	OPPONENTS	SCORE	GOALSCORERS	ATTENDANCE
Sep 6	LEICESTER FOSSE	W 2-1	Jobey, Devine (pen)	20,000
Sep 13	Wolverhampton Wanderers	W 2-1	Winship, Stonley (pen)	15,000
Sep 15	NOTTS COUNTY	W 3-0	Stonley 2, Grant G.	20,000
Sep 20	HULL CITY	D 0-0		25,000
Sep 27	Barnsley	L 0-1		11,000
Oct 4	BURY	L 0-1		30,000
Oct 11	Huddersfield Town	W 2-1	Stonley, Burrell	8,000
Oct 18	LINCOLN CITY	W 3-0	Flanagan, Stonley 2	25,000
Oct 25	Blackpool	D 1-1	Jobey	18,000
Nov 1	NOTTINGHAM FOREST	W 3-2	Rutherford 2, Flanagan	25,000
Nov 8	Fulham	L 1-6	Stonley	35,000
Nov 15	Grimsby Town	D 1-1	Devine (pen)	8,000
Nov 22	BIRMINGHAM	W 1-0	Flanagan	25,000
Nov 29	Bristol City	D 1-1	Hardinge	15,000
Dec 6	LEEDS CITY	W 1-0	Benson (pen)	18,000
Dec 13	Clapton Orient	L 0-1		27,000
Dec 20	GLOSSOP NORTH END	W 2-0	Stonley, Devine	14,500
Dec 25	Bradford Park Avenue	W 3-2	Stonley 3	22,000
Dec 26	BRADFORD PARK AVENUE	W 2-0	Flanagan, Hardinge	30,000
Dec 27	Leicester Fosse	W 2-0	Bell 2	10,000
Jan 1	Notts County	L 0-1		7,000
Jan 3	WOLVERHAMPTON WANDERERS	W 3-1	Rutherford 2, Hardinge	20,000
Jan 17	Hull City	W 2-1	Flanagan	10,000
Jan 24	BARNSLEY	W 1-0	Rutherford	19,000
Feb 7	Bury	D 1-1	Stonley	10,000
Feb 14	HUDDERSFIELD TOWN	L 0-1		25,000
Feb 21	Lincoln City	L 2-5	Slade, Hardinge	9,000
Feb 28	BLACKPOOL	W 2-1	Jobey, Slade	20,000
Mar 7	Nottingham Forest	D 0-0		10,000
Mar 14	FULHAM	W 2-0	Flanagan, Slade	30,000
Mar 28	Birmingham	L 0-2		18,000
Apr 4	BRISTOL CITY	D 1-1	Winship	12,000
Apr 10	Stockport County	L 0-2		15,000
Apr 11	Leeds City	D 0-0		22,000
Apr 13	STOCKPORT COUNTY	W 4-0	Flanagan 2, Benson, Rutherford	18,000
Apr 18	CLAPTON ORIENT	D 2-2	Flanagan 2	35,000
Apr 23	GRIMSBY TOWN	W 2-0	Stonley, Flanagan	25,000
Apr 25	Glossop North End	W 2-0	Slade, o.g.	4,000

FA Cup

Jan 10	Bradford City	L 0-2		18,000

League & Cup Appearances

PLAYER	LEAGUE	CUP COMPETITION FA CUP	TOTAL
Bell	1		1
Benson	25	1	26
Burrell	6		6
Caldwell	3		3
Devine	13		13
Fidler	12		12
Flanagan	24	1	25
Graham	13	1	14
Grant G.	12	1	13
Greenaway	8		8
Groves	3	1	4
Hardinge	29	1	30
Jobey	28		28
Lewis	26	1	27
Lievesley	35	1	36
McEachrane	2		2
McKinnon	24		24
Randall	1		1
Rutherford	21		21
Sands	33	1	34
Shaw	36	1	37
Slade	12		12
Spittle	1		1
Stonley	28	1	29
Thomson	7		7
Winship	15		15

Goalscorers

PLAYER	LEAGUE	CUP COMPETITION FA CUP	TOTAL
Stonley	13		13
Flanagan	12		12
Rutherford	6		6
Hardinge	4		4
Slade	4		4
Devine	3		3
Jobey	3		3
Bell	2		2
Benson	2		2
Winship	2		2
Burrell	1		1
Grant G.	1		1
Opps' o.gs.	1		1

Fact File

George Jobey scored Arsenal's first goal at Highbury in their opening day 2-1 win over Leicester Fosse on 6 September 1913. The stadium was still in the throes of building work. There were no exit gates and construction vehicles moved in and out of the ground while play was in progress.

MANAGER: George Morrell

CAPTAIN: Percy Sands/Joe Shaw

TOP SCORER: Stephen Stonley 13 (all League)

BIGGEST WIN: 4-0 v Stockport County, 13 April 1914, League

HIGHEST ATTENDANCE: 35,000 v Clapton Orient, 18 April 1914, League

MAJOR TRANSFERS IN: Joe Lievesley from Sheffield United, Wally Hardinge from Sheffield United, Jock Rutherford from Newcastle United

MAJOR TRANSFERS OUT: Charlie Randall to North Shields, John Peart to Croydon Common

Final Division Two Table

		P	W	D	L	F	A	Pts
1	NOTTS CO	38	23	7	8	77	36	53
2	BRADFORD PA	38	23	3	12	71	47	49
3	THE ARSENAL	38	20	9	9	54	38	49
4	LEEDS C	38	20	7	11	76	46	47
5	BARNSLEY	38	19	7	12	51	45	45
6	CLAPTON ORIENT	38	16	11	11	47	35	43
7	HULL C	38	16	9	13	53	37	41
8	BRISTOL C	38	16	9	13	52	50	41
9	WOLVERHAMPTON W	38	18	5	15	51	52	41
10	BURY	38	15	10	13	39	40	40
11	FULHAM	38	16	6	16	46	43	38
12	STOCKPORT CO	38	13	10	15	55	57	36
13	HUDDERSFIELD T	38	13	8	17	47	53	34
14	BIRMINGHAM	38	12	10	16	48	60	34
15	GRIMSBY T	38	13	8	17	42	58	34
16	BLACKPOOL	38	9	14	15	33	44	32
17	GLOSSOP	38	11	6	21	51	67	28
18	LEICESTER FOSSE	38	11	4	23	45	61	26
19	LINCOLN C	38	10	6	22	36	66	26
20	NOTTINGHAM F	38	7	9	22	37	76	23

Season 1914-15

Football League Division Two

DATE	OPPONENTS	SCORE	GOALSCORERS	ATTENDANCE
Sep 1	GLOSSOP NORTH END	W 3-0	King 2, Bradshaw	7,000
Sep 5	Wolverhampton Wanderers	L 0-1		8,000
Sep 8	Glossop North End	W 4-0	King 2, Flanagan, Bradshaw	7,000
Sep 12	FULHAM	W 3-0	King 2, Rutherford	10,000
Sep 19	Stockport County	D 1-1	King	6,000
Sep 26	HULL CITY	W 2-1	Hardinge 2	20,000
Oct 3	Leeds City	D 2-2	Bradshaw, Hardinge	12,000
Oct 10	CLAPTON ORIENT	W 2-1	King, Bradshaw	30,000
Oct 17	BLACKPOOL	W 2-0	King 2	17,000
Oct 24	Derby County	L 0-4		8,000
Oct 31	LINCOLN CITY	D 1-1	Hardinge	15,000
Nov 7	Birmingham	L 0-3		15,000
Nov 14	GRIMSBY TOWN	W 6-0	King 3, Bradshaw, Benson (pen), McKinnon	15,000
Nov 21	Nottingham Forest	D 1-1	Benson (pen)	3,000
Nov 28	BRISTOL CITY	W 3-0	Hardinge 2, King	7,000
Dec 5	Bury	. L 1-3	Bradshaw	5,000
Dec 12	PRESTON NORTH END	L 1-2	Hardinge	10,000
Dec 25	Leicester Fosse	W 4-1	Grant, King, Benson, Blyth	13,000
Dec 26	LEICESTER FOSSE	W 6-0	Lewis 3, McKinnon, King, Flanagan	6,000
Jan 1	Barnsley	L 0-1		5,000
Jan 2	WOLVERHAMPTON WANDERERS	W 5-1	King 4, Buckley	9,000
Jan 16	Fulham	W 1-0	Bradshaw	10,000
Jan 23	STOCKPORT COUNTY	W 3-1	Flanagan 2, Bradshaw	6,000
Feb 6	LEEDS CITY	W 2-0	Rutherford, Bradshaw	10,000
Feb 13	Clapton Orient	L 0-1		4,000
Feb 20	Blackpool	W 2-0	Winship, King	6,000
Feb 27	DERBY COUNTY	L 1-2	King (pen)	18,000
Mar 6	Lincoln City	L 0-1		6,000
Mar 13	BIRMINGHAM	W 1-0	Bradshaw	19,000
Mar 20	Grimsby Town	L 0-1		5,000
Mar 27	HUDDERSFIELD TOWN	L 0-3		14,000
Apr 2	Hull City	L 0-1		8,000
Apr 3	Bristol City	D 1-1	Winship	7,000
Apr 5	BARNSLEY	W 1-0	Lewis	15,000
Apr 10	BURY	W 3-1	Flanagan 2, Blyth	12,000
Apr 17	Preston North End	L 0-3		14,000
Apr 24	NOTTINGHAM FOREST	W 7-0	Benson 2, King 4, Rutherford	10,000

FA Cup

Jan 9	MERTHYR TYDFIL	(Rd1) W 3-0	King 3	9,000
Jan 30	Chelsea	(Rd2) L 0-1		40,372

League & Cup Appearances

PLAYER	LEAGUE	CUP COMPETITION FA CUP	TOTAL
Benson	27	1	28
Blyth	12		12
Bradshaw	29	2	31
Buckley	29	2	31
Flanagan	26	2	28
Fletcher	3		3
Ford	6	1	7
Graham	26		26
Grant	28	2	30
Greenaway	6		6
Groves	2		2
Hardinge	12		12
Kempton		1	1
King	37	2	39
Lewis	24	2	26
Liddell	2		2
Lievesley	38	1	39
McKinnon	21	2	23
Norman	4		4
Rutherford	26	2	28
Sands	10		10
Shaw	38	2	40
Winship	12		12

Goalscorers

PLAYER	LEAGUE	CUP COMPETITION FA CUP	TOTAL
King	26	3	29
Bradshaw	10		10
Hardinge	7		7
Flanagan	6		6
Benson	5		5
Lewis	4		4
Rutherford	3		3
Blyth	2		2
McKinnon	2		2
Winship	2		2
Buckley	1		1
Grant	1		1

Fact File

Manager George Morrell resigned at the end of the season as football was halted for the rest of World War I. Arsenal were in financial difficulties again because of the cost of the move to Highbury.

MANAGER: George Morrell

CAPTAIN: Joe Shaw

TOP SCORER: Henry King 29 (26 League)

BIGGEST WIN: 7-0 v Nottingham Forest, 24 April 1915, League

HIGHEST ATTENDANCE: 30,000 v Clapton Orient, 10 October 1914, League

MAJOR TRANSFERS IN: Henry King from Northampton Town, Chris Buckley from Aston Villa

MAJOR TRANSFER OUT: Stephen Stonley to Brentford

Final Division Two Table

		P	W	D	L	F	A	Pts
1	DERBY CO	38	23	7	8	71	33	53
2	PRESTON NE	38	20	10	8	61	42	50
3	BARNSLEY	38	22	3	13	51	51	47
4	WOLVERHAMPTON W	38	19	7	12	77	52	45
5	THE ARSENAL	38	19	5	14	69	41	43
6	BIRMINGHAM	38	17	9	12	62	39	43
7	HULL C	38	19	5	14	65	54	43
8	HUDDERSFIELD T	38	17	8	13	61	42	42
9	CLAPTON ORIENT	38	16	9	13	50	48	41
10	BLACKPOOL	38	17	5	16	58	57	39
11	BURY	38	15	8	15	61	56	38
12	FULHAM	38	15	7	16	53	47	37
13	BRISTOL C	38	15	7	16	62	56	37
14	STOCKPORT CO	38	15	7	16	54	60	37
15	LEEDS C	38	14	4	20	65	64	32
16	LINCOLN C	38	11	9	18	46	65	31
17	GRIMSBY T	38	11	9	18	48	76	31
18	NOTTINGHAM F	38	10	9	19	43	77	29
19	LEICESTER FOSSE	38	10	4	24	47	88	24
20	GLOSSOP	38	6	6	26	31	87	18

Season 1919-20

Football League Division One

DATE	OPPONENTS	SCORE	GOALSCORERS	ATTENDANCE
Aug 30	NEWCASTLE UNITED	L 0-1		40,000
Sep 1	Liverpool	W 3-2	White 2, Blyth	15,000
Sep 6	Newcastle United	L 1-3	Groves	45,000
Sep 8	LIVERPOOL	W 1-0	Rutherford	20,000
Sep 13	Sunderland	D 1-1	White	30,000
Sep 20	SUNDERLAND	W 3-2	White 3	42,000
Sep 27	Blackburn Rovers	D 2-2	White, Burgess	5,000
Oct 4	BLACKBURN ROVERS	L 0-1		30,000
Oct 11	Everton	W 3-2	White 2, Blyth	35,000
Oct 18	EVERTON	D 1-1	Groves	30,000
Oct 25	BRADFORD CITY	L 1-2	Graham (pen)	35,000
Nov 1	Bradford City	D 1-1	White	16,000
Nov 8	BOLTON WANDERERS	D 2-2	Pagnam, Rutherford	30,000
Nov 15	Bolton Wanderers	D 2-2	Hardinge, Pagnam	20,000
Nov 22	NOTTS COUNTY	W 3-1	Pagnam 2, Toner	25,000
Nov 29	Notts County	D 2-2	Buckley, Pagnam	6,000
Dec 6	CHELSEA	D 1-1	White	50,000
Dec 13	Chelsea	L 1-3	White	60,000
Dec 20	SHEFFIELD WEDNESDAY	W 3-1	Hardinge, Pagnam, Butler	30,000
Dec 25	Derby County	L 1-2	Pagnam (pen)	14,000
Dec 26	DERBY COUNTY	W 1-0	Groves	25,000
Dec 27	Sheffield Wednesday	W 2-1	Hardinge, White	23,000
Jan 3	MANCHESTER CITY	D 2-2	White, Lewis	32,000
Jan 17	Manchester City	L 1-4	Graham (pen)	25,000
Jan 24	ASTON VILLA	L 0-1		55,000
Feb 7	OLDHAM ATHLETIC	W 3-2	North, Graham, Blyth	32,000
Feb 11	Aston Villa	L 1-2	White	20,000
Feb 14	Oldham Athletic	L 0-3		14,000
Feb 21	MANCHESTER UNITED	L 0-3		25,000
Feb 28	Manchester United	W 1-0	Rutherford	30,000
Mar 6	Sheffield United	L 0-2		25,000
Mar 13	SHEFFIELD UNITED	W 3-0	Graham, Pagnam	35,000
Mar 20	Middlesbrough	L 0-1		22,000
Mar 27	MIDDLESBROUGH	W 2-1	Blyth, Groves	25,000
Apr 3	Burnley	L 1-2	Pagnam	20,000
Apr 5	WEST BROMWICH ALBION	W 1-0	Blyth	40,000
Apr 6	West Bromwich Albion	L 0-1		40,000
Apr 10	BURNLEY	W 2-0	Bradshaw, Pagnam	20,000
Apr 17	Preston North End	D 1-1	White	13,000
Apr 24	PRESTON NORTH END	D 0-0		35,000
Apr 28	Bradford Park Avenue	D 0-0		7,000
May 1	BRADFORD PARK AVENUE	W 3-0	Groves, Pagnam, Bradshaw	30,000

FA Cup

Jan 10	ROCHDALE	(Rd1) W 4-2	Rutherford, Groves, Graham, Pagnam	26,596
Jan 31	Bristol City	(Rd2) L 0-1		25,900

League & Cup Appearances

PLAYER	LEAGUE	CUP COMPETITION FA CUP	TOTAL
Baker	17		17
Blyth	29	1	30
Bradshaw	33	2	35
Buckley	23	1	24
Burgess	7		7
Butler	21	1	22
Coopland	1		1
Cownley	4		4
Dunn	16	1	17
Graham	22	2	24
Greenaway	3		3
Groves	29	2	31
Hardinge	13		13
Hutchins	18		18
Lewis C	5	1	6
McKinnon	41	2	43
North	4		4
Pagnam	25	2	27
Pattison	1		1
Peart	5		5
Rutherford	36	2	38
Shaw	33	2	35
Toner	15	1	16
Voysey	5		5
White	29	1	30
Whittaker	1		1
Williamson	26	1	27

Goalscorers

PLAYER	LEAGUE	CUP COMPETITION FA CUP	TOTAL
White	16		16
Pagnam	12	1	13
Groves	5	1	6
Blyth	5		5
Graham	4	1	5
Rutherford	3	1	4
Hardinge	3		3
Bradshaw	2		2
Buckley	1		1
Burgess	1		1
Butler	1		1
Lewis	1		1
North	1		1
Toner	1		1

Fact File

Arsenal's new manager was Leslie Knighton who had made a name for himself developing young talent as assistant manager of Manchester City. He took over a First Division club because Norris had successfully lobbied for Arsenal to be voted into the enlarged top division – at the expense of Tottenham – even though they only finished fifth in Division Two in 1915. The attendance of 55,000 for the visit of Aston Villa in January was a club record.

MANAGER: Leslie Knighton

CAPTAIN: Joe Shaw

TOP SCORER: Harry White 16 (all League)

BIGGEST WIN: 3-0 v Sheffield United, 13 March 1920, League

HIGHEST ATTENDANCE: 55,000 v Aston Villa, 24 January 1920, League

MAJOR TRANSFERS IN: Harry White from Brentford, Alf Baker from Huddersfield Town, Fred Pagnam from Liverpool

Final Division One Table

		P	W	D	L	F	A	Pts
1	WBA	42	28	4	10	104	47	60
2	BURNLEY	42	21	9	12	65	59	51
3	CHELSEA	42	22	5	15	56	51	49
4	LIVERPOOL	42	19	10	13	59	44	48
5	SUNDERLAND	42	22	4	16	72	59	48
6	BOLTON W	42	19	9	14	72	65	47
7	MANCHESTER C	42	18	9	15	71	62	45
8	NEWCASTLE U	42	17	9	16	44	39	43
9	ASTON VILLA	42	18	6	18	75	73	42
10	ARSENAL	42	15	12	15	56	58	42
11	BRADFORD PA	42	15	12	15	60	63	42
12	MANCHESTER U	42	13	14	15	54	50	40
13	MIDDLESBROUGH	42	15	10	17	61	65	40
14	SHEFFIELD U	42	16	8	18	59	69	40
15	BRADFORD C	42	14	11	17	54	63	39
16	EVERTON	42	12	14	16	69	68	38
17	OLDHAM ATH	42	15	8	19	49	52	38
18	DERBY CO	42	13	12	17	47	57	38
19	PRESTON NE	42	14	10	18	57	73	38
20	BLACKBURN R	42	13	11	18	64	77	37
21	NOTTS CO	42	12	12	18	56	74	36
22	SHEFFIELD W	42	7	9	26	28	64	23

Season 1920-21

Football League Division One

DATE	OPPONENTS	SCORE	GOALSCORERS	ATTENDANCE
Aug 28	Aston Villa	L 0-5		50,000
Aug 30	MANCHESTER UNITED	W 2-0	Pagnam, Smith	25,000
Sep 4	ASTON VILLA	L 0-1		45,000
Sep 6	Manchester United	D 1-1	White	30,000
Sep 11	MANCHESTER CITY	W 2-1	Pagnam, Groves	42,000
Sep 18	Manchester City	L 1-3	Blyth	30,000
Sep 25	MIDDLESBROUGH	D 2-2	Graham, Pagnam (pen)	40,000
Oct 2	Middlesbrough	L 1-2	White	25,000
Oct 9	BOLTON WANDERERS	D 0-0		38,000
Oct 16	Bolton Wanderers	D 1-1	White	35,000
Oct 23	Derby County	D 1-1	White	18,000
Oct 30	DERBY COUNTY	W 2-0	Pagnam, White	45,000
Nov 6	Blackburn Rovers	D 2-2	McKinnon, Buckley	20,000
Nov 13	BLACKBURN ROVERS	W 2-0	White, Pagnam	40,000
Nov 20	Huddersfield Town	W 4-0	Pagnam 2, Blyth, Graham (pen)	19,000
Nov 27	HUDDERSFIELD TOWN	W 2-0	Pagnam 2	35,000
Dec 4	Chelsea	W 2-1	Pagnam 2	60,000
Dec 11	CHELSEA	D 1-1	Blyth	50,000
Dec 18	Bradford City	L 1-3	Blyth	20,000
Dec 25	Everton	W 4-2	White, Toner, Blyth, Pagnam	35,000
Dec 27	EVERTON	D 1-1	Pagnam	40,000
Jan 1	BRADFORD CITY	L 1-2	Graham (pen)	20,000
Jan 15	Tottenham Hotspur	L 1-2	Rutherford	39,221
Jan 22	TOTTENHAM HOTSPUR	W 3-2	Rutherford 2, White	60,600
Jan 29	SUNDERLAND	L 1-2	Pagnam	40,000
Feb 5	Sunderland	L 1-5	Blyth	30,000
Feb 12	Oldham Athletic	D 1-1	Graham (pen)	18,313
Feb 19	OLDHAM ATHLETIC	D 2-2	Rutherford, Walden	40,000
Feb 26	Preston North End	W 1-0	White	25,000
Mar 12	Burnley	L 0-1		25,000
Mar 19	BURNLEY	D 1-1	Baker (pen)	45,000
Mar 26	SHEFFIELD UNITED	L 2-6	White, Baker	30,000
Mar 28	WEST BROMWICH ALBION	W 2-1	Graham (pen), Blyth	30,000
Mar 29	West Bromwich Albion	W 4-3	North 2, Hopkins, McKenzie	18,000
Apr 2	Sheffield United	D 1-1	Rutherford	35,000
Apr 9	BRADFORD PARK AVENUE	W 2-1	Toner, Rutherford	30,000
Apr 16	Bradford Park Avenue	W 1-0	Toner	14,000
Apr 23	NEWCASTLE UNITED	D 1-1	Rutherford	20,000
Apr 25	PRESTON NORTH END	W 2-1	Hopkins, McKenzie	12,000
Apr 30	Newcastle United	L 0-1		35,000
May 2	LIVERPOOL	D 0-0		17,000
May 7	Liverpool	L 0-3		20,000

FA Cup

Jan 8	Queens Park Rangers	(Rd1) L 0-2		18,000

League & Cup Appearances

PLAYER	LEAGUE	CUP COMPETITION FA CUP	TOTAL
Baker	37		37
Blyth	40	1	41
Bradshaw	21		21
Buckley	4		4
Burgess	4		4
Butler	6	1	7
Cownley	1		1
Dunn	9		9
Graham	30		30
Groves	13		13
Hopkins	8		8
Hutchins	39	1	40
McKenzie	5		5
McKinnon	37	1	38
North	8		8
Pagnam	25	1	26
Paterson	20		20
Pattison	6		6
Peart	1		1
Rutherford	32	1	33
Shaw	28	1	29
Smith	10		10
Toner	12	1	13
Voysey		1	1
Walden	2		2
White	26	1	27
Whittaker	5		5
Williamson	33	1	34

Goalscorers

PLAYER	LEAGUE	CUP COMPETITION FA CUP	TOTAL
Pagnam	14		14
White	10		10
Blyth	7		7
Rutherford	7		7
Graham	5		5
Toner	3		3
Baker	2		2
Hopkins	2		2
McKinnon	2		2
North	2		2
Buckley	1		1
Groves	1		1
McKenzie	1		1
Smith	1		1
Walden	1		1

Fact File

Tottenham gained promotion in 1919-20 and the stage was set for the first-ever North London derby. Spurs won 2-1 at White Hart Lane on 15 January. Arsenal won the return 3-2 a week later in front of a record crowd of 60,600.

MANAGER: Leslie Knighton

CAPTAIN: Joe Shaw

TOP SCORER: Fred Pagnam 14 (all League)

BIGGEST WIN: 4-0 v Huddersfield Town, 20 November 1920, League

HIGHEST ATTENDANCE: 60,600 v Tottenham Hotspur, 22 January 1921, League

MAJOR TRANSFERS OUT: Fred Pagnam to Cardiff City, Fred Groves to Brighton & Hove Albion

Final Division One Table

		P	W	D	L	F	A	Pts
1	BURNLEY	42	23	13	6	79	36	59
2	MANCHESTER C	42	24	6	12	70	50	54
3	BOLTON W	42	19	14	9	77	53	52
4	LIVERPOOL	42	18	15	9	63	35	51
5	NEWCASTLE UNITED	42	20	10	12	66	45	50
6	TOTTENHAM H	42	19	9	14	70	48	47
7	EVERTON	42	17	13	12	66	55	47
8	MIDDLESBROUGH	42	17	12	13	53	53	46
9	ARSENAL	42	15	14	13	59	63	44
10	ASTON VILLA	42	18	7	17	63	70	43
11	BLACKBURN R	42	13	15	14	57	59	41
12	SUNDERLAND	42	14	13	15	57	60	41
13	MANCHESTER U	42	15	10	17	64	68	40
14	WBA	42	13	14	15	54	58	40
15	BRADFORD C	42	12	15	15	61	63	39
16	PRESTON NE	42	15	9	18	61	65	39
17	HUDDERSFIELD T	42	15	9	18	42	49	39
18	CHELSEA	42	13	13	16	48	58	39
19	OLDHAM ATH	42	9	15	18	49	86	33
20	SHEFFIELD U	42	6	18	18	42	68	30
21	DERBY CO	42	5	16	21	32	58	26
22	BRADFORD PA	42	8	8	26	43	76	24

Season 1921-22

Football League Division One

DATE	OPPONENTS	SCORE	GOALSCORERS	ATTENDANCE
Aug 27	SHEFFIELD UNITED	L 1-2	White	40,000
Aug 29	Preston North End	L 2-3	White 2	25,000
Sep 3	Sheffield United	L 1-4	White	25,000
Sep 5	PRESTON NORTH END	W 1-0	White	20,000
Sep 10	Manchester City	L 0-2		25,000
Sep 17	MANCHESTER CITY	L 0-1		25,000
Sep 24	Everton	D 1-1	Bradshaw	30,000
Oct 1	EVERTON	W 1-0	White	35,000
Oct 8	Sunderland	L 0-1		30,000
Oct 15	SUNDERLAND	L 1-2	Bradshaw	40,000
Oct 22	Huddersfield Town	L 0-2		12,000
Oct 29	HUDDERSFIELD TOWN	L 1-3	North	30,000
Nov 5	Birmingham	W 1-0	North	30,000
Nov 12	BIRMINGHAM	W 5-2	Whittaker, Baker, Hopkins 2, North	30,000
Nov 19	Bolton Wanderers	L 0-1		20,000
Dec 3	Blackburn Rovers	W 1-0	Baker	25,000
Dec 10	BLACKBURN ROVERS	D 1-1	Hopkins	35,000
Dec 12	BOLTON WANDERERS	D 1-1	Butler	10,000
Dec 17	Oldham Athletic	L 1-2	Boreham	10,517
Dec 24	OLDHAM ATHLETIC	L 0-1		20,000
Dec 26	CARDIFF CITY	D 0-0		35,000
Dec 27	Cardiff City	L 3-4	White, Boreham	37,000
Dec 31	Chelsea	W 2-0	White, Boreham	40,000
Jan 14	CHELSEA	W 1-0	Boreham	40,000
Jan 21	BURNLEY	D 0-0		23,000
Feb 4	NEWCASTLE UNITED	W 2-1	Boreham, Toner	30,000
Feb 11	Newcastle United	L 1-3	Rutherford	30,000
Feb 20	Burnley	L 0-1		15,000
Feb 25	Liverpool	L 0-4		30,000
Mar 11	Manchester United	L 0-1		25,000
Mar 18	Aston Villa	L 0-2		30,000
Mar 22	LIVERPOOL	W 1-0	Baker	12,000
Mar 25	ASTON VILLA	W 2-0	White, Boreham	40,000
Apr 1	MIDDLESBROUGH	D 2-2	White, Boreham	30,000
Apr 5	MANCHESTER UNITED	W 3-1	White, Butler, Boreham	25,000
Apr 8	Middlesbrough	L 2-4	Baker, White	20,000
Apr 15	Tottenham Hotspur	L 0-2		40,394
Apr 17	West Bromwich Albion	W 3-0	Boreham, Young, Graham	19,000
Apr 18	WEST BROMWICH ALBION	D 2-2	White, Graham (pen)	22,000
Apr 22	TOTTENHAM HOTSPUR	W 1-0	Graham (pen)	42,000
Apr 29	Bradford City	W 2-0	White, Young	35,000
May 6	BRADFORD CITY	W 1-0	Blyth	32,000

FA Cup

DATE	OPPONENTS		SCORE	GOALSCORERS	ATTENDANCE
Jan 7	QUEENS PARK RANGERS	(Rd1)	D 0-0		31,000
Jan 11	Queens Park Rangers	(R)	W 2-1	Graham (pen), Milne	15,000
Jan 28	Bradford Park Avenue	(Rd2)	W 3-2	White 2, Blyth	10,000
Feb 18	LEICESTER CITY	(Rd3)	W 3-0	Rutherford, White 2	39,421
Mar 4	PRESTON NORTH END	(Rd4)	D 1-1	White	37,517
Mar 8	Preston North End	(R)	L 1-2	Blyth	30,000

League & Cup Appearances

PLAYER	LEAGUE	CUP COMPETITION FA CUP	TOTAL
Baker	32	6	38
Blyth	25	5	30
Boreham	22		22
Bradshaw	32	6	38
Burgess	2		2
Butler	25	3	28
Cowley	10		10
Creegan	5	1	6
Dunn	1		1
Earle	1		1
Graham	21	5	26
Henderson	5		5
Hutchins	37	3	40
Hopkins	11	1	12
McKenzie	3		3
McKinnon	17		17
Maxwell	1		1
Milne	4	3	7
North	11		11
Paterson	2		2
Pattison	2	1	3
Rutherford	36	4	40
Shaw	6		6
Toner	24	6	30
Turnbull	5	4	9
Voysey	1		1
White	35	6	41
Whittaker	36	6	42
Williamson	41	6	47
Young	9		9

Goalscorers

PLAYER	LEAGUE	CUP COMPETITION FA CUP	TOTAL
White	14	5	19
Boreham	10		10
Baker	4		4
Graham	3	1	4
Hopkins	3		3
North	3		3
Blyth	1	2	3
Bradshaw	2		2
Butler	2		2
Young	2		2
Rutherford	1	1	2
Toner	1		1
Whittaker	1		1

Fact File

Arsenal were in danger of relegation until late in the season when a closing run of four wins and a draw pulled them clear of trouble. They reached the FA Cup quarter-finals for only the third time in their history.

MANAGER: Leslie Knighton

CAPTAIN: Billy Blyth

TOP SCORER: Harry White 19 (14 League)

BIGGEST WIN: 5-2 v Birmingham City, 12 November 1921, League

HIGHEST ATTENDANCE: 42,000 v Tottenham Hotspur, 22 April 1922, League

MAJOR TRANSFERS IN: Billy Milne from Buckie Thistle, Bob John from Caerphilly Town

Final Division One Table

		P	W	D	L	F	A	Pts
1	LIVERPOOL	42	22	13	7	63	36	57
2	TOTTENHAM H	42	21	9	12	65	39	51
3	BURNLEY	42	22	5	15	72	54	49
4	CARDIFF C	42	19	10	13	61	53	48
5	ASTON VILLA	42	22	3	17	74	55	47
6	BOLTON W	42	20	7	15	68	59	47
7	NEWCASTLE U	42	18	10	14	59	45	46
8	MIDDLESBROUGH	42	16	14	12	79	69	46
9	CHELSEA	42	17	12	13	40	43	46
10	MANCHESTER C	42	18	9	15	65	70	45
11	SHEFFIELD U	42	15	10	17	59	54	40
12	SUNDERLAND	42	16	8	18	60	62	40
13	WBA	42	15	10	17	51	63	40
14	HUDDERSFIELD T	42	15	9	18	53	54	39
15	BLACKBURN R	42	13	12	17	54	57	38
16	PRESTON NE	42	13	12	17	42	65	38
17	ARSENAL	42	15	7	20	47	56	37
18	BIRMINGHAM	42	15	7	20	48	60	37
19	OLDHAM ATH	42	13	11	18	38	50	37
20	EVERTON	42	12	12	18	57	55	36
21	BRADFORD C	42	11	10	21	48	72	32
22	MANCHESTER U	42	8	12	22	41	73	28

Season 1922-23

Football League Division One

DATE	OPPONENTS	SCORE	GOALSCORERS	ATTENDANCE
Aug 26	Liverpool	L 2-5	Boreham, Young	43,000
Aug 28	BURNLEY	D 1-1	Young	25,000
Sep 2	LIVERPOOL	W 1-0	Hutchins	35,000
Sep 4	Burnley	L 1-4	Hopkins	20,000
Sep 9	Cardiff City	L 1-4	Whittaker	30,000
Sep 16	CARDIFF CITY	W 2-1	Young, Boreham	40,000
Sep 23	Tottenham Hotspur	W 2-1	Boreham 2	40,582
Sep 30	TOTTENHAM HOTSPUR	L 0-2		55,000
Oct 2	Sheffield United	L 1-2	Boreham	15,000
Oct 7	WEST BROMWICH ALBION	W 3-1	White, Voysey, Boreham	30,000
Oct 14	West Bromwich Albion	L 0-7		15,000
Oct 21	Newcastle United	D 1-1	Hopkins	30,000
Oct 28	NEWCASTLE UNITED	L 1-2	Roe	35,000
Nov 4	Everton	L 0-1		30,000
Nov 11	EVERTON	L 1-2	Blyth	30,000
Nov 18	Sunderland	D 3-3	Voysey 2, Turnbull	15,000
Nov 25	SUNDERLAND	L 2-3	Turnbull 2	30,000
Dec 2	Birmingham	L 2-3	Voysey, Turnbull	30,000
Dec 9	BIRMINGHAM	W 1-0	Graham (pen)	30,000
Dec 16	HUDDERSFIELD TOWN	D 1-1	Rutherford	25,000
Dec 23	Huddersfield Town	L 0-4		10,000
Dec 25	Bolton Wanderers	L 1-4	Turnbull	32,000
Dec 26	BOLTON WANDERERS	W 5-0	Turnbull 4, Blyth	35,000
Dec 30	STOKE	W 3-0	Blyth, Boreham, Turnbull	25,000
Jan 1	Blackburn Rovers	W 5-0	Turnbull 4, Baker	20,000
Jan 6	Stoke	L 0-1		15,000
Jan 20	MANCHESTER CITY	W 1-0	Turnbull	25,000
Jan 27	Manchester City	D 0-0		30,000
Feb 3	Nottingham Forest	L 1-2	Baker	15,000
Feb 10	NOTTINGHAM FOREST	W 2-0	Baker 2	20,000
Feb 17	Chelsea	D 0-0		50,000
Feb 24	CHELSEA	W 3-1	Blyth 2, Baker	30,000
Mar 3	Middlesbrough	L 0-2		20,000
Mar 10	MIDDLESBROUGH	W 3-0	Turnbull 3	25,000
Mar 17	OLDHAM ATHLETIC	W 2-0	Blyth, o.g.	30,000
Mar 24	Oldham Athletic	D 0-0		12,000
Mar 31	ASTON VILLA	W 2-0	Baker, Blyth	45,000
Apr 2	BLACKBURN ROVERS	D 1-1	McKenzie	32,000
Apr 7	Aston Villa	D 1-1	Blyth	18,000
Apr 14	PRESTON NORTH END	D 1-1	Boreham	23,000
Apr 21	Preston North End	W 2-1	Earle, Turnbull	15,000
Apr 28	SHEFFIELD UNITED	W 2-0	Turnbull, Blyth	25,000

FA Cup

Jan 13	Liverpool	(Rd1) D	0-0		37,000
Jan 17	LIVERPOOL	(R) L	1-4	Turnbull	39,000

League & Cup Appearances

PLAYER	LEAGUE	CUP COMPETITION FA CUP	TOTAL
Baker	29	2	31
Blyth	31	1	32
Boreham	27	2	29
Bradshaw	17		17
Butler	18	1	19
Clark	2		2
Dunn	17		17
Earle	1		1
Elvey	1		1
Graham	17		17
Henderson	2		2
Hopkins	2		2
Hutchins	10		10
John	24	2	26
Kennedy	24	2	26
McKenzie	7		7
Mackie	23	2	25
Milne	31	2	33
Paterson	26	2	28
Robson	20	2	22
Roe (Archie)	4		4
Rutherford	26		26
Toner	7		7
Townrow	1	1	2
Turnbull	35	2	37
Voysey	18	1	19
White	11		11
Whittaker	13		13
Williamson	5		5
Young	13		13

Goalscorers

PLAYER	LEAGUE	CUP COMPETITION FA CUP	TOTAL
Turnbull	20	1	21
Blyth	9		9
Boreham	8		8
Baker	6		6
Voysey	4		4
Young	3		3
Hopkins	2		2
Earle	1		1
Graham	1		1
Hutchins	1		1
McKenzie	1		1
Roe	1		1
Rutherford	1		1
White	1		1
Whittaker	1		1
Opps' o.gs.	1		1

Fact File

Top scorer Bobby Turnbull was typical of the signings that Knighton had to make because of lack of resources in the transfer market. The Scottish forward was playing in army football when Arsenal signed him. Highbury was the first English ground to play host to a European international team when the England v Belgium match was staged there in March 1923.

MANAGER: Leslie Knighton

CAPTAIN: Billy Blyth

TOP SCORER: Bobby Turnbull 21 (20 League)

BIGGEST WIN: 5-0 v Bolton Wanderers, 26 December 1922, League; 5-0 v Blackburn Rovers, 1 January 1923, League

HIGHEST ATTENDANCE: 55,000 v Tottenham Hotspur, 30 September 1922, League

MAJOR TRANSFER IN: Andy Kennedy from Crystal Palace

MAJOR TRANSFERS OUT: Joe North to Reading, Danny Burgess to West Ham United

Final Division One Table

		P	W	D	L	F	A	PTS
1	LIVERPOOL	42	26	8	8	70	31	60
2	SUNDERLAND	42	22	10	10	72	54	54
3	HUDDERSFIELD T	42	21	11	10	60	32	53
4	NEWCASTLE U	42	18	12	12	45	37	48
5	EVERTON	42	20	7	15	63	59	47
6	ASTON VILLA	42	18	10	14	64	51	46
7	WBA	42	17	11	14	58	49	45
8	MANCHESTER C	42	17	11	14	50	49	45
9	CARDIFF C	42	18	7	17	73	59	43
10	SHEFFIELD U	42	16	10	16	68	64	42
11	ARSENAL	42	16	10	16	61	62	42
12	TOTTENHAM H	42	17	7	18	50	50	41
13	BOLTON W	42	14	12	16	50	58	40
14	BLACKBURN R	42	14	12	16	47	62	40
15	BURNLEY	42	16	6	20	58	59	38
16	PRESTON NE	42	13	11	18	60	64	37
17	BIRMINGHAM	42	13	11	18	41	57	37
18	MIDDLESBROUGH	42	13	10	19	57	63	36
19	CHELSEA	42	9	18	15	45	53	36
20	NOTTINGHAM F	42	13	8	21	41	70	34
21	STOKE	42	10	10	22	47	67	30
22	OLDHAM ATH	42	10	10	22	35	65	30

227

Season 1923-24

Football League Division One

DATE	OPPONENTS	SCORE	GOALSCORERS	ATTENDANCE
Aug 25	NEWCASTLE UNITED	L 1-4	Turnbull	45,000
Aug 27	West Ham United	L 0-1		22,000
Sep 1	Newcastle United	L 0-1		40,000
Sep 8	West Bromwich Albion	L 0-4		25,000
Sep 10	WEST HAM UNITED	W 4-1	Earle 2, Woods, Graham	36,000
Sep 15	WEST BROMWICH ALBION	W 1-0	Voysey	36,000
Sep 22	Birmingham	W 2-0	Turnbull, Voysey	20,000
Sep 29	BIRMINGHAM	D 0-0		35,000
Oct 6	Manchester City	L 0-1		23,477
Oct 13	MANCHESTER CITY	L 1-2	Turnbull	32,000
Oct 20	Bolton Wanderers	W 2-1	Woods, Rutherford	20,000
Oct 27	BOLTON WANDERERS	D 0-0		30,000
Nov 3	MIDDLESBROUGH	W 2-1	Townrow, Woods	25,000
Nov 10	Middlesbrough	D 0-0		12,000
Nov 17	TOTTENHAM HOTSPUR	D 1-1	Townrow	50,000
Nov 24	Tottenham Hotspur	L 0-3		31,624
Dec 1	BLACKBURN ROVERS	D 1-1	Young, o.g.	20,000
Dec 8	Blackburn Rovers	L 0-2		20,000
Dec 15	HUDDERSFIELD TOWN	L 1-3	Young	25,000
Dec 22	Huddersfield Town	L 1-6	Baker	15,000
Dec 26	Notts County	W 2-1	Woods, Blyth	25,000
Dec 27	NOTTS COUNTY	D 0-0		16,000
Dec 29	CHELSEA	W 1-0	Turnbull	38,000
Jan 5	Chelsea	D 0-0		38,000
Jan 19	CARDIFF CITY	L 1-2	Turnbull	30,000
Jan 26	Cardiff City	L 0-4		20,000
Feb 9	Sheffield United	L 1-3	Blyth	10,000
Feb 16	ASTON VILLA	L 0-1		35,000
Feb 23	SHEFFIELD UNITED	L 1-3	Milne	18,000
Mar 1	LIVERPOOL	W 3-1	Woods 2, Rutherford	35,000
Mar 12	Aston Villa	L 1-2	Blyth	10,000
Mar 15	Nottingham Forest	L 1-2	Ramsay	14,000
Mar 22	NOTTINGHAM FOREST	W 1-0	Neil	20,000
Apr 2	Liverpool	D 0-0		30,000
Apr 5	BURNLEY	W 2-0	Ramsay, Neil	30,000
Apr 12	SUNDERLAND	W 2-0	Woods, Haden	18,000
Apr 18	Everton	L 1-3	Haden	30,000
Apr 19	Sunderland	D 1-1	Woods	20,000
Apr 21	EVERTON	L 0-1		25,000
Apr 26	Preston North End	W 2-0	Haden, Ramsay	12,000
Apr 28	Burnley	L 1-4	Woods	12,000
May 3	PRESTON NORTH END	L 1-2	Turnbull	25,000

FA Cup

Jan 12	LUTON TOWN	(Rd1) W 4-1	Blyth, Woods, Turnbull, Milne	37,500
Feb 2	Cardiff City	(Rd2) L 0-1		35,000

League & Cup Appearances

PLAYER	LEAGUE	CUP COMPETITION FA CUP	TOTAL
Baker	21	2	23
Blyth	27	2	29
Boreham	2		2
Butler	24	1	25
Clark	2		2
Earle	2		2
Graham	25	2	27
Haden	31	2	33
John	15		15
Jones F.	2		2
Kennedy	29	1	30
Mackie	31	2	33
Milne	36	2	38
Neil	11		11
Paterson	21	2	23
Ramsay	11		11
Robson	42	2	44
Rutherford	22		22
Toner	3		3
Townrow	7		7
Turnbull	18	1	19
Voysey	10		10
Wallington	1		1
Whittaker	8		8
Woods	36	1	37
Young	25	2	27

Goalscorers

PLAYER	LEAGUE	CUP COMPETITION FA CUP	TOTAL
Woods	9	1	10
Turnbull	6	1	7
Blyth	3	1	4
Haden	3		3
Ramsay	3		3
Earle	2		2
Neil	2		2
Rutherford	2		2
Townrow	2		2
Voysey	2		2
Young	2		2
Milne	1	1	2
Baker	1		1
Graham	1		1
Opps' o.gs.	1		1

Fact File

Arsenal were deep in relegation trouble for most of the season. The 2-0 win at Preston on 26 April saved them and they stayed up instead of London rivals Chelsea. Meanwhile, the legendary Herbert Chapman was leading Huddersfield Town to the first of three consecutive championships.

MANAGER: Leslie Knighton

CAPTAIN: Billy Blyth

TOP SCORER: Harry Woods 10 (9 League)

BIGGEST WIN: 4-1 v West Ham United, 10 September 1923, League; 4-1 v Luton Town, 12 January 1924, FA Cup

HIGHEST ATTENDANCE: 50,000, 17 November 1923, v Tottenham Hotspur, League

MAJOR TRANSFERS IN: Harry Woods from Newcastle United, Andy Neil from Brighton & Hove Albion, Jimmy Brain from Ton Pentre

Final Division One Table

		P	W	D	L	F	A	Pts
1	HUDDERSFIELD T	42	23	11	8	60	33	57
2	CARDIFF C	42	22	13	7	61	34	57
3	SUNDERLAND	42	22	9	11	71	54	53
4	BOLTON W	42	18	14	10	68	34	50
5	SHEFFIELD U	42	19	12	11	69	49	50
6	ASTON VILLA	42	18	13	11	52	37	49
7	EVERTON	42	18	13	11	62	53	49
8	BLACKBURN R	42	17	11	14	54	50	45
9	NEWCASTLE U	42	17	10	15	60	54	44
10	NOTTS CO	42	14	14	14	44	49	42
11	MANCHESTER C	42	15	12	15	54	71	42
12	LIVERPOOL	42	15	11	16	49	48	41
13	WEST HAM U	42	13	15	14	40	43	41
14	BIRMINGHAM	42	13	13	16	41	49	39
15	TOTTENHAM H	42	12	14	16	50	56	38
16	WBA	42	12	14	16	51	62	38
17	BURNLEY	42	12	12	18	55	60	36
18	PRESTON NE	42	12	10	20	52	67	34
19	ARSENAL	42	12	9	21	40	63	33
20	NOTTINGHAM F	42	10	12	20	42	64	32
21	CHELSEA	42	9	14	19	31	53	32
22	MIDDLESBROUGH	42	7	8	27	37	60	22

Season 1924-25

Football League Division One

DATE	OPPONENTS	SCORE	GOALSCORERS	ATTENDANCE
Aug 30	Nottingham Forest	W 2-0	Ramsay, Woods	20,000
Sep 1	MANCHESTER CITY	W 1-0	Neil	25,000
Sep 6	LIVERPOOL	W 2-0	Woods 2	45,000
Sep 13	Newcastle United	D 2-2	Rutherford, Woods	30,000
Sep 17	Manchester City	L 0-2		34,000
Sep 20	SHEFFIELD UNITED	W 2-0	Butler, Rutherford	40,000
Sep 27	West Ham United	L 0-1		31,000
Oct 4	BLACKBURN ROVERS	W 1-0	Neil	40,000
Oct 11	Huddersfield Town	L 0-4		15,000
Oct 13	BURY	L 0-1		20,000
Oct 18	ASTON VILLA	D 1-1	Butler	40,000
Oct 25	TOTTENHAM HOTSPUR	W 1-0	Brain	51,000
Nov 1	Bolton Wanderers	L 1-4	Brain	18,000
Nov 8	NOTTS COUNTY	L 0-1		35,000
Nov 15	Everton	W 3-2	Ramsay 2, Young	20,000
Nov 22	SUNDERLAND	D 0-0		35,000
Nov 29	Cardiff City	D 1-1	Young	20,000
Dec 6	PRESTON NORTH END	W 4-0	Woods 3, Toner	30,000
Dec 13	Burnley	L 0-1		6,000
Dec 20	LEEDS UNITED	W 6-1	Brain 4, Woods, Ramsay	30,000
Dec 25	Birmingham	L 1-2	Woods	36,000
Dec 26	BIRMINGHAM	L 0-1		40,000
Dec 27	NOTTINGHAM FOREST	W 2-1	Butler, Ramsay	12,000
Jan 3	Liverpool	L 1-2	Hoar	24,000
Jan 17	NEWCASTLE UNITED	L 0-2		30,000
Jan 24	Sheffield United	L 1-2	Ramsay	12,000
Feb 7	Blackburn Rovers	L 0-1		20,000
Feb 14	HUDDERSFIELD TOWN	L 0-5		25,000
Feb 28	Tottenham Hotspur	L 0-2		29,457
Mar 7	BOLTON WANDERERS	W 1-0	Blyth	35,000
Mar 14	Notts County	L 1-2	Brain	12,000
Mar 21	EVERTON	W 3-1	Woods 2, Baker	20,000
Mar 23	WEST HAM UNITED	L 1-2	Baker	10,000
Mar 28	Sunderland	L 0-2		18,000
Apr 1	Aston Villa	L 0-4		10,000
Apr 4	CARDIFF CITY	D 1-1	Brain	35,000
Apr 11	Preston North End	L 0-2		12,000
Apr 13	West Bromwich Albion	L 0-2		24,000
Apr 14	WEST BROMWICH ALBION	W 2-0	Brain, John	21,000
Apr 18	BURNLEY	W 5-0	Brain 3, Haden, Woods	25,000
Apr 25	Leeds United	L 0-1		20,000
May 2	Bury	L 0-2		15,000

FA Cup

Jan 14	West Ham United	(Rd1) D 0-0		26,000
Jan 21	WEST HAM UNITED	(R) D 2-2	Brain 2	34,160
Jan 26	West Ham United*	(2R) L 0-1		36,955

*Played at Stamford Bridge.

League & Cup Appearances

PLAYER	LEAGUE	CUP COMPETITION FA CUP	TOTAL
Baker	32	3	35
Blyth	17		17
Brain	28	3	31
Butler	39	3	42
Clark	2		2
Cock	2		2
Haden	15		15
Hoar	19	3	22
Hughes	1		1
John	39	3	42
Kennedy	40	3	43
Lewis	16	3	19
Mackie	19		19
Milne	32	2	34
Neil	16		16
Ramsay	30	3	33
Robson	26		26
Roe (Arthur)	1		1
Rutherford	20		20
Toner	26	3	29
Turnbull	1		1
Whittaker	1		1
Woods	32	3	35
Young	8	1	9

Goalscorers

PLAYER	LEAGUE	CUP COMPETITION FA CUP	TOTAL
Brain	12	2	14
Woods	12		12
Ramsay	6		6
Butler	3		3
Baker	2		2
Neil	2		2
Rutherford	2		2
Young	2		2
Blyth	1		1
Haden	1		1
Hoar	1		1
John	1		1
Toner	1		1

Fact File

Leslie Knighton was sacked after Arsenal again hovered close to relegation and Sir Henry Norris advertised for a manager who would not spend 'exorbitant transfer fees'. Knighton moved on to Bournemouth and later managed Birmingham City and Chelsea. Arsenal bought the Highbury ground outright for £64,000.

MANAGER: Leslie Knighton

CAPTAIN: Alf Baker

TOP SCORER: Jimmy Brain 14 (12 League)

BIGGEST WIN: 6-1 v Leeds United, 20 December 1924, League

HIGHEST ATTENDANCE: 51,000 v Tottenham Hotspur, 25 October 1924, League

MAJOR TRANSFER IN: Dan Lewis from Clapton Orient

Final Division One Table

		P	W	D	L	F	A	Pts
1	HUDDERSFIELD T	42	21	16	5	69	28	58
2	WBA	42	23	10	9	58	34	56
3	BOLTON W	42	22	11	9	76	34	55
4	LIVERPOOL	42	20	10	12	63	55	50
5	BURY	42	17	15	10	54	51	49
6	NEWCASTLE U	42	16	16	10	61	42	48
7	SUNDERLAND	42	19	10	13	64	51	48
8	BIRMINGHAM	42	17	12	13	49	53	46
9	NOTTS CO	42	16	13	13	42	31	45
10	MANCHESTER C	42	17	9	16	76	68	43
11	CARDIFF C	42	16	11	15	56	51	43
12	TOTTENHAM H	42	15	12	15	52	43	42
13	WEST HAM U	42	15	12	15	62	60	42
14	SHEFFIELD U	42	13	13	16	55	63	39
15	ASTON VILLA	42	13	13	16	58	71	39
16	BLACKBURN R	42	11	13	18	53	66	35
17	EVERTON	42	12	11	19	40	60	35
18	LEEDS U	42	11	12	19	46	59	34
19	BURNLEY	42	11	12	19	46	75	34
20	ARSENAL	42	14	5	23	46	58	33
21	PRESTON NE	42	10	6	26	37	74	26
22	NOTTINGHAM F	42	6	12	24	29	65	24

Season 1925-26

Football League Division One

DATE	OPPONENTS	SCORE	GOALSCORERS	ATTENDANCE
Aug 29	TOTTENHAM HOTSPUR	L 0-1		53,183
Aug 31	LEICESTER CITY	D 2-2	Neil, Brain	23,823
Sep 5	Manchester United	W 1-0	Brain	32,288
Sep 7	Leicester City	W 1-0	Brain	25,401
Sep 12	LIVERPOOL	D 1-1	Buchan	32,553
Sep 19	Burnley	D 2-2	Haden, Baker	12,334
Sep 21	WEST HAM UNITED	W 3-2	Buchan 2, Neil	24,800
Sep 26	LEEDS UNITED	W 4-1	Brain 2, Buchan, Neil	32,531
Oct 3	Newcastle United	L 0-7		40,683
Oct 5	West Ham United	W 4-0	Buchan 2, Brain 2	18,769
Oct 10	BOLTON WANDERERS	L 2-3	Buchan, Baker	41,076
Oct 17	CARDIFF CITY	W 5-0	Brain 3, Neil, Blyth	38,130
Oct 24	Sheffield United	L 0-4		27,555
Oct 31	EVERTON	W 4-1	Brain 3, Hoar	24,926
Nov 7	Manchester City	W 5-2	Brain 2, Buchan, Hoar, Haden	11,384
Nov 14	BURY	W 6-1	Brain 3, Buchan 2, Baker	22,566
Nov 21	Blackburn Rovers	W 3-2	Buchan, Brain, o.g.	11,386
Nov 28	SUNDERLAND	W 2-0	Buchan, Brain	44,870
Dec 5	Huddersfield Town	D 2-2	Neil, Buchan	22,115
Dec 12	WEST BROMWICH ALBION	W 1-0	Blyth	34,178
Dec 19	Birmingham	L 0-1		26,843
Dec 25	NOTTS COUNTY	W 3-0	Neil, Buchan, Hoar	33,398
Dec 26	Notts County	L 1-4	Baker	32,045
Jan 2	Tottenham Hotspur	D 1-1	Baker	43,221
Jan 16	MANCHESTER UNITED	W 3-2	Brain 2, Buchan	25,252
Jan 23	Liverpool	L 0-3		38,232
Feb 3	BURNLEY	L 1-2	Buchan	14,800
Feb 6	Leeds United	L 2-4	Brain, o.g.	26,239
Feb 13	NEWCASTLE UNITED	W 3-0	Buchan, Blyth, Paterson	48,346
Feb 27	Cardiff City	D 0-0		21,684
Mar 13	Everton	W 3-2	Brain 3	30,515
Mar 17	SHEFFIELD UNITED	W 4-0	Brain 2, Buchan, Blyth	15,609
Mar 20	MANCHESTER CITY	W 1-0	Blyth	34,974
Mar 27	Bury	D 2-2	Brain, Hulme	18,078
Apr 2	Aston Villa	L 0-3		26,177
Apr 3	BLACKBURN ROVERS	W 4-2	Baker, Blyth, Lawson, Buchan	31,031
Apr 5	ASTON VILLA	W 2-0	Brain 2	25,990
Apr 10	Sunderland	L 1-2	Brain	20,990
Apr 17	HUDDERSFIELD TOWN	W 3-1	Lawson, Hulme, Parker (pen)	34,110
Apr 24	West Bromwich Albion	L 1-2	Blyth	14,226
Apr 28	Bolton Wanderers	D 1-1	Parker	22,198
May 1	BIRMINGHAM	W 3-0	Brain 2, Parker (pen)	22,240

FA Cup

Jan 9	Wolverhampton Wanderers	(Rd3)	D 1-1	Brain	42,083
Jan 13	WOLVERHAMPTON W.	(R)	W 1-0	Baker	42,823
Jan 30	BLACKBURN ROVERS	(Rd4)	W 3-1	Haden, Brain, o.g.	44,836
Feb 20	Aston Villa	(Rd5)	D 1-1	Buchan	55,400
Feb 24	ASTON VILLA	(R)	W 2-0	Paterson, Brain	71,446
Mar 6	Swansea Town	(QF)	L 1-2	Mackie	25,198

League & Cup Appearances

PLAYER	LEAGUE	CUP COMPETITION FA CUP	TOTAL
Baker	31	6	37
Blyth	40	6	46
Brain	41	6	47
Buchan	39	6	45
Butler	41	6	47
Cock	1		1
Haden	25	3	28
Harper	19	6	25
Hoar	21	1	22
Hulme	15		15
John	29	6	35
Kennedy	16		16
Lawson	13	3	16
Lewis	14		14
Mackie	35	6	41
Milne	5		5
Neil	27	3	30
Parker	7		7
Paterson	1	3	4
Ramsay	16	3	19
Robson	9		9
Rutherford	3	1	4
Rutherford J.	1		1
Seddon	1		1
Toner	2		2
Voysey	1		1
Woods	2	1	3
Young	7		7

Goalscorers

PLAYER	LEAGUE	CUP COMPETITION FA CUP	TOTAL
Brain	34	3	37
Buchan	19	1	20
Blyth	7		7
Baker	6	1	7
Neil	6		6
Hoar	3		3
Parker	3		3
Haden	2	1	3
Hulme	2		2
Lawson	2		2
Paterson	1	1	2
Mackie		1	1
Opps' o.gs.	2	1	3

Fact File

Herbert Chapman quickly made his mark. Arsenal finished runners-up, their highest-ever league placing, with a record number of points. Jimmy Brain set a club scoring record and a record crowd packed Highbury for the FA Cup visit of Aston Villa. Winger Jock Rutherford became the oldest player to turn out for Arsenal. He was 41 years and 159 days when he made his last appearance, against Manchester City on 20 March 1926.

MANAGER: Herbert Chapman

CAPTAIN: Charlie Buchan

TOP SCORER: Jimmy Brain 37 (34 League)

BIGGEST WIN: 6-1 v Bury, 14 November 1925, League

HIGHEST ATTENDANCE: 71,446 v Aston Villa, 24 February 1926, FA Cup

MAJOR TRANSFERS IN: Charlie Buchan from Sunderland, Joe Hulme from Blackburn Rovers, Tom Parker from Southampton

Final Division One Table

		P	W	D	L	F	A	Pts
1	HUDDERSFIELD T	42	23	11	8	92	60	57
2	ARSENAL	42	22	8	12	87	63	52
3	SUNDERLAND	42	21	6	15	96	80	48
4	BURY	42	20	7	15	85	77	47
5	SHEFFIELD U	42	19	8	15	102	82	46
6	ASTON VILLA	42	16	12	14	86	76	44
7	LIVERPOOL	42	14	16	12	70	63	44
8	BOLTON W	42	17	10	15	75	76	44
9	MANCHESTER U	42	19	6	17	66	73	44
10	NEWCASTLE U	42	16	10	16	84	75	42
11	EVERTON	42	12	18	12	72	70	42
12	BLACKBURN R	42	15	11	16	91	80	41
13	WBA	42	16	8	18	79	78	40
14	BIRMINGHAM	42	16	8	18	66	81	40
15	TOTTENHAM H	42	15	9	18	66	79	39
16	CARDIFF C	42	16	7	19	61	76	39
17	LEICESTER C	42	14	10	18	70	80	38
18	WEST HAM U	42	15	7	20	63	76	37
19	LEEDS U	42	14	8	20	64	76	36
20	BURNLEY	42	13	10	19	85	108	36
21	MANCHESTER C	42	12	11	19	89	100	35
22	NOTTS CO	42	13	7	22	54	74	33

Season 1926-27

Football League Division One

DATE	OPPONENTS	SCORE	GOALSCORERS	ATTENDANCE
Aug 28	DERBY COUNTY	W 2-1	Parker (pen), Buchan	32,990
Sep 1	BOLTON WANDERERS	W 2-1	Hulme 2	23,002
Sep 4	Sheffield United	L 0-4		21,942
Sep 6	Bolton Wanderers	D 2-2	Brain, Hulme	19,117
Sep 11	LEICESTER CITY	D 2-2	Brain, Hulme	30,800
Sep 15	Manchester United	D 2-2	Brain 2	15,259
Sep 18	LIVERPOOL	W 2-0	Brain, Hoar	35,497
Sep 25	Leeds United	L 1-4	Buchan	20,544
Oct 2	NEWCASTLE UNITED	D 2-2	Buchan, Parker (pen)	38,842
Oct 9	Burnley	L 0-2		12,709
Oct 16	WEST HAM UNITED	D 2-2	Lambert, Brain	35,534
Oct 23	SHEFFIELD WEDNESDAY	W 6-2	Brain 4, Haden 2	27,846
Oct 30	Everton	L 1-3	Brain	34,153
Nov 6	BLACKBURN ROVERS	D 2-2	Brain, Buchan	29,439
Nov 13	Huddersfield Town	D 3-3	Blyth, Haden, Ramsay	16,219
Nov 20	SUNDERLAND	L 2-3	Buchan, Ramsay	20,087
Nov 27	West Bromwich Albion	W 3-1	Hulme, Haden, Brain	20,815
Dec 4	BURY	W 1-0	Brain	30,375
Dec 11	Birmingham	D 0-0		22,982
Dec 18	TOTTENHAM HOTSPUR	L 2-4	Butler, Brain	49,429
Dec 27	Cardiff City	L 0-2		25,386
Dec 28	MANCHESTER UNITED	W 1-0	Blyth	30,111
Jan 1	CARDIFF CITY	W 3-2	Brain 3	30,000
Jan 15	Derby County	W 2-0	Buchan, Parker	21,899
Jan 22	SHEFFIELD UNITED	D 1-1	Buchan	16,831
Feb 5	Liverpool	L 0-3		30,618
Feb 10	Leicester City	L 1-2	Brain	16,736
Feb 12	LEEDS UNITED	W 1-0	Buchan	25,961
Feb 26	BURNLEY	W 6-2	Brain 4, Buchan, Hoar	29,070
Mar 7	West Ham United	L 0-7		11,764
Mar 12	Sheffield Wednesday	L 2-4	Buchan, Brain	21,252
Mar 19	EVERTON	L 1-2	Buchan	33,788
Apr 2	HUDDERSFIELD TOWN	L 0-2		24,409
Apr 6	Newcastle United	L 1-6	Buchan	33,635
Apr 9	Sunderland	L 1-5	Shaw	23,163
Apr 15	ASTON VILLA	W 2-1	Brain 2	38,096
Apr 16	WEST BROMWICH ALBION	W 4-1	Brain, Parker (pen), Buchan 2	24,506
Apr 18	Aston Villa	W 3-2	John 2, Barley	22,542
Apr 28	Blackburn Rovers	W 2-1	Hulme, Brain	13,833
Apr 30	BIRMINGHAM	W 3-0	Brain, Tricker, John	22,619
May 4	Bury	L 2-3	Hulme 2	8,513
May 7	Tottenham Hotspur	W 4-0	Brain 2, Tricker 2	29,555

FA Cup

Jan 8	Sheffield United	(Rd3) W 3-2	Brain, Buchan, Hulme	28,137
Jan 29	Port Vale	(Rd4) D 2-2	Buchan, Brain	18,000
Feb 2	PORT VALE	(R) W 1-0	Buchan	35,781
Feb 19	LIVERPOOL	(Rd5) W 2-0	Brain, Buchan	43,000
Mar 5	WOLVERHAMPTON W.	(QF) W 2-1	Blyth, Butler	52,821
Mar 26	Southampton*	(SF) W 2-1	Hulme, Buchan	52,133
Apr 23	Cardiff City**	(F) L 0-1		91,206

*Played at Stamford Bridge. **Played at Wembley.

League & Cup Appearances

PLAYER	LEAGUE	CUP COMPETITION FA CUP	TOTAL
Baker	23	6	29
Barley	3	1	4
Blyth	33	7	40
Bowen	1		1
Brain	37	7	44
Buchan	33	7	40
Butler	31	7	38
Cope	11	5	16
Haden	17		17
Harper	23	1	24
Hoar	16	7	23
Hulme	37	7	44
John	41	7	48
Kennedy	11	1	12
Lambert	16		16
Lee	7		7
Lewis	17	6	23
Milne	6	1	7
Moody	2		2
Parker	42	7	49
Peel	9		9
Ramsay	12		12
Roberts	2		2
Seddon	17		17
Shaw	5		5
Tricker	4		4
Young	6		6

Goalscorers

PLAYER	LEAGUE	CUP COMPETITION FA CUP	TOTAL
Brain	31	3	34
Buchan	14	5	19
Hulme	8	2	10
Haden	4		4
Parker	4		4
John	3		3
Tricker	3		3
Blyth	2	1	3
Hoar	2		2
Ramsay	2		2
Butler	1	1	2
Barley	1		1
Lambert	1		1
Shaw	1		1

Fact File

Arsenal reached the FA Cup final for the first time, but lost to Cardiff City. The only goal came when a weak shot slipped off goalkeeper Dan Lewis's shiny new jersey and through his hands into the net. It then became Arsenal's custom for their goalkeeper to wear an old, unwashed jersey in Wembley finals.

MANAGER: Herbert Chapman

CAPTAIN: Charlie Buchan

TOP SCORER: Jimmy Brain 34 (31 League)

BIGGEST WIN: 6-2 v Sheffield Wednesday 23 October 1926, League; 6-2 v Burnley, 26 February 1927, League

HIGHEST ATTENDANCE: 52,821 v Wolverhampton Wanderers, 5 March 1927, FA Cup

MAJOR TRANSFERS IN: Herbie Roberts from Oswestry Town, Jack Lambert from Doncaster Rovers

MAJOR TRANSFERS OUT: Jock Robson to Bournemouth, Jimmy Ramsay to Kilmarnock, Harry Woods to Luton Town

Final Division One Table

		P	W	D	L	F	A	Pts
1	Newcastle U	42	25	6	11	96	58	56
2	Huddersfield T	42	17	17	8	76	60	51
3	Sunderland	42	21	7	14	98	70	49
4	Bolton W	42	19	10	13	84	62	48
5	Burnley	42	19	9	14	91	80	47
6	West Ham U	42	19	8	15	86	70	46
7	Leicester C	42	17	12	13	85	70	46
8	Sheffield U	42	17	10	15	74	86	44
9	Liverpool	42	18	7	17	69	61	43
10	Aston Villa	42	18	7	17	81	83	43
11	Arsenal	42	17	9	16	77	86	43
12	Derby Co	42	17	7	18	86	73	41
13	Tottenham H	42	16	9	17	76	78	41
14	Cardiff C	42	16	9	17	55	65	41
15	Manchester U	42	13	14	15	52	64	40
16	Sheffield W	42	15	9	18	75	92	39
17	Birmingham	42	17	4	21	64	73	38
18	Blackburn R	42	15	8	19	77	96	38
19	Bury	42	12	12	18	68	77	36
20	Everton	42	12	10	20	64	90	34
21	Leeds U	42	11	8	23	69	88	30
22	WBA	42	11	8	23	65	86	30

Season 1927-28

Football League Division One

DATE	OPPONENTS	SCORE	GOALSCORERS	ATTENDANCE
Aug 27	Bury	L 1-5	Brain	17,614
Aug 31	BURNLEY	W 4-1	Buchan, Brain 2, Blyth	19,910
Sep 3	SHEFFIELD UNITED	W 6-1	Hulme, Blyth, Buchan 2, Brain, Parker	30,910
Sep 5	Burnley	W 2-1	Blyth, Brain	14,668
Sep 10	Aston Villa	D 2-2	Blyth 2	42,136
Sep 17	SUNDERLAND	W 2-1	Baker, Brain	45,501
Sep 24	Derby County	L 0-4		16,539
Oct 1	WEST HAM UNITED	D 2-2	Brain 2	34,931
Oct 8	Portsmouth	W 3-2	Blyth, Hulme, Brain	27,261
Oct 15	LEICESTER CITY	D 2-2	Brain, Hoar	36,640
Oct 22	Sheffield Wednesday	D 1-1	Buchan	12,698
Oct 29	BOLTON WANDERERS	L 1-2	Buchan	35,787
Nov 5	Blackburn Rovers	L 1-4	Parker (pen)	9,656
Nov 12	MIDDLESBROUGH	W 3-1	Buchan 2, Hulme	25,921
Nov 19	Birmingham	D 1-1	Hoar	10,030
Dec 3	Huddersfield Town	L 1-2	Brain	15,140
Dec 10	NEWCASTLE UNITED	W 4-1	Hulme, Brain, Parker, Hoar	42,630
Dec 17	Manchester United	L 1-4	o.g.	18,120
Dec 24	EVERTON	W 3-2	Hulme, Buchan, Blyth	27,995
Dec 27	Liverpool	W 2-0	Hoar, Brain	41,024
Dec 31	BURY	W 3-1	Lambert, John, Parker (pen)	20,742
Jan 2	TOTTENHAM HOTSPUR	D 1-1	Hoar	13,518
Jan 7	Sheffield United	L 4-6	Hoar 2, Brain 2	18,158
Jan 21	ASTON VILLA	L 0-3		32,505
Feb 4	DERBY COUNTY	L 3-4	Brain 3	21,405
Feb 11	West Ham United	D 2-2	Brain 2	28,086
Feb 25	Leicester City	L 2-3	Hoar, Buchan	25,835
Mar 7	LIVERPOOL	W 6-3	Brain 3, Hulme, Buchan, Lambert	14,037
Mar 10	Bolton Wanderers	D 1-1	Buchan	15,546
Mar 14	Sunderland	L 1-5	Lambert	9,478
Mar 17	BLACKBURN ROVERS	W 3-1	Buchan 2, Hoar	33,446
Mar 28	PORTSMOUTH	L 0-2		15,416
Mar 31	BIRMINGHAM	D 2-2	Buchan 2	13,990
Apr 6	CARDIFF CITY	W 3-0	Hulme, Buchan, Brain	36,828
Apr 7	Tottenham Hotspur	L 0-2		39,193
Apr 9	Cardiff City	D 2-2	Tricker 2	17,699
Apr 14	HUDDERSFIELD TOWN	D 0-0		38,707
Apr 18	Middlesbrough	D 2-2	Baker, Hulme	16,731
Apr 21	Newcastle United	D 1-1	Shaw	22,819
Apr 28	MANCHESTER UNITED	L 0-1		22,452
May 2	SHEFFIELD WEDNESDAY	D 1-1	Brain	15,818
May 5	Everton	D 3-3	Shaw 2, o.g.	48,715

FA Cup

Jan 14	WEST BROMWICH ALBION	(Rd3)	W 2-0	Brain, Hulme	43,322
Jan 28	EVERTON	(Rd4)	W 4-3	Hulme 2, Brain, Buchan	44,328
Feb 18	ASTON VILLA	(Rd5)	W 4-1	Brain 2, Lambert, Hulme	58,505
Mar 3	STOKE CITY	(Rd6)	W 4-1	Blyth 2, Hoar 2	41,974
Mar 24	Blackburn Rovers*	(SF)	L 0-1		25,633

*Played at Filbert Street.

League & Cup Appearances

PLAYER	LEAGUE	CUP COMPETITION FA CUP	TOTAL
Baker	37	4	41
Barley	2		2
Blyth	39	5	44
Brain	39	5	44
Buchan	30	5	35
Butler	38	5	43
Clark	1		1
Cope	24	5	29
Hapgood	3		3
Hoar	38	5	43
Hulme	36	5	41
John	39	5	44
Lambert	16	1	17
Lewis	33	5	38
Moody	4		4
Parker	42	5	47
Paterson	5		5
Peel	13		13
Roberts	3		3
Seddon	4		4
Shaw	6		6
Thompson	1		1
Tricker	7		7

Goalscorers

PLAYER	LEAGUE	CUP COMPETITION FA CUP	TOTAL
Brain	25	4	29
Buchan	16	1	17
Hulme	8	4	12
Hoar	9	2	11
Blyth	7	2	9
Parker	4		4
Lambert	3	1	4
Shaw	3		3
Baker	2		2
Tricker	2		2
John	1		1
Opps' o.gs.	2		2

Fact File

That first trophy still proved elusive as the Gunners were beaten in the FA Cup semi-final. But one of the most important components of Chapman's great side – left back Eddie Hapgood – made his debut in the match at Birmingham City.

MANAGER: Herbert Chapman

CAPTAIN: Charlie Buchan

TOP SCORER: Jimmy Brain 29 (25 League)

BIGGEST WIN: 6-1 v Sheffield United, 3 September 1927, League

HIGHEST ATTENDANCE: 58,505 v Aston Villa, 18 February 1928, FA Cup

MAJOR TRANSFERS IN: Charlie Jones from Nottingham Forest, Eddie Hapgood from Kettering Town

MAJOR TRANSFER OUT: Sammy Haden to Notts County

Final Division One Table

		P	W	D	L	F	A	Pts
1	EVERTON	42	20	13	9	102	66	53
2	HUDDERSFIELD T	42	22	7	13	91	68	51
3	LEICESTER C	42	18	12	12	96	72	48
4	DERBY CO	42	17	10	15	96	83	44
5	BURY	42	20	4	18	80	80	44
6	CARDIFF C	42	17	10	15	70	80	44
7	BOLTON W	42	16	11	15	81	66	43
8	ASTON VILLA	42	17	9	16	78	73	43
9	NEWCASTLE U	42	15	13	14	79	81	43
10	ARSENAL	42	13	15	14	82	86	41
11	BIRMINGHAM	42	13	15	14	70	75	41
12	BLACKBURN R	42	16	9	17	66	78	41
13	SHEFFIELD U	42	15	10	17	79	86	40
14	SHEFFIELD W	42	13	13	16	81	78	39
15	SUNDERLAND	42	15	9	18	74	76	39
16	LIVERPOOL	42	13	13	16	84	87	39
17	WEST HAM U	42	14	11	17	81	88	39
18	MANCHESTER U	42	16	7	19	72	80	39
19	BURNLEY	42	16	7	19	82	98	39
20	PORTSMOUTH	42	16	7	19	66	90	39
21	TOTTENHAM H	42	15	8	19	74	86	38
22	MIDDLESBROUGH	42	11	15	16	81	88	37

Season 1928-29

Football League Division One

DATE	OPPONENTS	SCORE	GOALSCORERS	ATTENDANCE
Aug 25	Sheffield Wednesday	L 2-3	Jones C., Brain	23,684
Aug 28	DERBY COUNTY	L 1-3	Blyth	20,064
Sep 1	BOLTON WANDERERS	W 2-0	Peel, Brain	35,124
Sep 8	Portsmouth	L 0-2		24,846
Sep 15	BIRMINGHAM	D 0-0		30,118
Sep 22	Manchester City	L 1-4	Brain	36,223
Sep 26	Derby County	D 0-0		16,754
Sep 29	HUDDERSFIELD TOWN	W 2-0	Lambert, John	39,938
Oct 6	Everton	L 2-4	Brain, Jones C.	37,846
Oct 13	WEST HAM UNITED	L 2-3	Jones C. 2	43,327
Oct 20	Newcastle United	W 3-0	Thompson 2 (1pen), Brain	30,121
Oct 27	LIVERPOOL	D 4-4	Thompson 2 (pen), Brain, o.g.	33,782
Nov 3	Cardiff City	D 1-1	Jones C.	18,757
Nov 10	SHEFFIELD UNITED	W 2-0	Hulme, Jack	28,560
Nov 17	Bury	L 0-1		10,957
Nov 24	ASTON VILLA	L 2-5	Jack 2	30,491
Dec 1	Leicester City	D 1-1	Brain	26,851
Dec 8	MANCHESTER UNITED	W 3-1	Jack 2, Brain	18,923
Dec 15	Leeds United	D 1-1	Brain	20,293
Dec 22	BURNLEY	W 3-1	Hulme, Peel, Brain	14,990
Dec 25	Blackburn Rovers	L 2-5	Jack, Brain	30,828
Dec 26	SUNDERLAND	D 1-1	Peel	15,747
Dec 29	SHEFFIELD WEDNESDAY	D 2-2	Brain, Hulme	39,255
Jan 1	Sunderland	L 1-5	Parkin	32,843
Jan 5	Bolton Wanderers	W 2-1	Jack 2	17,597
Jan 19	PORTSMOUTH	W 4-0	Jack 2, Peel, Brain	32,224
Feb 2	MANCHESTER CITY	D 0-0		13,764
Feb 9	Huddersfield Town	W 1-0	Jack	14,697
Feb 23	West Ham United	W 4-3	Brain, Jack, Hoar, Hulme	28,931
Mar 9	Liverpool	W 4-2	Hulme 2, Brain, Jones C.	26,195
Mar 13	Birmingham	D 1-1	Jack	11,001
Mar 16	CARDIFF CITY	W 2-1	Brain, Jack	28,393
Mar 23	Sheffield United	D 2-2	Parker (pen), Jack	20,266
Mar 29	BLACKBURN ROVERS	W 1-0	Brain	39,038
Mar 30	BURY	W 7-1	Jack 4, Parkin 2, Thompson	22,577
Apr 2	NEWCASTLE UNITED	L 1-2	Jack	21,699
Apr 6	Aston Villa	L 2-4	Brain, Jack	26,664
Apr 13	LEICESTER CITY	D 1-1	Parker (pen)	19,139
Apr 20	Manchester United	L 1-4	Jack	22,858
Apr 22	EVERTON	W 2-0	Jack, Parker (pen)	11,696
Apr 27	LEEDS UNITED	W 1-0	Peel	21,645
May 4	Burnley	D 3-3	Jack 2, Brain	7,400

FA Cup

DATE	OPPONENTS		SCORE	GOALSCORERS	ATTENDANCE
Jan 12	STOKE CITY	(Rd3)	W 2-1	Brain, Hulme	30,762
Jan 26	MANSFIELD TOWN	(Rd4)	W 2-0	Jack, Peel	44,493
Feb 16	Swindon Town	(Rd5)	D 0-0		16,692
Feb 20	SWINDON TOWN	(R)	W 1-0	Brain	44,582
Mar 2	Aston Villa	(QF)	L 0-1		73,700

League & Cup Appearances

PLAYER	LEAGUE	CUP COMPETITION FA CUP	TOTAL
Baker	31	5	36
Barley	3	1	4
Blyth	21	1	22
Brain	37	5	42
Butler	22	1	23
Cope	23	1	24
Hapgood	17	4	21
Hoar	6	1	7
Hulme	41	5	46
Jack	31	5	36
John	34	3	37
Jones C.	39	3	42
Lambert	6		6
Lewis	32	5	37
Maycock	1		1
Parker	42	5	47
Parkin	5		5
Paterson	10		10
Peel	24	5	29
Roberts	20	4	24
Thompson	17		17
Tricker	1		1

Goalscorers

PLAYER	LEAGUE	CUP COMPETITION FA CUP	TOTAL
Jack	25	1	26
Brain	19	2	21
Hulme	6	1	7
Jones C.	6		6
Peel	5	1	6
Thompson	5		5
Parker	3		3
Parkin	3		3
Blyth	1		1
Hoar	1		1
John	1		1
Lambert	1		1
Opps' o.gs.	1		1

Fact File

Arsenal paid a British record transfer fee of £11,500 to Bolton for David Jack, to fill the gap left by Buchan's retirement. Jack made an immediate impact, finishing top scorer in his first season, including four goals in the win over Bury.

MANAGER: Herbert Chapman

CAPTAIN: Tom Parker

TOP SCORER: David Jack 26 (25 League)

BIGGEST WIN: 7-1 v Bury, 30 March 1929, League

HIGHEST ATTENDANCE: 44,582 v Swindon Town, 20 February 1929, FA Cup

MAJOR TRANSFER IN: David Jack from Bolton Wanderers

Final Division One Table

		P	W	D	L	F	A	Pts
1	SHEFFIELD W	42	21	10	11	86	62	52
2	LEICESTER C	42	21	9	12	96	67	51
3	ASTON VILLA	42	23	4	15	98	81	50
4	SUNDERLAND	42	20	7	15	93	75	47
5	LIVERPOOL	42	17	12	13	90	64	46
6	DERBY CO	42	18	10	14	86	71	46
7	BLACKBURN R	42	17	11	14	72	63	45
8	MANCHESTER C	42	18	9	15	95	86	45
9	ARSENAL	42	16	13	13	77	72	45
10	NEWCASTLE U	42	19	6	17	70	72	44
11	SHEFFIELD U	42	15	11	16	86	85	41
12	MANCHESTER U	42	14	13	15	66	76	41
13	LEEDS U	42	16	9	17	71	84	41
14	BOLTON W	42	14	12	16	73	80	40
15	BIRMINGHAM	42	15	10	17	68	77	40
16	HUDDERSFIELD T	42	14	11	17	70	61	39
17	WEST HAM U	42	15	9	18	86	96	39
18	EVERTON	42	17	4	21	63	75	38
19	BURNLEY	42	15	8	19	81	103	38
20	PORTSMOUTH	42	15	6	21	56	80	36
21	BURY	42	12	7	23	62	99	31
22	CARDIFF C	42	8	13	21	43	59	29

Season 1929-30

Football League Division One

DATE	OPPONENTS	SCORE	GOALSCORERS	ATTENDANCE
Aug 31	LEEDS UNITED	W 4-0	Jack 2, Hulme, Parker (pen)	41,885
Sep 4	Manchester City	L 1-3	Jack	38,458
Sep 7	Sheffield Wednesday	W 2-0	Jack, Hulme	31,735
Sep 11	MANCHESTER CITY	W 3-2	Jack 2, Johnstone	23,057
Sep 14	BURNLEY	W 6-1	Lambert 2, Hulme, Jack, James, o.g.	38,556
Sep 21	Sunderland	W 1-0	Lambert	34,804
Sep 24	Aston Villa	L 2-5	James, Thompson	33,850
Sep 28	BOLTON WANDERERS	L 1-2	Jones	42,723
Oct 5	Everton	D 1-1	Hulme	45,015
Oct 12	DERBY COUNTY	D 1-1	Parker (pen)	42,448
Oct 19	GRIMSBY TOWN	W 4-1	Lambert 3, Hulme	43,794
Oct 26	Manchester United	L 0-1		12,662
Nov 2	WEST HAM UNITED	L 0-1		44,828
Nov 9	Birmingham	W 3-2	Hulme 2, Jack	33,904
Nov 23	Blackburn Rovers	D 1-1	Halliday	25,591
Nov 27	MIDDLESBROUGH	L 1-2	Jack	28,326
Nov 30	NEWCASTLE UNITED	L 0-1		40,365
Dec 14	HUDDERSFIELD TOWN	W 2-0	Hulme, Jack	34,097
Dec 16	Sheffield United	L 1-4	Halliday	16,134
Dec 21	Liverpool	L 0-1		32,819
Dec 25	Portsmouth	W 1-0	James	27,475
Dec 26	PORTSMOUTH	L 1-2	Hulme	49,433
Dec 28	Leeds United	L 0-2		29,167
Jan 4	SHEFFIELD WEDNESDAY	L 2-3	Bastin, Parker	40,766
Jan 18	Burnley	D 2-2	Bastin, Jack	22,566
Feb 1	Bolton Wanderers	D 0-0		27,336
Feb 8	EVERTON	W 4-0	Lambert 3, Williams	27,302
Feb 19	Derby County	L 1-4	Halliday	11,136
Feb 22	Grimsby Town	D 1-1	Lambert	17,151
Mar 8	West Ham United	L 2-3	Jack	31,268
Mar 12	MANCHESTER UNITED	W 4-2	Bastin, Williams, Lambert, Hulme	18,082
Mar 15	BIRMINGHAM	W 1-0	James	32,174
Mar 29	BLACKBURN ROVERS	W 4-0	Williams, Hulme, Lambert 2	40,459
Apr 2	LIVERPOOL	L 0-1		18,824
Apr 5	Newcastle United	D 1-1	Halliday	36,309
Apr 9	Middlesbrough	D 1-1	Hulme	9,287
Apr 12	SHEFFIELD UNITED	W 8-1	Lambert 3, Johnstone 2, Hulme, Bastin, James	24,217
Apr 18	LEICESTER CITY	D 1-1	James	46,663
Apr 19	Huddersfield Town	D 2-2	Bastin, Hulme	11,988
Apr 21	Leicester City	D 6-6	Halliday 4, Bastin 2	27,241
Apr 28	SUNDERLAND	L 0-1		31,250
May 3	ASTON VILLA	L 2-4	Lambert 2	37,020

FA Cup

Jan 11	CHELSEA	(Rd3)	W 2-0	Lambert, Bastin	55,579
Jan 25	BIRMINGHAM CITY	(Rd4)	D 2-2	Bastin, Jack	43,274
Jan 29	Birmingham City	(R)	W 1-0	Baker (pen)	47,521
Feb 15	Middlesbrough	(Rd5)	W 2-0	Lambert, Bastin	42,073
Mar 1	West Ham United	(QF)	W 3-0	Lambert 2, Baker	40,797
Mar 22	Hull City*	(SF)	D 2-2	Jack, Bastin	47,549
Mar 26	Hull City**	(R)	W 1-0	Jack	46,200
Apr 26	Huddersfield Town†	(F)	W 2-0	Lambert, James	92,486

*Played at Elland Road. **Played at Villa Park. †Played at Wembley.

League & Cup Appearances

PLAYER	LEAGUE	CUP COMPETITION FA CUP	TOTAL
Baker	19	7	26
Bastin	21	8	29
Brain	6		6
Butler	2		2
Cope	1		1
Halliday	15		15
Hapgood	38	8	46
Haynes	13	1	14
Hulme	37	4	41
Humpish	3		3
Jack	33	8	41
James	31	6	37
John	34	5	39
Johnstone	7		7
Jones	31	4	35
Lambert	20	8	28
Lewis	30	6	36
Parker	41	8	49
Peel	1		1
Preedy	12	2	14
Roberts	26	5	31
Seddon	24	3	27
Thompson	5	1	6
Williams	12	4	16

Goalscorers

PLAYER	LEAGUE	CUP COMPETITION FA CUP	TOTAL
Lambert	18	5	23
Jack	13	3	16
Hulme	14		14
Bastin	7	4	11
Halliday	8		8
James	6	1	7
Johnstone	3		3
Parker	3		3
Williams	3		3
Baker		2	2
Jones	1		1
Thompson	1		1
Opps' o.gs.	1		1

Fact File

Arsenal celebrated their first major trophy at last, ironically against the team that Chapman had made the dominant force of the 1920s. Alex James caught Huddersfield napping for the first goal then set up the second for Jack Lambert. James was originally a goalscoring inside forward, but Chapman converted him into a legendary midfield general.

MANAGER: Herbert Chapman

CAPTAIN: Tom Parker

TOP SCORER: Jack Lambert 23 (18 League)

BIGGEST WIN: 8-1 v Sheffield United, 12 April 1930, League

HIGHEST ATTENDANCE: 55,579 v Chelsea, 11 January 1930, FA Cup

MAJOR TRANSFERS IN: Alex James from Preston North End, Cliff Bastin from Exeter City, Dave Halliday from Sunderland

MAJOR TRANSFERS OUT: Billy Blyth to Birmingham City, Sid Hoar to Clapton Orient

Final Division One Table

		P	W	D	L	F	A	Pts
1	SHEFFIELD W	42	26	8	8	105	57	60
2	DERBY CO	42	21	8	13	90	82	50
3	MANCHESTER C	42	19	9	14	91	81	47
4	ASTON VILLA	42	21	5	16	92	83	47
5	LEEDS U	42	20	6	16	79	63	46
6	BLACKBURN R	42	19	7	16	99	93	45
7	WEST HAM U	42	19	5	18	86	79	43
8	LEICESTER C	42	17	9	16	86	90	43
9	SUNDERLAND	42	18	7	17	76	80	43
10	HUDDERSFIELD T	42	17	9	16	63	69	43
11	BIRMINGHAM	42	16	9	17	67	62	41
12	LIVERPOOL	42	16	9	17	63	79	41
13	PORTSMOUTH	42	15	10	17	66	62	40
14	ARSENAL	42	14	11	17	78	66	39
15	BOLTON W	42	15	9	18	74	74	39
16	MIDDLESBROUGH	42	16	6	20	82	84	38
17	MANCHESTER U	42	15	8	19	67	88	38
18	GRIMSBY T	42	15	7	20	73	89	37
19	NEWCASTLE U	42	15	7	20	71	92	37
20	SHEFFIELD U	42	15	6	21	91	96	36
21	BURNLEY	42	14	8	20	79	97	36
22	EVERTON	42	12	11	19	80	92	35

Season 1930-31

Football League Division One

DATE	OPPONENTS	SCORE	GOALSCORERS	ATTENDANCE
Aug 30	Blackpool	W 4-1	Bastin 2 (1 pen), Jack 2	28,723
Sep 1	Bolton Wanderers	W 4-1	Lambert 3, Hulme	20,684
Sep 6	LEEDS UNITED	W 3-1	Lambert 2, Jack	40,828
Sep 10	BLACKBURN ROVERS	W 3-2	Bastin 2, Johnstone	20,863
Sep 13	Sunderland	W 4-1	Lambert 3, Hulme	26,525
Sep 15	Blackburn Rovers	D 2-2	Hulme, Lambert	25,572
Sep 20	LEICESTER CITY	W 4-1	Hulme, Lambert 2, Bastin	37,851
Sep 27	Birmingham	W 4-2	Lambert 3, Bastin	31,693
Oct 4	SHEFFIELD UNITED	D 1-1	Lambert	47,113
Oct 11	Derby County	L 2-4	Bastin, Roberts	29,783
Oct 18	Manchester United	W 2-1	Williams, Lambert	23,406
Oct 25	WEST HAM UNITED	D 1-1	Bastin	51,918
Nov 1	Huddersfield Town	D 1-1	Jack	25,772
Nov 8	ASTON VILLA	W 5-2	Bastin 2, Jack 2, Lambert	56,417
Nov 15	Sheffield Wednesday	W 2-1	Lambert 2	43,671
Nov 22	MIDDLESBROUGH	W 5-3	Lambert 3, Bastin 2 (1pen)	32,517
Nov 29	Chelsea	W 5-1	Jack 3, Lambert, Williams	74,667
Dec 13	Liverpool	D 1-1	Jack	44,342
Dec 20	NEWCASTLE UNITED	L 1-2	Jack	32,212
Dec 25	Manchester City	W 4-1	Bastin, Jack, Lambert, Hulme	56,750
Dec 26	MANCHESTER CITY	W 3-1	Hulme, Bastin, John	17,624
Dec 27	BLACKPOOL	W 7-1	Jack 3, Brain 3, Bastin	35,113
Jan 17	SUNDERLAND	L 1-2	James	35,975
Jan 28	GRIMSBY TOWN	W 9-1	Jack 4, Lambert 3, Bastin, Hulme	15,751
Jan 31	BIRMINGHAM	D 1-1	Lambert	30,913
Feb 5	Leicester City	W 7-2	Lambert 3, Bastin 2, Jack, Hulme	17,416
Feb 7	Sheffield United	D 1-1	Hulme	49,602
Feb 14	DERBY COUNTY	W 6-3	Bastin 3 (1 pen), James, Hulme, Jack	34,785
Feb 21	MANCHESTER UNITED	W 4-1	Hulme, Jack, Brain, Bastin	41,510
Feb 28	West Ham United	W 4-2	John, Jack 2, Bastin	30,361
Mar 7	HUDDERSFIELD TOWN	D 0-0		31,058
Mar 11	Leeds United	W 2-1	Bastin, James	12,212
Mar 14	Aston Villa	L 1-5	Jack	60,997
Mar 21	SHEFFIELD WEDNESDAY	W 2-0	Jack, Bastin	47,872
Mar 28	Middlesbrough	W 5-2	Lambert 3, Jack 2	23,476
Apr 3	Portsmouth	D 1-1	Bastin	31,398
Apr 4	CHELSEA	W 2-1	Hulme, Bastin	53,867
Apr 6	PORTSMOUTH	D 1-1	James	40,490
Apr 11	Grimsby Town	W 1-0	Lambert	22,394
Apr 18	LIVERPOOL	W 3-1	Lambert, Bastin, Jack	39,143
Apr 25	Newcastle United	W 3-1	Jones, Hulme 2	21,747
May 2	BOLTON WANDERERS	W 5-0	Lambert 2, Jack 2, James	35,406

FA Cup

Jan 10	ASTON VILLA	(Rd3) D 2-2	Lambert, Jack	40,864
Jan 14	Aston Villa	(R) W 3-1	Hulme 2, Jack	73,668
Jan 24	Chelsea	(Rd4) L 1-2	Bastin	62,945

League & Cup Appearances

PLAYER	LEAGUE	CUP COMPETITION FA CUP	TOTAL
Baker	1		1
Bastin	42	3	45
Brain	16	1	17
Cope	1		1
Hapgood	38	3	41
Harper	19	3	22
Haynes	2		2
Hulme	32	3	35
Jack	35	3	38
James	40	3	43
John	40	3	43
Johnstone	2		2
Jones	24		24
Keizer	12		12
Lambert	34	2	36
Male	3		3
Parker	41	3	44
Preedy	11		11
Roberts	40	3	43
Seddon	18	3	21
Thompson	2		2
Williams	9		9

Goalscorers

PLAYER	LEAGUE	CUP COMPETITION FA CUP	TOTAL
Lambert	38	1	39
Jack	31	2	33
Bastin	28	1	29
Hulme	14	2	16
James	5		5
Brain	4		4
John	2		2
Williams	2		2
Johnstone	1		1
Jones	1		1
Roberts	1		1

Fact File

Records tumbled as Arsenal won their first championship. Their points total was the highest ever recorded in the First Division. They set a club goals record that still stands and Jack Lambert set a club record for league goals with 38 during the season. The Gunners also fielded their first foreign player, Dutch goalkeeper Gerrie Keizer.

MANAGER: Herbert Chapman

CAPTAIN: Tom Parker

TOP SCORER: Jack Lambert 39 (38 League)

BIGGEST WIN: 9-1 v Grimsby Town, 28 January 1931, League

HIGHEST ATTENDANCE: 56,417 v Aston Villa, 8 November 1930, League

MAJOR TRANSFERS IN: Pat Beasley from Stourbridge

MAJOR TRANSFERS OUT: Jack Butler to Torquay United, Dave Halliday to Manchester City

Final Division One Table

		P	W	D	L	F	A	Pts
1	ARSENAL	42	28	10	4	127	59	66
2	ASTON VILLA	42	25	9	8	128	78	59
3	SHEFFIELD W	42	22	8	12	102	75	52
4	PORTSMOUTH	42	18	13	11	84	67	49
5	HUDDERSFIELD T	42	18	12	12	81	65	48
6	DERBY Co	42	18	10	14	94	79	46
7	MIDDLESBROUGH	42	19	8	15	98	90	46
8	MANCHESTER C	42	18	10	14	75	70	46
9	LIVERPOOL	42	15	12	15	86	85	42
10	BLACKBURN R	42	17	8	17	83	84	42
11	SUNDERLAND	42	16	9	17	89	85	41
12	CHELSEA	42	15	10	17	64	67	40
13	GRIMSBY T	42	17	5	20	82	87	39
14	BOLTON W	42	15	9	18	68	81	39
15	SHEFFIELD U	42	14	10	18	78	84	38
16	LEICESTER C	42	16	6	20	80	95	38
17	NEWCASTLE U	42	15	6	21	78	87	36
18	WEST HAM U	42	14	8	20	79	94	36
19	BIRMINGHAM	42	13	10	19	55	70	36
20	BLACKPOOL	42	11	10	21	71	125	32
21	LEEDS U	42	12	7	23	68	81	31
22	MANCHESTER U	42	7	8	27	53	115	22

235

Season 1931-32

Football League Division One

DATE	OPPONENTS	SCORE	GOALSCORERS	ATTENDANCE
Aug 29	WEST BROMWICH ALBION	L 0-1		52,478
Aug 31	Blackburn Rovers	D 1-1	Hulme	22,138
Sep 5	Birmingham	D 2-2	Lambert, Hulme	26,810
Sep 9	PORTSMOUTH	D 3-3	Lambert 2, Bastin	25,403
Sep 12	SUNDERLAND	W 2-0	Hulme 2	22,926
Sep 16	Portsmouth	W 3-0	Bastin 2, Parkin	22,977
Sep 19	Manchester City	W 3-1	Jack 2, Lambert	46,756
Sep 26	EVERTON	W 3-2	Hulme, Jack, Lambert	47,637
Oct 3	Grimsby Town	L 1-3	Lambert	17,840
Oct 10	Blackpool	W 5-1	Bastin 3 (1 pen), Hulme, Lambert	29,516
Oct 17	BOLTON WANDERERS	D 1-1	Hulme	42,141
Oct 24	Leicester City	W 2-1	Jack, o.g.	26,233
Oct 31	ASTON VILLA	D 1-1	Jack	54,951
Nov 7	Newcastle United	L 2-3	Lambert, Jack	28,949
Nov 14	WEST HAM UNITED	W 4-1	Jack 3, Hulme	41,028
Nov 21	Chelsea	L 1-2	Jack	64,427
Nov 28	LIVERPOOL	W 6-0	Jack 2, Lambert 3, Hulme	29,220
Dec 5	Sheffield Wednesday	W 3-1	Jack 2, Bastin	27,265
Dec 12	HUDDERSFIELD TOWN	D 1-1	Jack	39,748
Dec 19	Middlesbrough	W 5-2	Jack 2, Bastin 2, Lambert	17,083
Dec 25	Sheffield United	L 1-4	Hulme	49,737
Dec 26	SHEFFIELD UNITED	L 0-2		55,207
Jan 2	West Bromwich Albion	L 0-1		25,823
Jan 16	BIRMINGHAM	W 3-0	Hulme, Bastin, o.g.	37,843
Jan 30	MANCHESTER CITY	W 4-1	Parkin 3, James	39,834
Feb 6	Everton	W 3-1	Bastin, Hulme, John	56,698
Feb 17	GRIMSBY TOWN	W 4-0	Bastin, Jack, Parkin, James	20,980
Feb 20	BLACKPOOL	W 2-0	Jack, Parkin	39,045
Mar 2	Bolton Wanderers	L 0-1		20,922
Mar 5	LEICESTER CITY	W 2-1	Bastin (pen), Hulme	53,920
Mar 19	NEWCASTLE UNITED	W 1-0	Hulme	57,516
Mar 25	DERBY COUNTY	W 2-1	Lambert 2	56,435
Mar 26	West Ham United	D 1-1	Lambert	34,852
Mar 28	Derby County	D 1-1	Jack	25,790
Apr 2	CHELSEA	D 1-1	Lambert	56,124
Apr 6	Sunderland	L 0-2		30,443
Apr 9	Liverpool	L 1-2	Lambert	30,100
Apr 16	SHEFFIELD WEDNESDAY	W 3-1	John 2, Jack	25,220
Apr 25	Aston Villa	D 1-1	Parkin	25,959
Apr 27	Huddersfield Town	W 2-1	Coleman, Lambert	13,370
Apr 30	MIDDLESBROUGH	W 5-0	Bastin 2, Lambert 2, o.g.	30,714
May 7	BLACKBURN ROVERS	W 4-0	Lambert 2, Stockill, o.g.	23,127

FA Cup

Jan 9	DARWEN	(Rd3) W 11-1	Bastin 4, Jack 3, Lambert 2, Hulme 2	37,486
Jan 23	PLYMOUTH ARGYLE	(Rd4) W 4-2	Lambert 2, Hulme, o.g.	65,386
Feb 13	Portsmouth	(Rd5) W 2-0	Bastin, Hulme	38,918
Feb 27	Huddersfield Town	(QF) W 1-0	Roberts	67,037
Mar 12	Manchester City*	(SF) W 1-0	Bastin	50,337
Apr 23	Newcastle United**	(F) L 1-2	John	92,298

*Played at Villa Park. **Played at Wembley.

Fact File

Cliff 'Boy' Bastin had won every honour in the English game by the time he was 19. The left winger from Exeter gained an FA Cup winner's medal against Huddersfield in 1930, a championship medal the following season, then won the first of his 21 England caps, against Wales at Liverpool, in November 1931.

MANAGER: Herbert Chapman

CAPTAIN: Tom Parker

TOP SCORER: Jack Lambert 26 (22 League)

BIGGEST WIN: 11-1 v Darwen, 9 January 1932, FA Cup

HIGHEST ATTENDANCE: 65,386 v Plymouth Argyle, 23 January 1932, FA Cup

MAJOR TRANSFERS IN: Frank Moss from Oldham Athletic, Ernest Coleman from Grimsby Town

MAJOR TRANSFERS OUT: Jimmy Brain to Tottenham Hotspur, Bill Harper to Plymouth Argyle

League & Cup Appearances

PLAYER	LEAGUE	CUP COMPETITION FA CUP	TOTAL
Bastin	40	6	46
Beasley	3		3
Coleman	6		6
Compton	4		4
Cope	1		1
Hapgood	41	6	47
Harper	2		2
Haynes	7		7
Hulme	40	6	46
Jack	34	6	40
James	32	5	37
John	38	6	44
Jones	37	6	43
Lambert	36	5	41
Male	9	1	10
Moss	27	6	33
Parker	38	6	44
Parkin	9	1	10
Preedy	13		13
Roberts	35	6	41
Seddon	5		5
Stockill	3		3
Thompson	1		1
Williams	1		1

Goalscorers

PLAYER	LEAGUE	CUP COMPETITION FA CUP	TOTAL
Lambert	22	4	26
Jack	21	3	24
Bastin	15	6	21
Hulme	14	4	18
Parkin	7		7
John	3	1	4
James	2		2
Coleman	1		1
Stockill	1		1
Roberts		1	1
Opps' o.gs.	4	1	5

Final Division One Table

		P	W	D	L	F	A	PTS
1	EVERTON	42	26	4	12	116	64	56
2	ARSENAL	42	22	10	10	90	48	54
3	SHEFFIELD W	42	22	6	14	96	82	50
4	HUDDERSFIELD T	42	19	10	13	80	63	48
5	ASTON VILLA	42	19	8	15	104	72	46
6	WBA	42	20	6	16	77	55	46
7	SHEFFIELD U	42	20	6	16	80	75	46
8	PORTSMOUTH	42	19	7	16	62	62	45
9	BIRMINGHAM	42	18	8	16	78	67	44
10	LIVERPOOL	42	19	6	17	81	93	44
11	NEWCASTLE U	42	18	6	18	80	87	42
12	CHELSEA	42	16	8	18	69	73	40
13	SUNDERLAND	42	15	10	17	67	73	40
14	MANCHESTER C	42	13	12	17	83	73	38
15	DERBY CO	42	14	10	18	71	75	38
16	BLACKBURN R	42	16	6	20	89	95	38
17	BOLTON W	42	17	4	21	72	80	38
18	MIDDLESBROUGH	42	15	8	19	64	89	38
19	LEICESTER C	42	15	7	20	74	94	37
20	BLACKPOOL	42	12	9	21	65	102	33
21	GRIMSBY T	42	13	6	23	67	98	32
22	WEST HAM U	42	12	7	23	62	107	31

Season 1932-33

Football League Division One

DATE	OPPONENTS	SCORE	GOALSCORERS	ATTENDANCE
Aug 27	Birmingham	W 1-0	Stockill	31,592
Aug 31	WEST BROMWICH ALBION	L 1-2	Stockill	37,748
Sep 3	SUNDERLAND	W 6-1	Hulme 3, Coleman, Jack, Bastin	28,896
Sep 10	Manchester City	W 3-2	Jack, Coleman 2	36,542
Sep 14	West Bromwich Albion	D 1-1	Jack	45,038
Sep 17	BOLTON WANDERERS	W 3-2	Hulme, Coleman, Bastin	42,395
Sep 24	EVERTON	W 2-1	Jack, Coleman	51,182
Oct 1	Blackpool	W 2-1	Bastin, Coleman	30,218
Oct 8	DERBY COUNTY	D 3-3	Coleman 2, Hulme	32,055
Oct 15	Blackburn Rovers	W 3-2	Bastin, Jack, Coleman	28,799
Oct 22	Liverpool	W 3-2	Bastin 2, Coleman	38,548
Oct 29	LEICESTER CITY	W 8-2	Hulme 3, Bastin 2, Coleman 2, Jack	36,714
Nov 5	Wolverhampton Wanderers	W 7-1	Jack 3, Bastin 2, Lambert 2	43,570
Nov 12	NEWCASTLE UNITED	W 1-0	Hulme	56,498
Nov 19	Aston Villa	L 3-5	Jack, Lambert, Bastin	58,066
Nov 26	MIDDLESBROUGH	W 4-2	Coleman 2, Hulme, Jack	34,640
Dec 3	Portsmouth	W 3-1	Bastin 2, Jack	31,401
Dec 10	CHELSEA	W 4-1	Bastin 2, Coleman, Hulme	53,206
Dec 17	Huddersfield Town	W 1-0	Coleman	23,198
Dec 24	SHEFFIELD UNITED	W 9-2	Lambert 5, Bastin 3, Jack	41,520
Dec 26	LEEDS UNITED	L 1-2	Hulme	55,876
Dec 27	Leeds United	D 0-0		56,776
Dec 31	BIRMINGHAM	W 3-0	Jack, James, Bastin	37,800
Jan 2	Sheffield Wednesday	L 2-3	Jack, Bastin (pen)	64,492
Jan 7	Sunderland	L 2-3	Lambert 2	36,707
Jan 21	MANCHESTER CITY	W 2-1	Bastin	32,456
Feb 1	Bolton Wanderers	W 4-0	Coleman 3, Bastin	13,401
Feb 4	Everton	D 1-1	Coleman	55,463
Feb 11	BLACKPOOL	D 1-1	Coleman	35,180
Feb 22	Derby County	D 2-2	Jack, Bastin	23,148
Feb 25	BLACKBURN ROVERS	W 8-0	Coleman 3, Hulme 2, Bastin 2, Stockill	27,576
Mar 4	LIVERPOOL	L 0-1		42,868
Mar 11	Leicester City	D 1-1	James	32,228
Mar 18	WOLVERHAMPTON WANDERERS	L 1-2	Bowden	44,711
Mar 25	Newcastle United	L 1-2	Hulme	51,215
Apr 1	ASTON VILLA	W 5-0	Lambert 2, Jack, Bowden, James	54,265
Apr 8	Middlesbrough	W 4-3	Hulme 3, Bastin	22,137
Apr 14	SHEFFIELD WEDNESDAY	W 4-2	Hulme 2, Lambert, Bastin	61,945
Apr 15	PORTSMOUTH	W 2-0	Lambert, Bastin	42,809
Apr 22	Chelsea	W 3-1	Bastin, Jack	72,260
Apr 29	HUDDERSFIELD TOWN	D 2-2	Bastin 2	30,779
May 6	Sheffield United	L 1-3	Hill	18,620

FA Cup

Jan 14	Walsall	(Rd3) L 0-2		11,150

League & Cup Appearances

PLAYER	LEAGUE	CUP COMPETITION FA CUP	TOTAL
Bastin	42	1	43
Black		1	1
Bowden	7		7
Coleman	27		27
Compton	4		4
Cope	4		4
Hapgood	38		38
Haynes	6		6
Hill	26	1	27
Hulme	40		40
Jack	34	1	35
James	40	1	41
John	37		37
Jones	16		16
Lambert	12		12
Male	35	1	36
Moss	41	1	42
Parker	5		5
Parkin	5		5
Preedy	1		1
Roberts	36	1	37
Sidey	2	1	3
Stockill	4		4
Walsh		1	1
Warnes		1	1

Goalscorers

PLAYER	LEAGUE	CUP COMPETITION FA CUP	TOTAL
Bastin	33		33
Coleman	24		24
Hulme	20		20
Jack	18		18
Lambert	14		14
James	3		3
Stockill	3		3
Bowden	2		2
Hill	1		1

Fact File

Major rebuilding work at Highbury saw the completion of the new West Stand (now a listed building) which was opened by the Prince of Wales in December 1932. Chapman also persuaded London Transport to change the name of the nearby tube station from Gillespie Road to Arsenal.

MANAGER: Herbert Chapman

CAPTAIN: Eddie Hapgood

TOP SCORER: Cliff Bastin 33 (all League)

BIGGEST WIN: 8-0 v Blackburn Rovers, 25 February 1933, League

HIGHEST ATTENDANCE: 61,945 v Sheffield Wednesday, 14 April 1933, League

MAJOR TRANSFERS IN: Frank Hill from Aberdeen, Ray Bowden from Plymouth Argyle, Ralph Birkett from Torquay United

Final Division One Table

		P	W	D	L	F	A	Pts
1	ARSENAL	42	25	8	9	118	61	58
2	ASTON VILLA	42	23	8	11	92	67	54
3	SHEFFIELD W	42	21	9	12	80	68	51
4	WBA	42	20	9	13	83	70	49
5	NEWCASTLE U	42	22	5	15	71	63	49
6	HUDDERSFIELD T	42	18	11	13	66	53	47
7	DERBY CO	42	15	14	13	76	69	44
8	LEEDS U	42	15	14	13	59	62	44
9	PORTSMOUTH	42	18	7	17	74	76	43
10	SHEFFIELD U	42	17	9	16	74	80	43
11	EVERTON	42	16	9	17	81	74	41
12	SUNDERLAND	42	15	10	17	63	80	40
13	BIRMINGHAM	42	14	11	17	57	57	39
14	LIVERPOOL	42	14	11	17	79	84	39
15	BLACKBURN R	42	14	10	18	76	102	38
16	MANCHESTER C	42	16	5	21	68	71	37
17	MIDDLESBROUGH	42	14	9	19	63	73	37
18	CHELSEA	42	14	7	21	63	73	35
19	LEICESTER C	42	11	13	18	75	89	35
20	WOLVERHAMPTON W	42	13	9	20	80	96	35
21	BOLTON W	42	12	9	21	78	92	33
22	BLACKPOOL	42	14	5	23	69	85	33

Season 1933-34

Football League Division One

DATE	OPPONENTS	SCORE	GOALSCORERS	ATTENDANCE
Aug 26	BIRMINGHAM	D 1-1	Jack	44,662
Sep 2	Sheffield Wednesday	W 2-1	Bastin, Jack	23,186
Sep 6	WEST BROMWICH ALBION	W 3-1	Bastin 2 (1 pen), Lambert	34,688
Sep 9	MANCHESTER CITY	D 1-1	Coleman	43,412
Sep 13	West Bromwich Albion	L 0-1		29,429
Sep 16	Tottenham Hotspur	D 1-1	Bowden	56,612
Sep 23	Everton	L 1-3	Bowden	53,792
Sep 30	MIDDLESBROUGH	W 6-0	Birkett 2, Jack 2, Bastin, Bowden	28,293
Oct 7	Blackburn Rovers	D 2-2	Bastin, Bowden	31,636
Oct 14	NEWCASTLE UNITED	W 3-0	Birkett, Bowden, o.g.	32,821
Oct 21	LEICESTER CITY	W 2-1	Dunne 2	44,014
Oct 28	Aston Villa	W 3-2	Dunne 2, Bastin	54,323
Nov 4	PORTSMOUTH	D 1-1	Bastin	51,765
Nov 11	Wolverhampton Wanderers	W 1-0	Bowden	37,210
Nov 18	STOKE CITY	W 3-0	Hulme, Dunne, John	32,972
Nov 25	Huddersfield Town	W 1-0	Dunne	29,407
Dec 2	LIVERPOOL	W 2-1	Hulme, Dunne	38,362
Dec 9	Sunderland	L 0-3		35,166
Dec 16	CHELSEA	W 2-1	Beasley 2	43,897
Dec 23	Sheffield United	W 3-1	Beasley 2, Bowden	31,453
Dec 25	Leeds United	W 1-0	Bastin	33,193
Dec 26	LEEDS UNITED	W 2-0	Bowden, Dunne	22,817
Dec 30	Birmingham	D 0-0		34,771
Jan 6	SHEFFIELD WEDNESDAY	D 1-1	Dunne	45,156
Jan 20	Manchester City	L 1-2	Beasley	60,401
Jan 31	TOTTENHAM HOTSPUR	L 1-3	Bastin	68,828
Feb 3	EVERTON	L 1-2	Birkett	24,025
Feb 10	Middlesbrough	W 2-0	Birkett, Bowden	15,894
Feb 21	BLACKBURN ROVERS	W 2-1	Bastin, Beasley	29,886
Feb 24	Newcastle United	W 1-0	Beasley	40,065
Mar 8	Leicester City	L 1-4	Bowden	23,976
Mar 10	ASTON VILLA	W 3-2	Jack, Roberts, Hulme	41,169
Mar 24	WOLVERHAMPTON WANDERERS	W 3-2	Drake, James, Bastin	41,143
Mar 30	DERBY COUNTY	W 1-0	James	69,070
Mar 31	Stoke City	D 1-1	Bastin	43,163
Apr 2	Derby County	W 4-2	Drake 2, Bowden 2	32,180
Apr 7	HUDDERSFIELD TOWN	W 3-1	Beasley, Bowden, Drake	55,930
Apr 14	Liverpool	W 3-2	Beasley, Hulme 2	43,027
Apr 18	Portsmouth	L 0-1		28,442
Apr 21	SUNDERLAND	W 2-1	Drake, Beasley	37,783
Apr 28	Chelsea	D 2-2	James, Bastin	65,344
May 5	SHEFFIELD UNITED	W 2-0	Drake 2	25,265

FA Cup

DATE	OPPONENTS		SCORE	GOALSCORERS	ATTENDANCE
Jan 13	Luton Town	(Rd3)	W 1-0	Dunne	18,641
Jan 27	CRYSTAL PALACE	(Rd4)	W 7-0	Dunne 2, Bastin 2, Beasley 2, Birkett	56,177
Feb 17	DERBY COUNTY	(Rd5)	W 1-0	Jack	66,905
Mar 3	ASTON VILLA	(QF)	L 1-2	Dougall	67,366

League & Cup Appearances

PLAYER	LEAGUE	CUP COMPETITION FA CUP	TOTAL
Bastin	38	4	42
Beasley	23	4	27
Birkett	15	1	16
Bowden	32	2	34
Coleman	12	1	13
Cox	2		2
Dougall	5	2	7
Drake	10		10
Dunne	21	4	25
Hapgood	40	4	44
Haynes	1		1
Hill	25		25
Hulme	8		8
Jack	14	2	16
James	22		22
John	31	4	35
Jones	29	4	33
Lambert	3		3
Male	42	4	46
Moss	37	3	40
Parkin	5		5
Roberts	30	4	34
Sidey	12		12
Wilson	5	1	6

Goalscorers

PLAYER	LEAGUE	CUP COMPETITION FA CUP	TOTAL
Bastin	13	2	15
Bowden	13		13
Beasley	10	2	12
Dunne	9	3	12
Drake	7		7
Birkett	5	1	6
Jack	5	1	6
Hulme	5		5
James	3		3
Coleman	1		1
John	1		1
Lambert	1		1
Roberts	1		1
Dougall		1	1
Opps' o.gs.	1		1

Fact File

Outside left Cliff Bastin finished top scorer for the second season running, a rare feat for a winger. He was a prolific scorer for most of his career. His tally of 176 goals in 392 matches was an Arsenal record for more than 50 years, until Ian Wright passed it in 1997-98. His total of 33 goals in 1932-33 remains a record for a winger in the English game. David Jack retired at the end of the season to become manager of Southend United.

MANAGER: Herbert Chapman (Joe Shaw was caretaker after Chapman's death)

CAPTAIN: Eddie Hapgood

TOP SCORER: Cliff Bastin 15 (13 League)

BIGGEST WIN: 7-0 v Crystal Palace, 27 January 1934, FA Cup

HIGHEST ATTENDANCE: 69,070 v Derby County, 30 March 1934, League

MAJOR TRANSFERS IN: Jimmy Dunne from Sheffield United, Ted Drake from Southampton

MAJOR TRANSFER OUT: Jack Lambert to Fulham

Final Division One Table

		P	W	D	L	F	A	Pts
1	ARSENAL	42	25	9	8	75	47	59
2	HUDDERSFIELD T	42	23	10	9	90	61	56
3	TOTTENHAM H	42	21	7	14	79	56	49
4	DERBY CO	42	17	11	14	68	54	45
5	MANCHESTER C	42	17	11	14	65	72	45
6	SUNDERLAND	42	16	12	14	81	56	44
7	WBA	42	17	10	15	78	70	44
8	BLACKBURN R	42	18	7	17	74	81	43
9	LEEDS U	42	17	8	17	75	66	42
10	PORTSMOUTH	42	15	12	15	52	55	42
11	SHEFFIELD W	42	16	9	17	62	67	41
12	STOKE C	42	15	11	16	58	71	41
13	ASTON VILLA	42	14	12	16	78	75	40
14	EVERTON	42	12	16	14	62	63	40
15	WOLVERHAMPTON W	42	14	12	16	74	86	40
16	MIDDLESBROUGH	42	16	7	19	68	80	39
17	LEICESTER C	42	14	11	17	59	74	39
18	LIVERPOOL	42	14	10	18	79	87	38
19	CHELSEA	42	14	8	20	67	69	36
20	BIRMINGHAM	42	12	12	18	54	56	36
21	NEWCASTLE U	42	10	14	18	68	77	34
22	SHEFFIELD U	42	12	7	23	58	101	31

Season 1934-35

Football League Division One

DATE	OPPONENTS	SCORE	GOALSCORERS	ATTENDANCE
Aug 25	Portsmouth	D 3-3	Bowden, Drake, Bastin	39,710
Sep 1	LIVERPOOL	W 8-1	Drake 3, Bowden 3, Bastin, Crayston	54,062
Sep 5	BLACKBURN ROVERS	W 4-0	Drake 2, Bowden, Bastin	39,654
Sep 8	Leeds United	D 1-1	Drake	29,447
Sep 15	WEST BROMWICH ALBION	W 4-3	Bowden, James, Bastin, Drake	40,016
Sep 17	Blackburn Rovers	L 0-2		25,472
Sep 22	Sheffield Wednesday	D 0-0		24,751
Sep 29	BIRMINGHAM	W 5-1	Drake 4, Bastin	47,868
Oct 6	Stoke City	D 2-2	Bastin 2	45,348
Oct 13	MANCHESTER CITY	W 3-0	Bowden 2, Bastin	68,145
Oct 20	TOTTENHAM HOTSPUR	W 5-1	Drake 3, Beasley, o.g.	70,544
Oct 27	Sunderland	L 1-2	Drake	43,744
Nov 3	EVERTON	W 2-0	Bastin 2	50,350
Nov 10	Grimsby Town	D 2-2	Drake, Hulme	26,288
Nov 17	ASTON VILLA	L 1-2	Bastin (pen)	54,226
Nov 24	Chelsea	W 5-2	Drake 4, Hulme	43,419
Dec 1	WOLVERHAMPTON WANDERERS	W 7-0	Drake 4, Birkett 2, Bowden	39,532
Dec 8	Huddersfield Town	D 1-1	o.g.	36,113
Dec 15	LEICESTER CITY	W 8-0	Drake 3, Hulme 3, Bastin 2	23,689
Dec 22	Derby County	L 1-3	Bowden	26,091
Dec 25	PRESTON NORTH END	W 5-3	Hulme 2, Bowden, Bastin, o.g.	40,201
Dec 26	Preston North End	L 1-2	Hill	39,411
Dec 29	PORTSMOUTH	D 1-1	Drake	36,054
Jan 5	Liverpool	W 2-0	Drake, Hapgood	55,794
Jan 19	LEEDS UNITED	W 3-0	Bowden 2, Bastin	37,026
Jan 30	West Bromwich Albion	W 3-0	Drake, Bastin, Hulme	30,713
Feb 2	SHEFFIELD WEDNESDAY	W 4-1	James 3, Bastin	57,922
Feb 9	Birmingham	L 0-3		50,188
Feb 20	STOKE CITY	W 2-0	Davidson, Hill	27,067
Feb 23	Manchester City	D 1-1	Bowden	79,491
Mar 6	Tottenham Hotspur	W 6-0	Kirchen 2, Drake 2, Dougall, Bastin (pen)	47,714
Mar 9	SUNDERLAND	D 0-0		73,295
Mar 16	Everton	W 2-0	Moss, Drake	50,389
Mar 23	GRIMSBY TOWN	D 1-1	Drake	33,591
Mar 30	Aston Villa	W 3-1	Beasley, Drake, Bastin (pen)	59,572
Apr 6	CHELSEA	D 2-2	Drake, Compton (pen)	54,020
Apr 13	Wolverhampton Wanderers	D 1-1	Hill	40,888
Apr 19	MIDDLESBROUGH	W 8-0	Drake 4, Rogers 2, Bastin, Beasley	45,719
Apr 20	HUDDERSFIELD TOWN	W 1-0	Beasley	41,892
Apr 22	Middlesbrough	W 1-0	Drake	29,171
Apr 27	Leicester City	W 5-3	Beasley 2, Crayston 2, Davidson	26,958
May 4	DERBY COUNTY	L 0-1		36,421

FA Cup

Jan 12	Brighton & Hove Albion	(Rd3)	W 2-0	Hulme, Drake	22,343
Jan 26	Leicester City	(Rd4)	W 1-0	Hulme	39,494
Feb 16	Reading	(Rd5)	W 1-0	Bastin	30,621
Mar 2	Sheffield Wednesday	(QF)	L 1-2	o.g.	66,945

Fact File

Arsenal became only the second team, after Huddersfield Town, to win the championship for three consecutive seasons. Ted Drake set a club scoring record for league goals that still stands. The Gunners also provided a record seven players – Moss, Male, Hapgood, Copping, Bowden, Drake and Bastin – for the England team that beat World Cup winners Italy 3-2. The famous clock was installed at the south end of the stadium, known ever since as the 'Clock End'.

MANAGER: George Allison

CAPTAIN: Eddie Hapgood

TOP SCORER: Ted Drake 43 (42 League)

BIGGEST WIN: 8-0 v Leicester City 15 December 1934, League; 8-0 v Middlesbrough, 19 April 1935, League

HIGHEST ATTENDANCE: 73,295 v Sunderland, 9 March 1935, League

MAJOR TRANSFERS IN: Wilf Copping from Leeds United, Jack Crayston from Bradford Park Avenue, Alf Kirchen from Norwich City, Bobby Davidson from St Johnstone

MAJOR TRANSFER OUT: Ernest Coleman to Middlesbrough

League & Cup Appearances

PLAYER	LEAGUE	CUP COMPETITION FA CUP	TOTAL
Bastin	36	4	40
Beasley	20	2	22
Birkett	4	1	5
Bowden	24	2	26
Compton	5		5
Copping	31	4	35
Crayston	37	3	40
Davidson	11	1	12
Dougall	8		8
Drake	41	4	45
Dunne	1		1
Hapgood	34	3	37
Hill	15	1	16
Hulme	16	2	18
James	30	3	33
John	9	2	11
Kirchen	7		7
Male	39	4	43
Marshall	4		4
Moss	33	4	37
Roberts	36	4	40
Rogers	5		5
Sidey	6		6
Trim	1		1
Wilson	9		9

Goalscorers

PLAYER	LEAGUE	CUP COMPETITION FA CUP	TOTAL
Drake	42	1	43
Bastin	20	1	21
Bowden	14		14
Hulme	8	2	10
Beasley	6		6
James	4		4
Crayston	3		3
Hill	3		3
Birkett	2		2
Davidson	2		2
Kirchen	2		2
Rogers	2		2
Compton	1		1
Dougall	1		1
Hapgood	1		1
Moss	1		1
Opps' o.gs.	3	1	4

Final Division One Table

		P	W	D	L	F	A	Pts
1	ARSENAL	42	23	12	7	115	46	58
2	SUNDERLAND	42	19	16	7	90	51	54
3	SHEFFIELD W	42	18	13	11	70	64	49
4	MANCHESTER C	42	20	8	14	82	67	48
5	GRIMSBY T	42	17	11	14	78	60	45
6	DERBY CO	42	18	9	15	81	66	45
7	LIVERPOOL	42	19	7	16	85	88	45
8	EVERTON	42	16	12	14	89	88	44
9	WBA	42	17	10	15	83	83	44
10	STOKE C	42	18	6	18	71	70	42
11	PRESTON NE	42	15	12	15	62	67	42
12	CHELSEA	42	16	9	17	73	82	41
13	ASTON VILLA	42	14	13	15	74	88	41
14	PORTSMOUTH	42	15	10	17	71	72	40
15	BLACKBURN R	42	14	11	17	66	78	39
16	HUDDERSFIELD T	42	14	10	18	76	71	38
17	WOLVERHAMPTON W	42	15	8	19	88	94	38
18	LEEDS U	42	13	12	17	75	92	38
19	BIRMINGHAM	42	13	10	19	63	81	36
20	MIDDLESBROUGH	42	10	14	18	70	90	34
21	LEICESTER C	42	12	9	21	61	86	33
22	TOTTENHAM H	42	10	10	22	54	93	30**

Season 1935-36

Football League Division One

DATE	OPPONENTS	SCORE	GOALSCORERS	ATTENDANCE
Aug 31	SUNDERLAND	W 3-1	Drake 2, Bastin	66,428
Sep 3	Grimsby Town	L 0-1		25,978
Sep 7	Birmingham	D 1-1	Drake	42,804
Sep 11	GRIMSBY TOWN	W 6-0	Milne 3, Beasley, Bowden, Drake	33,633
Sep 14	SHEFFIELD WEDNESDAY	D 2-2	Drake, Milne	59,492
Sep 18	Leeds United	D 1-1	Drake	24,283
Sep 21	MANCHESTER CITY	L 2-3	Bastin (pen),James	61,290
Sep 28	Stoke City	W 3-0	Bastin 2, Crayston	45,570
Oct 5	BLACKBURN ROVERS	W 5-1	Bowden 3, Bastin, Milne	45,981
Oct 12	Chelsea	D 1-1	Crayston	82,905
Oct 19	Portsmouth	L 1-2	Milne	34,165
Oct 26	PRESTON NORTH END	W 2-1	Drake, Bastin	42,126
Nov 2	Brentford	L 1-2	Parkin	26,330
Nov 9	DERBY COUNTY	D 1-1	Drake	54,027
Nov 16	Everton	W 2-0	Drake, Bastin	46,990
Nov 23	WOLVERHAMPTON WANDERERS	W 4-0	Rogers, Drake 2, Hulme	39,860
Nov 30	Huddersfield Town	D 0-0		35,816
Dec 9	MIDDLESBROUGH	W 2-0	Rogers 2	23,365
Dec 14	Aston Villa	W 7-1	Drake 7	58,469
Dec 25	Liverpool	W 1-0	Hulme	45,899
Dec 26	LIVERPOOL	L 1-2	Hulme	57,035
Dec 28	Sunderland	L 4-5	Bowden, Drake, Bastin (pen), o.g.	58,773
Jan 4	BIRMINGHAM	D 1-1	Drake	44,534
Jan 18	Sheffield Wednesday	L 2-3	Drake, Roberts	35,576
Feb 1	STOKE CITY	W 1-0	Drake	49,347
Feb 8	Blackburn Rovers	W 1-0	Crayston	24,998
Feb 22	PORTSMOUTH	L 2-3	Compton, Dougall	21,728
Mar 4	Derby County	W 4-0	Dougall, Kirchen, Cox, Crayston	17,930
Mar 7	HUDDERSFIELD TOWN	D 1-1	Bastin	43,930
Mar 11	Manchester City	L 0-1		32,750
Mar 14	Preston North End	L 0-1		30,039
Mar 25	EVERTON	D 1-1	Hulme	18,593
Mar 28	Wolverhampton Wanderers	D 2-2	Beasley, Kirchen	32,330
Apr 1	BOLTON WANDERERS	D 1-1	Westcott	10,485
Apr 4	BRENTFORD	D 1-1	Dougall	28,303
Apr 10	WEST BROMWICH ALBION	W 4-0	Crayston, Dunne, Hulme, James	59,245
Apr 11	Middlesbrough	D 2-2	Bowden, Bastin (pen)	31,006
Apr 13	West Bromwich Albion	L 0-1		42,286
Apr 18	ASTON VILLA	W 1-0	Drake	55,431
Apr 27	CHELSEA	D 1-1	Drake	40,402
Apr 29	Bolton Wanderers	L 1-2	Hulme	29,479
May 2	LEEDS UNITED	D 2-2	Bastin, Kirchen	25,920

FA Cup

Jan 11	Bristol Rovers	(Rd3) W 5-1	Bastin 2, Drake 2, Bowden	24,234
Jan 25	Liverpool	(Rd4) W 2-0	Bowden, Hulme	53,720
Feb 15	Newcastle United	(Rd5) D 3-3	Bowden 2, Hulme	65,484
Feb 19	NEWCASTLE UNITED	(R) W 3-0	Bastin 2 (2pens), Beasley	62,391
Feb 29	BARNSLEY	(QF) W 4-1	Beasley 2, Bowden, Bastin (pen)	60,420
Mar 21	Grimsby Town*	(SF) W 1-0	Bastin	63,210
Apr 25	Sheffield United**	(F) W 1-0	Drake	93,384

*Played at Leeds Road. **Played at Wembley.

Fact File

Ted Drake set a top division scoring record that still stands when he scored all the goals in Arsenal's 7-1 win at Aston Villa in December. Drake's haul came from eight shots. The other one hit an upright! Arsenal's visit to Chelsea on 12 October attracted a crowd of 82,905, a new Football League attendance record.

MANAGER: George Allison

CAPTAIN: Eddie Hapgood

TOP SCORER: Ted Drake 27 (24 League)

BIGGEST WIN: 7-1 v Aston Villa, 14 December 1935, League

HIGHEST ATTENDANCE: 66,428 v Sunderland, 31 August 1935, League

MAJOR TRANSFERS IN: Jackie Milne from Middlesbrough, George Swindin from Bradford City

League & Cup Appearances

PLAYER	LEAGUE	CUP COMPETITION FA CUP	TOTAL
Bastin	31	7	38
Beasley	26	4	30
Bowden	22	7	29
Cartwright	5		5
Compton	12		12
Copping	33	7	40
Cox	5		5
Crayston	36	7	43
Davidson	13	1	14
Dougall	8		8
Drake	26	3	29
Dunne	6		6
Hapgood	33	7	40
Hill	10		10
Hulme	21	7	28
James	17	6	23
John	6		6
Joy	2		2
Kirchen	6		6
Male	35	7	42
Milne	14		14
Moss	5	2	7
Parkin	1		1
Roberts	26	5	31
Rogers	11		11
Sidey	11	2	13
Tuckett	2		2
Westcott	2		2
Wilson	37	5	42

Goalscorers

PLAYER	LEAGUE	CUP COMPETITION FA CUP	TOTAL
Drake	24	3	27
Bastin	11	6	17
Bowden	6	5	11
Hulme	6	2	8
Milne	6		6
Crayston	5		5
Beasley	2	3	5
Dougall	3		3
Kirchen	3		3
Rogers	3		3
James	2		2
Compton	1		1
Cox	1		1
Dunne	1		1
Parkin	1		1
Roberts	1		1
Westcott	1		1
Opps' o.gs.	1		1

Final Division One Table

		P	W	D	L	F	A	Pts
1	SUNDERLAND	42	25	6	11	109	74	56
2	DERBY CO	42	18	12	12	61	52	48
3	HUDDERSFIELD T	42	18	12	12	59	56	48
4	STOKE C	42	20	7	15	57	57	47
5	BRENTFORD	42	17	12	13	81	60	46
6	ARSENAL	42	15	15	12	78	48	45
7	PRESTON NE	42	18	8	16	67	64	44
8	CHELSEA	42	15	13	14	65	72	43
9	MANCHESTER C	42	17	8	17	68	60	42
10	PORTSMOUTH	42	17	8	17	54	67	42
11	LEEDS U	42	15	11	16	66	64	41
12	BIRMINGHAM	42	15	11	16	61	63	41
13	BOLTON W	42	14	13	15	67	76	41
14	MIDDLESBROUGH	42	15	10	17	84	70	40
15	WOLVERHAMPTON W	42	15	10	17	77	76	40
16	EVERTON	42	13	13	16	89	89	39
17	GRIMSBY T	42	17	5	20	65	73	39
18	WBA	42	16	6	20	89	88	38
19	LIVERPOOL	42	13	12	17	60	64	38
20	SHEFFIELD W	42	13	12	17	63	77	38
21	ASTON VILLA	42	13	9	20	81	110	35
22	BLACKBURN R	42	12	9	21	55	96	33

Season 1936-37

Football League Division One

DATE	OPPONENTS	SCORE	GOALSCORERS	ATTENDANCE
Aug 29	EVERTON	W 3-2	Hapgood, Bowden, James	50,321
Sep 3	Brentford	L 0-2		31,056
Sep 5	Huddersfield Town	D 0-0		32,013
Sep 9	BRENTFORD	D 1-1	Drake	44,010
Sep 12	SUNDERLAND	W 4-1	Crayston, Beasley, Bastin, Roberts	56,820
Sep 19	Wolverhampton Wanderers	L 0-2		53,097
Sep 26	DERBY COUNTY	D 2-2	Compton, Drake	61,390
Oct 3	Manchester United	L 0-2		55,884
Oct 10	SHEFFIELD WEDNESDAY	D 1-1	Drake	46,421
Oct 17	Charlton Athletic	W 2-0	Davidson, Compton	68,160
Oct 24	GRIMSBY TOWN	D 0-0		51,202
Oct 31	Liverpool	L 1-2	Kirchen	39,251
Nov 7	LEEDS UNITED	W 4-1	Kirchen, Drake, Milne, Davidson	32,535
Nov 14	Birmingham	W 3-1	Drake 2, Kirchen	39,940
Nov 21	MIDDLESBROUGH	W 5-3	Milne 2, Drake, Bastin, Bowden	44,829
Nov 28	West Bromwich Albion	W 4-2	Drake 2, Milne 2	27,609
Dec 5	MANCHESTER CITY	L 1-3	Drake	41,783
Dec 12	Portsmouth	W 5-1	Davidson 4, Drake	32,184
Dec 19	CHELSEA	W 4-1	Kirchen 2, Drake, Davidson	49,917
Dec 25	PRESTON NORTH END	W 4-1	Drake 2, Kirchen, Milne	42,781
Dec 26	Everton	D 1-1	Kirchen	59,440
Dec 28	Preston North End	W 3-1	Kirchen, Nelson, Milne	25,787
Jan 1	Bolton Wanderers	W 5-1	Drake 4, Milne	42,171
Jan 2	HUDDERSFIELD TOWN	D 1-1	Kirchen	44,224
Jan 9	Sunderland	D 1-1	Milne	54,694
Jan 23	WOLVERHAMPTON WANDERERS	W 3-0	Bastin (pen), Drake, Bowden	33,896
Feb 3	Derby County	L 4-5	Drake, Bastin (pen), Kirchen, o.g	22,064
Feb 6	MANCHESTER UNITED	D 1-1	Davidson	37,236
Feb 13	Sheffield Wednesday	D 0-0		35,813
Feb 24	CHARLTON ATHLETIC	D 1-1	Kirchen	60,568
Feb 27	Grimsby Town	W 3-1	Kirchen 3	18,216
Mar 10	LIVERPOOL	W 1-0	Kirchen	16,145
Mar 13	Leeds United	W 4-3	Kirchen 2, Bastin (pen), Bowden	25,148
Mar 20	BIRMINGHAM	D 1-1	Bowden	46,086
Mar 26	STOKE CITY	D 0-0		59,495
Mar 27	Middlesbrough	D 1-1	Bowden	44,523
Mar 29	Stoke City	D 0-0		51,480
Apr 3	WEST BROMWICH ALBION	W 2-0	Davidson, Nelson	38,773
Apr 10	Manchester City	L 0-2		74,918
Apr 17	PORTSMOUTH	W 4-0	Compton, 2, Nelson, Kirchen	29,098
Apr 24	Chelsea	L 0-2		53,325
May 1	BOLTON WANDERERS	D 0-0		22,875

FA Cup

Jan 16	Chesterfield	(Rd3)	W 5-1	Drake 2, Kirchen 2, Davidson	21,786
Jan 30	MANCHESTER UNITED	(Rd4)	W 5-0	Bastin, Davidson, Drake, Kirchen, o.g.	45,637
Feb 20	Burnley	(Rd5)	W 7-1	Drake 4, Crayston, Bastin, Kirchen	54,445
Mar 6	West Bromwich Albion	(QF)	L 1-3	Bastin	64,815

Fact File

Alex James retired at the end of the season, aged 35. He had been the midfield genius behind four championships and two FA Cup successes. Yet, despite his massive achievements with the Gunners, he was only capped eight times by Scotland.

MANAGER: George Allison
CAPTAIN: Eddie Hapgood
TOP SCORER: Ted Drake 27 (20 League)
BIGGEST WIN: 7-1 v Burnley, 20 February 1937, FA Cup
HIGHEST ATTENDANCE: 61,390 v Derby County, 26 September 1936, League
MAJOR TRANSFER IN: Frank Boulton from Bath City
MAJOR TRANSFERS OUT: Jimmy Dunne to Southampton, Frank Hill to Blackpool, Pat Beasley to Huddersfield Town

League & Cup Appearances

PLAYER	LEAGUE	CUP COMPETITION FA CUP	TOTAL
Bastin	33	4	37
Beasley	7		7
Biggs	1		1
Boulton	21	4	25
Bowden	28	2	30
Cartwright	2		2
Compton D.	14		14
Compton L.	15	2	17
Copping	38	4	42
Crayston	30	2	32
Davidson	28	2	30
Drake	26	3	29
Hapgood	32	2	34
Hulme	3		3
James	19	4	23
John	5		5
Joy	6		6
Kirchen	33	4	37
Male	37	4	41
Milne	19	3	22
Nelson	8		8
Roberts	30	4	34
Sidey	6		6
Swindin	19		19
Wilson	2		2

Goalscorers

PLAYER	LEAGUE	CUP COMPETITION FA CUP	TOTAL
Drake	20	7	27
Kirchen	18	4	22
Davidson	9	2	11
Milne	9		9
Bastin	5	3	8
Bowden	6		6
Compton	4		4
Nelson	3		3
Crayston	1	1	2
Beasley	1		1
Hapgood	1		1
James	1		1
Roberts	1		1
Opps' o.gs.	1	1	2

Final Division One Table

		P	W	D	L	F	A	Pts
1	MANCHESTER C	42	22	13	7	107	61	57
2	CHARLTON ATH	42	21	12	9	58	49	54
3	ARSENAL	42	18	16	8	80	49	52
4	DERBY CO	42	21	7	14	96	90	49
5	WOLVERHAMPTON W	42	21	5	16	84	67	47
6	BRENTFORD	42	18	10	14	82	78	46
7	MIDDLESBROUGH	42	19	8	15	74	71	46
8	SUNDERLAND	42	19	6	17	89	87	44
9	PORTSMOUTH	42	17	10	15	62	66	44
10	STOKE C	42	15	12	15	72	57	42
11	BIRMINGHAM	42	13	15	14	64	60	41
12	GRIMSBY T	42	17	7	18	86	81	41
13	CHELSEA	42	14	13	15	52	55	41
14	PRESTON NE	42	14	13	15	56	67	41
15	HUDDERSFIELD T	42	12	15	15	62	64	39
16	WBA	42	16	6	20	77	98	38
17	EVERTON	42	14	9	19	81	78	37
18	LIVERPOOL	42	12	11	19	62	84	35
19	LEEDS U	42	15	4	23	60	80	34
20	BOLTON W	42	10	14	18	43	66	34
21	MANCHESTER U	42	10	12	20	55	78	32
22	SHEFFIELD W	42	9	12	21	53	69	30

Season 1937-38

Football League Division One

DATE	OPPONENTS	SCORE	GOALSCORERS	ATTENDANCE
Aug 28	Everton	W 4-1	Drake 3, Bastin	53,856
Sep 1	HUDDERSFIELD TOWN	W 3-1	Drake, Crayston, Bastin	32,758
Sep 4	WOLVERHAMPTON WANDERERS	W 5-0	Drake 2, Crayston, Hulme, Bastin (pen)	67,311
Sep 8	Huddersfield Town	L 1-2	Bowden	28,405
Sep 11	Leicester City	D 1-1	Drake	39,106
Sep 15	Bolton Wanderers	L 0-1		39,750
Sep 18	SUNDERLAND	W 4-1	Milne, Drake, Hulme, Davidson	65,635
Sep 25	Derby County	L 0-2		33,101
Oct 2	MANCHESTER CITY	W 2-1	Milne, Kirchen	68,353
Oct 9	Chelsea	D 2-2	Kirchen 2	75,952
Oct 16	PORTSMOUTH	D 1-1	Hunt	45,150
Oct 23	Stoke City	D 1-1	Davidson	35,684
Oct 30	MIDDLESBROUGH	L 1-2	Milne	39,066
Nov 6	Grimsby Town	L 1-2	Jones L.	20,244
Nov 13	WEST BROMWICH ALBION	D 1-1	Compton L.	34,324
Nov 20	Charlton Athletic	W 3-0	Bastin, Drake, o.g.	55,078
Nov 27	LEEDS UNITED	W 4-1	Drake 2, Bastin (pen), Kirchen	34,350
Dec 4	Birmingham	W 2-1	Kirchen, Cartwright	18,440
Dec 11	PRESTON NORTH END	W 2-0	Bastin, Milne	35,679
Dec 18	Liverpool	L 0-2		32,093
Dec 25	Blackpool	L 1-2	Bastin (pen)	23,229
Dec 27	BLACKPOOL	W 2-1	Bastin, Cartwright	54,163
Jan 1	EVERTON	W 2-1	Lewis, Hunt	36,953
Jan 15	Wolverhampton Wanderers	L 1-3	Drake	39,383
Jan 29	Sunderland	D 1-1	Hunt	42,638
Feb 2	LEICESTER CITY	W 3-1	Drake, Bastin, Jones L.	23,839
Feb 5	DERBY COUNTY	W 3-0	Crayston 2, Lewis	47,263
Feb 16	Manchester City	W 2-1	Drake, Compton D.	34,299
Feb 19	CHELSEA	W 2-0	Griffiths, Drake	49,573
Feb 26	Portsmouth	D 0-0		43,991
Mar 5	STOKE CITY	W 4-0	Carr, Griffiths 2, Drake	35,296
Mar 12	Middlesbrough	L 1-2	Bastin	46,747
Mar 19	GRIMSBY TOWN	W 5-1	Bastin 2 (1pen), Griffiths 2, Jones L.	40,701
Mar 26	West Bromwich Albion	D 0-0		33,954
Apr 2	CHARLTON ATHLETIC	D 2-2	Drake, Carr	52,858
Apr 9	Leeds United	W 1-0	Bremner	29,365
Apr 15	BRENTFORD	L 0-2		51,299
Apr 16	BIRMINGHAM	D 0-0		35,161
Apr 18	Brentford	L 0-3		34,601
Apr 23	Preston North End	W 3-1	Carr 2, Bastin	42,684
Apr 30	LIVERPOOL	W 1-0	Carr	34,703
May 7	BOLTON WANDERERS	W 5-0	Bastin 2, Carr 2, Kirchen	40,500

FA Cup

DATE	OPPONENTS		SCORE	GOALSCORERS	ATTENDANCE
Jan 8	BOLTON WANDERERS	(Rd3)	W 3-1	Bastin 2, Kirchen	64,016
Jan 22	Wolverhampton Wanderers	(Rd4)	W 2-1	Kirchen, Drake	61,267
Feb 12	PRESTON NORTH END	(Rd5)	L 0-1		72,121

Fact File

Arsenal won the championship for the fifth time, with the joint lowest points total ever recorded for a 42-match season. Wing half Bob John, Arsenal's longest-serving player, retired at the age of 39. He made 467 league and FA Cup appearances in 16 years with the Gunners, a club record until it was surpassed by George Armstrong. He also played 15 times for Wales.

MANAGER: George Allison

CAPTAIN: Eddie Hapgood

TOP SCORER: Ted Drake 18 (17 League)

BIGGEST WIN: 5-0 v Wolverhampton Wanderers, 4 September 1937, League; 5-0 v Bolton Wanderers, 7 May 1938, League

HIGHEST ATTENDANCE: 72,121 v Preston North End, 12 February 1938, FA Cup

MAJOR TRANSFERS IN: Leslie Jones from Coventry City, George Drury from Sheffield Wednesday

MAJOR TRANSFERS OUT: Joe Hulme to Huddersfield Town, Jackie Milne to Middlesbrough, Bobby Davidson to Coventry City

League & Cup Appearances

PLAYER	LEAGUE	CUP COMPETITION FA CUP	TOTAL
Bastin	38	3	41
Biggs	2		2
Boulton	15	2	17
Bowden	10		10
Bremner	2		2
Carr	11		11
Cartwright	6		6
Collett	5		5
Compton D.	7		7
Compton L.	9		9
Copping	38	3	41
Crayston	31	3	34
Davidson	5		5
Drake	27	3	30
Drury	11		11
Griffiths	9		9
Hapgood	41	3	44
Hulme	7		7
Hunt	18	3	21
Jones L.	28	3	31
Joy	26	3	29
Kirchen	19	3	22
Lewis	4		4
Male	34	3	37
Milne	16		16
Roberts	13		13
Sidey	3		3
Swindin	17	1	18
Wilson	10		10

Goalscorers

PLAYER	LEAGUE	CUP COMPETITION FA CUP	TOTAL
Drake	17	1	18
Bastin	15	2	17
Kirchen	6	2	8
Carr	7		7
Griffiths	5		5
Crayston	4		4
Milne	4		4
Hunt	3		3
Jones L.	3		3
Cartwright	2		2
Davidson	2		2
Hulme	2		2
Lewis	2		2
Bowden	1		1
Bremner	1		1
Compton D.	1		1
Compton L.	1		1
Opps' o.gs.	1		1

Final Division One Table

		P	W	D	L	F	A	Pts
1	ARSENAL	42	21	10	11	77	44	52
2	WOLVERHAMPTON W	42	20	11	11	72	49	51
3	PRESTON NE	42	16	17	9	64	44	49
4	CHARLTON ATH	42	16	14	12	65	51	46
5	MIDDLESBROUGH	42	19	8	15	72	65	46
6	BRENTFORD	42	18	9	15	69	59	45
7	BOLTON W	42	15	15	12	64	60	45
8	SUNDERLAND	42	14	16	12	55	57	44
9	LEEDS U	42	14	15	13	64	69	43
10	CHELSEA	42	14	13	15	65	65	41
11	LIVERPOOL	42	15	11	16	65	71	41
12	BLACKPOOL	42	16	8	18	61	66	40
13	DERBY CO	42	15	10	17	66	87	40
14	EVERTON	42	16	7	19	79	75	39
15	HUDDERSFIELD T	42	17	5	20	55	68	39
16	LEICESTER C	42	14	11	17	54	75	39
17	STOKE C	42	13	12	17	58	59	38
18	BIRMINGHAM	42	10	18	14	58	62	38
19	PORTSMOUTH	42	13	12	17	62	68	38
20	GRIMSBY T	42	13	12	17	51	68	38
21	MANCHESTER C	42	14	8	20	80	77	36
22	WBA	42	14	8	20	74	91	36

Season 1938-39

Football League Division One

DATE	OPPONENTS	SCORE	GOALSCORERS	ATTENDANCE
Aug 27	PORTSMOUTH	W 2-0	Jones B., o.g.	54,940
Sep 3	Huddersfield Town	D 1-1	Jones B.	26,126
Sep 8	Brentford	L 0-1		38,535
Sep 10	EVERTON	L 1-2	Jones B.	64,555
Sep 14	DERBY COUNTY	L 1-2	Drake	25,756
Sep 17	Wolverhampton Wanderers	W 1-0	Cumner	45,364
Sep 24	ASTON VILLA	D 0-0		66,456
Oct 1	Sunderland	D 0-0		51,042
Oct 8	GRIMSBY TOWN	W 2-0	Bremner, Kirchen	39,174
Oct 15	Chelsea	L 2-4	Cumner, Kirchen	65,443
Oct 22	PRESTON NORTH END	W 1-0	o.g.	40,296
Oct 29	Bolton Wanderers	D 1-1	Jones B.	46,611
Nov 5	LEEDS UNITED	L 2-3	Bastin, Drake	39,092
Nov 12	Liverpool	D 2-2	Drake, Kirchen	42,540
Nov 19	LEICESTER CITY	D 0-0		36,407
Nov 26	Middlesbrough	D 1-1	Drury	29,147
Dec 3	BIRMINGHAM	W 3-1	Drake, Crayston, Nelson	33,710
Dec 10	Manchester United	L 0-1		42,008
Dec 17	STOKE CITY	W 4-1	Lewis 2, Bastin, Drury	30,006
Dec 24	Portsmouth	D 0-0		21,344
Dec 27	Charlton Athletic	L 0-1		51,479
Dec 31	HUDDERSFIELD TOWN	W 1-0	Drake	34,146
Jan 14	Everton	L 0-2		47,178
Jan 21	CHARLTON ATHLETIC	W 2-0	Crayston, Lewis	39,702
Jan 28	Aston Villa	W 3-1	Lewis 2, Kirchen	57,453
Feb 1	WOLVERHAMPTON WANDERS	D 0-0		33,103
Feb 4	SUNDERLAND	W 2-0	Bastin, Lewis	45,875
Feb 18	CHELSEA	W 1-0	Bremner	54,510
Feb 21	Grimsby Town	L 1-2	Kirchen	10,845
Feb 25	Preston North End	L 1-2	Lewis	29,678
Mar 4	BOLTON WANDERERS	W 3-1	Drake 2, o.g.	29,814
Mar 11	Leeds United	L 2-4	Drake, Compton L. (pen)	22,160
Mar 18	LIVERPOOL	W 2-0	Kirchen, Drake	31,495
Mar 25	Leicester City	W 2-0	Kirchen, Drake	22,565
Apr 1	MIDDLESBROUGH	L 1-2	Bremner	34,669
Apr 7	Blackpool	L 0-1		31,497
Apr 8	Birmingham	W 2-1	Kirchen, Drury	33,250
Apr 10	BLACKPOOL	W 2-1	Drake, Compton L. (pen)	30,760
Apr 15	MANCHESTER UNITED	W 2-1	Drake, Crayston	25,741
Apr 22	Stoke City	L 0-1		26,039
Apr 29	Derby County	W 2-1	Farr, Drake	10,186
May 6	BRENTFORD	W 2-0	Kirchen, Drake	30,928

FA Cup

Jan 7	Chelsea	(Rd3) L 1-2	Bastin	58,095

League & Cup Appearances

PLAYER	LEAGUE	CUP COMPETITION FA CUP	TOTAL
Bastin	23	1	24
Bremner	13		13
Carr	1		1
Cartwright	3		3
Collett	9		9
Compton D.	1		1
Compton L.	18		18
Copping	26	1	27
Crayston	34	1	35
Cumner	12		12
Curtis	2		2
Drake	38	1	39
Drury	23	1	24
Farr	2		2
Fields	3		3
Hapgood	38	1	39
Jones B.	30	1	31
Jones L.	18		18
Joy	39	1	40
Kirchen	27		27
Lewis	15	1	16
Male	28	1	29
Marks	2		2
Nelson	9		9
Pryde	4		4
Pugh	1		1
Swindin	21		21
Walsh	3		3
Wilson	19	1	20

Goalscorers

PLAYER	LEAGUE	CUP COMPETITION FA CUP	TOTAL
Drake	14		14
Kirchen	9		9
Lewis	7		7
Jones B.	4		4
Bastin	3	1	4
Bremner	3		3
Crayston	3		3
Drury	3		3
Compton L.	2		2
Cumner	2		2
Farr	1		1
Nelson	1		1
Opps' o.gs.	3		3

Fact File

Arsenal paid a British record fee of £14,000 to Wolverhampton Wanderers for Wales inside forward Bryn Jones, 23 days before the start of the season. George Allison and his staff saw Jones as the long-term replacement for Alex James. But the Welshman took time to settle in and the onset of war meant that Arsenal fans never saw him at his best. He played on for three postwar seasons, before joining Norwich City as player-coach in the summer of 1949.

MANAGER: George Allison
CAPTAIN: Eddie Hapgood
TOP SCORER: Ted Drake 14 (all League)
BIGGEST WIN: 4-1 v Stoke City, 17 December 1938, League
HIGHEST ATTENDANCE: 66,456 v Aston Villa, 24 September 1938, League
MAJOR TRANSFER IN: Bryn Jones from Wolverhampton Wanderers
MAJOR TRANSFER OUT: Wilf Copping to Leeds United

Final Division One Table

		P	W	D	L	F	A	Pts
1	EVERTON	42	27	5	10	88	52	59
2	WOLVERHAMPTON W	42	22	11	9	88	39	55
3	CHARLTON ATH	42	22	6	14	75	59	50
4	MIDDLESBROUGH	42	20	9	13	93	74	49
5	ARSENAL	42	19	9	14	55	41	47
6	DERBY CO	42	19	8	15	66	55	46
7	STOKE C	42	17	12	13	71	68	46
8	BOLTON W	42	15	15	12	67	58	45
9	PRESTON NE	42	16	12	14	63	59	44
10	GRIMSBY T	42	16	11	15	61	69	43
11	LIVERPOOL	42	14	14	14	62	63	42
12	ASTON VILLA	42	15	11	16	71	60	41
13	LEEDS U	42	16	9	17	59	67	41
14	MANCHESTER U	42	11	16	15	57	65	38
15	BLACKPOOL	42	12	14	16	56	68	38
16	SUNDERLAND	42	13	12	17	54	67	38
17	PORTSMOUTH	42	12	13	17	47	70	37
18	BRENTFORD	42	14	8	20	53	74	36
19	HUDDERSFIELD T	42	12	11	19	58	64	35
20	CHELSEA	42	12	9	21	64	80	33
21	BIRMINGHAM	42	12	8	22	62	84	32
22	LEICESTER C	42	9	11	22	48	82	29

Arsenal in Wartime 1939-45

The Football League and FA Cup were suspended for the duration of the World War II. League football did not resume until August 1946. Arsenal Stadium was closed and turned into an Air Raid Protection Centre. The Gunners played in regional competitions using White Hart Lane as their 'home' ground. Teams were hastily put together from players home on war leave and often included a host of 'guest' players from other clubs who were in the area and available. Among the famous names to guest for Arsenal during the war were Stanley Matthews, Bill Shankly and Stan Mortensen.

The FA Cup resumed in 1945-46. For the only time in the Cup's history, ties were played over two legs until the semi-finals.

1945-46

FA Cup

DATE	OPPONENTS	SCORE	GOALSCORERS	ATTENDANCE
Jan 5	West Ham United	(Rd3/1L) L 0-6		35,000
Jan 9	WEST HAM UNITED	(Rd3/2L)W 1-0	Cumner	21,733

Appearances

PLAYER	CUP COMPETITION FA CUP	TOTAL
Bastin	1	1
Collett	1	1
Cumner	1	1
Drury	1	1
Henley	1	1
Jones L.	1	1
Joy	2	2
Lewis	1	1
Logie	1	1
Male	1	1
Nelson	2	2
O'Flanagan	2	2
Scott	2	2
Swindin	2	2
Wade	2	2
Waller	1	1

Goalscorers

PLAYER	CUP COMPETITION FA CUP	TOTAL
Cumner	1	1

Three players that appeared in the one season after the war when FA Cup ties were played over two legs, until the semi-finals, l-r: Jimmy Logie, George Swindin, Reg Lewis.

Season 1946-47

Football League Division One

DATE	OPPONENTS	SCORE	GOALSCORERS	ATTENDANCE
Aug 31	Wolverhampton Wanderers	L 1-6	Lewis	50,845
Sep 4	BLACKBURN ROVERS	L 1-3	Lewis	28,700
Sep 7	SUNDERLAND	D 2-2	Lewis 2	53,377
Sep 11	Everton	L 2-3	Lewis 2	40,000
Sep 14	Aston Villa	W 2-0	Lewis, O'Flanagan	53,778
Sep 17	Blackburn Rovers	W 2-1	Lewis 2	24,563
Sep 21	DERBY COUNTY	L 0-1		60,643
Sep 28	Manchester United	L 2-5	Lewis, McPherson	62,718
Oct 5	Blackpool	L 1-2	Logie	24,039
Oct 12	BRENTFORD	D 2-2	Lewis, Logie	45,000
Oct 19	STOKE CITY	W 1-0	O'Flanagan	60,266
Oct 26	Chelsea	L 1-2	Lewis	56,568
Nov 2	SHEFFIELD UNITED	L 2-3	Lewis, Logie	41,730
Nov 9	Preston North End	L 0-2		29,971
Nov 16	LEEDS UNITED	W 4-2	Lewis 2 (1 pen), Logie, McPherson	36,377
Nov 23	Liverpool	L 2-4	Lewis, Logie	51,435
Nov 30	BOLTON WANDERERS	D 2-2	Lewis (pen), O'Flanagan	42,522
Dec 7	Middlesbrough	L 0-1		30,357
Dec 14	CHARLTON ATHLETIC	W 1-0	Rooke	38,606
Dec 21	Grimsby Town	D 0-0		13,308
Dec 25	PORTSMOUTH	W 2-1	Rooke, Logie	32,108
Dec 26	Portsmouth	W 2-0	Rooke 2	38,000
Dec 28	WOLVERHAMPTON WANDERERS	D 1-1	Rooke	58,075
Jan 4	Sunderland	W 4-1	Rooke 2, Lewis 2	36,812
Jan 18	ASTON VILLA	L 0-2		57,524
Feb 1	MANCHESTER UNITED	W 6-2	Rooke 3, Rudkin, Logie, McPherson	29,145
Feb 8	BLACKPOOL	D 1-1	Rooke	31,111
Feb 22	Stoke City	L 1-3	Rooke	30,000
Mar 1	CHELSEA	L 1-2	Rudkin	52,606
Mar 15	PRESTON NORTH END	W 4-1	Lewis 3, Rooke	45,775
Mar 22	Leeds United	D 1-1	Lewis	32,000
Apr 4	HUDDERSFIELD TOWN	L 1-2	Jones B.	46,105
Apr 5	Bolton Wanderers	W 3-1	Rooke 2, Lewis	34,398
Apr 7	Huddersfield Town	D 0-0		33,381
Apr 12	MIDDLESBROUGH	W 4-0	Rooke 4 (1 pen)	44,230
Apr 19	Charlton Athletic	D 2-2	McPherson, Logie	57,983
Apr 26	GRIMSBY TOWN	W 5-3	Lewis 4, Compton D.	42,100
May 10	Derby County	W 1-0	Rooke	19,153
May 24	LIVERPOOL	L 1-2	McPherson	44,265
May 26	Brentford	W 1-0	Sloan	17,599
May 31	EVERTON	W 2-1	Rooke, Lewis	23,785
Jun 7	Sheffield United	L 1-2	McPherson	14,939

FA Cup

Jan 11	Chelsea	(Rd3) D 1-1	McPherson	70,195
Jan 15	CHELSEA	(R) D 1-1	Rooke	53,350
Jan 20	Chelsea*	(2R) L 0-2		59,590

*Played at White Hart Lane.

League & Cup Appearances

PLAYER	LEAGUE	CUP COMPETITION FA CUP	TOTAL
Barnes	26	3	29
Bastin	6		6
Calverley	11		11
Collett	6		6
Compton D.	1		1
Compton L.	36	3	39
Curtis	11	1	12
Drury	4		4
Fields	8		8
Grant	2		2
Gudmundsson	2		2
Hodges	2		2
Jones B.	26	2	28
Joy	13		13
Lewis	28	3	31
Logie	35	3	38
McPherson	37	3	40
Male	15	2	17
Mercer	25	3	28
Morgan	2		2
Nelson	10		10
O'Flanagan	14		14
Platt	4		4
Rooke	24	3	27
Rudkin	5		5
Scott	28	1	29
Sloan	30	3	33
Smith A.	3		3
Swindin	38	3	41
Wade	2		2
Waller	8		8

Goalscorers

PLAYER	LEAGUE	CUP COMPETITION FA CUP	TOTAL
Lewis	29		29
Rooke	21	1	22
Logie	8		8
McPherson	6	1	7
O'Flanagan	3		3
Rudkin	2		2
Compton D.	1		1
Jones B.	1		1
Sloan	1		1

Fact File

Inside forward Albert Gudmundsson became the first Icelander to play for Arsenal when he made two league appearances in October. He later joined Milan after he was refused permission to play as a professional in the Football League. Kevin O'Flanagan, an Ireland international at football and rugby, made 14 appearances in the first half of the season. O'Flanagan, a Dublin doctor, was also Irish sprint and long jump champion!

MANAGER: George Allison

CAPTAIN: Les Compton/Joe Mercer

TOP SCORER: Reg Lewis 29 (all League)

BIGGEST WIN: 6-2 v Manchester United, 1 February 1947, League

HIGHEST ATTENDANCE: 60,266 v Stoke City, 19 October 1946, League

MAJOR TRANSFERS IN: Joe Mercer from Everton, Ian McPherson from Notts County, Ronnie Rooke from Fulham

MAJOR TRANSFER OUT: George Drury to West Bromwich Albion

Final Division One Table

		P	W	D	L	F	A	Pts
1	LIVERPOOL	42	25	7	10	84	52	57
2	MANCHESTER U	42	22	12	8	95	54	56
3	WOLVERHAMPTON W	42	25	6	11	98	56	56
4	STOKE C	42	24	7	11	90	53	55
5	BLACKPOOL	42	22	6	14	71	70	50
6	SHEFFIELD U	42	21	7	14	89	75	49
7	PRESTON NE	42	18	11	13	76	74	47
8	ASTON VILLA	42	18	9	15	67	53	45
9	SUNDERLAND	42	18	8	16	65	66	44
10	EVERTON	42	17	9	16	62	67	43
11	MIDDLESBROUGH	42	17	8	17	73	68	42
12	PORTSMOUTH	42	16	9	17	66	60	41
13	ARSENAL	42	16	9	17	72	70	41
14	DERBY CO	42	18	5	19	73	79	41
15	CHELSEA	42	16	7	19	69	84	39
16	GRIMSBY T	42	13	12	17	61	82	38
17	BLACKBURN R	42	14	8	20	45	53	36
18	BOLTON W	42	13	8	21	57	69	34
19	CHARLTON ATH	42	11	12	19	57	71	34
20	HUDDERSFIELD T	42	13	7	22	53	79	33
21	BRENTFORD	42	9	7	26	45	88	25
22	LEEDS U	42	6	6	30	45	90	18

Season 1947-48

Football League Division One

DATE	OPPONENTS	SCORE	GOALSCORERS	ATTENDANCE
Aug 23	SUNDERLAND	W 3-1	McPherson, Logie, Rooke	58,184
Aug 27	Charlton Athletic	W 4-2	McPherson, Roper, Lewis, Logie	60,000
Aug 30	Sheffield United	W 2-1	Rooke, Roper	39,130
Sep 3	CHARLTON ATHLETIC	W 6-0	Lewis 4, Rooke 2	54,684
Sep 6	MANCHESTER UNITED	W 2-1	Rooke, Lewis	64,905
Sep 10	BOLTON WANDERERS	W 2-0	McPherson, Rooke (pen)	46,969
Sep 13	Preston North End	D 0-0		40,061
Sep 20	STOKE CITY	W 3-0	Logie, McPherson 2	62,000
Sep 27	Burnley	W 1-0	Lewis	47,258
Oct 4	PORTSMOUTH	D 0-0		62,000
Oct 11	ASTON VILLA	W 1-0	Rooke	60,427
Oct 18	Wolverhampton Wanderers	D 1-1	Rooke (pen)	55,998
Oct 25	EVERTON	D 1-1	Lewis	56,645
Nov 1	Chelsea	D 0-0		67,277
Nov 8	BLACKPOOL	W 2-1	Rooke (pen), Roper	62,000
Nov 15	Blackburn Rovers	W 1-0	Rooke	37,423
Nov 22	HUDDERSFIELD TOWN	W 2-0	Rooke, Logie	47,514
Nov 29	Derby County	L 0-1		35,605
Dec 6	MANCHESTER CITY	D 1-1	Rooke	41,274
Dec 13	Grimsby Town	W 4-0	Rooke 2, Logie, Roper	20,000
Dec 20	Sunderland	D 1-1	Jones B.	58,391
Dec 25	Liverpool	W 3-1	Rooke 2, Roper	53,604
Dec 27	LIVERPOOL	L 1-2	Lewis	56,650
Jan 1	Bolton Wanderers	W 1-0	Lewis	30,028
Jan 3	SHEFFIELD UNITED	W 3 -2	Rooke 2, Lewis	48,993
Jan 17	Manchester United	D 1-1	Lewis	83,260
Jan 31	PRESTON NORTH END	W 3-0	Lewis 2, Rooke	63,162
Feb 7	Stoke City	D 0-0		44,836
Feb 14	BURNLEY	W 3-0	Rooke 2, Roper	62,125
Feb 28	Aston Villa	L 2-4	Rooke, o.g.	65,690
Mar 6	WOLVERHAMPTON WANDERERS	W 5-2	Rooke 2, Forbes, Roper, Logie	58,000
Mar 13	Everton	W 2-0	Compton D. 2	64,059
Mar 20	CHELSEA	L 0-2		56,596
Mar 26	MIDDLESBROUGH	W 7-0	Rooke 3, Compton D. 2, Roper, o.g.	57,557
Mar 27	Blackpool	L 0-3		32,678
Mar 29	Middlesbrough	D 1-1	Rooke	38,469
Apr 3	BLACKBURN ROVERS	W 2-0	Logie, Rooke	45,801
Apr 10	Huddersfield Town	D 1-1	Roper	38,110
Apr 17	DERBY COUNTY	L 1-2	Roper	49,677
Apr 21	Portsmouth	D 0-0		42,813
Apr 24	Manchester City	D 0-0		20,782
May 1	GRIMSBY TOWN	W 8-0	Rooke 4, Compton D. 2, Forbes, Logie (pen)	34,644

FA Cup

Jan 10	BRADFORD PARK AVENUE (Rd3)	L 0-1		47,738

League & Cup Appearances

PLAYER	LEAGUE	CUP COMPETITION FA CUP	TOTAL
Barnes	35		35
Compton D.	14		14
Compton L.	35	1	36
Fields	6		6
Forbes	11		11
Jones B.	7		7
Lewis	28	1	29
Logie	39	1	40
McPherson	29	1	30
Macaulay	40	1	41
Male	8	1	9
Mercer	40	1	41
Rooke	42	1	43
Roper	40	1	41
Scott	39	1	40
Sloan	3		3
Smith L.	1		1
Swindin	42	1	43
Wade	3		3

Goalscorers

PLAYER	LEAGUE	CUP COMPETITION FA CUP	TOTAL
Rooke	33		33
Lewis	14		14
Roper	10		10
Logie	8		8
Compton D.	6		6
McPherson	5		5
Forbes	2		2
Jones B.	1		1
Opps' o.gs.	2		2

Fact File

Arsenal's best-ever start to a season set up their sixth championship. They went 17 games unbeaten before losing 1-0 at Derby on 29 November. Skipper Joe Mercer had already won a championship medal, with Everton in 1939. Pre-war great George Male made eight appearances before retiring after the win over Grimsby. Arsenal's visit to runners-up Manchester United (played at Maine Road) attracted a still unbeaten record Football League attendance of 83,260.

MANAGER: Tom Whittaker

CAPTAIN: Joe Mercer

TOP SCORER: Ronnie Rooke 33 (all League)

BIGGEST WIN: 8-0 v Grimsby Town, 1 May 1948, League

HIGHEST ATTENDANCE: 64,905 v Manchester United, 6 September 1947, League

MAJOR TRANSFERS IN: Archie Macaulay from Brentford, Alex Forbes from Sheffield United, Don Roper from Southampton, Peter Goring from Cheltenham Town

MAJOR TRANSFER OUT: Paddy Sloan to Sheffield United

Final Division One Table

		P	W	D	L	F	A	Pts
1	ARSENAL	42	23	13	6	81	32	59
2	MANCHESTER U	42	19	14	9	81	48	52
3	BURNLEY	42	20	12	10	56	43	52
4	DERBY CO	42	19	12	11	77	57	50
5	WOLVERHAMPTON W	42	19	9	14	83	70	47
6	ASTON VILLA	42	19	9	14	65	57	47
7	PRESTON NE	42	20	7	15	67	68	47
8	PORTSMOUTH	42	19	7	16	68	50	45
9	BLACKPOOL	42	17	10	15	57	41	44
10	MANCHESTER C	42	15	12	15	52	47	42
11	LIVERPOOL	42	16	10	16	65	61	42
12	SHEFFIELD U	42	16	10	16	65	70	42
13	CHARLTON ATH	42	17	6	19	57	66	40
14	EVERTON	42	17	6	19	52	66	40
15	STOKE C	42	14	10	18	41	55	38
16	MIDDLESBROUGH	42	14	9	19	71	73	37
17	BOLTON W	42	16	5	21	46	58	37
18	CHELSEA	42	14	9	19	53	71	37
19	HUDDERSFIELD T	42	12	12	18	51	60	36
20	SUNDERLAND	42	13	10	19	56	67	36
21	BLACKBURN R	42	11	10	21	54	72	32
22	GRIMSBY T	42	8	6	28	45	111	22

Season 1948-49

Football League Division One

DATE	OPPONENTS	SCORE	GOALSCORERS	ATTENDANCE
Aug 21	Huddersfield Town	D 1-1	Rooke	30,620
Aug 25	STOKE CITY	W 3-0	Logie, Forbes, Roper	43,867
Aug 28	MANCHESTER UNITED	L 0-1		64,150
Aug 30	Stoke City	L 0-1		39,534
Sep 4	Sheffield United	D 1-1	o.g.	38,111
Sep 8	LIVERPOOL	D 1-1	Rooke	41,571
Sep 11	ASTON VILLA	W 3-1	Rooke 2 (2 pens), Roper	54,144
Sep 15	Liverpool	W 1-0	Lewis	46,714
Sep 18	Sunderland	D 1-1	Jones B.	64,436
Sep 25	WOLVERHAMPTON WANDERERS	W 3-1	Lewis 2, Compton D.	56,869
Oct 2	Bolton Wanderers	L 0-1		43,110
Oct 9	BURNLEY	W 3-1	Lewis 2, Logie	53,647
Oct 16	Preston North End	D 1-1	Rooke	31,443
Oct 23	EVERTON	W 5-0	Rooke 2, Logie 2, Forbes	49,048
Oct 30	Chelsea	W 1-0	Rooke (pen)	56,476
Nov 6	BIRMINGHAM CITY	W 2-0	Forbes, Lewis	61,511
Nov 13	Middlesbrough	W 1-0	Lewis	35,727
Nov 20	NEWCASTLE UNITED	L 0-1		68,283
Nov 27	Portsmouth	L 1-4	Lewis	42,687
Dec 4	MANCHESTER CITY	D 1-1	Rooke	48,960
Dec 11	Charlton Athletic	L 3-4	Roper, McPherson, Lewis	52,549
Dec 18	HUDDERSFIELD TOWN	W 3-0	Rooke 3	36,825
Dec 25	DERBY COUNTY	D 3-3	Logie, Rooke, McPherson	40,665
Dec 27	Derby County	L 1-2	Lewis	33,378
Jan 1	Manchester United	L 0-2		61,288
Jan 15	SHEFFIELD UNITED	W 5-3	Logie 2, Lishman, Rooke, McPherson	46,727
Jan 22	Aston Villa	L 0-1		69,161
Feb 5	SUNDERLAND	W 5-0	Lewis, Macaulay, Lishman, Vallance, McPherson	53,742
Feb 19	Wolverhampton Wanderers	W 3-1	Lewis 2, Logie	54,536
Feb 26	BOLTON WANDERERS	W 5-0	Logie 2, Lewis, Vallance, McPherson	50,263
Mar 5	Burnley	D 1-1	Lishman	20,303
Mar 12	PRESTON NORTH END	D 0-0		54,977
Mar 19	Newcastle United	L 2-3	Lewis, Forbes (pen)	55,148
Apr 2	Birmingham City	D 1-1	Lishman	38,503
Apr 9	MIDDLESBROUGH	D 1-1	Lishman	51,540
Apr 15	Blackpool	D 1-1	Lewis	28,718
Apr 16	Everton	D 0-0		56,987
Apr 18	BLACKPOOL	W 2-0	Lishman	45,047
Apr 23	CHELSEA	L 1-2	Compton D.	54,604
Apr 27	Manchester City	W 3-0	Lishman 2, Roper	27,955
May 4	PORTSMOUTH	W 3-2	Lishman 2, Logie	56,973
May 7	CHARLTON ATHLETIC	W 2-0	Roper, Lishman	47,564

FA Cup

Jan 8	TOTTENHAM HOTSPUR	(Rd3) W 3-0	McPherson, Roper, Lishman	47,314
Jan 29	Derby County	(Rd4) L 0-1		31,073

League & Cup Appearances

PLAYER	LEAGUE	CUP COMPETITION FA CUP	TOTAL
Barnes	40	2	42
Compton D.	6		6
Compton L.	40	1	41
Daniel	1		1
Fields	1		1
Forbes	25	1	26
Jones B.	8		8
Lewis	25	1	26
Lishman	23	2	25
Logie	35	2	37
McPherson	33	2	35
Macaulay	39	2	41
Mercer	33	2	35
Platt	10		10
Rooke	22	1	23
Roper	31	2	33
Scott	12		12
Smith L.	32	2	34
Swindin	32	2	34
Vallance	14		14

Goalscorers

PLAYER	LEAGUE	CUP COMPETITION FA CUP	TOTAL
Lewis	16		16
Rooke	14		14
Lishman	12	1	13
Logie	11		11
McPherson	5	1	6
Roper	5	1	6
Forbes	4		4
Compton D.	2		2
Vallance	2		2
Jones B.	1		1
Macaulay	1		1
Opps' o.gs.	1		1

Fact File

Tom Whittaker turned down an offer to take charge and rebuild the leading Italian club Torino, after their team was destroyed in the Superga air disaster. Arsenal and Tottenham were paired for the first time ever in the FA Cup third round draw. A massive crowd was expected, but thousands stayed away because they feared they wouldn't get in. The result was an attendance below Arsenal's home average for the season.

MANAGER: Tom Whittaker

CAPTAIN: Joe Mercer

TOP SCORER: Reg Lewis 16 (all League)

BIGGEST WIN: 5-0 v Everton, 23 October 1948, League; 5-0 v Sunderland, 5 February 1949, League; 5-0 v Bolton Wanderers, 26 February 1949, League

HIGHEST ATTENDANCE: 68,283 v Newcastle United, 20 November 1948, League

MAJOR TRANSFER IN: Doug Lishman from Walsall

Final Division One Table

		P	W	D	L	F	A	Pts
1	PORTSMOUTH	42	25	8	9	84	42	58
2	MANCHESTER U	42	21	11	10	77	44	53
3	DERBY CO	42	22	9	11	74	55	53
4	NEWCASTLE U	42	20	12	10	70	56	52
5	ARSENAL	42	18	13	11	74	44	49
6	WOLVERHAMPTON W	42	17	12	13	79	66	46
7	MANCHESTER C	42	15	15	12	47	51	45
8	SUNDERLAND	42	13	17	12	49	58	43
9	CHARLTON ATH	42	15	12	15	63	67	42
10	ASTON VILLA	42	16	10	16	60	76	42
11	STOKE C	42	16	9	17	66	68	41
12	LIVERPOOL	42	13	14	15	53	43	40
13	CHELSEA	42	12	14	16	69	68	38
14	BOLTON W	42	14	10	18	59	68	38
15	BURNLEY	42	12	14	16	43	50	38
16	BLACKPOOL	42	11	16	15	54	67	38
17	BIRMINGHAM C	42	11	15	16	36	38	37
18	EVERTON	42	13	11	18	41	63	37
19	MIDDLESBROUGH	42	11	12	19	46	57	34
20	HUDDERSFIELD T	42	12	10	20	40	69	34
21	PRESTON NE	42	11	11	20	62	75	33
22	SHEFFIELD U	42	11	11	20	57	78	33

Season 1949-50

Football League Division One

DATE	OPPONENTS	SCORE	GOALSCORERS	ATTENDANCE
Aug 20	BURNLEY	L 0-1		47,794
Aug 24	Chelsea	W 2-1	Lishman, Goring	63,124
Aug 27	Sunderland	L 2-4	Holton, o.g.	56,500
Aug 31	CHELSEA	L 2-3	Goring 2	52,901
Sep 3	LIVERPOOL	L 1-2	Lishman	51,866
Sep 7	West Bromwich Albion	W 2-1	Lewis, Barnes (pen)	43,000
Sep 10	Huddersfield Town	D 2-2	Lewis, Goring	20,882
Sep 14	WEST BROMWICH ALBION	W 4-1	Lewis, Goring, Roper, Barnes (pen)	40,755
Sep 17	Bolton Wanderers	D 2-2	Lewis, Barnes (pen)	33,867
Sep 24	BIRMINGHAM CITY	W 4-2	Goring 2, Logie, Lewis	50,850
Oct 1	Derby County	W 1-0	Lewis	30,417
Oct 8	EVERTON	W 5-2	Goring 2, Lewis 2, Roper	53,224
Oct 15	Middlesbrough	D 1-1	Roper	36,221
Oct 22	BLACKPOOL	W 1-0	Lewis	66,391
Oct 29	Newcastle United	W 3-0	Roper 3	54,670
Nov 5	FULHAM	W 2-1	McPherson, Barnes (pen)	40,593
Nov 12	Manchester City	W 2-0	Logie, Cox	28,288
Nov 19	CHARLTON ATHLETIC	L 2-3	Logie, Lewis	51,318
Nov 26	Aston Villa	D 1-1	Lewis	45,863
Dec 3	WOLVERHAMPTON WANDERERS	D 1-1	Roper	56,227
Dec 10	Portsmouth	L 1-2	Goring	39,537
Dec 17	Burnley	D 0-0		25,661
Dec 24	SUNDERLAND	W 5-0	Lewis, Forbes, Goring, Logie, McPherson	43,249
Dec 26	Manchester United	L 0-2		53,928
Dec 27	MANCHESTER UNITED	D 0-0		65,133
Dec 31	Liverpool	L 0-2		55,020
Jan 14	HUDDERSFIELD TOWN	W 1-0	Lewis	46,815
Jan 21	BOLTON WANDERERS	D 1-1	Lewis	47,493
Feb 4	Birmingham City	L 1-2	Goring	34,031
Feb 18	DERBY COUNTY	W 1-0	Logie	67,445
Feb 25	Everton	W 1-0	Cox	43,632
Mar 8	MIDDLESBROUGH	D 1-1	Forbes (pen)	34,464
Mar 11	Charlton Athletic	D 1-1	Compton D.	51,615
Mar 25	Fulham	D 2-2	Logie, Cox	35,703
Mar 29	ASTON VILLA	L 1-3	Lishman	24,736
Apr 1	MANCHESTER CITY	W 4-1	Lewis 2, Lishman, Goring	39,420
Apr 8	Blackpool	L 1-2	Goring	32,022
Apr 10	STOKE CITY	W 6-0	Goring 2, Lishman 2, Barnes (pen), o.g.	27,226
Apr 15	NEWCASTLE UNITED	W 4-2	Goring 3, Lewis	51,997
Apr 22	Wolverhampton Wanderers	L 0-3		53,082
May 3	PORTSMOUTH	W 2-0	Goring 2	63,124
May 10	Stoke City	W 5-2	Lishman 3, Lewis, McPherson	22,689

FA Cup

Jan 7	SHEFFIELD WEDNESDAY	(Rd3) W 1-0	Lewis	54,193
Jan 28	SWANSEA TOWN	(Rd4) W 2-1	Logie, Barnes (pen)	57,305
Feb 11	BURNLEY	(Rd5) W 2-0	Lewis, Compton D.	55,458
Mar 4	LEEDS UNITED	(QF) W 1-0	Lewis	62,573
Mar 18	Chelsea*	(SF) D 2-2	Cox, Compton L.	67,752
Mar 22	Chelsea**	(R) W 1-0	Cox	66,482
Apr 29	Liverpool†	(F) W 2-0	Lewis 2	100,000

*Played at White Hart Lane. **Played at White Hart Lane.
†Played at Wembley.

League & Cup Appearances

PLAYER	LEAGUE	CUP COMPETITION FA CUP	TOTAL
Barnes	38	7	45
Compton D.	11	5	16
Compton L.	35	7	42
Cox	32	7	39
Daniel	6		6
Forbes	23	6	29
Goring	29	6	35
Kelly	1		1
Lewis	31	7	38
Lishman	14		14
Logie	34	7	41
McPherson	27	2	29
Macaulay	24	1	25
Mercer	35	7	42
Platt	19		19
Roper	27	1	28
Scott	15	7	22
Shaw	5		5
Smith L.	31		31
Swindin	23	7	30
Vallance	1		1
Wade	1		1

Goalscorers

PLAYER	LEAGUE	CUP COMPETITION FA CUP	TOTAL
Lewis	19	5	24
Goring	21		21
Lishman	9		9
Logie	7	1	8
Roper	7		7
Barnes	5	1	6
Cox	3	2	5
McPherson	3		3
Forbes	2		2
Compton D.	1	1	2
Compton L.		1	1
Opps' o.gs.	2		2

MANAGER: Tom Whittaker

CAPTAIN: Joe Mercer

TOP SCORER: Reg Lewis 24 (19 League)

BIGGEST WIN: 6-0 v Stoke City, 10 April 1950, League

HIGHEST ATTENDANCE: 67,445 v Derby County, 18 February 1950, League

MAJOR TRANSFER IN: Freddie Cox from Tottenham Hotspur

Final Division One Table

		P	W	D	L	F	A	Pts
1	PORTSMOUTH	42	22	9	11	74	38	53
2	WOLVERHAMPTON W	42	20	13	9	76	49	53
3	SUNDERLAND	42	21	10	11	83	62	52
4	MANCHESTER U	42	18	14	10	69	44	50
5	NEWCASTLE U	42	19	12	11	77	55	50
6	ARSENAL	42	19	11	12	79	55	49
7	BLACKPOOL	42	17	15	10	46	35	49
8	LIVERPOOL	42	17	14	11	64	54	48
9	MIDDLESBROUGH	42	20	7	15	59	48	47
10	BURNLEY	42	16	13	13	40	40	45
11	DERBY CO	42	17	10	15	69	61	44
12	ASTON VILLA	42	15	12	15	61	61	42
13	CHELSEA	42	12	16	14	58	65	40
14	WBA	42	14	12	16	47	53	40
15	HUDDERSFIELD T	42	14	9	19	52	73	37
16	BOLTON W	42	10	14	18	45	59	34
17	FULHAM	42	10	14	18	41	54	34
18	EVERTON	42	10	14	18	42	66	34
19	STOKE C	42	11	12	19	45	75	34
20	CHARLTON ATH	42	13	6	23	53	65	32
21	MANCHESTER C	42	8	13	21	36	68	29
22	BIRMINGHAM C	42	7	14	21	31	67	28

Fact File

Arsenal won the FA Cup for the third time – without leaving London. They were drawn at home in the third, fourth, fifth and sixth rounds, met Chelsea twice at Tottenham in the semi-final and replay, then beat Liverpool at Wembley. Arsenal's equalizer in the 2-2 semi-final draw with Chelsea was a family affair. Denis Compton waved his brother Les forward for a late corner and the centre half headed in. It was Les's only goal in more than 200 postwar appearances. Legendary cricketer Denis retired from football at the end of the season. Skipper Joe Mercer was voted Footballer of the Year.

Season 1950-51

Football League Division One

DATE	OPPONENTS	SCORE	GOALSCORERS	ATTENDANCE
Aug 19	Burnley	W 1-0	Roper	32,957
Aug 23	CHELSEA	D 0-0		61,166
Aug 26	TOTTENHAM HOTSPUR	D 2-2	Roper, Barnes (pen)	64,600
Aug 30	Chelsea	W 1-0	Cox	48,792
Sep 2	SHEFFIELD WEDNESDAY	W 3-0	Logie 2, Lishman	45,647
Sep 6	EVERTON	W 2-1	Cox, Barnes (pen)	36,576
Sep 9	Middlesbrough	L 1-2	Lishman	46,119
Sep 13	Everton	D 1-1	Goring	47,518
Sep 16	HUDDERSFIELD TOWN	W 6-2	Goring 3, Logie 2, Lishman	51,518
Sep 23	Newcastle United	L 1-2	Logie	66,926
Sep 30	WEST BROMWICH ALBION	W 3-0	Lishman 2, Logie	51,928
Oct 7	Charlton Athletic	W 3-1	Goring, Forbes, Roper	63,539
Oct 14	MANCHESTER UNITED	W 3-0	Lishman, Goring, o.g.	66,150
Oct 21	Aston Villa	D 1-1	Logie	53,111
Oct 28	DERBY COUNTY	W 3-1	Logie, Forbes, Goring	62,889
Nov 4	Wolverhampton Wanderers	W 1-0	Lishman	55,548
Nov 11	SUNDERLAND	W 5-1	Lishman 4, Roper	68,682
Nov 18	Liverpool	W 3-1	Lishman, Logie, Roper	44,193
Nov 25	FULHAM	W 5-1	Lishman 3, Goring, Forbes	41,344
Dec 2	Bolton Wanderers	L 0-3		40,489
Dec 9	BLACKPOOL	D 4-4	Lishman, Forbes, Goring, Barnes (pen)	57,445
Dec 16	BURNLEY	L 0-1		32,374
Dec 23	Tottenham Hotspur	L 0-1		54,898
Dec 25	STOKE CITY	L 0-3		36,852
Dec 26	Stoke City	L 0-1		43,315
Dec 30	Sheffield Wednesday	W 2-0	Goring 2	39,583
Jan 13	MIDDLESBROUGH	W 3-1	Lewis 2, Goring	65,038
Jan 20	Huddersfield Town	D 2-2	Lewis 2	37,175
Feb 3	NEWCASTLE UNITED	D 0-0		55,073
Feb 17	West Bromwich Albion	L 0-2		35,851
Feb 24	CHARLTON ATHLETIC	L 2-5	Goring 2	58,137
Mar 3	Manchester United	L 1-3	Holton	46,202
Mar 10	ASTON VILLA	W 2-1	Lewis 2	43,747
Mar 17	Derby County	L 2-4	Lewis, Goring	22,168
Mar 23	PORTSMOUTH	L 0-1		52,051
Mar 24	WOLVERHAMPTON WANDERERS	W 2-1	Holton 2	54,213
Mar 26	Portsmouth	D 1-1	Marden	39,189
Mar 31	Sunderland	W 2-1	Marden, Roper	31,515
Apr 7	LIVERPOOL	L 1-2	Holton	34,664
Apr 14	Fulham	L 2-3	Holton, Lewis	34,111
Apr 21	BOLTON WANDERERS	D 1-1	Lishman	45,040
May 2	Blackpool	W 1-0	Roper	23,044

FA Cup

DATE	OPPONENTS		SCORE	GOALSCORERS	ATTENDANCE
Jan 6	CARLISLE UNITED	(Rd3)	D 0-0		57,932
Jan 11	Carlisle United	(R)	W 4-1	Lewis 2, Logie, Goring	21,215
Jan 27	NORTHAMPTON TOWN	(Rd4)	W 3-2	Lewis 2, Roper	72,408
Feb 10	Manchester United	(Rd5)	L 0-1		55,058

League & Cup Appearances

PLAYER	LEAGUE	CUP COMPETITION FA CUP	TOTAL
Barnes	35	4	39
Bowen	7		7
Compton L.	36	3	39
Cox	13	1	14
Daniel	5	1	6
Fields	1		1
Forbes	32	4	36
Goring	34	4	38
Holton	10		10
Kelsey	4		4
Lewis	14	4	18
Lishman	26		26
Logie	39	4	43
McPherson	26	3	29
Marden	11		11
Mercer	31	3	34
Milton	1		1
Platt	17	4	21
Roper	34	4	38
Scott	17		17
Shaw	16	1	17
Smith L	32	4	36
Swindin	21		21

Goalscorers

PLAYER	LEAGUE	CUP COMPETITION FA CUP	TOTAL
Lishman	17		17
Goring	15	1	16
Lewis	8	4	12
Logie	9	1	10
Roper	7	1	8
Holton	5		5
Forbes	4		4
Barnes	3		3
Cox	2		2
Marden	2		2
Opps' o.gs.	1		1

Fact File

The turning point of the season was the 3-0 home defeat by Stoke City on Christmas Day when leading scorer Doug Lishman was carried off with a broken leg. Lishman was in prolific form and finished top scorer for the season despite missing 16 league matches.

MANAGER: Tom Whittaker

CAPTAIN: Joe Mercer

TOP SCORER: Doug Lishman 17 (all League)

BIGGEST WIN: 6-2 v Huddersfield Town, 16 September 1950, League

HIGHEST ATTENDANCE: 72,408 v Northampton Town, 27 January 1951, FA Cup

MAJOR TRANSFERS IN: Dave Bowen from Northampton Town, Ben Marden from Chelmsford City

MAJOR TRANSFER OUT: Archie Macaulay to Fulham

Final Division One Table

		P	W	D	L	F	A	Pts
1	TOTTENHAM H	42	25	10	7	82	44	60
2	MANCHESTER U	42	24	8	10	74	40	56
3	BLACKPOOL	42	20	10	12	79	53	50
4	NEWCASTLE U	42	18	13	11	62	53	49
5	ARSENAL	42	19	9	14	73	56	47
6	MIDDLESBROUGH	42	18	11	13	76	65	47
7	PORTSMOUTH	42	16	15	11	71	68	47
8	BOLTON W	42	19	7	16	64	61	45
9	LIVERPOOL	42	16	11	15	53	59	43
10	BURNLEY	42	14	14	14	48	43	42
11	DERBY CO	42	16	8	18	81	75	40
12	SUNDERLAND	42	12	16	14	63	73	40
13	STOKE C	42	13	14	15	50	59	40
14	WOLVERHAMPTON W	42	15	8	19	74	61	38
15	ASTON VILLA	42	12	13	17	66	68	37
16	WBA	42	13	11	18	53	61	37
17	CHARLTON ATH	42	14	9	19	63	80	37
18	FULHAM	42	13	11	18	52	68	37
19	HUDDERSFIELD T	42	15	6	21	64	92	36
20	CHELSEA	42	12	8	22	53	65	32
21	SHEFFIELD W	42	12	8	22	64	83	32
22	EVERTON	42	12	8	22	48	86	32

Season 1951-52

Football League Division One

DATE	OPPONENTS	SCORE	GOALSCORERS	ATTENDANCE
Aug 18	HUDDERSFIELD TOWN	D 2-2	Marden, Holton	54,072
Aug 22	Chelsea	W 3-1	Holton, Marden, Roper	59,143
Aug 25	Wolverhampton Wanderers	L 1-2	Holton	40,931
Aug 29	CHELSEA	W 2-1	Holton, Lishman	48,768
Sep 1	SUNDERLAND	W 3-0	Lishman 3	66,137
Sep 5	LIVERPOOL	D 0-0		50,483
Sep 8	Aston Villa	L 0-1		56,860
Sep 12	Liverpool	D 0-0		39,853
Sep 15	DERBY COUNTY	W 3-1	Holton 2, Lishman	50,181
Sep 22	Manchester City	W 2-0	Holton, Lishman	48,367
Sep 29	TOTTENHAM HOTSPUR	D 1-1	Holton	72,164
Oct 6	Preston North End	L 0-2		38,321
Oct 13	BURNLEY	W 1-0	Lewis	48,531
Oct 20	Charlton Athletic	W 3-1	Holton, Milton	57,000
Oct 27	FULHAM	W 4-3	Lishman 3, Holton	54,178
Nov 3	Middlesbrough	W 3-0	Holton, Lishman, Milton	35,408
Nov 10	WEST BROMWICH ALBION	W 6-3	Lishman 3, Holton 2, Logie	53,432
Nov 17	Newcastle United	L 0-2		61,192
Nov 24	BOLTON WANDERERS	W 4-2	Lishman 3, Roper	53,790
Dec 1	Stoke City	L 1-2	Lewis	29,363
Dec 8	MANCHESTER UNITED	L 1-3	Logie	55,451
Dec 15	Huddersfield Town	W 3-2	Roper 2, Lewis	22,427
Dec 22	WOLVERHAMPTON WANDERERS	D 2-2	Lewis 2	45,644
Dec 25	PORTSMOUTH	W 4-1	Cox, Goring, Lewis, Logie	54,241
Dec 26	Portsmouth	D 1-1	Cox	41,305
Dec 29	Sunderland	L 1-4	Goring	47,045
Jan 5	ASTON VILLA	W 2-1	Roper 2	53,540
Jan 19	Derby County	W 2-1	Logie, Roper	28,791
Jan 26	MANCHESTER CITY	D 2-2	Lishman 2	54,527
Feb 9	Tottenham Hotspur	W 2-1	Roper, Forbes	66,438
Feb 16	PRESTON NORTH END	D 3-3	Lewis 2, Roper	61,849
Mar 1	Burnley	W 1-0	Milton	41,040
Mar 13	CHARLTON ATHLETIC	W 2-1	Goring 2	37,985
Mar 15	Fulham	D 0-0		44,088
Mar 22	MIDDLESBROUGH	W 3-1	Holton, Lishman, Milton	50,979
Apr 11	Blackpool	D 0-0		32,186
Apr 12	Bolton Wanderers	L 1-2	Forbes	44,722
Apr 14	BLACKPOOL	W 4-1	Lishman 2, Barnes (pen), o.g.	50,445
Apr 16	NEWCASTLE UNITED	D 1-1	Milton	53,203
Apr 19	STOKE CITY	W 4-1	Holton 2, Barnes (pen), Lishman	47,962
Apr 21	West Bromwich Albion	L 1-3	Lishman	29,700
Apr 26	Manchester United	L 1-6	Cox	53,651

FA Cup

Jan 12	Norwich City	(Rd3) W 5-0	Lishman 2, Logie, Goring, Roper	38,964
Feb 2	BARNSLEY	(Rd4) W 4-0	Lewis 3, Lishman	69,466
Feb 23	Leyton Orient	(Rd5) W 3-0	Lishman 2, Lewis	30,000
Mar 8	Luton Town	(QF) W 3-2	Cox 2, Milton	28,433
Apr 5	Chelsea*	(SF) D 1-1	Cox	68,084
Apr 7	Chelsea*	(R) W 3-0	Cox 2, Lishman	57,450
May 3	Newcastle United**	(F) L 0-1		100,000

*Played at White Hart Lane. **Played at Wembley.

League & Cup Appearances

PLAYER	LEAGUE	CUP COMPETITION FA CUP	TOTAL
Barnes	41	7	48
Bowen	8		8
Chenhall	3		3
Compton L.	4		4
Cox	25	7	32
Daniel	34	7	41
Forbes	38	5	43
Goring	16	3	19
Holton	28	1	29
Lewis	9	3	12
Lishman	38	7	45
Logie	34	6	40
Marden	7		7
Mercer	36	7	43
Milton	20	1	21
Robertson	1		1
Roper	30	7	37
Scott	4		4
Shaw	8	2	10
Smith L.	28	7	35
Swindin	42	7	49
Wade	8		8

Goalscorers

PLAYER	LEAGUE	CUP COMPETITION FA CUP	TOTAL
Lishman	23	6	29
Holton	17		17
Lewis	8	4	12
Roper	9	1	10
Cox	3	5	8
Milton	5	1	6
Goring	4	1	5
Logie	4	1	5
Barnes	2		2
Forbes	2		2
Marden	2		2
Opps' o.gs.	1		1

Fact File

Arsenal played the last 55 minutes of the FA Cup final with ten men – right back Walley Barnes having twisted a knee. George Robledo headed the winner five minutes from time. Floodlights were installed at Highbury as the authorities gave the go-ahead – more than 20 years after Herbert Chapman put forward the idea. The first game under lights was a 6-1 win over Israeli side Hapoel Tel Aviv in a friendly on 19 September 1951.

MANAGER: Tom Whittaker

CAPTAIN: Joe Mercer

TOP SCORER: Doug Lishman 29 (23 League)

BIGGEST WIN: 5-0 v Norwich City, 12 January 1952, FA Cup

HIGHEST ATTENDANCE: 72,164 v Tottenham Hotspur, 29 September 1951, League

MAJOR TRANSFERS OUT: Ian McPherson to Notts County, Laurie Scott to Crystal Palace (player-manager)

Final Division One Table

		P	W	D	L	F	A	Pts
1	MANCHESTER U	42	23	11	8	95	52	57
2	TOTTENHAM H	42	22	9	11	76	51	53
3	ARSENAL	42	21	11	10	80	61	53
4	PORTSMOUTH	42	20	8	14	68	58	48
5	BOLTON W	42	19	10	13	65	61	48
6	ASTON VILLA	42	19	9	14	79	70	47
7	PRESTON NE	42	17	12	13	74	54	46
8	NEWCASTLE U	42	18	9	15	98	73	45
9	BLACKPOOL	42	18	9	15	64	64	45
10	CHARLTON ATH	42	17	10	15	68	63	44
11	LIVERPOOL	42	12	19	11	57	61	43
12	SUNDERLAND	42	15	12	15	70	61	42
13	WBA	42	14	13	15	74	77	41
14	BURNLEY	42	15	10	17	56	63	40
15	MANCHESTER C	42	13	13	16	58	61	39
16	WOLVERHAMPTON W	42	12	14	16	73	73	38
17	DERBY CO	42	15	7	20	63	80	37
18	MIDDLESBROUGH	42	15	6	21	64	88	36
19	CHELSEA	42	14	8	20	52	72	36
20	STOKE C	42	12	7	23	49	88	31
21	HUDDERSFIELD T	42	10	8	24	49	82	28
22	FULHAM	42	8	11	23	58	77	27

Season 1952-53

Football League Division One

DATE	OPPONENTS	SCORE	GOALSCORERS	ATTENDANCE
Aug 23	Aston Villa	W 2-1	Lishman, Oakes	55,000
Aug 27	MANCHESTER UNITED	W 2-1	Cox, Goring	58,831
Aug 30	SUNDERLAND	L 1-2	Lishman	57,873
Sep 3	Manchester United	D 0-0		37,367
Sep 6	Wolverhampton Wanderers	D 1-1	Roper	43,371
Sep 10	PORTSMOUTH	W 3-1	Goring, Milton, Roper	40,743
Sep 13	CHARLTON ATHLETIC	L 3-4	Milton, Goring, Daniel	61,102
Sep 17	Portsmouth	D 2-2	Holton 2	37,256
Sep 20	Tottenham Hotspur	W 3-1	Goring, Milton, Logie	69,220
Sep 27	Derby County	L 0-2		24,582
Oct 4	BLACKPOOL	W 3-1	Roper 2, Logie	66,682
Oct 11	SHEFFIELD WEDNESDAY	D 2-2	Roper, Logie	55,678
Oct 25	NEWCASTLE UNITED	W 3-0	Roper 2, Lishman	63,744
Nov 1	West Bromwich Albion	L 0-2		41,000
Nov 8	MIDDLESBROUGH	W 2-1	Milton, Holton	49,564
Nov 15	Liverpool	W 5-1	Holton 3, Marden 2	45,010
Nov 22	MANCHESTER CITY	W 3-1	Logie 2, Lishman	39,161
Nov 29	Stoke City	D 1-1	Holton	24,033
Dec 13	Burnley	D 1-1	Milton	32,840
Dec 20	ASTON VILLA	W 3-1	Lishman, Holton, Roper	32,064
Dec 25	Bolton Wanderers	W 6-4	Holton 2, Milton, Logie, Roper, Daniel	47,344
Jan 3	Sunderland	L 1-3	Lishman	54,912
Jan 17	WOLVERHAMPTON WANDERERS	W 5-3	Lishman 2, Daniel, Logie, Milton	58,983
Jan 24	Charlton Athletic	D 2-2	Lishman, Roper	66,426
Feb 7	TOTTENHAM HOTSPUR	W 4-0	Holton 2, Lishman, Logie	69,051
Feb 18	DERBY COUNTY	W 6-2	Daniel 2, Holton 2, Lishman 2	32,681
Feb 21	Blackpool	L 2-3	Mercer, Goring	27,000
Mar 2	Sheffield Wednesday	W 4-1	Holton 4	30,452
Mar 7	CARDIFF CITY	L 0-1		59,580
Mar 14	Newcastle United	D 2-2	Lishman 2	51,560
Mar 19	PRESTON NORTH END	D 1-1	Mercer	33,697
Mar 21	WEST BROMWICH ALBION	D 2-2	Holton, Roper	50,078
Mar 28	Middlesbrough	L 0-2		35,000
Apr 3	Chelsea	D 1-1	Goring	72,614
Apr 4	LIVERPOOL	W 5-3	Roper 2, Lishman, Goring, o.g.	39,564
Apr 6	CHELSEA	W 2-0	Lishman, Marden	40,536
Apr 11	Manchester City	W 4-2	Goring 2, Logie, Roper	53,418
Apr 15	BOLTON WANDERERS	W 4-1	Lishman 2, Goring, Marden	35,006
Apr 18	STOKE CITY	W 3-1	Lishman 3	47,376
Apr 22	Cardiff City	D 0-0		57,800
Apr 25	Preston North End	L 0-2		40,000
May 1	BURNLEY	W 3-2	Forbes, Lishman, Logie	51,586

FA Cup

DATE	OPPONENTS		SCORE	GOALSCORERS	ATTENDANCE
Jan 10	DONCASTER ROVERS	(Rd3)	W 4-0	Holton, Lishman, Logie, Roper	57,443
Jan 31	BURY	(Rd4)	W 6-2	Holton, Lishman, Logie, Milton, Roper, o.g.	45,071
Feb 14	Burnley	(Rd5)	W 2-0	Holton, Lishman	52,122
Feb 29	BLACKPOOL	(QF)	L 1-2	Logie	69,158

League & Cup Appearances

PLAYER	LEAGUE	CUP COMPETITION FA CUP	TOTAL
Bowen	2		2
Chenhall	13		13
Cox	9		9
Daniel	41	4	45
Dodgin	1		1
Forbes	33	4	37
Goring	29		29
Holton	21	4	25
Kelsey	25	4	29
Lishman	39	4	43
Logie	32	4	36
Marden	8		8
Mercer	28	3	31
Milton	25	4	29
Oakes	2		2
Platt	3		3
Roper	41	4	45
Shaw	25	1	26
Smith L.	31	4	35
Swindin	14		14
Wade	40	4	44

Goalscorers

PLAYER	LEAGUE	CUP COMPETITION FA CUP	TOTAL
Lishman	22	3	25
Holton	19	3	22
Roper	14	2	16
Logie	10	3	13
Goring	10		10
Milton	7	1	8
Daniel	5		5
Marden	4		4
Mercer	2		2
Cox	1		1
Forbes	1		1
Oakes	1		1
Opps' o.gs.	1	1	2

Fact File

Arsenal clinched their seventh championship with a 3-2 win over Burnley on FA Cup final eve. Second-placed Preston had already finished their programme and Arsenal had to win to lift the title. Reg Lewis, one of the remaining links with the pre-war side, retired at the end of the season after a career stretching back to 1937. His best years were lost in wartime, but he still scored 116 goals for the Gunners, including both in the 1950 FA Cup final victory over Liverpool.

MANAGER: Tom Whittaker

CAPTAIN: Joe Mercer

TOP SCORER: Doug Lishman 25 (22 League)

BIGGEST WIN: 6-2 v Derby County, 18 February 1953, League; 6-2 v Bury, 31 January 1953, FA Cup

HIGHEST ATTENDANCE: 69,158 v Blackpool, 29 February 1953, FA Cup

MAJOR TRANSFER IN: Bill Dodgin from Fulham

Final Division One Table

		P	W	D	L	F	A	Pts
1	ARSENAL	42	21	12	9	97	64	54
2	PRESTON NE	42	21	12	9	85	60	54
3	WOLVERHAMPTON W	42	19	13	10	86	63	51
4	WBA	42	21	8	13	66	60	50
5	CHARLTON ATH	42	19	11	12	77	63	49
6	BURNLEY	42	18	12	12	67	52	48
7	BLACKPOOL	42	19	9	14	71	70	47
8	MANCHESTER U	42	18	10	14	69	72	46
9	SUNDERLAND	42	15	13	14	68	82	43
10	TOTTENHAM H	42	15	11	16	78	69	41
11	ASTON VILLA	42	14	13	15	63	61	41
12	CARDIFF C	42	14	12	16	54	46	40
13	MIDDLESBROUGH	42	14	11	17	70	77	39
14	BOLTON W	42	15	9	18	61	69	39
15	PORTSMOUTH	42	14	10	18	74	83	38
16	NEWCASTLE U	42	14	9	19	59	70	37
17	LIVERPOOL	42	14	8	20	61	82	36
18	SHEFFIELD W	42	12	11	19	62	72	35
19	CHELSEA	42	12	11	19	56	66	35
20	MANCHESTER C	42	14	7	21	72	87	35
21	STOKE C	42	12	10	20	53	66	34
22	DERBY CO	42	11	10	21	59	74	32

Season 1953-54

Football League Division One

DATE	OPPONENTS	SCORE	GOALSCORERS	ATTENDANCE
Aug 19	West Bromwich Albion	L 0-2		39,710
Aug 22	HUDDERSFIELD TOWN	D 0-0		54,847
Aug 24	Sheffield United	L 0-1		51,070
Aug 29	Aston Villa	L 1-2	Forbes	40,000
Sep 1	SHEFFIELD UNITED	D 1-1	o.g.	43,077
Sep 5	WOLVERHAMPTON WANDERERS	L 2-3	Roper, Holton	60,460
Sep 8	CHELSEA	L 1-2	Holton	55,086
Sep 12	Sunderland	L 1-7	Lishman	59,808
Sep 15	Chelsea	W 2-0	Lishman 2	60,652
Sep 19	MANCHESTER CITY	D 2-2	Lishman 2	65,869
Sep 26	Cardiff City	W 3-0	Lishman 2, o.g.	55,000
Oct 3	PRESTON NORTH END	W 3-2	Roper 2, Barnes (pen)	61,807
Oct 10	Tottenham Hotspur	W 4-1	Logie 2, Milton, Forbes	69,821
Oct 17	BURNLEY	L 2-5	Forbes, Roper	47,371
Oct 24	Charlton Athletic	W 5-1	Marden 3, Holton, Roper	60,245
Oct 31	SHEFFIELD WEDNESDAY	W 4-1	Holton 2, Logie 2	52,543
Nov 7	Manchester United	D 2-2	Holton, Roper	28,141
Nov 14	BOLTON WANDERERS	W 4-3	Holton 3, Lishman	52,319
Nov 21	Liverpool	W 2-1	Logie, Lishman	47,814
Nov 28	NEWCASTLE UNITED	W 2-1	Holton, Forbes	62,456
Dec 5	Middlesbrough	L 0-2		35,000
Dec 12	WEST BROMWICH ALBION	D 2-2	Lishman 2	55,264
Dec 19	Huddersfield Town	D 2-2	Milton, Lishman	34,018
Dec 26	Blackpool	D 2-2	Lishman, Roper	29,347
Dec 28	BLACKPOOL	D 1-1	Roper	62,900
Jan 16	Wolverhampton Wanderers	W 2-0	Logie, Lishman	45,974
Jan 23	SUNDERLAND	L 1-4	Holton	60,218
Feb 6	Manchester City	D 0-0		39,026
Feb 13	CARDIFF CITY	D 1-1	Lishman	45,497
Feb 24	Preston North End	W 1-0	Lishman	23,000
Feb 27	TOTTENHAM HOTSPUR	L 0-3		64,211
Mar 6	Burnley	L 1-2	Holton	22,726
Mar 13	CHARLTON ATHLETIC	D 3-3	Holton, Lishman, Dickson	41,256
Mar 20	Sheffield Wednesday	L 1-2	Holton	42,072
Mar 27	MANCHESTER UNITED	W 3-1	Logie 2, Holton	42,735
Apr 3	Bolton Wanderers	L 1-3	Holton	30,473
Apr 6	ASTON VILLA	D 1-1	Lawton	14,519
Apr 10	LIVERPOOL	W 3-0	Tapscott 2, Roper	33,178
Apr 16	PORTSMOUTH	W 3-0	Tapscott 2, Roper	44,948
Apr 17	Newcastle United	L 2-5	Milton, Holton	48,540
Apr 19	Portsmouth	D 1-1	Roper	30,958
Apr 24	MIDDLESBROUGH	W 3-1	Roper, Lishman, Tapscott	35,196

FA Cup

Jan 9	ASTON VILLA	(Rd3) W 5-1	Roper 2, Holton, Logie, Milton	50,990
Jan 30	NORWICH CITY	(Rd4) L 1-2	Logie	55,767

League & Cup Appearances

PLAYER	LEAGUE	CUP COMPETITION FA CUP	TOTAL
Barnes	19		19
Bowen	10		10
Dickson	24	2	26
Dodgin	39	2	41
Evans	10		10
Forbes	30	2	32
Goring	9		9
Holton	32	2	34
Kelsey	39	2	41
Lawton	9		9
Lishman	39	2	41
Logie	35	2	37
Marden	9		9
Mercer	19		19
Milton	21	2	23
Roper	39	2	41
Shaw	2		2
Smith L.	7	1	8
Sullivan	1		1
Swindin	2		2
Tapscott	5		5
Tilley	1		1
Wade	18	1	19
Walsh	10		10
Ward	3		3
Wills	30	2	32

Goalscorers

PLAYER	LEAGUE	CUP COMPETITION FA CUP	TOTAL
Lishman	18		18
Holton	17	1	18
Roper	12	2	14
Logie	8	2	10
Tapscott	5		5
Forbes	4		4
Milton	3	1	4
Marden	3		3
Barnes	1		1
Dickson	1		1
Lawton	1		1
Opps' o.gs.	2		2

Fact File

Joe Mercer was forced to end his distinguished career after suffering a broken leg in the home game against Liverpool on 10 April. Long-serving goalkeeper George Swindin also left the Gunners, nearly 18 years after signing from Bradford City. He was given a free transfer to become player-manager of Peterborough United. He returned as Arsenal boss six years later.

MANAGER: Tom Whittaker

CAPTAIN: Joe Mercer

TOP SCORER: Doug Lishman 18 (all League), Cliff Holton 18 (17 League)

BIGGEST WIN: 5-1 v Charlton Athletic, 24 October 1953, League; 5-1 v Aston Villa, 9 January 1954, FA Cup

HIGHEST ATTENDANCE: 65,869 v Manchester City, 19 September 1953, League

MAJOR TRANSFERS IN: Bill Dickson from Chelsea, Derek Tapscott from Barry Town, Tommy Lawton from Brentford

MAJOR TRANSFERS OUT: Freddie Cox to West Bromwich Albion, George Swindin to Peterborough United

Final Division One Table

		P	W	D	L	F	A	Pts
1	WOLVERHAMPTON W	42	25	7	10	96	56	57
2	WBA	42	22	9	11	86	63	53
3	HUDDERSFIELD T	42	20	11	11	78	61	51
4	MANCHESTER U	42	18	12	12	73	58	48
5	BOLTON W	42	18	12	12	75	60	48
6	BLACKPOOL	42	19	10	13	80	69	48
7	BURNLEY	42	21	4	17	78	67	46
8	CHELSEA	42	16	12	14	74	68	44
9	CHARLTON ATH	42	19	6	17	75	77	44
10	CARDIFF C	42	18	8	16	51	71	44
11	PRESTON NE	42	19	5	18	87	58	43
12	ARSENAL	42	15	13	14	75	73	43
13	ASTON VILLA	42	16	9	17	70	68	41
14	PORTSMOUTH	42	14	11	17	81	89	39
15	NEWCASTLE U	42	14	10	18	72	77	38
16	TOTTENHAM H	42	16	5	21	65	76	37
17	MANCHESTER C	42	14	9	19	62	77	37
18	SUNDERLAND	42	14	8	20	81	89	36
19	SHEFFIELD W	42	15	6	21	70	91	36
20	SHEFFIELD U	42	11	11	20	69	90	33
21	MIDDLESBROUGH	42	10	10	22	60	91	30
22	LIVERPOOL	42	9	10	23	68	97	28

Season 1954-55

Football League Division One

DATE	OPPONENTS	SCORE	GOALSCORERS	ATTENDANCE
Aug 21	NEWCASTLE UNITED	L 1-3	Lishman	65,334
Aug 25	Everton	L 0-1		69,134
Aug 28	West Bromwich Albion	L 1-3	Lishman	50,000
Aug 31	EVERTON	W 2-0	Lishman, Roper	42,146
Sep 4	TOTTENHAM HOTSPUR	W 2-0	Logie, Lishman	53,977
Sep 8	Manchester City	L 1-2	Lishman	38,146
Sep 11	SHEFFIELD UNITED	W 4-0	Forbes, Lishman, Tapscott, Roper	41,679
Sep 14	MANCHESTER CITY	L 2-3	Tapscott, Lishman	33,898
Sep 18	Preston North End	L 1-3	Logie	36,000
Sep 25	BURNLEY	W 4-0	Lawton 2, Lishman, Roper	46,190
Oct 2	Leicester City	D 3-3	Lawton 2, Logie	42,486
Oct 9	Sheffield Wednesday	W 2-1	Roper, Bloomfield	38,167
Oct 16	PORTSMOUTH	L 0-1		44,866
Oct 23	Aston Villa	L 1-2	Roper	40,000
Oct 30	SUNDERLAND	L 1-3	Roper	65,424
Nov 6	Bolton Wanderers	D 2-2	Goring, Lishman	31,222
Nov 13	HUDDERSFIELD TOWN	L 3-5	Milton 2, Lishman	42,950
Nov 20	Manchester United	L 1-2	Tapscott	33,373
Nov 27	WOLVERHAMPTON WANDERERS	D 1-1	Roper	55,055
Dec 4	Blackpool	D 2-2	Tapscott, Roper	16,348
Dec 11	CHARLTON ATHLETIC	W 3-1	Roper 2, Milton	40,498
Dec 18	Newcastle United	L 1-5	Wills (pen)	35,060
Dec 25	CHELSEA	W 1-0	Lawton	47,178
Dec 27	Chelsea	D 1-1	Tapscott	66,922
Jan 1	WEST BROMWICH ALBION	D 2-2	Tapscott, Lishman	40,246
Jan 15	Tottenham Hotspur	W 1-0	Lawton	36,263
Feb 5	PRESTON NORTH END	W 2-0	Tapscott, Roper	41,228
Feb 12	Burnley	L 0-3		24,940
Feb 19	LEICESTER CITY	D 1-1	Roper	27,384
Feb 26	SHEFFIELD WEDNESDAY	W 3-2	Tapscott 3	26,910
Mar 5	Charlton Athletic	D 1-1	Bloomfield	42,064
Mar 12	ASTON VILLA	W 2-0	Tapscott, Roper	30,136
Mar 19	Sunderland	W 1-0	Bloomfield	40,279
Mar 26	BOLTON WANDERERS	W 3-0	Lishman 2, Roper	33,852
Apr 2	Huddersfield Town	W 1-0	Roper	22,853
Apr 8	CARDIFF CITY	W 2-0	Tapscott 2	39,052
Apr 9	BLACKPOOL	W 3-0	Lishman 2, Roper	60,741
Apr 11	Cardiff City	W 2-1	Bloomfield, Lishman	38,000
Apr 16	Wolverhampton Wanderers	L 1-3	Lishman	34,985
Apr 18	Sheffield United	D 1-1	Roper	21,380
Apr 23	MANCHESTER UNITED	L 2-3	Lishman 2	42,754
Apr 30	Portsmouth	L 1-2	Herd	28,156

FA Cup

Jan 8	CARDIFF CITY	(Rd3)	W 1-0	Lawton	51,298
Jan 29	Wolverhampton Wanderers	(Rd4)	L 0-1		52,857

Fact File

Jimmy Logie moved on to Southern League club Gravesend after nearly 16 years with Arsenal. He signed from Scottish junior side Lochore Welfare in June 1939 and made more than 300 appearances. He was the midfield general of Tom Whittaker's successful side, and – like Alex James – was virtually ignored by Scotland. For all his achievements with the Gunners, he won only one cap. The North Bank roof was rebuilt at last, with money granted by the War Damages Commission. The roof was an exact copy of the pre-war construction which had been destroyed during the conflict.

MANAGER: Tom Whittaker

CAPTAIN: Jimmy Logie/Walley Barnes

TOP SCORER: Doug Lishman 19 (all League)

BIGGEST WIN: 4-0 v Sheffield United, 11 September 1954, League; 4-0 v Burnley, 25 September 1954, League

HIGHEST ATTENDANCE: 65,424 v Sunderland, 30 October 1954, League

MAJOR TRANSFERS IN: Jimmy Bloomfield from Brentford, Joe Haverty from St Patrick's Athletic, David Herd from Stockport County

MAJOR TRANSFERS OUT: Arthur Milton to Bristol City, Jimmy Logie to Gravesend

League & Cup Appearances

PLAYER	LEAGUE	CUP COMPETITION FA CUP	TOTAL
Barnes	25	2	27
Bloomfield	19		19
Bowen	21	2	23
Clapton	16		16
Dickson	4		4
Dodgin	3		3
Evans	21	2	23
Forbes	20		20
Fotheringham	27	2	29
Goring	41	2	43
Guthrie	2		2
Haverty	6	1	7
Herd	3		3
Holton	8	1	9
Kelsey	38	2	40
Lawton	18	2	20
Lishman	32	2	34
Logie	13		13
Marden	7		7
Milton	8	2	10
Oakes	9		9
Roper	35		35
Shaw	1		1
Sullivan	2		2
Swallow	1		1
Tapscott	37	2	39
Wade	14		14
Walsh	6		6
Wilkinson	1		1
Wills	24		24

Goalscorers

PLAYER	LEAGUE	CUP COMPETITION FA CUP	TOTAL
Lishman	19		19
Roper	17		17
Tapscott	13		13
Lawton	6	1	7
Bloomfield	4		4
Logie	3		3
Milton	3		3
Forbes	1		1
Goring	1		1
Herd	1		1
Wills	1		1

Final Division One Table

		P	W	D	L	F	A	Pts
1	CHELSEA	42	20	12	10	81	57	52
2	WOLVERHAMPTON W	42	19	10	13	89	70	48
3	PORTSMOUTH	42	18	12	12	74	62	48
4	SUNDERLAND	42	15	18	9	64	54	48
5	MANCHESTER U	42	20	7	15	84	74	47
6	ASTON VILLA	42	20	7	15	72	73	47
7	MANCHESTER C	42	18	10	14	76	69	46
8	NEWCASTLE U	42	17	9	16	89	77	43
9	ARSENAL	42	17	9	16	69	63	43
10	BURNLEY	42	17	9	16	51	48	43
11	EVERTON	42	16	10	16	62	68	42
12	HUDDERSFIELD T	42	14	13	15	63	68	41
13	SHEFFIELD U	42	17	7	18	70	86	41
14	PRESTON NE	42	16	8	18	83	64	40
15	CHARLTON ATH	42	15	10	17	76	75	40
16	TOTTENHAM H	42	16	8	18	72	73	40
17	WBA	42	16	8	18	76	96	40
18	BOLTON W	42	13	13	16	62	69	39
19	BLACKPOOL	42	14	10	18	60	64	38
20	CARDIFF C	42	13	11	18	62	76	37
21	LEICESTER C	42	12	11	19	74	86	35
22	SHEFFIELD W	42	8	10	24	63	100	26

Season 1955-56

Football League Division One

DATE	OPPONENTS	SCORE	GOALSCORERS	ATTENDANCE
Aug 20	Blackpool	L 1-3	Tapscott	30,928
Aug 23	CARDIFF CITY	W 3-1	Lawton 3	31,352
Aug 27	CHELSEA	D 1-1	Lawton	55,011
Aug 31	Manchester City	D 1-1	Roper, Lawton	36,955
Sep 3	Bolton Wanderers	L 1-4	Lawton	22,690
Sep 6	MANCHESTER CITY	D 0-0		30,864
Sep 10	Tottenham Hotspur	L 1-3	Roper	51,029
Sep 17	PORTSMOUTH	L 1-3	Lishman	48,816
Sep 24	Sunderland	L 1-3	Lishman	55,397
Oct 1	ASTON VILLA	W 1-0	Nutt	43,824
Oct 8	Everton	D 1-1	Lishman	47,794
Oct 15	NEWCASTLE UNITED	W 1-0	Roper	46,093
Oct 22	Luton Town	D 0-0		23,997
Oct 29	CHARLTON ATHLETIC	L 2-4	Lishman, Clapton	47,038
Nov 5	Manchester United	D 1-1	Lishman	41,586
Nov 12	SHEFFIELD UNITED	W 2-1	Groves, Roper	46,647
Nov 19	Preston North End	W 1-0	Holton	23,000
Nov 26	BURNLEY	L 0-1		37,583
Dec 3	Birmingham City	L 0-4		35,765
Dec 10	WEST BROMWICH ALBION	W 2-0	Tapscott, o.g.	33,217
Dec 17	BLACKPOOL	W 4-1	Groves, Holton, Tapscott, Bloomfield	45,086
Dec 24	Chelsea	L 0-2		43,022
Dec 26	Wolverhampton Wanderers	D 3-3	Groves 2, Bloomfield	43,738
Dec 27	WOLVERHAMPTON WANDERERS	D 2-2	Tapscott 2	61,814
Dec 31	BOLTON WANDERERS	W 3-1	Tapscott 2, Groves	42,677
Jan 14	TOTTENHAM HOTSPUR	L 0-1		59,603
Jan 21	Portsmouth	L 2-5	Tapscott 2	30,513
Feb 4	SUNDERLAND	W 3-1	Herd 2, Bloomfield	38,780
Feb 11	Aston Villa	D 1-1	Groves	28,000
Feb 21	EVERTON	W 3-2	Tapscott 2, Groves	16,039
Feb 25	Newcastle United	L 0-2		50,800
Mar 6	PRESTON NORTH END	W 3-2	Tapscott 2, Groves	34,672
Mar 10	Charlton Athletic	L 0-2		39,553
Mar 17	MANCHESTER UNITED	D 1-1	Holton	50,758
Mar 24	Sheffield United	W 2-0	Holton, Tapscott	26,556
Mar 31	LUTON TOWN	W 3-0	Holton 2, Haverty	45,968
Apr 2	HUDDERSFIELD TOWN	W 2-0	Haverty, Holton	30,836
Apr 3	Huddersfield Town	W 1-0	Clapton	24,469
Apr 7	Burnley	W 1-0	Swallow	24,403
Apr 14	BIRMINGHAM CITY	W 1-0	Tapscott	31,733
Apr 21	West Bromwich Albion	L 1-2	Tapscott	22,400
Apr 28	Cardiff City	W 2-1	Holton, Tapscott	20,000

FA Cup

Jan 7	BEDFORD TOWN	(Rd3) D 2-2	Tapscott, Groves	55,178
Jan 12	Bedford Town	(R) W 2-1	Groves, Tapscott	15,306
Jan 28	ASTON VILLA	(Rd4) W 4-1	Tapscott 2, Groves, Charlton	43,052
Feb 18	Charlton Athletic	(Rd5) W 2-0	Groves, Bloomfield	71,758
Mar 3	BIRMINGHAM CITY	(QF) L 1-3	Charlton	67,872

League & Cup Appearances

PLAYER	LEAGUE	CUP COMPETITION FA CUP	TOTAL
Barnes	8		8
Bloomfield	32	5	37
Bowen	22	2	24
Charlton	19	5	24
Clapton	39	4	43
Dickson	1		1
Dodgin	15	3	18
Evans	42	5	47
Forbes	5		5
Fotheringham	25	2	27
Goring	37	5	42
Groves	15	5	20
Haverty	8		8
Herd	5		5
Holton	31	3	34
Kelsey	32	4	36
Lawton	8		8
Lishman	15		15
Nutt	8	1	9
Roper	16	1	17
Sullivan	10	1	11
Swallow	1		1
Tapscott	31	5	36
Tiddy	21	4	25
Wills	15		15

Goalscorers

PLAYER	LEAGUE	CUP COMPETITION FA CUP	TOTAL
Tapscott	17	4	21
Groves	8	4	12
Holton	8		8
Lawton	6		6
Lishman	5		5
Roper	4		4
Bloomfield	3	1	4
Clapton	2		2
Haverty	2		2
Herd	2		2
Charlton		2	2
Nutt	1		1
Swallow	1		1
Opps' o.gs.	1		1

Fact File

This was a season of major change at Highbury: Walley Barnes retired; Doug Lishman was transferred; Jack Kelsey, Peter Goring, Don Roper and Cliff Holton were the only remaining links to the 1953 championship side as Tom Whittaker went for youth to lift the Gunners again but the manager's health was fading fast.

MANAGER: Tom Whittaker

CAPTAIN: Peter Goring/Cliff Holton/Don Roper

TOP SCORER: Derek Tapscott 21 (17 League)

BIGGEST WIN: 4-1 v Blackpool, 17 December 1955, League; 4-1 v Aston Villa, 28 January 1956, FA Cup

HIGHEST ATTENDANCE: 67,872 v Birmingham City, 3 March 1956, FA Cup

MAJOR TRANSFERS IN: Stan Charlton and Vic Groves from Leyton Orient, Dennis Evans from Ellesmere Port Town, Gordon Nutt and Mike Tiddy from Cardiff City

MAJOR TRANSFERS OUT: Ben Marden to Watford, Tommy Lawton to Kettering Town, Doug Lishman to Nottingham Forest

Final Division One Table

		P	W	D	L	F	A	Pts
1	MANCHESTER U	42	25	10	7	83	51	60
2	BLACKPOOL	42	20	9	13	86	62	49
3	WOLVERHAMPTON W	42	20	9	13	89	65	49
4	MANCHESTER C	42	18	10	14	82	69	46
5	ARSENAL	42	18	10	14	60	61	46
6	BIRMINGHAM C	42	18	9	15	75	57	45
7	BURNLEY	42	18	8	16	64	54	44
8	BOLTON W	42	18	7	17	71	58	43
9	SUNDERLAND	42	17	9	16	80	95	43
10	LUTON T	42	17	8	17	66	64	42
11	NEWCASTLE U	42	17	7	18	85	70	41
12	PORTSMOUTH	42	16	9	17	78	85	41
13	WBA	42	18	5	19	58	70	41
14	CHARLTON ATH	42	17	6	19	75	81	40
15	EVERTON	42	15	10	17	55	69	40
16	CHELSEA	42	14	11	17	64	77	39
17	CARDIFF C	42	15	9	18	55	69	39
18	TOTTENHAM H	42	15	7	20	61	71	37
19	PRESTON NE	42	14	8	20	73	72	36
20	ASTON VILLA	42	11	13	18	52	69	35
21	HUDDERSFIELD T	42	14	7	21	54	83	35
22	SHEFFIELD U	42	12	9	21	63	77	33

Season 1956-57

Football League Division One

DATE	OPPONENTS	SCORE	GOALSCORERS	ATTENDANCE
Aug 18	CARDIFF CITY	D 0-0		51,069
Aug 21	BURNLEY	W 2-0	Tiddy, Bloomfield	38,321
Aug 25	Birmingham City	L 2-4	Holton, Roper	37,200
Aug 28	Burnley	L 1-3	Tiddy	18,829
Sep 1	WEST BROMWICH ALBION	W 4-1	Roper 2, Tiddy, Tapscott	39,973
Sep 4	PRESTON NORTH END	L 1-2	Bloomfield	40,470
Sep 8	Portsmouth	W 3-2	Bloomfield, Tiddy, Holton	30,768
Sep 10	Preston North End	L 0-3		35,450
Sep 15	NEWCASTLE UNITED	L 0-1		46,318
Sep 22	Sheffield Wednesday	W 4-2	Bloomfield 2, Tapscott, Tiddy	40,629
Sep 29	MANCHESTER UNITED	L 1-2	Evans (pen)	62,429
Oct 6	MANCHESTER CITY	W 7-3	Holton 4, Evans (pen), Bloomfield, Haverty	33,651
Oct 13	Charlton Athletic	W 3-1	Tapscott 2, Clapton	40,051
Oct 20	TOTTENHAM HOTSPUR	W 3-1	Herd 2, Haverty	60,580
Oct 27	Everton	L 0-4		52,478
Nov 3	ASTON VILLA	W 2-1	Groves 2	40,045
Nov 10	Wolverhampton Wanderers	L 2-5	Tapscott, Haverty	34,019
Nov 17	BOLTON WANDERERS	W 3-0	Tapscott 2, Haverty	33,377
Nov 24	Leeds United	D 3-3	Tapscott 2, Holton	39,000
Dec 1	SUNDERLAND	D 1-1	Tapscott	36,442
Dec 8	Luton Town	W 2-1	Haverty, Tapscott	22,000
Dec 15	Cardiff City	W 3-2	Herd 2, Haverty	15,000
Dec 22	BIRMINGHAM CITY	W 4-0	Evans (pen), Holton, Bloomfield, o.g.	28,644
Dec 25	Chelsea	D 1-1	Bloomfield	32,094
Dec 26	CHELSEA	W 2-0	Clapton, Tapscott	22,526
Dec 29	West Bromwich Albion	W 2-0	Haverty, Tapscott	25,000
Jan 12	PORTSMOUTH	D 1-1	Herd	48,949
Jan 19	Newcastle United	L 1-3	Evans (pen)	45,990
Feb 2	SHEFFIELD WEDNESDAY	W 6-3	Herd 3, Tapscott 2, Bloomfield	40,217
Feb 9	Manchester United	L 2-6	Herd 2	60,384
Feb 23	EVERTON	W 2-0	Holton, Tapscott	30,562
Mar 9	LUTON TOWN	L 1-3	Tapscott	41,288
Mar 13	Tottenham Hotspur	W 3-1	Bowen 2, Tapscott	65,455
Mar 16	Aston Villa	D 0-0		40,000
Mar 20	Manchester City	W 3-2	Tiddy, Bloomfield, Tapscott	27,974
Mar 23	WOLVERHAMPTON WANDERERS	D 0-0		51,021
Mar 30	Bolton Wanderers	L 1-2	Tapscott	23,879
Apr 6	LEEDS UNITED	W 1-0	Herd	40,388
Apr 13	Sunderland	L 0-1		34,749
Apr 19	BLACKPOOL	D 1-1	Tapscott	50,270
Apr 20	CHARLTON ATHLETIC	W 3-1	Tapscott 2, Holton	26,364
Apr 22	Blackpool	W 4-2	Tapscott 2, Herd, Haverty	24,118

FA Cup

Jan 5	STOKE CITY	(Rd3) W 4-2	Herd 2, Tapscott, Haverty	56,173
Jan 26	Newport County	(Rd4) W 2-0	Tapscott, Herd	22,450
Feb 16	Preston North End	(Rd5) D 3-3	Clapton, Herd, o.g.	39,608
Feb 19	PRESTON NORTH END	(R) W 2-1	Dodgin, Herd	61,501
Mar 2	West Bromwich Albion	(QF) D 2-2	Herd, Charlton	58,000
Mar 5	WEST BROMWICH ALBION	(R) L 1-2	Holton	58,757

League & Cup Appearances

PLAYER	LEAGUE	CUP COMPETITION FA CUP	TOTAL
Barnwell	1		1
Bloomfield	42	6	48
Bowen	30	6	36
Charlton	40	6	46
Clapton	39	6	45
Dodgin	41	6	47
Evans	40	4	44
Goring	13		13
Groves	5	2	7
Haverty	28	4	32
Herd	22	6	28
Holton	39	6	45
Kelsey	30	3	33
Nutt	1		1
Roper	4		4
Sullivan	12	3	15
Swallow	4		4
Tapscott	38	6	44
Tiddy	15		15
Wills	18	2	20

Goalscorers

PLAYER	LEAGUE	CUP COMPETITION FA CUP	TOTAL
Tapscott	25	2	27
Herd	12	6	18
Holton	10	1	11
Bloomfield	10		10
Haverty	8	1	9
Tiddy	6		6
Evans	4		4
Roper	3		3
Clapton	2	1	3
Bowen	2		2
Groves	2		2
Charlton		1	1
Dodgin		1	1
Opps' o.gs.	1	1	2

Fact File

Tom Whittaker died of a heart attack in October 1956. He had earlier been diagnosed as suffering from nervous exhaustion. Jack Crayston, Whittaker's assistant since 1947, took over, with Bob Wall becoming club secretary. Whittaker had joined Arsenal as a player in 1919.

MANAGER: Tom Whittaker/Jack Crayston

CAPTAIN: Cliff Holton

TOP SCORER: Derek Tapscott 27 (25 League)

BIGGEST WIN: 7-3 v Manchester City, 6 October 1956, League

HIGHEST ATTENDANCE: 62,429 v Manchester United, 29 September 1956, League

MAJOR TRANSFERS OUT: Joe Wade to Hereford, Don Roper to Southampton

Final Division One Table

		P	W	D	L	F	A	Pts
1	MANCHESTER U	42	28	8	6	103	54	64
2	TOTTENHAM H	42	22	12	8	104	56	56
3	PRESTON NE	42	23	10	9	84	56	56
4	BLACKPOOL	42	22	9	11	93	65	53
5	ARSENAL	42	21	8	13	85	69	50
6	WOLVERHAMPTON W	42	20	8	14	94	70	48
7	BURNLEY	42	18	10	14	56	50	46
8	LEEDS U	42	15	14	13	72	63	44
9	BOLTON W	42	16	12	14	65	65	44
10	ASTON VILLA	42	14	15	13	65	55	43
11	WBA	42	14	14	14	59	61	42
12	BIRMINGHAM C=	42	15	9	18	69	69	39
12	CHELSEA=	42	13	13	16	73	73	39
14	SHEFFIELD W	42	16	6	20	82	88	38
15	EVERTON	42	14	10	18	61	79	38
16	LUTON T	42	14	9	19	58	76	37
17	NEWCASTLE U	42	14	8	20	67	87	36
18	MANCHESTER C	42	13	9	20	78	88	35
19	PORTSMOUTH	42	10	13	19	62	92	33
20	SUNDERLAND	42	12	8	22	67	88	32
21	CARDIFF C	42	10	9	23	53	88	29
22	CHARLTON ATH	42	9	4	29	62	120	22

Season 1957-58

Football League Division One

DATE	OPPONENTS	SCORE	GOALSCORERS	ATTENDANCE
Aug 24	Sunderland	W 1-0	Groves	56,493
Aug 27	WEST BROMWICH ALBION	D 2-2	Herd 2	45,988
Aug 31	LUTON TOWN	W 2-0	Groves, Holton	50,111
Sep 4	West Bromwich Albion	W 2-1	Bloomfield, Swallow	25,600
Sep 7	Blackpool	L 0-1		31,486
Sep 10	EVERTON	L 2-3	Groves 2	42,010
Sep 14	LEICESTER CITY	W 3-1	Groves 2, Herd	45,321
Sep 21	Manchester United	L 2-4	Tiddy, Herd	47,142
Sep 28	LEEDS UNITED	W 2-1	Herd 2	39,347
Oct 2	ASTON VILLA	W 4-0	Swallow, Tiddy, Bloomfield, Herd	18,472
Oct 5	Bolton Wanderers	W 1-0	Herd	20,212
Oct 12	Tottenham Hotspur	L 1-3	Holton	60,671
Oct 16	Everton	D 2-2	Bloomfield, Herd	54,345
Oct 19	BIRMINGHAM CITY	L 1-3	Swallow	39,006
Oct 26	Chelsea	D 0-0		66,007
Nov 2	MANCHESTER CITY	W 2-1	Tapscott, Bloomfield	43,664
Nov 9	Nottingham Forest	L 0-4		34,216
Nov 16	PORTSMOUTH	W 3-2	Herd 2, Clapton	40,528
Nov 23	Sheffield Wednesday	L 0-2		25,200
Nov 30	NEWCASTLE UNITED	L 2-3	Holton, Clapton	41,694
Dec 7	Burnley	L 1-2	Holton	18,530
Dec 14	PRESTON NORTH END	W 4-2	Nutt, Herd, Bloomfield, o.g.	31,830
Dec 21	SUNDERLAND	W 3-0	Herd 2, Groves	28,105
Dec 26	Aston Villa	L 0-3		41,000
Dec 28	Luton Town	L 0-4		27,291
Jan 11	BLACKPOOL	L 2-3	Herd 2	38,667
Jan 18	Leicester City	W 1-0	Groves	31,778
Feb 1	MANCHESTER UNITED	L 4-5	Bloomfield 2, Herd, Tapscott	63,578
Feb 18	BOLTON WANDERERS	L 1-2	Bloomfield	28,420
Feb 22	TOTTENHAM HOTSPUR	D 4-4	Clapton, Herd, Nutt, o.g.	59,116
Mar 1	Birmingham City	L 1-4	Bloomfield	26,824
Mar 8	CHELSEA	W 5-4	Herd 3, Clapton, Bloomfield	41,570
Mar 15	Manchester City	W 4-2	Bloomfield 3, Herd	31,645
Mar 19	Leeds United	L 0-2		26,000
Mar 22	SHEFFIELD WEDNESDAY	W 1-0	Herd	28,074
Mar 29	Portsmouth	L 4-5	Bloomfield, Clapton, Nutt, o.g.	23,000
Apr 7	WOLVERHAMPTON WANDERERS	L 0-2		51,318
Apr 8	Wolverhampton Wanderers	W 2-1	Groves, Wills (pen)	47,501
Apr 12	Newcastle United	D 3-3	Herd, Groves, Bloomfield	42,700
Apr 19	BURNLEY	D 0-0		31,440
Apr 21	NOTTINGHAM FOREST	D 1-1	Bloomfield	23,217
Apr 26	Preston North End	L 0-3		21,528

FA Cup

Jan 4	Northampton Town	(Rd3)	L 1-3	Clapton	21,344

League & Cup Appearances

PLAYER	LEAGUE	CUP COMPETITION	TOTAL
		FA CUP	
Biggs	2		2
Bloomfield	40	1	41
Bowen	30	1	31
Charlton	36		36
Clapton	28	1	29
Dodgin	23	1	24
Evans	32	1	33
Fotheringham	19		19
Goring	10		10
Groves	30	1	31
Haverty	15		15
Herd	39	1	40
Holton	26	1	27
Kelsey	38	1	39
Le Roux	5		5
Nutt	21	1	22
Petts	9		9
Standen	1		1
Sullivan	3		3
Swallow	7		7
Tapscott	8		8
Tiddy	12		12
Ward	10		10
Wills	18	1	19

Goalscorers

PLAYER	LEAGUE	CUP COMPETITION	TOTAL
		FA CUP	
Herd	24		24
Bloomfield	16		16
Groves	10		10
Clapton	5	1	6
Holton	4		4
Nutt	3		3
Swallow	3		3
Tapscott	2		2
Tiddy	2		2
Wills	1		1
Opps' o.gs.	3		3

Fact File

Arsenal goalkeeper Jack Kelsey was one of the stars of the World Cup finals in Sweden as Wales reached the last eight. The Brazilians nicknamed him 'O Maravilhoso' (The Marvellous One) after his brilliant performance against them in the quarter-finals. It took a late goal by Pele to beat him.

MANAGER: Jack Crayston
CAPTAIN: Dennis Evans
TOP SCORER: David Herd 24 (all League)
BIGGEST WIN: 4-0 v Aston Villa, 2 October 1957, League
HIGHEST ATTENDANCE: 63,578 v Manchester United, 1 February 1958, League

Final Division One Table

		P	W	D	L	F	A	Pts
1	WOLVERHAMPTON W	42	28	8	6	103	47	64
2	PRESTON NE	42	26	7	9	100	51	59
3	TOTTENHAM H	42	21	9	12	93	77	51
4	WBA	42	18	14	10	92	70	50
5	MANCHESTER C	42	22	5	15	104	100	49
6	BURNLEY	42	21	5	16	80	74	47
7	BLACKPOOL	42	19	6	17	80	67	44
8	LUTON T	42	19	6	17	69	63	44
9	MANCHESTER U	42	16	11	15	85	75	43
10	NOTTINGHAM F	42	16	10	16	69	63	42
11	CHELSEA	42	15	12	15	83	79	42
12	ARSENAL	42	16	7	19	73	85	39
13	BIRMINGHAM C	42	14	11	17	76	89	39
14	ASTON VILLA	42	16	7	19	73	86	39
15	BOLTON W	42	14	10	18	65	87	38
16	EVERTON	42	13	11	18	65	75	37
17	LEEDS U	42	14	9	19	51	63	37
18	LEICESTER C	42	14	5	23	91	112	33
19	NEWCASTLE U	42	12	8	22	73	81	32
20	PORTSMOUTH	42	12	8	22	73	88	32
21	SUNDERLAND	42	10	12	20	54	97	32
22	SHEFFIELD W	42	12	7	23	69	92	31

Season 1958-59

Football League Division One

DATE	OPPONENTS	SCORE	GOALSCORERS	ATTENDANCE
Aug 23	Preston North End	L 1-2	Bloomfield	30,578
Aug 26	BURNLEY	W 3-0	Bloomfield, Holton, Docherty	41,305
Aug 30	LEICESTER CITY	W 5-1	Holton 2, Evans, Clapton D., Nutt	35,411
Sep 2	Burnley	L 1-3	Groves	28,240
Sep 6	Everton	W 6-1	Groves, Herd 4, Bloomfield	40,557
Sep 9	BOLTON WANDERERS	W 6-1	Herd, Nutt 2, Bloomfield, Clapton D., Evans	45,255
Sep 13	TOTTENHAM HOTSPUR	W 3-1	Nutt, Herd 2	65,565
Sep 17	Bolton Wanderers	L 1-2	Bloomfield	42,391
Sep 20	MANCHESTER CITY	W 4-1	Herd 2, Evans (pen), Bloomfield	47,878
Sep 27	Leeds United	L 1-2	Herd	34,000
Oct 4	WEST BROMWICH ALBION	W 4-3	Henderson 2, Herd, o.g.	57,770
Oct 11	Manchester United	D 1-1	Ward	55,909
Oct 18	WOLVERHAMPTON WANDERERS	D 1-1	Biggs	49,393
Oct 22	Aston Villa	W 2-1	Ward, Nutt	30,000
Oct 25	Blackburn Rovers	L 2-4	Evans (pen), Ward	37,600
Nov 1	NEWCASTLE UNITED	W 3-2	Groves, Henderson 2	62,801
Nov 8	West Ham United	D 0-0		38,250
Nov 15	NOTTINGHAM FOREST	W 3-1	Herd, Henderson, o.g.	49,106
Nov 22	Chelsea	W 3-0	Henderson, Clapton D., Barnwell	57,910
Nov 29	BLACKPOOL	L 1-4	Clapton D.	54,792
Dec 6	Portsmouth	W 1-0	Nutt	33,321
Dec 13	ASTON VILLA	L 1-2	Henderson	32,170
Dec 20	PRESTON NORTH END	L 1-2	Henderson	32,860
Dec 26	Luton Town	L 3-6	Julians, Evans (pen), Bloomfield	21,870
Dec 27	LUTON TOWN	W 1-0	Bloomfield	56,501
Jan 3	Leicester City	W 3-2	Julians 2, Bloomfield	33,979
Jan 17	EVERTON	W 3-1	Groves 2, Bloomfield	39,474
Jan 31	Tottenham Hotspur	W 4-1	Groves, Herd, Henderson 2	60,241
Feb 7	Manchester City	D 0-0		31,819
Feb 21	West Bromwich Albion	D 1-1	Julians	32,700
Feb 24	LEEDS UNITED	W 1-0	Herd	30,244
Feb 28	MANCHESTER UNITED	W 3-2	Barnwell 2, Herd	67,386
Mar 7	Wolverhampton Wanderers	L 1-6	Haverty	40,080
Mar 14	BLACKBURN ROVERS	D 1-1	Wills (pen)	40,155
Mar 21	Newcastle United	L 0-1		32,620
Mar 28	WEST HAM UNITED	L 1-2	Henderson	52,452
Apr 4	Nottingham Forest	D 1-1	Haverty	32,558
Apr 11	CHELSEA	D 1-1	Ward	40,900
Apr 14	Birmingham City	L 1-4	Clapton D.	25,791
Apr 18	Blackpool	W 2-1	Haverty, Julians	17,118
Apr 25	PORTSMOUTH	W 5-2	Groves 3, Henderson, o.g.	24,569
May 4	BIRMINGHAM CITY	W 2-1	Clapton D., Groves	26,129

FA Cup

DATE	OPPONENTS		SCORE	GOALSCORERS	ATTENDANCE
Jan 10	Bury	(Rd3)	W 1-0	Herd	29,880
Jan 24	Colchester United	(Rd4)	D 2-2	Groves 2	16,000
Jan 28	COLCHESTER UNITED	(R)	W 4-0	Herd 2, Julians, Evans	62,686
Feb 14	SHEFFIELD UNITED	(Rd5)	D 2-2	Evans (pen), Julians	55,407
Feb 18	Sheffield United	(R)	L 0-3		48,763

Fact File

Arsenal's 6-1 win at Everton in September could have finished in double figures. Two more 'goals' were disallowed for offside and Vic Groves hit the bar three times.

MANAGER: George Swindin   **CAPTAIN:** Vic Groves/David Bowen

TOP SCORER: David Herd 18 (15 League)

BIGGEST WIN: 6-1 v Everton, 6 September 1958, League; 6-1 v Bolton Wanderers, 9 September 1958, League

HIGHEST ATTENDANCE: 67,386 v Manchester United, 28 February 1959, League

MAJOR TRANSFERS IN: Tommy Docherty from Preston North End, Jackie Henderson from Portsmouth, Len Julians from Leyton Orient, Billy McCullough from Portadown, Mel Charles from Swansea Town

MAJOR TRANSFERS OUT: Jim Fotheringham to Heart of Midlothian, Mike Tiddy to Brighton & Hove Albion, Cliff Holton to Watford, Stan Charlton to Leyton Orient

League & Cup Appearances

PLAYER	LEAGUE	CUP COMPETITION FA CUP	TOTAL
Barnwell	16		16
Biggs	2		2
Bloomfield	29	2	31
Bowen	16	5	21
Charlton	4		4
Clapton D.	39	5	44
Docherty	38	4	42
Dodgin	39	3	42
Evans	37	4	41
Fotheringham	1		1
Goring	2		2
Goulden	1		1
Goy	2		2
Groves	33	4	37
Haverty	10	1	11
Henderson	21	4	25
Herd	26	5	31
Holton	3		3
Julians	10	4	14
Kelsey	27	5	32
McCullough	10	1	11
Nutt	16		16
Petts	3		3
Standen	13		13
Ward	31	3	34
Wills	33	5	38

Goalscorers

PLAYER	LEAGUE	CUP COMPETITION FA CUP	TOTAL
Herd	15	3	18
Henderson	12		12
Groves	10	2	12
Bloomfield	10		10
Evans	5	2	7
Julians	5	2	7
Clapton D.	6		6
Nutt	6		6
Ward	4		4
Barnwell	3		3
Haverty	3		3
Holton	3		3
Biggs	1		1
Docherty	1		1
Wills	1		1
Opps' o.gs.	3		3

Final Division One Table

		P	W	D	L	F	A	Pts
1	WOLVERHAMPTON W	42	28	5	9	110	49	61
2	MANCHESTER U	42	24	7	11	103	66	55
3	ARSENAL	42	21	8	13	88	68	50
4	BOLTON W	42	20	10	12	79	66	50
5	WBA	42	18	13	11	88	68	49
6	WEST HAM U	42	21	6	15	85	70	48
7	BURNLEY	42	19	10	13	81	70	48
8	BLACKPOOL	42	18	11	13	66	49	47
9	BIRMINGHAM C	42	20	6	16	84	68	46
10	BLACKBURN R	42	17	10	15	76	70	44
11	NEWCASTLE U	42	17	7	18	80	80	41
12	PRESTON NE	42	17	7	18	70	77	41
13	NOTTINGHAM F	42	17	6	19	71	74	40
14	CHELSEA	42	18	4	20	77	98	40
15	LEEDS U	42	15	9	18	57	74	39
16	EVERTON	42	17	4	21	71	87	38
17	LUTON T	42	12	13	17	68	71	37
18	TOTTENHAM H	42	13	10	19	85	95	36
19	LEICESTER C	42	11	10	21	67	98	32
20	MANCHESTER C	42	11	9	22	64	95	31
21	ASTON VILLA	42	11	8	23	58	87	30
22	PORTSMOUTH	42	6	9	27	64	112	21

Season 1959-60

Football League Division One

DATE	OPPONENTS	SCORE	GOALSCORERS	ATTENDANCE
Aug 22	SHEFFIELD WEDNESDAY	L 0-1		47,585
Aug 26	Nottingham Forest	W 3-0	Clapton D. 3	32,386
Aug 29	Wolverhampton Wanderers	D 3-3	Clapton D., Herd 2	45,885
Sep 1	NOTTINGHAM FOREST	D 1-1	Herd	41,585
Sep 5	TOTTENHAM HOTSPUR	D 1-1	Barnwell	61,011
Sep 9	Bolton Wanderers	W 1-0	Herd	32,571
Sep 12	MANCHESTER CITY	W 3-1	Clapton D., Barnwell, Haverty	38,392
Sep 15	BOLTON WANDERERS	W 2-1	Herd, Clapton D.	38,795
Sep 19	Blackburn Rovers	D 1-1	Herd	31,800
Sep 26	BLACKPOOL	W 2-1	Barnwell, Herd	47,473
Oct 3	Everton	L 1-3	Barnwell	40,587
Oct 10	Manchester United	L 2-4	Henderson, Herd	51,872
Oct 17	PRESTON NORTH END	L 0-3		44,073
Oct 24	Leicester City	D 2-2	Barnwell, Bloomfield	29,152
Oct 31	BIRMINGHAM CITY	W 3-0	Herd, Barnwell, Henderson	34,605
Nov 7	Leeds United	L 2-3	Herd, Henderson	21,500
Nov 14	WEST HAM UNITED	L 1-3	Bloomfield	49,760
Nov 21	Chelsea	W 3-1	Haverty 2, Bloomfield	52,748
Nov 28	WEST BROMWICH ALBION	L 2-4	Groves, Bloomfield	41,157
Dec 5	Newcastle United	L 1-4	Haverty	39,940
Dec 12	BURNLEY	L 2-4	Haverty, Bloomfield	26,249
Dec 19	Sheffield Wednesday	L 1-5	Julians	25,135
Dec 26	LUTON TOWN	L 0-3		31,466
Dec 27	Luton Town	W 1-0	Julians	27,055
Jan 2	WOLVERHAMPTON WANDERERS	D 4-4	Evans, Haverty, Charles, Wills (pen)	47,854
Jan 16	Tottenham Hotspur	L 0-3		58,962
Jan 23	Manchester City	W 2-1	Charles, o.g.	28,441
Feb 6	BLACKBURN ROVERS	W 5-2	Charles 3, Haverty, Herd	35,633
Feb 13	Blackpool	L 1-2	Charles	14,868
Feb 20	EVERTON	W 2-1	Charles 2	28,872
Feb 27	NEWCASTLE UNITED	W 1-0	Barnwell	47,657
Mar 5	Preston North End	W 3-0	Haverty, Henderson, Bloomfield	23,635
Mar 15	LEICESTER CITY	D 1-1	Herd	27,838
Mar 19	Burnley	L 2-3	Henderson 2	20,166
Mar 26	LEEDS UNITED	D 1-1	Herd	19,735
Apr 2	West Ham United	D 0-0		29,000
Apr 9	CHELSEA	L 1-4	Bloomfield	40,700
Apr 15	FULHAM	W 2-0	Henderson, Herd	37,873
Apr 16	Birmingham City	L 0-3		27,216
Apr 18	Fulham	L 0-3		31,058
Apr 23	MANCHESTER UNITED	W 5-2	Bloomfield 3, Clapton D., Ward	41,057
Apr 30	West Bromwich Albion	L 0-1		25,600

FA Cup

DATE	OPPONENTS		SCORE	GOALSCORERS	ATTENDANCE
Jan 9	Rotherham United	(Rd3)	D 2-2	Julians, o.g.	24,750
Jan 13	ROTHERHAM UNITED	(R)	D 1-1	Bloomfield	57,598
Jan 18	Rotherham United*	(2R)	L 0-2		56,290

*Played at Hillsborough.

League & Cup Appearances

PLAYER	LEAGUE	CUP COMPETITION FA CUP	TOTAL
Barnwell	28	3	31
Bloomfield	36	3	39
Charles	20	1	21
Clapton D.	23	2	25
Clapton D.P.	3		3
Docherty	24	3	27
Dodgin	30	1	31
Evans	7	2	9
Everitt	5		5
Groves	30		30
Haverty	35	2	37
Henderson	31	3	34
Herd	31	1	32
Julians	8	2	10
Kelsey	22		22
Magill	17	3	20
McCullough	33		33
Nutt	3		3
Petts	7		7
Snedden	1	1	2
Standen	20	3	23
Ward	15		15
Wills	33	3	36

Goalscorers

PLAYER	LEAGUE	CUP COMPETITION FA CUP	TOTAL
Herd	14		14
Bloomfield	10	1	11
Haverty	8		8
Charles	8		8
Barnwell	7		7
Clapton D.	7		7
Henderson	7		7
Julians	2	1	3
Evans	1		1
Groves	1		1
Ward	1		1
Wills	1		1
Opps' o.gs.	1	1	2

Fact File

Mel Charles, Arsenal's major signing at the end of the 1958-59 season, was the younger brother of Leeds, Juventus and Wales legend, John Charles. Like his brother, he could play at centre half or centre forward. But his Arsenal career was wrecked by cartilage injuries. He needed a knee operation in September 1959, only a month after making his debut, and had a second operation at the end of the season. He returned to Wales with Cardiff City in February 1962.

MANAGER: George Swindin

CAPTAIN: Vic Groves/Tommy Docherty

TOP SCORER: David Herd 14 (all League)

BIGGEST WIN: 5-2 v Blackburn Rovers, 6 February 1960, League; 5-2 v Manchester United, 23 April 1960, League

HIGHEST ATTENDANCE: 61,011 v Tottenham Hotspur, 5 September 1959, League

MAJOR TRANSFERS IN: Jimmy Magill from Portadown, Terry Neill from Bangor City

Final Division One Table

		P	W	D	L	F	A	Pts
1	BURNLEY	42	24	7	11	85	61	55
2	WOLVERHAMPTON W	42	24	6	12	106	67	54
3	TOTTENHAM H	42	21	11	10	86	50	53
4	WBA	42	19	11	12	83	57	49
5	SHEFFIELD W	42	19	11	12	80	59	49
6	BOLTON W	42	20	8	14	59	51	48
7	MANCHESTER U	42	19	7	16	102	80	45
8	NEWCASTLE U	42	18	8	16	82	78	44
9	PRESTON NE	42	16	12	14	79	76	44
10	FULHAM	42	17	10	15	73	80	44
11	BLACKPOOL	42	15	10	17	59	71	40
12	LEICESTER C	42	13	13	16	66	75	39
13	ARSENAL	42	15	9	18	68	80	39
14	WEST HAM U	42	16	6	20	75	91	38
15	EVERTON	42	13	11	18	73	78	37
16	MANCHESTER C	42	17	3	22	78	84	37
17	BLACKBURN R	42	16	5	21	60	70	37
18	CHELSEA	42	14	9	19	76	91	37
19	BIRMINGHAM C	42	13	10	19	63	80	36
20	NOTTINGHAM F	42	13	9	20	50	74	35
21	LEEDS U	42	12	10	20	65	92	34
22	LUTON T	42	9	12	21	50	73	30

Season 1960-61

Football League Division One

DATE	OPPONENTS	SCORE	GOALSCORERS	ATTENDANCE
Aug 20	Burnley	L 2-3	Herd, Bloomfield	23,653
Aug 23	PRESTON NORTH END	W 1-0	Everitt	31,612
Aug 27	NOTTINGHAM FOREST	W 3-0	Henderson, Skirton 2	28,878
Aug 30	Preston North End	L 0-2		20,105
Sep 3	Manchester City	D 0-0		36,656
Sep 6	BIRMINGHAM CITY	W 2-0	Herd, Kane	20,285
Sep 10	TOTTENHAM HOTSPUR	L 2-3	Herd, Ward	60,088
Sep 14	Birmingham City	L 0-2		22,904
Sep 17	NEWCASTLE UNITED	W 5-0	Herd 3, Strong, Clapton	34,885
Sep 24	Cardiff City	L 0-1		35,000
Oct 1	WEST BROMWICH ALBION	W 1-0	Herd	27,176
Oct 8	Leicester City	L 1-2	Henderson	22,501
Oct 15	ASTON VILLA	W 2-1	Herd, Strong	34,048
Oct 22	Blackburn Rovers	W 4-2	Strong 2, Charles, Herd	21,500
Oct 29	MANCHESTER UNITED	W 2-1	Barnwell, Herd	45,715
Nov 5	West Ham United	L 0-6		29,375
Nov 12	CHELSEA	L 1-4	Charles	38,886
Nov 19	Blackpool	D 1-1	Herd	15,417
Nov 26	EVERTON	W 3-2	Herd 3	36,709
Dec 3	Wolverhampton Wanderers	L 3-5	Herd 2, Barnwell	25,658
Dec 10	BOLTON WANDERERS	W 5-1	Barnwell, Strong 2, Eastham 2	30,818
Dec 17	BURNLEY	L 2-5	Strong, Herd	37,209
Dec 23	Sheffield Wednesday	D 1-1	Neill	29,311
Dec 26	SHEFFIELD WEDNESDAY	D 1-1	Eastham	43,995
Dec 31	Nottingham Forest	W 5-3	Herd 3, Eastham, Henderson	30,735
Jan 14	MANCHESTER CITY	W 5-4	Herd 3, Henderson, Clapton	36,440
Jan 21	Tottenham Hotspur	L 2-4	Henderson, Haverty	65,251
Feb 4	Newcastle United	D 3-3	Strong 2, Eastham	34,780
Feb 11	CARDIFF CITY	L 2-3	Herd 2	33,754
Feb 18	West Bromwich Albion	W 3-2	Haverty 2, Skirton	21,500
Feb 25	LEICESTER CITY	L 1-3	Henderson	31,721
Mar 4	Aston Villa	D 2-2	Haverty, Barnwell	35,000
Mar 11	BLACKBURN ROVERS	D 0-0		34,250
Mar 18	Manchester United	D 1-1	Charles	29,732
Mar 25	WEST HAM UNITED	D 0-0		27,665
Mar 31	Fulham	D 2-2	Herd 2	35,476
Apr 1	Bolton Wanderers	D 1-1	Henderson	18,618
Apr 3	FULHAM	W 4-2	Henderson 2, Barnwell 2	20,142
Apr 8	BLACKPOOL	W 1-0	Herd	36,301
Apr 15	Chelsea	L 1-3	Strong	38,233
Apr 22	WOLVERHAMPTON WANDERERS	L 1-5	Henderson	34,429
Apr 29	Everton	L 1-4	Herd	39,810

FA Cup

Jan 7	Sunderland	(Rd3) L 1-2	Herd	58,575

League & Cup Appearances

PLAYER	LEAGUE	CUP COMPETITION FA CUP	TOTAL
Bacuzzi	13		13
Barnwell	26	1	27
Bloomfield	12		12
Charles	19	1	20
Clapton	18		18
Clapton D.P.	1		1
Docherty	21		21
Eastham	19	1	20
Everitt	4		4
Griffiths	1		1
Groves	32	1	33
Haverty	12		12
Henderson	39	1	40
Herd	40	1	41
Kane	4		4
Kelsey	37	1	38
McClelland	4		4
McCullough	41	1	42
Magill	6	1	7
Neill	14	1	15
O'Neill	2		2
Petts	1		1
Skirton	16		16
Snedden	23		23
Standen	1		1
Strong	19	1	20
Ward	9		9
Wills	24		24
Young	4		4

Goalscorers

PLAYER	LEAGUE	CUP COMPETITION FA CUP	TOTAL
Herd	29	1	30
Henderson	10		10
Strong	10		10
Barnwell	6		6
Eastham	5		5
Haverty	4		4
Charles	3		3
Skirton	3		3
Clapton	2		2
Bloomfield	1		1
Everitt	1		1
Kane	1		1
Neill	1		1
Ward	1		1

Fact File

George Eastham spent months out of the game before joining Arsenal, because Newcastle stopped him playing even though they would not let him join another club. Eastham and the PFA chairman Jimmy Hill later won a landmark High Court judgement against football's contract system and the maximum wage of £20 a week for players, regardless of their status. Mr Justice Wilberforce ruled that both were a 'restraint of trade'. This judgement was one of the earliest steps towards freedom of contract for players.

MANAGER: George Swindin

CAPTAIN: Vic Groves

TOP SCORER: David Herd 30 (29 League)

BIGGEST WIN: 5-0 v Newcastle United, 17 September 1960, League

HIGHEST ATTENDANCE: 60,088 v Tottenham Hotspur, 10 September 1960, League

MAJOR TRANSFERS IN: George Eastham from Newcastle United, Jack McClelland from Glenavon

MAJOR TRANSFERS OUT: Jimmy Bloomfield to Birmingham City, Tommy Docherty to Chelsea

Final Division One Table

		P	W	D	L	F	A	Pts
1	TOTTENHAM H	42	31	4	7	115	55	66
2	SHEFFIELD W	42	23	12	7	78	47	58
3	WOLVERHAMPTON W	42	25	7	10	103	75	57
4	BURNLEY	42	22	7	13	102	77	51
5	EVERTON	42	22	6	14	87	69	50
6	LEICESTER C	42	18	9	15	87	70	45
7	MANCHESTER U	42	18	9	15	88	76	45
8	BLACKBURN R	42	15	13	14	77	76	43
9	ASTON VILLA	42	17	9	16	78	77	43
10	WBA	42	18	5	19	67	71	41
11	ARSENAL	42	15	11	16	77	85	41
12	CHELSEA	42	15	7	20	98	100	37
13	MANCHESTER C	42	13	11	18	79	90	37
14	NOTTINGHAM F	42	14	9	19	62	78	37
15	CARDIFF C	42	13	11	18	60	85	37
16	WEST HAM U	42	13	10	19	77	88	36
17	FULHAM	42	14	8	20	72	95	36
18	BOLTON W	42	12	11	19	58	73	35
19	BIRMINGHAM C	42	14	6	22	62	84	34
20	BLACKPOOL	42	12	9	21	68	73	33
21	NEWCASTLE U	42	11	10	21	86	109	32
22	PRESTON NE	42	10	10	22	43	71	30

Season 1961-62

Football League Division One

DATE	OPPONENTS	SCORE	GOALSCORERS	ATTENDANCE
Aug 19	BURNLEY	D 2-2	Charles 2	42,856
Aug 23	Leicester City	W 1-0	Eastham	29,396
Aug 26	Tottenham Hotspur	L 3-4	Charles 2, Skirton	59,371
Aug 30	LEICESTER CITY	D 4-4	MacLeod, Eastham, Skirton, Charles	35,055
Sep 2	Bolton Wanderers	L 1-2	Charles	18,414
Sep 9	MANCHESTER CITY	W 3-0	Griffiths, Skirton, o.g.	41,478
Sep 16	West Bromwich Albion	L 0-4		20,560
Sep 20	Sheffield Wednesday	D 1-1	Charles	35,903
Sep 23	BIRMINGHAM CITY	D 1-1	Skirton	31,749
Sep 30	Everton	L 1-4	Charles	43,289
Oct 7	BLACKPOOL	W 3-0	Charles 2, Ward	41,166
Oct 14	Blackburn Rovers	D 0-0		14,000
Oct 21	MANCHESTER UNITED	W 5-1	Skirton 2, Eastham, Barnwell, Ward	54,099
Oct 28	Cardiff City	D 1-1	Charles	25,400
Nov 4	CHELSEA	L 0-3		37,590
Nov 11	Aston Villa	L 1-3	Skirton	24,200
Nov 14	SHEFFIELD WEDNESDAY	W 1-0	Strong	19,331
Nov 21	NOTTINGHAM FOREST	W 2-1	Strong, MacLeod	34,217
Nov 28	Wolverhampton Wanderers	W 3-2	Ward 2, Skirton	28,882
Dec 2	WEST HAM UNITED	D 2-2	Strong, Skirton	47,206
Dec 9	Sheffield United	L 1-2	Strong	19,213
Dec 16	Burnley	W 2-0	Skirton, Charles	22,887
Dec 23	TOTTENHAM HOTSPUR	W 2-1	Charles, Skirton	63,440
Dec 26	FULHAM	W 1-0	Charles	32,969
Jan 13	BOLTON WANDERERS	L 1-2	Charles	33,351
Jan 20	Manchester City	L 2-3	Skirton 2	20,414
Feb 3	WEST BROMWICH ALBION	L 0-1		29,597
Feb 10	Birmingham City	L 0-1		27,797
Feb 24	Blackpool	W 1-0	Strong	13,728
Mar 3	BLACKBURN ROVERS	D 0-0		25,744
Mar 17	CARDIFF CITY	D 1-1	Strong	25,059
Mar 24	Chelsea	W 3-2	Skirton, Barnwell, MacLeod	31,016
Mar 31	ASTON VILLA	L 4-5	Skirton 2, Strong 2	20,107
Apr 7	Nottingham Forest	W 1-0	Strong	21,129
Apr 11	Fulham	L 2-5	Skirton, MacLeod	26,517
Apr 14	WOLVERHAMPTON WANDERERS	W 3-1	Skirton, Strong 2	24,367
Apr 16	Manchester United	W 3-2	Eastham, Skirton, o.g.	24,788
Apr 20	Ipswich Town	D 2-2	MacLeod, Eastham	30,649
Apr 21	West Ham United	D 3-3	Clapton, Strong, MacLeod	31,912
Apr 23	IPSWICH TOWN	L 0-3		44,694
Apr 28	SHEFFIELD UNITED	W 2-0	Barnwell, Eastham	18,761
May 1	EVERTON	L 2-3	Griffiths, Armstrong	20,034

FA Cup

Jan 6	BRADFORD CITY	(Rd3)	W 3-0	Charles 2, o.g.	40,232
Jan 31	Manchester United	(Rd4)	L 0-1		54,082

League & Cup Appearances

PLAYER	LEAGUE	CUP COMPETITION FA CUP	TOTAL
Armstrong	4		4
Bacuzzi	22	2	24
Barnwell	14	2	16
Brown	41	2	43
Charles	21	2	23
Clamp	18	2	20
Clapton	5		5
Clarke	1		1
Eastham	38	2	40
Griffiths	14		14
Groves	16		16
Henderson	12		12
Kelsey	35	2	37
MacLeod	37	2	39
McClelland	4		4
McCullough	40	2	42
McKechnie	3		3
Magill	21		21
Neill	20		20
Petts	12		12
Skirton	38	2	40
Snedden	15	2	17
Strong	20		20
Ward	11		11

Goalscorers

PLAYER	LEAGUE	CUP COMPETITION FA CUP	TOTAL
Skirton	19		19
Charles	15	2	17
Strong	12		12
Eastham	6		6
MacLeod	6		6
Ward	4		4
Barnwell	3		3
Griffiths	2		2
Armstrong	1		1
Clapton	1		1
Opps' o.gs.	2	1	3

Fact File

When George Swindin resigned near the end of the season, Arsenal turned to Wolves and England great Billy Wright to succeed him. The move was viewed as a big gamble at the time. Wright had been working for the FA, with responsibility for England's Under-23 and youth teams. But he had virtually no management or coaching experience and, unlike Allison, Whittaker, Crayston and Swindin, no previous links with Arsenal.

MANAGER: George Swindin

CAPTAIN: Vic Groves/George Eastham

TOP SCORER: Alan Skirton 19 (all League)

BIGGEST WIN: 5-1 v Manchester United, 21 October 1961, League

HIGHEST ATTENDANCE: 63,440 v Tottenham Hotspur, 23 December 1961, League

MAJOR TRANSFERS IN: Laurie Brown from Northampton Town, Eddie Clamp from Wolverhampton Wanderers, Johnny MacLeod from Hibernian

MAJOR TRANSFERS OUT: David Herd to Manchester United, Joe Haverty to Blackburn Rovers, Mel Charles to Cardiff City

Final Division One Table

		P	W	D	L	F	A	Pts
1	IPSWICH T	42	24	8	10	93	67	56
2	BURNLEY	42	21	11	10	101	67	53
3	TOTTENHAM H	42	21	10	11	88	69	52
4	EVERTON	42	20	11	11	88	54	51
5	SHEFFIELD U	42	19	9	14	61	69	47
6	SHEFFIELD W	42	20	6	16	72	58	46
7	ASTON VILLA	42	18	8	16	65	56	44
8	WEST HAM U	42	17	10	15	76	82	44
9	WBA	42	15	13	14	83	67	43
10	ARSENAL	42	16	11	15	71	72	43
11	BOLTON W	42	16	10	16	62	66	42
12	MANCHESTER C	42	17	7	18	78	81	41
13	BLACKPOOL	42	15	11	16	70	75	41
14	LEICESTER C	42	17	6	19	72	71	40
15	MANCHESTER U	42	15	9	18	72	75	39
16	BLACKBURN R	42	14	11	17	50	58	39
17	BIRMINGHAM C	42	14	10	18	65	81	38
18	WOLVERHAMPTON W	42	13	10	19	73	86	36
19	NOTTINGHAM F	42	13	10	19	63	79	36
20	FULHAM	42	13	7	22	66	74	33
21	CARDIFF C	42	9	14	19	50	81	32
22	CHELSEA	42	9	10	23	63	94	28

Season 1962-63

Football League Division One

DATE	OPPONENTS	SCORE	GOALSCORERS	ATTENDANCE
Aug 18	Leyton Orient	W 2-1	Strong, Baker	26,300
Aug 21	BIRMINGHAM CITY	W 2-0	Strong, McCullough	34,004
Aug 25	MANCHESTER UNITED	L 1-3	Clamp	62,308
Aug 29	Birmingham City	D 2-2	Strong 2	27,135
Sep 1	Burnley	L 1-2	Skirton	26,231
Sep 4	ASTON VILLA	L 1-2	Skirton	33,861
Sep 8	SHEFFIELD WEDNESDAY	L 1-2	Baker	31,115
Sep 10	Aston Villa	L 1-3	Strong	36,705
Sep 15	Fulham	W 3-1	Skirton, MacLeod, Baker	31,442
Sep 22	LEICESTER CITY	D 1-1	Baker	31,291
Sep 29	Bolton Wanderers	L 0-3		16,572
Oct 6	Tottenham Hotspur	D 4-4	Court 2, MacLeod, Strong	61,749
Oct 13	WEST HAM UNITED	D 1-1	Baker	49,597
Oct 27	WOLVERHAMPTON WANDERERS	W 5-4	Baker 3, Eastham 2	43,002
Nov 3	Blackburn Rovers	D 5-5	Baker 2, Skirton 2, Eastham	15,400
Nov 10	SHEFFIELD UNITED	W 1-0	Strong	25,503
Nov 14	Liverpool	L 1-2	Strong	38,452
Nov 17	Nottingham Forest	L 0-3		24,804
Nov 24	IPSWICH TOWN	W 3-1	Baker, Armstrong, Barnwell	25,056
Dec 1	Manchester City	W 4-2	MacLeod 2, Baker, Strong	25,454
Dec 8	BLACKPOOL	W 2-0	Strong, o.g.	23,767
Dec 15	LEYTON ORIENT	W 2-0	Baker 2	29,075
Feb 9	Leicester City	L 0-2		26,320
Feb 16	BOLTON WANDERERS	W 3-2	MacLeod, Brown, Armstrong	25,204
Feb 23	TOTTENHAM HOTSPUR	L 2-3	Strong, Baker	59,980
Mar 2	West Ham United	W 4-0	Baker 2, McCullough, Strong	31,467
Mar 9	LIVERPOOL	D 2-2	MacLeod, McCullough	30,496
Mar 23	BLACKBURN ROVERS	W 3-1	Strong 2, MacLeod	21,467
Mar 26	EVERTON	W 4-3	Strong, Baker, MacLeod, Skirton	38,061
Mar 30	Ipswich Town	D 1-1	o.g.	16,686
Apr 6	NOTTINGHAM FOREST	D 0-0		25,134
Apr 8	Wolverhampton Wanderers	L 0-1		18,593
Apr 12	WEST BROMWICH ALBION	W 3-2	Strong 2, Skirton	28,219
Apr 13	Sheffield United	D 3-3	Baker, Anderson, Barnwell	21,487
Apr 15	West Bromwich Albion	W 2-1	Baker 2	16,600
Apr 20	MANCHESTER CITY	L 2-3	MacLeod, Strong	20,539
Apr 24	Everton	D 1-1	Strong	56,034
Apr 27	Blackpool	L 2-3	Sammels, Skirton	13,864
May 6	Manchester United	W 3-2	Baker, Strong, Skirton	36,000
May 11	BURNLEY	L 2-3	Skirton, Baker	23,256
May 14	FULHAM	W 3-0	Baker 3	17,839
May 18	Sheffield Wednesday	W 3-2	Baker, Eastham, Court	20,514

FA Cup

Date	Opponents	Round	Score	Goalscorers	Attendance
Jan 30	OXFORD UNITED	(Rd3)	W 5-1	Baker 2, Strong 2, MacLeod	14,649
Mar 12	SHEFFIELD WEDNESDAY	(Rd4)	W 2-0	MacLeod, Strong	40,367
Mar 16	LIVERPOOL	(Rd5)	L 1-2	MacLeod	55,245

League & Cup Appearances

PLAYER	LEAGUE	CUP COMPETITION FA CUP	TOTAL
Anderson	5		5
Armstrong	16		16
Bacuzzi	6		6
Baker	39	3	42
Barnwell	34	3	37
Brown	38	3	41
Clamp	4		4
Clarke	5		5
Court	6	1	7
Eastham	33	3	36
Groves	9		9
MacLeod	33	3	36
McClelland	33	3	36
McCullough	42	3	45
McKechnie	9		9
Magill	36	3	39
Neill	17		17
Sammels	2		2
Skirton	28	2	30
Smithson	2		2
Snedden	27	3	30
Strong	36	3	39
Ward	2		2

Goalscorers

PLAYER	LEAGUE	CUP COMPETITION FA CUP	TOTAL
Baker	29	2	31
Strong	18	3	21
MacLeod	9	3	12
Skirton	10		10
Eastham	4		4
Court	3		3
McCullough	3		3
Armstrong	2		2
Barnwell	2		2
Anderson	1		1
Brown	1		1
Clamp	1		1
Sammels	1		1
Opps' o.gs.	2		2

Fact File

Billy Wright's first move in the transfer market was to bring England centre forward Joe Baker back to Britain from Italian club Torino. Baker was a rarity, an Englishman who spoke with a Scots accent. He was born in Liverpool but brought up in Lanarkshire. He even played for Scotland Schoolboys before making his name with Hibernian. Baker made an immediate impression and finished top scorer in all his four seasons with the Gunners.

MANAGER: Billy Wright

CAPTAIN: George Eastham

TOP SCORER: Joe Baker 31 (29 League)

BIGGEST WIN: 5-1 v Oxford United, 30 January 1963, FA Cup

HIGHEST ATTENDANCE: 62,308 v Manchester United, 25 August 1962, League

MAJOR TRANSFER IN: Joe Baker from Torino

MAJOR TRANSFER OUT: Danny Clapton to Luton Town

Final Division One Table

		P	W	D	L	F	A	Pts
1	EVERTON	42	25	11	6	84	42	61
2	TOTTENHAM H	42	23	9	10	111	62	55
3	BURNLEY	42	22	10	10	78	57	54
4	LEICESTER C	42	20	12	10	79	53	52
5	WOLVERHAMPTON W	42	20	10	12	93	65	50
6	SHEFFIELD W	42	19	10	13	77	63	48
7	ARSENAL	42	18	10	14	86	77	46
8	LIVERPOOL	42	17	10	15	71	59	44
9	NOTTINGHAM F	42	17	10	15	67	69	44
10	SHEFFIELD U	42	16	12	14	58	60	44
11	BLACKBURN R	42	15	12	15	79	71	42
12	WEST HAM U	42	14	12	16	73	69	40
13	BLACKPOOL	42	13	14	15	58	64	40
14	WBA	42	16	7	19	71	79	39
15	ASTON VILLA	42	15	8	19	62	68	38
16	FULHAM	42	14	10	18	50	71	38
17	IPSWICH T	42	12	11	19	59	78	35
18	BOLTON W	42	15	5	22	55	75	35
19	MANCHESTER U	42	12	10	20	67	81	34
20	BIRMINGHAM C	42	10	13	19	63	90	33
21	MANCHESTER C	42	10	11	21	58	102	31
22	LEYTON ORIENT	42	6	9	27	37	81	21

Season 1963-64

Football League Division One

DATE	OPPONENTS	SCORE	GOALSCORERS	ATTENDANCE
Aug 24	WOLVERHAMPTON WANDERERS	L 1-3	Strong	50,302
Aug 27	WEST BROMWICH ALBION	W 3-2	Baker 2, Strong	31,381
Aug 31	Leicester City	L 2-7	Barnwell (pen), MacLeod	29,620
Sep 4	West Bromwich Albion	L 0-4		24,500
Sep 7	BOLTON WANDERERS	W 4-3	Skirton 2, Baker, Ure	26,016
Sep 10	ASTON VILLA	W 3-0	Baker 3	29,189
Sep 14	Fulham	W 4-1	Strong 2, Baker, MacLeod	34,910
Sep 21	MANCHESTER UNITED	W 2-1	Eastham, Baker	56,776
Sep 28	Burnley	W 3-0	Strong 2, Eastham	20,618
Oct 2	Everton	L 1-2	Strong	51,829
Oct 5	IPSWICH TOWN	W 6-0	Strong 3, Baker 2, MacLeod	31,803
Oct 9	Stoke City	W 2-1	Baker 2	31,014
Oct 15	TOTTENHAM HOTSPUR	D 4-4	Eastham 2, Baker, Strong	67,986
Oct 19	Aston Villa	L 1-2	MacLeod	22,981
Oct 26	NOTTINGHAM FOREST	W 4-2	Strong 2, Anderson, o.g.	41,124
Nov 2	Sheffield United	D 2-2	Baker, Strong	33,908
Nov 5	BIRMINGHAM CITY	W 4-1	Baker 3, Strong	23,499
Nov 9	WEST HAM UNITED	D 3-3	MacLeod, Eastham, Anderson	52,742
Nov 16	Chelsea	L 1-3	Eastham	47,050
Nov 23	BLACKPOOL	W 5-3	Strong 2, Barnwell, Brown, Eastham	33,847
Nov 30	Blackburn Rovers	L 1-4	Baker	21,000
Dec 7	LIVERPOOL	D 1-1	Baker	40,551
Dec 10	EVERTON	W 6-0	Baker 2, Eastham 2, Armstrong, Strong	33,644
Dec 14	Wolverhampton Wanderers	D 2-2	Strong 2	18,952
Dec 21	LEICESTER CITY	L 0-1		28,019
Dec 28	Birmingham City	W 4-1	MacLeod 2, Baker, Armstrong	23,329
Jan 11	Bolton Wanderers	D 1-1	Baker	14,651
Jan 18	FULHAM	D 2-2	Baker, Strong	35,895
Feb 1	Manchester United	L 1-3	McCullough	48,340
Feb 8	BURNLEY	W 3-2	Strong, Armstrong, Anderson	30,863
Feb 18	Ipswich Town	W 2-1	Eastham, Strong	17,486
Feb 22	Tottenham Hotspur	L 1-3	Strong	57,358
Feb 29	STOKE CITY	D 1-1	Baker	26,208
Mar 7	Nottingham Forest	L 0-2		18,416
Mar 14	CHELSEA	L 2-4	Neill, Baker	25,513
Mar 21	West Ham United	D 1-1	Skirton	28,170
Mar 24	SHEFFIELD WEDNESDAY	D 1-1	Strong	18,221
Mar 28	SHEFFIELD UNITED	L 1-3	Strong	21,001
Mar 30	Sheffield Wednesday	W 4-0	Skirton 3, Court	26,433
Apr 4	Blackpool	W 1-0	Skirton	14,067
Apr 11	BLACKBURN ROVERS	D 0-0		26,164
Apr 18	Liverpool	L 0-5		48,623

FA Cup

Jan 4	WOLVERHAMPTON W.	(Rd3)	W 2-1	Strong, Baker	40,803
Jan 25	West Bromwich Albion	(Rd4)	D 3-3	MacLeod, Armstrong, Baker	39,597
Jan 29	WEST BROMWICH ALBION	(R)	W 2-0	Armstrong, Strong	57,698
Feb 15	LIVERPOOL	(Rd5)	L 0-1		61,295

Inter-Cities' Fairs Cup

Sep 25	Staevnet	(Rd1/1L)	W 7-1	Strong 3, Baker 3, MacLeod	15,000
Oct 22	STAEVNET	(Rd1/2L)	L 2-3	Skirton, Barnwell	13,569
Nov 13	RFC LIEGE	(Rd2/1L)	D 1-1	Anderson	22,003
Dec 18	RFC Liege	(Rd2/2L)	L 1-3	McCullough	10,000

Fact File

Arsenal's seventh place in 1962-63 qualified them for European football for the first time. Their Fairs Cup first round opponents, Staevnet, were a combined team formed from Copenhagen clubs.

MANAGER: Billy Wright

CAPTAIN: George Eastham

TOP SCORER: Joe Baker 31 (26 League), Geoff Strong 31 (26 League)

BIGGEST WIN: 7-1 v Staevnet, 25 September 1963, Fairs Cup

HIGHEST ATTENDANCE: 67,986 v Tottenham Hotspur, 15 October 1963, League

MAJOR TRANSFERS IN: Ian Ure from Dundee, Jim Furnell from Liverpool

MAJOR TRANSFER OUT: Laurie Brown to Tottenham Hotspur

League & Cup Appearances

PLAYER	LEAGUE	CUP COMPETITION		TOTAL
		FA CUP	ICFC	
Anderson	10		1	11
Armstrong	28	4	3	35
Bacuzzi	5			5
Baker	39	4	2	45
Barnwell	19	1	3	23
Brown	22		3	25
Clarke	5			5
Court	8		2	10
Eastham	38	4	3	45
Furnell	21	4	1	26
Groves	15	3	2	20
MacLeod	30	3	3	36
McClelland	5			5
McCullough	40	4	4	48
McKechnie	11		2	13
Magill	35	4	4	43
Neill	11			11
Radford	1			1
Simpson	6			6
Skirton	15	1	1	17
Snedden	14	4	1	19
Strong	38	4	4	46
Ure	41	4	4	49
Wilson	5		1	6

Goalscorers

PLAYER	LEAGUE	CUP COMPETITION		TOTAL
		FA CUP	ICFC	
Baker	26	2	3	31
Strong	26	2	3	31
Eastham	10			10
MacLeod	7	1	1	9
Skirton	7		1	8
Armstrong	3	2		5
Anderson	3		1	4
Barnwell	2		1	3
McCullough	1		1	2
Brown	1			1
Court	1			1
Neill	1			1
Ure	1			1
Opps' o.gs.	1			1

Final Division One Table

		P	W	D	L	F	A	Pts
1	LIVERPOOL	42	26	5	11	92	45	57
2	MANCHESTER U	42	23	7	12	90	62	53
3	EVERTON	42	21	10	11	84	64	52
4	TOTTENHAM H	42	22	7	13	97	81	51
5	CHELSEA	42	20	10	12	72	56	50
6	SHEFFIELD W	42	19	11	12	84	67	49
7	BLACKBURN R	42	18	10	14	89	65	46
8	ARSENAL	42	17	11	14	90	82	45
9	BURNLEY	42	17	10	15	71	64	44
10	WBA	42	16	11	15	70	61	43
11	LEICESTER C	42	16	11	15	61	58	43
12	SHEFFIELD U	42	16	11	15	61	64	43
13	NOTTINGHAM F	42	16	9	17	64	68	41
14	WEST HAM U	42	14	12	16	69	74	40
15	FULHAM	42	13	13	16	58	65	39
16	WOLVERHAMPTON W	42	12	15	15	70	80	39
17	STOKE C	42	14	10	18	77	78	38
18	BLACKPOOL	42	13	9	20	52	73	35
19	ASTON VILLA	42	11	12	19	62	71	34
20	BIRMINGHAM C	42	11	7	24	54	92	29
21	BOLTON W	42	10	8	24	48	80	28
22	IPSWICH T	42	9	7	26	56	121	25

Season 1964-65

Football League Division One

DATE	OPPONENTS	SCORE	GOALSCORERS	ATTENDANCE
Aug 22	Liverpool	L 2-3	Baker, Strong	47,620
Aug 25	SHEFFIELD WEDNESDAY	D 1-1	Simpson	35,590
Aug 29	ASTON VILLA	W 3-1	Armstrong, MacLeod, Strong	28,732
Sep 2	Sheffield Wednesday	L 1-2	Baker	22,555
Sep 5	Wolverhampton Wanderers	W 1-0	Skirton	23,000
Sep 9	BLACKBURN ROVERS	D 1-1	Baker	29,510
Sep 12	SUNDERLAND	W 3-1	Eastham 2, Strong	34,291
Sep 16	Blackburn Rovers	W 2-1	Armstrong, Baker	17,675
Sep 19	Leicester City	W 3-2	Baker, Court, Eastham	21,364
Sep 26	CHELSEA	L 1-3	Court	54,936
Oct 6	NOTTINGHAM FOREST	L 0-3		35,041
Oct 10	Tottenham Hotspur	L 1-3	Baker	55,959
Oct 17	BURNLEY	W 3-2	Baker, Simpson, Sammels	24,962
Oct 24	Sheffield United	L 0-4		16,906
Oct 31	EVERTON	W 3-1	Baker 2, Anderson	33,561
Nov 7	Birmingham City	W 3-2	Baker, Eastham, Sammels	20,210
Nov 11	Leeds United	L 1-3	Sammels	38,620
Nov 14	WEST HAM UNITED	L 0-3		36,026
Nov 21	West Bromwich Albion	D 0-0		18,000
Nov 28	MANCHESTER UNITED	L 2-3	Anderson, Eastham	59,637
Dec 5	Fulham	W 4-3	Baker 2, Skirton, Armstrong	13,764
Dec 12	LIVERPOOL	D 0-0		25,171
Dec 19	Aston Villa	L 1-3	Baker	16,000
Dec 26	STOKE CITY	W 3-2	Baker, Sammels, McLintock	27,663
Dec 28	Stoke City	L 1-4	Sammels	20,491
Jan 2	WOLVERHAMPTON WANDERERS	W 4-1	Radford 3, Baker	25,261
Jan 16	Sunderland	W 2-0	Radford, Baker	42,158
Jan 23	LEICESTER CITY	W 4-3	Baker 2, Eastham, Armstrong	31,063
Feb 6	Chelsea	L 1-2	Radford	46,798
Feb 13	LEEDS UNITED	L 1-2	Eastham	32,132
Feb 20	FULHAM	W 2-0	Radford, Baker	22,101
Feb 23	TOTTENHAM HOTSPUR	W 3-1	Baker 2, Radford	48,367
Feb 27	Burnley	L 1-2	Court	12,841
Mar 6	SHEFFIELD UNITED	D 1-1	Ure	22,001
Mar 13	Nottingham Forest	L 0-3		24,497
Mar 27	West Ham United	L 1-2	Baker	24,665
Apr 3	WEST BROMWICH ALBION	D 1-1	Eastham	18,797
Apr 6	BIRMINGHAM CITY	W 3-0	Baker, Skirton, McLintock	16,048
Apr 16	Blackpool	D 1-1	Eastham	18,620
Apr 19	BLACKPOOL	W 3-1	Baker 2, Neill	17,063
Apr 24	Everton	L 0-1		32,643
Apr 26	Manchester United	L 1-3	Eastham	51,625

FA Cup

DATE	OPPONENTS		SCORE	GOALSCORERS	ATTENDANCE
Jan 9	Darlington	(Rd3)	W 2-0	Radford, Armstrong	19,717
Jan 30	Peterborough United	(Rd4)	L 1-2	Radford	32,000

League & Cup Appearances

PLAYER	LEAGUE	CUP COMPETITION FA CUP	TOTAL
Anderson	10		10
Armstrong	40	2	42
Baker	42	2	44
Baldwin	1		1
Burns	24	2	26
Clarke	15	2	17
Court	33	2	35
Eastham	42	2	44
Ferry	11		11
Furnell	18		18
Howe	40	2	42
MacLeod	1		1
McCullough	30		30
McLintock	25	2	27
Magill	1		1
Neill	29		29
Radford	13	2	15
Sammels	17		17
Simpson	6		6
Skirton	22	2	24
Snedden	3		3
Strong	12		12
Tawse	5		5
Ure	22	2	24

Goalscorers

PLAYER	LEAGUE	CUP COMPETITION FA CUP	TOTAL
Baker	25		25
Eastham	10		10
Radford	7	2	9
Sammels	5		5
Armstrong	4	1	5
Court	3		3
Skirton	3		3
Strong	3		3
Anderson	2		2
McLintock	2		2
Simpson	2		2
MacLeod	1		1
Neill	1		1
Ure	1		1

Fact File

Arsenal's FA Cup defeat by Peterborough, then in the Third Division, increased the pressure on Billy Wright. The shock was of almost Walsall proportions, especially as John Radford had given Arsenal the lead. This was also the season that two key figures in Arsenal's 1970-71 'Double' success arrived – Don Howe and Frank McLintock.

MANAGER: Billy Wright

CAPTAIN: George Eastham

TOP SCORER: Joe Baker 25 (all League)

BIGGEST WIN: 4-1 v Wolverhampton Wanderers, 2 January 1965, League

HIGHEST ATTENDANCE: 59,637 v Manchester United, 28 November 1964, League

MAJOR TRANSFERS IN: Don Howe from West Bromwich Albion, Frank McLintock from Leicester City

MAJOR TRANSFERS OUT: Johnny MacLeod to Aston Villa, Jack McClelland to Fulham, Geoff Strong to Liverpool

Final Division One Table

		P	W	D	L	F	A	Pts
1	MANCHESTER U	42	26	9	7	89	39	61
2	LEEDS U	42	26	9	7	83	52	61
3	CHELSEA	42	24	8	10	89	54	56
4	EVERTON	42	17	15	10	69	60	49
5	NOTTINGHAM F	42	17	13	12	71	67	47
6	TOTTENHAM H	42	19	7	16	87	71	45
7	LIVERPOOL	42	17	10	15	67	73	44
8	SHEFFIELD W	42	16	11	15	57	55	43
9	WEST HAM U	42	19	4	19	82	71	42
10	BLACKBURN R	42	16	10	16	83	79	42
11	STOKE C	42	16	10	16	67	66	42
12	BURNLEY	42	16	10	16	70	70	42
13	ARSENAL	42	17	7	18	69	75	41
14	WBA	42	13	13	16	70	65	39
15	SUNDERLAND	42	14	9	19	64	74	37
16	ASTON VILLA	42	16	5	21	57	82	37
17	BLACKPOOL	42	12	11	19	67	78	35
18	LEICESTER C	42	11	13	18	69	85	35
19	SHEFFIELD U	42	12	11	19	50	64	35
20	FULHAM	42	11	12	19	60	78	34
21	WOLVERHAMPTON W	42	13	4	25	59	89	30
22	BIRMINGHAM C	42	8	11	23	64	96	27

Season 1965-66

Football League Division One

DATE	OPPONENTS	SCORE	GOALSCORERS	ATTENDANCE
Aug 21	STOKE CITY	W 2-1	Baker 2	30,107
Aug 25	Northampton Town	D 1-1	Baldwin	17,352
Aug 28	Burnley	D 2-2	Eastham, Baker	16,737
Sep 4	CHELSEA	L 1-3	Baker	45,456
Sep 7	Nottingham Forest	W 1-0	Sammels	30,431
Sep 11	Tottenham Hotspur	D 2-2	Baker, o.g.	53,962
Sep 14	NOTTINGHAM FOREST	W 1-0	Eastham	34,542
Sep 18	Everton	L 1-3	Baker	38,935
Sep 25	MANCHESTER UNITED	W 4-2	Baker, Radford, Armstrong, Eastham	56,757
Sep 28	NORTHAMPTON TOWN	D 1-1	Radford	33,240
Oct 2	Newcastle United	W 1-0	McLintock	42,790
Oct 9	FULHAM	W 2-1	Sammels, Baker	32,318
Oct 16	Blackpool	L 3-5	Armstrong, Radford, o.g.	19,533
Oct 23	BLACKBURN ROVERS	D 2-2	McLintock, Baker	27,703
Oct 30	Leicester City	L 1-3	Armstrong	22,528
Nov 6	SHEFFIELD UNITED	W 6-2	Baker 2, Skirton 2, Armstrong 2	28,541
Nov 13	Leeds United	L 0-2		36,383
Nov 20	WEST HAM UNITED	W 3-2	Skirton 2, Baker	35,855
Dec 4	ASTON VILLA	D 3-3	Skirton 2, Eastham	25,880
Dec 11	Liverpool	L 2-4	Radford, Baldwin	43,727
Dec 27	Sheffield Wednesday	L 0-4		33,101
Dec 28	SHEFFIELD WEDNESDAY	W 5-2	Eastham 2, Skirton, Sammels, Baker	21,035
Jan 1	Fulham	L 0-1		25,801
Jan 8	LIVERPOOL	L 0-1		43,917
Jan 15	Blackburn Rovers	L 1-2	Radford	12,532
Jan 29	Stoke City	W 3-1	Radford 2, Howe	21,883
Feb 5	BURNLEY	D 1-1	Sammels	28,652
Feb 19	Chelsea	D 0-0		48,641
Mar 5	BLACKPOOL	D 0-0		21,881
Mar 8	TOTTENHAM HOTSPUR	D 1-1	Court	51,805
Mar 12	EVERTON	L 0-1		24,821
Mar 19	Manchester United	L 1-2	Walley	47,246
Mar 26	NEWCASTLE UNITED	L 1-3	o.g.	13,979
Apr 5	WEST BROMWICH ALBION	D 1-1	Skirton	8,738
Apr 11	West Bromwich Albion	D 4-4	Baldwin 2, Radford, Armstrong	20,000
Apr 12	West Ham United	L 1-2	Baldwin	26,022
Apr 20	Sunderland	W 2-0	Skirton, Sammels	32,349
Apr 23	SUNDERLAND	D 1-1	Sammels	25,699
Apr 25	Sheffield United	L 0-3		15,045
Apr 30	Aston Villa	L 0-3		18,866
May 5	LEEDS UNITED	L 0-3		4,554
May 7	LEICESTER CITY	W 1-0	o.g.	16,435

FA Cup

Jan 22	Blackburn Rovers	(Rd3) L 0-3		22,951

League & Cup Appearances

PLAYER	LEAGUE	CUP COMPETITION FA CUP	TOTAL
Armstrong	39	1	40
Baker	24	1	25
Baldwin	8		8
Burns	7		7
Court	38		38
Eastham	37	1	38
Furnell	31	1	32
Howe	29	1	30
McCullough	17		17
McGill	2		2
McLintock	36	1	37
Neill	39	1	40
Neilson	2		2
Pack	1		1
Radford	32		32
Sammels	32	1	33
Simpson	5 (3)		5 (3)
Skirton	23 (1)	1	24 (1)
Storey	28	1	29
Ure	21		21
Walley	7 (3)	1	8 (3)
Wilson	4		4

Goalscorers

PLAYER	LEAGUE	CUP COMPETITION FA CUP	TOTAL
Baker	13		13
Skirton	9		9
Radford	8		8
Armstrong	6		6
Eastham	6		6
Sammels	6		6
Baldwin	5		5
McLintock	2		2
Court	1		1
Howe	1		1
Walley	1		1
Opps' o.gs.	4		4

Fact File

Billy Wright quit as Arsenal slipped to 14th place, their lowest since 1930. The attendance of 4,554 for Leeds' visit on 5 May was the lowest-ever for a senior competitive game at Highbury. It was a wet night and the game clashed with live TV coverage of the Cup-Winners' Cup final between Liverpool and Borussia Dortmund. The few who attended made their feelings clear. After Leeds had gone 3-0 up, a fan with a bugle even played 'The Last Post' for Arsenal.

MANAGER: Billy Wright

CAPTAIN: George Eastham/Terry Neill

TOP SCORER: Joe Baker 13 (all League)

BIGGEST WIN: 6-2 v Sheffield United, 6 November 1965, League

HIGHEST ATTENDANCE: 56,757 v Manchester United, 25 September 1965, League

MAJOR TRANSFERS OUT: Jimmy Magill to Brighton, Billy McCullough to Millwall, Joe Baker to Nottingham Forest

Final Division One Table

		P	W	D	L	F	A	Pts
1	LIVERPOOL	42	26	9	7	79	34	61
2	LEEDS U	42	23	9	10	79	38	55
3	BURNLEY	42	24	7	11	79	47	55
4	MANCHESTER U	42	18	15	9	84	59	51
5	CHELSEA	42	22	7	13	65	53	51
6	WBA	42	19	12	11	91	69	50
7	LEICESTER C	42	21	7	14	80	65	49
8	TOTTENHAM H	42	16	12	14	75	66	44
9	SHEFFIELD U	42	16	11	15	56	59	43
10	STOKE C	42	15	12	15	65	64	42
11	EVERTON	42	15	11	16	56	62	41
12	WEST HAM U	42	15	9	18	70	83	39
13	BLACKPOOL	42	14	9	19	55	65	37
14	ARSENAL	42	12	13	17	62	75	37
15	NEWCASTLE U	42	14	9	19	50	63	37
16	ASTON VILLA	42	15	6	21	69	80	36
17	SHEFFIELD W	42	14	8	20	56	66	36
18	NOTTINGHAM F	42	14	8	20	56	72	36
19	SUNDERLAND	42	14	8	20	51	72	36
20	FULHAM	42	14	7	21	67	85	35
21	NORTHAMPTON T	42	10	13	19	55	92	33
22	BLACKBURN R	42	8	4	30	57	88	20

Season 1966-67

Football League Division One

DATE	OPPONENTS	SCORE	GOALSCORERS	ATTENDANCE
Aug 20	Sunderland	W 3-1	Skirton 2, Armstrong	33,304
Aug 23	WEST HAM UNITED	W 2-1	Radford, Baldwin	40,614
Aug 27	ASTON VILLA	W 1-0	Baldwin	26,762
Aug 29	West Ham United	D 2-2	McLintock, Sammels	34,964
Sep 3	Tottenham Hotspur	L 1-3	Sammels	56,271
Sep 6	SHEFFIELD WEDNESDAY	D 1-1	Sammels	28,898
Sep 10	Manchester City	D 1-1	Sammels	27,948
Sep 17	BLACKPOOL	D 1-1	Coakley	28,946
Sep 24	Chelsea	L 1-3	Addison	48,001
Oct 1	LEICESTER CITY	L 2-4	Addison, Graham	33,945
Oct 8	NEWCASTLE UNITED	W 2-0	Boot, o.g.	24,595
Oct 15	Leeds United	L 1-3	Boot	31,481
Oct 22	WEST BROMWICH ALBION	L 2-3	Armstrong 2	31,606
Oct 29	Manchester United	L 0-1		45,387
Nov 5	LEEDS UNITED	L 0-1		24,227
Nov 12	Everton	D 0-0		45,745
Nov 19	FULHAM	W 1-0	McLintock	25,755
Nov 26	Nottingham Forest	L 1-2	Neilson	20,482
Dec 3	BURNLEY	D 0-0		23,220
Dec 10	Sheffield United	D 1-1	Graham	15,488
Dec 17	SUNDERLAND	W 2-0	McLintock, Sammels	20,482
Dec 26	SOUTHAMPTON	W 4-1	Radford 2, Armstrong 2	29,527
Dec 27	Southampton	L 1-2	Addison	27,781
Dec 31	Aston Villa	W 1-0	McLintock	19,431
Jan 7	TOTTENHAM HOTSPUR	L 0-2		49,851
Jan 14	MANCHESTER CITY	W 1-0	McLintock	22,392
Jan 21	Blackpool	W 3-0	Sammels 2, Neilson	12,028
Feb 4	CHELSEA	W 2-1	Graham, Armstrong	52,467
Feb 11	Leicester City	L 1-2	Graham	24,587
Feb 25	Newcastle United	L 1-2	Graham	27,460
Mar 3	MANCHESTER UNITED	D 1-1	Sammels	63,563
Mar 8	West Bromwich Albion	W 1-0	McLintock	16,500
Mar 25	SHEFFIELD UNITED	W 2-0	Sammels, McLintock	23,099
Mar 27	Liverpool	D 0-0		46,168
Mar 28	LIVERPOOL	D 1-1	Graham	35,877
Apr 1	Stoke City	D 2-2	Graham 2	14,606
Apr 19	Fulham	D 0-0		27,690
Apr 22	NOTTINGHAM FOREST	D 1-1	Storey	36,196
Apr 25	EVERTON	W 3-1	Sammels, Graham, McLintock	20,567
Apr 29	Burnley	W 4-1	Addison, Graham, Armstrong, Simpson	10,947
May 6	STOKE CITY	W 3-1	Radford, McLintock, o.g.	24,611
May 13	Sheffield Wednesday	D 1-1	Graham	23,222

FA Cup

Jan 28	Bristol Rovers	(Rd3) W 3-0	Graham, Neilson, Armstrong	35,420
Feb 18	Bolton Wanderers	(Rd4) D 0-0		31,870
Feb 22	BOLTON WANDERERS	(R) W 3-0	Radford 3	47,050
Mar 11	Birmingham City	(Rd5) L 0-1		40,665

League Cup

Sep 13	GILLINGHAM	(Rd2) D 1-1	Baldwin	13,029
Sep 22	Gillingham	(R) D 1-1	Baldwin	20,566
Sep 28	GILLINGHAM	(2R) W 5-0	Baldwin 2, McLintock 2, Coakley	18,409
Oct 5	WEST HAM UNITED	(Rd3) L 1-3	Jenkins	33,647

League & Cup Appearances

PLAYER	LEAGUE	CUP COMPETITION		TOTAL
		FA CUP	LC	
Addison	17	2		19
Armstrong	40	4	3	47
Baldwin	8		3	11
Boot	3 (1)		1	4 (1)
Coakley	9		4	13
Court	10 (3)	1		11 (3)
Furnell	42	4	4	50
Graham	33	4		37
Howe	1		1	2
Jenkins			2	2
McGill	4 (4)		2	6 (4)
McLintock	40	3	2	45
McNab	25 (1)	1		26 (1)
Neill	34	4	3	41
Neilson	12	3		15
Radford	30	3	1	34
Sammels	42	4	4	50
Simpson	34 (2)	4		40 (2)
Skirton	2			2
Storey	34	4	3	41
Tyrer			1 (1)	1 (1)
Ure	37	3	4	44
Walley	3 (1)		3	6 (1)
Woodward	1		1	2

Goalscorers

PLAYER	LEAGUE	CUP COMPETITION		TOTAL
		FA CUP	LC	
Graham	11	1		12
McLintock	9		2	11
Sammels	10			10
Armstrong	7	1		8
Radford	4	3		7
Baldwin	2		4	6
Addison	4			4
Neilson	2	1		3
Boot	2			2
Skirton	2			2
Coakley	1		1	2
Simpson	1			1
Storey	1			1
Jenkins			1	1
Opps' o.gs.	2			2

Fact File

Bertie Mee had been the club physio before taking the manager's job, prompting media comments about Arsenal 'sending for the medicine man'. A young striker called George Graham arrived from Chelsea in a swop deal with Tommy Baldwin. Arsenal entered the League Cup for the first time.

MANAGER: Bertie Mee **CAPTAIN:** Frank McLintock

TOP SCORER: George Graham 12 (11 League)

BIGGEST WIN: 5-0 v Gillingham, 28 September 1966, League Cup

HIGHEST ATTENDANCE: 63,563 v Manchester United, 3 March 1966, League

MAJOR TRANSFERS IN: Colin Addison from Nottingham Forest, George Graham from Chelsea, Bob McNab from Huddersfield Town

MAJOR TRANSFERS OUT: George Eastham to Stoke City, Alan Skirton to Blackpool, Tommy Baldwin to Chelsea

Final Division One Table

		P	W	D	L	F	A	Pts
1	MANCHESTER U	42	24	12	6	84	45	60
2	NOTTINGHAM F	42	23	10	9	64	41	56
3	TOTTENHAM H	42	24	8	10	71	48	56
4	LEEDS U	42	22	11	9	62	42	55
5	LIVERPOOL	42	19	13	10	64	47	51
6	EVERTON	42	19	10	13	65	46	48
7	ARSENAL	42	16	14	12	58	47	46
8	LEICESTER C	42	18	8	16	78	71	44
9	CHELSEA	42	15	14	13	67	62	44
10	SHEFFIELD U	42	16	10	16	52	59	42
11	SHEFFIELD W	42	14	13	15	56	47	41
12	STOKE C	42	17	7	18	63	58	41
13	WBA	42	16	7	19	77	73	39
14	BURNLEY	42	15	9	18	66	76	39
15	MANCHESTER C	42	12	15	15	43	52	39
16	WEST HAM U	42	14	8	20	80	84	36
17	SUNDERLAND	42	14	8	20	58	72	36
18	FULHAM	42	11	12	19	71	83	34
19	SOUTHAMPTON	42	14	6	22	74	92	34
20	NEWCASTLE U	42	12	9	21	39	81	33
21	ASTON VILLA	42	11	7	24	54	85	29
22	BLACKPOOL	42	6	9	27	41	76	21

Season 1967-68

Football League Division One

DATE	OPPONENTS	SCORE	GOALSCORERS	ATTENDANCE
Aug 19	STOKE CITY	W 2-0	Graham, Sammels	27,048
Aug 22	Liverpool	L 0-2		52,033
Aug 26	Nottingham Forest	L 0-2		33,991
Aug 28	LIVERPOOL	W 2-0	Sammels, o.g.	33,420
Sep 2	COVENTRY CITY	D 1-1	Graham	30,404
Sep 6	West Bromwich Albion	W 3-1	Armstrong, Sammels, Addison	19,232
Sep 9	Sheffield United	W 4-2	Addison, Graham 2, McLintock	14,939
Sep 16	TOTTENHAM HOTSPUR	W 4-0	Radford, Neill (pen), Graham, Addison	62,836
Sep 23	MANCHESTER CITY	W 1-0	Radford	41,466
Sep 30	Newcastle United	L 1-2	Graham	33,350
Oct 7	Manchester United	L 0-1		60,197
Oct 14	SUNDERLAND	W 2-1	Radford, Graham	30,864
Oct 23	Wolverhampton Wanderers	L 2-3	Graham, Armstrong	36,664
Oct 28	FULHAM	W 5-3	Radford 3, Addison 2	29,974
Nov 4	Leeds United	L 1-3	McLintock	31,632
Nov 11	EVERTON	D 2-2	Johnston, Sammels	36,371
Nov 18	Leicester City	D 2-2	Radford, Johnston	28,150
Nov 25	WEST HAM UNITED	D 0-0		42,029
Dec 2	Burnley	L 0-1		15,381
Dec 16	Stoke City	W 1-0	Graham	16,119
Dec 23	NOTTINGHAM FOREST	W 3-0	Graham 2, Armstrong	32,512
Dec 26	Chelsea	L 1-2	Neill (pen)	51,672
Dec 30	CHELSEA	D 1-1	Radford	47,157
Jan 6	Coventry City	D 1-1	Graham	32,839
Jan 13	SHEFFIELD UNITED	D 1-1	Graham	27,447
Jan 20	Tottenham Hotspur	L 0-1		57,885
Feb 3	Manchester City	D 1-1	Graham	42,392
Feb 10	NEWCASTLE UNITED	D 0-0		36,996
Feb 24	MANCHESTER UNITED	L 0-2		46,417
Mar 16	WOLVERHAMPTON WANDERERS	L 0-2		25,983
Mar 23	Fulham	W 3-1	Graham, Gould, Court	20,612
Mar 29	West Ham United	D 1-1	Armstrong	33,986
Apr 6	Everton	L 0-2		40,029
Apr 10	Southampton	L 0-2		23,207
Apr 13	LEICESTER CITY	W 2-1	Gould, Graham	19,108
Apr 15	SOUTHAMPTON	L 0-3		23,165
Apr 20	Sunderland	L 0-2		31,255
Apr 27	BURNLEY	W 2-0	Court, Armstrong	15,278
Apr 30	SHEFFIELD WEDNESDAY	W 3-2	Court, Radford, Gould	11,262
May 4	Sheffield Wednesday	W 2-1	Radford, Gould	25,066
May 7	LEEDS UNITED	W 4-3	Gould, McLintock, Johnston, o.g.	25,043
May 11	WEST BROMWICH ALBION	W 2-1	Gould, McLintock	24,896

FA Cup

Jan 27	Shrewsbury Town	(Rd3) D 1-1	Radford	18,280
Jan 30	SHREWSBURY TOWN	(R) W 2-0	Sammels, Jenkins	41,958
Feb 17	Swansea Town	(Rd4) W 1-0	Gould	31,919
Mar 9	BIRMINGHAM CITY	(Rd5) D 1-1	Radford	45,515
Mar 12	Birmingham City	(R) L 1-2	Gould	51,586

League Cup

Sep 12	Coventry City	(Rd2) W 2-1	Sammels, Graham	22,605
Oct 11	READING	(Rd3) W 1-0	Simpson	27,866
Nov 1	BLACKBURN ROVERS	(Rd4) W 2-1	Graham, Addison	20,044
Nov 29	Burnley	(QF) D 3-3	Graham 2, McLintock	16,033
Dec 5	BURNLEY	(R) W 2-1	Radford, Neill	36,570
Jan 17	HUDDERSFIELD TOWN	(SF/1L) W 3-2	Graham, Radford, McNab	39,986
Feb 6	Huddersfield Town	(SF/2L) W 3-1	Sammels, Jenkins, McLintock	27,312
Mar 2	Leeds United*	(F) L 0-1		97,887

*Played at Wembley.

MANAGER: Bertie Mee

CAPTAIN: Frank McLintock

TOP SCORER: George Graham 21 (16 League)

BIGGEST WIN: 5-3 v Fulham, 28 October 1967, League

HIGHEST ATTENDANCE: 62,836 v Tottenham Hotspur, 16 September 1967, League

MAJOR TRANSFER IN: Bobby Gould from Coventry City

MAJOR TRANSFER OUT: Colin Addison to Sheffield United

League & Cup Appearances

PLAYER	LEAGUE	CUP COMPETITION		TOTAL
		FA CUP	LC	
Addison	10 (1)		2	12 (1)
Armstrong	42	5	8	55
Court	15 (1)	0 (1)		15 (2)
Davidson	0 (1)			0 (1)
Furnell	29	4	8	41
Gould	15 (1)	3		18 (1)
Graham	38	5	8	51
Jenkins	2 (1)	2	2	6 (1)
Johnston	17 (1)		3 (1)	20 (2)
McLintock	38	5	8	51
McNab	30	3	5	38
Neill	38	4 (1)	7 (1)	49 (2)
Radford	39	5	8	52
Rice	2 (4)		1	3 (4)
Sammels	34 (1)	5	8	47 (1)
Simpson	40	5	8	53
Storey	39	5	7	51
Ure	21	3	5	29
Wilson	13	1		14

Goalscorers

PLAYER	LEAGUE	CUP COMPETITION		TOTAL
		FA CUP	LC	
Graham	16		5	21
Radford	10	2	2	14
Gould	6	2		8
Sammels	4	1	2	7
Addison	5		1	6
McLintock	4		2	6
Armstrong	5			5
Court	3			3
Johnston	3			3
Neill	2		1	3
Jenkins		1	1	2
McNab			1	1
Simpson			1	1
Opps' o.gs.	2			2

Fact File

On a sartorial note, Arsenal reverted to the red shirts with white sleeves introduced by Herbert Chapman. The Gunners had worn plain red shirts for two seasons – a move designed to break with the traditions some believed were weighing down on the club.

Final Division One Table

		P	W	D	L	F	A	Pts
1	MANCHESTER C	42	26	6	10	86	43	58
2	MANCHESTER U	42	24	8	10	89	55	56
3	LIVERPOOL	42	22	11	9	71	40	55
4	LEEDS U	42	22	9	11	71	41	53
5	EVERTON	42	23	6	13	67	40	52
6	CHELSEA	42	18	12	12	62	68	48
7	TOTTENHAM H	42	19	9	14	70	59	47
8	WBA	42	17	12	13	75	62	46
9	ARSENAL	42	17	10	15	60	56	44
10	NEWCASTLE U	42	13	15	14	54	67	41
11	NOTTINGHAM FOREST	42	14	11	17	52	64	39
12	WEST HAM U	42	14	10	18	73	69	38
13	LEICESTER C	42	13	12	17	64	69	38
14	BURNLEY	42	14	10	18	64	71	38
15	SUNDERLAND	42	13	11	18	51	61	37
16	SOUTHAMPTON	42	13	11	18	66	83	37
17	WOLVERHAMPTON W	42	14	8	20	66	75	36
18	STOKE C	42	14	7	21	50	73	35
19	SHEFFIELD W	42	11	12	19	51	63	34
20	COVENTRY C	42	9	15	18	51	71	33
21	SHEFFIELD U	42	11	10	21	49	70	32
22	FULHAM	42	10	7	25	56	98	27

Season 1968-69

Football League Division One

DATE	OPPONENTS	SCORE	GOALSCORERS	ATTENDANCE
Aug 10	Tottenham Hotspur	W 2-1	Radford, o.g.	56,280
Aug 13	LEICESTER CITY	W 3-0	Court, Gould 2	32,164
Aug 17	LIVERPOOL	D 1-1	Radford	43,535
Aug 21	Wolverhampton Wanderers	D 0-0		36,006
Aug 24	Ipswich Town	W 2-1	Radford, Jenkins	25,825
Aug 27	MANCHESTER CITY	W 4-1	Jenkins 2, Sammels, Radford	40,776
Aug 31	QUEENS PARK RANGERS	W 2-1	McLintock, Neill (pen)	44,407
Sep 7	Southampton	W 2-1	Radford 2	25,126
Sep 14	STOKE CITY	W 1-0	Neill	28,275
Sep 21	Leeds United	L 0-2		39,946
Sep 28	SUNDERLAND	D 0-0		35,277
Oct 5	Manchester United	D 0-0		61,843
Oct 9	Manchester City	D 1-1	Radford	33,830
Oct 12	COVENTRY CITY	W 2-1	Court, Radford	35,240
Oct 19	West Bromwich Albion	L 0-1		29,324
Oct 26	WEST HAM UNITED	D 0-0		59,533
Nov 9	NEWCASTLE UNITED	D 0-0		34,277
Nov 16	Nottingham Forest	W 2-0	Armstrong, Radford	24,550
Nov 23	CHELSEA	L 0-1		45,588
Nov 30	Burnley	W 1-0	Robertson	16,264
Dec 7	EVERTON	W 3-1	Radford, Court, Graham	40,108
Dec 14	Coventry City	W 1-0	Gould	27,332
Dec 21	WEST BROMWICH ALBION	W 2-0	Gould, o.g.	30,765
Dec 26	MANCHESTER UNITED	W 3-0	Armstrong, Court, Radford	62,300
Jan 11	SHEFFIELD WEDNESDAY	W 2-0	Gould, Radford	39,008
Jan 18	Newcastle United	L 1-2	Gould	34,227
Feb 1	NOTTINGHAM FOREST	D 1-1	Gould	35,585
Feb 15	BURNLEY	W 2-0	Gould 2	27,614
Feb 18	IPSWICH TOWN	L 0-2		23,891
Mar 1	Sheffield Wednesday	W 5-0	Radford 3, Sammels, Gould	21,436
Mar 22	Queens Park Rangers	W 1-0	Armstrong	23,076
Mar 24	TOTTENHAM HOTSPUR	W 1-0	Sammels	43,972
Mar 29	SOUTHAMPTON	D 0-0		28,990
Mar 31	Liverpool	D 1-1	Robertson	44,843
Apr 5	Sunderland	D 0-0		23,214
Apr 7	WOLVERHAMPTON WANDERERS	W 3-1	Robertson, Armstrong, Graham	31,011
Apr 8	Leicester City	D 0-0		35,573
Apr 12	LEEDS UNITED	L 1-2	Graham	44,715
Apr 14	Chelsea	L 1-2	Court	38,905
Apr 19	Stoke City	W 3-1	Armstrong, Court, o.g.	14,996
Apr 21	West Ham United	W 2-1	Sammels, Graham	34,941
Apr 29	Everton	L 0-1		39,689

FA Cup

Jan 4	Cardiff City	(Rd3) D 0-0		55,316
Jan 7	CARDIFF CITY	(R) W 2-0	Armstrong, Gould	52,681
Jan 25	CHARLTON ATHLETIC	(Rd4) W 2-0	Sammels, Robertson	55,760
Feb 12	West Bromwich Albion	(Rd5) L 0-1		46,000

League Cup

Sep 4	SUNDERLAND	(Rd2) W 1-0	Neill	28,460
Sep 25	Scunthorpe United	(Rd3) W 6-1	Jenkins 3, Gould, Sammels, Court	17,450
Oct 15	LIVERPOOL	(Rd4) W 2-1	Simpson, Radford	39,299
Oct 29	BLACKPOOL	(QF) W 5-1	Armstrong 2, Radford, Gould, Simpson	32,321
Nov 20	TOTTENHAM HOTSPUR	(SF/1L) W 1-0	Radford	55,237
Dec 4	Tottenham Hotspur	(SF/2L) D 1-1	Radford	55,923
Mar 15	Swindon Town*	(F) L 1-3	Gould	98,189

*Played at Wembley.

League & Cup Appearances

PLAYER	LEAGUE	CUP COMPETITION		TOTAL
		FA CUP	LC	
Armstrong	26 (3)	2 (1)	6	34 (4)
Court	40	4	6 (1)	50 (1)
Gould	33 (5)	4	5 (2)	42 (7)
Graham	23 (3)	1	3 (2)	27 (5)
Jenkins	14		2	16
Johnston	0 (3)			0 (3)
McLintock	37	4	7	48
McNab	42	4	7	53
Neill	21 (1)		4	25 (1)
Radford	31 (3)	4	6	41 (3)
Robertson	18 (1)	2		20 (1)
Sammels	36	3	5	44
Simpson	34	4	7	45
Storey	42	4	7	53
Ure	23	4	5	32
Wilson	42	4	7	53

Goalscorers

PLAYER	LEAGUE	CUP COMPETITION		TOTAL
		FA CUP	LC	
Radford	15		4	19
Gould	10	1	3	14
Armstrong	5	1	2	8
Court	6		1	7
Sammels	4	1	1	6
Jenkins	3		3	6
Graham	4			4
Robertson	3	1		4
Neill	2		1	3
Simpson			2	2
McLintock	1			1
Opps' o.gs.	3			3

Fact File

A unique swop deal between North London's great rivals took place in October. Winger Jimmy Robertson moved to Arsenal from Tottenham with striker David Jenkins going in the opposite direction. Arsenal found a new goalkeeper, but he'd been with them for years. Bob Wilson, who had been playing for the reserves while teaching at nearby Holloway school, took over the keeper's jersey and played in every game. Wilson had made his league debut, as an amateur, against Nottingham Forest in October 1963.

Final Division One Table

		P	W	D	L	F	A	PTS
1	LEEDS U	42	27	13	2	66	26	67
2	LIVERPOOL	42	25	11	6	63	24	61
3	EVERTON	42	21	15	6	77	36	57
4	ARSENAL	42	22	12	8	56	27	56
5	CHELSEA	42	20	10	12	73	53	50
6	TOTTENHAM H	42	14	17	11	61	51	45
7	SOUTHAMPTON	42	16	13	13	57	48	45
8	WEST HAM U	42	13	18	11	66	50	44
9	NEWCASTLE U	42	15	14	13	61	55	44
10	WBA	42	16	11	15	64	67	43
11	MANCHESTER U	42	15	12	15	57	53	42
12	IPSWICH T	42	15	11	16	59	60	41
13	MANCHESTER C	42	15	10	17	64	55	40
14	BURNLEY	42	15	9	18	55	82	39
15	SHEFFIELD W	42	10	16	16	41	54	36
16	WOLVERHAMPTON W	42	10	15	17	41	58	35
17	SUNDERLAND	42	11	12	19	43	67	34
18	NOTTINGHAM F	42	10	13	19	45	57	33
19	STOKE C	42	9	15	18	40	63	33
20	COVENTRY C	42	10	11	21	46	64	31
21	LEICESTER C	42	9	12	21	39	68	30
22	QPR	42	4	10	28	39	95	18

MANAGER: Bertie Mee

CAPTAIN: Frank McLintock

TOP SCORER: John Radford 19 (15 League)

BIGGEST WIN: 6-1 v Scunthorpe United, 25 September 1968, League Cup

HIGHEST ATTENDANCE: 62,300 v Manchester United, 26 December 1968, League

MAJOR TRANSFER IN: Jimmy Robertson from Tottenham Hotspur

MAJOR TRANSFERS OUT: Jim Furnell to Rotherham United, David Jenkins to Tottenham Hotspur

Season 1969-70

Football League Division One

DATE	OPPONENTS	SCORE	GOALSCORERS	ATTENDANCE
Aug 9	EVERTON	L 0-1		44,364
Aug 13	Leeds United	D 0-0		37,164
Aug 16	West Bromwich Albion	W 1-0	George	32,215
Aug 19	LEEDS UNITED	D 1-1	Rice	44,923
Aug 23	NOTTINGHAM FOREST	W 2-1	McNab, Graham	30,290
Aug 25	West Ham United	D 1-1	o.g.	39,590
Aug 30	Newcastle United	L 1-3	Robertson	47,208
Sep 6	SHEFFIELD WEDNESDAY	D 0-0		28,605
Sep 13	Burnley	W 1-0	Graham	14,721
Sep 16	TOTTENHAM HOTSPUR	L 2-3	Robertson, Radford	55,280
Sep 20	MANCHESTER UNITED	D 2-2	Graham, Sammels	59,489
Sep 27	Chelsea	L 0-3		46,370
Oct 4	COVENTRY CITY	L 0-1		28,877
Oct 7	WEST BROMWICH ALBION	D 1-1	Radford	21,165
Oct 11	Stoke City	D 0-0		25,801
Oct 18	Sunderland	D 1-1	Sammels	17,864
Oct 25	IPSWICH TOWN	D 0-0		22,458
Nov 1	Crystal Palace	W 5-1	Radford 3, Armstrong, Graham	34,894
Nov 8	DERBY COUNTY	W 4-0	Sammels 2, George, Armstrong	49,763
Nov 15	Wolverhampton Wanderers	L 0-2		26,796
Nov 22	MANCHESTER CITY	D 1-1	Neill (pen)	42,923
Nov 29	Liverpool	W 1-0	Robertson	40,295
Dec 6	SOUTHAMPTON	D 2-2	Sammels, Radford	24,509
Dec 13	BURNLEY	W 3-2	Robertson, Radford, Armstrong	21,404
Dec 20	Sheffield Wednesday	D 1-1	Sammels	17,101
Dec 26	Nottingham Forest	D 1-1	McNab	38,915
Dec 27	NEWCASTLE UNITED	D 0-0		39,637
Jan 10	Manchester United	L 1-2	Marinello	41,055
Jan 17	CHELSEA	L 0-3		53,793
Jan 31	Coventry City	L 0-2		31,661
Feb 7	STOKE CITY	D 0-0		26,601
Feb 14	Everton	D 2-2	George, Radford	48,564
Feb 18	Manchester City	D 1-1	Graham	25,508
Feb 21	Derby County	L 2-3	Radford, Roberts	35,284
Feb 28	SUNDERLAND	W 3-1	Storey (pen), Kennedy, Kelly	21,826
Mar 14	LIVERPOOL	W 2-1	Sammels, Radford	32,295
Mar 21	Southampton	W 2-0	Sammels, George	23,902
Mar 28	WOLVERHAMPTON WANDERERS	D 2-2	Graham 2	32,353
Mar 30	CRYSTAL PALACE	W 2-0	Radford, George	34,144
Mar 31	Ipswich Town	L 1-2	George	25,713
Apr 4	WEST HAM UNITED	W 2-1	Kelly, Radford	36,212
May 2	Tottenham Hotspur	L 0-1		146,949

FA Cup

Jan 3	BLACKPOOL	(Rd 3)	D 1-1	Radford	32,210
Jan 15	Blackpool	(R)	L 2-3	Sammels, Radford	24,801

League Cup

Sep 2	Southampton	(Rd2)	D 1-1	McNab	21,111
Sep 4	SOUTHAMPTON	(R)	W 2-0	Graham 2	26,362
Sep 24	EVERTON	(Rd3)	D 0-0		36,102
Oct 1	Everton	(R)	L 0-1		41,140

Inter-Cities' Fairs Cup

Sep 9	GLENTORAN	(Rd1/1L)	W 3-0	Graham 2, Gould	24,292
Sep 29	Glentoran	(Rd1/2L)	L 0-1		13,000
Oct 29	Sporting Lisbon	(Rd2/1L)	D 0-0		32,000
Nov 26	SPORTING LISBON	(Rd2/2L)	W 3-0	Graham 2, Radford	35,253
Dec 17	Rouen	(Rd3/1L)	D 0-0		12,093
Jan 13	ROUEN	(Rd3/2L)	W 1-0	Sammels	38,018
Mar 11	Dinamo Bacau	(QF/1L)	W 2-0	Sammels, Radford	20,000
Mar 18	DINAMO BACAU	(QF/2L)	W 7-1	Radford 2, George 2, Sammels 2, Graham	35,342
Apr 8	AJAX	(SF/1L)	W 3-0	George 2, Sammels	46,271
Apr 15	Ajax	(SF/2L)	L 0-1		32,000
Apr 22	Anderlecht	(F/1L)	L 1-3	Kennedy	37,000
Apr 28	ANDERLECHT	(F/2L)	W 3-0	Kelly, Radford, Sammels	51,612

MANAGER: Bertie Mee   **CAPTAIN:** Frank McLintock

TOP SCORER: John Radford 19 (12 League)

BIGGEST WIN: 7-1 v Dinamo Bacau, 18 March 1970, Fairs Cup

HIGHEST ATTENDANCE: 59,489 v Manchester United, 20 September 1969, League

MAJOR TRANSFERS IN: John Roberts from Northampton Town, Geoff Barnett from Everton, Peter Marinello from Hibernian

MAJOR TRANSFERS OUT: Ian Ure to Manchester United, Jimmy Robertson to Ipswich Town

---

League & Cup Appearances

PLAYER	LEAGUE	CUP COMPETITION			TOTAL
		FA CUP	LC	ICFC	
Armstrong	17	2	1	8 (2)	28 (2)
Barnett	11		2		13
Court	18 (3)	1	3 (1)	6	28 (4)
George	21 (7)	1	2	8	32 (7)
Gould	9 (2)		1 (1)	2	12 (3)
Graham	36	2	4	10 (1)	52 (1)
Kelly	14 (2)		6 (2)		20 (4)
Kennedy	2 (2)		0 (2)		2 (4)
Marinello	14		4		18
McLintock	30		4	7	41
McNab	37	1	4	11	53
Neill	17	2	1	5	25
Nelson	4	1		1 (1)	6 (1)
Radford	39	2	3	11	55
Rice	7		1	1	9
Roberts	11		2		13
Robertson	27	2	4	5	38
Sammels	36	2	2	12	52
Simpson	39	2	4	12	57
Storey	39	2	4	11	56
Ure	3				3
Webster	3		2	1	6
Wilson	28	2	2	9	41

Goalscorers

PLAYER	LEAGUE	CUP COMPETITION			TOTAL
		FA CUP	LC	ICFC	
Radford	12	2		5	19
Sammels	8	1		6	15
Graham	7		2	5	14
George	6			4	10
Robertson	4				4
Armstrong	3				3
Kelly	2		1		3
McNab	2		1		3
Kennedy	1		1		2
Marinello	1				1
Neill	1				1
Rice	1				1
Roberts	1				1
Storey	1				1
Gould			1		1
Opps' o.gs.	1				1

Fact File

Bertie Mee moved fast to sign an experienced keeper after Bob Wilson was injured at Burnley in September. Arsenal's only back-up was 19-year-old Malcolm Webster, who made his league debut in the North London Derby.

Final Division One Table

		P	W	D	L	F	A	Pts
1	EVERTON	42	29	8	5	72	34	66
2	LEEDS U	42	21	15	6	84	49	57
3	CHELSEA	42	21	13	8	70	50	55
4	DERBY CO	42	22	9	11	64	37	53
5	LIVERPOOL	42	20	11	11	65	42	51
6	COVENTRY C	42	19	11	12	58	48	49
7	NEWCASTLE U	42	17	13	12	57	35	47
8	MANCHESTER U	42	14	17	11	66	61	45
9	STOKE C	42	15	15	12	56	52	45
10	MANCHESTER C	42	16	11	15	55	48	43
11	TOTTENHAM H	42	17	9	16	54	55	43
12	ARSENAL	42	12	18	12	51	49	42
13	WOLVERHAMPTON W	42	12	16	14	55	57	40
14	BURNLEY	42	12	15	15	56	61	39
15	NOTTINGHAM F	42	10	18	14	50	71	38
16	WBA	42	14	9	19	58	66	37
17	WEST HAM U	42	12	12	18	51	60	36
18	IPSWICH T	42	10	11	21	40	63	31
19	SOUTHAMPTON	42	6	17	19	46	67	29
20	CRYSTAL PALACE	42	6	15	21	34	68	27
21	SUNDERLAND	42	6	14	22	30	68	26
22	SHEFFIELD W	42	8	9	25	40	71	25

Season 1970-71

Football League Division One

DATE	OPPONENTS	SCORE	GOALSCORERS	ATTENDANCE
Aug 15	Everton	D 2-2	George, Graham	49,684
Aug 17	West Ham United	D 0-0		39,904
Aug 22	MANCHESTER UNITED	W 4-0	Radford 3, Graham	54,117
Aug 25	HUDDERSFIELD TOWN	W 1-0	Kennedy	34,848
Aug 29	Chelsea	L 1-2	Kelly	53,722
Sep 1	LEEDS UNITED	D 0-0		47,749
Sep 5	TOTTENHAM HOTSPUR	W 2-0	Armstrong 2	48,713
Sep 12	Burnley	W 2-1	Kennedy, Radford	12,675
Sep 19	WEST BROMWICH ALBION	W 6-2	Kennedy 2, Graham 2, Armstrong, o.g.	33,326
Sep 26	Stoke City	L 0-5		18,153
Oct 3	NOTTINGHAM FOREST	W 4-0	Kennedy 3, Armstrong	32,053
Oct 10	Newcastle United	D 1-1	Graham	38,024
Oct 17	EVERTON	W 4-0	Kennedy 2, Kelly, Storey (pen)	50,012
Oct 24	Coventry City	W 3-1	Kennedy, Radford, Graham	30,017
Oct 31	DERBY COUNTY	W 2-0	Kelly, Radford	43,013
Nov 7	Blackpool	W 1-0	Radford	17,115
Nov 14	CRYSTAL PALACE	D 1-1	Radford	34,503
Nov 21	Ipswich Town	W 1-0	Armstrong	22,856
Nov 28	LIVERPOOL	W 2-0	Graham, Radford	45,097
Dec 5	Manchester City	W 2-0	Armstrong, Radford	33,027
Dec 12	WOLVERHAMPTON WANDERERS	W 2-1	Radford, Graham	38,816
Dec 19	Manchester United	W 3-1	McLintock, Graham, Kennedy	33,182
Dec 26	SOUTHAMPTON	D 0-0		34,169
Jan 9	WEST HAM UNITED	W 2-0	Graham, Kennedy	49,007
Jan 16	Huddersfield Town	L 1-2	Kennedy	30,455
Jan 30	Liverpool	L 0-2		43,847
Feb 6	MANCHESTER CITY	W 1-0	Radford	46,122
Feb 20	IPSWICH TOWN	W 3-2	George, Radford, McLintock	39,822
Feb 27	Derby County	L 0-2		35,875
Mar 2	Wolverhampton Wanderers	W 3-0	Armstrong, Kennedy, Radford	33,644
Mar 13	Crystal Palace	W 2-0	Graham, Sammels	35,022
Mar 20	BLACKPOOL	W 1-0	Storey	37,372
Apr 3	CHELSEA	W 2-0	Kennedy 2	62,087
Apr 6	COVENTRY CITY	W 1-0	Kennedy	37,029
Apr 10	Southampton	W 2-1	Radford, McLintock	30,231
Apr 13	Nottingham Forest	W 3-0	McLintock, Kennedy, George	40,727
Apr 17	NEWCASTLE UNITED	W 1-0	George	48,106
Apr 20	BURNLEY	W 1-0	George (pen)	47,484
Apr 24	West Bromwich Albion	D 2-2	McLintock, o.g.	36,858
Apr 26	Leeds United	L 0-1		48,350
May 1	STOKE CITY	W 1-0	Kelly	55,011
May 3	Tottenham Hotspur	W 1-0	Kennedy	51,992

FA Cup

Jan 6	Yeovil Town	(Rd3) W 3-0	Radford 2, Kennedy	14,374
Jan 23	Portsmouth	(Rd4) D 1-1	Storey (pen)	39,659
Feb 1	PORTSMOUTH	(R) W 3-2	George, Simpson, Storey (pen)	47,865
Feb 17	Manchester City	(Rd5) W 2-1	George 2	45,105
Mar 6	Leicester City	(QF) D 0-0		42,000
Mar 15	LEICESTER CITY	(R) W 1-0	George	57,443
Mar 27	Stoke City*	(SF) D 2-2	Storey 2 (1 pen)	53,436
Mar 31	Stoke City**	(R) W 2-0	Graham, Kennedy	62,500
May 8	Liverpool†	(F) W 2-1	Kelly, George	100,000

*Played at Hillsborough. **Played at Villa Park. †Played at Wembley.

League Cup

Sep 8	Ipswich Town	(Rd2) D 0-0		21,564
Sep 28	IPSWICH TOWN	(R) W 4-0	Kennedy 2, Radford, Roberts	26,379
Oct 6	Luton Town	(Rd3) W 1-0	Graham	27,023
Oct 28	Crystal Palace	(Rd4) D 0-0		40,451
Nov 9	CRYSTAL PALACE	(R) L 0-2		45,026

Inter-Cities' Fairs Cup

Sep 16	Lazio	(Rd1/1L) D 2-2	Radford 2	60,000
Sep 23	LAZIO	(Rd1/2L) W 2-0	Radford, Armstrong	53,013
Oct 21	Sturm Graz	(Rd2/1L) L 0-1		13,000
Nov 4	STURM GRAZ	(Rd2/2L) W 2-0	Kennedy, Storey (pen)	37,667
Dec 2	BEVEREN	(Rd3/1L) W 4-0	Kennedy 2, Sammels, Graham	33,444
Dec 16	Beveren	(Rd3/2L) D 0-0		16,000
Mar 9	KOLN	(QF/1L) W 2-1	McLintock, Storey	40,007
Mar 23	Koln	(QF/2L) L 0-1		50,000

League & Cup Appearances

PLAYER	LEAGUE	CUP COMPETITION			TOTAL
		FA CUP	LC	ICFC	
Armstrong	42	9	5	8	64
George	17	7 (1)		2 (1)	26 (2)
Graham	36 (2)	6	5	7 (1)	54 (3)
Kelly	21 (2)	(2)	5	4	30 (4)
Kennedy	41	9	5	8	63
McLintock	42	9	5	7	63
Marinello	1 (2)			0 (1)	1 (3)
McNab	40	9	5	8	62
Nelson	2 (2)		1	0 (1)	3 (3)
Radford	41	9	4	8	62
Rice	41	9	5	8	63
Roberts	18		5	5	28
Sammels	13 (2)	5 (1)		3	21 (3)
Simpson	25	9		4	38
Storey	40	9	5	8	62
Wilson	42	9	5	8	64

Goalscorers

PLAYER	LEAGUE	CUP COMPETITION			TOTAL
		FA CUP	LC	ICFC	
Kennedy	19	2	2	3	26
Radford	15	2	1	3	21
Graham	11	1	1	1	14
George	5	5			10
Armstrong	7			1	8
Storey	2	4		2	8
McLintock	5			1	6
Kelly	4	1			5
Sammels	1			1	2
Roberts			1		1
Simpson		1			1
Opps' o.gs.	2				2

Fact File

Arsenal won the 'Double' using only 16 players. Skipper Frank McLintock was voted Footballer of the Year.

MANAGER: Bertie Mee   **CAPTAIN:** Frank McLintock

TOP SCORER: Ray Kennedy 26 (19 League)

BIGGEST WIN: 6-2 v West Bromwich Albion, 19 September 1970, League

HIGHEST ATTENDANCE: 62,087 v Chelseal, 3 April 1971, League

MAJOR TRANSFERS OUT: Terry Neill to Hull City, David Court to Luton Town, Bobby Gould to Wolverhampton Wanderers, Malcolm Webster to Fulham

Final Division One Table

		P	W	D	L	F	A	Pts
1	ARSENAL	42	29	7	6	71	29	65
2	LEEDS U	42	27	10	5	72	30	64
3	TOTTENHAM H	42	19	14	9	54	33	52
4	WOLVERHAMPTON W	42	22	8	12	64	54	52
5	LIVERPOOL	42	17	17	8	42	24	51
6	CHELSEA	42	18	15	9	52	42	51
7	SOUTHAMPTON	42	17	12	13	56	44	46
8	MANCHESTER U	42	16	11	15	65	66	43
9	DERBY Co	42	16	10	16	56	54	42
10	COVENTRY C	42	16	10	16	37	38	42
11	MANCHESTER C	42	12	17	13	47	42	41
12	NEWCASTLE U	42	14	13	15	44	46	41
13	STOKE C	42	12	13	17	44	48	37
14	EVERTON	42	12	13	17	54	60	37
15	HUDDERSFIELD T	42	11	14	17	40	49	36
16	NOTTINGHAM F	42	14	8	20	42	61	36
17	WBA	42	10	15	17	58	75	35
18	CRYSTAL PALACE	42	12	11	19	39	57	35
19	IPSWICH T	42	12	10	20	42	48	34
20	WEST HAM U	42	10	14	18	47	60	34
21	BURNLEY	42	7	13	22	29	63	27
22	BLACKPOOL	42	4	15	23	34	66	23

Season 1971-72

Football League Division One

DATE	OPPONENTS	SCORE	GOALSCORERS	ATTENDANCE
Aug 14	CHELSEA	W 3-0	McLintock, Kennedy, Radford	49,174
Aug 17	Huddersfield Town	W 1-0	Kennedy	21,279
Aug 20	Manchester United*	L 1-3	McLintock	27,649
Aug 24	SHEFFIELD UNITED	L 0-1		45,395
Aug 28	STOKE CITY	L 0-1		37,637
Sep 4	West Bromwich Albion	W 1-0	Roberts	29,922
Sep 11	LEEDS UNITED	W 2-0	Graham, Storey (pen)	51,196
Sep 18	Everton	L 1-2	Kennedy	39,710
Sep 25	LEICESTER CITY	W 3-0	Radford 2, Rice	40,201
Oct 2	Southampton	W 1-0	Simpson	23,738
Oct 9	NEWCASTLE UNITED	W 4-2	Graham, Kennedy, Armstrong, Kelly	40,509
Oct 16	Chelsea	W 2-1	Kennedy 2	52,338
Oct 23	Derby County	L 1-2	Graham	36,480
Oct 30	IPSWICH TOWN	W 2-1	George, o.g.	39,065
Nov 6	Liverpool	L 2-3	Kennedy, o.g.	46,929
Nov 13	MANCHESTER CITY	L 1-2	Nelson	47,443
Nov 20	Wolverhampton Wanderers	L 1-5	Kennedy	28,251
Nov 24	Tottenham Hotspur	D 1-1	Kennedy	52,884
Nov 27	CRYSTAL PALACE	W 2-1	Kelly, Radford	32,461
Dec 4	West Ham United	D 0-0		35,155
Dec 11	COVENTRY CITY	W 2-0	Radford 2	28,599
Dec 18	WEST BROMWICH ALBION	W 2-0	Roberts 2	28,177
Dec 27	Nottingham Forest	D 1-1	Graham	42,750
Jan 1	EVERTON	D 1-1	Simpson	47,031
Jan 8	Stoke City	D 0-0		18,965
Jan 22	HUDDERSFIELD TOWN	W 1-0	Armstrong	36,670
Jan 29	Sheffield United	W 5-0	George 2, Graham, Simpson, Kennedy	30,778
Feb 12	DERBY COUNTY	W 2-0	George 2 (1 pen)	52,055
Feb 19	Ipswich Town	W 1-0	George	28,657
Mar 4	Manchester City	L 0-2		44,213
Mar 11	Newcastle United	L 0-2		31,920
Mar 25	Leeds United	L 0-3		45,055
Mar 28	SOUTHAMPTON	W 1-0	Marinello	27,172
Apr 1	NOTTINGHAM FOREST	W 3-0	Kennedy, George (pen), Graham	33,895
Apr 4	Leicester City	D 0-0		27,431
Apr 8	WOLVERHAMPTON WANDERERS	W 2-1	Graham 2	38,189
Apr 11	Crystal Palace	D 2-2	Radford, Ball	34,384
Apr 22	WEST HAM UNITED	W 2-1	Ball 2	45,251
Apr 25	MANCHESTER UNITED	W 3-0	Radford, Kennedy, Simpson	49,125
May 2	Coventry City	W 1-0	McLintock	23,509
May 8	LIVERPOOL	D 0-0		39,285
May 11	TOTTENHAM HOTSPUR	L 0-2		42,038

*Played at Anfield.

FA Cup

Jan 15	Swindon Town	(Rd3) W 2-0	Armstrong, Ball	32,000
Feb 5	Reading	(Rd4) W 2-1	Rice, o.g.	25,756
Feb 26	Derby County	(Rd5) D 2-2	George 2	39,622
Feb 29	DERBY COUNTY	(R) D 0-0		63,077
Mar 13	Derby County**	(2R) W 1-0	Kennedy	36,534
Mar 18	Orient	(QF) W 1-0	Ball	31,768
Apr 15	Stoke City†	(SF) D 1-1	Armstrong	56,576
Apr 19	Stoke City††	(R) W 2-1	George, Radford	38,970
May 6	Leeds United#	(F) L 0-1		100,000

**Played at Filbert Street. †Played at Villa Park. ††Played at Goodison Park. #Played at Wembley.

League Cup

Sep 8	BARNSLEY	(Rd2) W 1-0	Kennedy	27,294
Oct 6	NEWCASTLE UNITED	(Rd3) W 2-0	Radford 2, Kennedy, Graham	34,071
Oct 26	SHEFFIELD UNITED	(Rd4) D 0-0		44,061
Nov 8	Sheffield United	(R) L 0-2		35,461

European Cup

Sep 15	Stromsgodset	(Rd1/1L) W 3-1	Simpson, Marinello, Kelly	23,000
Sep 29	STROMSGODSET	(Rd1/2L) W 4-0	Radford 2, Kennedy, Armstrong	27,176
Oct 20	Grasshoppers	(Rd2/1L) W 2-0	Kennedy, Graham	23,000
Nov 3	GRASSHOPPERS	(Rd2/2L) W 3-0	Kennedy, George, Radford	31,105
Mar 8	Ajax	(QF/1L) L 1-2	Kennedy	63,000
Mar 22	AJAX	(QF/2L) L 0-1		56,155

Fact File

Brendon Batson became Arsenal's first black first-team player when he appeared as substitute at Newcastle on 11 March 1972.

League & Cup Appearances

PLAYER	LEAGUE	CUP COMPETITION			TOTAL
		FA CUP	LC	EC	
Armstrong	41 (1)	9	3	5	58 (1)
Ball	18	9			27
Barnett	5	2	1		8
Batson	0 (2)				0 (2)
Davies	0 (1)			0 (1)	0 (2)
George	20 (3)	8	2	5	35 (3)
Graham	39 (1)	9	4	6	58 (1)
Kelly	22 (1)	3	3	3	31 (1)
Kennedy	37	6 (2)	4	6	53 (2)
McLintock	37	9	4	5	55
McNab	20	3	1 (1)	1 (1)	25 (2)
Marinello	4 (4)		1	2	7 (4)
Nelson	24.	6	3	5	38
Radford	34	4 (1)	4	5	47 (1)
Rice	42	9	4	6	61
Roberts	21 (2)		4	4 (1)	29 (3)
Simpson	32 (2)	9	1	4 (1)	46 (3)
Storey	29	6 (1)	2	3	40 (1)
Wilson	37	7	3	6	53

Goalscorers

PLAYER	LEAGUE	CUP COMPETITION			TOTAL
		FA CUP	LC	EC	
Kennedy	12	1	2	4	19
Radford	8	1	2	3	14
George	7	3		1	11
Graham	8		1	1	10
Ball	3	2			5
Simpson	4			1	5
Armstrong	2	2		1	5
McLintock	3				3
Roberts	3				3
Kelly	2		1		3
Marinello	1			1	2
Rice	1	1			2
Nelson	1				1
Storey	1				1
Opps' o.gs.	2	1			3

MANAGER: Bertie Mee

CAPTAIN: Frank McLintock

TOP SCORER: Ray Kennedy 19 (12 League)

BIGGEST WIN: 5-0 v Sheffield United, 29 January 1972, League

HIGHEST ATTENDANCE: 63,007 v Derby County, 29 February 1972, FA Cup

MAJOR TRANSFER IN: Alan Ball from Everton

MAJOR TRANSFER OUT: Jon Sammels to Leicester City

Final Division One Table

		P	W	D	L	F	A	PTS
1	DERBY CO	42	24	10	8	69	33	58
2	LEEDS U	42	24	9	9	73	31	57
3	LIVERPOOL	42	24	9	9	64	30	57
4	MANCHESTER C	42	23	11	8	77	45	57
5	ARSENAL	42	22	8	12	58	40	52
6	TOTTENHAM H	42	19	13	10	63	42	51
7	CHELSEA	42	18	12	12	58	49	48
8	MANCHESTER U	42	19	10	13	69	61	48
9	WOLVERHAMPTON W	42	18	11	13	65	57	47
10	SHEFFIELD U	42	17	12	13	61	60	46
11	NEWCASTLE UNITED	42	15	11	16	49	52	41
12	LEICESTER C	42	13	13	16	41	46	39
13	IPSWICH T	42	11	16	15	39	53	38
14	WEST HAM U	42	12	12	18	47	51	36
15	EVERTON	42	9	18	15	37	48	36
16	WBA	42	12	11	19	42	54	35
17	STOKE C	42	10	15	17	39	56	35
18	COVENTRY C	42	9	15	18	44	67	33
19	SOUTHAMPTON	42	12	7	23	52	80	31
20	CRYSTAL PALACE	42	8	13	21	39	65	29
21	NOTTINGHAM F	42	8	9	25	47	81	25
22	HUDDERSFIELD T	42	6	13	23	27	59	25

Season 1972-73

Football League Division One

DATE	OPPONENTS	SCORE	GOALSCORERS	ATTENDANCE
Aug 12	Leicester City	W 1-0	Ball (pen)	28,009
Aug 15	WOLVERHAMPTON WANDERERS	W 5-2	Radford 2, Kennedy, Simpson, McNab	38,524
Aug 19	STOKE CITY	W 2-0	Kennedy 2	42,146
Aug 22	Coventry City	D 1-1	Rice	24,670
Aug 26	Manchester United	D 0-0		48,108
Aug 29	WEST HAM UNITED	W 1-0	Ball (pen)	43,802
Sep 2	CHELSEA	D 1-1	o.g.	46,675
Sep 9	Newcastle United	L 1-2	Kennedy	23,849
Sep 16	LIVERPOOL	D 0-0		47,597
Sep 23	Norwich City	L 2-3	Storey, Radford	32,273
Sep 26	BIRMINGHAM CITY	W 2-0	Storey, George	30,003
Sep 30	SOUTHAMPTON	W 1-0	Graham	34,694
Oct 7	Sheffield United	L 0-1		24,478
Oct 14	IPSWICH TOWN	W 1-0	Graham	34,196
Oct 21	Crystal Palace	W 3-2	George (pen), Radford, Rice	35,865
Oct 28	MANCHESTER CITY	D 0-0		45,536
Nov 4	COVENTRY CITY	L 0-2		33,699
Nov 11	Wolverhampton Wanderers	W 3-1	Radford 2, Marinello	25,988
Nov 18	EVERTON	W 1-0	Radford	35,728
Nov 25	Derby County	L 0-5		31,034
Dec 2	LEEDS UNITED	W 2-1	Ball (pen), Radford	39,108
Dec 9	Tottenham Hotspur	W 2-1	Storey, Radford	47,505
Dec 16	WEST BROMWICH ALBION	W 2-1	Radford, o.g.	27,119
Dec 23	Birmingham City	D 1-1	Kelly	32,721
Dec 26	NORWICH CITY	W 2-0	Radford, Ball	39,038
Dec 30	Stoke City	D 0-0		24,586
Jan 6	MANCHESTER UNITED	W 3-1	Kennedy, Armstrong, Ball	56,194
Jan 20	Chelsea	W 1-0	Kennedy	36,292
Jan 27	NEWCASTLE UNITED	D 2-2	Kennedy, Ball	37,906
Feb 10	Liverpool	W 2-0	Ball (pen), Radford	49,898
Feb 17	LEICESTER CITY	W 1-0	o.g.	42,047
Feb 28	West Bromwich Albion	L 0-1		23,515
Mar 3	SHEFFIELD UNITED	W 3-2	George 2, Ball	33,346
Mar 10	Ipswich Town	W 2-1	Radford, Ball (pen)	34,646
Mar 24	Manchester City	W 2-1	George, Kennedy	32,031
Mar 26	CRYSTAL PALACE	W 1-0	Ball	41,879
Mar 31	DERBY COUNTY	L 0-1		45,217
Apr 14	TOTTENHAM HOTSPUR	D 1-1	Storey	50,863
Apr 21	Everton	D 0-0		42,888
Apr 23	Southampton	D 2-2	George, Radford	23,919
Apr 28	West Ham United	W 2-1	Kennedy, Radford	37,366
May 9	Leeds United	L 1-6	Armstrong	25,088

FA Cup

Jan 13	LEICESTER CITY	(Rd3) D 2-2	Kennedy, Armstrong	36,433
Jan 17	Leicester City	(R) W 2-1	Radford, Kelly	32,973
Feb 3	BRADFORD CITY	(Rd4) W 2-0	Ball, George	40,407
Feb 24	Carlisle United	(Rd5) W 2-1	Ball, McLintock	23,922
Mar 17	Chelsea	(QF) D 2-2	Ball, George	37,685
Mar 20	CHELSEA	(R) W 2-1	Ball (pen), Kennedy	62,746
Apr 7	Sunderland*	(SF) L 1-2	George	53,301

*Played at Hillsborough

League Cup

Sep 5	EVERTON	(Rd2) W 1-0	Storey	35,230
Oct 3	ROTHERHAM UNITED	(Rd3) W 5-0	Radford 2, George, Storey, Marinello	25,241
Oct 31	Sheffield United	(Rd4) W 2-1	Radford, George	20,128
Nov 21	NORWICH CITY	(QF) L 0-3		37,671

League & Cup Appearances

PLAYER	LEAGUE	CUP COMPETITION		TOTAL
		FA CUP	LC	
Armstrong	29 (1)	7		36 (1)
Ball	40	7	3	50
Barnett	20	1	4	25
Batson	3			3
Blockley	20	4		24
George	18 (9)	4	3	25 (9)
Graham	14 (2)		3	17 (2)
Hornsby	1			1
Kelly	27	7	2	36
Kennedy	34	7	1	42
McLintock	27 (2)	3	4	34 (2)
McNab	42	7	3	52
Marinello	13	0 (1)	4	17 (1)
Nelson	2 (4)	0 (1)	1	3 (5)
Price	0 (1)			0 (1)
Radford	38	3 (1)	4	45 (1)
Rice	39	7	4	50
Roberts	6 (1)		1	7 (1)
Simpson	27	7	3	37
Storey	40	7	4	51
Wilson	22	6		28

Goalscorers

PLAYER	LEAGUE	CUP COMPETITION		TOTAL
		FA CUP	LC	
Radford	15	1	3	19
Ball	10	4		14
Kennedy	9	2		11
George	6	3	2	11
Storey	4		2	6
Armstrong	2	1		3
Graham	2			2
Rice	2			2
Kelly	1	1		2
Marinello	1		1	2
McNab	1			1
Simpson	1			1
McLintock		1		1
Opps' o.gs.	3			3

Fact File

'Double' team skipper Frank McLintock made the last of his 403 appearances for the Gunners in the 1-0 home defeat by Derby on March 31. McLintock was signed from Leicester City on 5 October 1964. He was given a free transfer and was quickly snapped up by promoted Queens Park Rangers.

Final Division One Table

		P	W	D	L	F	A	Pts
1	LIVERPOOL	42	25	10	7	72	42	60
2	ARSENAL	42	23	11	8	57	43	57
3	LEEDS U	42	21	11	10	71	45	53
4	IPSWICH T	42	17	14	11	55	45	48
5	WOLVERHAMPTON W	42	18	11	13	66	54	47
6	WEST HAM U	42	17	12	13	67	53	46
7	DERBY CO	42	19	8	15	56	54	46
8	TOTTENHAM H	42	16	13	13	58	48	45
9	NEWCASTLE UNITED	42	16	13	13	60	51	45
10	BIRMINGHAM C	42	15	12	15	53	54	42
11	MANCHESTER C	42	15	11	16	57	60	41
12	CHELSEA	42	13	14	15	49	51	40
13	SOUTHAMPTON	42	11	18	13	47	52	40
14	SHEFFIELD U	42	15	10	17	51	59	40
15	STOKE C	42	14	10	18	61	56	38
16	LEICESTER C	42	10	17	15	40	46	37
17	EVERTON	42	13	11	18	41	49	37
18	MANCHESTER U	42	12	13	17	44	60	37
19	COVENTRY C	42	13	9	20	40	55	35
20	NORWICH C	42	11	10	21	36	63	32
21	CRYSTAL PALACE	42	9	12	21	41	58	30
22	WBA	42	9	10	23	38	62	28

MANAGER: Bertie Mee

CAPTAIN: Frank McLintock

TOP SCORER: John Radford 19 (15 League)

BIGGEST WIN: 5-0 v Rotherham United, 3 October 1972, League Cup

HIGHEST ATTENDANCE: 62,746 v Chelsea, 20 March 1973, FA Cup

MAJOR TRANSFER IN: Jeff Blockley from Coventry City

MAJOR TRANSFERS OUT: John Roberts to Birmingham City, George Graham to Manchester United, Frank McLintock to Queens Park Rangers

Season 1973-74

Football League Division One

DATE	OPPONENTS	SCORE	GOALSCORERS	ATTENDANCE
Aug 25	MANCHESTER UNITED	W 3-0	Kennedy, Radford, Ball	51,501
Aug 28	LEEDS UNITED	L 1-2	Blockley	47,429
Sep 1	Newcastle United	D 1-1	George	28,697
Sep 4	Sheffield United	L 0-5		27,839
Sep 8	LEICESTER CITY	L 0-2		28,558
Sep 11	SHEFFIELD UNITED	W 1-0	Kennedy	29,434
Sep 15	Norwich City	W 4-0	George, McNab, Ball (pen), Kennedy	29,278
Sep 22	STOKE CITY	W 2-1	Radford, Ball	30,578
Sep 29	Everton	L 0-1		31,359
Oct 6	BIRMINGHAM CITY	W 1-0	Kennedy	23,915
Oct 13	Tottenham Hotspur	L 0-2		41,855
Oct 20	IPSWICH TOWN	D 1-1	Simpson	28,344
Oct 27	Queens Park Rangers	L 0-2		29,115
Nov 3	LIVERPOOL	L 0-2		39,837
Nov 10	Manchester City	W 2-1	Kelly, Hornsby	31,041
Nov 17	CHELSEA	D 0-0		38,677
Nov 24	West Ham United	W 3-1	George, Ball 2	28,287
Dec 1	COVENTRY CITY	D 2-2	Hornsby, Nelson	22,340
Dec 4	WOLVERHAMPTON WANDERERS	D 2-2	George, Hornsby	13,482
Dec 8	Derby County	D 1-1	o.g.	25,161
Dec 15	Burnley	L 1-2	Radford	13,200
Dec 22	EVERTON	W 1-0	Ball	19,886
Dec 26	Southampton	D 1-1	Ball	24,133
Dec 29	Leicester City	L 0-2		25,860
Jan 1	NEWCASTLE UNITED	L 0-1		29,258
Jan 12	NORWICH CITY	W 2-0	Ball 2	22,084
Jan 19	Manchester United	D 1-1	Kennedy	38,589
Feb 2	BURNLEY	D 1-1	Ball	20,789
Feb 5	Leeds United	L 1-3	Ball	26,778
Feb 16	TOTTENHAM HOTSPUR	L 0-1		38,804
Feb 23	Birmingham City	L 1-3	Kennedy	29,822
Mar 2	SOUTHAMPTON	W 1-0	Ball	19,210
Mar 16	Ipswich Town	D 2-2	Kennedy, Simpson	22,297
Mar 23	MANCHESTER CITY	W 2-0	Radford 2	25,319
Mar 30	Stoke City	D 0-0		18,532
Apr 6	WEST HAM UNITED	D 0-0		37,868
Apr 13	Chelsea	W 3-1	Kennedy 2, Radford	29,152
Apr 15	Wolverhampton Wanderers	L 1-3	Kennedy	25,881
Apr 20	DERBY COUNTY	W 2-0	Ball (pen), George	26,017
Apr 24	Liverpool	W 1-0	Kennedy	47,997
Apr 27	Coventry City	D 3-3	Rice, Kennedy, Radford	19,945
Apr 30	QUEENS PARK RANGERS	D 1-1	Brady	40,396

FA Cup

Jan 5	Norwich City	(Rd3) W 1-0	Kelly	21,500
Jan 26	ASTON VILLA	(Rd4) D 1-1	Kennedy	41,682
Jan 30	Aston Villa	(R) L 0-2		47,821

League Cup

Oct 2	TRANMERE ROVERS	(Rd2) L 0-1		20,337

League & Cup Appearances

PLAYER	LEAGUE	CUP COMPETITION		TOTAL
		FA CUP	LC	
Armstrong	40 (1)	3	1	44 (1)
Ball	36	3	1	40
Batson	3 (2)			3 (2)
Blockley	26	3	1	30
Brady	9 (4)	0 (1)		9 (5)
Chambers	1	0 (1)		1 (1)
George	28			28
Hornsby	6 (3)			6 (3)
Kelly	35 (2)	3	1	39 (2)
Kennedy	42	3	1	46
McNab	23	3	1	27
Nelson	18 (1)			18 (1)
Powling	2			2
Price	3 (1)			3 (1)
Radford	32	3	1	36
Rice	41	3	1	45
Rimmer	1			1
Simpson	34 (4)	3	1	38 (4)
Storey	41	3	1	45
Wilson	41	3	1	45

Goalscorers

PLAYER	LEAGUE	CUP COMPETITION		TOTAL
		FA CUP	LC	
Ball	13			13
Kennedy	12	1		13
Radford	7			7
George	5			5
Hornsby	3			3
Simpson	2			2
Kelly	1	1		2
Blockley	1			1
Brady	1			1
McNab	1			1
Nelson	1			1
Rice	1			1
Opps' o.gs.	1			1

Fact File

Bob Wilson retired at the end of the season, to pursue a career in television. Barcelona, including the Dutch greats Johan Cruyff and Johan Neeskens, were the visitors for George Armstrong's testimonial on 12 March which attracted a bumper crowd of 36,099.

MANAGER: Bertie Mee

CAPTAIN: Alan Ball

TOP SCORER: Alan Ball 13 (all League), Ray Kennedy 13 (12 League)

BIGGEST WIN: 4-0 v Norwich City, 15 September 1973, League

HIGHEST ATTENDANCE: 51,501 v Manchester United, 25 August 1973, League

MAJOR TRANSFER IN: Jimmy Rimmer from Manchester United

MAJOR TRANSFER OUT: Peter Marinello to Portsmouth

Final Division One Table

		P	W	D	L	F	A	Pts
1	Leeds U	42	24	14	4	66	31	62
2	Liverpool	42	22	13	7	52	31	57
3	Derby Co	42	17	14	11	52	42	48
4	Ipswich T	42	18	11	13	67	58	47
5	Stoke C	42	15	16	11	54	42	46
6	Burnley	42	16	14	12	56	53	46
7	Everton	42	16	12	14	50	48	44
8	QPR	42	13	17	12	56	52	43
9	Leicester C	42	13	16	13	51	41	42
10	Arsenal	42	14	14	14	49	51	42
11	Tottenham H	42	14	14	14	45	50	42
12	Wolverhampton W	42	13	15	14	49	49	41
13	Sheffield U	42	14	12	16	44	49	40
14	Manchester C	42	14	12	16	39	46	40
15	Newcastle United	42	13	12	17	49	48	38
16	Coventry C	42	14	10	18	43	54	38
17	Chelsea	42	12	13	17	56	60	37
18	West Ham U	42	11	15	16	55	60	37
19	Birmingham C	42	12	13	17	52	64	37
20	Southampton	42	11	14	17	47	68	36
21	Manchester U	42	10	12	20	38	48	32
22	Norwich C	42	7	15	20	37	62	29

Season 1974-75

Football League Division One

DATE	OPPONENTS	SCORE	GOALSCORERS	ATTENDANCE
Aug 17	Leicester City	W 1-0	Kidd	26,448
Aug 20	IPSWICH TOWN	L 0-1		31,027
Aug 24	MANCHESTER CITY	W 4-0	Kidd 2, Radford 2	27,143
Aug 27	Ipswich Town	L 0-3		28,036
Aug 31	Everton	L 1-2	Kidd	42,438
Sep 7	BURNLEY	L 0-1		23,586
Sep 14	Chelsea	D 0-0		34,596
Sep 21	LUTON TOWN	D 2-2	Kidd 2	21,629
Sep 28	Birmingham City	L 1-3	George	25,584
Oct 5	Leeds United	L 0-2		32,784
Oct 12	QUEENS PARK RANGERS	D 2-2	Kidd, Radford	29,690
Oct 16	Manchester City	L 1-2	Radford	26,658
Oct 19	Tottenham Hotspur	L 0-2		36,194
Oct 26	WEST HAM UNITED	W 3-0	Radford, Brady, Kidd	41,004
Nov 2	WOLVERHAMPTON WANDERERS	D 0-0		27,572
Nov 9	Liverpool	W 3-1	Ball 2, Brady	43,850
Nov 16	DERBY COUNTY	W 3-1	Ball 2 (1 pen), Kidd	32,286
Nov 23	Coventry City	L 0-3		15,669
Nov 30	MIDDLESBROUGH	W 2-0	Brady, Ball (pen)	25,283
Dec 7	Carlisle United	L 1-2	Kidd	12,926
Dec 14	LEICESTER CITY	D 0-0		20,849
Dec 21	Stoke City	W 2-0	Kidd 2	23,292
Dec 26	CHELSEA	L 1-2	Ball	33,784
Dec 28	Sheffield United	D 1-1	George	19,967
Jan 11	CARLISLE UNITED	W 2-1	Radford, Cropley	21,538
Jan 18	Middlesbrough	D 0-0		27,996
Feb 1	LIVERPOOL	W 2-0	Ball 2 (1 pen)	43,028
Feb 8	Wolverhampton Wanderers	L 0-1		19,807
Feb 22	Derby County	L 1-2	Radford	24,002
Mar 1	EVERTON	L 0-2		32,216
Mar 15	BIRMINGHAM CITY	D 1-1	Kidd	17,845
Mar 18	NEWCASTLE UNITED	W 3-0	Kidd, Ball (pen), Rostron	16,540
Mar 22	Burnley	D 3-3	Rostron, Hornsby 2	17,539
Mar 25	Luton Town	L 0-2		22,101
Mar 29	STOKE CITY	D 1-1	Kelly	26,852
Mar 31	SHEFFIELD UNITED	W 1-0	Kidd	24,338
Apr 8	COVENTRY CITY	W 2-0	Kidd 2	17,291
Apr 12	LEEDS UNITED	L 1-2	Kidd	36,619
Apr 19	Queens Park Rangers	D 0-0		24,362
Apr 23	Newcastle United	L 1-3	Hornsby	21,895
Apr 26	TOTTENHAM HOTSPUR	W 1-0	Kidd	43,752
Apr 28	West Ham United	L 0-1		30,195

FA Cup

Jan 4	YORK CITY	(Rd3)	D 1-1	Kelly	27,029
Jan 7	York City	(R)	W 3-1	Kidd 3	15,362
Jan 25	Coventry City	(Rd4)	D 1-1	Ball	31,165
Jan 29	COVENTRY CITY	(R)	W 3-0	Armstrong 2, Matthews	30,867
Feb 15	LEICESTER CITY	(Rd5)	D 0-0		43,841
Feb 19	Leicester City	(R)	D 1-1	Radford	35,009
Feb 24	Leicester City	(2R)	W 1-0	Radford	39,025
Mar 8	WEST HAM UNITED	(QF)	L 0-2		56,742

League Cup

Sep 10	LEICESTER CITY	(Rd2)	D 1-1	Kidd	20,788
Sep 18	Leicester City	(R)	L 1-2	Brady	17,303

League & Cup Appearances

PLAYER	LEAGUE	CUP COMPETITION		TOTAL
		FA CUP	LC	
Armstrong	21 (3)	7 (1)	2	30 (4)
Ball	30	8		38
Barnett	2			2
Blockley	6		2	8
Brady	30 (2)	2 (3)	2	34 (5)
Cropley	7	2		9
George	9 (1)	1	1	11 (1)
Hornsby	12			12
Kelly	32	2	2	36
Kidd	40	8	2	50
McNab	18	8		26
Mancini	26	8		34
Matthews	20	4 (1)	2	26 (1)
Nelson	19 (1)		1	20 (1)
Powling	5 (3)	1		6 (3)
Price	0 (1)			0 (1)
Radford	29	7	2	38
Rice	32	8		40
Rimmer	40	8	2	50
Ross	1 (1)			1 (1)
Rostron	6			6
Simpson	39 (1)	7		48 (1)
Stapleton	1			1
Storey	37	7	2	46

Goalscorers

PLAYER	LEAGUE	CUP COMPETITION		TOTAL
		FA CUP	LC	
Kidd	19	3	1	23
Ball	9	1		10
Radford	7	2		9
Brady	3		1	4
Hornsby	3			3
George	2			2
Rostron	2			2
Kelly	1	1		2
Armstrong		2		2
Cropley	1			1
Matthews		1		1

Fact File

Another 'Double' hero, Ray Kennedy, left Highbury for Liverpool in the summer of 1974. He was converted from a striker into a midfield player at Anfield and played in three European Cup victories.

MANAGER: Bertie Mee

CAPTAIN: Alan Ball

TOP SCORER: Brian Kidd 23 (19 League)

BIGGEST WIN: 4-0 v Manchester City, 24 August 1974, League

HIGHEST ATTENDANCE: 56,742 v West Ham United, 8 March 1975, FA Cup

MAJOR TRANSFERS IN: Brian Kidd from Manchester United, Terry Mancini from Queens Park Rangers, Alex Cropley from Hibernian

MAJOR TRANSFERS OUT: Ray Kennedy to Liverpool, Jeff Blockley to Leicester City

Final Division One Table

		P	W	D	L	F	A	Pts
1	DERBY CO	42	21	11	10	67	49	53
2	LIVERPOOL	42	20	11	11	60	39	51
3	IPSWICH T	42	23	5	14	66	44	51
4	EVERTON	42	16	18	8	56	42	50
5	STOKE C	42	17	15	10	64	48	49
6	SHEFFIELD U	42	18	13	11	58	51	49
7	MIDDLESBROUGH	42	18	12	12	54	40	48
8	MANCHESTER C	42	18	10	14	54	54	46
9	LEEDS U	42	16	13	13	57	49	45
10	BURNLEY	42	17	11	14	68	67	45
11	QPR	42	16	10	16	54	54	42
12	WOLVERHAMPTON W	42	14	11	17	57	54	39
13	WEST HAM U	42	13	13	16	58	59	39
14	COVENTRY C	42	12	15	15	51	62	39
15	NEWCASTLE UNITED	42	15	9	18	59	72	39
16	ARSENAL	42	13	11	18	47	49	37
17	BIRMINGHAM C	42	14	9	19	53	61	37
18	LEICESTER C	42	12	12	18	46	60	36
19	TOTTENHAM H	42	13	8	21	52	63	34
20	LUTON T	42	11	11	20	47	65	33
21	CHELSEA	42	9	15	18	42	72	33
22	CARLISLE U	42	12	5	25	43	59	29

Season 1975-76

Football League Division One

DATE	OPPONENTS	SCORE	GOALSCORERS	ATTENDANCE
Aug 16	Burnley	D 0-0		18,603
Aug 19	Sheffield United	W 3-1	Brady, Rice, Kidd	23,344
Aug 23	STOKE CITY	L 0-1		28,025
Aug 26	NORWICH CITY	W 2-1	Ball (pen), Kelly	22,613
Aug 30	Wolverhampton Wanderers	D 0-0		18,144
Sep 6	LEICESTER CITY	D 1-1	Stapleton	22,005
Sep 13	Aston Villa	L 0-2		34,474
Sep 20	EVERTON	D 2-2	Kidd, Stapleton	24,864
Sep 27	Tottenham Hotspur	D 0-0		37,092
Oct 4	MANCHESTER CITY	L 2-3	Ball, Cropley	24,928
Oct 11	COVENTRY CITY	W 5-0	Cropley 2, Ball, Kidd 2	19,234
Oct 18	Manchester United	L 1-3	Kelly	52,958
Oct 25	MIDDLESBROUGH	W 2-1	Stapleton, Cropley	23,591
Nov 1	Newcastle United	L 0-2		32,824
Nov 8	DERBY COUNTY	L 0-1		32,012
Nov 15	Birmingham City	L 1-3	Ball	21,652
Nov 22	MANCHESTER UNITED	W 3-1	Ball, Armstrong, o.g.	40,102
Nov 29	West Ham United	L 0-1		31,012
Dec 2	Liverpool	D 2-2	Ball (pen), Kidd	27,447
Dec 6	LEEDS UNITED	L 1-2	Brady	36,003
Dec 13	Stoke City	L 1-2	Armstrong	18,628
Dec 20	BURNLEY	W 1-0	Radford	16,459
Dec 26	Ipswich Town	L 0-2		28,457
Dec 27	QUEENS PARK RANGERS	W 2-0	Ball, Kidd	39,021
Jan 10	ASTON VILLA	D 0-0		24,501
Jan 17	Leicester City	L 1-2	Ross	21,331
Jan 31	SHEFFIELD UNITED	W 1-0	Brady	14,477
Feb 7	Norwich City	L 1-3	Kidd	23,038
Feb 18	Derby County	L 0-2		24,875
Feb 21	BIRMINGHAM CITY	W 1-0	Brady	20,907
Feb 24	LIVERPOOL	W 1-0	Radford	36,127
Feb 28	Middlesbrough	W 1-0	Radford	20,000
Mar 13	Coventry City	D 1-1	Powling	13,938
Mar 16	NEWCASTLE UNITED	D 0-0		18,424
Mar 20	WEST HAM UNITED	W 6-1	Kidd 3, Ball 2 (1 pen), Armstrong	34,011
Mar 27	Leeds United	L 0-3		26,657
Apr 3	TOTTENHAM HOTSPUR	L 0-2		42,134
Apr 10	Everton	D 0-0		20,774
Apr 13	WOLVERHAMPTON WANDERERS	W 2-1	Brady, Mancini	19,518
Apr 17	IPSWICH TOWN	L 1-2	Stapleton	26,973
Apr 19	Queens Park Rangers	L 1-2	Kidd	30,362
Apr 24	Manchester City	L 1-3	Armstrong	31,003

FA Cup

Jan 3	Wolverhampton Wanderers	(Rd3) L 0-3		22,215

League Cup

Sep 9	Everton	(Rd2) D 2-2	Cropley, Stapleton	17,174
Sep 23	EVERTON	(R) L 0-1		21,813

League & Cup Appearances

PLAYER	LEAGUE	CUP COMPETITION		TOTAL
		FA CUP	LC	
Armstrong	28 (1)	1		29 (1)
Ball	39	1	2	42
Barnett	1			1
Brady	41 (1)	1	1	43 (1)
Cropley	20		2	22
Hornsby	4			4
Kelly	17		2	19
Kidd	37	1	2	40
Mancini	26		2	28
Matthews	0 (1)			0 (1)
Nelson	36	1	2	39
O'Leary	27	1	2	30
Powling	28 (1)	1		29 (1)
Radford	15		1	16
Rice	42	1	2	45
Rimmer	41	1	2	44
Ross	17			17
Rostron	2 (3)		1	3 (3)
Simpson	7 (2)			7 (2)
Stapleton	23 (2)	1	1 (1)	25 (3)
Storey	11	1		12

Goalscorers

PLAYER	LEAGUE	CUP COMPETITION		TOTAL
		FA CUP	LC	
Kidd	11			11
Ball	9			9
Brady	5			5
Cropley	4		1	5
Stapleton	4		1	5
Armstrong	4			4
Radford	3			3
Kelly	2			2
Mancini	1			1
Powling	1			1
Rice	1			1
Ross	1			1
Opps' o.gs.	1			1

Fact File

Arsenal's 17th place was their lowest position since 1924-5. Safety was only assured with four games to go, thanks to a 2-1 win over Wolverhampton Wanderers. Bertie Mee announced his retirement at the end of the campaign after ten seasons in charge.

MANAGER: Bertie Mee

CAPTAIN: Alan Ball

TOP SCORER: Brian Kidd 11 (all League)

BIGGEST WIN: 6-1 v West Ham United, 20 March 1976, League

HIGHEST ATTENDANCE: 42,134 v Tottenham Hotspur, 3 April 1976, League

MAJOR TRANSFER OUT: Charlie George to Derby County, Bob McNab to Wolverhampton Wanderers

Final Division One Table

		P	W	D	L	F	A	Pts
1	LIVERPOOL	42	23	14	5	66	31	60
2	QPR	42	24	11	7	67	33	59
3	MANCHESTER U	42	23	10	10	68	42	56
4	DERBY CO	42	21	11	10	75	58	53
5	LEEDS U	42	21	9	12	65	46	51
6	IPSWICH T	42	16	14	12	54	48	46
7	LEICESTER C	42	13	19	10	48	51	45
8	MANCHESTER C	42	16	12	15	64	46	43
9	TOTTENHAM H	42	14	15	13	63	63	43
10	NORWICH C	42	16	10	16	58	58	42
11	EVERTON	42	15	12	15	60	66	42
12	STOKE C	42	15	11	16	48	50	41
13	MIDDLESBROUGH	42	15	10	17	46	45	40
14	COVENTRY C	42	13	14	15	47	57	40
15	NEWCASTLE U	42	15	9	18	71	62	39
16	ASTON VILLA	42	11	17	14	51	59	39
17	ARSENAL	42	13	10	19	47	53	36
18	WEST HAM U	42	13	10	19	48	71	36
19	BIRMINGHAM C	42	13	7	22	57	75	33
20	WOLVERHAMPTON W	42	10	10	22	51	68	30
21	BURNLEY	42	9	10	23	43	66	28
22	SHEFFIELD U	42	6	10	26	33	82	22

Season 1976-77

Football League Division One

DATE	OPPONENTS	SCORE	GOALSCORERS	ATTENDANCE
Aug 21	BRISTOL CITY	L 0-1		41,082
Aug 25	Norwich City	W 3-1	Nelson, Macdonald, Stapleton	26,769
Aug 28	Sunderland	D 2-2	Ross, Macdonald	41,211
Sep 4	MANCHESTER CITY	D 0-0		35,132
Sep 11	West Ham United	W 2-0	Ross, Stapleton	32,415
Sep 18	EVERTON	W 3-1	Brady, Stapleton, Macdonald	34,076
Sep 25	Ipswich Town	L 1-3	o.g.	25,505
Oct 2	QUEENS PARK RANGERS	W 3-2	Rice, Brady, Stapleton	39,442
Oct 16	STOKE CITY	W 2-0	Rice, Macdonald	28,745
Oct 20	Aston Villa	L 1-5	Ball	33,860
Oct 23	Leicester City	L 1-4	Stapleton	19,351
Oct 30	Leeds United	L 1-2	Matthews	33,556
Nov 6	BIRMINGHAM CITY	W 4-0	Stapleton, Nelson, Macdonald (pen), Ross	23,063
Nov 20	LIVERPOOL	D 1-1	Armstrong	45,016
Nov 27	Coventry City	W 2-1	Macdonald, Stapleton	18,313
Dec 4	NEWCASTLE UNITED	W 5-3	Macdonald 3, Ross, Stapleton	34,053
Dec 15	Derby County	D 0-0		24,016
Dec 18	MANCHESTER UNITED	W 3-1	Macdonald 2, Brady	39,572
Dec 27	Tottenham Hotspur	D 2-2	Macdonald 2	47,751
Jan 3	LEEDS UNITED	D 1-1	Macdonald	44,090
Jan 15	NORWICH CITY	W 1-0	Rice	30,537
Jan 18	Birmingham City	D 3-3	Macdonald 3	23,247
Jan 27	Bristol City	L 0-2		26,282
Feb 5	SUNDERLAND	D 0-0		30,925
Feb 12	Manchester City	L 0-1		45,368
Feb 15	Middlesbrough	L 0-3		26,083
Feb 19	WEST HAM UNITED	L 2-3	Brady, Stapleton	38,221
Mar 1	Everton	L 1-2	Macdonald	29,802
Mar 5	IPSWICH TOWN	L 1-4	Macdonald (pen)	34,688
Mar 8	WEST BROMWICH ALBION	L 1-2	Macdonald	19,517
Mar 12	Queens Park Rangers	L 1-2	Young	26,191
Mar 23	Stoke City	D 1-1	Price	13,951
Apr 2	LEICESTER CITY	W 3-0	Rix, O'Leary 2	23,013
Apr 9	West Bromwich Albion	W 2-0	Stapleton, Macdonald	24,275
Apr 11	TOTTENHAM HOTSPUR	W 1-0	Macdonald	47,432
Apr 16	Liverpool	L 0-2		48,174
Apr 23	COVENTRY CITY	W 2-0	Stapleton, Macdonald	22,790
Apr 25	ASTON VILLA	W 3-0	Macdonald, Armstrong, Nelson	24,011
Apr 30	Newcastle United	W 2-0	Macdonald, Matthews	44,763
May 3	DERBY COUNTY	D 0-0		26,659
May 7	MIDDLESBROUGH	D 1-1	Stapleton	23,911
May 14	Manchester United	L 2-3	Brady, Stapleton	53,232

FA Cup

Jan 8	Notts County	(Rd3) W 1-0	Ross	17,328
Jan 29	COVENTRY CITY	(Rd4) W 3-1	Macdonald 2, Stapleton	41,078
Feb 26	Middlesbrough	(Rd5) L 1-4	Macdonald	35,028

League Cup

Aug 31	Carlisle United	(Rd2) W 3-2	Ross 2, Macdonald	21,550
Sep 21	Blackpool	(Rd3) D 1-1	Armstrong	18,983
Sep 28	BLACKPOOL	(R) D 0-0		27,195
Oct 5	BLACKPOOL	(2R) W 2-0	Stapleton, O'Leary	26,791
Oct 26	CHELSEA	(Rd4) W 2-1	Ross, Stapleton	52,285
Dec 1	Queens Park Rangers	(QF) L 1-2	Stapleton	27,621

MANAGER: Terry Neill

CAPTAIN: Alan Ball/Pat Rice

TOP SCORER: Malcolm Macdonald 29 (25 League)

BIGGEST WIN: 5-3 v Newcastle United, 4 December 1976, League

HIGHEST ATTENDANCE: 52,285 v Chelsea, 26 October 1976, League Cup

MAJOR TRANSFERS IN: Malcolm Macdonald from Newcastle United, Pat Howard from Newcastle United, Alan Hudson from Stoke City, Willie Young from Tottenham Hotspur

MAJOR TRANSFERS OUT: Brian Kidd to Manchester City, Eddie Kelly to Queens Park Rangers, Alex Cropley to Aston Villa, Alan Ball to Southampton, John Radford to West Ham United, Peter Storey to Fulham

League & Cup Appearances

PLAYER	LEAGUE	CUP COMPETITION		TOTAL
		FA CUP	LC	
Armstrong	37	2	6	45
Ball	14		6	20
Brady	37 (1)	3	6	46 (1)
Cropley	2 (1)			2 (1)
Howard	15 (1)		4	19 (1)
Hudson	19	3		22
Macdonald	41	3	6	50
Matthews	14 (3)	0 (1)	1	15 (4)
Nelson	31 (1)	3	5	39 (1)
O'Leary	33	3	4	40
Powling	11 (1)		1	12 (1)
Price	6 (2)			6 (2)
Radford	1 (1)			1 (1)
Rice	42	3	6	51
Rimmer	42	3	6	51
Rix	4 (3)			4 (3)
Ross	29	3	5	37
Rostron	4 (2)	1		5 (2)
Simpson	19	3	3	25
Stapleton	40	3	6	49
Storey	7 (4)	0 (1)	1 (1)	8 (6)
Young	14			14

Goalscorers

PLAYER	LEAGUE	CUP COMPETITION		TOTAL
		FA CUP	LC	
Macdonald	25	3	1	29
Stapleton	13	1	3	17
Ross	4	1	3	8
Brady	5			5
Nelson	3			3
Rice	3			3
Armstrong	2		1	3
O'Leary	2		1	3
Matthews	2			2
Ball	1			1
Price	1			1
Rix	1			1
Young	1			1
Opps' o.gs.	1			1

Fact File

Terry Neill left Tottenham to take charge at Arsenal. He was the first man to manage both North London clubs – a feat later achieved by George Graham. Arsenal's eight consecutive defeats (seven league, one FA Cup) between 12 February and 12 March 1977 was the worst losing run in their history.

Final Division One Table

		P	W	D	L	F	A	Pts
1	LIVERPOOL	42	23	11	8	62	33	57
2	MANCHESTER C	42	21	14	7	60	34	56
3	IPSWICH T	42	22	8	12	66	39	56
4	ASTON VILLA	42	22	7	13	76	50	51
5	NEWCASTLE U	42	18	13	11	64	49	49
6	MANCHESTER U	42	18	11	13	71	62	47
7	WBA	42	16	13	13	62	56	45
8	ARSENAL	42	16	11	15	64	59	43
9	EVERTON	42	14	14	14	62	64	42
10	LEEDS U	42	15	12	15	48	51	42
11	LEICESTER C	42	12	18	12	47	60	42
12	MIDDLESBROUGH	42	14	13	15	40	45	41
13	BIRMINGHAM C	42	13	12	17	63	61	38
14	QPR	42	13	12	17	47	52	38
15	DERBY CO	42	9	19	14	50	55	37
16	NORWICH C	42	14	9	19	47	64	37
17	WEST HAM U	42	11	14	17	46	65	36
18	BRISTOL C	42	11	13	18	38	48	35
19	COVENTRY C	42	10	15	17	48	59	35
20	SUNDERLAND	42	11	12	19	46	54	34
21	STOKE C	42	10	14	18	28	51	34
22	TOTTENHAM H	42	12	9	21	48	72	33

Season 1977-78

Football League Division One

DATE	OPPONENTS	SCORE	GOALSCORERS	ATTENDANCE
Aug 20	Ipswich Town	L 0-1		30,384
Aug 23	EVERTON	W 1-0	Powling	32,924
Aug 27	Wolverhampton Wanderers	D 1-1	Powling	22,909
Sep 3	NOTTINGHAM FOREST	W 3-0	Stapleton 2, Brady (pen)	40,810
Sep 10	Aston Villa	L 0-1		36,929
Sep 17	LEICESTER CITY	W 2-1	Stapleton, Macdonald	27,371
Sep 24	Norwich City	L 0-1		19,312
Oct 1	WEST HAM UNITED	W 3-0	Stapleton, Rice, Brady (pen)	41,245
Oct 4	LIVERPOOL	D 0-0		47,110
Oct 8	Manchester City	L 1-2	Macdonald	43,177
Oct 15	QUEENS PARK RANGERS	W 1-0	Macdonald	36,290
Oct 22	Bristol City	W 2-0	Rix, Macdonald	25,497
Oct 29	BIRMINGHAM CITY	D 1-1	Rice	31,355
Nov 5	Manchester United	W 2-1	Macdonald, Stapleton	53,055
Nov 12	COVENTRY CITY	D 1-1	o.g.	31,653
Nov 19	Newcastle United	W 2-1	Stapleton, Sunderland	22,880
Nov 26	DERBY COUNTY	L 1-3	Nelson	31,989
Dec 3	Middlesbrough	W 1-0	o.g.	17,422
Dec 10	LEEDS UNITED	D 1-1	Young	40,162
Dec 17	Coventry City	W 2-1	Stapleton 2	20,993
Dec 26	CHELSEA	W 3-0	Price, Rix, O'Leary	46,074
Dec 27	West Bromwich Albion	W 3-1	Macdonald, Brady (pen), Sunderland	27,723
Dec 31	Everton	L 0-2		47,039
Jan 2	IPSWICH TOWN	W 1-0	Price	43,705
Jan 14	WOLVERHAMPTON WANDERERS	W 3-1	Brady, Macdonald, Stapleton	34,784
Jan 21	Nottingham Forest	L 0-2		35,743
Feb 4	ASTON VILLA	L 0-1		30,127
Feb 11	Leicester City	D 1-1	Brady (pen)	15,780
Feb 25	West Ham United	D 2-2	Macdonald 2	31,675
Feb 28	NORWICH CITY	D 0-0		23,506
Mar 4	MANCHESTER CITY	W 3-0	Sunderland, Young, Price	34,003
Mar 18	BRISTOL CITY	W 4-1	Stapleton 2, Sunderland, Price	28,463
Mar 21	Birmingham City	D 1-1	Brady (pen)	22,087
Mar 25	WEST BROMWICH ALBION	W 4-0	Macdonald 3, Young	36,763
Mar 27	Chelsea	D 0-0		40,764
Apr 1	MANCHESTER UNITED	W 3-1	Macdonald 2, Brady	40,739
Apr 11	Queens Park Rangers	L 1-2	Brady (pen)	25,683
Apr 15	NEWCASTLE UNITED	W 2-1	Brady, Price	33,353
Apr 22	Leeds United	W 3-1	Stapleton, Macdonald, o.g.	33,263
Apr 25	Liverpool	L 0-1		38,318
Apr 29	MIDDLESBROUGH	W 1-0	Stapleton	32,138
May 9	Derby County	L 0-3		21,189

FA Cup

Jan 7	Sheffield United	(Rd3) W 5-0	Macdonald 2, Stapleton 2, O'Leary	32,156
Jan 28	WOLVERHAMPTON WANDERERS	(Rd4) W 2-1	Sunderland, Macdonald	49,373
Feb 18	WALSALL	(Rd5) W 4-1	Stapleton 2, Macdonald, Sunderland	43,789
Mar 11	Wrexham	(QF) W 3-2	Macdonald, Sunderland, Young	25,547
Apr 8	Orient*	(SF) W 3-0	Macdonald 2, Rix	49,698
May 6	Ipswich Town**	(F) L 0-1		100,000

*Played at Stamford Bridge. **Played at Wembley.

League Cup

Aug 30	MANCHESTER UNITED	(Rd2) W 3-2	Macdonald 2, Brady	36,171
Oct 25	SOUTHAMPTON	(Rd3) W 2-0	Brady (pen), Stapleton	40,749
Nov 29	HULL CITY	(Rd4) W 5-1	Matthews 2, Brady, Macdonald, Stapleton	25,922
Jan 18	Manchester City	(QF) D 0-0		42,435
Jan 24	MANCHESTER CITY	(R) W 1-0	Brady	57,960
Feb 7	Liverpool	(SF/1L) L 1-2	Macdonald	44,764
Feb 14	LIVERPOOL	(SF/2L) D 0-0		49,561

MANAGER: Terry Neill

CAPTAIN: Pat Rice

TOP SCORER: Malcolm Macdonald 26 (15 League)

BIGGEST WIN: 5-0 v Sheffield United, 7 January 1978, FA Cup

HIGHEST ATTENDANCE: 57,960 v Manchester City, 24 January 1978, League Cup

MAJOR TRANSFERS IN: Pat Jennings from Tottenham Hotspur, Steve Walford from Tottenham Hotspur, Mark Heeley from Peterborough United, Alan Sunderland from Wolverhampton Wanderers

MAJOR TRANSFERS OUT: George Armstrong to Leicester City, Trevor Ross to Everton

League & Cup Appearances

PLAYER	LEAGUE	CUP COMPETITION		TOTAL
		FA CUP	LC	
Brady	39	6	7	52
Devine	3			3
Harvey	1			1
Heeley	3 (2)			3 (2)
Hudson	17	4	3 (1)	24 (1)
Jennings	42	6	7	55
Macdonald	39	6	7	52
Matthews	4 (3)		3	7 (3)
Nelson	41	6	7	54
O'Leary	41	6	6	53
Powling	4		1	5
Price	38 (1)	6	6	50 (1)
Rice	38	6	7	51
Rix	37 (2)	4 (1)	7	48 (3)
Ross	10		1	11
Simpson	6 (3)		1 (1)	7 (4)
Stapleton	39	5	7	51
Sunderland	23	5		28
Walford	2 (3)			2 (3)
Young	35	6	7	48

Goalscorers

PLAYER	LEAGUE	CUP COMPETITION		TOTAL
		FA CUP	LC	
Macdonald	15	7	4	26
Stapleton	13	4	2	19
Brady	9		4	13
Sunderland	4	3		7
Price	5			5
Young	3	1		4
Rix	2	1		3
Powling	2			2
Rice	2			2
O'Leary	1	1		2
Matthews			2	2
Nelson	1			1
Opps' o.gs.	3			3

Fact File

Terry Neill stepped in to sign goalkeeper Pat Jennings when question marks were raised over his future at Tottenham. Jennings retired at the age of 39, eight years later, after more than 300 appearances for the Gunners.

Final Division One Table

		P	W	D	L	F	A	Pts
1	NOTTINGHAM F	42	25	14	3	69	24	64
2	LIVERPOOL	42	24	9	9	65	34	57
3	EVERTON	42	22	11	9	76	45	55
4	MANCHESTER C	42	20	12	10	74	51	52
5	ARSENAL	42	21	10	11	60	37	52
6	WBA	42	18	14	10	62	53	50
7	COVENTRY C	42	18	12	12	75	62	48
8	ASTON VILLA	42	18	10	14	57	42	46
9	LEEDS U	42	18	10	14	63	53	46
10	MANCHESTER U	42	16	10	16	67	63	42
11	BIRMINGHAM C	42	16	9	17	55	60	41
12	DERBY CO	42	14	13	15	54	59	41
13	NORWICH C	42	11	18	13	52	66	40
14	MIDDLESBROUGH	42	12	15	15	42	54	39
15	WOLVERHAMPTON W	42	12	12	18	51	64	36
16	CHELSEA	42	11	14	17	46	69	36
17	BRISTOL C	42	11	13	18	49	53	35
18	IPSWICH T	42	11	13	18	47	61	35
19	QPR	42	9	15	18	47	64	33
20	WEST HAM U	42	12	8	22	52	69	32
21	NEWCASTLE U	42	6	10	26	42	78	22
22	LEICESTER C	42	5	12	25	26	70	22

Season 1978-79

Football League Division One

DATE	OPPONENTS	SCORE	GOALSCORERS	ATTENDANCE
Aug 19	LEEDS UNITED	D 2-2	Brady 2 (1 pen)	42,057
Aug 22	Manchester City	D 1-1	Macdonald	39,506
Aug 26	Everton	L 0-1		41,179
Sep 2	QUEENS PARK RANGERS	W 5-1	Rix 2, Brady, Stapleton 2	33,883
Sep 9	Nottingham Forest	L 1-2	Brady	28,124
Sep 16	BOLTON WANDERERS	W 1-0	Stapleton	31,120
Sep 23	MANCHESTER UNITED	D 1-1	Price	45,393
Sep 30	Middlesbrough	W 3-2	O'Leary, Price, Walford	14,404
Oct 7	ASTON VILLA	D 1-1	Sunderland	34,537
Oct 14	Wolverhampton Wanderers	L 0-1		19,664
Oct 21	SOUTHAMPTON	W 1-0	Brady	33,074
Oct 28	Bristol City	W 3-1	Brady 2 (1 pen), Stapleton	27,016
Nov 4	IPSWICH TOWN	W 4-1	Stapleton 3, Nelson	35,269
Nov 11	Leeds United	W 1-0	Gatting	33,961
Nov 18	EVERTON	D 2-2	Brady 2 (1 pen)	39,801
Nov 25	Coventry City	D 1-1	Stapleton	26,786
Dec 2	LIVERPOOL	W 1-0	Price	51,902
Dec 9	Norwich City	D 0-0		20,165
Dec 16	DERBY COUNTY	W 2-0	Price, Stapleton	26,943
Dec 23	Tottenham Hotspur	W 5-0	Sunderland 3, Stapleton, Brady	42,273
Dec 26	WEST BROMWICH ALBION	L 1-2	Brady (pen)	40,055
Dec 30	BIRMINGHAM CITY	W 3-1	Stapleton, Rice, Sunderland	27,877
Jan 13	NOTTINGHAM FOREST	W 2-1	Price, Stapleton	52,158
Feb 3	Manchester United	W 2-0	Sunderland 2	45,460
Feb 10	MIDDLESBROUGH	D 0-0		28,371
Feb 13	Queens Park Rangers	W 2-1	Price, Brady	21,125
Feb 24	WOLVERHAMPTON WANDERERS	L 0-1		32,215
Mar 3	Southampton	L 0-2		25,052
Mar 10	BRISTOL CITY	W 2-0	Rix, Stapleton	24,288
Mar 17	Ipswich Town	L 0-2		26,407
Mar 24	MANCHESTER CITY	D 1-1	Sunderland	35,014
Mar 26	Bolton Wanderers	L 2-4	Price, Heeley	20,704
Apr 3	COVENTRY CITY	D 1-1	Nelson	30,091
Apr 7	Liverpool	L 0-3		47,297
Apr 10	TOTTENHAM HOTSPUR	W 1-0	Stapleton	53,896
Apr 14	West Bromwich Albion	D 1-1	Brady	28,353
Apr 16	CHELSEA	W 5-2	Stapleton 2, O'Leary, Price, Sunderland	37,232
Apr 21	Derby County	L 0-2		18,674
Apr 25	Aston Villa	L 1-5	Stapleton	26,168
Apr 28	NORWICH CITY	D 1-1	Walford	28,885
May 5	Birmingham City	D 0-0		14,015
May 14	Chelsea	D 1-1	Macdonald	30,705

FA Cup

Jan 6	Sheffield Wednesday	(Rd3)	D 1-1	Sunderland	33,635
Jan 9	SHEFFIELD WEDNESDAY	(R)	D 1-1	Brady	37,987
Jan 15	Sheffield Wednesday*	(2R)	D 2-2	Brady, Sunderland	25,011
Jan 17	Sheffield Wednesday*	(3R)	D 3-3	Stapleton 2, Young	17,088
Jan 22	Sheffield Wednesday*	(4R)	W 2-0	Gatting, Stapleton	30,275
Jan 27	NOTTS COUNTY	(Rd4)	W 2-0	Young, Talbot	39,195
Feb 26	Nottingham Forest	(Rd5)	W 1-0	Stapleton	35,906
Mar 19	Southampton	(QF)	D 1-1	Price	24,536
Mar 21	SOUTHAMPTON	(R)	W 2-0	Sunderland 2	44,820
Mar 31	Wolverhampton Wanderers**	(SF)	W 2-0	Stapleton, Sunderland	46,244
May 12	Manchester United†	(F)	W 3-2	Talbot, Stapleton, Sunderland	100,000

* Played at Filbert Street. **Played at Villa Park. †Played at Wembley.

League Cup

Aug 29	Rotherham United	(Rd2)	L 1-3	Stapleton	10,481

UEFA Cup

Sep 13	LOKOMOTIV LEIPZIG	(Rd1/1L)	W 3-0	Stapleton 2, Sunderland	34,183
Sep 27	Lokomotiv Leipzig	(Rd1/2L)	W 4-1	Stapleton 2, Brady, Sunderland	22,000
Oct 19	Hajduk Split	(Rd2/1L)	L 1-2	Brady	25,000
Nov 1	HAJDUK SPLIT	(Rd2/2L)	W 1-0	Young	41,812
Nov 22	Red Star Belgrade	(Rd3/1L)	L 0-1		51,000
Dec 6	RED STAR BELGRADE	(Rd3/2L)	D 1-1	Sunderland	41,452

MANAGER: Terry Neill

CAPTAIN: Pat Rice

TOP SCORER: Frank Stapleton 28 (17 League)

BIGGEST WIN: 5-0 v Tottenham Hotspur, 23 December 1978, League

HIGHEST ATTENDANCE: 53,896 v Tottenham Hotspur, 10 April 1979, League

MAJOR TRANSFER IN: Brian Talbot from Ipswich Town

MAJOR TRANSFERS OUT: John Matthews to Sheffield United, Alan Hudson to Seattle Sounders

League & Cup Appearances

PLAYER	LEAGUE	CUP COMPETITION			TOTAL
		FA CUP	LC	UEFA	
Barron	3				3
Brady	37	10	1	4	52
Brignall	0 (1)				0 (1)
Devine	7			1	8
Gatting	19 (2)	6		2 (1)	27 (3)
Harvey	1 (1)			1	2 (1)
Heeley	6 (4)			4 (1)	10 (5)
Jennings	39	11	1	6	57
Kosmina	0 (1)			1 (2)	1 (3)
McDermott	0 (2)				0 (2)
Macdonald	4		1	0 (1)	5 (1)
Nelson	33	10	1	6	50
O'Leary	37	11	1	5	54
Price	39	11	1	6	57
Rice	39	11	1	6	57
Rix	39	11	1	6	57
Stapleton	41	11	1	6	59
Stead	1 (1)				1 (1)
Sunderland	37	11	1	4	53
Talbot	20	6			26
Vaessen	1			0 (2)	1 (2)
Walford	26 (7)	2 (4)		2 (1)	30 (12)
Young	33	10	1	6	50

Goalscorers

PLAYER	LEAGUE	CUP COMPETITION			TOTAL
		FA CUP	LC	UEFA	
Stapleton	17	6	1	4	28
Sunderland	9	6		3	18
Brady	13	2		2	17
Price	8	1			9
Rix	3				3
Young		2		1	3
Macdonald	2				2
Nelson	2				2
O'Leary	2				2
Walford	2				2
Talbot		2			2
Gatting	1	1			2
Heeley	1				1
Rice	1				1

Fact File

Arsenal fans thought Christmas had come early after the Gunners' 5-0 win at Tottenham on 23 December. It was their biggest win at White Hart Lane since March 1935. Arsenal needed four replays, their longest-ever FA Cup sequence, before knocking out Sheffield Wednesday, then a Third Division side.

Final Division One Table

		P	W	D	L	F	A	Pts
1	LIVERPOOL	42	30	8	4	85	16	68
2	NOTTINGHAM F	42	21	18	3	61	26	60
3	WBA	42	24	11	7	72	35	59
4	EVERTON	42	17	17	8	52	40	51
5	LEEDS U	42	18	14	10	70	52	50
6	IPSWICH T	42	20	9	13	63	49	49
7	ARSENAL	42	17	14	11	61	48	48
8	ASTON VILLA	42	15	16	11	59	49	46
9	MANCHESTER U	42	15	15	12	60	63	45
10	COVENTRY C	42	14	16	12	58	68	44
11	TOTTENHAM H	42	13	15	14	48	61	41
12	MIDDLESBROUGH	42	15	10	17	57	50	40
13	BRISTOL C	42	15	10	17	47	51	40
14	SOUTHAMPTON	42	12	16	14	47	53	40
15	MANCHESTER C	42	13	13	16	58	56	39
16	NORWICH C	42	7	23	12	51	57	37
17	BOLTON W	42	12	11	19	54	75	35
18	WOLVERHAMPTON W	42	13	8	21	44	68	34
19	DERBY CO	42	10	11	21	44	71	31
20	QPR	42	6	13	23	45	73	25
21	BIRMINGHAM C	42	6	10	26	37	64	22
22	CHELSEA	42	5	10	27	44	92	20

Season 1979-80

Football League Division One

DATE	OPPONENTS	SCORE	GOALSCORERS	ATTENDANCE
Aug 18	Brighton & Hove Albion	W 4-0	Sunderland 2, Stapleton, Brady (pen)	28,604
Aug 21	IPSWICH TOWN	L 0-2		33,255
Aug 25	MANCHESTER UNITED	D 0-0		44,380
Sep 1	Leeds United	D 1-1	Nelson	23,245
Sep 8	Derby County	L 2-3		16,429
Sep 15	MIDDLESBROUGH	W 2-0	Sunderland, Stapleton	30,341
Sep 22	Aston Villa	D 0-0		27,277
Sep 29	WOLVERHAMPTON WANDERERS	L 2-3	Stapleton, Hollins	41,844
Oct 6	MANCHESTER CITY	D 0-0		34,688
Oct 9	Ipswich Town	W 2-1	Sunderland, Rix	21,527
Oct 13	Bolton Wanderers	D 0-0		17,032
Oct 20	STOKE CITY	D 0-0		31,591
Oct 27	Bristol City	W 1-0	Sunderland	23,029
Nov 3	BRIGHTON & HOVE ALBION	W 3-0	Rix, Brady (pen), Sunderland	34,400
Nov 10	Crystal Palace	L 0-1		42,887
Nov 17	EVERTON	W 2-0	Stapleton 2	33,450
Nov 24	LIVERPOOL	D 0-0		55,546
Dec 1	Nottingham Forest	D 1-1	Stapleton	27,925
Dec 8	COVENTRY CITY	W 3-1	Stapleton, Sunderland, O'Leary	27,563
Dec 15	West Bromwich Albion	D 2-2	Nelson, Stapleton	18,280
Dec 21	NORWICH CITY	D 1-1	Stapleton	18,869
Dec 26	TOTTENHAM HOTSPUR	W 1-0	Sunderland	44,560
Dec 29	Manchester United	L 0-3		54,295
Jan 1	Southampton	W 1-0	Young	22,473
Jan 12	LEEDS UNITED	L 0-1		35,945
Jan 19	DERBY COUNTY	W 2-0	Brady (pen), Young	22,091
Feb 9	ASTON VILLA	W 3-1	Sunderland 2, Rix	33,816
Feb 23	BOLTON WANDERERS	W 2-0	Young, Stapleton	24,383
Mar 1	Stoke City	W 3-2	Sunderland, Price, Brady	19,752
Mar 11	BRISTOL CITY	D 0-0		21,559
Mar 15	Manchester City	W 3-0	Brady 2 (1pen), Stapleton	33,792
Mar 22	CRYSTAL PALACE	D 1-1	Brady	37,606
Mar 28	Everton	W 1-0	Gatting	28,184
Apr 2	Norwich City	L 1-2	Rix	16,923
Apr 5	SOUTHAMPTON	D 1-1	Sunderland	34,593
Apr 7	Tottenham Hotspur	W 2-1	Vaessen, Sunderland	41,369
Apr 19	Liverpool	D 1-1	Talbot	46,878
Apr 26	WEST BROMWICH ALBION	D 1-1	Stapleton	30,027
May 3	Coventry City	W 1-0	Vaessen	16,817
May 5	NOTTINGHAM FOREST	D 0-0		34,632
May 16	Wolverhampton Wanderers	W 2-1	Walford, Stapleton	23,619
May 19	Middlesbrough	L 0-5		15,603

FA Cup

Jan 5	Cardiff City	(Rd3) D 0-0		21,972
Jan 8	CARDIFF CITY	(R) W 2-1	Sunderland 2	36,155
Jan 26	BRIGHTON & HOVE ALBION	(Rd4) W 2-0	Nelson, Talbot	43,202
Feb 16	Bolton Wanderers	(Rd5) D 1-1	Stapleton	23,530
Feb 19	BOLTON WANDERERS	(R) W 3-0	Sunderland 2, Stapleton	40,564
Mar 8	Watford	(QF) W 2-1	Stapleton 2	27,975
Apr 12	Liverpool*	(SF) D 0-0		50,174
Apr 16	Liverpool**	(R) D 1-1	Sunderland	40,679
Apr 28	Liverpool**	(2R) D 1-1	Sunderland	42,975
May 1	Liverpool †	(3R) W 1-0	Talbot	35,335
May 10	West Ham United††	(F) L 0-1		100,000

*Played at Hillsborough. **Played at Villa Park. †Played at Coventry. ††Played at Wembley.

League Cup

Aug 29	Leeds United	(Rd2/1L) D 1-1	Stapleton	21,972
Sep 4	LEEDS UNITED	(Rd2/2L) W 7-0	Sunderland 3, Brady 2 (2 pen), Nelson, Stapleton	36,155
Sep 25	SOUTHAMPTON	(Rd3) W 2-1	Stapleton, Brady	37,348
Oct 30	Brighton & Hove Albion	(Rd4) D 0-0		25,231
Nov 13	BRIGHTON & HOVE ALBION	(R) W 4-0	Stapleton 2, Vaessen 2	30,351
Dec 4	SWINDON TOWN	(QF) D 1-1	Sunderland (pen)	38,024
Dec 11	Swindon Town	(R) L 3-4	Brady 2, Talbot	21,795

European Cup-Winners' Cup

Sep 19	FENERBAHCE	(Rd1/1L) W 2-0	Sunderland, Young	34,973
Oct 3	Fenerbahce	(Rd1/2L) D 0-0		30,000
Oct 24	MAGDEBURG	(Rd2/1L) W 2-1	Young, Sunderland	34,575
Nov 7	Magdeburg	(Rd2/2L) D 2-2	Price, Brady	22,000
Mar 5	IFK GOTEBORG	(QF/1L) W 5-1	Sunderland 2, Price, Brady, Young	36,323
Mar 19	IFK Goteborg	(QF/2L) D 0-0		40,044
Apr 9	JUVENTUS	(SF/1L) D 1-1	o.g.	51,998
Apr 23	Juventus	(SF/2L) W 1-0	Vaessen	66,386
May 14	Valencia#	(F) D 0-0		40,000

#Played in Brussels. Lost 4-5 on penalties.

League & Cup Appearances

PLAYER	LEAGUE	CUP COMPETITION			TOTAL
		FA CUP	LC	ECWC	
Barron	5				5
Brady	34	9	6	9	58
Davis	1 (1)				1 (1)
Devine	20	5	3	5	33
Gatting	9 (5)	2 (1)	1 (1)	1	13 (7)
Hollins	23 (3)	2	5 (1)	4 (3)	34 (7)
Jennings	37	11	7	9	64
McDermott	0 (1)			0 (1)	0 (2)
Nelson	35	6 (1)	6	7	54 (1)
O'Leary	34	9	6	9	58
Price	21 (1)	9	2	5 (1)	37 (2)
Rice	26	10	4	5 (1)	45 (1)
Rix	38	11	7	9	65
Stapleton	39	11	7	9	66
Sunderland	36 (1)	11	6	7	60 (1)
Talbot	42	11	7	9	69
Vaessen	8 (6)		1	1 (2)	10 (8)
Walford	16 (3)	3 (1)	3	1 (1)	23 (5)
Young	38	11	6	9	64

Goalscorers

PLAYER	LEAGUE	CUP COMPETITION			TOTAL
		FA CUP	LC	ECWC	
Sunderland	14	6	4	4	28
Stapleton	14	4	5		23
Brady	7		5	2	14
Young	3			3	6
Vaessen	2		2	1	5
Rix	4				4
Nelson	2	1	1		4
Talbot	1	2	1		4
Price	1			2	3
O'Leary	1				1
Gatting	1				1
Hollins	1				1
Walford	1				1
Opps' o.gs.				1	1

Fact File

Arsenal became the first British team to win at Juventus in European competition after Paul Vaessen headed the only goal in the European Cup-Winners' Cup semi-final second leg. Arsenal's 7-0 second round second leg win over Leeds United was their biggest-ever League Cup victory.

Final Division One Table

		P	W	D	L	F	A	Pts
1	LIVERPOOL	42	25	10	7	81	30	60
2	MANCHESTER U	42	24	10	8	65	35	58
3	IPSWICH T	42	22	9	11	68	39	53
4	ARSENAL	42	18	16	8	52	36	52
5	NOTTINGHAM F	42	20	8	14	63	43	48
6	WOLVERHAMPTON W	42	19	9	14	58	47	47
7	ASTON VILLA	42	16	14	12	51	50	46
8	SOUTHAMPTON	42	18	9	15	65	53	45
9	MIDDLESBROUGH	42	16	12	14	50	44	44
10	WBA	42	11	19	12	54	50	41
11	LEEDS U	42	13	14	15	46	50	40
12	NORWICH C	42	13	14	15	58	66	40
13	CRYSTAL PALACE	42	12	16	14	41	50	40
14	TOTTENHAM H	42	15	10	17	52	62	40
15	COVENTRY C	42	16	7	19	56	66	39
16	BRIGHTON & HA	42	11	15	16	47	57	37
17	MANCHESTER C	42	12	13	17	43	66	37
18	STOKE C	42	13	10	19	44	58	36
19	EVERTON	42	9	17	16	43	51	35
20	BRISTOL C	42	9	13	20	37	66	31
21	DERBY CO	42	11	8	23	47	67	30
22	BOLTON W	42	5	15	22	38	73	25

Season 1980-81

Football League Division One

DATE	OPPONENTS	SCORE	GOALSCORERS	ATTENDANCE
Aug 16	West Bromwich Albion	W 1-0	Stapleton	22,364
Aug 19	SOUTHAMPTON	D 1-1	Stapleton	43,050
Aug 23	Coventry City	L 1-3	Stapleton	15,399
Aug 30	TOTTENHAM HOTSPUR	W 2-0	Price, Stapleton	54,045
Sep 6	Manchester City	D 0-0	Young	32,233
Sep 13	STOKE CITY	W 2-0	Hollins,Sansom	27,183
Sep 20	Middlesbrough	L 1-2	Rix	14,680
Sep 27	NOTTINGHAM FOREST	W 1-0	Rix	37,582
Oct 4	LEICESTER CITY	W 1-0	Stapleton	28,490
Oct 7	Birmingham City	L 1-3	Sunderland	15,511
Oct 11	Manchester United	D 0-0		49,036
Oct 18	SUNDERLAND	D 2-2	Gatting, Young	32,135
Oct 21	NORWICH CITY	W 3-1	Talbot, McDermott, Sansom	21,839
Oct 25	Liverpool	D 1-1	Sunderland	40,310
Nov 1	BRIGHTON & HOVE ALBION	W 2-0	Rix, McDermott	28,569
Nov 8	Leeds United	W 5-0	Hollins 2, Gatting, Talbot, Sunderland	20,855
Nov 11	Southampton	L 1-3	Rix	21,244
Nov 15	WEST BROMWICH ALBION	D 2-2	Sunderland, o.g.	25,858
Nov 22	EVERTON	W 2-1	McDermott, Sunderland	30,911
Nov 29	Aston Villa	D 1-1	Talbot	30,140
Dec 6	WOLVERHAMPTON WANDERERS	D 1-1	Stapleton	26,050
Dec 13	Sunderland	L 0-2		21,595
Dec 20	MANCHESTER UNITED	W 2-1	Rix, Vaessen	33,730
Dec 26	Crystal Palace	D 2-2	Stapleton, McDermott	29,850
Dec 27	IPSWICH TOWN	D 1-1	Sunderland	42,818
Jan 10	Everton	W 2-1	Gatting, Vaessen	29,362
Jan 17	Tottenham Hotspur	L 0-2		32,994
Jan 31	COVENTRY CITY	D 2-2	Talbot, Stapleton	24,876
Feb 7	Stoke City	D 1-1	Stapleton	14,428
Feb 21	Nottingham Forest	L 1-3	Stapleton	25,357
Feb 24	MANCHESTER CITY	W 2-0	Talbot, Sunderland	24,790
Feb 28	MIDDLESBROUGH	D 2-2	Stapleton, Hollins (pen)	24,504
Mar 7	Leicester City	L 0-1		20,198
Mar 21	Norwich City	D 1-1	Talbot	19,569
Mar 28	LIVERPOOL	W 1-0	Sunderland	47,058
Mar 31	BIRMINGHAM CITY	W 2-1	Stapleton, O'Leary	17,431
Apr 4	Brighton & Hove Albion	W 1-0	Hollins	21,015
Apr 11	LEEDS UNITED	D 0-0		29,339
Apr 18	Ipswich Town	W 2-0	Sansom, Nicholas P.	30,935
Apr 20	CRYSTAL PALACE	W 3-2	Talbot, Davis, Young	24,346
Apr 25	Wolverhampton Wanderers	W 2-1	Stapleton, o.g.	15,160
May 2	ASTON VILLA	W 2-0	Young, McDermott	57,472

FA Cup

Jan 3	Everton	(Rd3) L 0-2		34,236

League Cup

Aug 26	Swansea City	(Rd2/1L) D 1-1	Stapleton	17,036
Sep 2	SWANSEA CITY	(Rd2/2L) W 3-1	Hollins (pen) Sunderland, Walford	26,399
Sep 22	Stockport County	(Rd3) W 3-1	Hollins, Sunderland, Stapleton	11,635
Nov 4	Tottenham Hotspur	(Rd4) L 0-1		42,511

Fact File

Clive Allen signed for Arsenal and left them without ever playing a competitive game for the club. The 19-year-old was signed from Queens Park Rangers for £1.25 million after finishing First Division top scorer in 1979-80 – then, after a handful of friendly appearances, was sold on to Crystal Palace in the deal that brought Kenny Sansom to Highbury.

MANAGER: Terry Neill

CAPTAIN: David O'Leary

TOP SCORER: Frank Stapleton 16 (14 League)

BIGGEST WIN: 5-0 v Leeds United, 8 November 1980, League

HIGHEST ATTENDANCE: 57,472 v Aston Villa, 2 May 1981, League

MAJOR TRANSFERS IN: Clive Allen from Queens Park Rangers, George Wood from Everton, Kenny Sansom from Crystal Palace, Peter Nicholas from Crystal Palace

MAJOR TRANSFERS OUT: Liam Brady to Juventus, Clive Allen to Crystal Palace, Pat Rice to Watford, Steve Walford to Norwich City

League & Cup Appearances

PLAYER	LEAGUE	CUP COMPETITION		TOTAL
		FA CUP	LC	
Davis	9 (1)			9 (1)
Devine	38 (1)	1	4	43 (1)
Gatting	22 (1)	1	2	25 (1)
Hollins	38	1	4	43
Jennings	31	1	2	34
McDermott	16 (7)	0 (1)	0 (1)	16 (9)
Nelson	0 (1)			0 (1)
Nicholas P.	8			8
O'Leary	24	1	2	27
Price	9 (3)		2	11 (3)
Rice	0 (2)			0 (2)
Rix	35	1	4	40
Sansom	42	1	4	47
Stapleton	40	1	4	45
Sunderland	34	1	4	39
Talbot	40	1	4	45
Vaessen	5 (2)			5 (2)
Walford	20		2	22
Wood	11		2	13
Young	40	1	4	45

Goalscorers

PLAYER	LEAGUE	CUP COMPETITION		TOTAL
		FA CUP	LC	
Stapleton	14		2	16
Sunderland	7		2	9
Talbot	7			7
Hollins	5		2	7
McDermott	5			5
Rix	5			5
Young	4			4
Gatting	3			3
Sansom	3			3
Vaessen	2			2
Davis	1			1
Nicholas P.	1			1
O'Leary	1			1
Price	1			1
Walford		1		1
Opps' o.gs.	2			2

Final Division One Table

		P	W	D	L	F	A	Pts
1	ASTON VILLA	42	26	8	8	72	40	60
2	IPSWICH T	42	23	10	9	77	43	56
3	ARSENAL	42	19	15	8	61	45	53
4	WBA	42	20	12	10	60	42	52
5	LIVERPOOL	42	17	17	8	62	46	51
6	SOUTHAMPTON	42	20	10	12	76	56	50
7	NOTTINGHAM F	42	19	12	11	62	44	50
8	MANCHESTER U	42	15	18	9	51	36	48
9	LEEDS U	42	17	10	15	39	47	44
10	TOTTENHAM H	42	14	15	13	70	68	43
11	STOKE C	42	12	18	12	51	60	42
12	MANCHESTER C	42	14	11	17	56	59	39
13	BIRMINGHAM C	42	13	12	17	50	61	38
14	MIDDLESBROUGH	42	16	5	21	53	61	37
15	EVERTON	42	13	10	19	55	58	36
16	COVENTRY C	42	13	10	19	48	68	36
17	SUNDERLAND	42	14	7	21	52	53	35
18	WOLVERHAMPTON W	42	13	9	20	43	55	3
19	BRIGHTON & HA	42	14	7	21	54	67	35
20	NORWICH C	42	13	7	22	49	73	33
21	LEICESTER C	42	13	6	23	40	67	32
22	CRYSTAL PALACE	42	6	7	29	47	83	19

Season 1981-82

Football League Division One

DATE	OPPONENTS	SCORE	GOALSCORERS	ATTENDANCE
Aug 29	STOKE CITY	L 0-1		28,012
Sep 2	West Bromwich Albion	W 2-0	Talbot, Sunderland	17,104
Sep 5	Liverpool	L 0-2		35,269
Sep 12	SUNDERLAND	D 1-1	Sunderland	26,527
Sep 19	Leeds United	D 0-0		21,410
Sep 22	BIRMINGHAM CITY	W 1-0	Talbot	19,588
Sep 26	MANCHESTER UNITED	D 0-0		39,797
Oct 3	Notts County	L 1-2	Hawley	10,840
Oct 10	Swansea City	L 0-2		20,591
Oct 17	MANCHESTER CITY	W 1-0	Meade	25,466
Oct 24	Ipswich Town	L 1-2	Sunderland	24,362
Oct 31	COVENTRY CITY	W 1-0	o.g.	23,102
Nov 7	Aston Villa	W 2-0	Talbot, Rix	27,316
Nov 21	Nottingham Forest	W 2-1	Talbot, Sunderland	20,912
Nov 28	EVERTON	W 1-0	McDermott	25,860
Dec 5	West Ham United	W 2-1	Hollins (pen), Whyte	33,833
Jan 20	Stoke City	W 1-0	Sunderland	9,625
Jan 23	Southampton	L 1-3	O'Leary	22,263
Jan 26	BRIGHTON & HOVE ALBION	D 0-0		17,922
Jan 30	LEEDS UNITED	W 1-0	Vaessen	22,408
Feb 2	WOLVERHAMPTON WANDERERS	W 2-1	Rix, Vaessen	15,163
Feb 6	Sunderland	D 0-0		16,345
Feb 13	NOTTS COUNTY	W 1-0	Meade	18,229
Feb 16	MIDDLESBROUGH	W 1-0	Rix	13,738
Feb 20	Manchester United	D 0-0		43,833
Feb 27	SWANSEA CITY	L 0-2		29,724
Mar 6	Manchester City	D 0-0		30,288
Mar 13	IPSWICH TOWN	W 1-0	Robson	25,977
Mar 16	WEST BROMWICH ALBION	D 2-2	Meade, Sunderland	15,799
Mar 20	Coventry City	L 0-1		11,965
Mar 27	ASTON VILLA	W 4-3	Sunderland, Rix 2, Meade	24,756
Mar 29	Tottenham Hotspur	D 2-2	Sunderland 2	40,940
Apr 3	Wolverhampton Wanderers	D 1-1	Davis	11,532
Apr 10	Brighton & Hove Albion	L 1-2	Talbot	21,019
Apr 12	TOTTENHAM HOTSPUR	L 1-3	Hawley	48,897
Apr 17	NOTTINGHAM FOREST	W 2-0	Talbot, Rix	21,986
Apr 24	Everton	L 1-2	Rix	19,136
May 1	WEST HAM UNITED	W 2-0	Rix, Sunderland	34,977
May 4	Birmingham City	W 1-0	Whyte	13,133
May 8	Middlesbrough	W 3-1	Talbot, Davis, Rix	9,565
May 11	LIVERPOOL	D 1-1	Sunderland	30,932
May 15	SOUTHAMPTON	W 4-1	Davis 2, Robson, Hawley	28,534

FA Cup

Jan 2	Tottenham Hotspur	(Rd3)	L	0-1	38,421

League Cup

Oct 6	Sheffield United	(Rd2/1L)	L 0-1		19,101
Oct 27	SHEFFIELD UNITED	(Rd2/2L)	W 2-0	Sunderland, Young	22,301
Nov 10	Norwich City	(Rd3)	W 1-0	Nicholas P.	19,899
Dec 1	LIVERPOOL	(Rd4)	D 0-0		37,917
Dec 8	Liverpool	(R)	L 0-3		21,375

UEFA Cup

Sep 16	Panathinaikos	(Rd1/1L)	W 2-0	McDermot, Meade	20,000
Sep 30	PANATHINAIKOS	(Rd1/2L)	W 1-0	Talbot	23,513
Oct 20	Winterslag	(Rd2/1L)	L 0-1		10,000
Nov 3	WINTERSLAG*	(Rd2/2L)	W 2-1	Hollins, Rix	22,930

*Lost on away goals.

Fact File

The departure of Frank Stapleton, following the loss of Liam Brady, was evident in Arsenal's goal tally – 56 in 52 league and cup matches. Five different players had spells as Alan Sunderland's strike partner.

MANAGER: Terry Neill

CAPTAIN: David O'Leary

TOP SCORER: Alan Sunderland 12 (11 League)

BIGGEST WIN: 4-1 v Southampton, 15 May 1982, League

HIGHEST ATTENDANCE: 48,897 v Tottenham Hotspur, 12 April 1982, League

MAJOR TRANSFERS OUT: Frank Stapleton to Manchester United, Willie Young to Nottingham Forest

League & Cup Appearances

PLAYER	LEAGUE	CUP COMPETITION			TOTAL
		FA CUP	LC	UEFA	
Davis	37 (1)	1	4	1 (1)	43 (2)
Devine	10 (1)		1	2	13 (1)
Gorman	4				4
Hankin			0 (2)		0 (2)
Hawley	12 (2)		1		13 (2)
Hollins	40	1	5	4	50
Jennings	16	1	4	4	25
McDermott	9 (4)		3	3 (1)	15 (5)
Meade	8 (8)	0 (1)	1 (1)	2 (1)	11 (11)
Nicholas P.	28 (3)	1	5	4	38 (3)
O'Leary	40	1	5	4	50
Rix	39	1	4	4	48
Robson	20	1	1		22
Sansom	42	1	5	4	52
Sunderland	38	1	5	2	46
Talbot	42	1	5	4	52
Vaessen	9 (1)		0 (1)	2	11 (2)
Whyte	32	1	3	1 (1)	37 (1)
Wood	26		1		27
Young	10		2	3	15

Goalscorers

PLAYER	LEAGUE	CUP COMPETITION			TOTAL
		FA CUP	LC	UEFA	
Sunderland	11		1		12
Rix	9			1	10
Talbot	7			1	8
Meade	4			1	5
Davis	4				4
Hawley	3				3
Robson	2				2
Vaessen	2				2
Whyte	2				2
Hollins	1			1	2
McDermott	1			1	2
O'Leary	1				1
Nicholas P.			1		1
Young			1		1
Opps' o.g.s.	1				1

Final Division One Table

		P	W	D	L	F	A	Pts
1	LIVERPOOL	42	26	9	7	80	32	87
2	IPSWICH T	42	26	5	11	75	53	83
3	MANCHESTER U	42	22	12	8	59	29	78
4	TOTTENHAM H	42	20	11	11	67	48	71
5	ARSENAL	42	20	11	11	48	37	71
6	SWANSEA C	42	21	6	15	58	51	69
7	SOUTHAMPTON	42	19	9	14	72	67	66
8	EVERTON	42	17	13	12	56	50	64
9	WEST HAM U	42	14	16	12	66	57	58
10	MANCHESTER C	42	15	13	14	49	50	58
11	ASTON VILLA	42	15	12	15	55	53	57
12	NOTTINGHAM F	42	15	12	15	42	48	57
13	BRIGHTON & HA	42	13	13	16	43	52	52
14	COVENTRY C	42	13	11	18	56	62	50
15	NOTTS CO	42	13	8	21	61	69	47
16	BIRMINGHAM C	42	10	14	18	53	61	44
17	WBA	42	11	11	20	46	57	44
18	STOKE C	42	12	8	22	44	63	44
19	SUNDERLAND	42	11	11	20	38	58	44
20	LEEDS U	42	10	12	20	39	61	42
21	WOLVERHAMPTON W	42	10	10	22	32	63	40
22	MIDDLESBROUGH	42	8	15	19	34	52	39

Season 1982-83

Football League Division One

DATE	OPPONENTS	SCORE	GOALSCORERS	ATTENDANCE
Aug 28	Stoke City	L 1-2	Sunderland	15,532
Aug 31	NORWICH CITY	D 1-1	Woodcock	22,652
Sep 4	LIVERPOOL	L 0-2		36,429
Sep 7	Brighton & Hove Albion	L 0-1		13,507
Sep 11	Coventry City	W 2-0	Chapman, Woodcock	10,246
Sep 18	NOTTS COUNTY	W 2-0	Rix, Hollins (pen)	20,556
Sep 25	Manchester United	D 0-0		43,198
Oct 2	WEST HAM UNITED	L 2-3	Talbot, Davis	30,484
Oct 9	Ipswich Town	W 1-0	Woodcock	20,792
Oct 16	WEST BROMWICH ALBION	W 2-0	Sunderland, Woodcock	21,666
Oct 23	Nottingham Forest	L 0-3		17,161
Oct 30	BIRMINGHAM CITY	D 0-0		20,699
Nov 6	Luton Town	D 2-2	Rix, Talbot	16,597
Nov 13	EVERTON	D 1-1	McDermott	23,067
Nov 20	Swansea City	W 2-1	Woodcock, Chapman	12,389
Nov 27	WATFORD	L 2-4	Robson, Talbot	34,287
Dec 4	Manchester City	L 1-2	McDermott	23,057
Dec 7	ASTON VILLA	W 2-1	Whyte, Woodcock	17,384
Dec 18	Sunderland	L 0-3		11,753
Dec 27	TOTTENHAM HOTSPUR	W 2-0	Sunderland, Woodcock	51,497
Dec 28	Southampton	D 2-2	Woodcock, Chapman	22,025
Jan 1	SWANSEA CITY	W 2-1	Sunderland, Woodcock	25,237
Jan 3	Liverpool	L 1-3	Talbot	37,713
Jan 15	STOKE CITY	W 3-0	Rix, Petrovic, Hollins (pen)	19,428
Jan 22	Notts County	L 0-1		9,731
Feb 5	BRIGHTON & HOVE ALBION	W 3-1	Meade 2, Rix	17,972
Feb 26	West Bromwich Albion	D 0-0		13,923
Mar 5	NOTTINGHAM FOREST	D 0-0		21,698
Mar 15	Birmingham City	L 1-2	Sunderland	11,276
Mar 19	LUTON TOWN	W 4-1	Woodcock 3, Davis	23,987
Mar 22	IPSWICH TOWN	D 2-2	Rix, Whyte	17,639
Mar 26	Everton	W 3-2	Sunderland, Robson, Woodcock	16,318
Apr 2	SOUTHAMPTON	D 0-0		24,911
Apr 4	Tottenham Hotspur	L 0-5		43,642
Apr 9	COVENTRY CITY	W 2-1	Rix, Woodcock	19,152
Apr 20	Norwich City	L 1-3	Davis	16,858
Apr 23	MANCHESTER CITY	W 3-0	Talbot 3	16,810
Apr 30	Watford	L 1-2	McDermott	20,043
May 2	MANCHESTER UNITED	W 3-0	O'Leary, Talbot 2	23,602
May 7	SUNDERLAND	L 0-1		18,053
May 10	West Ham United	W 3-1	Whyte, Petrovic, McDermott	28,930
May 14	Aston Villa	L 1-2	Davis	24,647

FA Cup

Jan 8	BOLTON WANDERERS	(Rd3) W 2-1	Davis, Rix	22,576
Jan 29	LEEDS UNITED	(Rd4) D 1-1	Sunderland	33,930
Feb 2	Leeds United	(R) D 1-1	Rix	24,410
Feb 9	LEEDS UNITED	(2R) W 2-1	Woodcock, Rix	26,802
Feb 19	Middlesbrough	(Rd5) D 1-1	Rix	20,580
Feb 28	MIDDLESBROUGH	(R) W 3-2	Talbot, Woodcock, Davis	28,689
Mar 12	ASTON VILLA	(QF) W 2-0	Woodcock, Petrovic	41,774
Apr 16	Manchester United*	(SF) L 1-2	Woodcock	46,535

*Played at Villa Park.

League Cup

Oct 5	CARDIFF CITY	(Rd2/1L) W 2-1	Hollins, Davis	15,115
Oct 26	Cardiff City	(Rd2/2L) W 3-1	Sunderland, Woodcock, Davis	11,632
Nov 9	Everton	(Rd3) D 1-1	Robson	13,089
Nov 23	EVERTON	(R) W 3-0	Sunderland	19,547
Nov 30	HUDDERSFIELD TOWN	(Rd4) W 1-0	Sunderland (pen)	17,742
Jan 18	SHEFFIELD WEDNESDAY	(QF) W 1-0	Woodcock	30,937
Feb 15	MANCHESTER UNITED	(SF1/1L) L 2-4	Nicholas P., Woodcock	43,136
Feb 23	Manchester United	(SF2/2L) L 1-2	Meade	56,635

UEFA Cup

Sep 14	Spartak Moscow	(Rd1/1L) L 2-3	Robson, Chapman	68,500
Sep 29	SPARTAK MOSCOW	(Rd1/2L) L 2-5	Chapman, o.g.	28,445

MANAGER: Terry Neill

CAPTAIN: David O'Leary

TOP SCORER: Tony Woodcock 21 (14 League)

BIGGEST WIN: 4-1 v Luton Town, 19 March 1983, League

HIGHEST ATTENDANCE: 51,497 v Tottenham Hotspur, 27 December 1982, League

MAJOR TRANSFERS IN: Tony Woodcock from Koln, Lee Chapman from Stoke City, Vladimir Petrovic from Red Star Belgrade

League & Cup Appearances

PLAYER	LEAGUE	CUP COMPETITION			TOTAL
		FA CUP	LC	UEFA	
Chapman	12 (7)		(1)	(2)	2	14 (10)
Davis	40 (1)	5 (1)	6 (2)	2	53 (4)
Devine	8 (1)				8 (1)
Hawley	2 (4)				2 (4)
Hill	7				7
Hollins	22 (1)	8	5	2	37 (1)
Jennings	19	7	4		30
Kay	7				7
McDermott	7 (2)			0 (1)	7 (3)
Meade	2 (2)	1	2		5 (2)
Nicholas P.	21	7	3		31
O'Leary	36	5	7	2	50
O'Shea	6		3		9
Petrovic	10 (3)	6	3		19 (3)
Rix	36	8	8	2	54
Robson	31	8	8	2	49
Sansom	40	8	8	2	58
Sunderland	25	5	6	0 (1)	36 (1)
Talbot	38 (4)	7	7	2	54 (4)
Whyte	36	4	6	2	48
Wood	23	1	4	2	30
Woodcock	34	8	8	2	52

Goalscorers

PLAYER	LEAGUE	CUP COMPETITION			TOTAL
		FA CUP	LC	UEFA	
Woodcock	14	4	3		21
Sunderland	6	1	5		12
Talbot	9	1			10
Rix	6	4			10
Davis	4	2	2		8
Chapman	3			2	5
McDermott	4				4
Robson	2	1	1		4
Whyte	3				3
Hollins	2		1		3
Meade	2	1			3
Petrovic	2	1			3
O'Leary	1				1
Nicholas P.			1		1
Opps' o.gs.			1	1	1

Fact File

Arsenal signed Yugoslavia midfielder Vladimir Petrovic in the summer of 1982, but administrative problems with the transfer meant he had to wait until 1 January to make his debut for the Gunners. He moved on to Belgian club Royal Antwerp at the end of the season.

Final Division One Table

		P	W	D	L	F	A	Pts
1	LIVERPOOL	42	24	10	8	87	37	82
2	WATFORD	42	22	5	15	74	57	71
3	MANCHESTER U	42	19	13	8	56	38	70
4	TOTTENHAM H	42	20	9	13	65	50	69
5	NOTTINGHAM F	42	20	9	13	62	50	69
6	ASTON VILLA	42	21	5	16	62	50	68
7	EVERTON	42	18	10	14	66	48	64
8	WEST HAM U	42	20	4	.18	68	62	64
9	IPSWICH T	42	15	13	14	64	50	58
10	ARSENAL	42	16	10	16	58	56	58
11	WBA	42	15	12	15	51	49	57
12	SOUTHAMPTON	42	15	12	15	54	58	57
13	STOKE C	42	16	9	17	53	64	57
14	NORWICH C	42	14	12	16	52	58	54
15	NOTTS CO	42	15	7	20	55	71	52
16	SUNDERLAND	42	12	14	16	48	61	50
17	BIRMINGHAM C	42	12	15	16	40	55	50
18	LUTON T	42	12	13	17	65	84	49
19	COVENTRY C	42	13	9	20	48	59	48
20	MANCHESTER C	42	13	8	21	47	70	47
21	SWANSEA C	42	10	11	21	51	69	41
22	BRIGHTON & HA	42	9	13	20	38	68	40

Season 1983-84

Football League Division One

DATE	OPPONENTS	SCORE	GOALSCORERS	ATTENDANCE
Aug 27	LUTON TOWN	W 2-1	Woodcock, McDermott	39,348
Aug 29	Wolverhampton Wanderers	W 2-1	Nicholas C.	18,571
Sep 3	Southampton	L 0-1		19,377
Sep 6	MANCHESTER UNITED	L 2-3	Woodcock, Talbot	42,704
Sep 10	LIVERPOOL	L 0-2		41,896
Sep 17	Notts County	W 4-0	Rix, Woodcock, Talbot, o.g.	10,217
Sep 24	NORWICH CITY	W 3-0	Chapman, Sunderland 2	24,438
Oct 1	Queens Park Rangers	L 0-2		26,293
Oct 15	COVENTRY CITY	L 0-1		20,290
Oct 22	NOTTINGHAM FOREST	W 4-1	Woodcock 2, Hill, Sunderland	22,870
Oct 29	Aston Villa	W 6-2	Woodcock 5, McDermott	23,678
Nov 5	SUNDERLAND	L 1-2	Woodcock	26,064
Nov 12	Ipswich Town	L 0-1		21,652
Nov 19	EVERTON	W 2-1	Sunderland, Robson	24,330
Nov 26	Leicester City	L 0-3		14,777
Dec 3	WEST BROMWICH ALBION	L 0-1		22,271
Dec 10	West Ham United	L 1-3	Whyte	25,118
Dec 17	WATFORD	W 3-1	Meade 3	25,104
Dec 26	Tottenham Hotspur	W 4-2	Nicholas C. 2, Meade 2	38,756
Dec 27	BIRMINGHAM CITY	D 1-1	Nicholas (pen)	25,642
Dec 31	SOUTHAMPTON	D 2-2	Cork, Nicholas C. (pen)	27,596
Jan 2	Norwich City	D 1-1	Woodcock	20,482
Jan 14	Luton Town	W 2-1	Sansom, Woodcock	16,320
Jan 21	NOTTS COUNTY	D 1-1	Nicholas C.	20,110
Jan 28	Stoke City	L 0-1		12,840
Feb 4	QUEENS PARK RANGERS	L 0-2		31,014
Feb 11	Liverpool	L 1-2	Rix	34,642
Feb 18	ASTON VILLA	D 1-1	Rix	26,640
Feb 25	Nottingham Forest	W 1-0	Mariner	20,045
Mar 3	Sunderland	D 2-2	Nicholas C. (pen), Woodcock	15,370
Mar 10	IPSWICH TOWN	W 4-1	Mariner 2, Talbot, Woodcock	24,000
Mar 17	Manchester United	L 0-4		48,942
Mar 24	WOLVERHAMPTON WANDERERS	W 4-1	Robson, Woodcock, Nicholas C. (pen), Rix	18,612
Mar 31	Coventry City	W 4-1	Talbot, Whyte, Robson, Mariner	10,550
Apr 7	STOKE CITY	W 3-1	Nicholas C., Mariner, Woodcock	21,211
Apr 9	Everton	D 0-0		21,174
Apr 21	TOTTENHAM HOTSPUR	W 3-2	Robson, Nicholas C., Woodcock	48,831
Apr 23	Birmingham City	D 1-1	Woodcock	11,164
Apr 28	LEICESTER CITY	W 2-1	Woodcock, Davis	24,143
May 5	West Bromwich Albion	W 3-1	Talbot, Mariner, Robson	13,566
May 7	WEST HAM UNITED	D 3-3	Talbot, Woodcock, Mariner	33,347
May 12	Watford	L 1-2	Robson	22,007

FA Cup

Jan 7	Middlesbrough	(Rd3) L 2-3	Woodcock, Nicholas C.	17,813

League Cup

Oct 4	Plymouth Argyle	(Rd2/1L) D 1-1	Rix	20,983
Oct 25	PLYMOUTH ARGYLE	(Rd2/2L) W 1-0	Sunderland	22,640
Nov 9	Tottenham Hotspur	(Rd3) W 2-1	Nicholas C., Woodcock	48,200
Nov 29	WALSALL	(Rd4) L 1-2	Robson	22,406

League & Cup Appearances

PLAYER	LEAGUE	CUP COMPETITION FA CUP	LC	TOTAL
Adams	3			3
Allinson	7 (2)		1	8 (2)
Caton	26	1		27
Chapman	3 (1)			3 (1)
Cork	5 (2)	1		6 (2)
Davis	31 (4)	1	4	36 (4)
Gorman	1 (1)			1 (1)
Hill	37	1	4	42
Jennings	38	1	4	43
Kay	6 (1)			6 (1)
Lukic	4			4
McDermott	6 (7)			6 (7)
Madden	2			2
Mariner	15			15
Meade	9 (4)	1		10 (4)
Nicholas C.	41	1	4	46
O'Leary	36	1	4	41
Rix	34	1	3	38
Robson	28		4	32
Sansom	40	1	4	45
Sparrow	2			2
Sunderland	11 (1)	1	4	15 (1)
Talbot	26 (1)	0 (1)	0 (1)	26 (3)
Whyte	14 (1)		4	18 (1)
Woodcock	37	1	4	42

Goalscorers

PLAYER	LEAGUE	CUP COMPETITION FA CUP	LC	TOTAL
Woodcock	21	1	1	23
Nicholas C.	11	1	1	13
Mariner	7			7
Robson	6		1	7
Talbot	6			6
Meade	5			5
Rix	4		1	5
Sunderland	4		1	5
McDermott	2			2
Whyte	2			2
Chapman	1			1
Cork	1			1
Davis	1			1
Hill	1			1
Sansom	1			1
Opps' o.gs.	1			1

Fact File

Arsenal reached the FA Youth Cup semi-finals with a team including Tony Adams, Martin Keown, Gus Caesar, David Rocastle, Mickey Thomas, Niall Quinn and Martin Hayes.

MANAGER: Terry Neill/Don Howe

CAPTAIN: Graham Rix

TOP SCORER: Tony Woodcock 23 (21 League)

BIGGEST WIN: 6-2 v Aston Villa, 29 October 1983, League

HIGHEST ATTENDANCE: 48,831 v Tottenham Hotspur, 21 April 1984, League

MAJOR TRANSFERS IN: Charlie Nicholas from Celtic, John Lukic from Leeds United, Ian Allinson from Colchester United, Tommy Caton from Manchester City, Paul Mariner from Ipswich Town

MAJOR TRANSFERS OUT: Peter Nicholas to Crystal Palace, Alan Sunderland to Ipswich Town, Lee Chapman to Sunderland

Final Division One Table

		P	W	D	L	F	A	Pts
1	Liverpool	42	22	14	6	73	32	80
2	Southampton	42	22	11	9	66	38	77
3	Nottingham F	42	22	8	12	76	45	74
4	Manchester U	42	20	14	8	71	41	74
5	QPR	42	22	7	13	67	37	73
6	Arsenal	42	18	9	15	74	60	63
7	Everton	42	16	14	12	44	42	62
8	Tottenham H	42	17	10	15	64	65	61
9	West Ham U	42	17	9	16	60	55	60
10	Aston Villa	42	17	9	16	59	61	60
11	Watford	42	16	9	17	68	77	57
12	Ipswich T	42	15	8	19	55	57	53
13	Sunderland	42	13	13	16	42	53	52
14	Norwich C	42	12	15	15	48	49	51
15	Leicester C	42	13	12	17	65	68	51
16	Luton T	42	14	9	19	53	66	51
17	WBA	42	14	9	19	48	62	51
18	Stoke C	42	13	11	18	44	63	50
19	Coventry C	42	13	11	18	57	77	50
20	Birmingham C	42	12	12	18	39	50	48
21	Notts Co	42	10	11	21	50	72	41
22	Wolverhampton W	42	6	11	25	27	80	29

Season 1984-85

Football League Division One

DATE	OPPONENTS	SCORE	GOALSCORERS	ATTENDANCE
Aug 25	CHELSEA	D 1-1	Mariner	45,329
Aug 29	Nottingham Forest	L 0-2		17,972
Sep 1	Watford	W 4-3	Nicholas 2, Talbot, Woodcock	21,320
Sep 4	NEWCASTLE UNITED	W 2-0	Talbot, Anderson	37,078
Sep 8	LIVERPOOL	W 3-1	Talbot 2, Woodcock	50,006
Sep 15	Ipswich Town	L 1-2	Nicholas	24,508
Sep 22	STOKE CITY	W 4-0	Woodcock 2 (1 pen), Mariner, Sansom	26,758
Sep 29	Coventry City	W 2-1	Woodcock, Mariner	14,394
Oct 6	EVERTON	W 1-0	Nicholas (pen)	37,049
Oct 13	Leicester City	W 4-1	Talbot 2 (1 pen), Anderson, Rix	19,944
Oct 20	SUNDERLAND	W 3-2	Caton, Allinson, Talbot	36,944
Oct 27	West Ham United	L 1-3	Allinson	33,218
Nov 2	Manchester United	L 2-4	Allinson, Woodcock	32,379
Nov 10	ASTON VILLA	D 1-1	Mariner	33,193
Nov 17	QUEENS PARK RANGERS	W 1-0	Woodcock	34,953
Nov 25	Sheffield Wednesday	L 1-2	Woodcock	25,575
Dec 1	LUTON TOWN	W 3-1	Allinson, Woodcock, Anderson	26,366
Dec 8	Southampton	L 0-1		20,243
Dec 15	WEST BROMWICH ALBION	W 4-0	Allinson 2, Talbot, Davis (pen)	23,728
Dec 22	WATFORD	D 1-1	Allinson	31,302
Dec 26	Norwich City	L 0-1		17,702
Dec 29	Newcastle United	W 3-1	Nicholas 2, Talbot	27,349
Jan 1	TOTTENHAM HOTSPUR	L 1-2	Woodcock	48,714
Jan 19	Chelsea	D 1-1	Mariner	34,752
Feb 2	COVENTRY CITY	W 2-1	Meade, Allinson	21,791
Feb 12	Liverpool	L 0-3		28,645
Feb 23	MANCHESTER UNITED	L 0-1		48,612
Mar 2	WEST HAM UNITED	W 2-1	Mariner, Robson	25,818
Mar 9	Sunderland	D 0-0		27,694
Mar 13	Aston Villa	D 0-0		15,487
Mar 16	LEICESTER CITY	W 2-1	Williams, Meade	20,663
Mar 19	IPSWICH TOWN	D 1-1	Meade	18,365
Mar 23	Everton	L 0-2		36,387
Mar 30	Stoke City	L 0-2		7,371
Apr 6	NORWICH CITY	W 2-0	Nicholas, Robson	19,597
Apr 13	NOTTINGHAM FOREST	D 1-1	Allinson	24,152
Apr 17	Tottenham Hotspur	W 2-0	Nicholas, Talbot	40,399
Apr 20	Queens Park Rangers	L 0-1		20,189
Apr 27	SHEFFIELD WEDNESDAY	W 1-0	Mariner	23,803
May 4	Luton Town	L 1-3	Nicholas (pen)	12,251
May 6	SOUTHAMPTON	W 1-0	Rix	21,214
May 11	West Bromwich Albion	D 2-2	Allinson, o.g.	13,485

FA Cup

Jan 5	Hereford United	(Rd3) D 1-1	Woodcock	15,777
Jan 22	HEREFORD UNITED	(R) W 7-2	Mariner 2, Talbot 2, Nicholas, Allinson, Woodcock	26,023
Jan 26	York City	(Rd4) L 0-1		10,840

League Cup

Sep 25	BRISTOL ROVERS	(Rd2/1L) W 4-0	Woodcock, Anderson, Nicholas 2	23,871
Oct 9	Bristol Rovers	(Rd2/2L) D 1-1	Caton	10,408
Oct 31	Oxford United	(Rd3) L 2-3	Rix, Allinson	14,393

Fact File

Arsenal had topped the table in mid-October before falling away. A home defeat by Tottenham ended their flickering title hopes. Worse followed in the FA Cup at snowy York, where Keith Houchen's last-minute penalty sent the Fourth Division side into the fifth round at the Gunners' expense.

MANAGER: Don Howe

CAPTAIN: Graham Rix/Kenny Sansom

TOP SCORER: Tony Woodcock 13 (10 League)

BIGGEST WIN: 7-2 v Hereford United, 22 January 1985, FA Cup

HIGHEST ATTENDANCE: 50,006 v Liverpool, 8 September 1984, League

MAJOR TRANSFERS IN: Viv Anderson from Nottingham Forest, Steve Williams from Southampton

MAJOR TRANSFER OUT: Brian McDermott to Oxford United

League & Cup Appearances

PLAYER	LEAGUE	CUP COMPETITION		TOTAL
		FA CUP	LC	
Adams	15 (1)	1	0 (1)	16 (2)
Allinson	20 (7)	0 (2)	1	21 (9)
Anderson	41	3	3	47
Caton	35	3	3	41
Davis	21 (3)			21 (3)
Hill	2			2
Jennings	15		3	18
Lukic	27	3		30
Mariner	34 (2)	3	2	39 (2)
Meade	6 (2)			6 (2)
Nicholas C.	35 (3)	3	3	41 (3)
O'Leary	36	3	3	42
Rix	18		3	21
Robson	40	3	3	46
Sansom	39	2	3	44
Talbot	37 (4)	3	3	43 (4)
Williams	14 (1)		3	17 (1)
Woodcock	27	3	3	33

Goalscorers

PLAYER	LEAGUE	CUP COMPETITION		TOTAL
		FA CUP	LC	
Woodcock	10	2	1	13
Talbot	10	2		12
Nicholas	9	1	2	12
Allinson	10	1		11
Mariner	7	2		9
Anderson	3		1	4
Meade	3			3
Rix	2		1	3
Robson	2			2
Caton	1		1	2
Davis	1			1
Sansom	1			1
Williams	1			1
Opps' o.gs.	1			1

Final Division One Table

		P	W	D	L	F	A	PTS
1	EVERTON	42	28	6	8	88	43	90
2	LIVERPOOL	42	22	11	9	68	35	77
3	TOTTENHAM H	42	23	8	11	78	51	77
4	MANCHESTER U	42	22	10	10	77	47	76
5	SOUTHAMPTON	42	19	11	12	56	47	68
6	CHELSEA	42	18	12	12	63	48	66
7	ARSENAL	42	19	9	14	61	49	66
8	SHEFFIELD W	42	17	14	11	58	45	65
9	NOTTINGHAM F	42	19	7	16	56	48	64
10	ASTON VILLA	42	15	11	16	60	60	56
11	WATFORD	42	14	13	15	81	71	55
12	WBA	42	16	7	19	58	62	55
13	LUTON T	42	15	9	18	57	61	54
14	NEWCASTLE U	42	13	13	16	55	70	52
15	LEICESTER C	42	15	6	21	65	73	51
16	WEST HAM U	42	13	12	17	51	68	51
17	IPSWICH T	42	13	11	18	46	57	50
18	COVENTRY C	42	15	5	22	47	64	50
19	QPR	42	13	11	18	53	72	50
20	NORWICH C	42	13	10	19	46	64	49
21	SUNDERLAND	42	10	10	22	40	62	40
22	STOKE C	42	3	8	31	24	91	17

Season 1985-86

Football League Division One

DATE	OPPONENTS	SCORE	GOALSCORERS	ATTENDANCE
Aug 17	Liverpool	L 0-2		38,261
Aug 20	SOUTHAMPTON	W 3-2	Caton, Robson, Woodcock	21,895
Aug 24	MANCHESTER UNITED	L 1-2	Allinson (pen)	37,145
Aug 27	Luton Town	D 2-2	Woodcock, o.g.	10,012
Aug 31	LEICESTER CITY	W 1-0	Woodcock	18,207
Sep 3	Queens Park Rangers	W 1-0	Allinson	15,993
Sep 7	Coventry City	W 2-0	Woodcock, Nicholas C.	12,189
Sep 14	SHEFFIELD WEDNESDAY	W 1-0	Allinson (pen)	23,108
Sep 21	Chelsea	L 1-2	Nicholas C.	33,341
Sep 28	NEWCASTLE UNITED	D 0-0		24,104
Oct 5	ASTON VILLA	W 3-2	Woodcock, Anderson, Whyte	18,881
Oct 12	West Ham United	D 0-0		24,057
Oct 19	IPSWICH TOWN	W 1-0	Davis	19,523
Oct 26	Nottingham Forest	L 2-3	Rix, Davis	17,756
Nov 2	MANCHESTER CITY	W 1-0	Davis	22,264
Nov 9	Everton	L 1-6	Nicholas C.	28,620
Nov 16	OXFORD UNITED	W 2-1	Davis, Woodcock	19,632
Nov 23	West Bromwich Albion	D 0-0		9,165
Nov 30	BIRMINGHAM CITY	D 0-0		16,673
Dec 7	Southampton	L 0-3		15,052
Dec 14	LIVERPOOL	W 2-0	Nicholas C., Quinn	35,048
Dec 21	Manchester United	W 1-0	Nicholas C.	44,386
Dec 28	QUEENS PARK RANGERS	W 3-1	Rix, Nicholas C., Woodcock	25,770
Jan 1	TOTTENHAM HOTSPUR	D 0-0		45,109
Jan 18	Leicester City	D 2-2	Robson, Nicholas C.	11,246
Feb 1	LUTON TOWN	W 2-1	Allinson (pen), Rix	22,473
Mar 1	Newcastle United	L 0-1		21,860
Mar 8	Aston Villa	W 4-1	Nicholas C., Hayes, Rocastle, o.g.	10,584
Mar 11	Ipswich Town	W 2-1	Nicholas C., Woodcock	13,967
Mar 15	WEST HAM UNITED	W 1-0	Woodcock	31,240
Mar 22	COVENTRY CITY	W 3-0	Woodcock, Hayes, o.g.	17,189
Mar 29	Tottenham Hotspur	L 0-1		33,427
Mar 31	WATFORD	L 0-2		19,599
Apr 1	Watford	L 0-3		18,635
Apr 5	Manchester City	W 1-0	Robson	19,590
Apr 8	NOTTINGHAM FOREST	D 1-1	Allinson (pen)	15,098
Apr 12	EVERTON	L 0-1		28,251
Apr 16	Sheffield Wednesday	L 0-2		16,344
Apr 26	WEST BROMWICH ALBION	D 2-2	Robson, Allinson (pen)	14,843
Apr 29	CHELSEA	W 2-0	Anderson, Nicholas C.	24,025
May 3	Birmingham City	W 1-0	Woodcock	6,234
May 5	Oxford United	L 0-3		13,651

FA Cup

Jan 4	Grimsby Town	(Rd3) W 4-3	Rix, Nicholas C. 3	12,829
Jan 25	ROTHERHAM UNITED	(Rd4) W 5-1	Rix, Nicholas C., Allinson 2 (1 pen), Robson	28,490
Feb 15	Luton Town	(Rd5) D 2-2	Allinson, Rocastle	15,799
Mar 3	LUTON TOWN	(R) D 0-0		26,547
Mar 5	Luton Town	(2R) L 0-3		13,251

League Cup

Sep 25	Hereford United	(Rd2/1L) D 0-0		6,049
Oct 8	HEREFORD UNITED	(Rd2/2L) W 2-1	Anderson, Nicholas C.	15,789
Oct 30	Manchester City	(Rd3) W 2-1	Nicholas C., Allinson	18,279
Nov 19	SOUTHAMPTON	(Rd4) D 0-0		18,244
Nov 26	Southampton	(R) W 3-1	Hayes, Nicholas C., Robson	14,010
Jan 22	Aston Villa	(QF) D 1-1	Nicholas C.	26,093
Feb 4	ASTON VILLA	(R) L 1-2	Mariner	33,091

League & Cup Appearances

PLAYER	LEAGUE	CUP COMPETITION		TOTAL
		FA CUP	LC	
Adams	10			10
Allinson	28 (5)	5	5 (1)	38 (6)
Anderson	39	5	7	51
Caesar	2			2
Caton	20		7	27
Davis	28 (1)	1	5	34 (1)
Hayes	11	1	2	14
Keown	22	5		27
Lukic	40	5	6	51
Mariner	3 (6)	2 (1)	1 (1)	6 (8)
Nicholas C.	41	5	7	53
O'Leary	35	5	7	47
Quinn	10 (2)	2 (1)	2	14 (3)
Rix	38	4	5	47
Robson	26 (1)	1	4	31 (1)
Rocastle	13 (3)	5	2 (1)	20 (4)
Sansom	42	5	7	54
Whyte	4 (3)		1	5 (3)
Williams	17	3	3	23
Wilmot	2		1	3
Woodcock	31 (2)	1 (1)	5 (2)	37 (5)

Goalscorers

PLAYER	LEAGUE	CUP COMPETITION		TOTAL
		FA CUP	LC	
Nicholas C.	10	4	4	18
Woodcock	11			11
Allinson	6	3	1	10
Robson	4	1	1	6
Rix	3	2		5
Davis	4			4
Anderson	2		1	3
Hayes	2		1	3
Rocastle	1	1		2
Caton	1			1
Quinn	1			1
Whyte	1			1
Mariner			1	1
Opps' o.gs.	3			3

Fact File

Don Howe asked to be released from his contract in March 1986, amid rumours that Arsenal were in talks with Terry Venables, then at Barcelona. Howe's assistant Terry Burton and chief scout Steve Burtenshaw ran the team until the end of the season.

MANAGER: Don Howe **CAPTAIN:** Kenny Sansom
TOP SCORER: Charlie Nicholas 18 (10 League)
BIGGEST WIN: 5-1 v Rotherham United, 25 January 1986, FA Cup
HIGHEST ATTENDANCE: 45,109 v Tottenham Hotspur, 1 January 1986, League
MAJOR TRANSFERS OUT: Raphael Meade to Sporting Lisbon, Colin Hill to Maritimo de Funchal

Final Division One Table

		P	W	D	L	F	A	Pts
1	LIVERPOOL	42	26	10	6	89	37	88
2	EVERTON	42	26	8	8	87	41	86
3	WEST HAM U	42	26	6	10	74	40	84
4	MANCHESTER U	42	22	10	10	70	36	76
5	SHEFFIELD W	42	21	10	11	63	54	73
6	CHELSEA	42	20	11	11	57	56	71
7	ARSENAL	42	20	9	13	49	47	69
8	NOTTINGHAM F	42	19	11	12	69	53	68
9	LUTON T	42	18	12	12	61	44	66
10	TOTTENHAM H	42	19	8	15	74	52	65
11	NEWCASTLE U	42	17	12	13	67	72	63
12	WATFORD	42	16	11	15	69	62	59
13	QPR	42	15	7	20	53	64	52
14	SOUTHAMPTON	42	12	10	20	51	62	46
15	MANCHESTER C	42	11	12	19	43	57	45
16	ASTON VILLA	42	10	14	18	51	67	44
17	COVENTRY C	42	11	10	21	48	71	43
18	OXFORD U	42	10	12	20	62	80	42
19	LEICESTER C	42	10	12	20	54	76	42
20	IPSWICH T	42	11	8	23	32	55	41
21	BIRMINGHAM C	42	8	5	29	30	73	29
22	WBA	42	4	12	26	35	89	24

Season 1986-87

Football League Division One

DATE	OPPONENTS	SCORE	GOALSCORERS	ATTENDANCE
Aug 23	MANCHESTER UNITED	W 1-0	Nicholas	41,382
Aug 26	Coventry City	L 1-2	Anderson	11,182
Aug 30	Liverpool	L 1-2	Adams	38,637
Sep 2	SHEFFIELD WEDNESDAY	W 2-0	Adams, Quinn	20,101
Sep 6	TOTTENHAM HOTSPUR	D 0-0		44,707
Sep 13	Luton Town	D 0-0		9,876
Sep 20	OXFORD UNITED	D 0-0		20,676
Sep 27	Nottingham Forest	L 0-1		25,371
Oct 4	Everton	W 1-0	Williams	30,007
Oct 11	WATFORD	W 3-1	Groves, Hayes (pen), Quinn	24,076
Oct 18	Newcastle United	W 2-1	Anderson, Williams	22,368
Oct 25	CHELSEA	W 3-1	Rocastle, Hayes 2 (1 pen)	32,990
Nov 1	Charlton Athletic	W 2-0	Adams, Hayes	19,614
Nov 8	WEST HAM UNITED	D 0-0		36,084
Nov 15	Southampton	W 4-0	Hayes (pen), Quinn, Groves, Anderson	18,728
Nov 22	MANCHESTER CITY	W 3-0	Quinn, Anderson, Adams	29,009
Nov 29	Aston Villa	W 4-0	Hayes, Rocastle, Groves, o.g.	21,658
Dec 6	QUEENS PARK RANGERS	W 3-1	Hayes 2, Quinn	34,049
Dec 13	Norwich City	D 1-1	Hayes (pen)	21,049
Dec 20	LUTON TOWN	W 3-0	Quinn, Adams, Hayes	28,217
Dec 26	Leicester City	D 1-1	Hayes (pen)	19,205
Dec 27	SOUTHAMPTON	W 1-0	Quinn	38,138
Jan 1	WIMBLEDON	W 3-1	Nicholas 2, Hayes (pen)	36,144
Jan 4	Tottenham Hotspur	W 2-1	Adams, Davis	37,723
Jan 18	COVENTRY CITY	D 0-0		17,561
Jan 24	Manchester United	L 0-2		51,367
Feb 14	Sheffield Wednesday	D 1-1	Quinn	24,792
Feb 25	Oxford United	D 0-0		13,296
Mar 7	Chelsea	L 0-1		29,301
Mar 10	LIVERPOOL	L 0-1		47,777
Mar 17	NOTTINGHAM FOREST	D 0-0		18,352
Mar 21	Watford	L 0-2		18,172
Mar 28	EVERTON	L 0-1		36,218
Apr 8	West Ham United	L 1-3	Hayes (pen)	26,174
Apr 11	CHARLTON ATHLETIC	W 2-1	Davis, Hayes	26,111
Apr 14	NEWCASTLE UNITED	L 0-1		17,353
Apr 18	Wimbledon	W 2-1	Davis, Merson	8,515
Apr 20	LEICESTER CITY	W 4-1	Davis, Hayes 2 (1 pen), Nicholas	18,767
Apr 25	Manchester City	L 0-3		18,072
May 2	ASTON VILLA	W 2-1	Hayes 2 (1 pen)	18,463
May 4	Queens Park Rangers	W 4-1	Rix 2, Merson, Hayes	13,387
May 9	NORWICH CITY	L 1-2	Merson	24,001

FA Cup

Jan 10	Reading	(Rd3) W 3-1	Nicholas 2, Hayes (pen)	16,822
Jan 31	PLYMOUTH ARGYLE	(Rd4) W 6-1	Nicholas, Davis, Quinn, Rocastle, Anderson 2	39,029
Feb 21	BARNSLEY	(Rd5) W 2-0	Hayes (pen), Nicholas	28,302
Mar 14	WATFORD	(QF) L 1-3	Allinson	43,276

League Cup

Sep 23	HUDDERSFIELD TOWN	(Rd2/1L) W 2-0	Davis, Quinn	15,194
Oct 7	Huddersfield Town	(Rd2/2L) D 1-1	Hayes	8,713
Oct 28	MANCHESTER CITY	(Rd3) W 3-1	Rocastle, Hayes (pen), Davis	21,604
Nov 18	CHARLTON ATHLETIC	(Rd4) W 2-0	Quinn, o.g.	28,301
Jan 21	NOTTINGHAM FOREST	(QF) W 2-0	Nicholas, Hayes	38,617
Feb 8	TOTTENHAM HOTSPUR	(SF/1L) L 0-1		41,306
Mar 1	Tottenham Hotspur	(SF/2L) W 2-1	Anderson, Quinn	37,099
Mar 4	Tottenham Hotspur	(R) W 2-1	Allinson, Rocastle	41,055
Apr 5	Liverpool*	(F) W 2-1	Nicholas 2	96,000

*Played at Wembley

MANAGER: George Graham

CAPTAIN: Kenny Sansom

TOP SCORER: Martin Hayes 24 (19 League)

BIGGEST WIN: 6-1 v Plymouth Argyle, 31 January 1987, FA Cup

HIGHEST ATTENDANCE: 47,777 v Liverpool, 10 March 1987, League

MAJOR TRANSFERS IN: Perry Groves from Colchester United, Alan Smith from Leicester City

MAJOR TRANSFERS OUT: Tony Woodcock to Koln, Martin Keown to Aston Villa, Paul Mariner to Portsmouth, Tommy Caton to Oxford United

League & Cup Appearances

PLAYER	LEAGUE	CUP COMPETITION		TOTAL
		FA CUP	LC	
Adams	42	4	9	55
Allinson	5 (9)	2	1 (4)	8 (13)
Anderson	40	4	8	52
Caesar	6 (9)	0 (1)	1	7 (10)
Davis	39	3	9	51
Groves	19 (6)	2 (1)	4 (2)	25 (8)
Hayes	31 (4)	4	7 (1)	42 (5)
Lukic	36	4	9	49
Merson	5 (2)			5 (2)
Nicholas	25 (3)	2 (2)	6	33 (5)
O'Leary	39	4	9	52
Quinn	35	4	9	48
Rix	13 (5)		1 (2)	14 (7)
Robson	5			5
Rocastle	36	4	8	48
Sansom	35	4	9	48
Thomas	12	0 (2)	2 (2)	14 (4)
Williams	33 (1)	3	7	43 (1)
Wilmot	6			6

Goalscorers

PLAYER	LEAGUE	CUP COMPETITION		TOTAL
		FA CUP	LC	
Hayes	19	2	3	24
Quinn	8	1	3	12
Nicholas	4	4	3	11
Anderson	4	2	1	7
Davis	4	1	2	7
Adams	6			6
Rocastle	2	1	2	5
Groves	3			3
Merson	3			3
Rix	2			2
Williams	2			2
Allinson		1	1	2
Opps' o.gs.	1		1	2

Fact File

Arsenal won the League Cup for the first time, after overcoming Spurs in a semi-final trilogy. They were 2-0 down on aggregate at half-time of the second leg at White Hart Lane before fighting back to force a replay. The Gunners were never ahead in the tie until David Rocastle's winner in the closing minutes of the third game. Top scorer Martin Hayes made a habit of netting from the penalty spot. Twelve of his 24 goals were penalties.

Final Division One Table

		P	W	D	L	F	A	PTS
1	EVERTON	42	26	8	8	76	31	86
2	LIVERPOOL	42	23	8	11	72	42	77
3	TOTTENHAM H	42	21	8	13	68	43	71
4	ARSENAL	42	20	10	12	58	35	70
5	NORWICH CITY	42	17	17	8	53	51	68
6	WIMBLEDON	42	19	9	14	57	50	66
7	LUTON TOWN	42	18	12	12	47	45	66
8	NOTTINGHAM F	42	18	11	13	64	51	65
9	WATFORD	42	18	9	15	67	54	63
10	COVENTRY C	42	17	12	13	50	45	63
11	MANCHESTER U	42	14	14	14	52	45	56
12	SOUTHAMPTON	42	14	10	18	69	68	52
13	SHEFFIELD W	42	13	13	16	58	59	52
14	CHELSEA	42	13	13	16	53	64	52
15	WEST HAM U	42	14	10	18	52	67	52
16	QPR	42	13	11	18	48	64	50
17	NEWCASTLE U	42	12	11	19	47	65	47
18	OXFORD U	42	11	13	18	44	69	46
19	CHARLTON ATH	42	11	11	20	45	55	44
20	LEICESTER C	42	11	9	22	54	76	42
21	MANCHESTER C	42	8	15	19	36	57	39
22	ASTON VILLA	42	8	12	22	45	79	36

The Essential History of Arsenal

Season 1987-88

Football League Division One

DATE	OPPONENTS	SCORE	GOALSCORERS	ATTENDANCE
Aug 15	LIVERPOOL	L 1-2	Davis	54,703
Aug 19	Manchester United	D 0-0		42,890
Aug 22	Queens Park Rangers	L 0-2		18,981
Aug 29	PORTSMOUTH	W 6-0	Smith 3, Adams, Rocastle, Davis	30,865
Aug 31	Luton Town	D 1-1	Davis	8,745
Sep 12	Nottingham Forest	W 1-0	Smith	18,490
Sep 19	WIMBLEDON	W 3-0	Rocastle, Smith, Thomas (pen)	27,752
Sep 26	WEST HAM UNITED	W 1-0	Sansom	40,127
Oct 3	Charlton Athletic	W 3-0	Thomas, Adams, Groves	15,326
Oct 10	OXFORD UNITED	W 2-0	Davis, Williams	25,244
Oct 18	Tottenham Hotspur	W 2-1	Rocastle, Thomas	36,680
Oct 24	DERBY COUNTY	W 2-1	Richardson, Thomas (pen)	32,374
Oct 31	Newcastle United	W 1-0	Smith	23,622
Nov 3	CHELSEA	W 3-1	Richardson 2, o.g.	40,230
Nov 14	Norwich City	W 4-2	Rocastle 2, Thomas, Groves	20,558
Nov 21	SOUTHAMPTON	L 0-1		32,477
Nov 28	Watford	L 0-2		19,598
Dec 5	SHEFFIELD WEDNESDAY	W 3-1	Groves, Richardson, Merson	23,670
Dec 13	Coventry City	D 0-0		17,557
Dec 19	EVERTON	D 1-1	Rocastle	34,857
Dec 26	NOTTINGHAM FOREST	L 0-2		31,211
Dec 28	Wimbledon	L 1-3	Quinn	12,473
Jan 1	Portsmouth	D 1-1	Smith	17,366
Jan 2	QUEENS PARK RANGERS	D 0-0		28,271
Jan 16	Liverpool	L 0-2		44,294
Jan 24	MANCHESTER UNITED	L 1-2	Quinn	29,392
Feb 13	LUTON TOWN	W 2-1	Thomas, Rocastle	22,615
Feb 27	CHARLTON ATHLETIC	W 4-0	Merson 2, Thomas, Smith	25,394
Mar 6	TOTTENHAM HOTSPUR	W 2-1	Smith, Groves	37,143
Mar 19	NEWCASTLE UNITED	D 1-1	Groves	25,889
Mar 26	Derby County	D 0-0		18,382
Mar 30	Oxford United	D 0-0		9,088
Apr 2	Chelsea	D 1-1	o.g.	26,084
Apr 4	NORWICH CITY	W 2-0	Smith, Groves	19,341
Apr 9	Southampton	L 2-4	Davis, o.g.	14,521
Apr 12	West Ham United	W 1-0	Thomas	26,746
Apr 15	WATFORD	L 0-1		19,541
Apr 30	Sheffield Wednesday	D 3-3	Merson 2, Smith	16,681
May 2	COVENTRY CITY	D 1-1	Marwood (pen)	16,963
May 7	Everton	W 2-1	Thomas, Hayes	22,445

FA Cup

Jan 9	MILLWALL	(Rd3) W 2-0	Hayes, Rocastle	42,083
Jan 30	Brighton & Hove Albion	(Rd4) W 2-1	Richardson, Groves	26,467
Feb 20	MANCHESTER UNITED	(Rd5) W 2-1	Smith, o.g.	54,161
Mar 12	NOTTINGHAM FOREST	(QF) L 1-2	Rocastle	50,157

League Cup

Sep 23	Doncaster Rovers	(Rd2/1L) W 3-0	Groves, Smith, Williams	5,469
Oct 6	DONCASTER ROVERS	(Rd2/2L) W 1-0	Rocastle	18,321
Oct 27	BOURNEMOUTH	(Rd3) W 3-0	Richardson, Smith, Thomas (pen)	26,050
Nov 17	STOKE CITY	(Rd4) W 3-0	O'Leary, Rocastle, Richardson	30,058
Jan 20	Sheffield Wednesday	(QF) W 1-0	Winterburn	34,535
Feb 7	Everton	(SF/1L) W 1-0	Groves	25,476
Feb 24	EVERTON	(SF/2L) W 3-1	Thomas, Rocastle, Smith	51,148
Apr 24	Luton Town*	(F) L 2-3	Hayes, Smith	95,732

*Played at Wembley.

League & Cup Appearances

PLAYER	LEAGUE	CUP COMPETITION		TOTAL
		FA CUP	LC	
Adams	39	4	8	51
Caesar	17 (5)		2 (1)	19 (6)
Campbell	0 (1)			0 (1)
Davis	28 (1)	0 (1)	5 (1)	33 (3)
Dixon	6			6
Groves	28 (6)	3 (1)	7 (1)	38 (8)
Hayes	17 (10)	3 (1)	3 (2)	23 (13)
Lukic	40	4	8	52
Marwood	4			4
Merson	7 (8)	1	0 (1)	8 (9)
Nicholas	3			3
O'Leary	23	4	6	33
Quinn	6 (5)	1 (1)	1 (2)	8 (8)
Richardson	24 (5)	4	6 (1)	34 (6)
Rix	7 (3)	1 (1)	2	10 (4)
Rocastle	40	4	8	52
Sansom	34	4	8	46
Smith	36 (3)	3	8	47 (3)
Thomas	36 (1)	2	7	45 (1)
Williams	29	2	5	36
Winterburn	16 (1)	4	4	24 (1)

Goalscorers

PLAYER	LEAGUE	CUP COMPETITION		TOTAL
		FA CUP	LC	
Smith	11	1	4	16
Rocastle	7	2	3	12
Thomas	9		2	11
Groves	6	1	2	9
Richardson	4	1	2	7
Davis	5			5
Merson	5			5
Hayes	1	1	1	3
Adams	2			2
Quinn	2			2
Williams	1		1	2
Marwood	1			1
Sansom	1			1
O'Leary			1	1
Winterburn			1	1
Opps' o.gs.	3	1		4

Fact File

Charlie Nicholas, signed from Celtic in a blaze of publicity in 1983, left Arsenal after four and a half seasons. His last appearance came in the 2-0 defeat at Queens Park Rangers in August 1987. He did not play for the first team again before his transfer to Aberdeen in January 1988.

MANAGER: George Graham **CAPTAIN:** Kenny Sansom/Tony Adams
TOP SCORER: Alan Smith 16 (11 League)
BIGGEST WIN: 6-0 v Portsmouth, 29 August 1987, League
HIGHEST ATTENDANCE: 54,703 v Liverpool, 15 August 1987, League
MAJOR TRANSFERS IN: Nigel Winterburn from Wimbledon, Kevin Richardson from Watford, Lee Dixon from Stoke City, Brian Marwood from Sheffield Wednesday
MAJOR TRANSFER OUT: Charlie Nicholas to Aberdeen

Final Division One Table

		P	W	D	L	F	A	Pts
1	Liverpool	40	26	12	2	87	24	90
2	Manchester U	40	23	12	5	71	38	81
3	Nottingham F	40	20	13	7	67	39	73
4	Everton	40	19	13	8	53	27	70
5	QPR	40	19	10	11	48	38	67
6	Arsenal	40	18	12	10	58	39	66
7	Wimbledon	40	14	15	11	58	47	57
8	Newcastle U	40	14	14	12	55	53	56
9	Luton T	40	14	11	15	57	58	53
10	Coventry C	40	13	14	13	46	53	53
11	Sheffield W	40	15	8	17	52	66	53
12	Southampton	40	12	14	14	49	53	50
13	Tottenham H	40	12	11	17	38	48	47
14	Norwich C	40	12	9	19	40	52	45
15	Derby Co	40	10	13	17	35	45	43
16	West Ham U	40	9	15	16	40	52	42
17	Charlton Ath	40	9	15	16	38	52	42
18	Chelsea	40	9	15	16	50	68	42
19	Portsmouth	40	7	14	19	36	66	35
20	Watford	40	7	11	22	27	51	32
21	Oxford U	40	6	13	21	44	80	31

Season 1988-89

Football League Division One

DATE	OPPONENTS	SCORE	GOALSCORERS	ATTENDANCE
Aug 27	Wimbledon	W 5-1	Smith 3, Marwood, Merson	15,710
Sep 3	ASTON VILLA	L 2-3	Marwood, Smith	37,417
Sep 10	Tottenham Hotspur	W 3-2	Winterburn, Marwood, Smith	32,621
Sep 17	SOUTHAMPTON	D 2-2	Marwood (pen), Smith	31,384
Sep 24	Sheffield Wednesday	L 1-2	Smith	17,830
Oct 1	West Ham United	W 4-1	Smith 2, Thomas, Rocastle	27,658
Oct 22	QUEENS PARK RANGERS	W 2-1	Adams, Smith	33,202
Oct 25	Luton Town	D 1-1	Smith	10,548
Oct 29	COVENTRY CITY	W 2-0	Thomas, Adams	31,273
Nov 6	Nottingham Forest	W 4-1	Smith, Bould, Adams, Marwood	19,038
Nov 12	Newcastle United	W 1-0	Bould	24,003
Nov 19	MIDDLESBROUGH	W 3-0	Merson 2, Rocastle	32,294
Nov 26	Derby County	L 1-2	Thomas	21,209
Dec 4	LIVERPOOL	D 1-1	Smith	31,863
Dec 10	Norwich City	D 0-0		23,069
Dec 17	MANCHESTER UNITED	W 2-1	Thomas, Merson	37,422
Dec 26	Charlton Athletic	W 3-2	Marwood 2 (1 pen), Merson	18,439
Dec 31	Aston Villa	W 3-0	Smith, Rocastle, Groves	32,486
Jan 2	TOTTENHAM HOTSPUR	W 2-0	Merson, Thomas	45,129
Jan 14	Everton	W 3-1	Merson, Smith, Richardson	34,825
Jan 21	SHEFFIELD WEDNESDAY	D 1-1	Merson	33,490
Feb 4	WEST HAM UNITED	W 2-1	Groves, Smith	40,139
Feb 11	Millwall	W 2-1	Marwood, Smith	21,854
Feb 18	Queens Park Rangers	D 0-0		20,543
Feb 21	Coventry City	L 0-1		21,390
Feb 25	LUTON TOWN	W 2-0	Groves, Smith	31,012
Feb 28	MILLWALL	D 0-0		37,524
Mar 11	NOTTINGHAM FOREST	L 1-3	Smith	39,639
Mar 21	CHARLTON ATHLETIC	D 2-2	Rocastle, Davis	30,259
Mar 25	Southampton	W 3-1	Groves, Rocastle, Merson	19,202
Apr 2	Manchester United	D 1-1	Adams	37,977
Apr 8	EVERTON	W 2-0	Dixon, Quinn	37,608
Apr 15	NEWCASTLE UNITED	W 1-0	Marwood	38,023
May 1	NORWICH CITY	W 5-0	Winterburn, Smith 2, Rocastle, Thomas	28,449
May 6	Middlesbrough	W 1-0	Hayes	21,803
May 13	DERBY COUNTY	L 1-2	Smith	41,008
May 17	WIMBLEDON	D 2-2	Winterburn, Merson	39,132
May 26	Liverpool	W 2-0	Smith, Thomas	41,728

FA Cup

Jan 8	West Ham United	(Rd3) D 2-2	Merson 2	22,017
Jan 11	WEST HAM UNITED	(R) L 0-1		44,124

League Cup

Sep 28	Hull City	(Rd2/1L) W 2-1	Winterburn, Marwood	11,450
Oct 11	HULL CITY	(Rd2/2L) W 3-0	Merson, Smith 2	17,885
Nov 2	Liverpool	(Rd3) D 1-1	Rocastle	31,951
Nov 9	LIVERPOOL	(R) D 0-0		54,029
Nov 23	Liverpool*	(2R) L 1-2	Merson	21,708

*Played at Aston Villa.

League & Cup Appearances

PLAYER	LEAGUE	CUP COMPETITION		TOTAL
		FA CUP	LC	
Adams	36	2	5	43
Bould	26 (4)	1	5	32 (4)
Caesar	2			2
Davis	11 (1)	0 (2)	2	13 (3)
Dixon	31 (2)	1	5	37 (2)
Groves	6 (15)	0 (2)	1 (1)	7 (18)
Hayes	3 (14)		0 (4)	3 (18)
Lukic	38	2	5	45
Marwood	31	2	5	38
Merson	29 (8)	2	4	35 (8)
O'Leary	26	2		28
Quinn	2 (1)			2 (1)
Richardson	32 (2)	2	3 (2)	37 (4)
Rocastle	38	2	5	45
Smith	36	2	5	43
Thomas	33 (4)	2	5	40 (4)
Winterburn	38	2	5	45

Goalscorers

PLAYER	LEAGUE	CUP COMPETITION		TOTAL
		FA CUP	LC	
Smith	23		2	25
Merson	10	2	2	14
Marwood	9		1	10
Thomas	7			7
Rocastle	6		1	7
Adams	4			4
Groves	4			4
Winterburn	3		1	4
Bould	2			2
Davis	1			1
Dixon	1			1
Hayes	1			1
Quinn	1			1
Richardson	1			1

Fact File

Mickey Thomas scored probably the most dramatic goal in league history to give George Graham a rare 'double' – championship victories as a player and manager with the same club. Alan Smith finished First Division top scorer with 23 league goals. The Clock End was covered with a cantilever roof and executive boxes were installed.

MANAGER: George Graham
CAPTAIN: Tony Adams
TOP SCORER: Alan Smith 25 (23 League)
BIGGEST WIN: 5-0 v Norwich City, 1 May 1989, League
HIGHEST ATTENDANCE: 54,029 v Liverpool, 9 November 1988, League Cup
MAJOR TRANSFER IN: Steve Bould from Stoke City
MAJOR TRANSFERS OUT: Steve Williams to Luton Town, Kenny Sansom to Newcastle United

Final Division One Table

		P	W	D	L	F	A	Pts
1	ARSENAL	38	22	10	6	73	36	76
2	LIVERPOOL	38	22	10	6	65	28	76
3	NOTTINGHAM F	38	17	13	8	64	43	64
4	NORWICH C	38	17	11	10	48	45	62
5	DERBY CO	38	17	7	14	40	38	58
6	TOTTENHAM H	38	15	12	11	60	46	57
7	COVENTRY C	38	14	13	11	47	42	55
8	EVERTON	38	14	12	12	50	45	54
9	QPR	38	14	11	13	43	37	53
10	MILLWALL	38	14	11	13	47	52	53
11	MANCHESTER U	38	13	12	13	45	35	51
12	WIMBLEDON	38	14	9	15	50	46	51
13	SOUTHAMPTON	38	10	15	13	52	66	45
14	CHARLTON ATH	38	10	12	16	44	58	42
15	SHEFFIELD W	38	10	12	16	34	51	42
16	LUTON T	38	10	11	17	42	52	41
17	ASTON VILLA	38	9	13	16	45	56	40
18	MIDDLESBROUGH	38	9	12	17	44	61	39
19	WEST HAM U	38	10	8	20	37	62	38
20	NEWCASTLE U	38	7	10	21	32	63	31

Season 1989-90

Football League Division One

DATE	OPPONENTS	SCORE	GOALSCORERS	ATTENDANCE
Aug 19	Manchester United	L 1-4	Rocastle	47,245
Aug 22	COVENTRY CITY	W 2-0	Thomas, Marwood	33,886
Aug 26	WIMBLEDON	D 0-0		32,279
Sep 9	SHEFFIELD WEDNESDAY	W 5-0	Merson, Smith, Thomas, Adams, Marwood	30,058
Sep 16	Nottingham Forest	W 2-1	Marwood, Merson	22,216
Sep 23	CHARLTON ATHLETIC	W 1-0	Marwood (pen)	34,583
Sep 30	Chelsea	D 0-0		31,833
Oct 14	MANCHESTER CITY	W 4-0	Groves 2, Merson, Thomas	40,414
Oct 18	Tottenham Hotspur	L 1-2	Thomas	33,944
Oct 21	Everton	L 0-3		32,917
Oct 28	DERBY COUNTY	D 1-1	Smith	33,189
Nov 4	NORWICH CITY	W 4-3	Quinn, O'Leary, Dixon 2 (1 pen)	35,338
Nov 11	Millwall	W 2-1	Quinn, Thomas	17,265
Nov 18	QUEENS PARK RANGERS	W 3-0	Dixon (pen), Smith, Jonsson	38,236
Nov 26	Liverpool	L 1-2	Smith	35,983
Dec 3	MANCHESTER UNITED	W 1-0	Groves	34,484
Dec 9	Coventry City	W 1-0	Merson	16,255
Dec 16	LUTON TOWN	W 3-2	Smith, Marwood, Merson	28,761
Dec 26	Southampton	L 0-1		20,229
Dec 30	Aston Villa	L 1-2	Adams	40,665
Jan 1	CRYSTAL PALACE	W 4-1	Smith 2, Dixon, Adams	38,711
Jan 13	Wimbledon	L 0-1		13,793
Jan 20	TOTTENHAM HOTSPUR	W 1-0	Adams	46,132
Feb 17	Sheffield Wednesday	L 0-1		20,640
Feb 27	Charlton Athletic	D 0-0		17,504
Mar 3	Queens Park Rangers	L 0-2		18,067
Mar 7	NOTTINGHAM FOREST	W 3-0	Groves, Adams, Campbell	31,879
Mar 10	Manchester City	D 1-1	Marwood	29,087
Mar 17	CHELSEA	L 0-1		33,805
Mar 24	Derby County	W 3-1	Hayes 2, Campbell	17,514
Mar 31	EVERTON	W 1-0	Smith	35,223
Apr 11	ASTON VILLA	L 0-1		30,060
Apr 14	Crystal Palace	D 1-1	Hayes	28,094
Apr 18	LIVERPOOL	D 1-1	Merson	33,395
Apr 21	Luton Town	L 0-2		11,595
Apr 28	MILLWALL	W 2-0	Davis, Merson	25,607
May 2	SOUTHAMPTON	W 2-1	Dixon (pen), Rocastle	23,732
May 5	Norwich City	D 2-2	Smith 2	19,256

FA Cup

Date	Opponent		Score	Goalscorers	Attendance
Jan 6	Stoke City	(Rd3)	W 1-0	Quinn	23,827
Jan 27	QUEENS PARK RANGERS	(Rd4)	D 0-0		43,483
Jan 31	Queens Park Rangers	(R)	L 0-2		21,547

League Cup

Date	Opponent		Score	Goalscorers	Attendance
Sep 19	PLYMOUTH ARGYLE	(Rd2/1L)	W 2-0	Smith, o.g.	26,865
Oct 3	Plymouth Argyle	(Rd2/2L)	W 6-1	Thomas 3, Smith, Groves, o.g.	17,360
Oct 25	LIVERPOOL	(Rd3)	W 1-0	Smith	40,814
Nov 22	Oldham Athletic	(Rd4)	L 1-3	Quinn	14,924

League & Cup Appearances

PLAYER	LEAGUE	CUP COMPETITION		TOTAL
		FA CUP	LC	
Adams	38	3	4	45
Ampadu	0 (2)			0 (2)
Bould	19	3		22
Caesar	0 (3)		0 (1)	0 (4)
Campbell	8 (7)			8 (7)
Davis	8 (3)	2		10 (3)
Dixon	38	3	4	45
Groves	20 (10)	3	1 (2)	24 (12)
Hayes	8 (4)		2	10 (4)
Jonsson	0 (6)	0 (1)	1	1 (7)
Lukic	38	3	4	45
Marwood	17		1	18
Merson	21 (8)	1 (2)	2 (1)	24 (11)
O'Leary	28 (6)	3	4	35 (6)
Pates	1 (1)			1 (1)
Quinn	6	1	2	9
Richardson	32 (1)	3	4	39 (1)
Rocastle	28 (5)	2 (1)	4	34 (6)
Smith	37 (1)	2	3 (1)	42 (2)
Thomas	35 (1)	2 (1)	4	41 (2)
Winterburn	36	2	4	42

Goalscorers

PLAYER	LEAGUE	CUP COMPETITION		TOTAL
		FA CUP	LC	
Smith	10		3	13
Thomas	5		3	8
Merson	7			7
Marwood	6			6
Adams	5			5
Dixon	5			5
Groves	4		1	5
Quinn	2	1	1	4
Hayes	3			3
Campbell	2			2
Rocastle	2			2
Davis	1			1
Jonsson	1			1
O'Leary	1			1
Opps' o.gs.			2	2

Fact File

Arsenal were unable to play in the European Cup because of the five-year European ban imposed on English clubs after the Heysel stadium tragedy. David O'Leary broke George Armstrong's club appearance record. By the end of the season, he had made 646 appearances. He also scored the penalty shootout decider against Romania to send Ireland into the 1990 World Cup quarter-finals.

MANAGER: George Graham

CAPTAIN: Tony Adams

TOP SCORER: Alan Smith 13 (10 League)

BIGGEST WIN: 6-1 v Plymouth Argyle, 3 October 1989, League Cup

HIGHEST ATTENDANCE: 46,132 v Tottenham Hotspur, 20 January 1990, League

MAJOR TRANSFER IN: Colin Pates from Charlton Athletic

MAJOR TRANSFER OUT: Niall Quinn to Manchester City

Final Division One Table

		P	W	D	L	F	A	PTS
1	LIVERPOOL	38	23	10	5	78	37	79
2	ASTON VILLA	38	21	7	10	57	38	70
3	TOTTENHAM H	38	19	6	13	59	47	63
4	ARSENAL	38	18	8	12	54	38	62
5	CHELSEA	38	16	12	10	58	50	60
6	EVERTON	38	17	8	13	57	46	59
7	SOUTHAMPTON	38	15	10	13	71	63	55
8	WIMBLEDON	38	13	16	9	47	40	55
9	NOTTINGHAM F	38	15	9	14	55	47	54
10	NORWICH CITY	38	13	14	11	44	42	53
11	QPR	38	13	11	14	45	44	50
12	COVENTRY CITY	38	14	7	17	39	59	49
13	MANCHESTER U	38	13	9	16	46	47	48
14	MANCHESTER C	38	12	12	14	43	52	48
15	CRYSTAL P	38	13	9	16	42	66	48
16	DERBY C	38	13	7	18	43	40	46
17	LUTON T	38	10	13	15	43	57	43
18	SHEFFIELD W	38	11	10	17	35	51	43
19	CHARLTON ATH	38	7	9	22	31	57	30
20	MILLWALL	38	5	11	22	39	65	26

Season 1990-91

Football League Division One

DATE	OPPONENTS	SCORE	GOALSCORERS	ATTENDANCE
Aug 25	Wimbledon	W 3-0	Merson, Smith, Groves	13,733
Aug 29	LUTON TOWN	W 2-1	Merson, Thomas	32,723
Sep 1	TOTTENHAM HOTSPUR	D 0-0		40,009
Sep 8	Everton	D 1-1	Groves	29,919
Sep 15	CHELSEA	W 4-1	Limpar, Dixon (pen), Merson, Rocastle	40,475
Sep 22	Nottingham Forest	W 2-0	Rocastle, Limpar	26,013
Sep 29	Leeds United	D 2-2	Limpar 2	30,085
Oct 6	NORWICH CITY	W 2-0	Davis 2	36,737
Oct 20	Manchester United	W 1-0	Limpar	47,232
Oct 27	SUNDERLAND	W 1-0	Dixon (pen)	38,485
Nov 3	Coventry City	W 2-0	Limpar 2	15,336
Nov 10	Crystal Palace	D 0-0		28,282
Nov 17	SOUTHAMPTON	W 4-0	Smith 2, Merson, Limpar	36,229
Nov 24	Queens Park Rangers	W 3-1	Merson, Smith, Campbell	18,555
Dec 2	LIVERPOOL	W 3-0	Merson, Dixon (pen), Smith	40,419
Dec 8	Luton Town	D 1-1	Smith	12,506
Dec 15	WIMBLEDON	D 2-2	Merson, Adams	30,164
Dec 23	Aston Villa	D 0-0		22,687
Dec 26	DERBY COUNTY	W 3-0	Smith 2, Merson	25,558
Dec 29	SHEFFIELD UNITED	W 4-1	Dixon (pen), Smith 2, Thomas	37,810
Jan 1	Manchester City	W 1-0	Smith	30,579
Jan 12	Tottenham Hotspur	D 0-0		34,753
Jan 19	EVERTON	W 1-0	Merson	35,349
Feb 2	Chelsea	L 1-2	Smith	29,094
Feb 23	CRYSTAL PALACE	W 4-0	O'Leary, Merson, Smith, Campbell	42,162
Mar 3	Liverpool	W 1-0	Merson	37,221
Mar 17	LEEDS UNITED	W 2-0	Campbell 2	26,218
Mar 20	NOTTINGHAM FOREST	D 1-1	Campbell	34,152
Mar 23	Norwich City	D 0-0		20,131
Mar 30	Derby County	W 2-0	Smith 2	18,397
Apr 3	ASTON VILLA	W 5-0	Campbell 2, Smith 2, Davis	41,868
Apr 6	Sheffield United	W 2-0	Campbell, Smith	26,920
Apr 9	Southampton	D 1-1	o.g.	21,300
Apr 17	MANCHESTER CITY	D 2-2	Campbell, Merson	38,412
Apr 23	QUEENS PARK RANGERS	W 2-0	Dixon (pen), Merson	42,393
May 4	Sunderland	D 0-0		27,606
May 6	MANCHESTER UNITED	W 3-1	Smith 3 (1 pen)	40,229
May 11	COVENTRY CITY	W 6-1	Limpar 3, Smith, Groves, o.g.	41,039

FA Cup

Jan 5	SUNDERLAND	(Rd3)	W 2-1	Smith, Limpar	35,128
Jan 27	LEEDS UNITED	(Rd4)	D 0-0		30,905
Jan 30	Leeds United	(R)	D 1-1	Limpar	27,763
Feb 13	LEEDS UNITED	(2R)	D 0-0		30,433
Feb 16	Leeds United	(3R)	W 2-1	Merson, Dixon	27,190
Feb 27	Shrewsbury Town	(Rd5)	W 1-0	Thomas	12,536
Mar 9	CAMBRIDGE UNITED	(QF)	W 2-1	Campbell, Adams	42,960
Apr 14	Tottenham Hotspur*	(SF)	L 1-3	Smith	77,893

*Played at Wembley.

League Cup

Sep 25	Chester City	(Rd2/1L)	W 1-0	Merson	4,135
Oct 9	CHESTER CITY	(Rd2/2L)	W 5-0	Groves 2, Adams, Smith, Merson	22,890
Oct 30	Manchester City	(Rd3)	W 2-1	Groves, Adams	26,825
Nov 28	MANCHESTER UNITED	(Rd4)	L 2-6	Smith 2	40,884

League & Cup Appearances

PLAYER	LEAGUE	CUP COMPETITION			TOTAL
		FA CUP	LC		
Adams	30	3	4		37
Bould	38	8	4		50
Campbell	15 (7)	4 (2)	0 (4)		19 (13)
Cole	0 (1)				0 (1)
Davis	36 (1)	6 (1)	4		46 (2)
Dixon	38	8	4		50
Groves	13 (9)	3 (1)	4		20 (10)
Hillier	9 (7)	3 (1)	2		14 (8)
Jonsson	2				2
Limpar	32 (2)	5	2		39 (2)
Linighan	7 (3)	3 (1)			10 (4)
Merson	36 (1)	8	4		48 (1)
O'Leary	11 (10)	5 (1)	0 (1)		16 (12)
Pates	0 (1)				0 (1)
Rocastle	13 (3)	0 (1)	2		15 (4)
Seaman	38	8	4		50
Smith	35 (2)	8	4		47 (2)
Thomas	27 (4)	8	2		37 (4)
Winterburn	38	8	4		50

Goalscorers

PLAYER	LEAGUE	CUP COMPETITION		TOTAL
		FA CUP	LC	
Smith	22	2	3	27
Merson	13	1	2	16
Limpar	11	2		13
Campbell	9	1		10
Dixon	5	1		6
Groves	3		3	6
Adams	1	1	2	4
Davis	3			3
Thomas	2	1		3
Rocastle	2			2
O'Leary	1			1
Opps' o.gs.	2			2

Fact File

Arsenal paid a British record fee for a goalkeeper – £1.3 million to Queens Park Rangers for David Seaman. The Gunners won their ninth title despite having two points deducted because of an on-field brawl in the 1-0 win at Manchester United on 20 October. Alan Smith finished First Division top scorer with 22 goals.

Final Division One Table

		P	W	D	L	F	A	Pts
1	ARSENAL	38	24	13	1	74	18	83
2	LIVERPOOL	38	23	7	8	77	40	76
3	CRYSTAL PALACE	38	20	9	9	50	41	69
4	LEEDS U	38	19	7	12	65	47	64
5	MANCHESTER C	38	17	11	10	64	53	62
6	MANCHESTER U	38	16	12	10	58	45	59
7	WIMBLEDON	38	14	14	10	53	46	56
8	NOTTINGHAM F	38	14	12	12	65	50	54
9	EVERTON	38	13	12	13	50	46	51
10	TOTTENHAM H	38	11	16	11	51	50	49
11	CHELSEA	38	13	10	15	58	69	49
12	QPR	38	12	10	16	44	53	46
13	SHEFFIELD U	38	13	7	18	36	55	46
14	SOUTHAMPTON	38	12	9	17	58	69	45
15	NORWICH C	38	13	6	19	41	64	45
16	COVENTRY C	38	11	11	16	42	49	44
17	ASTON VILLA	38	9	14	15	46	58	41
18	LUTON T	38	10	7	21	42	61	37
19	SUNDERLAND	38	8	10	20	38	60	34
20	DERBY CO	38	5	9	24	37	75	24

ARSENAL TWO POINTS DEDUCTED, MANCHESTER UNITED ONE POINT DEDUCTED FOR DISCIPLINARY REASONS.

MANAGER: George Graham

CAPTAIN: Tony Adams

TOP SCORER: Alan Smith 27 (22 League)

BIGGEST WIN: 6-1 v Coventry City, 11 May 1991, League

HIGHEST ATTENDANCE: 42,960 v Cambridge United, 9 March 1991, FA Cup

MAJOR TRANSFERS IN: David Seaman from Queens Park Rangers, Andy Linighan from Norwich City, Anders Limpar from Cremonese

MAJOR TRANSFERS OUT: Martin Hayes to Celtic, Brian Marwood to Sheffield United, John Lukic to Leeds United

Season 1991-92

Football League Division One

DATE	OPPONENTS	SCORE	GOALSCORERS	ATTENDANCE
Aug 17	QUEENS PARK RANGERS	D 1-1	Merson	38,099
Aug 20	Everton	L 1-3	Winterburn	31,200
Aug 24	Aston Villa	L 1-3	Smith	29,684
Aug 27	LUTON TOWN	W 2-0	Smith, Merson	25,898
Aug 31	MANCHESTER CITY	W 2-1	Smith, Limpar	35,009
Sep 3	Leeds United	D 2-2	Smith 2	29,396
Sep 7	COVENTRY CITY	L 1-2	Adams	28,142
Sep 14	Crystal Palace	W 4-1	Campbell 2, Smith, Thomas	24,228
Sep 21	SHEFFIELD UNITED	W 5-2	Dixon (pen), Campbell, Rocastle, Smith, Groves	30,244
Sep 28	Southampton	W 4-0	Wright 3, Rocastle	18,050
Oct 5	CHELSEA	W 3-2	Dixon (pen), Wright, Campbell	42,074
Oct 19	Manchester United	D 1-1	Rocastle	46,594
Oct 26	NOTTS COUNTY	W 2-0	Wright, Smith	30,011
Nov 2	WEST HAM UNITED	L 0-1		33,534
Nov 16	Oldham Athletic	D 1-1	Wright	15,681
Nov 23	Sheffield Wednesday	D 1-1	Bould	32,174
Dec 1	TOTTENHAM HOTSPUR	W 2-0	Wright, Campbell	38,892
Dec 8	Nottingham Forest	L 2-3	Smith, Merson	22,095
Dec 21	EVERTON	W 4-2	Wright 4	29,684
Dec 26	Luton Town	L 0-1		12,665
Dec 28	Manchester City	L 0-1		32,325
Jan 1	WIMBLEDON	D 1-1	Merson	26,339
Jan 11	ASTON VILLA	D 0-0		31,413
Jan 18	Queens Park Rangers	D 0-0		20,497
Jan 29	Liverpool	L 0-2		33,753
Feb 1	MANCHESTER UNITED	D 1-1	Rocastle	41,703
Feb 8	Notts County	W 1-0	Smith	11,221
Feb 11	NORWICH CITY	D 1-1	Merson	22,352
Feb 15	SHEFFIELD WEDNESDAY	W 7-1	Campbell 2, Limpar 2, Smith, Wright, Merson	26,805
Feb 22	Tottenham Hotspur	D 1-1	Wright	33,124
Mar 10	OLDHAM ATHLETIC	W 2-1	Merson, Wright	22,096
Mar 14	West Ham United	W 2-0	Wright 2	22,640
Mar 22	LEEDS UNITED	D 1-1	Merson	27,844
Mar 28	Wimbledon	W 3-1	Parlour, Wright, Campbell	11,299
Mar 31	NOTTINGHAM FOREST	D 3-3	Dixon (pen), Merson, Adams	27,036
Apr 4	Coventry City	W 1-0	Campbell	14,133
Apr 8	Norwich City	W 3-1	Wright 2 (1 pen), Campbell	12,971
Apr 11	CRYSTAL PALACE	W 4-1	Merson 3, Campbell	36,016
Apr 18	Sheffield United	D 1-1	Campbell	25,034
Apr 20	LIVERPOOL	W 4-0	Wright 2, Hillier, Limpar	38,517
Apr 25	Chelsea	D 1-1	Dixon	26,003
May 2	SOUTHAMPTON	W 5-1	Wright 3 (pen), Campbell, Smith	37,702

FA Cup

Jan 4	Wrexham	(Rd3)	L 1-2	Smith	13,343

League Cup

Sep 25	Leicester City	(Rd2/1L)	D 1-1	Wright	20,679
Oct 8	LEICESTER CITY	(Rd2/2L)	W 2-0	Merson, Wright	28,580
Oct 30	Coventry City	(Rd3)	L 0-1		15,337

European Cup

Sep 18	AUSTRIA MEMPHIS	(Rd1/1L)	W 6-1	Smith 4, Linighan, Limpar	24,124
Oct 2	Austria Memphis	(Rd1/2L)	L 0-1		11,000
Oct 23	Benfica	(Rd2/1L)	D 1-1	Campbell	80,000
Nov 6	BENFICA	(Rd2/2L)	L 1-3	Pates	35,815

Fact File

Ian Wright grabbed a hat-trick in the last game of the season to finish First Division top scorer. He scored 24 league goals after his arrival from Crystal Palace in September 1991.

MANAGER: George Graham

CAPTAIN: Tony Adams

TOP SCORER: Ian Wright 26 (24 League)

BIGGEST WIN: 7-1 v Sheffield Wednesday, 15 February 1992, League

HIGHEST ATTENDANCE: 42,074 v Chelsea, 5 October 1991, League

MAJOR TRANSFERS IN: Ian Wright from Crystal Palace, Jimmy Carter from Millwall, Pal Lydersen from Start Kristiansand

MAJOR TRANSFER OUT: Mickey Thomas to Liverpool

League & Cup Appearances

PLAYER	LEAGUE	FA CUP	LC	EC	TOTAL
Adams	35	1	3	4	43
Bould	24 (1)		0 (1)		24 (2)
Campbell	22 (9)	1	2	4	29 (9)
Carter	5 (1)	1			6 (1)
Davis	12		2	3	17
Dixon	38	1	3	4	46
Groves	5 (8)	0 (1)	1 (2)	0 (4)	6 (15)
Heaney	0 (1)				0 (1)
Hillier	27	1			28
Limpar	23 (6)		1	3	27 (6)
Linighan	15 (2)		1 (1)	2	18 (3)
Lydersen	5 (2)				5 (2)
Morrow	0 (2)				0 (2)
Merson	41 (1)	1	3	4	49 (1)
O'Leary	11 (14)	1	0 (1)	1	13 (15)
Parlour	2 (4)				2 (4)
Pates	9 (2)		2	2	13 (2)
Rocastle	36 (3)	1	3	4	44 (3)
Seaman	42	1	3	4	50
Smith	33 (6)	1	2	4	40 (6)
Thomas	6 (4)		2	1 (1)	9 (5)
Winterburn	41	1	2	4	48
Wright	30		3		33

Goalscorers

PLAYER	LEAGUE	FA CUP	LC	EC	TOTAL
Wright	24		2		26
Smith	12	1		4	17
Campbell	13			1	14
Merson	12		1		13
Limpar	4			1	5
Dixon	4				4
Rocastle	4				4
Adams	2				2
Bould	1				1
Groves	1				1
Hillier	1				1
Parlour	1				1
Thomas	1				1
Winterburn	1				1
Linighan				1	1
Pates				1	1

Final Division One Table

		P	W	D	L	F	A	Pts
1	LEEDS U	42	22	16	4	74	37	82
2	MANCHESTER U	42	21	15	6	63	33	78
3	SHEFFIELD W	42	21	12	9	62	49	75
4	ARSENAL	42	19	15	8	81	46	72
5	MANCHESTER C	42	20	10	12	61	48	70
6	LIVERPOOL	42	16	16	10	47	40	64
7	ASTON VILLA	42	17	9	16	48	44	60
8	NOTTINGHAM F	42	16	11	15	60	58	59
9	SHEFFIELD U	42	16	9	17	65	63	57
10	CRYSTAL PALACE	42	14	15	13	53	61	57
11	QPR	42	12	18	12	48	47	54
12	EVERTON	42	13	14	15	52	51	53
13	WIMBLEDON	42	13	14	15	53	53	53
14	CHELSEA	42	13	14	15	50	60	53
15	TOTTENHAM H	42	15	7	20	58	63	52
16	SOUTHAMPTON	42	14	10	18	39	55	52
17	OLDHAM ATH	42	14	9	19	63	67	51
18	NORWICH C	42	11	12	19	47	63	45
19	COVENTRY C	42	11	11	20	35	44	44
20	LUTON T	42	10	12	20	38	71	42
21	NOTTS CO	42	10	10	22	40	62	40
22	WEST HAM U	42	9	11	22	37	59	38

Season 1992-93

FA Premier League

DATE	OPPONENTS	SCORE	GOALSCORERS	ATTENDANCE
Aug 15	NORWICH CITY	L 2-4	Bould, Campbell	24,030
Aug 18	Blackburn Rovers	L 0-1		16,454
Aug 23	Liverpool	W 2-0	Limpar, Wright	34,961
Aug 26	OLDHAM ATHLETIC	W 2-0	Winterburn, Wright	20,796
Aug 29	SHEFFIELD WEDNESDAY	W 2-0	Parlour, Merson	23,389
Sep 2	Queens Park Rangers	D 0-0		20,868
Sep 5	Wimbledon	L 2-3	Wright 2	12,906
Sep 12	BLACKBURN ROVERS	L 0 1		28,643
Sep 19	Sheffield United	D 1-1	Wright	19,105
Sep 28	MANCHESTER CITY	W 1-0	Wright	21,504
Oct 3	CHELSEA	W 2-1	Merson, Wright	27,780
Oct 17	Nottingham Forest	W 1-0	Smith	24,862
Oct 24	EVERTON	W 2-0	Wright, Limpar	28,052
Nov 2	Crystal Palace	W 2-1	Merson, Wright	20,734
Nov 7	COVENTRY CITY	W 3-0	Smith, Wright, Campbell	27,693
Nov 21	Leeds United	L 0-3		30,516
Nov 28	MANCHESTER UNITED	L 0-1		29,739
Dec 5	Southampton	L 0-2		17,286
Dec 12	Tottenham Hotspur	L 0-1		33,707
Dec 19	MIDDLESBROUGH	D 1-1	Wright	23,197
Dec 26	IPSWICH TOWN	D 0-0		26,198
Dec 28	Aston Villa	L 0-1		35,170
Jan 9	SHEFFIELD UNITED	D 1-1	Hillier	23,818
Jan 16	Manchester City	W 1-0	Merson	25,047
Jan 31	LIVERPOOL	L 0-1		27,580
Feb 10	WIMBLEDON	L 0-1		18,253
Feb 20	Oldham Athletic	W 1-0	Linighan	12,311
Feb 24	LEEDS UNITED	D 0-0		21,061
Mar 1	Chelsea	L 0-1		17,725
Mar 3	Norwich City	D 1-1	Wright	14,802
Mar 13	Coventry City	W 2-0	Campbell, Wright	15,437
Mar 20	SOUTHAMPTON	W 4-3	Linighan, Merson, Carter 2	24,149
Mar 24	Manchester United	D 0-0		37,301
Apr 6	Middlesbrough	L 0-1		12,726
Apr 10	Ipswich Town	W 2-1	Smith, Merson	20,358
Apr 12	ASTON VILLA	L 0-1		27,123
Apr 21	NOTTINGHAM FOREST	D 1-1	Wright	19,024
May 1	Everton	D 0-0		19,044
May 4	QUEENS PARK RANGERS	D 0-0		18,817
May 6	Sheffield Wednesday	L 0-1		23,645
May 8	CRYSTAL PALACE	W 3-0	Wright, Dickov, Campbell	25,225
May 11	TOTTENHAM HOTSPUR	L 1-3	Dickov	26,393

FA Cup

Jan 2	Yeovil Town	(Rd3) W 3-1	Wright 3	8,612
Jan 25	LEEDS UNITED	(Rd4) D 2-2	Parlour, Merson	26,516
Feb 3	Leeds United	(R) W 3-2	Smith, Wright 2	26,449
Feb 13	NOTTINGHAM FOREST	(Rd5) W 2-0	Wright 2	27,591
Mar 6	Ipswich Town	(QF) W 4-2	Adams, Wright (pen), o.g. Campbell	22,054
Apr 4	Tottenham Hotspur*	(SF) W 1-0	Adams	76,263
May 15	Sheffield Wednesday*	(F) D 1-1	Wright	79,347
May 20	Sheffield Wednesday*	(R) W 2-1	Wright, Linighan	62,267

*Played at Wembley.

League Cup

Sep 2	MILLWALL	(Rd2/1L) D 1-1	Campbell	20,940
Oct 7	Millwall**	(Rd2/2L) D 1-1	Campbell	16,994
Oct 28	Derby County	(Rd3) D 1-1	Campbell	22,208
Dec 1	DERBY COUNTY	(R) W 2-1	Wright, Campbell	24,587
Jan 6	Scarborough	(Rd4) W 1-0	Winterburn	6,261
Jan 12	NOTTINGHAM FOREST	(QF) W 2-0	Wright 2	25,600
Feb 7	Crystal Palace	(SF/1L) W 3-1	Wright (pen), Smith 2	26,508
Mar 10	CRYSTAL PALACE	(SF/2L) W 2-0	Linighan, Wright	28,584
Apr 18	Sheffield Wednesday*	(F) W 2-1	Merson, Morrow	74,007

**Arsenal won 3-1 on penalties. *Played at Wembley.

Fact File

Arsenal become the first team to win the FA Cup and the Football League Cup in the same season.

MANAGER: George Graham
CAPTAIN: Tony Adams
TOP SCORER: Ian Wright 30 (15 League)
MAJOR TRANSFERS IN: John Jensen from Brondby, Martin Keown from Everton
MAJOR TRANSFERS OUT: David Rocastle to Leeds, Andy Cole to Bristol City

League & Cup Appearances

PLAYER	LEAGUE	CUP COMPETITION		TOTAL
		FA CUP	LC	
Adams	33 (2)	8	9	50 (2)
Bould	24	1	5	30
Campbell	32 (5)	4 (3)	5 (4)	41 (12)
Carter	11 (5)	1 (1)	1	13 (6)
Davis	6	3	2	11
Dickov	1 (2)			1 (2)
Dixon	29	8	7	44
Flatts	6 (4)		1	7 (4)
Groves	0 (1)			0 (1)
Heaney	3 (2)			3 (2)
Hillier	27 (3)	4 (1)	7 (1)	38 (5)
Jensen	29 (3)	4	3	36 (3)
Keown	15 (1)			15 (1)
Limpar	12 (11)	2	4	18 (11)
Linighan	19 (2)	7	4	30 (2)
Lydersen	7 (1)		1	8 (1)
McGowan	0 (2)			0 (2)
Marshall	2			2
Merson	32 (1)	8	9	49 (1)
Miller	3 (1)			3 (1)
Morrow	13 (3)	2 (2)	4 (1)	19 (6)
O'Leary	6 (5)	1 (3)	2	9 (8)
Parlour	16 (5)	4	3 (1)	23 (6)
Pates	2 (5)			2 (5)
Seaman	39	8	9	56
Selley	9	3	1	13
Smith	27 (4)	5 (2)	7	39 (6)
Winterburn	29	8	7	44
Wright	30 (1)	7	8	45 (1)

Goalscorers

PLAYER	LEAGUE	CUP COMPETITION		TOTAL
		FA CUP	LC	
Wright	15	10	5	30
Campbell	4	1	4	9
Merson	6	1	1	8
Smith	3	1	2	6
Linighan	2	1	1	4
Carter	2			2
Dickov	2			2
Limpar	2			2
Parlour	1	1		2
Winterburn	1		1	2
Adams		2		2
Bould	1			1
Hillier	1			1
Morrow			1	1
Opps' o.gs.		1		1

Final Premier League Table

		P	W	D	L	F	A	Pts
1	MANCHESTER U	42	24	12	6	67	31	84
2	ASTON VILLA	42	21	11	10	57	40	74
3	NORWICH C	42	21	9	12	61	65	72
4	BLACKBURN R	42	20	11	11	68	46	71
5	QPR	42	17	12	13	63	55	63
6	LIVERPOOL	42	16	11	15	62	55	59
7	SHEFFIELD W	42	15	14	13	55	51	59
8	TOTTENHAM H	42	16	11	15	60	66	59
9	MANCHESTER C	42	15	12	15	56	51	57
10	ARSENAL	42	15	11	16	40	38	56
11	CHELSEA	42	14	14	14	51	54	56
12	WIMBLEDON	42	14	12	16	56	55	54
13	EVERTON	42	15	8	19	53	55	53
14	SHEFFIELD U	42	14	10	18	54	53	52
15	COVENTRY C	42	13	13	16	52	57	52
16	IPSWICH T	42	12	16	14	50	55	52
17	LEEDS U	42	12	15	15	57	62	51
18	SOUTHAMPTON	42	13	11	18	54	61	50
19	OLDHAM ATH	42	13	10	19	63	74	49
20	CRYSTAL PALACE	42	11	16	15	48	61	49
21	MIDDLESBROUGH	42	11	11	20	54	75	44
22	NOTTINGHAM F	42	10	10	22	41	62	40

Season 1993-94

FA Premier League

DATE	OPPONENTS	SCORE	GOALSCORERS	ATTENDANCE
Aug 14	COVENTRY CITY	L 0-3		26,397
Aug 16	Tottenham Hotspur	W 1-0	Wright	28,355
Aug 21	Sheffield Wednesday	W 1-0	Wright	26,023
Aug 24	LEEDS UNITED	W 2-1	o.g., Merson	29,042
Aug 28	EVERTON	W 2-0	Wright 2	29,063
Sep 1	Blackburn Rovers	D 1-1	Campbell	14,051
Sep 11	IPSWICH TOWN	W 4-0	Wright, Campbell 3	28,563
Sep 19	Manchester United	L 0-1		44,009
Sep 25	SOUTHAMPTON	W 1-0	Merson	26,902
Oct 2	Liverpool	D 0-0		42,750
Oct 16	MANCHESTER CITY	D 0-0		29,567
Oct 23	Oldham Athletic	D 0-0		12,105
Oct 30	NORWICH CITY	D 0-0		30,516
Nov 6	ASTON VILLA	L 1-2	Wright	31,773
Nov 20	Chelsea	W 2-0	Smith, Wright (pen)	26,839
Nov 24	West Ham United	D 0-0		20,279
Nov 27	NEWCASTLE UNITED	W 2-1	Wright, Smith	36,091
Dec 4	Coventry City	L 0-1		12,722
Dec 6	TOTTENHAM HOTSPUR	D 1-1	Wright	35,669
Dec 12	SHEFFIELD WEDNESDAY	W 1-0	Wright	22,026
Dec 18	Leeds United	L 1-2	Campbell	37,515
Dec 2	Swindon Town	W 4-0	Campbell 3, Wright	17,651
Dec 2	SHEFFIELD UNITED	W 3-0	Campbell 2, Wright	27,035
Jan	Wimbledon	W 3-0	Campbell, Parlour, Wright	16,584
Jan 3	QUEENS PARK RANGERS	D 0-0		34,935
Jan 15	Manchester City	D 0-0		24,642
Jan 22	OLDHAM ATHLETIC	D 1-1	Wright (pen)	26,524
Feb 13	Norwich City	D 1-1	Campbell	17,667
Feb 19	Everton	D 1-1	Merson	19,891
Feb 26	BLACKBURN ROVERS	W 1-0	Merson	35,030
Mar 5	Ipswich Town	W 5-1	Wright 3 (1 pen), Parlour, o.g.	18,656
Mar 19	Southampton	W 4-0	Wright 3 (1 pen), Campbell	16,790
Mar 22	MANCHESTER UNITED	D 2-2	o.g., Merson	36,203
Mar 26	LIVERPOOL	W 1-0	Merson	35,556
Apr 2	SWINDON TOWN	D 1-1	Smith	31,634
Apr 4	Sheffield United	D 1-1	Campbell	20,019
Apr 16	CHELSEA	W 1-0	Wright	34,314
Apr 19	WIMBLEDON	D 1-1	Bould	21,292
Apr 23	Aston Villa	W 2-1	Wright 2 (1 pen)	31,580
Apr 27	Queens Park Rangers	D 1-1	Merson	11,442
Apr 30	WEST HAM UNITED	L 0-2		33,701
May 7	Newcastle United	L 0-2		32,216

FA Cup

Jan 10	Millwall	(Rd/3) W 1-0	Adams	20,093
Jan 31	Bolton Wanderers	(Rd4) D 2-2	Wright, Adams	18,891
Feb 9	BOLTON WANDERERS	(R) L 1-3	Smith	33,863

League Cup

Sep 21	Huddersfield Town	(Rd2/1L) W 5-0	Wright 3, Campbell, Merson	14,275
Oct 5	HUDDERSFIELD TOWN	(Rd2/2L) D 1-1	Smith	18,789
Oct 26	NORWICH CITY	(Rd3) D 1-1	Wright	24,539
Nov 10	Norwich City	(R) W 3-0	Wright 2, Merson	16,319
Nov 30	ASTON VILLA	(Rd4) L 0-1		26,453

European Cup-Winners' Cup

Sep 15	Odense	(Rd1/1L) W 2-1	Wright, Merson	9,580
Sep 29	ODENSE	(Rd1/2L) D 1-1	Campbell	25,689
Oct 20	STANDARD LIEGE	(Rd2/1L) W 3-0	Wright 2, Merson	25,258
Nov 3	Standard Liege	(Rd2/2L) W 7-0	Smith, Selley, Adams,	15,000
			Campbell 2, Merson, McGoldrick	
Mar 2	Torino	(QF/1L) D 0-0		32,480
Mar 15	TORINO	(QF/2L) W 1-0	Adams	34,678
Mar 29	Paris Saint-Germain	(SF/1L) D 1-1	Wright	46,000
Apr 12	PARIS SAINT-GERMAIN	(SF/2L) W 1-0	Campbell	34,212
May 4	Parma*	(F) W 1-0	Smith	33,765

*Played in Copenhagen.

MANAGER: George Graham   **CAPTAIN:** Tony Adams

TOP SCORER: Ian Wright 34 (23 League)

BIGGEST WIN: 7-0 v Standard Liege, 3 November 1993, European Cup-Winners' Cup

HIGHEST ATTENDANCE: 36,203 v Manchester United, 22 March 1994, League

MAJOR TRANSFERS IN: Eddie McGoldrick from Crystal Palace

MAJOR TRANSFERS OUT: Colin Pates to Brighton & Hove Albion, Anders Limpar to Everton

League & Cup Appearances

PLAYER	LEAGUE	CUP COMPETITION			TOTAL
		FA CUP	LC	ECWC	
Adams	35	3	2	8	48
Bould	23 (2)	3	3	5 (1)	34 (3)
Campbell	28 (9)	3	2 (2)	6 (2)	39 (13)
Davis	21 (1)		1 (2)	9	31 (3)
Dickov	0 (1)				0 (1)
Dixon	32 (1)	3	4	8	47 (1)
Flatts	2 (1)				2 (1)
Heaney	1		0 (1)		1 (1)
Hillier	11 (4)	3	0 (1)	2 (1)	16 (6)
Jensen	27	0 (1)	5	8	40 (1)
Keown	23 (10)	2 (1)	3	4 (3)	32 (14)
Limpar	9 (1)		2		11 (1)
Linighan	20 (1)		4	1 (1)	25 (2)
McGoldrick	23 (3)	1 (1)	4	3 (2)	31 (6)
Merson	24 (9)	2 (1)	4	8	38 (10)
Miller	3 (1)				3 (1)
Morrow	7 (4)		1	1	9 (4)
Parlour	24 (3)	3	2		29 (3)
Seaman	39	3	5	9	56
Selley	16 (2)		1 (1)	5 (2)	22 (5)
Smith	21 (4)	1 (1)	4 (1)	7 (2)	33 (8)
Winterburn	34	3	4	9	50
Wright	39	3	4	6	52

Goalscorers

PLAYER	LEAGUE	CUP COMPETITION			TOTAL
		FA CUP	LC	ECWC	
Wright	23	1	6	4	34
Campbell	14		1	4	19
Merson	7		2	3	12
Smith	3	1	1	2	7
Adams		2		2	4
Parlour	2				2
Bould	1				1
McGoldrick				1	1
Selley				1	1
Opps' o.gs.	3				3

Fact File

The North Bank stand opened on the first day of the 1993-94 season. The Clock End conversion was completed in November, bringing the ground capacity to around 38,400. The Gunners were also the first British club to install giant video screens. Arsenal's 7-0 win at Standard Liege was their biggest in European competition. The Gunners won the FA Youth Cup, beating Millwall 5-3 on aggregate in the final.

Final Premier League Table

		P	W	D	L	F	A	Pts
1	MANCHESTER U	42	27	11	4	80	38	92
2	BLACKBURN R	42	25	9	8	63	36	84
3	NEWCASTLE U	42	23	8	11	82	41	77
4	ARSENAL	42	18	17	7	53	28	71
5	LEEDS U	42	18	16	8	65	39	70
6	WIMBLEDON	42	18	11	13	56	53	65
7	SHEFFIELD W	42	16	16	10	76	54	64
8	LIVERPOOL	42	17	9	16	59	55	60
9	QPR	42	16	12	14	62	61	60
10	ASTON VILLA	42	15	12	15	46	50	57
11	COVENTRY C	42	14	14	14	43	45	56
12	NORWICH C	42	12	17	13	65	61	53
13	WEST HAM U	42	13	13	16	47	58	52
14	CHELSEA	42	13	12	17	49	53	51
15	TOTTENHAM H	42	11	12	19	54	59	45
16	MANCHESTER C	42	9	18	15	38	49	45
17	EVERTON	42	12	8	22	42	63	44
18	SOUTHAMPTON	42	12	7	23	49	66	43
19	IPSWICH T	42	9	16	17	35	58	43
20	SHEFFIELD U	42	8	18	16	42	60	42
21	OLDHAM ATH	42	9	13	20	42	68	40
22	SWINDON T	42	5	15	22	47	100	30

Season 1994-95

FA Premier League

DATE	OPPONENTS	SCORE	GOALSCORERS	ATTENDANCE
Aug 20	MANCHESTER CITY	W 3-0	Campbell, o.g., Wright	38,368
Aug 23	Leeds United	L 0-1		34,218
Aug 28	Liverpool	L 0-3		30,017
Aug 31	BLACKBURN ROVERS	D 0-0		37,629
Sep 10	Norwich City	D 0-0		17,768
Sep 18	NEWCASTLE UNITED	L 2-3	Adams, Wright	36,819
Sep 25	West Ham United	W 2-0	Adams, Wright	18,498
Oct 1	CRYSTAL PALACE	L 1-2	Wright	34,136
Oct 8	Wimbledon	W 3-1	Wright, Smith, Campbell	10,842
Oct 15	CHELSEA	W 3-1	Wright 2, Campbell	38,234
Oct 23	COVENTRY CITY	W 2-1	Wright 2	31,725
Oct 29	Everton	D 1-1	Schwarz	32,003
Nov 6	SHEFFIELD WEDNESDAY	D 0-0		33,705
Nov 19	Southampton	L 0-1		15,201
Nov 23	Leicester City	L 1-2	Wright (pen)	20,774
Nov 26	MANCHESTER UNITED	D 0-0		38,301
Dec 3	Nottingham Forest	D 2-2	Keown, Davis	21,662
Dec 12	Manchester City	W 2-1	Smith, Schwarz	20,580
Dec 17	LEEDS UNITED	L 1-3	Linighan	38,098
Dec 26	ASTON VILLA	D 0-0		34,452
Dec 28	Ipswich Town	W 2-0	Wright, Campbell	22,054
Dec 31	QUEENS PARK RANGERS	L 1-3	Jensen	32,393
Jan 2	Tottenham Hotspur	L 0-1		28,747
Jan 14	EVERTON	D 1-1	Wright	34,743
Jan 21	Coventry City	W 1-0	Hartson	14,468
Jan 24	SOUTHAMPTON	D 1-1	Hartson	27,213
Feb 4	Sheffield Wednesday	L 1-3	Linighan	23,468
Feb 11	LEICESTER CITY	D 1-1	Merson	31,373
Feb 21	NOTTINGHAM FOREST	W 1-0	Kiwomya	35,441
Feb 25	Crystal Palace	W 3-0	Merson, Kiwomya 2	17,092
Mar 5	WEST HAM UNITED	L 0-1		36,295
Mar 8	Blackburn Rovers	L 1-3	Morrow	23,452
Mar 19	Newcastle United	L 0-1		35,611
Mar 22	Manchester United	L 0-3		43,623
Apr 1	NORWICH CITY	W 5-1	Hartson 2, Dixon, Merson, o.g.	36,942
Apr 8	Queens Park Rangers	L 1-3	Adams	16,341
Apr 12	LIVERPOOL	L 0-1		38,036
Apr 15	IPSWICH TOWN	W 4-1	Merson, Wright 3	36,818
Apr 17	Aston Villa	W 4-0	Wright 2, Hartson 2	32,005
Apr 29	TOTTENHAM HOTSPUR	D 1-1	Wright (pen)	38,377
May 4	WIMBLEDON	D 0-0		32,822
May 14	Chelsea	L 1-2	Hartson	29,542

FA Cup

Jan 7	Millwall	(Rd3)	D 0-0		17,715
Jan 18	MILLWALL	(R)	L 0-2		32,319

League Cup

Sep 21	Hartlepool United	(Rd2/1L)	W 5-0	Adams, Smith, Wright 2, Merson	4,421
Oct 5	HARTLEPOOL UNITED	(Rd2/2L)	W 2-0	Campbell, Dickov	20,520
Oct 26	Oldham Athletic	(Rd3)	D 0-0		9,303
Nov 9	OLDHAM ATHLETIC	(R)	W 2-0	Dickov 2	22,746
Nov 30	SHEFFIELD WEDNESDAY	(Rd4)	W 2-0	Morrow, Wright	27,390
Jan 11	Liverpool	(QF)	L 0-1		35,026

European Cup-Winners' Cup

Sep 15	Omonia Nicosia	(Rd1/1L)	W 3-1	Merson 2, Wright	20,000
Sep 29	OMONIA NICOSIA	(Rd1/2L)	W 3-0	Wright 2, Schwarz	24,265
Oct 20	Brondby	(Rd2/1L)	W 2-1	Wright, Smith	13,406
Nov 3	BRONDBY	(Rd2/2L)	D 2-2	Wright (pen), Selley	32,290
Mar 2	AUXERRE	(QF/1L)	D 1-1	Wright (pen)	35,508
Mar 16	Auxerre	(QF/2L)	W 1-0	Wright	22,000
Apr 6	SAMPDORIA	(SF/1L)	W 3-2	Bould 2, Wright	38,089
Apr 20	Sampdoria*	(SF/2L)	L 2-3	Wright, Schwarz	34,353
May 10	Real Zaragoza**	(F)	L 1-2	Hartson	42,424

*Arsenal won 3-2 on penalties. **Played in Paris.

Fact File

George Graham was dismissed amid 'bung' allegations relating to the transfer of John Jensen. He was subsequently banned from football for a year.

MANAGER: George Graham, Stewart Houston caretaker

CAPTAIN: Tony Adams   **TOP SCORER:** Ian Wright 30 (18 League)

MAJOR TRANSFERS IN: Stefan Schwarz from Benfica, Vince Bartram from Bournemouth, John Hartson from Luton Town, Chris Kiwomya from Ipswich Town, Glenn Helder from Vitesse Arnhem

---

League & Cup Appearances

PLAYER	LEAGUE	CUP COMPETITION			TOTAL
		FA CUP	LC	ECWC	
Adams	27	0 (1)	4	8	39 (1)
Bartram	11	0 (1)			11 (1)
Bould	30 (1)	1	5	5	41 (1)
Campbell	19 (4)	1 (1)	5	1 (1)	26 (6)
Carter	2 (1)				2 (1)
Clarke	0 (1)				0 (1)
Davis	3 (1)		2		5 (1)
Dickov	4 (5)		2 (2)		6 (7)
Dixon	39	2	5	9	55
Flatts	1 (2)	0 (1)			1 (3)
Hartson	14 (1)			4 (1)	18 (2)
Helder	12 (1)				12 (1)
Hillier	5 (4)	2	2	2 (2)	11 (6)
Hughes	1				1
Jensen	24	2	1 (1)	5	32 (1)
Keown	24 (7)	1 (1)	3 (2)	5	33 (10)
Kiwomya	5 (9)			1 (2)	6 (11)
Linighan	13 (7)	2	2	3	20 (7)
McGoldrick	9 (2)		3 (2)	1 (1)	13 (5)
McGowan	1				1
Merson	24		2	8	34
Morrow	11 (4)	1	1 (1)	0 (4)	13 (9)
Parlour	22 (8)	2	5	7 (1)	36 (9)
Schwarz	34	1	4	8	47
Seaman	31	2	6	9	48
Selley	10 (3)		3	1	14 (3)
Shaw	0 (1)				0 (1)
Smith	17 (2)	1	3	4	25 (2)
Winterburn	39	2	5	9	55
Wright	30 (1)	2	3	9	44 (1)

Goalscorers

PLAYER	LEAGUE	CUP COMPETITION			TOTAL
		FA CUP	LC	ECWC	
Wright	18		3	9	30
Hartson	7			1	8
Merson	4		1	2	7
Campbell	4		1		5
Adams	3		1		4
Schwarz	2			2	4
Smith	2		1	1	4
Kiwomya	3				3
Dickov			3		3
Linighan	2				2
Bould				2	2
Morrow	1		1		2
Davis	1				1
Dixon	1				1
Jensen	1				1
Keown	1				1
Selley				1	1
Opps' o.gs.	2				2

Final Premier League Table

		P	W	D	L	F	A	Pts
1	BLACKBURN R	42	27	8	7	80	39	89
2	MANCHESTER U	42	26	10	6	77	28	88
3	NOTTINGHAM F	42	22	11	9	72	43	77
4	LIVERPOOL	42	21	11	10	65	37	74
5	LEEDS U	42	20	13	9	59	38	73
6	NEWCASTLE U	42	20	12	10	67	47	72
7	TOTTENHAM H	42	16	14	12	66	58	62
8	QPR	42	17	9	16	61	59	60
9	WIMBLEDON	42	15	11	16	48	65	56
10	SOUTHAMPTON	42	12	18	12	61	63	54
11	CHELSEA	42	13	15	14	50	55	54
12	ARSENAL	42	13	12	17	52	49	51
13	SHEFFIELD W	42	13	12	17	49	57	51
14	WEST HAM U	42	13	11	18	44	48	50
15	EVERTON	42	11	17	14	44	51	50
16	COVENTRY C	42	12	14	16	44	62	50
17	MANCHESTER C	42	12	13	17	53	64	49
18	ASTON VILLA	42	11	15	16	51	56	48
19	CRYSTAL PAL	42	11	12	19	34	49	45
20	NORWICH C	42	10	13	19	37	54	43
21	LEICESTER C	42	6	11	25	45	80	29
22	IPSWICH T	42	7	6	29	36	93	27

Season 1995-96

FA Premier League

DATE	OPPONENTS	SCORE	GOALSCORERS	ATTENDANCE
Aug 20	MIDDLESBROUGH	D 1-1	Wright	37,308
Aug 23	Everton	W 2-0	Platt, Wright	35,775
Aug 26	Coventry City	D 0-0		20,065
Aug 29	NOTTINGHAM FOREST	D 1-1	Platt	38,248
Sep 10	Manchester City	W 1-0	Wright	23,994
Sep 16	WEST HAM UNITED	W 1-0	Wright (pen)	38,065
Sep 23	SOUTHAMPTON	W 4-2	Bergkamp 2, Adams, Wright	38,136
Sep 30	Chelsea	L 0-1		31,048
Oct 14	Leeds United	W 3-0	Merson, Bergkamp, Wright	38,552
Oct 21	ASTON VILLA	W 2-0	Merson, Wright	38,271
Oct 30	Bolton Wanderers	L 0-1		18,682
Nov 4	MANCHESTER UNITED	W 1-0	Bergkamp	38,317
Nov 18	Tottenham Hotspur	L 1-2	Bergkamp	32,894
Nov 21	SHEFFIELD WEDNESDAY	W 4-2	Bergkamp, Winterburn, Dickov, Hartson	34,556
Nov 26	BLACKBURN ROVERS	D 0-0		37,695
Dec 2	Aston Villa	D 1-1	Platt	37,770
Dec 9	Southampton	D 0-0		15,238
Dec 16	CHELSEA	D 1-1	Dixon	38,295
Dec 23	Liverpool	L 1-3	Wright (pen)	39,806
Dec 26	QUEENS PARK RANGERS	W 3-0	Wright, Merson 2	38,259
Dec 30	WIMBLEDON	L 1-3	Wright	37,640
Jan 2	Newcastle United	L 0-2		36,530
Jan 13	Middlesbrough	W 3-2	Merson, Platt, Helder	29,359
Jan 20	EVERTON	L 1-2	Wright	38,275
Feb 3	COVENTRY CITY	D 0-0		35,623
Feb 10	Nottingham Forest	W 1-0	Bergkamp	27,222
Feb 24	West Ham United	W 1-0	Hartson	24,217
Mar 2	Queens Park Rangers	D 1-1	Bergkamp	17,970
Mar 5	MANCHESTER CITY	W 3-1	Hartson 2, Dixon	34,519
Mar 16	Wimbledon	W 3-0	Winterburn, Platt, Bergkamp	18,335
Mar 20	Manchester United	L 0-1		50,028
Mar 23	NEWCASTLE UNITED	W 2-0	Marshall, Wright	38,271
Apr 6	LEEDS UNITED	W 2-1	Wright 2	37,619
Apr 8	Sheffield Wednesday	L 0-1		24,349
Apr 15	TOTTENHAM HOTSPUR	D 0-0		38,273
Apr 27	Blackburn Rovers	D 1-1	Wright (pen)	29,834
May 1	LIVERPOOL	D 0-0		38,323
May 5	BOLTON WANDERERS	W 2-1	Platt, Bergkamp	38,104

FA Cup

Jan 6	SHEFFIELD UNITED	(Rd3)	D 1-1	Wright	33,453
Jan 17	Sheffield United	(R)	L 0-1		22,255

League Cup

Sep 19	Hartlepool United	(Rd2/1L)	W 3-0	Adams 2, Wright	4,945
Oct 3	HARTLEPOOL UNITED	(Rd2/2L)	W 5-0	Wright 3, Bergkamp 2	27,194
Oct 24	Barnsley	(Rd3)	W 3-0	Bould, Bergkamp, Keown	18,429
Nov 29	SHEFFIELD WEDNESDAY	(Rd4)	W 2-1	Wright (pen), Hartson	35,361
Jan 10	NEWCASTLE UNITED	(QF)	W 2-0	Wright 2	37,857
Feb 14	ASTON VILLA	(SF/1L)	D 2-2	Bergkamp	37,562
Feb 21	Aston Villa*	(SF/2L)	D 0-0		39,334

*Arsenal lost on away goals.

League & Cup Appearances

PLAYER	LEAGUE	CUP COMPETITION		TOTAL
		FA CUP	LC	
Adams	21	2	5	28
Bergkamp	33	1	7	41
Bould	19		5	24
Clarke	4 (2)	1 (1)		5 (3)
Dickov	1 (6)			1 (6)
Dixon	38	2	7	47
Hartson	15 (4)	1	1 (2)	17 (6)
Helder	15 (9)	2	4 (2)	21 (11)
Hillier	3 (2)		2	5 (2)
Hughes	0 (1)		0 (1)	0 (2)
Jensen	13 (2)	2	5 (1)	20 (3)
Keown	34	2	5	41
Linighan	17 (1)	0 (1)	2	19 (2)
McGoldrick	0 (1)			0 (1)
McGowan	1	1		2
Marshall	10 (1)			10 (1)
Merson	38	2	7	47
Morrow	3 (1)		1	4 (1)
Parlour	20 (2)		3 (1)	23 (3)
Platt	27 (2)	1	2 (1)	30 (3)
Rose	1 (3)			1 (3)
Seaman	38	2	7	47
Shaw	0 (3)			0 (3)
Winterburn	36	1	7	44
Wright	31	2	7	40

Goalscorers

PLAYER	LEAGUE	CUP COMPETITION		TOTAL
		FA CUP	LC	
Wright	15	1	7	23
Bergkamp	11		5	16
Platt	6			6
Merson	5			5
Hartson	4		1	5
Adams	1		2	3
Dixon	2			2
Winterburn	2			2
Dickov	1			1
Helder	1			1
Marshall	1			1
Bould			1	1
Keown			1	1

Fact File

The Gunners gained a UEFA Cup place after late goals by summer signings Dennis Bergkamp and David Platt beat Bruce Rioch's old club Bolton 2-1 on the last day of the Premiership season.

MANAGER: Bruce Rioch

CAPTAIN: Tony Adams

TOP SCORER: Ian Wright 23 (15 League)

BIGGEST WIN: 5-0 v Hartlepool United, 3 October 1995, League Cup

HIGHEST ATTENDANCE: 38,323 v Liverpool, 1 May 1996, League

MAJOR TRANSFERS IN: Dennis Bergkamp from Internazionale, David Platt from Sampdoria,

MAJOR TRANSFERS OUT: Stefan Schwarz to Fiorentina, Kevin Campbell to Nottingham Forest, John Jensen to Brondby

Final Premier League Table

		P	W	D	L	F	A	PTS
1	MANCHESTER U	38	25	7	6	73	35	82
2	NEWCASTLE U	38	24	6	8	66	37	78
3	LIVERPOOL	38	20	11	7	70	34	71
4	ASTON VILLA	38	18	9	11	52	35	63
5	ARSENAL	38	17	12	9	49	32	63
6	EVERTON	38	17	10	11	64	44	61
7	BLACKBURN R	38	18	7	13	61	47	61
8	TOTTENHAM H	38	16	13	9	50	38	61
9	NOTTINGHAM F	38	15	13	10	50	54	58
10	WEST HAM U	38	14	9	15	43	52	51
11	CHELSEA	38	12	14	12	46	44	50
12	MIDDLESBROUGH	38	11	10	17	35	50	43
13	LEEDS U	38	12	7	19	40	57	43
14	WIMBLEDON	38	10	11	17	55	70	41
15	SHEFFIELD W	38	10	10	18	48	61	40
16	COVENTRY C	38	8	14	16	42	60	38
17	SOUTHAMPTON	38	9	11	18	34	52	38
18	MANCHESTER C	38	9	11	18	33	58	38
19	QPR	38	9	6	23	38	57	33
20	BOLTON W	38	8	5	25	39	71	29

Season 1996-97

FA Premier League

DATE	OPPONENTS	SCORE	GOALSCORERS	ATTENDANCE
Aug 17	WEST HAM UNITED	W 2-0	Hartson, Bergkamp (pen)	38,056
Aug 19	Liverpool	L 0-2		38,103
Aug 24	Leicester City	W 2-0	Bergkamp (pen), Wright	20,429
Sep 4	CHELSEA	D 3-3	Merson, Keown, Wright	38,132
Sep 7	Aston Villa	D 2-2	Merson, Linighan	37,944
Sep 16	SHEFFIELD WEDNESDAY	W 4-1	Platt, Wright 3	33,461
Sep 21	Middlesbrough	W 2-0	Hartson, Wright	29,629
Sep 28	SUNDERLAND	W 2-0	Hartson, Parlour	38,016
Oct 12	Blackburn Rovers	W 2-0	Wright 2	24,303
Oct 19	COVENTRY CITY	D 0-0		38,140
Oct 26	LEEDS UNITED	W 3-0	Dixon, Bergkamp, Wright	38,076
Nov 2	Wimbledon	D 2-2	Wright, Merson	25,521
Nov 16	Manchester United	L 0-1		55,210
Nov 24	TOTTENHAM HOTSPUR	W 3-1	Wright, Adams, Bergkamp	38,264
Nov 30	Newcastle United	W 2-1	Dixon, Wright	36,565
Dec 4	SOUTHAMPTON	W 3-1	Merson, Wright (pen), Shaw	38,033
Dec 7	DERBY COUNTY	D 2-2	Adams, Vieira	38,018
Dec 21	Nottingham Forest	L 1-2	Wright	27,384
Dec 26	Sheffield Wednesday	D 0-0		23,245
Dec 28	ASTON VILLA	D 2-2	Wright, Merson	38,130
Jan 1	MIDDLESBROUGH	W 2-0	Bergkamp, Wright	37,573
Jan 11	Sunderland	L 0-1		21,154
Jan 19	EVERTON	W 3-1	Bergkamp, Vieira, Merson	38,095
Jan 29	West Ham United	W 2-1	Parlour, Wright	24,382
Feb 1	Leeds United	D 0-0		35,502
Feb 15	Tottenham Hotspur	D 0-0		33,039
Feb 19	MANCHESTER UNITED	L 1-2	Bergkamp	38,172
Feb 23	WIMBLEDON	L 0-1		37,854
Mar 1	Everton	W 2-0	Bergkamp, Wright	36,980
Mar 8	NOTTINGHAM FOREST	W 2-0	Bergkamp 2 (1 pen)	38,206
Mar 15	Southampton	W 2-0	Hughes, Shaw	15,144
Mar 24	LIVERPOOL	L 1-2	Wright	38,068
Apr 5	Chelsea	W 3-0	Wright, Platt, Bergkamp	28,182
Apr 12	LEICESTER CITY	W 2-0	Adams, Platt	38,044
Apr 19	BLACKBURN ROVERS	D 1-1	Platt	38,086
Apr 21	Coventry City	D 1-1	Wright	19,998
May 3	NEWCASTLE UNITED	L 0-1		38,179
May 11	Derby County	W 3-1	Wright 2, Bergkamp	18,287

FA Cup

Jan 4	SUNDERLAND	(Rd3) D 1-1	Hartson	37,793
Jan 15	Sunderland	(R) W 2-0	Bergkamp, Hughes	15,277
Feb 4	LEEDS UNITED	(Rd4) L 0-1		38,115

League Cup

Oct 23	Stoke City	(Rd3) D 1-1	Wright	20,804
Nov 13	STOKE CITY	(R) W 5-2	Wright 2 (1 pen), Platt, Bergkamp, Merson	33,962
Nov 27	Liverpool	(Rd4) L 2-4	Wright 2 (2 pen)	32,814

UEFA Cup

Sep 10	BORUSSIA MÖNCHENGLADBACH	(Rd1/1L) L 2-3	Merson, Wright	36,894
Sep 25	Borussia Mönchengladbach	(Rd1/2L) L 2-3	Wright, Merson	34,000

Fact File

Arsène Wenger became Arsenal's first non-British manager. On Wenger's advice, the Gunners had already signed Remi Garde from Strasbourg and a 20-year-old Milan reserve called Patrick Vieira.

MANAGER: Stewart Houston/Pat Rice caretakers, Arsène Wenger
CAPTAIN: Tony Adams   **TOP SCORER:** Ian Wright 30 (23 League)
BIGGEST WIN: 5-2 v Stoke City, 13 November 1996, League Cup
HIGHEST ATTENDANCE: 38,264 v Tottenham Hotspur, 24 November 1996, League
MAJOR TRANSFERS IN: John Lukic from Leeds United, Patrick Vieira from Milan, Remi Garde from Strasbourg, Nicolas Anelka from Paris Saint-Germain
MAJOR TRANSFERS OUT: David Hillier to Portsmouth, Paul Dickov to Manchester City, Andy Linighan to Crystal Palace, John Hartson to West Ham United, Stephen Morrow to Queens Park Rangers

League & Cup Appearances

PLAYER	LEAGUE	CUP COMPETITION			TOTAL
		FA CUP	LC	UEFA	
Adams	27 (1)	3	3	1	34 (1)
Anelka	0 (4)				0 (4)
Bergkamp	28 (1)	2	2	1	33 (1)
Bould	33	3	3	1 (1)	40 (1)
Dickov	0 (1)				0 (1)
Dixon	31 (1)	1	3	1	36 (1)
Garde	7 (4)				7 (4)
Harper	1				1
Hartson	14 (5)	1 (1)	1 (2)	2	18 (8)
Helder	0 (2)			0 (2)	0 (4)
Hillier	0 (2)				0 (2)
Hughes	9 (5)	2 (1)			11 (6)
Keown	33	3	3	2	41
Linighan	10 (1)			2	12 (1)
Lukic	15	1	1		17
McGowan	1				1
Marshall	6 (2)				6 (2)
Merson	32	3	3	2	40
Morrow	5 (9)	2	0 (2)		7 (11)
Parlour	17 (13)	3	0 (1)	1 (1)	21 (15)
Platt	27 (1)	1	3	2	33 (1)
Rose	1				1
Seaman	22	2	2	2	28
Selley	0 (1)				0 (1)
Shaw	1 (7)	0 (1)			1 (8)
Vieira	30 (1)	3	3	1	37 (1)
Winterburn	38	2	3	2	45
Wright	30 (5)	1	3	2	36 (5)

Goalscorers

PLAYER	LEAGUE	CUP COMPETITION			TOTAL
		FA CUP	LC	UEFA	
Wright	23		5	2	30
Bergkamp	12	1	1		14
Merson	6		1	2	9
Platt	4		1		5
Hartson	3	1			4
Adams	3				3
Dixon	2				2
Parlour	2				2
Shaw	2				2
Vieira	2				2
Hughes	1	1			2
Keown	1				1
Linighan	1				1

Final Premier League Table

		P	W	D	L	F	A	Pts
1	MANCHESTER U	38	21	12	5	76	44	75
2	NEWCASTLE U	38	19	11	8	73	40	68
3	ARSENAL	38	19	11	8	62	32	68
4	LIVERPOOL	38	19	11	8	62	37	68
5	ASTON VILLA	38	17	10	11	47	34	61
6	CHELSEA	38	16	11	11	58	55	59
7	SHEFFIELD W	38	14	15	9	50	51	57
8	WIMBLEDON	38	15	11	12	49	46	56
9	LEICESTER C	38	12	11	15	46	54	47
10	TOTTENHAM H	38	13	7	18	44	51	46
11	LEEDS U	38	11	13	14	28	38	46
12	DERBY CO	38	11	13	14	45	58	46
13	BLACKBURN R	38	9	15	14	42	43	42
14	WEST HAM U	38	10	12	16	39	48	42
15	EVERTON	38	10	12	16	44	57	42
16	SOUTHAMPTON	38	10	11	17	50	56	41
17	COVENTRY C	38	9	14	15	38	54	41
18	SUNDERLAND	38	10	10	18	35	53	40
19	MIDDLESBROUGH	38	10	12	16	51	60	39
20	NOTTINGHAM F	38	6	16	16	31	59	34

MIDDLESBROUGH DEDUCTED THREE POINTS FOR FAILURE TO FULFIL A FIXTURE ON A GIVEN DATE.

Season 1997-98

Premier League

DATE	OPPONENTS	SCORE	GOALSCORERS	ATTENDANCE
Aug 9	Leeds United	D 1-1	Wright	37,993
Aug 11	COVENTRY CITY	W 2-0	Wright 2	37,324
Aug 23	Southampton	W 3-1	Overmars, Bergkamp 2	15,246
Aug 27	Leicester City	D 3-3	Bergkamp 3	21,089
Aug 30	TOTTENHAM HOTSPUR	D 0-0		38,102
Sep 13	BOLTON WANDERERS	W 4-1	Wright 3, Parlour	38,138
Sep 21	Chelsea	W 3-2	Bergkamp 2, Winterburn	33,012
Sep 24	WEST HAM UNITED	W 4-0	Bergkamp, Overmars 2, Wright (pen)	38,012
Sep 27	Everton	D 2-2	Wright, Overmars	35,457
Oct 4	BARNSLEY	W 5-0	Parlour, Platt, Wright, Bergkamp 2	38,049
Oct 18	Crystal Palace	D 0-0		26,180
Oct 26	ASTON VILLA	D 0-0		38,061
Nov 1	Derby County	L 0-3		30,004
Nov 9	MANCHESTER UNITED	W 3-2	Anelka, Vieira, Platt	38,205
Nov 22	Sheffield Wednesday	L 0-2		34,373
Nov 30	LIVERPOOL	L 0-1		38,094
Dec 6	Newcastle United	W 1-0	Wright	36,751
Dec 13	BLACKBURN ROVERS	L 1-3	Overmars	38,147
Dec 26	LEICESTER CITY	W 2-1	Platt, o.g.	38,023
Dec 28	Tottenham Hotspur	D 1-1	Parlour	29,610
Jan 10	LEEDS UNITED	W 2-1	Overmars 2	38,018
Jan 17	Coventry City	D 2-2	Bergkamp, Anelka	22,864
Jan 31	SOUTHAMPTON	W 3-0	Adams, Anelka, Bergkamp	38,056
Feb 8	CHELSEA	W 2-0	Hughes 2	38,083
Feb 21	CRYSTAL PALACE	W 1-0	Grimandi	38,094
Mar 2	West Ham United	D 0-0		25,717
Mar 11	Wimbledon	W 1-0	Wreh	22,291
Mar 14	Manchester United	W 1-0	Overmars	55,174
Mar 28	SHEFFIELD WEDNESDAY	W 1-0	Bergkamp	38,087
Mar 31	Bolton Wanderers	W 1-0	Wreh	25,000
Apr 11	NEWCASTLE UNITED	W 3-1	Vieira, Anelka 2	38,102
Apr 13	Blackburn Rovers	W 4-1	Bergkamp, Parlour 2, Anelka	28,212
Apr 18	WIMBLEDON	W 5-0	Adams, Petit, Bergkamp, Wreh, Overmars	38,024
Apr 25	Barnsley	W 2-0	Bergkamp, Overmars	18,691
Apr 29	DERBY COUNTY	W 1-0	Petit	38,121
May 3	EVERTON	W 4-0	o.g., Overmars 2, Adams	38,269
May 6	Liverpool	L 0-4		44,417
May 10	Aston Villa	L 0-1		39,372

FA Cup

Jan 3	PORT VALE	(Rd3)	D 0-0		37,471
Jan 14	Port Vale	(R)	D 1-1*	Bergkamp	14,964
Jan 24	Middlesbrough	(Rd4)	W 2-0	Overmars, Parlour	28,264
Feb 15	CRYSTAL PALACE	(Rd5)	D 0-0		37,164
Feb 25	Crystal Palace	(R)	W 2-1	Anelka, Bergkamp	15,674
Mar 8	WEST HAM UNITED	(QF)	D 1-1	Bergkamp (pen)	38,077
Mar 17	West Ham United	(R)	D 1-1**	Anelka	25,859
Apr 5	Wolverhampton Wanderers†		W 1-0	Wreh	39,372
May 15	Newcastle United††	(F)	W 2-0	Overmars, Anelka	79,183

*Arsenal won 4-3 on penalties. **Arsenal won 4-3 on penalties.
†Played at Villa. ††Played at Wembley.

League Cup

Oct 14	BIRMINGHAM CITY	(Rd3)	W 4-1	Boa Morte 2, Platt (pen), Mendez	27,097
Nov 18	COVENTRY CITY	(Rd4)	W 1-0	Bergkamp	30,199
Jan 6	West Ham United	(QF)	W 2-1	Wright, Overmars	24,770
Jan 28	CHELSEA	(SF/1L)	W 2-1	Overmars, Hughes	38,114
Feb 18	Chelsea	(SF/2L)	L 1-3	Bergkamp (pen)	34,330

UEFA Cup

Sep 16	PAOK Salonika	(Rd1/1L)	L 0-1		33,117
Sep 30	PAOK SALONIKA	(Rd1/2L)	D 1-1	Bergkamp	37,982

MANAGER: Arsène Wenger **CAPTAIN:** Tony Adams

TOP SCORER: Dennis Bergkamp 22 (16 League)

BIGGEST WIN: 5-0 v Wimbledon, 18 April 1998, League

HIGHEST ATTENDANCE: 38,269 v Everton, 3 May 1998, League

MAJOR TRANSFERS IN: Matthew Upson from Luton Town, Marc Overmars from Ajax, Luis Boa Morte from Sporting Lisbon, Manu Petit and Gilles Grimandi from Monaco, Christopher Wreh from Guingamp, Alex Manninger from Casino Graz

MAJOR TRANSFERS OUT: Paul Merson to Middlesbrough, Glenn Helder to NAC Breda, Chris Kiwomya to Queens Park Rangers, Vince Bartram to Gillingham

---

League & Cup Appearances

PLAYER	LEAGUE	CUP COMPETITION			TOTAL
		FA CUP	LC	UEFA	
Adams	26	6	2	2	36
Anelka	16 (10)	8 (1)	3	1 (1)	28 (12)
Bergkamp	28	7	4	1	40
Boa Morte	4 (11)	1 (3)	1	0 (1)	6 (15)
Bould	21 (3)	4 (1)	3	2	30 (4)
Crowe		0 (1)	0 (1)		(2)
Dixon	26 (2)	7	3	2	38 (2)
Garde	6 (4)	1			7 (4)
Grimandi	16 (6)	3 (2)	4		23 (8)
Hughes	7 (10)	3 (3)	3 (2)		13 (15)
Keown	18	7		2	27
McGowan	0 (1)				0 (1)
Manninger	7	5	4		16
Marshall	1 (2)		1 (1)		2 (3)
Mendez	1 (2)		2		3 (2)
Muntasser			0 (1)		0 (1)
Overmars	32	8 (1)	3	2	45 (1)
Parlour	34	7	4	2	47
Petit	32	7	3	2	44
Platt	11 (20)	1 (3)	2 (2)	0 (2)	14 (27)
Rankin	0 (1)				(1)
Seaman	31	4	1	2	38
Upson	5	1	2		8
Vernazza	1		1		2
Vieira	31 (2)	8 (1)	2	2	43 (3)
Winterburn	35 (1)	8	3	2	48 (1)
Wreh	7 (9)	2 (4)	1 (2)	(1)	10 (16)
Wright	22 (1)	1	1	2	26 (2)

Goalscorers

PLAYER	LEAGUE	CUP COMPETITION			TOTAL
		FA CUP	LC	UEFA	
Bergkamp	16	3	2	1	22
Overmars	12	2	2		16
Wright	10		1		11
Anelka	6	3			9
Parlour	5	1			6
Platt	3		1		4
Wreh	3	1			4
Adams	3				3
Hughes	2		1		3
Petit	2				2
Vieira	2				2
Boa Morte			2		2
Grimandi	1				1
Winterburn	1				1
Mendez			1		1
Opps' o.gs.	2				2

Fact File

Arsenal won their second 'Double'. Ian Wright passed Cliff Bastin's all-time goals record. David Seaman broke Jack Kelsey's record for appearances in goal.

Final Premier League Table

		P	W	D	L	F	A	PTS
1	ARSENAL	38	23	9	6	68	33	78
2	MANCHESTER U	38	23	8	7	73	26	77
3	LIVERPOOL	38	18	11	9	68	42	65
4	CHELSEA	38	20	3	15	71	43	63
5	LEEDS U	38	17	8	13	57	46	59
6	BLACKBURN R	38	16	10	12	57	52	58
7	ASTON VILLA	38	17	6	15	49	48	57
8	WEST HAM U	38	16	8	14	56	57	56
9	DERBY CO	38	16	7	15	52	49	55
10	LEICESTER C	38	13	14	11	51	41	53
11	COVENTRY C	38	12	16	10	46	44	52
12	SOUTHAMPTON	38	14	6	18	50	55	48
13	NEWCASTLE U	38	11	11	16	35	44	44
14	TOTTENHAM H	38	11	11	16	44	56	44
15	WIMBLEDON	38	10	14	14	34	46	44
16	SHEFFIELD W	38	12	8	18	52	67	44
17	EVERTON	38	9	13	16	41	56	40
18	BOLTON W	38	9	13	16	41	61	40
19	BARNSLEY	38	10	5	23	37	82	35
20	CRYSTAL PAL	38	8	9	21	37	71	33

Season 1998-99

Premier League

DATE	OPPONENTS	SCORE	GOALSCORERS	ATTENDANCE
Aug 17	NOTTINGHAM FOREST	W 2-1	Petit, Overmars	38,064
Aug 22	Liverpool	D 0-0		44,429
Aug 29	CHARLTON ATHLETIC	D 0-0		38,014
Sep 9	Chelsea	D 0-0		34,644
Sep 12	Leicester City	D 1-1	Hughes	21,628
Sep 20	MANCHESTER UNITED	W 3-0	Adams, Anelka, Ljungberg	38,142
Sep 26	Sheffield Wednesday	L 0-1		27,949
Oct 4	NEWCASTLE UNITED	W 3-0	Bergkamp 2 (1 pen), Anelka	38,102
Oct 17	SOUTHAMPTON	D 1-1	Anelka	38,027
Oct 25	Blackburn Rovers	W 2-1	Anelka, Petit	27,012
Oct 31	Coventry City	W 1-0	Anelka	23,040
Nov 8	EVERTON	W 1-0	Anelka	38,088
Nov 14	TOTTENHAM HOTSPUR	D 0-0		38,278
Nov 21	Wimbledon	L 0-1		26,003
Nov 29	MIDDLESBROUGH	D 1-1	Anelka	38,075
Dec 5	Derby County	D 0-0		29,018
Dec 13	Aston Villa	L 2-3	Bergkamp 2	39,217
Dec 20	LEEDS UNITED	W 3-1	Bergkamp, Vieira, Petit	38,025
Dec 26	WEST HAM UNITED	W 1-0	Overmars	38,098
Dec 28	Charlton Athletic	W 1-0	Overmars (pen)	20,043
Jan 9	LIVERPOOL	D 0-0		38,107
Jan 16	Nottingham Forest	W 1-0	Keown	26,021
Jan 31	CHELSEA	W 1-0	Bergkamp	38,121
Feb 6	West Ham United	W 4-0	Bergkamp, Overmars, Anelka, Parlour	26,042
Feb 17	Manchester United	D 1-1	Anelka	55,171
Feb 20	LEICESTER CITY	W 5-0	Anelka 3, Parlour 2	38,069
Feb 28	Newcastle United	D 1-1	Anelka	36,708
Mar 9	SHEFFIELD WEDNESDAY	W 3-0	Bergkamp 2, Kanu	37,792
Mar 13	Everton	W 2-0	Parlour, Bergkamp (pen)	38,049
Mar 21	COVENTRY CITY	W 2-0	Parlour, Overmars	38,073
Apr 3	Southampton	D 0-0		15,255
Apr 6	BLACKBURN ROVERS	W 1-0	Bergkamp	37,762
Apr 19	WIMBLEDON	W 5-1	Parlour, Vieira, o.g., Bergkamp, Kanu	37,982
Apr 24	Middlesbrough	W 6-1	Overmars (pen), Anelka 2, Kanu 2, Vieira	34,630
May 2	DERBY COUNTY	W 1-0	Anelka	37,323
May 5	Tottenham Hotspur	W 3-1	Petit, Anelka, Kanu	36,019
May 11	Leeds United	L 0-1		40,142
May 16	ASTON VILLA	W 1-0	Kanu	38,308

FA Cup

Jan 4	Preston North End	(Rd3)	W 4-2	Boa Morte, Petit 2, Overmars	21,099
Jan 24	Wolverhampton Wanderers	(Rd4)	W 2-1	Overmars, Bergkamp	27,511
Feb 23	SHEFFIELD UNITED*	(Rd5)	W 2-1*	Overmars, Bergkamp	37,161
Mar 6	DERBY COUNTY	(QF)	W 1-0	Kanu	38,046
Apr 12	Manchester United**	(SF)	D 0-0		39,217
Apr 14	Manchester United**	(R)	L 1-2	Bergkamp	30,223

*After Arsenal's 2-1 win on 13 February was declared a void match.
**Played at Villa Park.

League Cup

Oct 28	Derby County	(Rd3)	W 2-1	o.g., Vivas	25,621
Nov 11	CHELSEA	(Rd4)	L 0-5		37,652

European Champions League

Sep 16	Lens	(Gp)	D 1-1	Overmars	33,371
Sep 30	PANATHINAIKOS	(Gp)	W 2-1	Adams, Keown	73,455
Oct 21	DYNAMO KIEV	(Gp)	D 1-1	Bergkamp	73,256
Nov 4	Dynamo Kiev	(Gp)	L 1-3	Hughes	53,000
Nov 25	LENS	(Gp)	L 0-1		73,707
Dec 9	Panathinaikos	(Gp)	W 3-1	Anelka, Boa Morte, Mendez	50,000

Arsenal played their Champions League home games at Wembley.
They were eliminated after the first group stage.

MANAGER: Arsène Wenger

CAPTAIN: Tony Adams

TOP SCORER: Nicolas Anelka 18 (17 League)

BIGGEST WIN: 6-1 v Middlesbrough, 24 April 1999, League

HIGHEST ATTENDANCE: 73,707 v Lens, 25 November 1999, Champions League

MAJOR TRANSFERS IN: Nelson Vivas from Lugano, Freddie Ljungberg from Halmstad, Nwankwo Kanu from Internazionale

MAJOR TRANSFER OUT: Ian Wright to West Ham United

League & Cup Appearances

PLAYER	LEAGUE	CUP COMPETITION			TOTAL
		FA CUP	LC	ECL	
Adams	26	5		4	35
Anelka	34 (1)	5		5	44 (1)
Bergkamp	28 (1)	5	1	3	37 (1)
Black M.				0 (1)	0 (1)
Boa Morte	2 (6)	1	2	2 (1)	7 (6)
Bould	14 (5)	2 (1)		2 (1)	18 (7)
Caballero	0 (1)	0 (1)			0 (2)
Crowe			0 (1)		0 (1)
Diawara	2 (10)	0 (2)			2 (12)
Dixon	36	5		5	46
Garde	6 (4)	1 (2)	2	3 (2)	12 (8)
Grimandi	3 (5)	0 (1)	2	1 (1)	6 (7)
Grondin	1		2	1	4
Hughes	4 (9)	2 (1)	2	2 (2)	10 (12)
Kanu	5 (7)	(4)			5 (11)
Keown	34	4		5	43
Ljungberg	10 (6)	2 (1)	2		14 (7)
Manninger	6	2	2		10
Mendez	0 (1)	1	1 (1)	1	3 (2)
Overmars	37	5 (1)		4	46 (1)
Parlour	35	6		4	45
Petit	26 (1)	3		3	32 (1)
Riza			0 (1)		0 (1)
Seaman	32	4		6	42
Upson	0 (5)	1	2	1	4 (5)
Vernazza				1	1
Vieira	34	4		3	41
Vivas	10 (13)	3 (2)	2	2 (3)	17 (18)
Winterburn	30	5		5	40
Wreh	3 (9)		2	3	8 (9)

Goalscorers

PLAYER	LEAGUE	CUP COMPETITION			TOTAL
		FA CUP	LC	ECL	
Anelka	17			1	18
Bergkamp	12	3		1	16
Overmars	6	3		1	10
Kanu	6	1			7
Parlour	6				6
Petit	4	2			6
Vieira	3				3
Adams	1			1	2
Hughes	1			1	2
Keown	1			1	2
Boa Morte		1		1	2
Ljungberg	1				1
Mendez				1	1
Vivas			1		1
Opps' o.gs.		1	1		2

Fact File

No championship but Arsenal set a Premiership defensive record, conceding 17 league goals all season.

Final Premier League Table

		P	W	D	L	F	A	Pts
1	MANCHESTER U	38	22	13	3	80	37	79
2	ARSENAL	38	22	12	4	59	17	78
3	CHELSEA	38	20	15	3	57	30	67
4	LEEDS U	38	18	13	7	62	34	67
5	WEST HAM U	38	16	9	13	46	53	57
6	ASTON VILLA	38	15	10	13	51	46	55
7	LIVERPOOL	38	15	9	14	68	49	54
8	DERBY CO	38	13	13	12	40	45	52
9	MIDDLESBROUGH	38	12	15	11	48	54	51
10	LEICESTER C	38	12	13	13	40	46	49
11	TOTTENHAM H	38	11	14	13	47	50	47
12	SHEFFIELD W	38	13	7	18	41	42	46
13	NEWCASTLE U	38	11	13	14	48	54	46
14	EVERTON	38	11	10	17	42	47	43
15	COVENTRY C	38	11	9	18	39	51	42
16	WIMBLEDON	38	10	12	16	40	63	42
17	SOUTHAMPTON	38	11	8	19	37	64	41
18	CHARLTON ATH	38	8	12	18	41	56	36
19	BLACKBURN R	38	7	14	17	38	52	35
20	NOTTINGHAM F	38	7	9	22	35	69	30

Season 1999-2000

Premier League

DATE		OPPONENTS	SCORE	GOALSCORERS	ATTENDANCE
Aug	7	LEICESTER CITY	W 2-1	o.g., Bergkamp	38,026
Aug	10	Derby County	W 2-1	Petit, Bergkamp	25,901
Aug	14	Sunderland	D 0-0		41,680
Aug	22	MANCHESTER UNITED	L 1-2	Ljungberg	38,147
Aug	25	BRADFORD CITY	W 2-0	Vieira, Kanu (pen)	38,073
Aug	28	Liverpool	L 0-2		44,886
Sep	11	ASTON VILLA	W 3-1	Suker 2, Kanu	38,093
Sep	18	Southampton	W 1-0	Henry	15,242
Sep	25	WATFORD	W 1-0	Kanu	38,127
Oct	3	West Ham United	L 1-2	Suker	26,009
Oct	16	EVERTON	W 4-1	Dixon, Suker 2, Kanu	38,042
Oct	23	Chelsea	W 3-2	Kanu 3	34,958
Oct	30	NEWCASTLE UNITED	D 0-0		38,106
Nov	7	Tottenham Hotspur	L 1-2	Vieira	36,085
Nov	20	MIDDLESBROUGH	W 5-1	Overmars 3, Bergkamp 2	38,082
Nov	28	DERBY COUNTY	W 2-1	Henry 2	37,964
Dec	4	Leicester City	W 3-0	Grimandi, o.g., Overmars	20,495
Dec	18	WIMBLEDON	D 1-1	Henry	38,052
Dec	26	Coventry City	L 2-3	Ljungberg, Suker	22,757
Dec	28	LEEDS UNITED	W 2-0	Ljungberg, Henry	38,096
Jan	3	Sheffield Wednesday	D 1-1	Petit	26,155
Jan	15	SUNDERLAND	W 4-1	Henry 2, Suker 2	38,039
Jan	24	Manchester United	D 1-1	Ljungberg	58,293
Feb	5	Bradford City	L 1-2	Henry	18,276
Feb	13	LIVERPOOL	L 0-1		38,098
Feb	26	SOUTHAMPTON	W 3-1	Ljungberg 2, Bergkamp	38,044
Mar	5	Aston Villa	D 1-1	Dixon	36,930
Mar	12	Middlesbrough	L 1-2	Bergkamp	34,244
Mar	19	TOTTENHAM HOTSPUR	W 2-1	o.g., Henry (pen)	38,131
Mar	26	COVENTRY CITY	W 3-0	Henry, Grimandi, Kanu	38,027
Apr	1	Wimbledon	W 3-1	Kanu 2, Henry (pen)	25,858
Apr	16	Leeds United	W 4-0	Henry, Keown, Kanu, Overmars	39,307
Apr	23	Watford	W 3-2	Henry 2, Parlour	19,670
Apr	29	Everton	W 1-0	Overmars	35,919
May	2	WEST HAM UNITED	W 2-1	Overmars, Petit	38,093
May	6	CHELSEA	W 2-1	Henry 2	38,119
May	9	SHEFFIELD WEDNESDAY	D 3-3	Dixon, Silvinho, Henry	37,271
May	14	Newcastle United	L 2-4	Kanu, Malz	36,450

FA Cup

Dec	13	BLACKPOOL	(Rd3) W 3-1	Grimandi, Adams, Overmars	34,143
Jan	9	LEICESTER CITY	(Rd4) D 0-0		35,710
Jan	19	Leicester City	(R) D 0-0*		15,235

*Arsenal lost 6-5 on penalties.

League Cup

Oct	12	PRESTON NORTH END	(Rd3) W 2-1	Kanu, Malz	15,239
Nov	30	Middlesbrough	(Rd4) D 2-2*	Henry, Suker	23,157

*Arsenal lost 3-1 on penalties.

European Champions League

Sep	14	Fiorentina	(P1/Gp) D 0-0		40,000
Sep	22	AIK SOLNA	(P1/Gp) W 3-1	Ljungberg, Henry, Suker	71,227
Sep	29	Barcelona	(P1/Gp) D 1-1	Kanu	85,000
Oct	19	BARCELONA	(P1/Gp) L 2-4	Bergkamp, Overmars	73,091
Oct	27	FIORENTINA	(P1/Gp) L 0-1		73,336
Nov	2	AIK Solna	(P1/Gp) W 3-2	Overmars 2, Suker	33,005

Home games played at Wembley. Arsenal failed to qualify for the second group phase but gained a place in the UEFA Cup as third team in their group.

UEFA Cup

Nov	25	NANTES	(Rd3/1L) W 3-0	Overmars (pen), Winterburn, Bergkamp	36,118
Dec	9	Nantes	(Rd3/2L) D 3-3	Grimandi, Henry, Overmars	28,000
Mar	2	DEPORTIVO LA CORUNA	(R4/1L) W 5-1	Dixon, Henry 2, Kanu, Bergkamp	37,831
Mar	9	Deportivo La Coruna	(Rd4/2L) L 1-2	Henry	20,000
Mar	16	WERDER BREMEN	(QF/1L) W 2-0	Henry, Ljungberg	38,009
Mar	23	Werder Bremen	(QF/2L) W 4-2	Parlour 3, Henry	33,875
Apr	6	LENS	(SF/1L) W 1-0	Bergkamp	38,102
Apr	20	Lens	(SF2/2L) W 2-1	Henry, Kanu	41,043
May	17	Galatasaray*	(F) D 0-0		38,919

*Played in Copenhagen. Arsenal lost 4-1 on penalties.

MANAGER: Arsène Wenger **CAPTAIN:** Tony Adams

MAJOR TRANSFERS IN: Thierry Henry from Juventus, Oleg Luzhny from Dynamo Kiev, Silvinho from Corinthians, Davor Suker from Real Madrid

MAJOR TRANSFERS OUT: Steve Bould to Sunderland, Nicolas Anelka to Real Madrid, Luis Boa Morte to Southampton, Stephen Hughes to Everton

---

League & Cup Appearances

PLAYER	LEAGUE	CUP COMPETITION				TOTAL
		FA CUP	LC	ECL	UEFA	
Adams	21	1 (1)		5	6	33 (1)
Barrett	0 (2)					0 (2)
Bergkamp	23 (5)			5	6	34 (5)
Black M.	0 (1)		1			1 (1)
Boa Morte	0 (2)					0 (2)
Cole	1		0 (1)			1 (1)
Dixon	28	3		5	8	44
Gray	0 (1)					0 (1)
Grimandi	27 (1)	3	1	3	6 (1)	40 (2)
Henry	26 (5)	3	2 (4)	7 (1)		38 (10)
Hughes	1 (1)	0 (2)	0 (1)			1 (4)
Kanu	24 (7)	0 (2)	1	4 (2)	5 (4)	34 (11)
Keown	27	2		5	4	38
Ljungberg	22 (4)	2		4 (2)	7 (1)	35 (7)
Luzhny	16 (5)	1	2	2	4	25 (5)
McGovern	0 (1)					0 (1)
Malz	2 (3)	2		0 (1)	0 (1)	6 (5)
Manninger	14 (1)	1	1	4	2	22 (1)
Overmars	22 (9)	1	0 (1)	6	5 (3)	34 (13)
Parlour	29 (1)	1		3	6 (2)	41 (3)
Pennant			0 (1)			0 (1)
Petit	24 (2)	3		2	7 (1)	36 (3)
Seaman	24	2		2	7	36
Silvinho	23 (8)	3	2	0 (1)	7 (1)	35 (10)
Suker	8 (14)	3	1	3 (3)	0 (7)	15 (24)
Upson	5 (3)		2	1 (1)		8 (4)
Vernazza	1 (1)		2		0 (1)	3 (2)
Vieira	29 (1)	2		6	8	45 (1)
Vivas	1 (4)		1	0 (2)	0 (1)	2 (7)
Weston	1		0 (1)			1 (1)
Winterburn	19 (9)		1	6	3 (1)	29 (10)
Wreh			0 (1)			0 (1)

Goalscorers

PLAYER	LEAGUE	CUP COMPETITION				TOTAL
		FA CUP	LC	ECL	UEFA	
Henry	17		1	1	7	26
Kanu	12		1	1	2	16
Overmars	7	1		3	2	13
Suker	8		1	2		11
Bergkamp	6			1	3	10
Ljungberg	6			1	1	8
Dixon	4				1	5
Grimandi	2	1			1	4
Parlour	1				3	4
Petit	3					3
Vieira	2					2
Malz	1		1			2
Keown	1			1		2
Silvinho	1					1
Adams		1				1
Winterburn					1	1
Opps' o.g.	2					2

Final Premier League Table

		P	W	D	L	F	A	Pts
1	MANCHESTER U	38	28	7	3	97	45	91
2	ARSENAL	38	22	7	9	73	43	73
3	LEEDS U	38	21	6	11	58	43	69
4	LIVERPOOL	38	19	10	9	51	30	67
5	CHELSEA	38	18	11	9	53	34	65
6	ASTON VILLA	38	15	13	10	46	35	58
7	SUNDERLAND	38	16	10	12	57	56	58
8	LEICESTER C	38	16	7	15	55	55	55
9	WEST HAM U	38	15	10	13	52	53	55
10	TOTTENHAM H	38	15	8	15	57	49	53
11	NEWCASTLE UNITED	38	14	10	14	63	54	52
12	MIDDLESBROUGH	38	14	10	14	46	52	52
13	EVERTON	38	12	14	12	59	49	50
14	COVENTRY C	38	12	8	18	47	54	44
15	SOUTHAMPTON	38	12	8	18	45	62	44
16	DERBY CO	38	9	11	18	44	57	38
17	BRADFORD C	38	9	9	20	38	68	36
18	WIMBLEDON	38	7	12	19	46	74	33
19	SHEFFIELD W	38	8	7	23	38	70	31
20	WATFORD	38	6	6	26	35	77	24

Season 2000-01

Premier League

DATE	OPPONENTS	SCORE	GOALSCORERS	ATTENDANCE
Aug 19	Sunderland	L 0-1		46,347
Aug 21	LIVERPOOL	W 2-0	Lauren, Henry	38,014
Aug 26	CHARLTON ATHLETIC	W 5-3	Henry 2, Vieira 2, Silvinho	38,025
Sep 6	Chelsea	D 2-2	Henry, Silvinho	34,923
Sep 9	Bradford City	D 1-1	Cole	17,160
Sep 16	COVENTRY CITY	W 2-1	Wiltord, Vernazza	37,794
Sep 23	Ipswich Town	D 1 1	Bergkamp	22,030
Oct 1	MANCHESTER UNITED	W 1-0	Henry	38,146
Oct 14	ASTON VILLA	W 1-0	Henry	38,042
Oct 21	West Ham United	W 2-1	Pires, o.g.	26,034
Oct 28	MANCHESTER CITY	W 5-0	Cole, Henry 2, Bergkamp, Wiltord	38,049
Nov 4	Middlesbrough	W 1-0	Henry (pen)	29,541
Nov 11	DERBY COUNTY	D 0-0		37,679
Nov 18	Everton	L 0-2		33,106
Nov 26	Leeds United	L 0-1		38,084
Dec 2	SOUTHAMPTON	W 1-0	o.g.	38,036
Dec 9	NEWCASTLE UNITED	W 5-0	Parlour 3, Henry, Kanu	38,052
Dec 18	Tottenham Hotspur	D 1-1	Vieira	36,062
Dec 23	Liverpool	L 0-4		44,144
Dec 26	LEICESTER CITY	W 6-1	Ljungberg, Henry 3, Vieira, Adams	38,007
Dec 30	SUNDERLAND	D 2-2	Dixon, Vieira	38,026
Jan 1	Charlton Athletic	L 0-1		20,043
Jan 13	CHELSEA	D 1-1	Pires	38,071
Jan 20	Leicester City	D 0-0		21,872
Jan 30	BRADFORD CITY	W 2-0	Lauren, Parlour	37,318
Feb 3	Coventry City	W 1-0	Bergkamp	22,035
Feb 10	IPSWICH TOWN	W 1-0	Henry	38,011
Feb 25	Manchester United	L 1-6	Henry	67,535
Mar 3	WEST HAM UNITED	W 3-0	Wiltord 3	38,071
Mar 18	Aston Villa	D 0-0		36,111
Mar 31	TOTTENHAM HOTSPUR	W 2-0	Pires, Henry	38,121
Apr 11	Manchester City	W 4-0	Kanu, Ljungberg 2, Wiltord	33,444
Apr 14	MIDDLESBROUGH	L 0-3		37,879
Apr 21	EVERTON	W 4-1	Wiltord, Ljungberg, Henry, Grimandi	38,029
Apr 28	Derby County	W 2-1	Kanu, Pires	29,567
May 5	LEEDS UNITED	W 2-1	Ljungberg, Wiltord	38,142
May 15	Newcastle United	D 0-0		50,729
May 19	Southampton	L 2-3	Cole, Ljungberg	15,252

FA Cup

Jan 6	Carlisle United	(Rd3) W 1-0	Wiltord	15,300
Jan 27	Queens Park Rangers	(Rd4) W 6-0	o.g. 2, Wiltord 2, Bergkamp, Pires	19,003
Feb 18	CHELSEA	(Rd5) W 3-1	Wiltord 2, Henry (pen)	38,096
Mar 10	BLACKBURN ROVERS	(QF) W 3-0	Adams, Pires, Wiltord	36,604
Apr 8	Tottenham Hotspur*	(SF) W 2-1	Vieira, Pires	63,541
May 12	Liverpool**	(F) L 1-2	Ljungberg	72,500

*Played at Old Trafford. **Played at Millennium Stadium.

League Cup

Nov 1	IPSWICH TOWN	(Rd3) L 1-2	Stepanovs	26,105

European Champions League

Sep 12	Sparta Prague	(P1/Gp) W 1-0	Silvinho	17,666
Sep 20	SHAKHTAR DONETSK	(P1/Gp) W 3-2	Keown 2, Wiltord	34,922
Sep 27	LAZIO	(P1/Gp) W 2-0	Ljungberg 2	34,521
Oct 17	Lazio	(P1/Gp) D 1-1	Pires	42,500
Oct 25	SPARTA PRAGUE	(P1/Gp) W 4-2	Dixon, Lauren, Parlour, Kanu	34,479
Nov 7	Shakhtar Donetsk	(P1/Gp) L 0-3		32,000
Nov 22	Spartak Moscow	(P2/Gp) L 1-4	Silvinho	70,000
Dec 5	BAYERN MUNICH	(P2/Gp) D 2-2	Henry, Kanu	35,318
Feb 13	Olympique Lyons	(P2/Gp) W 1-0	Henry	39,541
Feb 21	OLYMPIQUE LYONS	(P2/Gp) D 1-1	Bergkamp	34,303
Mar 6	Spartak Moscow	(P2/Gp) W 1-0	Henry	35,196
Mar 14	Bayern Munich	(P2/Gp) L 0-1		58,000
Apr 4	VALENCIA	(QF/1L) W 2-1	Henry, Parlour	35,104
Apr 17	Valencia	(QF/2L) L 0-1†		47,700

†Arsenal lost on away goals.

MANAGER: Arsène Wenger **CAPTAIN:** Tony Adams

MAJOR TRANSFERS IN: Lauren from Mallorca, Robert Pires from Olympique Marseille, Sylvain Wiltord from Bordeaux, Edu from Corinthians

MAJOR TRANSFERS OUT: Manu Petit and Marc Overmars to Barcelona, Davor Suker and Nigel Winterburn to West Ham United

---

League & Cup Appearances

PLAYER	LEAGUE	CUP COMPETITION			TOTAL
		FA CUP	LC	ECL	
Adams	26	4		8	38
Barrett			1		1
Bergkamp	19 (6)	4 (1)		3 (2)	26 (9)
Canoville			0 (1)		0 (1)
Cole	15 (2)	5 (1)	1	8 (1)	29 (4)
Danilevicius	0 (2)	0 (1)			0 (3)
Dixon	26 (3)	6		11	43 (3)
Edu	2 (3)				2 (3)
Grimandi	28 (2)	2 (1)		8	38 (3)
Henry	27 (8)	3 (1)		14	44 (9)
Kanu	13 (14)	0 (1)		11 (3)	24 (18)
Keown	28	2		9	39
Lauren	15 (3)	4		6 (5)	25 (8)
Ljungberg	25 (5)	4 (1)		10 (3)	39 (9)
Lukic	3		1		4
Luzhny	16 (3)	2		8	26 (3)
Malz	0 (1)	0 (2)			0 (3)
Manninger	11	1		2	14
Mendez			0 (1)		0 (1)
Parlour	28 (5)	3 (1)		9 (1)	40 (7)
Pennant			1		1
Pires	29 (4)	6		11 (1)	46 (5)
Seaman	24	5		10	39
Silvinho	23 (1)	1 (2)		6 (1)	30 (4)
Stepanovs	9	3		1	13
Taylor			1	1	2
Upson	0 (2)		1	1	2 (2)
Vernazza			1	0 (1)	1 (3)
Vieira	28 (2)	5 (1)		12	45 (3)
Vivas	3 (9)	1 (2)	1	3 (4)	8 (15)
Volz			1		1
Weston			1		1
Wiltord	20 (7)	5 (1)	1	2 (11)	28 (19)
Wreh			0 (1)		0 (1)

Goalscorers

PLAYER	LEAGUE	CUP COMPETITION			TOTAL
		FA CUP	LC	ECL	
Henry	17	1		4	22
Wiltord	8	6		1	15
Ljungberg	6	1		2	9
Pires	4	3		1	8
Vieira	5	1			6
Parlour	4			2	6
Bergkamp	3	1		1	5
Kanu	3			2	5
Silvinho	2			2	4
Cole	3				3
Lauren	2			1	3
Adams	1	1			2
Dixon	1			1	2
Keown				2	2
Grimandi	1				1
Vernazza	1				1
Stepanovs			1		1
Opps' o.gs.	2	2			4

Final Premier League Table

		P	W	D	L	F	A	Pts
1	MANCHESTER U	38	24	8	6	79	31	80
2	ARSENAL	38	20	10	8	63	38	70
3	LIVERPOOL	38	20	9	9	71	39	69
4	LEEDS U	38	20	8	10	64	43	68
5	IPSWICH T	38	20	6	12	57	42	66
6	CHELSEA	38	17	10	11	68	45	61
7	SUNDERLAND	38	15	12	11	46	41	57
8	ASTON VILLA	38	13	15	10	46	43	54
9	CHARLTON ATH	38	14	10	14	50	57	52
10	SOUTHAMPTON	38	14	10	14	40	48	52
11	NEWCASTLE U	38	14	9	15	44	50	51
12	TOTTENHAM H	38	13	10	15	47	54	49
13	LEICESTER CITY	38	14	6	18	39	51	48
14	MIDDLESBROUGH	38	9	15	14	44	44	42
15	WEST HAM U	38	10	12	16	45	50	42
16	EVERTON	38	11	9	18	45	59	42
17	DERBY CO	38	10	12	16	37	59	42
18	MANCHESTER C	38	8	10	20	41	65	34
19	COVENTRY C	38	8	10	20	36	63	34
20	BRADFORD C	38	5	11	22	30	70	26

Season 2001-02

Premier League

DATE	OPPONENTS	SCORE	GOALSCORERS	ATTENDANCE
Aug 18	Middlesbrough	W 4-0	Pires (pen), Henry, Bergkamp 2	31,557
Aug 21	LEEDS UNITED	L 1-2	Wiltord	38,062
Aug 25	LEICESTER CITY	W 4-0	Ljungberg, Wiltord, Henry, Kanu	37,909
Sep 8	Chelsea	D 1-1	Henry	40,855
Sep 15	Fulham	W 3-1	Henry, Ljungberg, Bergkamp	20,805
Sep 22	BOLTON WANDERERS	D 1-1	Jeffers	38,014
Sep 29	Derby County	W 2-0	Henry 2 (1pen)	29,200
Oct 13	Southampton	W 2-0	Henry, Pires	29,759
Oct 20	BLACKBURN ROVERS	D 3-3	Pires, Henry, Bergkamp	38,108
Oct 27	Sunderland	D 1-1	Kanu	48,029
Nov 4	CHARLTON ATHLETIC	L 2-4	Henry 2 (1pen)	38,010
Nov 17	Tottenham Hotspur	D 1-1	Pires	36,049
Nov 25	MANCHESTER UNITED	W 3-1	Henry 2, Ljungberg	38,174
Dec 1	Ipswich Town	W 2-0	Henry (pen), Ljungberg	24,666
Dec 9	ASTON VILLA	W 3-2	Wiltord, Henry 2	38,074
Dec 15	West Ham United	D 1-1	Cole	34,523
Dec 18	NEWCASTLE UNITED	L 1-3	Pires	38,012
Dec 23	Liverpool	W 2-1	Ljungberg, Henry (pen)	44,297
Dec 26	CHELSEA	W 2-1	Campbell, Wiltord	38,079
Dec 29	MIDDLESBROUGH	W 2-1	Cole, Pires	37,948
Jan 13	LIVERPOOL	D 1-1	Ljungberg	38,132
Jan 20	Leeds United	D 1-1	Pires	40,143
Jan 23	Leicester City	W 3-1	Henry, Wiltord, Van Bronckhorst	21,344
Jan 30	Blackburn Rovers	W 3-2	Bergkamp 2, Henry	25,893
Feb 2	SOUTHAMPTON	D 1-1	Wiltord	38,024
Feb 10	Everton	W 1-0	Wiltord	30,859
Feb 23	FULHAM	W 4-1	Vieira, Lauren, Henry 2	38,029
Mar 2	Newcastle United	W 2-0	Bergkamp, Campbell	52,067
Mar 5	DERBY COUNTY	W 1-0	Pires	37,878
Mar 17	Aston Villa	W 2-1	Edu, Pires	41,520
Mar 30	SUNDERLAND	W 3-0	Vieira, Bergkamp, Wiltord	38,047
Apr 1	Charlton Athletic	W 3-0	Henry 2, Ljungberg	26,339
Apr 6	TOTTENHAM HOTSPUR	W 2-1	Ljungberg, Lauren (pen)	38,186
Apr 21	IPSWICH TOWN	W 2-0	Ljungberg 2	38,058
Apr 24	WEST HAM UNITED	W 2-0	Ljungberg, Kanu	38,038
Apr 29	Bolton Wanderers	W 2-0	Wiltord, Ljungberg	27,351
May 8	Manchester United	W 1-0	Wiltord	67,580
May 11	EVERTON	W 4-3	Henry 2, Bergkamp, Jeffers	38,254

FA Cup

Jan 5	Watford	(Rd3) W 4-2	Henry, Ljungberg, Kanu, Bergkamp	20,105
Jan 27	LIVERPOOL	(Rd4) W 1-0	Bergkamp	38,092
Feb 16	GILLINGHAM	(Rd5) W 5-2	Wiltord 2, Parlour, Adams, Kanu	38,003
Mar 9	Newcastle United	(QF) D 1-1	Edu	51,027
Mar 23	NEWCASTLE UNITED	(R) W 3-0	Pires, Bergkamp, Campbell	38,073
Apr 14	Middlesbrough*	(SF) W 1-0	o.g.	61,168
May 4	Chelsea**	(F) W 2-0	Parlour, Ljungberg	76,963

*Played at Old Trafford. **Played at Millennium Stadium.

League Cup

Nov 5	MANCHESTER UNITED	(Rd3) W 4-0	Wiltord 3 (1pen), Kanu (pen)	30,693
Nov 27	GRIMSBY TOWN	(Rd4) W 2-0	Wiltord, Edu	16,917
Dec 11	Blackburn Rovers	(QF) L 0-4		13,278

European Champions League

Sep 11	Real Mallorca	(P1/GpC) L 0-1		22,000
Sep 19	SCHALKE	(P1/GpC) W 3-2	Henry 2 (1pen), Ljungberg	35,361
Sep 26	Panathinaikos	(P1/GpC) L 0-1		17,200
Oct 16	PANATHINAIKOS	(P1/GpC) W 2-1	Henry 2 (1pen)	35,432
Oct 24	REAL MALLORCA	(P1/GpC) W 3-1	Pires, Bergkamp, Henry	34,764
Oct 30	Schalke	(P1/GpC) L 1-3	Wiltord	53,500
Nov 21	Deportivo La Coruna	(P2/GpD) L 0-2		32,800
Dec 4	JUVENTUS	(P2/GpD) W 3-1	Ljungberg 2, Henry	35,421
Feb 19	Bayer Leverkusen	(P2/GpD) D 1-1	Pires	22,200
Feb 27	BAYER LEVERKUSEN	(P2/GpD) W 4-1	Pires, Vieira, Henry, Bergkamp	35,019
Mar 12	DEPORTIVO LA CORUNA	(P2/GpD) L 0-2		35,392
Mar 20	Juventus	(P2/GpD) L 0-1		8,562

Arsenal were eliminated after the second group phase.

League & Cup Appearances

PLAYER	LEAGUE	CUP COMPETITION			TOTAL
		FA CUP	LC	ECL	
Adams	10	3			13
Aliadiere	0 (1)		0 (2)		0 (2)
Bergkamp	22 (11)	4 (2)	1	3 (3)	30 (16)
Campbell	29 (2)	7		10	46 (2)
Cole	29	4		6 (1)	39 (1)
Dixon	3 (10)	2 (2)		2	7 (12)
Edu	8 (6)	4 (1)	3	2 (3)	17 (10)
Grimandi	11 (15)	1 (3)	2	5 (3)	19 (21)
Halls			0 (3)		0 (3)
Henry	31 (2)	4 (1)		11	46 (3)
Inamoto			2	0 (2)	2 (2)
Itonga			0 (1)		0 (1)
Jeffers	2 (4)	1 (1)		0 (2)	3 (7)
Juan		1	1		2
Kanu	9 (14)	3 (2)	2	4 (5)	18 (21)
Keown	21 (1)	3 (1)	2	4 (2)	30 (4)
Lauren	27	3		11	41
Ljungberg	24 (1)	5		8 (1)	37 (2)
Luzhny	15 (3)	4	1	3	23 (3)
Parlour	25 (2)	2 (2)	1	5 (3)	33 (7)
Pennant			3	0 (2)	3 (2)
Pires	27 (1)	3 (2)		12	42 (3)
Ricketts			0 (1)		0 (1)
Seaman	17	1		7	25
Stepanovs	6	1	2 (1)	3 (1)	12 (2)
Svard			0 (1)		0 (1)
Tavlaridis			3		3
Taylor	9 (1)	1	2	1 (1)	13 (2)
Upson	10 (4)	0 (1)	1	5 (1)	16 (6)
Van Bronckhorst	13 (8)	2	3	6 (1)	24 (9)
Vieira	35 (1)	7		11	53 (1)
Wiltord	23 (10)	6 (1)	3	9 (2)	41 (13)
Wright	12	5	1	4	22

Goalscorers

PLAYER	LEAGUE	CUP COMPETITION			TOTAL
		FA CUP	LC	ECL	
Henry	24	1		7	32
Ljungberg	12	2		3	17
Wiltord	10	2	4	1	17
Bergkamp	9	3		2	14
Pires	9	1		3	13
Kanu	3	2	1		6
Campbell	2	1			3
Vieira	2			1	3
Edu	1	1	1		3
Cole	2				2
Jeffers	2				2
Lauren	2				2
Parlour		2			2
Adams		1			1
Van Bronckhorst	1				1
Opps' o.gs.		1			1

Final Premier League Table

		P	W	D	L	F	A	Pts
1	ARSENAL	38	26	9	3	79	36	87
2	LIVERPOOL	38	24	8	6	67	30	80
3	MANCHESTER U	38	24	5	9	87	45	77
4	NEWCASTLE U	38	21	8	9	74	52	71
5	LEEDS U	38	18	12	8	53	37	66
6	CHELSEA	38	17	13	8	66	38	64
7	WEST HAM U	38	15	8	15	48	57	53
8	ASTON VILLA	38	12	14	12	46	47	50
9	TOTTENHAM H	38	14	8	16	49	53	50
10	BLACKBURN R	38	12	10	16	55	51	46
11	SOUTHAMPTON	38	12	9	17	46	54	45
12	MIDDLESBROUGH	38	12	9	17	35	47	45
13	FULHAM	38	10	14	14	36	44	44
14	CHARLTON ATH	38	10	14	14	38	49	44
15	EVERTON	38	11	10	17	45	57	43
16	BOLTON W	38	9	13	16	44	62	40
17	SUNDERLAND	38	10	10	18	29	51	40
18	IPSWICH T	38	9	9	20	41	64	36
19	DERBY CO	38	8	6	24	33	63	30
20	LEICESTER C	38	5	13	20	30	64	28

Season 2002-03

Premier League

DATE	OPPONENTS	SCORE	GOALSCORERS	ATTENDANCE
Aug 18	BIRMINGHAM CITY	W 2-0	Henry, Wiltord	38,018
Aug 24	West Ham United	D 2-2	Henry, Wiltord	35,048
Aug 27	WEST BROMWICH ALBION	W 5-2	Cole, Lauren, Wiltord 2, Aliadiere	37,920
Sep 1	Chelsea	D 1-1	Toure	40,037
Sep 10	MANCHESTER CITY	W 2-1	Wiltord, Henry	37,878
Sep 14	Charlton Athletic	W 3-0	Henry, Wiltord, Edu	26,080
Sep 21	BOLTON WANDERERS	W 2-1	Henry, Kanu	37,974
Sep 28	Leeds United	W 4-1	Kanu 2, Toure, Henry	40,199
Oct 6	SUNDERLAND	W 3-1	Kanu 2, Vieira	37,902
Oct 19	Everton	L 1-2	Ljungberg	39,038
Oct 26	BLACKBURN ROVERS	L 1-2	Edu	38,064
Nov 3	Fulham	W 1-0	o.g.	18,800
Nov 9	NEWCASTLE UNITED	W 1-0	Wiltord	38,121
Nov 16	TOTTENHAM HOTSPUR	W 3-0	Henry, Ljungberg, Wiltord	38,152
Nov 23	Southampton	L 2-3	Bergkamp, Pires	31,797
Nov 30	ASTON VILLA	W 3-1	Henry 2 (1pen), Pires	38,090
Dec 7	Manchester United	L 0-2		67,650
Dec 15	Tottenham Hotspur	D 1-1	Pires (pen)	36,076
Dec 21	MIDDLESBROUGH	W 2-0	Campbell, Pires	38,003
Dec 26	West Bromwich Albion	W 2-1	Jeffers, Henry	27,025
Dec 29	LIVERPOOL	D 1-1	Henry (pen)	38,074
Jan 1	CHELSEA	W 3-2	o.g., van Bronckhorst, Henry	38,096
Jan 12	Birmingham City	W 4-0	Henry 2, Pires, o.g.	29,505
Jan 19	WEST HAM UNITED	W 3-1	Henry 3 (1pen)	38,053
Jan 29	Liverpool	D 2-2	Pires, Bergkamp	43,668
Feb 1	FULHAM	W 2-1	Pires 2	38,050
Feb 9	Newcastle United	D 1-1	Henry	52,157
Feb 22	Manchester City	W 5-1	Bergkamp, Pires, Henry, Campbell, Vieira	34,960
Mar 2	CHARLTON ATHLETIC	W 2-0	Jeffers, Pires	38,015
Mar 15	Blackburn Rovers	L 0-2		29,840
Mar 23	EVERTON	W 2-1	Cygan, Vieira	38,042
Apr 5	Aston Villa	D 1-1	Ljungberg	42,602
Apr 16	MANCHESTER UNITED	D 2-2	Henry 2	38,164
Apr 19	Middlesbrough	W 2-0	Wiltord, Henry	34,724
Apr 26	Bolton Wanderers	D 2-2	Wiltord, Pires	27,253
May 4	LEEDS UNITED	L 2-3	Henry, Bergkamp	38,127
May 7	SOUTHAMPTON	W 6-1	Pires 3, Pennant 3	38,052
May 11	Sunderland	W 4-0	Henry, Ljungberg 3	40,188

FA Cup

Jan 4	OXFORD UNITED	(Rd3) W 2-0	Bergkamp, o.g.	35,432
Jan 25	Farnborough Town*	(Rd4) W 5-1	Campbell, Jeffers 2, Bergkamp, Lauren	35,108
Feb 15	Manchester United	(Rd5) W 2-0	Edu, Wiltord	67,209
Mar 8	CHELSEA	(QF) D 2-2	Jeffers, Henry	35,788
Mar 25	Chelsea	(R) W 3-1	o.g., Wiltord, Lauren	41,456
Apr 13	Sheffield United**	(SF) W 1-0	Ljungberg	59,170
May 17	Southampton†	(F) W 1-0	Pires	73,726

*Played at Highbury, Farnborough waived home advantage.
**Played at Old Trafford. †Played at Millennium Stadium.

League Cup

Nov 6	SUNDERLAND	(Rd3) L 2-3	Pires, Jeffers	19,059

European Champions League

Sep 17	BORUSSIA DORTMUND	(P1/GpA) W 2-0	Bergkamp, Ljungberg	34,907
Sep 25	PSV Eindhoven	(P1/GpA) W 4-0	Gilberto, Ljungberg, Henry 2	29,500
Oct 2	Auxerre	(P1/GpA) W 1-0	Gilberto	19,454
Oct 22	AUXERRE	(P1/GpA) L 1-2	Kanu	35,206
Oct 30	Borussia Dortmund	(P1/GpA) L 1-2	Henry	51,000
Nov 12	PSV EINDHOVEN	(P1/GpA) D 0-0		35,274
Nov 27	Roma	(P2/GpB) W 3-1	Henry 3	49,860
Dec 10	VALENCIA	(P2/GpB) D 0-0		34,793
Feb 18	AJAX	(P2/GpB) D 1-1	Wiltord	35,427
Feb 26	Ajax	(P2/GpB) D 0-0		51,503
Mar 11	ROMA	(P2/GpB) D 1-1	Vieira	35,472
Mar 19	Valencia	(P2/GpB) L 1-2	Henry	44,151

Arsenal were eliminated after the second group phase.

► Fact File

Arsenal became the first team for 21 years – since Tottenham in 1982 – to successfully defend the FA Cup. Their 1-0 win over Southampton was their ninth FA Cup triumph, in a record 16th final. The Gunners had emulated the 1978-80 squad by reaching three consecutive finals.

League & Cup Appearances

PLAYER	LEAGUE	CUP COMPETITION			TOTAL
		FA CUP	LC	ECL	
Aliadiere	0 (3)				0 (3)
Bentley		0 (1)			0 (1)
Bergkamp	23 (6)	2 (2)		6 (1)	31 (9)
Campbell	33	5		10	48
Cole	30 (1)	3		9	42 (1)
Cygan	16 (2)	2		9 (2)	27 (4)
Edu	12 (6)	5 (1)		1 (3)	18 (10)
Garry	1		0 (1)		1 (1)
Gilberto	32 (3)	1 (2)		11 (1)	44 (6)
Henry	37	2 (3)		12	51 (3)
Hoyte	0 (1)				0 (1)
Jeffers	2 (14)	6	1	1 (4)	10 (18)
Kanu	9 (7)	1	1	2 (6)	13 (13)
Keown	22 (2)	5		4 (1)	31 (3)
Lauren	26 (1)	6		9 (1)	41 (2)
Ljungberg	19 (1)	3 (1)		7 (1)	29 (3)
Luzhny	11 (6)	2	1	3 (1)	17 (7)
Parlour	14 (5)	6		0 (2)	20 (7)
Pennant	1 (4)		1	0 (1)	2 (5)
Pires	21 (5)	5 (1)	1	8 (1)	35 (7)
Seaman	28	5		9	42
Shaaban	3			2	5
Stepanovs	2		1	1	4
Svard		1	1		2
Tavlaridis	0 (1)		1		1 (1)
Taylor	7 (1)	2		1 (1)	11 (2)
Toure	9 (17)	3 (2)	1	3 (4)	16 (23)
Upson		1			1
Van Bronckhorst	9 (11)	3 (2)	1	2 (2)	15 (15)
Vieira	24	5		12	41
Volz			0 (1)		0 (1)
Wiltord	27 (7)	3 (4)		10 (2)	40 (13)

Goalscorers

PLAYER	LEAGUE	CUP COMPETITION			TOTAL
		FA CUP	LC	ECL	
Henry	24	1		7	32
Pires	14	1	1		16
Wiltord	10	2		1	13
Ljungberg	6	1		2	9
Bergkamp	4	2		1	7
Kanu	5			1	6
Jeffers	2	3	1		6
Vieira	3			1	4
Pennant	3				3
Campbell	2	1			3
Edu	2	1			3
Lauren	1	2			3
Toure	2				2
Gilberto				2	2
Aliadiere	1				1
Cole	1				1
Cygan	1				1
Van Bronckhorst	1				1
Opps' o.gs.	3	2			5

Final Premier League Table

		P	W	D	L	F	A	Pts
1	MANCHESTER U	38	25	8	5	74	34	83
2	ARSENAL	38	23	9	6	85	42	78
3	NEWCASTLE U	38	21	6	11	63	48	69
4	CHELSEA	38	19	10	9	68	38	67
5	LIVERPOOL	38	18	10	10	61	41	64
6	BLACKBURN R	38	16	12	10	52	43	60
7	EVERTON	38	17	8	13	48	49	59
8	SOUTHAMPTON	38	13	13	12	43	46	52
9	MANCHESTER C	38	15	6	17	47	54	51
10	TOTTENHAM H	38	14	8	16	51	62	50
11	MIDDLESBROUGH	38	13	10	15	48	44	49
12	CHARLTON ATH	38	14	7	17	45	56	49
13	BIRMINGHAM C	38	13	9	16	41	49	48
14	FULHAM	38	13	9	16	41	50	48
15	LEEDS U	38	14	5	19	58	57	47
16	ASTON VILLA	38	12	9	17	42	47	45
17	BOLTON W	38	10	14	14	41	51	44
18	WEST HAM U	38	10	12	16	42	59	42
19	WEST BROMWICH ALB	38	6	8	24	29	65	26
20	SUNDERLAND	38	4	7	27	21	65	19

Complete Players' Career Records

Records cover Royal Arsenal, Woolwich Arsenal and Arsenal players up to and including season 2002-03.

Player	Birthplace	From	Year Joined	Year Left	To	League Apps	Sub	Goals
Adams, T	Romford	youth team	1983	2002	retired	500	4	32
Addison, C	Taunton	Nottingham Forest	1966	1967	Sheffield United	27	1	9
Aliadiere, J	Rambouillet	youth team	1999		still at club		4	1
Allinson, I	Stevenage	Colchester United	1983	1987	Stoke City	60	23	16
Ambler, C	Hampshire	Tottenham Hotspur	1891-94	1895	not known	1		
Ampadu, K	Bradford	youth team	1988	1991	West Bromwich Albion		2	
Anderson, E	Beith	St Mirren	1903	1904	Fulham	2		
Anderson, J	not known	Crook Town	1896	1903	Portsmouth	144		10
Anderson, T	Woking	youth team	1959	1965	Norwich City	25		6
Anderson, V	Nottingham	Nottingham Forest	1984	1987	Manchester United	120		9
Anderson, W	not known	Sheffield United	1901	1903	Plymouth Argyle	28		10
Anelka, N	Versailles	Paris Saint-Germain	1997	1999	Real Madrid	50	15	23
Armstrong, G	Hebburn	youth team	1961	1977	Leicester City	490	10	53
Arnold, T	Coventry	Coventry City	1905	1907	Coventry City	2		
Ashcroft, J	Liverpool	Gravesend United	1900	1908	Blackburn Rovers	273		
Aston, J	Walsall	Walsall	1899	1900	Small Heath	11		3
Bacuzzi, D	Islington	Eastbourne United	1958	1964	Manchester City	46		
Baker, A	Ilkeston	Huddersfield Town	1919	1931	retired	310		23
Baker, J	Liverpool	Torino	1962	1966	Nottingham Forest	144		93
Baldwin, T	Gateshead	Gateshead	1962	1966	Chelsea	17		7
Ball, A	Farnworth	Everton	1971	1976	Southampton	177		45
Bannister, B	Burnley	Bolton Wanderers	1902	1904	Leicester City	18		
Barbour, H	Glasgow	Airdrie	1888	1893	not known			
Barley, J	Staveley	Staveley Town	1925	1929	Reading	8		1
Barnes, W	Brecon	Southampton	1943	1955	retired	267		11
Barnett, G	Northwich	Everton	1969	1976	Minnesota Kicks (USA)	39		
Barnwell, J	Newcastle	youth team	1955	1964	Nottingham Forest	138		23
Barrett, G	Dublin	youth team	1997	2003	Coventry City		2	
Barron, P	Woolwich	Plymouth Argyle	1978	1980	Crystal Palace	8		
Bartram, V	Birmingham	AFC Bournemouth	1994	1997	Gillingham	11		
Bassett, S	Blackheath	Maidstone	1906	1910	Exeter City	1		
Bastin, C	Exeter	Exeter City	1929	1946	retired	350		150
Bates, M	not known	Nottingham Forest	1888	1891	not known			
Bateup, E	Horley	Faversham	1905-08 &	1910-11	Burslem Port Vale	34		
Batson, B	Trinidad	youth team	1969	1974	Cambridge United	6	4	
Beardsley, F	Ilkeston	Nottingham Forest	1886	1891	not known			
Beasley, P	Stourbridge	Stourbridge	1931	1936	Huddersfield Town	79		19
Bee, E	Nottingham	not known	1890	1893	not known			
Bell, C	Dumfries	Carlisle City	1913	1914	Chesterfield	1		2
Bellamy, J	Bethnal Green	Reading	1903	1907	Portsmouth	29		4
Beney, A	Hastings	Hastings	1909	1910	Carlisle United	16		6
Benson, B	Swalewell	Sheffield United	1913	1916	died 1916	52		7
Bentley, D	Peterborough	youth team	2002		still at club			
Bergkamp, D	Amsterdam	Internazionale	1995		still at club	204	30	73
Bigden, J	London	West Ham United	1904	1908	Bury	75		1
Biggs, A	Wootton	as an amateur	1933	1937	Heart of Midlothian	3		
Biggs, T	Greenford	Hounslow Town	1955	1958	Leyton Orient	4		1
Birkett, R	Torquay	Torquay United	1933	1935	Middlesbrough	19		7
Black, M	Chigwell	youth team	1995	1999	Southend United			
Black, Tommy	Glasgow	Strathclyde	1931	1933	Plymouth Argyle			
Black, Tommy	Chigwell	youth team	1996	2000	Crystal Palace		1	
Blackwood, J	Glasgow	Celtic	1900	1901	Reading	17		6
Blair, J	Dumfries	Kilmarnock	1905	1906	Manchester City	13		3
Blockley, J	Leicester	Coventry City	1972	1975	Leicester City	52		1
Bloomfield, J	Kensington	Brentford	1954	1960	Birmingham City	210		54
Blyth, B	Dalkeith	Manchester City	1914	1929	Birmingham City	314		45
Boa Morte, L	Lisbon	Sporting Lisbon	1997	1999	Southampton	6	19	
Boot, M	Leicester	Enderby Town	1963	1967	Port Elizabeth (S Africa)	3	1	2
Booth, C	Gainsborough	Wolverhampton W	1892	1894	Loughborough Town	16		2
Boreham, R	High Wycombe	Wycombe Wanderers	1921	1925	contract cancelled	51		18
Bould, S	Stoke	Stoke City	1988	1999	Sunderland	271	16	5
Boulton, F	Yate	Bath City	1936	1938	Derby County	36		
Bowden, R	Looe	Plymouth Argyle	1933	1937	Newcastle United	123		42
Bowen, D	Nantyffyllon	Northampton Town	1950	1959	Northampton Town	146		2
Bowen, E	Goldthorpe	Waith Athletic	1926	1928	Northampton Town	1		
Boyd, H	Pollokshaws	West Bromwich Albion	1894	1897	Newton Heath	40		32
Boylan, PA	Greenock	Greenock Volunteers	1896	1897	Greenock Morton	11		
Boyle, J	Glasgow	Celtic	1893	1897	Dartford	61		7
Bradshaw, F	Sheffield	Everton	1914	1923	retired	132		14
Bradshaw, B	Burnley	Burnley Belvedere	1900	1904	Fulham	4		2
Brady, L	Dublin	youth team	1971	1980	Juventus	227	8	43

League = Football League and Premiership. **FAC** = FA Cup. **FLC** = Football League Cup. **Europe** = European Cup, Champions League, Cup-Winners' Cup, UEFA Cup and Inter-Cities' Fairs Cup.

FAC Apps	Sub	Goals	FLC Apps	Sub	Goals	Europe Apps	Sub	Goals	Totals Apps	Sub	Goals
53	1	8	58	1	5	48		3	659	6	48
2			2		1				31	1	10
				2					6		1
7	2	4	8	5	3				75	30	23
1									2		
										2	
									2		
9		1							153		11
1		1				1		1	27		8
12		3	18		3				150		15
2		1							30		11
13	1	3	3			6	1	1	72	17	27
58	2	10	35		3	24	2	2	607	14	68
									2		
30									303		
4		2							15		5
2									48		
41		3							351		26
10		4				2		3	156		100
			3		4				20		11
28		7	12						217		52
4									22		
5		4							5		4
2									10		1
25		1							292		12
3			5			2			49		
10						3		1	151		24
			1						1	2	
									8		
				1					11	1	
									1		
42		26						392		176	
3									3		
2									36		
									6	4	
2									2		
10		5							89		24
4									4		
									1		2
									29		4
1									17		6
2									54		7
	1									1	
26	5	13	15		8	28	6	10	273	41	104
12									87		1
									3		
									4		1
2		1							21		8
						1				1	
1									1		
			1						1	1	
1		1							18		7
									13		3
7			3						62		1
17		2							227		56
29		6							343		51
2	3	1	3	2		2	2	1	13	24	4
			1						4	1	2
10		8							26		10
2									53		18
27	2		33	1		17	5	2	348	23	8
6									42		
13		5							136		47
16									162		2
									1		
1									41		32
									11		
5		2							66		7
10									142		14
									4		2
31	4	2	23	10		13		4	294	12	59

Player	Birthplace	From	Year Joined	Year Left	To	League Apps	Sub	Goals
Brain, J	Bristol	Ton Pentre	1923	1931	Tottenham Hotspur	204		125
Bremner, G	Glasgow	Cartha Athletic	1937	1946	Motherwell	15		4
Briercliffe, T	not known	Stalybridge Rovers	1901	1905	Plymouth Argyle	122		33
Briggs, S	Stamford Hill	Tottenham Hotspur	1893	1894	amateur football	2		
Brignall, S	Tenterden	youth team	1975	1979	contract cancelled		1	
Brock, J	not known	East Stirlingshire	1896	1898	Cowes	57		20
Brown, L	Shildon	Northampton Town	1961	1964	Tottenham Hotspur	101		2
Bryan, T	not known	Woolwich	1894	1894	Royal Ordnance	9		1
Buchan, C	Plumstead	Sunderland	1925	1928	retired	102		49
Buchan, J	Perth	Hibernian	1904	1905	Manchester City	8		
Buchanan, B	Johnstone	Burnley	1894	1896	Southampton St Mary's	42		16
Buckenham, B	Woolwich	army football	1909	1910	Southampton	21		5
Buckley, C	Urmston	Aston Villa	1914	1921	retired	56		3
Buist, G	not known	Greenock Morton	1896	1897	not known	6		
Buist Bobby	Glasgow	Clyde	1891	1894	Leith Athletic	17		1
Burdett, G	Tottenham	army football	1910	1912	army football	28		
Burgess, D	Goldenhill, Staffs	Goldenhill Wanderers	1919	1922	West Ham United	13		1
Burns, T	Edenbridge	Tonbridge United	1963	1966	Brighton & Hove Albion	31		
Burrell, G	Newcastle	Leyton	1912	1914	South Shields	23		3
Burrows, L	Ashton-under-Lyne	Woolwich Poly	1892	1895	Tottenham Hotspur	10		
Busby, W	Wellingborough	Queens Park Rangers	1903	1905	Leyton	5		2
Butler, J	Colombo, Ceylon	Fulham Wednesday	1914	1930	Torquay United	267		7
Caballero, F	Argentina	Cerro Porteno, Paraguay	1998	1999	released 1999		1	
Caesar, G	Tottenham	youth team	1982	1991	Cambridge United	27	17	
Caie, A	Aberdeen	Victoria United	1897	1897	Bristol City	8		4
Calder, L	Southampton	amateur	1911	1913	not known	1		
Caldwell, Jimmy	Falkirk	Everton	1913	1914	Reading	3		
Caldwell John	Ayr	Hibernian	1894	1898	Brighton United	93		2
Calverley, A	Huddersfield	Mansfield Town	1947	1947	Preston North End	11		
Calvert, F	Southend	army football	1911	1912	army football	2		1
Campbell, K	Lambeth	youth team	1985	1995	Nottingham Forest	124	42	46
Campbell, S	Newham	Tottenham Hotspur	2001		still at club	62	2	4
Carr, E	Ludworth	amateur	1935	1945	Huddersfield Town	12		7
Carter, J	Hammersmith	Liverpool	1991	1995	Portsmouth	18	7	2
Cartwright, S	Kiveton Park	High Moor	1931	1946	retired	16		2
Carver, G	not known	not known	1896	1900	not known	1		
Cassidy, H	not known	army football	1897	1897	army football	1		
Caton, T	Kirkby	Manchester City	1983	1987	Oxford United	81		2
Chalmers, J	Rutherglen	Clyde	1910	1912	Greenock Morton	48		21
Chambers, B	Newcastle	Sunderland	1973	1974	Luton Town	1		
Chapman, L	Lincoln	Stoke City	1982	1983	Sunderland	15	8	4
Charles, M	Swansea	Swansea Town	1959	1962	Cardiff City	60		26
Charlton, S	Exeter	Leyton Orient	1955	1958	Leyton Orient	99		
Charteris, J	Kirkcaldy	Motherwell	1888	1890	retired through injury			
Chenhall, J	Bristol	Maidenhead United	1944	1953	Fulham	16		
Chisholm, N	Arbroath	London Caledonians	1907	1910	not known	3		
Christmas, A	Wolverhampton	Kidderminster	1890	1891	Cray Wanderers			
Clamp, E	Coalville	Wolverhampton W	1961	1962	Stoke City	22		1
Clapton, Danny	Stepney	Leytonstone	1953	1962	Luton Town	207		25
Clapton Dennis	Hackney	Bexleyheath	1957	1961	Northampton Town	4		
Clark, A	Shoreham	Brentford	1927	1928	Luton Town	1		
Clark, Jim	not known	Bostal Rovers	1897	1900	Plumstead	6		
Clark, John	Coatbridge	Boness	1923	1926	Luton Town	4		
Clarke, A	Haverhill	youth team	1989	1997	Southend United	4	3	
Clarke, F	Kilpike, N Ireland	Glenavon	1960	1965	Glenavon	26		
Coakley, T	Bellshill	Motherwell	1966	1967	Detroit Cougars (USA)	9		1
Cock, D	Hayle	Notts County	1925	1925	Clapton Orient	3		
Cole, Andy	Nottingham	youth team	1988	1992	Bristol City		1	
Cole, Ashley	Stepney	youth team	1997		still at club	75	3	6
Coleman, E	Blidworth	Grimsby Town	1932	1934	Middlesbrough	45		26
Coleman, J	Kettering	Northampton Town	1902	1908	Everton	172		79
Coles, F	Nottingham	Nottingham Forest	1900	1904	Grimsby Town	78		2
Collett, E	Sheffield	as an amateur	1933	1949	retired	20		
Common, A	Sunderland	Middlesbrough	1910	1912	Preston North End	77		23
Compton, D	Hendon	Nunhead	1932	1950	retired	54		15
Compton, L	Woodford	Hampstead Town	1931	1952	retired	253		5
Connolly, P	Kirkcaldy	Kirkcaldy Wanderers	1888	1893	not known			
Connor, J	Lochee	Bristol City	1902	1902	Brentford	14		2
Cooper, J	Wolverhampton	Wolverhampton W	1893	1894	not known	6		
Coopland, W	Sheffield	Birleycarr	1920	1923	Exeter City	1		
Cope, H	Sheffield	Notts County	1926	1933	Bristol Rovers	65		
Copping, W	Middlecliffe	Leeds United	1934	1939	Leeds United	166		
Cork, D	Doncaster	youth team	1978	1985	Huddersfield Town	5	2	1
Cottrell, E	Grantham	Sheppey United	1898	1901	Watford	24		12
Court, D	Mitcham	youth team	1959	1970	Luton Town	168	7	17
Cownley, F	Swallownest	Nottingham Forest	1919	1923	not known	15		
Cox, F	Reading	Tottenham Hotspur	1949	1953	West Bromwich Albion	79		9
Cox, G	Warnham	Horsham	1933	1936	Fulham	7		1
Crawford, G	Ayrshire	Sheffield United	1891	1898	Millwall	122		13
Crawford, H	Dundee	Hebburn Argyle	1911	1913	Reading	26		
Crayston, J	Grange-over-Sands	Bradford Park Avenue	1934	1947	joined coaching staff	168		16

FAC Apps	Sub	Goals	FLC Apps	Sub	Goals	Europe Apps	Sub	Goals	Totals Apps	Sub	Goals
27		14							231		139
									15		4
11		1							133		34
									2		
										1	
6		3							63		23
5						3			109		2
									9		1
18		7							120		56
									8		
2									44		16
									21		5
3									59		3
									6		
10									27		1
									28		
									13		1
2									33		
1									24		3
									10		
1									6		2
29		1							296		8
	1			1						3	
1			3	2					30	20	
									8		4
									1		
									3		
4									97		2
									11		
									2		1
13	6	2	14	10	6	13	4	5	164	62	59
12		2				20			94	2	6
									12		7
2	1		1						21	8	2
									16		2
									1		
									1		
4			10		1				95		3
3		1							51		22
				1					1	1	
	1			2		2		2	17	11	6
4		2							64		28
11		3							110		3
1									1		
									16		
									3		
									1		
2									24		1
18		2							225		27
									4		
									1		
									6		
									4		
1	1								5	4	
2									28		
			4		1				13		2
									3		
										1	
12	1		1	1		23	2		111	7	6
									46		26
24		5							196		84
8									86		2
									21		
3									80		23
5		1							59		16
17		1							270		6
6		2							6		2
2		1							16		3
2		2							8		2
									1		
11									76		
19									185		
1									6	2	1
									24		12
9	1		9	2	1	8			194	10	18
									15		
15		7							94		16
									7		1
16		4							138		17
1									27		
16		1							184		17

Player	Birthplace	From	Year Joined	Year Left	To	League Apps	Sub	Goals
Creegan, W	Salford	amateur	1921	1923	not known	5		
Cropley, A	Aldershot	Hibernian	1974	1976	Aston Villa	29	1	5
Cross, A	Dartford	Dartford	1900	1910	Dartford	132		
Crowe, A	not known	North Woolwich Invicta	1903	1906	not known	6		4
Crowe, J	Sidcup	youth team	1996	1999	Portsmouth			
Crozier, J	not known	Partick Thistle	1894	1895	Partick Thistle	1		
Cumner, H	Cwmaman	Hull City	1938	1946	Notts County	12		2
Curle, B	Glasgow	Rutherglen	1908	1910	not known	3		
Curtis, G	West Thurrock	Anglo Purfleet	1936	1947	Southampton	13		
Cygan, P	Lens	Lille	2002		still at club	16	2	1
Dailly, H	Scotland	Dundee North End	1898	1899	Dundee	8		4
Daniel, R	Swansea	Swansea Town	1946	1953	Sunderland	87		5
Davidson, A	Strathclyde	not known	1904	1905	not known	1		
Davidson, B	Crieff	St Johnstone	1935	1937	Coventry City	57		13
Davidson, R	Islington	youth team	1964	1969	Portsmouth		1	
Davie, G	not known	Renton	1891	1892	not known			
Davies, F	Smethwick	Birmingham St George's	1893	1899	Nottingham Forest	137		8
Davies, P	St Asaph	youth team	1968	1972	Charlton Athletic		1	
Davis, P	Dulwich	youth team	1978	1995	Brentford	331	20	30
Devine, A	Fife	Bradford City	1913	1914	Bradford City	24		5
Devine, D	Dumbarton	Dumbarton Athletic	1892	1893	Partick Thistle	2		
Devine, John	Dublin	youth team	1974	1983	Norwich City	86	3	
Devlin, Jimmy	not known	Sunderland	1897	1898	Airdrieonians	1		1
Diawara, K	Toulon	Bordeaux	1999	1999	contract cancelled	2	10	
Dick, J	Eaglesham	Airdrieonians	1898	1912	retired	262		12
Dickov, P	Glasgow	youth team	1988	1996	Manchester City	6	15	3
Dickson, B	Lurgan	Chelsea	1953	1956	Mansfield Town	29		1
Dixon, L	Manchester	Stoke City	1988	2002	retired	439	19	25
Docherty, T	Glasgow	Preston North End	1958	1961	Chelsea	83		1
Dodgin, B	Wardley Colliery	Fulham	1952	1961	Fulham	191		
Dougall, P	Denny, Stirling	Southampton	1933	1937	Everton	21		4
Drain, T	Pollokshaws	Exeter City	1909	1910	not known	2		
Drake, T	Southampton	Southampton	1934	1939	retired	168		124
Drury, G	Hucknall	Sheffield Wednesday	1938	1946	West Bromwich Albion	38		3
Ducat, A	Brixton	Southend United	1905	1912	Aston Villa	175		19
Duff, Hugh	not known	Millwall	1895-98	1900	Millwall	1		1
Duncan, D	Antrim	Fulham	1912	1913	not known	3		1
Dunn, S	Darlaston, Staffs	army football	1919	1922	retired	43		
Dunne, J	Dublin	Sheffield United	1933	1936	Southampton	28		10
Dunsbee, C	not known	Kidderminster	1899	1900	not known	8		
Dwight, F	not known	Fulham	1903	1905	Nelson	1		
Dyer, F	Bishopbriggs	West Bromwich Albion	1892	1893	Manchester City			
Earle, S	Stratford	Clapton (amateur)	1922	1924	West Ham United	4		3
Eastham, G	Blackpool	Newcastle United	1960	1966	Stoke City	207		41
Edgar, J	Scotland	Parkhead	1901	1902	Aberdeen	10		1
Edu	Sao Paulo	Corinthians	2001		still at club	22	15	3
Elliott, A	Nottingham	Accrington Stanley	1892	1894	not known	24		10
Elvey, J	Luton	Bolton Wanderers	1922	1923	not known	1		
Evans, D	Ellesmere Port	Ellesmere Port Town	1951	1963	retired through injury	189		10
Evans, B	not known	amateur	1912	1913	not known	1		
Everitt, M	Clacton	Clacton Town	1956	1961	Northampton Town	9		1
Fairclough, O	not known	army football	1895	1897	New Brompton	26		
Farmer, G	not known	Belper Town	1896	1896	not known	1		
Farr, A	Larkhall	Margate (nursery club)	1937	1940	Airdrieonians	2		1
Farrell, P	Belfast	Celtic	1897	1898	Brighton United	19		2
Ferguson, J	Scotland	Cambuslang Hibernian	1906	1907	not known	1		
Ferry, G	Sunderland	youth team	1960	1965	Leyton Orient	11		
Fidler, J	Sheffield	Queens Park Rangers	1913	1914	Port Vale	25		
Fields, A	Canning Town	Margate (nursery club)	1936	1952	retired	19		
Fisher, G	not known	trialist	1909	1909	Manchester United	2		
Fitchie, T	Edinburgh	Fulham	1901-06	1909	Glossop North End	56		27
Flanagan, J	Birmingham	Fulham	1910	1917	not known	114		28
Flatts, M	Islington	youth team	1987	1996	Watford	9	7	
Fletcher, A	Ripley	Glossop North End	1914	1915	not known	3		
Forbes, A	Dundee	Sheffield United	1948	1956	Leyton Orient	217		20
Ford, G	Woolwich	Dartford	1912	1915	not known	9		
Foster, R	not known	not known	1889	1889	not known			
Fotheringham, J	Hamilton	amateur	1949	1959	Heart of Midlothian	72		
Foxall, A	Sheffield	Queens Park Rangers	1901	1902	Gainsborough Trinity	31		3
Freeman, B	Handsworth	Aston Villa	1905	1908	Everton	44		21
Furnell, J	Manchester	Liverpool	1963	1968	Rotherham United	141		
Fyfe, J	Scotland	Alloa Athletic	1898	1898	returned to Scotland	7		
Garbutt, B	Stockport	Reading	1905	1908	Blackburn Rovers	52		8
Garde, R	L'Arbresle	Strasbourg	1996	1999	retired	19	12	
Garry, R	Hornchurch	youth team	2002		still at club	1		
Garton, J	Castle Donnington	amateur	1899	1899	not known	5		
Gatting, S	Park Royal	youth team	1974	1981	Brighton & Hove Albion	50	8	5
Gaudie, R	Guisborough	Sheffield United	1899	1901	retired through illness	47		23
Gemmell, D	Glasgow	Sheffield Wednesday	1892	1894	not known	5		
George, C	Islington	youth team	1966	1975	Derby County	113	20	31
Gilberto	Brazil	Atlético Mineiro	2002		still at club	32	3	

FAC Apps	Sub	Goals	FLC Apps	Sub	Goals	Europe Apps	Sub	Goals	Totals Apps	Sub	Goals
1									6		
2			2		1				33	1	6
17									149		
									6		4
	1			2						3	
									1		
1		1							13		3
									3		
1									14		
2						9	2		27	4	1
									8		4
12									99		5
									1		
3		2							60		15
										1	
4	3								4		3
13		2							150		10
								1		2	
22	5	3	46	5	4	15	1		414	31	37
									24		5
2									4		
6			8			8			108	3	
									1		1
1	2								3	12	
22		1							284		13
			2	2	3				8	17	6
2									31		1
52	2	1	45			57		2	593	21	28
7									90		1
16		1							207		1
2		1							23		5
									2		
14		12							182		136
2									40		3
13		2							188		21
1	1								2		2
2	1								5		2
1									44		
4		3							32		13
3									11		
									1		
5									5		
									4		3
13						3			223		41
1									11		1
9	2	2	3		1	3	6		37	23	6
10		9							34		19
									1		
18		2							207		12
1									2		
									9		1
1									27		
1		1							2		1
									2		1
3		1							22		3
									1		
									11		
									25		
									19		
									2		
7		3							63		30
7									121		28
	1			1					10	8	
									3		
22									239		20
1									10		
2									2		
4									76		
									31		3
5		3							49		24
13			12			1			167		
									7		
13		6							65		14
3	2		2			3	2		27	16	
				1					1	1	
									5		
9	1	1	3	1		3	1		65	11	6
3									50		23
3									8		
21	1	11	8		2	15	1	5	157	22	49
1	2					11	1	2	44	6	2

Player	Birthplace	From	Year Joined	Year Left	To	League Apps	Sub	Goals
Gilmer, B	not known	Royal Ordnance	1895	1896	not known	3		
Gloak, D	not known	not known	1889	1891	not known			
Gooing, B	Penistone	Chesterfield	1901	1905	Northampton Town	94		45
Gordon, B	Leith	Leicester Fosse	1895	1896	Reading	20		6
Goring, P	Bishop Cleeve	Cheltenham Town	1948	1960	Boston United	220		51
Gorman, P	Dublin	youth team	1979	1984	Birmingham City	5	1	
Gould, B	Coventry	Coventry City	1968	1970	Wolverhampton W	57	8	16
Goulden, R	Ilford	amateur	1953	1961	Southend United	1		
Goy, P	Beverley	amateur	1953	1960	Southend United	2		
Graham, A	Hurlford, Lanark	Larkhill United	1911	1924	Brentford	166		17
Graham, G	Bargeddie	Chelsea	1966	1972	Manchester United	219	8	59
Graham, J	Derby	Millwall Athletic	1899	1900	Brentford	1		
Graham, T	Balloch	Vale of Leven	1891	1892	not known			
Grant, C	Waith-on-Dearne	Lincoln City	1946	1946	Fulham	2		
Grant, G	Plumstead	Invicta	1910	1919	Millwall	54		4
Grant, J	not known	amateur	1912	1912	Southport Central	4		3
Gray, A	Govan	Hibernian	1904	1912	Fulham	184		
Gray, J	Lewisham	youth team	1998	2000	Crystal Palace		1	
Greenaway, D	Coaldyke	Shettleston	1908	1921	retired	161		13
Grice, N	not known	Ealing	1906	1906	not known	1		
Grieve, T	not known	Gravesend	1900	1904	Watford	6		
Griffiths, A	Wrexham	Wrexham	1961	1962	Wrexham	15		2
Griffiths, M	Merthyr Tydfil	amateur	1936	1938	Leicester City	9		5
Grimandi, G	Gap	Monaco	1997	2002	Colorado Rapids (USA)	85	29	4
Grondin, D	Paris	Saint-Etienne	1998	1999	Saint-Etienne	1		
Groves, F	Shadwell	Glossop North End	1912	1921	Brighton & Hove Albion	50		6
Groves, P	Bow	Colchester United	1986	1992	Southampton	91	65	21
Groves, V	Stepney	Leyton Orient	1955	1964	Canterbury City	185		31
Gudmundsson, A	Iceland	Rangers	1946	1947	Milan	2		
Guthrie, R	Hartlepool	Tow Law Town	1952	1956	Hartlepool United	2		
Haden, S	Barnsley	Castleford Town	1922	1927	Notts County	88		10
Halliday, D	Dumfries	Sunderland	1929	1930	Manchester City	15		8
Halls, J	Islington	youth team	1998		still at club			
Hamilton, T	not known	Stockton	1898	1900	Gravesend	7		
Hankin, R	Wallsend	Vancouver Whitecaps	1981	1982	contract cancelled			
Hanks, E	not known	army football	1912	1913	Southend United	4		1
Hannah, D	Raffrey, N Ireland	Dundee	1897	1899	not known	46		17
Hannigan, R	not known	Notts County	1899	1899	Burnley	1		
Hapgood, E	Bristol	Kettering Town	1927	1945	retired	393		2
Harding, E	not known	amateur	1896	1896	not known			
Hardinge, W	Greenwich	Sheffield United	1913	1921	retired	54		14
Hare, C	Yardley	Aston Villa	1895	1896	Small Heath	19		7
Harper, L	Chelsea	Sittingbourne Town	1994	1997	Queens Park Rangers	1		
Harper, B	Tarbrax, Lanarkshire	Hibernian	1925-27	1931	Plymouth Argyle	63		
Hartley, A	Dumbarton	Southampton	1899	1899	Burnley	5		1
Hartson, J	Swansea	Luton Town	1995	1997	West Ham United	43	10	14
Harvey, J	Lurgan	Glenavon	1977	1980	Hereford United	2	1	
Hatfield, T	not known	not known	1895	1896	Tottenham Hotspur	2		
Haverty, J	Dublin	St Patrick's Athletic	1954	1961	Blackburn Rovers	114		25
Hawley, J	Patrington	Sunderland	1981	1983	Hong Kong	14	6	3
Hayes, M	Walthamstow	youth team	1981	1990	Celtic	70	32	26
Haynes, A	Oxford	Oxford City	1928	1933	Crystal Palace	29		
Haywood, A	Burton-on Trent	Swadlincote	1896	1899	Glossop North End	84		31
Heaney, N	Middlesbrough	youth team	1987	1994	Southampton	4	3	
Heath, J	Bristol	Wolverhampton W	1893-95	1899	Gravesend United	10		5
Heeley, M	Peterborough	Peterborough United	1977	1980	Northampton Town	9	6	1
Helder, G	Leiden	Vitesse Arnhem	1995	1997	NAC Breda	27	12	1
Henderson, Jackie	Bishopbriggs	Wolverhampton W	1958	1962	Fulham	103		29
Henderson, Jimmy	Dumfries	Rangers	1892	1895	returned to Scotland	38		19
Henderson, B	Carlisle	Carlisle United	1921	1923	Luton Town	7		
Henley, L	Lambeth	as an amateur	1938	1946	Reading			
Henry, T	Paris	Juventus	1999		still at club	121	15	82
Heppinstall, F	Barnsley	Swindon Town	1909	1911	Stalybridge Celtic	23		
Herd, D	Hamilton	Stockport County	1954	1961	Manchester United	166		97
Hill, C	Uxbridge	youth team	1979	1986	Maritimo	46		1
Hill, F	Forfar	Aberdeen	1932	1936	Blackpool	76		4
Hillier, D	Blackheath	youth team	1985	1996	Portsmouth	82	22	2
Hoar, S	Leagrave	Luton Town	1924	1929	Clapton Orient	100		16
Hoare, G	Blackheath	Bromley	1907-09	1912	Glossop North End	30		12
Hodges, C	Hackney	amateur	1944	1946	Brighton& Hove Albion	2		
Hollins, J	Guildford	Queens Park Rangers	1979	1983	Chelsea (coaching staff)	123	4	9
Holton, C	Oxford	Oxford City	1947	1958	Watford	198		83
Hopkins, J	Belfast	Belfast United	1919	1923	Brighton & Hove Albion	21		7
Hornsby, B	Cambridge	youth team	1970	1976	Shrewsbury Town	23	3	6
Horsington, R	not known	Swindon Town	1889	1890	not known			
Howard, P	Barnsley	Newcastle United	1976	1977	Birmingham City	15	1	
Howat, D	Preston	Preston North End	1889	1896	Third Lanark	56		2
Howe, D	Wolverhampton	West Bromwich Albion	1964	1967	joined coaching staff	70		1
Hoyte, J	Waltham Forest	youth team	2001		still at club		1	
Hudson, A	Chelsea	Stoke City	1976	1978	Seattle Sounders (USA)	36		
Hughes, J	Manchester	Guildford	1925	1925	retired through injury	1		

FAC Apps	Sub	Goals	FLC Apps	Sub	Goals	Europe Apps	Sub	Goals	Totals Apps	Sub	Goals
									3		
1									1		
12		3							106		48
									20		6
20		2							240		53
									5	1	
7		3	6	3	3	2		1	72	11	23
									1		
									2		
13		3							179		20
27		2	27	2	9	23	2	7	296	12	77
									1		
1									1		
									2		
3									57		4
									4		3
16									200		
										1	
9									170		13
									1		
									6		
									15		2
									9		5
10	7	1	9			23	5	1	127	41	6
			2			1			4		
3		1							53		7
11	6	1	18	8	6			4	120	83	28
16		6				2			203		37
									2		
									2		
5		1							93		11
									15		8
				3						3	
									7		
				2						2	
									4		1
4									50		17
1									2		
41									434		2
1									1		
1									55		14
1									20		7
									1		
10									73		
4									9		1
2	1	1	2	4	1	8	1	1	55	16	17
						1			3	1	
									2		
8		1							122		26
			1						15	6	3
8	1	3	14	7	5				92	40	34
1									30		
7		5							91		36
					1				4	4	
2		2							12		7
						4	1		13	7	1
2			4	2				2	33	16	1
8									111		29
9		12							47		31
									7		
									1		
12	5	3	2		1	44	5	26	179	25	112
									23		
14		10							180		107
1			4						51		1
2									78		4
13	2		13	2		4	4		112	30	2
17		2							117		18
4		1							34		13
									2		
12			19	1	3	10	3	1	164	8	13
18		5							216		88
1									22		7
									23	3	6
4									4		
			4						19	1	
16		1							72		3
3			1						74		1
									1		
7			3	1					46	1	
									1		

Player	Birthplace	From	Year Joined	Year Left	To	League Apps	Sub	Goals
Hughes, S	Wokingham	youth team	1992	1999	Everton	22	26	4
Hulme, J	Stafford	Blackburn Rovers	1926	1938	Huddersfield Town	333		107
Humpish, A	Heaton-on-Tyne	Wigan Borough	1930	1930	Bristol City	3		
Hunt, F	not known	Darwen	1897-1900	1903	Fulham	72		30
Hunt, G	Barnsley	Tottenham Hotspur	1937	1938	Bolton Wanderers	18		3
Hunter, J	Johnstone	Heart of Midlothian	1904	1905	Portsmouth	22		4
Hutchins, A	Bishop's Waltham	Croydon Common	1919	1923	Charlton Athletic	104		1
Hynds, T	not known	Manchester City	1906	1907	Leeds City	13		
Inamoto, J	Osaka	Gamba Osaka	2001	2002	Fulham			
Itonga, C	Zaire	youth team	1999	2002	Kettering Town			
Jack, D	Bolton	Bolton Wanderers	1928	1934	retired	181		113
Jackson, J	Cambuslang	Newcastle United	1899	1905	Leyton	183		
James, A	Mossend	Preston North End	1929	1937	retired	231		26
Jacques, GH	not known	Rushden	1894	1894	not known	2		2
Jeffers, F	Liverpool	Everton	2001		still at club	4	18	4
Jeffrey, B	Dalderby	Burnley	1892	1894	Southampton	22		
Jenkins, D	Bristol	youth team	1962	1968	Tottenham Hotspur	16	1	3
Jenkyns, CL	Builth Wells	Small Heath	1895	1896	Newton Heath	27		6
Jennings, P	Newry	Tottenham Hotspur	1977	1985	retired	237		
Jensen, J	Copenhagen	Brondby	1992	1996	Brondby	93	5	1
Jobey, G	Hebden	Newcastle United	1913	1914	Bradford Park Avenue	28		3
John, B	Barry Dock	Caerphilly Town	1922	1937	retired	421		12
Johnston, G	Glasgow	Cardiff City	1967	1969	Birmingham City	17	4	3
Johnstone, W	Fife	Reading	1929	1931	Oldham Athletic	9		4
Jones, B	Merthy Tydfil	Wolverhampton W	1938	1949	Norwich City	71		7
Jones, C	Troedyrhiw	Nottingham Forest	1928	1934	Notts County (manager)	176		8
Jones, F	Clerkenwell	Navy football	1923	1924	Aberdare Athletic	2		
Jones, L	Aberdare	Coventry City	1937	1946	Swansea Town	46		3
Jonsson, S	Akranes, Iceland	Sheffield Wednesday	1989	1991	retired through injury	2	6	1
Joy, B	Fulham	Fulham	1935	1946	retired	86		
Juan	Sao Paulo	Sao Paulo	2001		still at club			
Julian, J	Boston	Boston Town	1889	1892	Luton Town			
Julians, L	Tottenham	Leyton Orient	1958	1960	Nottingham Forest	18		7
Kane, E	not known	army football	1896	1897	army football	1		
Kane, P	Govan	Northampton Town	1960	1963	Northampton Town	4		1
Kanu, N	Owerri, Nigeria	Internazionale	1999		still at club	60	49	29
Kay, J	Chester-le-Street	youth team	1979	1984	Wimbledon	13	1	
Keizer, G	Amsterdam	Millwall	1930	1931	Charlton Athletic	12		
Kelly, E	Glasgow	youth team	1966	1976	Queens Park Rangers	168	7	13
Kelly, N	Dublin	Glentoran	1947	1950	Crystal Palace	1		
Kelsey, J	Swansea	Winch Wen	1949	1962	retired through injury	327		
Kemp, F	Tottenham	Barking	1905	1906	West Ham United	2		
Kempton, Arthur	West Thurrock	Tufnell Park	1914	1921	Reading			
Kennedy, Andy	Belfast	Crystal Palace	1922	1928	Everton	122		
Kennedy, R	Seaton Delaval	youth team	1968	1974	Liverpool	156	2	53
Keown, M	Oxford	youth team/Everton	1982-86 & 1993		still at club	301	21	4
Kidd, B	Manchester	Manchester United	1974	1976	Manchester City	77		30
King, T	Blyth	Leyton	1912	1914	Clapton Orient	11		
King, H	Evesham	Northampton Town	1914	1919	Leicester City	37		26
Kington, E	not known	Charlton United	1895	1898	not known			
Kirchen, A	Shouldham, Norfolk	Norwich City	1935	1943	retired	92		38
Kirk, F	not known	not known	1892	1894	Royal Ordnance	1		
Kiwomya, C	Huddersfield	Ipswich Town	1995	1998	Queens Park Rangers	5	9	3
Kosmina, J	Adelaide	Polonia (Australia)	1978	1979	Port Adelaide (Australia)	5	1	
Kyle, P	Rutherglen	Tottenham Hotspur	1906	1908	Aston Villa	52		21
Laidlaw, J	Scotland	Newcastle United	1901	1901	returned to Scotland	3		2
Lambert, J	Rotherham	Doncaster Rovers	1926	1933	Fulham	143		98
Lauren	Cameroon	Mallorca	2000		still at club	68	4	5
Lawrence, T	not known	Northampton Town	1902	1903	Fulham	20		3
Lawrence, W	not known	Crystal Palace	1909	1910	Crystal Palace	25		5
Lawson, H	Luton	amateur	1924	1927	Brentford	13		2
Lawton, T	Bolton	Brentford	1953	1956	Kettering Town	35		13
Leather, J	not known	Macclesfield Town	1896	1898	Queens Park Rangers	8		
Lee, H	Erith	Sittingbourne Town	1905	1909	Bury	41		15
Lee, J	Blyth	Horden Athletic	1926	1928	Chesterfield	7		
Le Roux, D	Natal, S Africa	Queens Park, Durban	1957	1958	returned to S Africa	5		
Lewis, C	Plumstead	Maidstone United	1907	1921	Margate	206		30
Lewis, D	Mardy	Clapton Orient	1924	1931	Gillingham	142		
Lewis, R	Bilston	Margate (nursery side)	1937	1953	retired	154		103
Liddell, N	Sunderland	Southend United	1914	1919	Southend Utd (manager)	2		
Lievesley, J	Staveley	Sheffield United	1913	1915	retired	73		
Limpar, A	Solna, Sweden	Cremonese	1990	1994	Everton	76	20	17
Linighan, A	Hartlepool	Norwich City	1990	1997	Crystal Palace	101	17	5
Linward, B	Hull	West Ham United	1902	1905	Norwich City	47		10
Lishman, D	Birmingham	Walsall	1948	1956	Nottingham Forest	226		125
Ljungberg, F	Halmstad	Halmstad	1998		still at club	100	17	31
Lloyd, F	not known	Wednesbury	1899	1900	Aston Villa	18		3
Logan, H	Glasgow	Sunderland	1910	1911	not known	11		
Logan, P	Glasgow	Notts County	1899-1900	1901	Brentford	28		7
Logie, J	Edinburgh	Lochore Welfare	1939	1955	Gravesend & Northfleet	296		68
Low, A	Scotland	Ashfield	1906	1908	Partick Thistle	3		

FAC Apps	Sub	Goals	FLC Apps	Sub	Goals	Europe Apps	Sub	Goals	Totals Apps	Sub	Goals
7	7	1	5	3	1	2	3	1	36	39	7
39		17							372		124
									3		
9		5							81		35
3									21		3
									22		4
4									108		1
4		1							17		1
			2				2		2	2	
				1						1	
25		10							206		123
21		1							204		1
28		1							259		27
									2		2
7	1	3	1		1	1	6		13	25	8
9									31		
2		1	6		5				24	1	9
									27		6
38			32			19			326		
8	1		14	2		14			129	8	1
									28		3
46		1							467		13
			3	1					20	5	3
									9		4
3									74		7
17									193		8
									2		
4									50		3
	1		1						3	7	1
6									92		
1			1						2		
4									4		
6		3							24		10
									1		
									4		1
4	10	3	4		2	26	20	6	94	79	40
									13	1	
									12		
15	2	4	15			13	2	2	211	11	19
									1		
24									351		
									2		
1									1		
7									129		
25	2	6	11		4	14	2	8	206	6	71
36	3		18	2	1	42	7	3	397	33	8
9		3	4		1				90		34
2									13		
2		3							39		29
1									1		
7		6							99		44
									1		
						1	2		6	11	3
						1	2		1	3	
8		2							60		23
									3		2
16		11							159		109
13		2				26	6	1	107	10	8
3									23		3
1									26		5
3									16		2
2		1							37		14
2									10		
									41		15
									7		
									5		
14		4							220		34
25									167		
21		13							175		116
									2		
2									75		
7		2	9			3		1	95	20	20
12	2	1	13	1	1	8	1	1	134	21	8
3									50		10
17		10							243		135
16	3	4	2			36	8	9	154	28	44
1									19		3
									11		
1									29		7
30		8							326		76
									3		

Player	Birthplace	From	Year Joined	Year Left	To	League Apps	Sub	Goals
Low, T	Cambuslang	Dundee	1900	1901	not known	24		1
Lukic, J	Chesterfield	Leeds United	1983-90 & 1996	2001	retired	241		
Luzhny, O	Kiev	Dynamo Kiev	1999	2003	Wolverhampton W	58	17	
Lydersen, P	Kristiansand	Start Kristiansand	1991	1995	Start Kristiansand	12	3	
MacLeod, J	Edinburgh	Hibernian	1961	1964	Aston Villa	101		23
McAuley, J	not known	Greenock Morton	1897	1898	not known	23		1
McAvoy, F	Ayr	Ayr	1895	1898	Brighton United	45		8
McAvoy, J	Scotland	Celtic	1898	1899	Grimsby Town	25		
McBean, J	Kirkcaldy	Kirkcaldy Wanderers	1889	1892	not known			
McClelland, J	Lurgan	Glenavon	1960	1964	Fulham	46		
McConnell, A	Glenbuck	Everton	1897	1899	Queens Park Rangers	37		1
McCowie, A	Cambuslang	Liverpool	1899	1900	Middlesbrough	28		7
McCullough, B	Woodburn, NI	Portadown	1958	1966	Millwall	253		4
McDermott, B	Slough	youth team	1977	1984	Oxford United	38	23	12
McDonald, D	Glasgow	Bo'ness	1909	1911	West Hartlepool	26		
McDonald, H	Kilwinning	Beith	1906-08 & 1910-13	Fulham	94			
McEachrane, R	Inverness	West Ham United	1902	1915	retired	313		
McFarlane, S	Airdrie	Airdrieonians	1896	1897	Airdrieonians	5		
McGeoch, A	Scotland	Dunblane	1897	1899	Dundee	35		13
McGibbon, C	Portsmouth	army football	1905	1910	Leyton	4		3
McGill, J	Partick	youth team	1965	1967	Huddersfield Town	6	4	
McGoldrick, E	Islington	Crystal Palace	1993	1996	Corby Town (manager)	32	6	
McGovern, B	Dublin	youth team	1997	2000	Norwich City		1	
McGowan, G	Blackheath	youth team	1991	1998	Luton Town	3	3	
McKechnie, I	Bellshill	youth team	1958	1964	Southend United	23		
McKellar, M	Campsie, Stirling	Kirkintilloch Harp	1909	1910	not known	3		1
McKenzie, A	Leith	Armiston Rangers	1920	1923	Blackpool	15		2
McKinnon, A	Paisley	Petershill	1908	1922	Charlton Athletic	211		4
McLaughlan, J	Edinburgh	Bathgate	1911	1913	Watford	16		3
McLintock, F	Glasgow	Leicester City	1964	1973	Queens Park Rangers	312	2	26
McNab, B	Huddersfield	Huddersfield Town	1966	1975	Wolverhampton W	277	1	4
McNab, W	Scotland	Burnley	1893	1894	not known	2		1
McNichol, D	Dumbarton	St Bernard's	1899	1903	Aberdeen	101		1
McPhee, J	Scotland	not known	1898	1899	not known	7		
McPherson, I	Glasgow	Notts County	1946	1951	Notts County	152		19
McQuilkie, J	Scotland	Renton	1892	1893	not known			
Macaulay, A	Falkirk	Brentford	1947	1950	Fulham	103		1
Macdonald, M	Fulham	Newcastle United	1976	1979	retired through injury	84		42
Mackie, A	Monkstown, NI	Forth River	1922	1928	Portsmouth	108		
Madden, D	Stepney	Southampton	1983	1984	Charlton Athletic	2		
Magill, J	Lurgan	Portadown	1959	1965	Brighton & Hove Albion	116		
Main, A	Scotland	Hibernian	1899	1903	Motherwell	63		14
Male, G	West Ham	Clapton	1929	1948	retired	285		
Malz, S	Ludwigshafen	Munich 1860	1999	2001	Kaiserslautern	2	4	1
Mancini, T	St Pancras	Queens Park Rangers	1974	1976	Aldershot	52		1
Manninger, A	Salzburg	Casino Graz	1997	2002	Espanyol	38	1	
Marden, B	Fulham	Chelmsford City	1950	1955	Watford	42		11
Marinello, P	Edinburgh	Hibernian	1970	1973	Portsmouth	32	6	3
Mariner, P	Bolton	Ipswich Town	1984	1986	Portsmouth	52	8	14
Marks, G	Salisbury	Salisbury Corinthians	1936	1946	Blackburn Rovers	2		
Marshall, J	Avonbridge	Rangers	1934	1935	West Ham United	4		
Marshall, S	Edinburgh	youth team	1988	1998	Southampton	19	5	1
Marwood, B	Seaham Harbour	Sheffield Wednesday	1988	1990	Sheffield United	52		16
Matthews, J	Camden	youth team	1971	1978	Sheffield United	38	7	2
Maxwell, J	Kilmarnock	Sheffield Wednesday	1908	1909	returned to Scotland	2		
Maxwell, J	Glasgow	Dunfermline Athletic	1921	1921	not known	1		
Maycock, B	Burton-on-Trent	Gresley Rovers	1928	1931	retired			
Meade, R	Islington	youth team	1978	1985	Sporting Lisbon	25	16	14
Meade, T	Plumstead	amateur	1893	1897	Tottenham Hotspur	11		5
Meggs, J	not known	City Ramblers	1889	1891	not known			
Mendez, A	Nurnberg	Feucht (Germany)	1997	2002	Racing Ferrol	1	3	
Mercer, J	Ellesmere Port	Everton	1946	1954	retired through injury	247		2
Merson, P	Harlesden	youth team	1984	1997	Middlesbrough	289	38	78
Miller, A	Epping	youth team	1984	1994	Middlesbrough	6	2	
Mills, S	Derby	Loughborough Town	1895	1896	Heanor Town	24		3
Milne, J	Stirling	Blackburn Rovers	1935	1937	Middlesbrough	49		19
Milne, B	Buckie	Buckie Thistle	1921	1927	assistant trainer	114		1
Milton, A	Bristol	amateur	1945	1955	Bristol City	75		18
Mitchell, A	Scotland	Albion Rovers	1898	1899	not known	10		2
Moir, J	Inverbervie	Sunderland	1898	1900	Gravesend United	41		
Monteith, J	Ireland	Celtic	1897	1898	Belfast Distillery	6		1
Moody, J	Heeley	Hathersage, Derby	1925	1928	Bradford Park Avenue	6		
Mordue, J	County Durham	Barnsley	1907	1908	Sunderland	26		1
Morgan, S	Abergwynifi	Gwynifi Welfare	1938	1948	Walsall	2		
Morrow, S	Carrickfergus	Youth team	1987	1997	Queens Park Rangers	39	23	1
Mortimer, P	Calton	Leith Athletic	1894	1896	not known	48		23
Moss, F	Leyland	Oldham Athletic	1931	1937	Hearts (manager)	143		1
Muntasser, J	Tripoli, Libya	Atalanta Bergamo	1997	1998	Bristol City			
Murphy, J	not known	Stoke City	1899	1900	Raith Rovers	27		
Murrell, J	Hounslow	army football	1898	1900	Clapton Orient	6		
Neave, D	Arbroath	Arbroath	1904	1912	Merthyr Town	154		30

FAC Apps	Sub	Goals	FLC Apps	Sub	Goals	Europe Apps	Sub	Goals	Totals Apps	Sub	Goals
2		1							26		2
22			33			1			297		
9			4			20	1		91	18	
			1						13	3	
8	4		3			1			112		28
4	1								27		2
3	2								48		10
1									26		
6									6		
3									49		
1									38		1
5									33		7
11						4		1	268		5
	1		3	1		3	3	1	44	28	13
1									27		
9									103		
33									346		
									5		
4		1							39		14
									4		3
			2						8	4	
1	1		7	2		4	3	1	44	12	1
										1	
1									4	3	
						2			25		
2		1							5		2
									15		2
6									217		4
									16		3
36		1	34		4	19		1	401	2	32
39			26	1	2	20	1		362	3	6
									2		1
11									112		1
1									8		
11		2							163		21
2									2		
4									107		
9		10	14		5			1	107	1	57
10		1							118		1
									2		
11						4			131		
6									69		14
29									314		
2	2		2		1		2		6	8	2
8			2						62		1
9			7			8			62	1	
									42		11
	1		5		1	6	1	1	43	8	5
5	1	2	3	1	1				60	10	17
									2		
									4		
			1	1					20	6	1
			6		1				60		17
4	2	1	6		2				48	9	5
									2		
									1		
1									1		
2	1		3	1	1	2	1	1	32	19	16
3		2							14		7
5		4							5		4
1			3	2	1	1		1	6	5	2
26									273		2
28	3	4	38	2	10	23	1	7	378	44	99
									6	2	
1									25		3
3									52		19
10		2							124		3
9		3							84		21
									10		2
4									45		
									6		1
									6		
2									28		1
									2		
5	2		7	4	2	1	4		52	33	3
									48		23
16									159		1
				1						1	
5									32		
									6		
14		2							168		32

Player	Birthplace	From	Year Joined	Year Left	To	League Apps	Sub	Goals
Neil, A	Kilmarnock	Brighton & Hove Albion	1924	1926	Brighton & Hove Albion	54		10
Neill, T	Belfast	Bangor	1959	1970	Hull City	240	1	8
Neilson, G	Glasgow	youth team	1964	1968	Brentford	14		2
Nelson, D	Douglas Water, Scot.	St Bernard's	1936	1946	Fulham	27		4
Nelson, S	Belfast	youth team	1966	1981	Brighton & Hove Albion	245	10	10
Nicholas, C	Glasgow	Celtic	1983	1988	Aberdeen	145	6	34
Nicholas, P	Newport	Crystal Palace	1981	1983	Crystal Palace	57	3	1
Norman, J	Hackney	amateur	1914	1919	retired	4		
North, J	Burton-on Trent	Sheffield United	1919	1922	Reading	23		6
Nutt, G	Birmingham	Cardiff City	1955	1960	Southend United	49		10
Oakes, D	Rhyl	amateur	1945	1955	retired through injury	11		1
O'Brien, P	not known	Glasgow Northern	1894	1897	Bristol City	63		27
Offer, H	Devizes	Swindon Town	1889	1891	not known			
O'Flanagan, K	Dublin	Bohemians	1945	1949	retired	14		3
O'Leary D	Stoke Newington	youth team	1973	1993	Leeds United	523	35	11
Oliver, H	Holloway	not known	1909	1910	not known	1		
O'Neill, F	Dublin	Home Farm	1958	1961	Shamrock Rovers	2		
Ord, R	Northumberland	Middlesbrough Ironopolis	1897	1900	Luton Town	89		
O'Shea, D	Kennington	youth team	1978	1984	Exeter City	6		
Overmars, M	Emst, Holland	Ajax	1997	2000	Barcelona	91	9	25
Owens, I	Darlington	Crook Town	1901	1902	Plymouth Argyle	9		2
Pack, R	Islington	youth team	1962	1966	Portsmouth	1		
Pagnam, F	Poulton-le-Fylde	Liverpool	1919	1921	Cardiff City	50		26
Parker, T	Woolston, Hants	Southampton	1926	1933	Norwich City (manager)	258		17
Parkin, R	Crook	Esh Winning (Co. Durham)	1928	1936	Middlesbrough	25		11
Parlour, R	Romford	youth team	1988		still at club	266	48	22
Paterson, J	London	Queens Park (Glasgow)	1920	1926	retired	70		1
Paterson, B	Dunfermline	Dundee	1928	1929	Airdrieonians	15		
Pates, C	Carshalton	Charlton Athletic	1990	1993	Brighton & Hove Albion	12	9	
Pattison, G	North Shields	Wallsend	1920	1922	West Ham United	9		
Payne, G	Hitchin	Leyton	1912	1918	retired after war wound	3		
Peachey, CB	not known	Chiswick Park	1891	1892	not known			
Peart, J	Tewkesbury	amateur	1910	1921	Margate	63		
Peel, H	Bradford	Bradford Park Avenue	1926	1929	Bradford City	47		5
Pennant, J	Nottingham	Notts County	1999		still at club	1	4	3
Petit, M	Dieppe	Monaco	1997	2000	Barcelona	82	3	9
Petrovic, V	Belgrade	Red Star Belgrade	1982	1983	Antwerp	10	3	2
Petts, J	Edmonton	youth team	1954	1962	Reading	32		
Pires, R	Reims	Marseille	2000		still at club	77	10	27
Place, W	Burnley	Burnley	1900	1902	not known	42		6
Platt, D	Chadderton, Lancs	Sampdoria	1995	1998	retired	65	23	13
Platt, T	Woolstanton, Staffs	Colchester United	1938	1953	Portsmouth	53		
Powell, J	Bristol	army football	1892	1896	died 1896	86		1
Powling, R	Barking	youth team	1971	1981	retired through injury	50	5	3
Pratt, T	Fleetwood, Lancs	Preston North End	1903	1904	Fulham	8		2
Preedy, C	Neemuch, India	Wigan Borough	1929	1933	Luton Town	37		
Price, D	Caterham	youth team	1970	1981	Crystal Palace	116	10	16
Pryde, D	Newton Grange	not known	1935	1946	Torquay United	4		
Pugh, S	Dartford	Margate (nursery team)	1936	1939	killed in war action	1		
Quayle, J	Charlton	Northfleet	1910	1911	retired through injury	1		
Quinn, N	Dublin	youth team	1983	1990	Manchester City	59	8	14
Radford, J	Hemsworth, Yorks	youth team	1962	1976	West Ham United	375	4	111
Ramsay, J	Clydebank	Kilmarnock	1924	1926	Kilmarnock	69		11
Randall, C	County Durham	Newcastle United	1911	1914	North Shields	43		12
Rankin, A	Glasgow	Glasgow Northern	1891	1893	not known			
Rankin, I	Edmonton	youth team	1995	1998	Bradford City		1	
Ransom, F	Ireland	not known	1900	1905	Southend United	1		
Raybould, S	Chesterfield	Sunderland	1908	1909	retired	26		6
Reece, G	not known	Soho Villa (Birmingham)	1895	1895	not known	1		
Rice, P	Belfast	youth team	1964	1980	Watford	391	6	12
Richardson, K	Newcastle	Watford	1987	1990	Real Sociedad	88	8	5
Ricketts, R	Clapham	youth team	1999	2002	Tottenham Hotspur			
Rimmer, J	Southport	Manchester United	1974	1977	Aston Villa	124		
Rippon, W	Beighton, Yorks	Bristol City	1910	1911	Brentford	9		2
Rix, G	Doncaster	youth team	1974	1988	Caen	338	13	41
Riza, O	Edmonton	youth team	1998	1999	West Ham United			
Roberts, H	Oswestry	Oswestry Town	1926	1938	retired through injury	297		4
Roberts, J	Abercynon	Northampton Town	1969	1972	Birmingham City	56	3	4
Robertson, A	not known	Preston North End	1891	1892	not known			
Robertson, H	Glasgow	Westburn	1889	1890	not known			
Robertson, Jimmy	Cardonald	Tottenham Hotspur	1968	1970	Ipswich Town	45	1	7
Robertson, Jim	Falkirk	Dunipace Thistle	1948	1953	Brentford	1		
Robson, J	Innerleithen	Innerleithen	1921	1926	Bournemouth	97		
Robson, S	Billericay	youth team	1980	1987	West Ham United	150	1	16
Rocastle, D	Lewisham	youth team	1983	1992	Leeds United	204	14	24
Rodger, J	Scotland	Renton	1907	1909	not known	1		
Roe, Archie	Hull	Castleford Town	1922	1923	Lincoln City	4		1
Roe, Arthur	South Normanton	Luton Town	1925	1925	contract cancelled	1		
Rogers, T	Chirk	Wrexham	1935	1936	Newcastle United	16		5
Rooke, R	Guildford	Fulham	1946	1949	Crystal Palace	88		68
Roose, D	Wrexham	Aston Villa	1911	1912	not known	13		

FAC Apps	Sub	Goals	FLC Apps	Sub	Goals	Europe Apps	Sub	Goals	Totals Apps	Sub	Goals
3									57		10
12	1		15	1	2	5			272	3	10
3		1							17		3
2									29		4
33	2	1	27		1	19	2		324	14	12
11	2	10	20		10				176	8	54
8			8		2	4			77	3	3
									4		
									23		6
2									51		10
									11		1
4		2							67		29
3		1							3		1
2									16		3
66	4	1	68	2	2	21			678	41	14
									1		
									2		
10									99		
			3						9		
15	2	7	3	1	2	17	3	6	126	15	40
2									11		2
									1		
3		1							53		27
34									292		17
1									26		11
38	3	4	20	3		37	11	5	361	65	31
7		1							77		2
									15		
			2			2		1	16	9	1
1									10		
									3		
1									1		
3									66		
5		1							52		6
			5	1				3	6	8	3
13		2	3			14	1		112	4	11
6		1	3						19	3	3
									32		
14	3	5	1		1	31	2	4	123	15	37
3		1							45		7
3	3		7	3	2	2	2		77	31	15
4									57		
6		1							92		2
2			2						54	5	3
2									10		2
2									39		
26		1	11			11	1	2	164	11	19
									4		
									1		
									1		
8	2	2	14	2	4				81	12	20
42	2	15	34		12	24		11	475	6	149
6									75		11
1									44		12
3									3		
										1	
									1		
4		1							30		7
									1		
67		1	36			26	1		520	7	13
9		1	13	3	2				110	11	8
				1						1	
12			10						146		
									9		2
42	2	7	45	2	2	21		1	446	17	51
				1						1	
36		1							333		5
			12		1	9	1		77	4	5
									1		
4		4							4		4
4		1	4			5			58	1	8
									1		
4									101		
13		1	20		3	2		1	185	1	21
18	2	4	32	1	6	4			258	17	34
									1		
2									6		1
									1		
									16		5
5		1							93		69
									13		

Player	Birthplace	From	Year Joined	Year Left	To	League Apps	Sub	Goals
Roper, D	Botley, Hants	Southampton	1947	1957	Southampton	297		88
Rose, M	Dartford	youth team	1994	1997	Queens Park Rangers	2	3	
Ross, T	Ashton-under-Lyne	youth team	1972	1977	Everton	57	1	5
Rostron, W	Sunderland	youth team	1972	1977	Sunderland	12	5	2
Rudkin, T	Worksop	Peterborough United	1947	1947	Southampton	5		2
Russell, A	Woolwich	Bostal Rovers	1895	1896	not known			
Russell, J	Carstairs	St Mirren	1896	1897	Bristol South End	23		4
Rutherford, Jock	Percy Main	Newcastle United	1913	1926	Clapton Orient	222		25
Rutherford, John	South Shields	Ilford	1924	1927	West Ham United	1		
Sammels, J	Ipswich	youth team	1961	1971	Leicester City	212	3	39
Sanders, M	not known	Preston North End	1899	1900	not known	4		1
Sands, P	Norwood	Cheltenham Town	1902	1919	Southend United	327		10
Sansom, K	Camberwell	Crystal Palace	1980	1988	Newcastle United	314		6
Satterthwaite, C	Cockermouth	West Ham United	1904	1910	retired	129		45
Sattherthwaite, J	Cockermouth	Workington	1906	1908	Grimsby Town	5		1
Schwarz, S	Kulldal, Sweden	Benfica	1994	1995	Fiorentina	34		2
Scott, B	not known	Notts All Saints	1888	1890	not known			
Scott, L	Sheffield	Bradford City	1937	1951	Crystal Palace	115		
Seaman, D	Rotherham	Queens Park Rangers	1990	2003	Manchester City	405		
Seddon, B	Clapton	Gillingham	1924	1932	Grimsby Town	69		
Selley, I	Chertsey	youth team	1988	1997	Fulham	35	6	
Shaaban, R	Stockholm	Djurgarden	2002		still at club	3		
Shanks, T	Wexford	Brentford	1903	1904	Brentford	44		28
Sharp, J	Alyth, Perth	Fulham	1905	1908	Rangers	103		4
Sharpe, B	not known	Loughborough Town	1894	1895	Glossop North End	13		4
Shaw, A	Limehouse	Brentford	1948	1955	Watford	57		
Shaw, B	Sheffield	Sheffield United	1891	1892	not known			
Shaw, H	not known	Haverton Hill, Durham	1898	1900	not known	26		9
Shaw, Jim	Goldenhill, Staffs	Frickley Athletic	1926	1930	Brentford	11		4
Shaw, Joe	Bury	Accrington Stanley	1907	1923	reserve team manager	309		
Shaw, P	Maidenhead	youth team	1988	1997	Millwall	1	11	2
Shaw, W	Birmingham	Birmingham St George's	1893	1895	not known	19		11
Shortt, M	Dumfries	Dumfries	1910	1911	Kilmarnock	4		
Shrewsbury, T	not known	Darwen	1896	1900	not known	3		
Sidey, N	London	Nunhead	1929	1939	retired	40		
Silvinho	São Paulo	Corinthians	1999	2001	Celta Vigo	47	8	3
Simpson, P	Gorleston, Norfolk	youth team	1960	1978	New England Teamen (US)	353	17	10
Sinclair, F	Glasgow	Rangers	1896	1897	Bristol City	26		
Skirton, A	Bath	Bath City	1959	1966	Blackpool	144	1	53
Slade, D	Southampton	Lincoln City	1913	1914	Fulham	12		4
Sloan, P	Lurgan	Tranmere Rovers	1946	1948	Sheffield United	33		1
Smith, Alan	Newcastle	as an amateur	1946	1946	Brentford	3		
Smith, Alan	Birmingham	Leicester City	1987	1995	retired through injury	242	22	86
Smith, J	Preston	Fulham	1920	1921	free transfer	10		1
Smith, L	Mexborough	Denaby United	1939	1954	Watford	162		
Smithson, R	Leicester	youth team	1959	1964	Oxford United	2		
Snedden, J	Bonnybridge	youth team	1958	1965	Charlton Athletic	83		
Sparrow, B	Bethnal Green	youth team	1977	1984	Crystal Palace	2		
Spicer, T	not known	Brighton United	1900	1901	Leyton	4		
Spittle, B	Southfields	Southfields Juniors	1912	1919	Leicester City	7		
Standen, J	Edmonton	Rickmansworth Town	1952	1960	Luton Town	35		
Stapleton, F	Dublin	youth team	1972	1981	Manchester United	223	2	75
Stead, K	West Ham	Tottenham Hotspur	1977	1979	Oxford City	1	1	
Stepanovs, I	Ogre, Latvia	Skonto Riga	2000		still at club	17		
Steven, A	Scotland	Bathgate	1897	1898	Dartford	5		1
Steven, R	Glasgow	Rangers	1909	1910	retired	7		1
Stevenson, R	Barrhead	Third Lanark	1894	1895	Thames Ironworks	7		
Stewart, B	Dundee	Kidderminster	1889	1893	not known			
Stockill, R	York	Scarborough	1931	1934	Derby County	7		4
Stonley, S	Sunderland	Newcastle City	1913	1914	Brentford	38		14
Storer, H	Ripley	Loughborough Town	1894	1895	Liverpool	40		
Storey, P	Farnham	youth team	1961	1977	Fulham	387	4	9
Storrs, JA	not known	army football	1893	1895	retired	12		
Strong, G	Kirkheaton	Stanley United	1957	1964	Liverpool	125		69
Stuart, J	Coatbridge	Blackburn Rovers	1897	1897	New Brompton	2		1
Suker, H	Osijek, Croatia	Real Madrid	1999	2000	West Ham United	8	14	8
Sullivan, C	Bristol	Bristol City	1954	1958	retired through injury	28		
Sunderland, A	Conisbrough, Yorks.	Wolverhampton W	1977	1984	Ipswich Town	204	2	55
Sebastian, Svard	Copenhagen	FC Kobnhavn	2000		still at club			
Swallow, R	Southwark	youth team	1952	1958	Derby County	13		4
Swan, A	Dalbeattie	Barnsley	1901	1901	Stockport County	7		2
Swindin, G	Doncaster	Bradford City	1936	1954	Peterborough Utd (p/m)	271		
Talbot, A	not known	Hednesford Town	1896	1897	not known	5		
Talbot, B	Ipswich	Ipswich Town	1979	1985	Watford	245	9	40
Tapscott, D	Barry	Barry Town	1953	1958	Cardiff City	119		62
Tavlaridis, S	Serres, Greece	Iraklis Saloniki	2001		still at club		1	
Taylor, S	Romford	youth team	1997		still at club	16	2	
Tawse, B	Aberdeenshire	youth team	1963	1965	Brighton & Hove Albion	5		
Templeton, B	Coylton	Newcastle United	1904	1906	Celtic	33		1
Tennant, J	Parkhead	St Bernard's	1899	1901	Middlesbrough	51		8
Theobald, S	Plumstead	St Andrew's Woolwich	1900	1909	not known	24		

FAC Apps	Sub	Goals	FLC Apps	Sub	Goals	Europe Apps	Sub	Goals	Totals Apps	Sub	Goals
22		7							319		95
									2	3	
3	1		6		3				66	1	9
1			1						14	5	2
									5		2
1									1		
2									25		4
10		2							232		27
									1		
20	1	3	19		3	15		7	266	4	52
									4		1
23		2							350		12
26			48			6			394		6
12		3							141		48
									5		1
1			4			10		2	49		4
3		4							3		4
11									126		
48			38			69			560		
6									75		
3			5	1		8	2	2	51	9	2
						2			5		
4		1							48		29
13		1							116		5
1									14		4
4									61		
1									1		
4									30		9
									11		4
17									326		
	1								1	12	2
5		1							24		12
									4		
3									6		
3									43		
4	2		2			13	3	2	66	13	5
53		1	32	1	3	20	1	1	458	19	15
2									28		
8						1		1	153	1	54
									12		4
3									36		1
									3		
23	3	6	36	2	16	15	2	7	316	29	115
									10		1
18									180		
									2		
10						1			94		
									2		
									4		
									7		
3									38		
32		15	26	1	14	15		4	296	3	108
									1	1	
4			4	1	1	4	1		29	2	1
1		1							6		2
									7		1
									7		
2									2		
									7		4
1									39		14
1									41		
49	2	4	36	1	2	22		2	494	7	17
4									16		
8		5				4		3	137		77
									2		1
3			1		1	3	10	2	15	24	11
4									32		
34		16	26		13	13	1	7	277	3	91
1			1	1					2	1	
									13		4
									7		2
23									294		
									5		
29	1	7	26	1	1	15		1	315	11	49
13		6							132		68
			4						4	1	
3			4			3	2		26	4	
									5		
8									41		1
3		2							54		10
									24		

Player	Birthplace	From	Year Joined	Year Left	To	League Apps	Sub	Goals
Thomas, M	Lambeth	youth team	1983	1991	Liverpool	149	14	24
Thompson, L	Sheffield	Swansea Town	1928	1933	Crystal Palace	26		6
Thomson, M	Maryhill	Maryhill	1908	1914	Swindon Town	89		1
Thorpe, H	Barrowhill, Derbys	Chesterfield	1903	1904	Fulham	10		
Tiddy, M	Helston	Cardiff City	1955	1958	Brighton & Hove Albion	48		8
Tilley, P	Lurgan	Witton Albion	1952	1953	Bury	1		
Toner, J	Castlewellan, N Ire.	Belfast United	1919	1926	St Johnstone	89		6
Toure, K	Ivory Coast	ASEC Mimosas	2002		still at club	9	17	2
Townrow, F	West Ham	amateur	1921	1926	Dundee	8		2
Tricker, R	Karachi	Charlton Athletic	1927	1929	Clapton Orient	12		5
Trim, R	Portsmouth	Bournemouth	1933	1937	Nottingham Forest	1		
Tuckett, E	Guisborough	Scarborough	1932	1937	Bradford City	2		
Turnbull, B	Dumbarton	army football	1921	1924	Charlton Athletic	59		26
Turner, P	Scotland	St Bernard's	1900	1901	Luton Town	33		5
Tyrer, A	Liverpool	Mansfield Town	1965	1967	Bury			
Upson, M	Stowmarket	Luton Town	1997	2003	Birmingham City	20	14	
Ure, I	Ayr	Dundee	1963	1969	Manchester United	168		2
Vaessen, P	Bermondsey	youth team	1977	1982	retired through injury	23	9	6
Vallance, T	Stoke	Stoke City	1946	1953	not known	15		2
Van Bronckhorst, G	Rotterdam	Rangers	2001		still at club	22	19	2
Vaughan, J	not known	not known	1900	1903	Millwall Athletic			
Vernazza, P	Islington	youth team	1997	2000	Watford	2	3	1
Vieira, P	Dakar, Senegal	Milan	1996		still at club	211	7	19
Vivas, N	Argentina	Lugano	1998	2001	Internazionale	14	26	
Volz, M	Siegen, Germany	youth team	1999					
Voysey, C	New Cross	Navy football	1919	1926	not known	35		6
Wade, J	Shoreditch	Hoxton Manor	1944	1956	Hereford United	86		
Walden, H	Manchester	Bradford City	1920	1921	Bradford Park Avenue	2		1
Walford, S	Highgate	Tottenham Hotspur	1977	1981	Norwich City	64	13	3
Waller, H	Ashington	Ashington	1937	1947	Leyton Orient	8		
Walley, T	Caernarvon	Caernarvon Town	1964	1967	Watford	10	4	1
Wallington, E	Rickmansworth	Watford	1923	1924	not known	1		
Walsh, B	Aldershot	Chase of Chertsey	1949	1955	Cardiff City	17		
Walsh, C	London	Hampstead Town	1930	1933	Brentford			
Walsh, W	Pontlottyn	Margate (nursery side)	1935	1939	Derby County	3		
Ward, A	Barnsley	Burton Wanderers	1895	1896	not known	7		
Ward, G	Stepney	youth team	1952	1963	Leyton Orient	81		10
Warnes, B	Rotherhithe	amateur	1925	1933	Norwich City	1		
Watson, B	Middlesbrough	Middlesbrough	1903	1905	Leeds City	9		1
Webster, M	Rossington, Yorks	youth team	1966	1970	Fulham	3		
Westcott, R	Wallasey	Banbury Spencer	1935	1936	retired through injury	2		1
Weston, R	Kingston	youth team	1999	2000	Cardiff City	1		
White, H	Watford	Brentford	1919	1923	Blackpool	101		40
White, W	not known	Heart of Midlothian	1897	1899	New Brompton	39		16
Whitfield, J	not known	Houghton-le-Wear	1896	1897	not known	2		
Whittaker, T	Aldershot	army football	1919	1925	retired through injury	64		2
Whyte, C	Islington	youth team	1977	1986	New York Express (US)	86	4	8
Wilkinson, J	Middlewich	Witton Albion	1953	1956	Sheffield United	1		
Williams, C	Welling	Erith	1891	1894	Manchester City	19		
Williams, T	not known	not known	1889	1890	not known			
Williams, J	Rotherham	Stoke City	1929	1932	Middlesbrough	22		5
Williams, S	Hammersmith	Southampton	1984	1988	Luton Town	93	2	4
Williams, W	not known	Bostal Rovers	1893	1895	not known	1		
Williamson, E	Murton, Co. Durham	Croydon Common	1919	1923	Norwich City	105		
Wills, L	Hackney	Eton Manor	1949	1962	Romford	195		4
Wilmot, R	Newport	youth team	1977	1989	Plymouth Argyle	8		
Wilson, A	Wishaw	Greenock Morton	1933	1941	St Mirren	82		
Wilson, J	not known	Erith	1896	1897	Watford	1		
Wilson, O	not known	Leyton	1912	1913	not known	1		
Wilson, R	Chesterfield	amateur	1963	1974	retired	234		
Wiltord, S	Neuilly-sur-Marne	Bordeaux	2000		still at club	70	24	28
Winship, T	Newcastle	Wallsend Park Villa	1910	1915	Darlington	55		7
Winterburn, N	Nuneaton	Wimbledon	1987	2000	West Ham United	429	11	8
Wolfe, G	London	Folkestone	1900	1903	Swindon Town	5		
Wood, G	Douglas, Lanark	Everton	1980	1983	Crystal Palace	60		
Woodcock, T	Eastwood	Köln (Germany)	1982	1986	Koln	129	2	56
Woods, H	St Helens	Newcastle United	1923	1926	Luton Town	70		21
Woodward, J	Glasgow	youth team	1966	1971	York City	2	1	
Worrall, A	not known	Burton Swifts	1894	1894	Nelson	4		1
Wreh, C	Monrovia, Liberia	Monaco	1997	2000	Al-Hilal (Saudi Arabia)	10	18	3
Wright, I	Woolwich	Crystal Palace	1991	1998	West Ham United	212	9	128
Wright, R	Ipswich	Ipswich Town	2001	2002	Everton	12		
Young, Allan	Edmonton	youth team	1956	1961	Chelsea	4		
Young Andy	Darlington	Aston Villa	1922	1927	Bournemouth	68		9
Young, W	Edinburgh	Tottenham Hotspur	1977	1981	Nottingham Forest	170		11

FAC Apps	Sub	Goals	FLC Apps	Sub	Goals	Europe Apps	Sub	Goals	Totals Apps	Sub	Goals
14	3	1	22	2	5	1	1		186	20	30
1									27		6
5									94		1
									10		
4									52		8
									1		
11									100		6
3	2		1			3	4		16	23	2
1									9		2
									12		5
									1		
									2		
7		2							66		28
3									36		5
			1	1					1	1	
3	1		8			8	2		39	17	
16			14			4			202		2
			1	1	2	3	4	1	27	14	9
									15		2
5	2		4			8	3		39	24	2
1									1		
			4			1	2		7	5	1
35	2	2	5			55		2	306	9	23
5	4		4		1	6	10		29	40	1
			1	1					1	1	
2									37		6
7									93		
									2		1
5	5		5		1	3	2		77	20	4
1									9		
1			3						14	4	1
									1		
									17		
1									1		
									3		
									7		
3									84		10
									1		
1									10		1
			2			1			6		
									2		1
			1	1					2	1	
8		5							109		45
3									42		16
									2		
6									70		2
5			14			3	1		108	5	8
									1		
4									23		
1									1		
4									26		5
11			15		1				119	2	5
									1		
8									113		
13									208		4
			1						9		
7									89		
									1		
									1		
32			18			24			308		
14	6	10	4		4	21	15	3	109	45	45
1									56		7
47			49		3	42	1	1	567	12	12
									5		
1			7			2			70		
13	1	7	20	2	5	2			164	5	68
5		1							75		22
			1						3	1	
									4		1
2	4	1	3	4		3	1		18	27	4
16		12	29		29	21		15	278	9	184
5			1			4			22		
									4		
3									71		9
28		3	20		1	18		4	236		19

OTHER TITLES IN THE SERIES

The Essential History of...

Football

Blackburn Rovers	Mike Jackman	*0 7553 1022 5*
Celtic	Graham McColl/George Sheridan	*0 7553 1141 8*
Charlton Athletic	Paul Clayton	*0 7553 1020 9*
England	Andrew Mourant/Jack Rollin	*0 7553 1142 6*
Everton	Mark Platt	*0 7553 1274 0**
Leeds United	Andrew Mourant	*0 7553 1170 1**
Leicester City	Tony Matthews	*0 7553 1023 3*
Liverpool	Alex Murphy/Eric Doig	*0 7553 1268 6*
Manchester City	Ian Penney	*0 7553 1168 X**
Manchester United	Ivan Ponting/Cliff Butler	*0 7553 1269 4*
Middlesbrough	Richard Jones	*0 7553 1143 4*
Newcastle United	Paul Joannou/Bill Swann/Steve Corke	*0 7553 1270 8*
Rangers	Stephen Halliday	*0 7553 1145 0*
West Bromwich Albion	Gavin McOwan	*0 7553 1146 9*
West Ham United	Kirk Blows/Tony Hogg	*0 7553 1169 8**

Rugby Union

England	Ian Malin/John Griffiths	*0 7553 1271 6*
Scotland	Nick Oswald/John Griffiths	*0 7553 1272 4*
Wales	Steve Lewis/John Griffiths	*0 7553 1273 2*

* Trade paperback editions

Please contact your local WHSmith store for details about ordering any of these titles.